Juan Domínguez de Mendoza

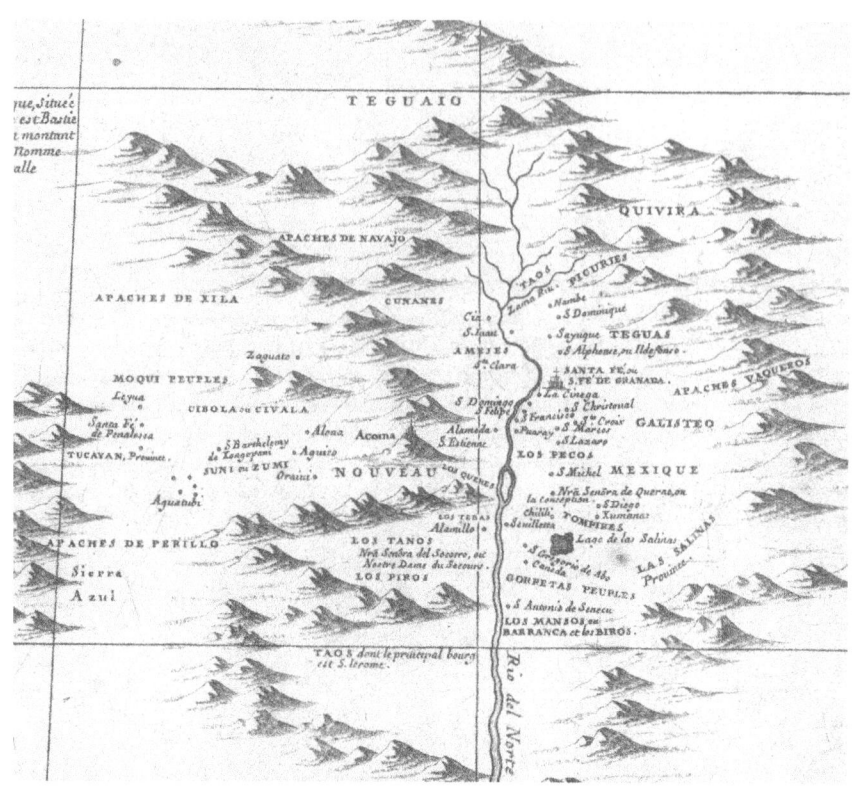

MAP 1. Detail of the Coronelli-Tillemon map of New Mexico in the mid-seventeenth century based on the information provided to French authorities by don Diego de Peñalosa y Briceño, governor of New Mexico (1661–1664). Although most place names are familiar and are depicted in the relative geographical location of seventeenth-century places and settlements, some place names are unfamiliar, such as Sayuque above San Ildefonso, S. Estienne (San Estéban) below Alameda, and Zaguato in the west. Missing from the map are the pueblos of Isleta, Tesuque, and Pecos, although a region labeled "Los Pecos" is shown. The Pueblo of Zía (Cia) is placed above that of San Juan along the Chama River instead of to the south and east of San Felipe. The pueblo of San Diego de los Jemez is shown in the east instead of the west. The Pueblo of Sandia is listed by the name of its patron saint, San Francisco. S. Dominque, listed below Nambé, is the pueblo of Jacona. S. Michel shown below Los Pecos is the pueblo of Tajique. The pueblo of Acoma is depicted with a structure atop a large *monte*. The Villa de Santa Fe is associated with Santa Fe de Granada, a designation not found in surviving seventeenth-century records of New Mexico. Fr. Vicenzo María Coronelli (1650–1718), augmented by Jean Nicolás du Tralage, Sieur de Tillemon (d. 1699), and published by Jean Baptiste Nolin (1648–1708), *Le Nouveau Mexique appele aussi Nouvelle Grenade et Marata; Avec partie de Californie*, ca. 1688, Paris. Library of Congress, Geography and Map Division, Washington, D.C.

Juan Domínguez de Mendoza

SOLDIER AND FRONTIERSMAN
OF THE SPANISH SOUTHWEST,
1627–1693

Edited by
France V. Scholes
Marc Simmons
José Antonio Esquibel

Translated by
Eleanor B. Adams

Coronado Historical Series VII
University of New Mexico Press | Albuquerque

© 2012 by the University of New Mexico Press
All rights reserved. Published 2012
Printed in the United States of America

First paperback printing 2023

LIBRARY OF CONGRESS CATALOGING-IN-PUBLICATION DATA

Juan Domínguez de Mendoza: soldier and frontiersman of the Spanish
    Southwest, 1627–1693/edited by France V. Scholes, Marc Simmons,
    and José Antonio Esquibel; translated by Eleanor B. Adams.
    p. cm.
Includes bibliographical references and index.
ISBN 978-0-8263-5115-9 (cloth: alk. paper)
ISBN 978-0-8263-5116-6 (paper)
ISBN 978-0-8263-5117-3 (electronic)

1. Domínguez de Mendoza, Juan, 1627–1693.
2. Spaniards—New Mexico—History—17th century—Sources.
3. Pueblo Indians—New Mexico—History—17th century—Sources.
4. Pueblo Revolt, 1680—Sources.
5. New Mexico—History—To 1848—Sources.
I. Scholes, France V. (France Vinton), 1897–1979.
II. Simmons, Marc.
III. Esquibel, José Antonio.

F799.J798 2012
978.9'04—dc23

2011044548

Contents

Illustrations, Maps, Tables, and Charts / xi
Foreword / xiii
   Marc Simmons
Preface / xxi
   France V. Scholes
A Question of Forgeries or Reconstructed Documents / xxvii
Introduction / 1
   France V. Scholes, Marc Simmons, and José Antonio Esquibel

PART ONE: MILITARY SERVICE RECORDS OF JUAN DOMÍNGUEZ DE MENDOZA AND RELATED DOCUMENTS

   Translations by Eleanor B. Adams
DOCUMENT 1: Proof of Lineage of Elena de la Cruz,
   1625 [Summary] / 69
DOCUMENT 2: Commission as Alférez Real, Santa Fe,
   October 12, 1643 / 70
DOCUMENT 3: Commission as Captain of Infantry, Santa Fe,
   December 7, 1644 / 73
DOCUMENT 4: Title of Captain and Commander, Santa Fe,
   April 14, 1646 / 78
DOCUMENT 5: Appointment as Lieutenant Governor and
   Captain General, Santa Fe, April 15, 1650 / 81
DOCUMENT 6: Commission as Captain of Cavalry, Santa Fe,
   November 10, 1652 / 83
DOCUMENT 7: Certification of Services, Santa Fe, January 12, 1653 / 86
DOCUMENT 8: Certification of Services, Santa Fe, September 13, 1653 / 88
DOCUMENT 9: Title of Maestre de Campo, Santa Fe, October 15, 1658 / 90
DOCUMENT 10: Commission as Captain of Mounted Harquebusiers, Santa
   Fe, August 30, 1659 / 93
DOCUMENT 11: Appointment as Alcalde Mayor of the
   Jurisdictions of Sandia and Isleta and as Lieutenant Captain
   General in the Río Abajo, Santa Fe, November 19, 1659 / 96

Document 12: Appointment as Escudero of the Encomienda of Sargento Mayor Francisco Gómez Robledo, Santa Fe, May 7, 1662 / 99

Document 13: Title of Lieutenant Captain General and Visitador General, October 6, 1663 / 102

Document 14: Decree of Governor Peñalosa, Santa Fe, January 7, 1664 / 104

Document 15: Appointment as Lieutenant of the Governor and Captain General in the Jurisdictions of the Río Abajo, Santa Fe, June 25, 1665 / 105

Document 16: Appointment as Visitador of the Mission Supply Caravan, Santa Fe, October 16, 1665 / 107

Document 17: Appointment as Visitador of Trading Caravan, Santa Fe, December 16, 1666 / 109

Document 18: Appointment as Lieutenant of the Governor and Captain General, Santa Fe, February 10, 1667 / 112

Document 19: Edict Concerning a Council of War and Petition for Horses and Provisions for a Campaign against the Apaches, Santa Fe and Santo Domingo, February 18–26, 1668 / 118

Document 20: Title of Encomienda, Santa Fe, May 1, 1669 / 129

Document 21: Documents Concerning Provisions and Livestock Given by the Conventos for an Expedition against the Apaches, June 16–July 4, 1669 / 132

Document 22: Commission as Maestre de Campo in Campaign, Santa Fe, September 11, 1670 / 139

Document 23: Commission as Sargento Mayor of the Kingdom, Santa Fe, June 27, 1671 / 142

Document 24: Commission as Maestre de Campo General of the Kingdom, Santa Fe, July 27, 1671 / 144

Document 25: Appointment as Lieutenant of the Governor and Captain General, Santa Fe, August 2, 1671 / 147

Document 26: Certification of Services, Santa Fe, January 26, 1672 / 149

Document 27: Commission as Alférez Real Granted to Don Baltasar Domínguez de Mendoza. Santa Fe, December 27, 1672 / 151

Document 28: Commission as Maestre de Campo in Campaign, San Juan de los Caballeros, July 15, 1673 / 153

Document 29: Commission as Captain of Cavalry Granted to Don Baltasar Domínguez de Mendoza, Santa Fe, October 20, 1674 / 156

Document 30: Commission as Maestre de Campo in a Campaign against the Faraon Apaches, Pecos, January 5, 1675 / 157

DOCUMENT 31: Commission as Military Commander and Chief, Santa Fe, September 24, 1675 / 160
DOCUMENT 32: Commission as Military Commander and Chief, Estancia de San Antonio, July 1, 1676 / 163
DOCUMENT 33: Commission as Lieutenant Captain General in Campaign, Santa Fe, July 12, 1678 / 164
DOCUMENT 34: Instructions as Lieutenant Captain General, Santa Fe, July 12, 1678 / 168
DOCUMENT 35: Commission as Lieutenant Captain General in Campaign, Santa Fe, October 28, 1678 / 171
DOCUMENT 36: Instructions as Lieutenant Captain General, Santa Fe, October 28, 1678 / 173
DOCUMENT 37: Title of Encomienda of the Pueblo of Isleta, Santa Fe, November 26, 1678 / 175
DOCUMENT 38: Commission as Maestre de Campo in Campaign, Santa Fe, August 17, 16[79] / 177
DOCUMENT 39: Commission as Lieutenant General of Cavalry, Ancón de Fray García, November 9, 1681 / 179
DOCUMENT 40: Certification of Services, El Paso, October 13, 1683 / 181
DOCUMENT 41: Statement Made by Juan Sabeata before Governor Jironza Petríz de Cruzate, El Paso, October 20, 1683 / 182
DOCUMENT 42: Commission as Commander of the Expedition to Texas, El Paso, November 29, 1683 / 187
DOCUMENT 43: Instruction for the Expedition to Texas, El Paso, November 29, 1683 / 190
DOCUMENT 44: Certification, June 23, 1684 / 193
DOCUMENT 45: Journal of the Expedition to Texas, 1683–1684 / 196
DOCUMENT 46: Certification of Documents Showing the Services of Maestre de Campo Don Juan Domínguez de Mendoza, El Paso, October 3, 1684 / 214
DOCUMENT 47: Certification of the Personal Appearance and Services of Maestre de Campo Don Juan Domínguez de Mendoza and His Two Sons, Don Baltasar and Don Juan, Issued by the Cabildo, Justicia, and Regimiento of the Villa de Santa Fe, El Paso, October 8, 1684 / 221
DOCUMENT 48: Excerpt from a Letter of Governor Domingo Jironza Petríz de Cruzate to the Viceroy, El Paso, August 26, 1685 / 225
DOCUMENT 49: First Memorial of Juan Domínguez de Mendoza to the Viceroy, Mexico City, November 18, 1685 / 227
DOCUMENT 50: Second Memorial of Juan Domínguez de Mendoza [Mexico City], November 18, 1685 / 231

DOCUMENT 51: Criminal Case against Maestre de Campo Juan Domínguez de Mendoza and the Others Who Fled with Him, Guadalupe del Paso, September 28–October 6, 1685 / 234

DOCUMENT 52: Attested Copy of a Document Issued by the Cabildo of Santa Fe, October 3, 1684, Certifying the Titles of Offices of Juan Domínguez de Mendoza, Mexico City, April 23–24, 1686 / 248

DOCUMENT 53: Petition of Fray Nicolás López to the Viceroy with the Reply of the Fiscal and Decision of the Junta General, Mexico City, March 26, 1686 / 253

DOCUMENT 54: Copy of the Sentence Pronounced in the Proceedings against Maestre de Campo Juan Domínguez de Mendoza, Mexico City, April 30, 1687 / 258

DOCUMENT 55: Testimony Concerning the Conduct of Juan Domínguez de Mendoza during the Expedition of 1681–1682, [El Paso del Norte], May 19–June 12, 1687 / 260

DOCUMENT 56: Permission for Maestre de Campo Don Juan Domínguez de Mendoza to Bring His Wife and Family from El Paso del Río del Norte, Mexico City, July 23, 1688, and Presentation of License of Baltasar Domínguez de Mendoza, Nuestra Señora de Guadalupe del Paso del Río del Norte, March 1, 1689 / 267

DOCUMENT 57: Decree of Governor Domingo Jironza Petríz de Cruzate, El Paso, March 1, 1689 / 269

DOCUMENT 58: Information Given by Maestre de Campo Don Juan Domínguez de Mendoza, Mexico City, June 6, 1693 / 270

DOCUMENT 59: License for Maestre de Campo Juan Domínguez de Mendoza to Go to Spain, Mexico City, June 12, 1693 / 273

DOCUMENT 60: Résumé of Papers Presented by Baltasar Domínguez de Mendoza, Madrid, August 19, 1694 / 275

DOCUMENT 61: Report of the Council of the Indies Concerning Petitions Made by Baltasar Domínguez de Mendoza, Madrid, October 1, 1694 / 277

DOCUMENT 62: Petition of Baltasar Domínguez de Mendoza to the Crown Asking for the Corregimiento of Tlajomulco and Caxititlan, [Madrid, November] 1694 / 279

DOCUMENT 63: Petition of Baltasar Domínguez de Mendoza Asking for Admission to One of the Military Orders, [Madrid], March 1695 / 281

DOCUMENT 64: Royal Cédula to the Viceroy of New Spain Recommending Don Baltasar Domínguez de Mendoza, Madrid, April 21, 1695 / 284

DOCUMENT 65: Papers Concerning the Return of Baltasar Domínguez de Mendoza to New Spain, May 26–July 8, 1695 [Summary] / 285

DOCUMENT 66: License Granted to Baltasar Domínguez de Mendoza to Travel in the Fleet of General Don Ignacio de Barrios Leal, July 8, 1695, Cádiz / 285

DOCUMENT 67: Certification of Services of Don Juan Domínguez de Mendoza, the Younger, Santa Fe, September 18, 1701 / 286

PART TWO: SUPPLEMENTAL DOCUMENTS

Translations by France V. Scholes, Eleanor B. Adams, and José Antonio Esquibel

SUPPLEMENTAL DOCUMENT 1: The State of the Conversions, Churches and Conventos of the Custodia de San Pablo in New Mexico in the Matter of Granting Forty Friars, Circa 1641 / 291

SUPPLEMENTAL DOCUMENT 2: List of Administrators of Justice and War during the Tenure of Governor Don Bernardo López de Mendizábal, Santa Fe, 1659–1661 / 296

SUPPLEMENTAL DOCUMENT 3: List of Papers of Merits and Services of New Mexico Vecinos, Santa Fe, July 11, 1662 / 297

SUPPLEMENTAL DOCUMENT 4: Merits and Services of Don Diego de Guadalajara Bernardo de Quirós, Lieutenant Governor of Nueva Vizcaya, Madrid, January 4, 1664 / 301

SUPPLEMENTAL DOCUMENT 5: Certification of the Number of Friars Serving in the Conventos of the Custody of New Mexico, Mexico City, December 6, 1667 / 304

SUPPLEMENTAL DOCUMENT 6: Account of the Services of Don Fernando de Villanueva, Governor and Captain General of the Provinces of New Mexico by Appointment of the Marqués de Mancera, Viceroy of New Spain, October 30, 1671 / 310

SUPPLEMENTAL DOCUMENT 7: Letter of the Viceroy to the King Regarding Aid to New Mexico to Quell the Invasion of the Apache Nation, Mexico City, January 13, 1678 / 315

SUPPLEMENTAL DOCUMENT 8: Excerpt from a Petition of Fray Nicolás López to the Viceroy, Mexico City, June 7, 1685 / 317

SUPPLEMENTAL DOCUMENT 9: Letter of Fray Nicolás López to the Secretary of the Council of the Indies, Don Antonio Ortiz de Otalora, Mexico City, April 24, 1686 / 321

SUPPLEMENTAL DOCUMENT 10: Memorial of Fray Nicolás López to
   His Majesty, Mexico City, April 24, 1686 / 323
SUPPLEMENTAL DOCUMENT 11: Account of the Services of Don Domingo
   Jironza Petríz de Cruzate, Former Governor and Captain General of
   the Provinces of New Mexico, January 12, 1693 / 332

PART THREE: IN SERVICE TO THE SPANISH CROWN:
   THE FAMILY OF DOMÍNGUEZ DE MENDOZA

José Antonio Esquibel

Background / 347
Paternal and Maternal Ancestry of the Domínguez
   de Mendoza Clan / 348
The Domínguez de Mendoza Family in New Spain / 355
The Domínguez de Mendoza Family in New Mexico / 356
Juan Domínguez de Mendoza and Doña Isabel de Chaves
   y Bohórquez / 360
Francisco Domínguez de Mendoza and Juana de Rueda / 365
Tomé Domínguez de Mendoza and Doña Catalina López Mederos / 371
Doña Damiana Ramírez de Mendoza and Álvaro de Paredes / 378
Doña Leonor Ramírez de Mendoza and Cristóbal de Anaya Almazán / 380
Doña Elena Domínguez de Mendoza and Don Pedro II
   Durán y Chaves / 388
José Domínguez de Mendoza and Juana Domínguez / 393
Epilogue / 395

WORKS CITED 417
INDEX 431

Illustrations, Maps, Tables, and Charts

ILLUSTRATIONS

FIGURE 1: Acoma Pueblo looking east / 24
FIGURE 2: Cover sheet for the Juan Domínguez de Mendoza documents / 52
FIGURE 3: Appointment of Juan Domínguez de Mendoza as lieutenant governor / 113
FIGURE 4: Pueblo of Zuni / 161
FIGURE 5: View of Santa Fe / 382

MAPS

MAP 1: Detail Coronelli-Tilleron Map of Seventeenth-Century New Mexico / ii
MAP 2: Coronelli-Tillimon Map of New Mexico, ca. 1688 / 68
MAP 3: Las Provincias del Nuevo México / 298

TABLES

TABLE 1: Personal Service Records of Juan Domínguez de Mendoza Preserved in the Biblioteca Nacional de España, Madrid, MSS 19258 / xxiii
TABLE 2: Chronological Sequence of Commissions/Titles of Juan Domínguez de Mendoza, 1643–1686 / 8

CHARTS

CHART 1: The Geneology and Family of Tomé Domínguez and Elena de la Cruz y Mendoza / 358
CHART 2: The Geneology and Family of Juan Domínguez de Mendoza and Isabel Durán y Cháves / 362
CHART 3: Descendants of Baltasar Domínguez de Mendoza and María Francisca de Alburu / 364
CHART 4: Durán y Chaves–Domínguez de Mendoza / 391

Foreword

Marc Simmons

WITH THE PUBLICATION OF THIS BOOK, THE FINAL VOLUME IN THE CORONADO HISTORICAL SERIES, A PROJECT BEGUN MORE THAN SEVEN decades ago has at last been brought to a conclusion. The New Mexico state legislature in 1935 created the Coronado Cuarto Centennial Commission, whose purpose was to plan and carry out a commemorative program honoring the four hundredth anniversary of the landmark Francisco Vásquez de Coronado expedition.

An initial legislative appropriation of $35,000 to underwrite a statewide celebration was soon augmented by a general federal subsidy of $200,000, ensuring that the broad program of activities would be well funded. Much of the money was dedicated to showy public events, such as fiestas, historical exhibits, art shows, and, especially, an elaborate pageant titled the Coronado Entrada, which over a two-year period toured New Mexico, Arizona, Texas, Colorado, Oklahoma, and Kansas. Those were the states, it was then thought, that Coronado had passed through. Other monies went for the placing of historical monuments.[1]

There were knowledgeable persons, however, who believed that the anniversary observance should direct at least a portion of its bountiful resources to the production of "a substantial cultural dividend" that would outlast the popular displays. Among them were George P. Hammond, a professor of history and dean of the Graduate School at the University of New Mexico; another faculty member, the prominent George I. Sánchez; and the university president James F. Zimmerman, who was elected president of the Cuarto Centennial Commission. Their zeal and seriousness of purpose would lead to the publication by the University of New Mexico Press of the prestigious Coronado Historical Series.[2]

The official program published under the auspices of the Commission carried this notice concerning the pending series:

Texts will be published giving in complete form valuable and scientific information relating to the Southwest in general. These will preserve for permanent use historical and cultural facts about the period covered by the Coronado expedition.[3]

As plans progressed, it became clear that focusing all the titles on the brief period of the expedition was wholly unrealistic. Therefore, the concept was expanded to include works that dealt with people and events of the later colonial years, representing the aftermath of the Coronado enterprise. Of the books that eventually appeared, all but *Pfefferkorn's Description of Sonora* were centered upon New Mexican subjects.

Dr. Hammond became the series' general editor and began to solicit manuscripts. Twelve volumes, treating ten subjects, were finally approved. The distinguished father of borderland studies, Herbert Eugene Bolton of the University of California, accepted an invitation to write volume 1, a biography intended to serve as the series' cornerstone. It appeared, belatedly, in 1949 under the title *Coronado on the Turquoise Trail: Knight of Pueblos and Plains*. Volume 2 actually saw print in the anniversary year of 1940; this is Hammond and Agapito Rey's *Narratives of the Coronado Expedition, 1540–1542*. It comprised a collection of the main Spanish documents, translated, that dealt with the subject, together with a lengthy interpretive introduction. Except for Bolton's Coronado biography, that format was followed by the remaining books of the series that were published periodically over the next quarter century.

On January 8, 1940, Professor France Vinton Scholes of the University of New Mexico History Department signed a memorandum of agreement with editor Hammond, by which he would submit, as early as possible in that year, a finished manuscript that would become volume 7. For that he was to be paid the sum of $300, plus the costs of obtaining documentary photostats.

Dr. Hammond evidently had not discussed the subject of the book beforehand with his author. Therefore, since Scholes was a recognized authority on the Franciscan missionaries, Hammond assumed he would take some aspect of that topic, and for purposes of completing the memorandum he supplied a general title of his own for volume 7, "The Spanish Missions in New Mexico." However, in an appended note, he invited Scholes to furnish him with the correct title. This Prof. Scholes did, at the bottom of the memorandum, adding in script, "Juan Domínguez de Mendoza: Soldier and Frontiersman of the Southwest," indicating that he had settled on a topic far removed from Spanish missions.[4]

Scholes had come to the University of New Mexico in 1925, fresh out of Harvard, and was soon specializing in the history of the Franciscans and seventeenth-century New Mexico. Shortly, he began spending his summers in the archives of Mexico and Spain in pursuit of relevant documents. During a visit in 1928 to Madrid's National Library (today the Biblioteca Nacional de España, Madrid), he stumbled upon a bound volume of original documents (MSS 19258) bearing the title "Relación de servicios personales del Maestre de Campo don Juan Domingues y Mendoza hechos en las Provincias de la Nueva México, 1686" ("Personal Services of the Maestre de Campo don Juan Domínguez de Mendoza Rendered in the Provinces of New Mexico, 1686").

This treasure trove of papers, fifty-one items in all, represented a running record of Domínguez de Mendoza's career on the Upper Rio Grande, extending from the 1640s down to the mid-1680s, when he made his final departure from New Mexico. At the very end of his life, he carried these documents to Spain, where he hoped to gain an audience with the Royal Council of the Indies, or even the king, so that he might ask for the governorship of New Mexico or some other high political office, as reward for his years of faithful service.

Reading through the Domínguez de Mendoza papers, perhaps the first American ever to do so, Scholes recognized their historical importance. He took copious notes but quickly became aware that he needed photostats of the entire run, something difficult for individuals to obtain from the ponderous Spanish bureaucracy of that time.[5]

The following March, however, Roscoe R. Hill was in Madrid copying documents for the Library of Congress related to the history of America, a project made possible by Rockefeller funding. Probably at the request of Scholes, he secured film negative copies of Domínguez de Mendoza's personal military service records.[6] From these, Scholes subsequently was able to get his own set of positive photostats. His intention from the beginning was to see them published, and the Coronado Historical Series seemed to offer a convenient opportunity.

George Hammond on March 26, 1940, wrote to Scholes, saying:

> I am glad to know that the Domínguez de Mendoza documents will make a grand book. In fact, the same reaction is coming from each of the other contributors for their particular volume. Bolton has worked up tremendous enthusiasm over his volume, all of the which augurs well for the whole series.

Hammond also acknowledged that he had received specimen pages of the Scholes manuscript, confirming that it was already in progress.[7] The optimistic tone of the letter gives no indication that the editor had any qualms about the future delivery of that manuscript. But in fact, when France V.

Scholes died on February 11, 1979, at age eighty-two, the book was still not finished, leaving the Coronado Historical Series incomplete, to the distress of the eighty-three-year-old Hammond. The circumstances surrounding the failure, and how the present writer became involved in its aftermath, form the subject of the remainder of this foreword.

During the middle years of his career, 1931 to 1946, Scholes served as a member of the Division of Historical Research for the Carnegie Institution in Washington, D.C. At Harvard's Peabody Museum in 1934, he happened to be introduced to Eleanor B. Adams, a studious scholar who was pursuing graduate studies in Spanish literature at the University of Madrid. In conversation, he suggested that with her background and knowledge of Spanish paleography, she ought to abandon literature and move into history. Shortly, she joined him at the Carnegie Institution, remarking long afterward, "I walked all unsuspecting into my life's work [coming] into the profession of history by the backdoor."[8] Until Scholes's death, he and Miss Adams (as she was always known) collaborated on numerous books and projects dealing with the colonial era.

The year 1940 ended without Scholes meeting his contractual deadline for Hammond; neither did he submit a manuscript in 1941 or 1942. How much actual work he had done on Juan Domínguez de Mendoza during those years is not known. He would have started on the task of transcribing the documents to produce clean typescripts of the Spanish for the next stage, which was the translation. There is no evidence, nevertheless, that he had proceeded very far.

In the Scholes Collection at the University of New Mexico Library is found a copy of a typed statement to Eleanor Adams acknowledging the sum of $300 paid for translations of documents to appear in the Coronado Historical Series, volume 7. A note at the bottom reads: "Payment of this sum to Miss Eleanor B. Adams will liquidate all obligation to me under the terms of my contract with the Coronado Cuarto Centennial Commission." The document is dated April 12, 1943.[9]

By turning over the $300 he had originally received from Dr. Hammond to his research associate, Scholes seemed to be divesting himself of any responsibility for completion of the Juan Domínguez de Mendoza book. Miss Adams would undertake the translations, which formed the core of the proposed volume. But, perhaps as partial compensation for failing to perform the job himself, he is thought to have informally promised editor Hammond that he would go ahead and contribute the interpretive introduction, as well as the historical annotations. On that, he labored sporadically until shortly before his passing.

In the course of his periodic stays at the Carnegie Institution, and before his full-time return to the University of New Mexico in 1946, Scholes developed new research interests in colonial New Spain, particularly in the life of Hernán Cortés, about whom he planned to write a multivolume biography. Thus, his earlier enthusiasm for seventeenth-century New Mexico, which had led him to publish important studies in the 1920s and 1930s, seemed to wane. But not so his interest in "Johnny Domínguez," Scholes's pet name for his subject, which he commonly used in conversation with his graduate students. This writer, one of those students, recalls Prof. Scholes in 1958 referring to Domínguez de Mendoza as the most prominent citizen-soldier of his century and the only person of his rank and social status for whom we have a significant body of documentation.

Not long after Scholes's memorial service in 1979, I received a letter from his only child, Marianne Scholes Spores, asking me to drop by her house in Albuquerque, as she wished to discuss the disposition of her father's Johnny Domínguez papers. On my visit, I made a quick examination, and among other things I found carbon copies of Miss Adams's translations of the Domínguez de Mendoza Servicios Personales and other collateral documents that she apparently had given to Scholes many years before, for his use in writing the introduction. She had also returned the Library of Congress photostats he had obtained back in 1928, and which he had loaned her.

Marianne Scholes Spores on that occasion requested that I take the hefty box of Domínguez de Mendoza materials, go through the papers at my leisure, and give her my opinion as to what might be done with them. Subsequently, I received a letter from her relating that she had spoken to Miss Adams, who professed no longer to have an interest in the Domínguez de Mendoza project; therefore, Spores hinted that I should take it over myself, so that the Johnny Domínguez story might at last be told. I agreed with some hesitation.[10]

As it happened, I had several of my own projects needing attention, and the Domínguez de Mendoza box sat on a bottom shelf in my library for another twenty years, gathering dust. In 1995, Marianne Scholes Spores died, to be followed a year later by Miss Adams. I began to think that unless, late in life, I found a way to pick up the baton, Johnny Domínguez was destined to be consigned to oblivion.

Then in the spring of 2000 I received a visit from the noted genealogical researcher José Antonio Esquibel. In the course of our conversation, he mentioned that he was looking for a new research project and had considered a study of the notorious and ill-fated Governor Bernardo López de Mendizábal (1659–1661), a man to whom Scholes had given much attention in his seminal work *Troublous Times in New Mexico, 1659–1670*.[11]

A light bulb went on in my head. I hastened to the rear of my library stacks and brought forth the long-neglected Domínguez de Mendoza documents. Esquibel and I pored over them for hours, growing increasingly excited. Johnny Domínguez, we concluded, had been as substantial a historical figure as Dr. Scholes had always claimed. Together, we agreed to bring the body of material into publishable form, thereby belatedly closing the books on the final Coronado Cuarto Centennial project.

Besides the Adams translations, the inherited papers yielded numerous handwritten sheets by Scholes representing a long series of false starts or incomplete attempts to produce the introduction to volume 7, for which he remained committed. To the degree possible, I have incorporated the meat from those fragments into the introduction composed for this book. Thus, it can be considered truly a joint effort, with France V. Scholes receiving top billing, as is proper, inasmuch as he initiated this project so long ago and lived close to Johnny Domínguez for more than forty years.

Eleanor B. Adams, however, must receive the lion's share of the credit for her authoritative translations that lend this book its value as a work of history. All too often, the achievement of translators is not rightfully acknowledged, and they go unrecognized. Esquibel is listed as collaborator. He made new translations, from the Library of Congress photostats, of a few of Miss Adams's pages that were lost. Furthermore, he translated, in consultation with myself, several pertinent documents, not part of the original Scholes–Adams package, but which we saw fit to include. The genealogical section, tracing the ancestry of the Domínguez de Mendoza family, is entirely the work of Mr. Esquibel. In the text, his name appears on his translations. All notations are by Scholes, except those marked in brackets E & S, identifying Esquibel and Simmons as authors.

Scholes's original intention was to write an extended introduction that could serve as a summary history of New Mexico in the latter seventeenth century, structured around the pivotal figure of Juan Domínguez de Mendoza. For reasons of economy, I abandoned that ambitious design and narrowed the scope to place more emphasis on Domínguez de Mendoza himself, and less on broad provincial affairs that would have touched on him only indirectly.

I have no way of knowing whether my mentor, Dr. France Vinton Scholes, would have approved of this alteration of his plan. But since he as well as his daughter, Marianne, Miss Adams, and Dr. Hammond are now gone, it is left to me to determine the configuration of the "the Johnny Domínguez book." I can only hope that all of them might have found the final product acceptable.

Notes

1. On the "History of the Coronado Celebrations." See George P. Hammond, *Coronado's Seven Cities* (Albuquerque: University of New Mexico Press, 1940), 75–82.
2. George P. Hammond provides background on the anniversary publications in his *Reminiscences* (privately printed, 1986), 97–98.
3. The program, printed in Roswell, New Mexico, in 1940, was titled *Coronado Magazine*. See p. 5. The commission also published (ca. 1938) a forty-page handbook, *Coronado Cuarto Centennial, What Will It Mean to New Mexico*, to serve as a guide for local communities and private groups wishing to organize their own commemorative events.
4. The memorandum is in the France V. Scholes Collection, Box 1, Center for Southwest Research, University of New Mexico Library, Albuquerque, cited hereinafter as the Scholes Coll.
5. See Document 46, October 3, 1684, infra, note 11.
6. Thomas P. Martin, "Spanish Archive Materials and Related Materials in the Other National Archives Copied for the Library of Congress by the Rockerfeller Project, 1927–1929," *Hispanic American Historical Review* 10 (February 1930): 96.
7. The letter is in the Scholes Coll., Box 1.
8. Eleanor B. Adams, "The Historical Society of New Mexico Honors France Vinton Scholes for Outstanding Achievement in Spanish Colonial History, 1970," *The Americas* 27 (January 1971): 226. Also see Richard E. Greenleaf, "France V. Scholes: Historian's Historian, 1897–1979," *New Mexico Historical Review* 75, no. 3 (July 2000): 325.
9. Scholes failed to sign the file copy of this item, but it is clear that he prepared it.
10. Personal correspondence, Marianne Scholes Spores to Marc Simmons, July 4, 1979, and June 17, 1981, in possession of the editor. Miss Adams's original copies of the translations appear to have been lost. At least they were not found among her papers at her death in 1996, according to the executor of her estate, Prof. John L. Kessell.
11. Initially published serially in the *New Mexico Historical Review*, 1937 to 1941, and afterward issued as a separate monograph (Albuquerque: University of New Mexico Press, 1942).

Preface

France V. Scholes

Writings on the history of New Mexico in the seventeenth century have related chiefly to such topics as the founding of missions, the conflicts between secular and religious authorities, the successful revolt of the Pueblo Indians, and the reconquest of the Pueblo area during the last decade of the century.

The services of fray Estéban de Perea, fray Alonso de Benavides, fray Alonso de Posada, fray Francisco de Ayeta, and other Franciscan friars are well known. Governors like Pedro de Peralta, Juan de Eulate, Luis de Rosas, Bernardo López de Mendizábal, and Diego de Peñalosa, who came into conflict with the ecclesiastical leaders, are now familiar figures. The tragic administration of Governor Antonio de Otermín and the successes of Governor Diego de Vargas are highlights in the annals of the Spanish province.

Little attention has been paid, however, to the exploits of the loyal soldiers and frontiersmen who formed the backbone of the nonaboriginal colony, defended the missions against attack by marauding Apaches and Navajos, and laid the foundations of European society in an isolated outpost of the far-flung empire of Spain in North America.

It is fitting, therefore, that one volume of the Coronado Historical Series should recognize the services and exploits of a prominent soldier-colonist of New Mexico in colonial days, one of the soldiers and frontiersmen who, quite as much as governors and friars, helped to lay the foundations of Hispano-Indian society in New Mexico.

For most of the soldier-colonists who served the area in the seventeenth century, we have relatively little information. But for one man, who achieved somewhat greater prominence than the others, an extensive quantity of papers has been preserved in the archives of Mexico and Spain. This individual was Juan Domínguez de Mendoza, who served in New Mexico from age thirteen to fifty-six, and rose step by step from the rank of common soldier to the highest post in the province that was open to him.

The story of his career, as set forth in this volume, shows that he was no gallant knight of the frontier, but rather a rough soldier, restless and ambitious, a product of his environment. Indeed, the record shows that he was not above resorting to fraud and forgery in an effort to advance his ambitions. But withal, he stood as a pillar of strength during the troubled days before the 1680 Pueblo Revolt. In 1683, he became commander of an important expedition of exploration into central Texas. For some forty years, he served his majesty, the Catholic king, with little reward of material character. It was Domínguez de Mendoza and men like him who kept the gold and red ensign of Spain flying in the northernmost outpost of empire in America. In recounting his story, we pay homage to all the colonists and soldiers, known and unknown, in seventeenth-century New Mexico.

Most of the documents were translated by Miss Eleanor B. Adams, subject to my final revisions. Miss Adams made valuable suggestions on many points that made their way into the historical introduction and notations. Initially, Dean George P. Hammond of the University of New Mexico, general editor of the Coronado Historical Series, and Professor Lansing B. Bloom gave generous assistance during preparation of the volume. Dr. Herbert E. Bolton was consulted concerning the itinerary of the Domínguez de Mendoza expedition of 1683–1684.

Translations or summaries of fifty-one of the documents made from photographs of the Domínguez de Mendoza Servicios Personales (personal services) records in the Library of Congress, originally in the Biblioteca Nacional de Madrid, are presented here. They are arranged in chronological order, rather than in the order in which they occur in the bound manuscript.

Most of the documents consist of appointments of Domínguez de Mendoza to civil and military offices. They contain an unfortunate amount of legal verbiage and are sometimes dull reading, but they have genuine value, not only for understanding the career of Domínguez de Mendoza, but also as a source for the administrative and military history of the province of New Mexico. They illustrate governmental procedures and the way in which administrative and military appointments were made, the manner in which local military campaigns were conducted, and certain facets of the encomienda system. Some of the documents provide new sources and new points of view on Domínguez de Mendoza's role in the attempted reconquest of 1681–1682, especially his conduct of the Cochiti incident. But most important of all, they throw a flood of light on the growing Apache–Navajo menace that threatened the security of the province prior to the Pueblo Revolt of 1680.

TABLE 1

Personal Service Records of Juan Domínguez de Mendoza Preserved in the Biblioteca Nacional de España, Madrid, MSS 19258

A portfolio of the records of *servicios y méritos* was compiled and kept by Juan Domínguez de Mendoza for the purpose of seeking favors in the form of high-level administrative and military positions from representatives of the royal government in the name of the king of Castilla y León. The portfolio consists of fifty-one documents dating from 1625 to 1701. In 1929, copies of this portfolio were brought to the U.S. Library of Congress by Roscoe R. Hill at the request of France V. Scholes, who located the documents in Madrid in the previous year. (E & S)

Manuscript folio #	Date	Title	Document # in this Volume
2–5	October 3, 1684	Certification of Documents Showing the Services of the Maestre de Campo Don Juan Domínguez de Mendoza	46
6–7	October 8, 1684	Certification of the Personal Appearance and Services of the Maestre de Campo Don Juan Domínguez y Mendoza and His Two Sons, Don Baltasar and Don Juan, Issued by the Cabildo, Justicia and Regimiento of the Villa de Santa Fe	47
8–11	November 29, 1683	Commission as Commander of the Expedition to Texas	42
12–14	October 12, 1643	Commission as Alférez Real	2
15–16	December 7, 1644	Commission as Captain of Infantry	3
17–18	April 14, 1646	Title of Captain and Commander	4
19–20	April 15, 1650	Appointment as Lieutenant Governor and Captain General	5
21	September 13, 1653	Certification of Services	8
22–23	November 10, 1652	Commission as Captain of Cavalry	6
24–25	January 12, 1653	Certification of Services	7
26–28	October 15, 1658	Title of Maestre de Campo	9
29	November 19, 1659	Appointment as Alcalde Mayor of the Jurisdictions of Sandia and Isleta and as Lieutenant General of the Río Abajo	11
30	August 30, 1659	Commission as Captain of Mounted Harquebusiers	10
31–32	May 7, 1662	Appointment as Escudero of the Encomienda of Sargento Mayor Francisco Gómez Robledo	12

Manuscript folio #	Date	Title	Document # in this Volume
33–34	October 6, 1663	Title of Lieutenant Captain General and Visitador General	13
35–36	January 7, 1664	Decree of Governor Peñalosa	14
37–38	June 25, 1665	Appointment as Lieutenant of the Governor and Captain General in the Jurisdiction of the Río Abajo	15
39–40	October 16, 1665	Appointment as Visitador of the Mission Supply Caravan	16
41–43	December 16, 1666	Appointment as Visitador of the Trading Caravan	17
44–47	February 10, 1667	Appointment as Lieutenant of the Governor and Captain General	18
48–49	January 26, 1672	Certification of Services	26
50–52	September 11, 1670	Commission as Maestre de Campo in Campaign	22
53–54	June 27, 1671	Commission as Sargento Mayor of the Kingdom	23
55–57	May 1, 1669	Title of Encomienda	20
58–59	July 15, 1673	Commission as Maestre de Campo in Campaign	28
60–61	January 5, 1675	Commission as Maestre de Campo in a Campaign against the Faraon Apaches	30
62–66	July 27, 1671	Commission as Maestre de Campo General of the Kingdom	24
67–69	August 5, 1671	Appointment as Lieutenant of the Governor and Captain General	25
70–71	October 20, 1674	Commission as Captain of Cavalry Granted to Baltasar Domínguez de Mendoza	29
72–73	December 27, 1672	Commission as Alférez Real Granted to Don Baltasar Domínguez de Mendoza	27
74–76	July 1, 1676	Commission as Military Commander and Chief	32
77–81	September 24, 1675	Commission as Military Commander and Chief	31
82–84	June 12, 1693	License for Maestre de Campo Juan Domínguez de Mendoza to Go to Spain	59
85	September 18, 1701	Certification of Services of Don Juan Domínguez de Mendoza	67

Manuscript folio #	Date	Title	Document # in this Volume
86–87	May 26–July 8, 1695	Papers Concerning the Return of Baltasar Domínguez de Mendoza to New Spain	65
88–91	August 19, 1694	Résumé of Papers Presented by Baltasar Domínguez de Mendoza	60
92–93	April 21, 1695	Royal Cédula to the Viceroy of New Spain Recommending don Baltasar Domínguez de Mendoza	64
94–95	November 9, 1681	Commission as Lieutenant General of the Calvary	39
96–97	August 17, 16[79]	Commission as Maestre de Campo in Campaign	38
98–104	April 30, 1687	Copy of the Sentence Pronounced in the Proceedings Against Maestre de Campo Juan Domínguez de Mendoza	54
105	March 1, 1689	Decree of Governor Domingo Jironza Petríz de Cruzate	57
106–112	1625	Proof of Lineage of Elena de la Cruz	1
113–121		*Possibly the missing prueba (proof of lineage) documents on the Domínguez family (see note 13 of Document 46, in which Scholes indicates a jump in foliation)*	
122–123	October 13, 1683	Certification of Services	40
124–127		*Blank or missing folios*	
128–130	October 28, 1678	Commission as Lieutenant Captain General	35
131–133	October 28, 1678	Instruction as Lieutenant Captain General	36
134–136	July 12, 1678	Instruction as Lieutenant Captain General	34
137–138	November 26, 1678	Title of Encomienda of the Pueblo of Isleta	37
139–141	July 12, 1678	Commission as Lieutenant Captain General in Campaign	33
142–145	May 19–June 12, 1687	Testimony concerning the Conduct of Juan Domínguez de Mendoza during the Expeditions of 1681–1682	55
146–151		*Blank or missing folios*	
152–154	November 29, 1683	Instruction for the Expedition to Texas	43
155–161	June 6, 1693	Information Given by Maestre de Campo Don Juan Domínguez de Mendoza	58

A Question of Forgeries or Reconstructed Documents

Eleven of the fifty-one documents that make up the portfolio of the military service record of Juan Domínguez de Mendoza deserve special attention because of the fact that there are inconsistencies that draw into question their authenticity.[1] These inconsistencies are addressed more specifically in the notes provided for each document. The general reasoning and the various steps that led to the conclusion that the documents were forged or reconstructed are described here. To facilitate this analysis, the documents in question are divided into two groups, A and B, on the basis of handwriting styles. Group A comprises Documents 2, 6, 27, and 29, and Group B includes Documents 3, 4, 5, 7, 9, 13, and 26.

The documents in Group A are all in the same handwriting, but the handwriting is so much like that found in several documents of undoubted authenticity in Domínguez de Mendoza's papers that at first it did not arouse suspicion. Later on, when a study was being made of certain documents relating to the Domínguez de Mendoza family that are now in the Spanish Archives of New Mexico at the New Mexico State Archives and Records Center in Santa Fe, it was noted that the handwriting in the Group A documents is almost certainly the same as that of a petition of Juan's son, Baltasar Domínguez de Mendoza, dated 1694 and written in his own hand.[2] This naturally suggested the possibility that the Group A documents were forgeries written by Baltasar Domínguez de Mendoza, or perhaps a clumsy attempt on the part of Baltasar to reconstruct lost or damaged records as a result of the passage of time, the Pueblo Revolt of 1680, or the shipwreck of 1693 in which Juan Domínguez de Mendoza and Baltasar lost "everything they had with them" while on the way to Spain. With the ensuing death of his father in Madrid, Baltasar remained to petition the king for favors, in which case it was Baltasar who submitted the portfolio of his father's military service records that are preserved in the Biblioteca Nacional de Madrid.

The first example of the documents in question, Document 2, purports to be an appointment of Juan Domínguez de Mendoza as *alférez real* by Governor Alonso Pacheco de Heredia on October 12, 1643. Domínguez de Mendoza was sixteen years old at the time and had served in the province for hardly a year, inasmuch as he had come with Pacheco de Heredia about November 1 of the preceding year. It may be possible that the young soldier, as a newcomer to the province, may have given such a good account of himself in various campaigns during the first year he was in New Mexico that the governor decided to reward him by appointment as alférez real, but there is at least a reasonable doubt that Pacheco de Heredia would have selected a person so young for this permanent post of honor and trust.

In Document 6, the second of Group A, we find an obvious error in date. This document, supposedly executed by Governor Juan de Samaniego y Jaca, is dated November 10, 1652, but we know from records of salary payments in the treasury accounts that Samaniego y Jaca did not leave Mexico City on his journey to New Mexico until November 16, 1652.[3] This error in date might be regarded as a careless mistake on the part of the scribe if it stood alone, but in view of the fact that there are other errors of date in the documents in Group B, this particular case cannot be immediately dismissed in this manner. Finally, Documents 27 and 29 in Group A are appointments of Baltasar Domínguez de Mendoza to the offices of alférez real and captain of cavalry, respectively. At the time of the first, dated December 27, 1672, Baltasar was not more than thirteen years old; and at the time of the second, dated October 20, 1674, he was not more than fifteen. Here again we have some doubt as to whether such a young soldier would be given rank of this kind in preference to others of more mature years.

It is true that in Baltasar's case we are dealing with a boy who had been born and raised in the province and was the son of a prominent soldier. On the other hand, it is impossible to avoid the suspicion that Baltasar, who as we believe, had a hand in the forgery of the documents in both Group A and Group B, may have seized the opportunity to record for himself an appointment as alférez real as the first step in his military career to match that recorded for his father in Document 2. The appointment as captain of cavalry in Document 29 would mark the next step in his career. It is admitted, however, that the evidence of forgery in the documents in Group A, as noted above, is by no means conclusive, but in light of other evidence pointing to forgery or reconstruction of documents in Groups A and B, the points discussed above cannot be ignored.

The documents in Group B, dating from 1644 to 1672, are all written in the same handwriting but not the same as that in Group A. The handwriting of Group B is in an open, clear, bold style, necessitating the use of a heavy pen, and bears no resemblance whatsoever to the writing in any other documents in the entire series comprising the Biblioteca Nacional manuscript. Five of the documents in Group B contain obvious errors of date. For example, Document 3, a commission as captain of infantry dated December 7, 1644, contains a reference to an event in 1646, yet there is a later reference to such an appointment in Document 11 (November 9, 1659), which is not considered a possible forgery, which suggests that Document 3 is a reconstruction of the original commission record. Document 4 was supposedly executed by Governor Luis de Guzmán y Figueroa, but the document is dated April 14, 1646, two months before Guzmán y Figueroa was appointed governor, and more than a year before he took office in Santa Fe on May 5, 1647.[4] Document 7, which bears the signature of Governor Juan de Samaniego y Jaca, is dated January 12, 1653, whereas Samaniego y Jaca did not take office until April 23, 1653. Document 9, dated October 15, 1658, refers to the death of fray Pedro de Ayala at Hawikuh, which actually occurred on October 7, 1672. In Document 26 Governor Juan Rodríguez de Medrano Messía certified the services of Domínguez de Mendoza, but the document is dated January 26, 1672, whereas the treasury accounts show that his term of office ended on July 20, 1671. These errors of date, as well as other points of internal evidence that will be discussed in the notes, and the fact that the documents are all in the same handwriting, led to the tentative conclusion that all of the documents in Group B are forgeries, or at the very least they are inaccurate reconstructions.

A detailed examination of the papers in Groups A and B and a careful comparison with genuine documents in this series antedating 1684 revealed other interesting points that strengthen the forgery/reconstruction thesis and helped to fix the date when these documents were made. In all except one of the suspected documents (Document 13, Group B) there is a line or two at the end, following the signatures, giving a brief statement of the character or purpose of the documents. For example, on Document 2, Group A, we find: "*Su SS^a Yso merced de alferez R^1 del Reino a D^n Ju^o Domingues y Mendoza.*" The handwriting here and in other cases is apparently that of Baltasar Domínguez de Mendoza. In the document of undoubted authenticity similar statements indicating the character or purpose of the documents are found in only two cases (Document 12 and Document 42), and the handwriting is not Baltasar's. Document 42, dated November 29, 1683, gives the appointment of Juan Domínguez de Mendoza as commander of the expedition to Texas. Speculating on the foregoing, a hypothesis was formed that the documents in question were made in 1684 after Domínguez de Mendoza returned from Texas, and that Baltasar, who apparently had a hand in making them, may have noted the line at the bottom of the 1683 document, which was the most recent in his father's personal papers, and used this as a precedent to write a similar statement on all but one of the documents that were being forged or reconstructed.

The hypothesis concerning the date of the forged documents and the general thesis of the forgery itself were strengthened by other evidence. In all of the genuine documents antedating 1684, the family name is written "Domínguez de Mendoza." Moreover, Juan Domínguez de Mendoza's own signatures on Document 14 and Document 32, dated January 7, 1664, and July 1, 1676, respectively, are written "'Domínguez de Mendoza."

In the documents of Groups A and B, however, we find that the family name is written "Domínguez y Mendoza," except in Document 2, Group A, and the one with the earliest date. Here the "de" form is used, but at the end of the document Domínguez de Mendoza signed "D. Juan Dominguez y Mendoza." This suggested that Document 2 was the first to be forged or reconstructed, and that Baltasar and the person who wrote out the papers in Group B took note of the signature with an "y" and incorporated this form in all other documents of the forged/reconstructed series. When the complete file of papers was presented to the exiled Santa Fe cabildo at El Paso del Norte for certification, the scribe of the cabildo apparently noticed the "y" form in the signature on Document 2, the earliest in date in the entire file and consequently probably placed at the beginning, and incorporated this form in the texts of the certifications dated October 3 and 8, 1684. Later documents in the Domínguez de Mendoza papers, drawn up in Mexico and in Spain, sometimes employed the "de" form and sometimes the "y" form. This might also indicate, alternatively, that either form was acceptable and that consistency of usage was not particularly important.

A few comments should be made concerning the signatures of the governors and their secretaries on the documents in Groups A and B and the wax seals of the governors that are attached to all of them. With regard to the seals, it is impossible to form any conclusions. In some cases the photographer making the copies of the originals did not turn back the pointed ends of the paper covering the seals before photocopying the documents. In other cases, where we have both genuine and suspect documents bearing the signature and seals of the same governor, the photographs do not show the details of the seals clearly enough to make comparison possible. Concerning the signatures of Governors Argüello Carvajal, Guzmán y Figueroa, and Ugarte de la Concha, we do not possess authentic contemporary originals with which to compare the signatures on these documents. In the case of Governors Manso, Medrano Messía, and Miranda, for whom we have authentic signatures, both in the Domínguez de Mendoza papers and in other manuscripts, there is so much similarity between signatures on the suspect documents and those in the authentic papers that the former could easily pass as genuine. Only a qualified handwriting expert could give a competent opinion in these cases.

In the case of Peñalosa's signature on Document 13, Group B, dated October 6, 1663, there seems to be one obvious point of difference in comparison with the authentic signatures, of which a large number are available. In the authentic signatures there is a forward upsweep of the pen at the beginning of the word "Don," which is lacking in the signature on Document 13.

With regard to the signature of the secretaries of war and government, for which we have genuine originals for comparison, in all cases but one their appearance would arouse no doubt, and here again only an expert could give a valid opinion. But with regard to the signature of Juan Lucero de Godoy on Document 13, Group B, an interesting point was noted in the rubric. This rubric is similar in appearance to his customary one, but a tracing reveals a basic difference, for although the beginning of the outline follows the same direction as in Lucero de Godoy's genuine rubric, at one point instead of a downward right-to-left stroke of the pen, there is an upward turn that creates an extra closed loop and reverses the direction of the pen from there on, although the general appearance of the design is preserved. This is a point of considerable significance. Although on superficial examination the rubrics of a given individual often appear to be different, a careful tracing of the outline will reveal that the basic form is the same and that the pen follows the same course. Occasionally, an individual might change his rubric completely or, even less often, add or reduce it, but while he was using a particular rubric, we should expect it invariably to follow the same outline, even though accidents, such as a different pen, haste, or other circumstances might result in a superficial difference in appearance. Lucero de Godoy's rubric in Document 13 was presumably written on October 6, 1663. Other signatures of Lucero de Godoy are available for a period of several years both before and after this date, and they all follow the same outline. The one in Document 13 is the only example we have of a deviation from the usual course of the pen.

While the weight of evidence points to the Group A and B documents as being forgeries, the possibility exists that they were clumsy reconstructions of titles and commissions that Juan Domínguez de Mendoza had actually been granted early in his career. The originals having been lost in the flight from upper New Mexico, Domínguez de Mendoza could have seen to the creation of new versions, the contents based upon his own shaky memory and including added embellishments designed to strengthen his petition to the viceroy and Crown for the governorship of New Mexico; or Baltasar Domínguez de Mendoza could have reconstructed documents that were lost or damaged during the 1693 shipwreck on the way to Spain.

The future discovery of new documentation related to these matters or critical textual analysis of the supposed Domínguez de Mendoza "forgeries" by

Spanish philologists might yet clarify the problem of authenticity. Fortunately, the questionable documents form a minor part of the Domínguez de Mendoza service record, so that what remains casts welcome light on the history of seventeenth-century New Mexico.

Notes

1. Scholes's written analysis and discussion of the documents in question was only in draft form and incomplete. The editors of this volume added some additional conclusions based on a review of the records, including the possibility that some or all of the documents in question may represent attempts to reconstruct lost or destroyed documents in order to present as complete a portfolio as possible to royal officials in Spain. The main additions to the draft text by Scholes are found at the end of paragraph two of this section, beginning with "... or perhaps a clumsy attempt ... ," and the last two paragraphs of this section. In addition, further analysis revealed that there is a reference in a document considered genuine to a commission as captain of infantry (Document 11, November 19, 1659). Document 3 (December 7, 1644), a document in question, purports to relate to a commission as captain of infantry. The reference in Document 11 appears to support the premise that at least one of the documents in question was a reconstruction of an earlier record of commission that was lost or destroyed. Scholes aptly points out inconsistencies in the questionable documents.

2. Document 62, Petition of Baltasar Domínguez de Mendoza to the Crown, Asking for the Corregimiento of Tlajomulco and Caxititlan, 1694.

3. France V. Scholes, "Royal Treasury Records Relating to the Province of New Mexico, 1596–1683," *New Mexico Historical Review* 50 (April 1975): 20.

4. Ibid.

Introduction

France V. Scholes, Marc Simmons, and José Antonio Esquibel

From Merchant Family to Frontier Soldiers, 1625–1658

Juan Domínguez de Mendoza is worthy of an honored place in the ranks of Spanish soldiers and settlers who helped defend the borderlands province of New Mexico in the seventeenth century. He was born in Mexico City in 1627, receiving the sacrament of baptism on May 30 of that year, with Hernán Vásquez and María de Villegas as his godparents.[1]

Juan's father, Tomé Domínguez, in 1625 was a merchant in Mexico City in partnership with his brother Juan Matheo, who was mentioned shortly afterward as vending wine in the Calle de Tacuba.[2] It is perhaps a safe guess that Juan Domínguez de Mendoza was named for his uncle Juan. One source of evidence points to the father, Tomé, as being about forty-six years of age in 1633.

Juan's mother, Elena de la Cruz, also known as Elena Ramírez de Mendoza, came from a good family, resident in the port of Veracruz on the Mexico Gulf Coast. Her parents, Benito de París and Leonor Francisca de Mendoza, at an unknown date left their native Spain and immigrated to New Spain. In 1625 Elena received formal certification as to her *limpieza de sangre*, that is, that her ancestry was untainted by non-Christian blood, an important qualification for her sons should they ever aspire to high government or ecclesiastical posts. That document was issued nine years after her marriage to Tomé Domínguez, which occurred on August 29, 1616.[3]

Ultimately, the couple had fourteen children, the first born near Puebla, and the remainder in Mexico City, where they moved by 1623. At least three of the sons—Tomé Jr. (usually called *el mozo*, meaning "the younger"), Juan, and Francisco—would relocate in New Mexico with their parents, as did four of the daughters, Damiana, Leonor, Francisca, and Elena, the last one named for her mother.[4]

During the decade 1620–1630, New Mexico affairs were receiving widespread attention in the viceregal capital, especially the rapid progress of the Franciscan *doctrinas* within numerous Pueblo communities, including the building of *conventos* and churches. Merchant Tomé Domínguez apparently became interested in trade with that province, and what followed would change the course of his family history.

By the early 1630s, Tomé established a close relationship with veteran New Mexican missionary fray Estéban de Perea, who had first gone to the Upper Rio Grande in 1610. The Spanish-born friar became the first head (*custos*) of the Franciscan order in New Mexico in 1617, serving a five-year term. The years 1627–1628 found him in Mexico City, purchasing and assembling provisions for shipment north on the next Franciscan supply caravan. It is thought that Tomé Domínguez may have initially made Perea's acquaintance at that time, but if he sold him wine or other supplies, the specific records that might confirm this have not yet been found.[5]

Since the royal treasury was funding New Mexico's booming evangelization program and expending large sums on food, clothing, hardware, medicines, books, paper, and ecclesiastical furnishings, as well as on wagons and draft animals, opportunities were plentiful for enterprising businessmen to become involved and reap profits. Not only could they expect to make large sales to purchasing agents, such as Perea, but they could also attach their own wagon loads of merchandise to the Franciscans' northbound caravans, which were protected by a military escort.

That is what Tomé Domínguez did in 1631. So far as we know, it was his first venture into the New Mexico market, and he found the commercial possibilities attractive. When he returned home in the second half of that year, he carried a packet (*pliego*) of official dispatches consigned to his care by Father Perea and destined for the Holy Office of the Inquisition. Perea was the agent for the Inquisition in New Mexico. Tomé's role as a messenger can be interpreted as a measure of the confidence placed in him by the Franciscan priest. Indeed, in a letter, Perea identified him as "a trustworthy resident of Mexico City."[6] By 1633, Domínguez was back in New Mexico, where he spent several months before joining the return caravan. Once more Father Perea placed important documents in his hands for delivery to the Inquisition. Their friendship, now firmly established, was no doubt mutually advantageous.[7]

Tomé Domínguez had fallen into debt, however, and being unable to satisfy as many as four of his creditors, among them the estate of one Pedro de Ibarra, to which he owed 1,100 pesos, he was arrested and imprisoned in Mexico City on June 27, 1634. By late the following year, he had been released and was heading back to New Mexico, apparently making his third trip to that distant land.[8]

By now, it was clear that Domínguez had gained prestige and influence in the local New Mexican power structure. He was in the Villa de Santa Fe in October 1636 when he auctioned eight oxen from the estate of Francisco Gómez de Torres.[9] A couple of months later, as the Franciscan supply caravan assembled at the Indian pueblo of Socorro in preparation for its return home to Mexico City during mid-December 1636, Tomé Domínguez, by order of the provisional governor Francisco Martínez de Baeza, was commissioned as captain and *cabo de despacho* (special-duties officer) of the military escort guarding the wagon train on the months-long journey to the viceregal capital of New Spain. Further, Governor Martínez de Baeza placed him in charge of his personal shipment of local products that he was sending out of the province to be sold.[10]

By June 1637 creditors in Mexico City once again sought justice in the failure of Tomé Domínguez to pay his debts. The estate of Hernán Delgado, a deceased surgeon, represented by Juan Gutiérrez and his wife, Francisca Delgado, the daughter of Hernán, petitioned officials for the settlement of Domínguez's outstanding obligations.[11] In time Domínguez resolved his financial difficulties well enough to avoid further imprisonment. His commercial connection to New Mexico apparently offered the attractive prospect of improving his financial and social standing, and this connection set the course for the future legacy of his family.

Domínguez took up permanent residence in New Mexico, although he may have kept a home in Mexico City, since for the next few years he continued to shuttle back and forth in handling his trading ventures. On his trip north in 1642, he sponsored two families willing to settle on the frontier, and subsequently he brought others. His descendants would claim that Tomé had been "one of the first conquerors and settlers of New Mexico, which he entered with thirty families whom he took at his own expense."[12]

It would seem that Tomé Domínguez, having become a citizen of the New Mexican kingdom more than forty years after its founding by Juan de Oñate in 1598, could in no way claim the accolades attached to the title of "a first conqueror and settler." Furthermore, had he actually introduced thirty families at one time, this would have been an event of such magnitude as to leave a blazing mark on the historical record. Clearly, his sponsorship of several smaller parties, over a number of years, became condensed in the minds of his progeny, emerging as a single grand colonizing effort.

When Tomé brought his family members to the raw New Mexico frontier, he settled them upon an estancia situated two leagues north of Sandia

Pueblo. Estancias were mixed farming and stock-raising operations, with the latter activity usually predominating. The Domínguez estate was in the center of a highly fertile area of the Middle Rio Grande Valley. Its adobe house was sufficiently large enough to accommodate the many people, including three priests, who assembled there in February 1660 for the marriage of eldest daughter Damiana to Álvaro de Paredes, a native of Mexico City.[13]

The question arises as to why Tomé Domínguez decided to leave Mexico City, the center of commerce, finance, and government, to relocate in the undeveloped and dangerous kingdom of New Mexico, a place at the end of the earth and lacking in all civilized amenities. Of conditions there in 1639, Governor Martínez de Baeza painted a bleak picture. "It is a land that is very cold in the winter and very hot in summer," he wrote in a report to the viceregal government.[14] Two hundred leagues of empty desert separated the Pueblo of Senecú in the Socorro Valley from the mining town of San José del Parral, the northernmost community in the neighboring kingdom of Nueva Vizcaya. The isolation was crippling to the economy.

Between Senecú and Santa Fe, a distance of fifty leagues, could be found only ten or twelve Spanish farms. The land along the Rio Grande was exceedingly productive, the few settlers irrigating and growing wheat and corn. "They also raise cattle and sheep as in Spain," added the governor. But that positive note was offset by the perennial problem of raiding Apaches, who kept the country in turmoil. They were "warlike and, as barbarians, make unexpected attacks" on the Pueblo Indians, asserted Martínez de Baeza. He further lamented that only two hundred settlers were available who could bear arms, yet they did a good job of punishing the marauders during campaigns.[15]

The administrative center of the colony, the capital of the Villa de Santa Fe, had no more than fifty households; thus, it rated only as "a moderate settlement," in the governor's words. Except for the Indian pueblos, New Mexico held no other communities.[16] So what was the attraction for Tomé Domínguez?

The answer is not readily available. The little wealth in New Mexico, in the form of local products such as hides, salt, piñon nuts, rough textiles, and livestock on the hoof, while perhaps making an occasional trading expedition there worthwhile, could scarcely have justified a successful merchant giving up his business in a metropolis like Mexico City and withdrawing to the thoroughly unpromising domain of the Rio Grande, on the outer margins of the viceroyalty.

Records of the period, however, indicate that Domínguez's commercial dealings had soured, no doubt because of his serious debts. That being the case, poor beleaguered New Mexico, with which he had become familiar in recent years, and where he had valuable contacts, might have seemed like a good place to escape his creditors and get a new start.

Moreover, he may have reckoned that the kingdom of New Mexico was bound to turn around, grow, and prosper, and that by his being in on the ground floor his own fortunes would advance. As one of a crowd of merchants in Mexico City, Tomé was a very small fish in an enormous pond, but in New Mexican society, as he discovered on his previous business trips, he was automatically ranked as a big fish. His instincts, if those are what were guiding him, were right on target, for in the last decade and a half of his life on the Rio Grande, he saw improvement in his personal finances, and marriages of his children into prominent families of the local gentry, and two of his sons began their rise to positions of leadership in the kingdom.

Sometime in the 1650s, one of the sons, Tomé el Mozo, moved south with his family and established a prosperous estancia four leagues below the Isleta Pueblo church, in the vicinity of today's village of Tomé.[17] His father, Tomé el Viejo (the elder), died during 1660 or the early months of 1661, and his mother soon afterward. Tomé Domínguez de Mendoza, and his wife, Catalina López Mederos, had five sons, Tomé III, Juan, Diego, Francisco, and Antonio, along with one daughter, Juana. While building his flourishing estate in the Isleta jurisdiction, Tomé served in various public offices, both civil and military. Among his appointments, on at least two occasions, was that of acting governor.[18]

Juan Domínguez de Mendoza, at some undetermined date, developed his own estancia, located three leagues below the Tiwa pueblo of Alameda and five leagues above Isleta. Juan's property, which he called the Hacienda de Atrisco, was on the west bank of the Rio Grande, evidently within the present boundaries of the city of Albuquerque.[19] According to available records, after Tomé went down to Isleta, he and Juan took opposite sides in the festering Church–state conflict, a bitterly fought episode that will be described shortly. Whether the brothers' partisanship had a serious impact upon their personal relations is unknown.[20]

The date of Juan Domínguez de Mendoza's marriage to the prominent doña Isabel Durán y Chaves, also known as doña Isabel Chaves de Bohórquez, has not surfaced. She was the daughter of don Pedro Durán y Chaves by a first wife whose name is not known from surviving records, but whose second wife was doña Elena Domínguez de Mendoza, a sister of Juan and Tomé.[21] The estate of don Pedro Durán y Chaves was located south of the pueblo of Sandia, and her uncle, don Fernando Durán y Chaves, maintained an estate at El Tunque, north of the pueblo of Sandia in the same area as several members of the Domínguez de Mendoza family.[22]

Doña Isabel was also a first cousin of Cristóbal Durán y Chaves, who married Juan Domínguez de Mendoza's niece, doña Catalina Domínguez de Mendoza y López Mederos, daughter of Tomé Domínguez de Mendoza. Suffice it to say that this complicated matrimonial picture cemented the firm alliance between the influential Domínguez de Mendoza and Durán y Chaves families, a union that often, although not invariably, led to cooperation in matters of politics and business.[23]

Juan Domínguez de Mendoza and doña Isabel Durán y Chaves, as best as can be determined, had four children. Their eldest son, Baltasar, was born about 1659, and a younger son named Juan was born about 1664. In addition, the couple had at least two daughters, María, who wed Diego Lucero de Godoy, and a second daughter, name unknown, but who became the wife of Diego de Hinojos.[24]

The large, even baronial, Hacienda de Atrisco, with its orchard and garden, and including its surrounding pastureland, served as the residence for Juan Domínguez de Mendoza's immediate family and his retainers. At the time of the 1680 Pueblo Revolt, the substantial house at Atrisco briefly became a refuge for survivors, whom Domínguez de Mendoza sheltered and fed before the general flight southward. As soon as the structure was abandoned, Indian rebels moved in to sack and burn it, as happened to estates throughout the Upper Rio Grande Valley.[25]

Almost from the time of his arrival in New Mexico in the early 1640s, down to the catastrophe of the Pueblo Revolt, Juan Domínguez de Mendoza was regularly engaged in exploring expeditions and punitive campaigns against hostile Indians, prompting historians John L. Kessell and Rick Hendricks to characterize him as "the colony of New Mexico's most experienced military veteran."[26] As a result, details contained in his personal service record reveal valuable information on the mechanics and structure involved in defending the province during the seventeenth century.

Prior to the revolt, there were no standing troops in New Mexico. Rather, all able-bodied men, Spaniards and Pueblo Indians, were required to serve as temporary militia, "at their own cost," whenever called up for duty. When poor citizens and Indians lacked food and horses for a campaign, the governors were in the habit of making levies upon the Franciscan conventos to furnish both, as a contribution to the protection and welfare of the realm and as a service to the Crown. Companies of militia draftees were formed at the beginning of each campaign and disbanded at its conclusion. The only recompense the men might receive was a share of any spoils seized.[27]

Military officers were drawn from the small provincial upper class and received their appointments directly from the governor. The ranks, beginning with alférez (ensign), extended upward through *teniente, capitán, sargento mayor, maestre de campo* (field marshal), lieutenant general, and general. Upon the organization of a campaign, the governor at Santa Fe summoned the officers-to-be and handed over their commissions, which had the words *de campaña* after the rank, indicating that the appointment was valid only for the duration of the mission at hand. Once it was completed, the officer received a formal discharge, surrendering his commissioned rank, returning to his current military rank or back to civilian status if not a career soldier.[28]

The officer of highest rank for any particular operation became the troop commander. Beside his commission, he was issued a set of campaign instructions that outlined the objectives and the procedures to be followed. When his assignment was complete, he obtained, along with his discharge of commission, a formal certification to that effect, which could include recognition of his success, or alternatively a reprimand for any dereliction of duty. A positive certification was highly coveted by men like the ambitious Juan Domínguez de Mendoza, since it could be used in seeking favors from the king, such as preferment for political office.[29]

Another category of officership, beyond that of campaign officer, also existed. A new governor, upon assuming his executive chair, was permitted to commission a small cadre of staff officers who held their position until the end of the governor's term, or upon dismissal by the same governor. They assisted him in a variety of ceremonial and administrative functions. The alférez real, or royal standard bearer, for instance, was an honorific rank and title bestowed upon the keeper and raiser of His Majesty's flag. It was a highly visible and sought-after post. Both Juan Domínguez de Mendoza and his son Baltasar submitted papers claiming to have been awarded the office and rank of alférez real in their youth.[30] The authenticity of their documents, however, remains questionable.

In the course of his long career, through the administrations of fifteen different governors, Domínguez de Mendoza held practically every military rank available, multiple times (see Table 2 for an account of his appointments and ranks). As a staff officer, usually with a commission of maestre de campo, but sometimes with that of a lieutenant general, he served as provincial royal inspector (*visitador*), as inspector of the Franciscan supply caravan, and four times as lieutenant governor of New Mexico. The one thing that he most craved that eluded him to the end of his life was the governorship, which normally carried with it the superior military rank of captain general.[31]

In the service records of Juan Domínguez de Mendoza is a series of documents dating 1643 to 1653 in the form of commissions and certifications, which purport to show several staff and field (campaign) ranks granted him

TABLE 2
Chronological sequence of commissions/titles of Juan Domínguez de Mendoza, 1643–1686

Date	Holding Rank	Commission/Title	Governor	Other titles mentioned and # of years in New Mexico
*10-12-43	*Alférez*	*Alférez Real*	Pacheco	More than 3 years in NM (ca. 1640)
*12-7-44	Captain	Captain of Infantry for the and royal standard of the *Casas Reales*	Argüello	More than 10 years in NM (ca. 1634 or earlier)
*4-14-46	*Maestre de Campo*	Captain and Commander of all military forces	Gúzman	
*4-15-50	Captain	Lieutenant general, *justicia mayor*, and captain general for inspection of the Río Abajo area	Ugarte	
*11-10-52	*Alférez*	Captain of Cavalry	Samaniego	*Alférez Real* under Samaniego; more than 10 years in New Mexico (ca. 1642 or earlier)
*1-12-53	Captain	Certification of services (no other titles)	Samaniego	
9-13-53	*Alférez*	Certification of services (no other titles)	Ugarte	
10-15-58	*Maestre de Campo* and *visitador general*	*Maestre de Campo*	Manso	
8-30-59	*Alférez*	Captain of mounted harquebusiers	López de Mendizábal	Held many times the office of lieutenant governor and captain general

Date	Rank	Office	Governor	Notes
11-19-59	Captain	Alcalde mayor and lieutenant general of Río Abajo	López de Mendizábal	Held many times the offices of alférez, commander and captain of Spanish Infantry
5-7-62	Captain	Escudero	Peñalosa	
10-6-63	Maestre de Campo	Lt. Captain General and Vistador	Peñalosa	Served 25 years (ca. 1638) in New Mexico; ordinary soldier, sargento, alférez, captain of infantry, many times sargento mayor of the kingdom, maestre de campo of the kingdom, maestre de campo of campaign three times, military commander and chief in active wars, many times lt. governor and captain general and visitador of the kingdom
1-7-64	Captain alcalde ordinario of Villa de Santa Fe, lt. governor visitador general	,	Peñalosa	
6-25-65	General	Lt. Governor and Captain General of Río Arriba	Villanueva	Served as alférez, captain, vistador general, lt. governor, alcalde ordinario de primer voto
12-16-66	General	Lt. Governor and captain general of the Río Abajo, Villanueva		
2-10-67	General	Lt. Governor and Captain General of these provinces	Villanueva	
5-1-69	Captain	Encomendero	Medrano	Served more than 25 years as soldier (since ca. 1644) as alférez, captain, lt. governor of these provinces, alcalde ordinario of Santa Fe, and as commander in campaign

* Denotes questionable document; presumed fraudulent or perhaps a reconstructed record.

Date	Holding Rank	Commission/Title	Governor	Other titles mentioned and # of years in New Mexico
9-11-70	Captain	Maestre de Campo of the tercio (regiment)	Medrano	Served more than 20 years as soldier (since ca.1650) sargento, alférez, captain of infantry, commander and chief of different troops
6-27-71	Maestre de Campo	Sargento Mayor of the kingdom	Medrano	Served His Majesty more than 26 years (since ca. 1645)
6-27-71	General	Maestre de Campo and General of kingdom	Miranda	Alférez in campaign under Argüello, lt. governor under Peñalosa, Alcalde ordinario during Miranda's 1st term, lt. governor and visitador of royal supply train under Villanueva, maestre de campo of campaign, sargento mayor and encomendero under Medrano
8-5-71	General, maestre de campo of the kingdom	Lt. Governor and Captain General	Miranda	
1-26-72	Maestre de Campo, encomendero	Certification of Services	Medrano	Served as maestre de campo of kingdom within the last three years; hidalgo
7-15-73	Maestre de Campo	Maestre de Campo in Campaign	Miranda	Served his Majesty more than thirty years (ca. 1643); held the posts of alférez, captain of infantry and cavalry, sargento mayor, maestre de campo of the kingdom, lt. governor under Miranda, and civil posts, including alcalde ordinario of the Villa de Santa Fe

1-5-75	Maestre de Campo	Maestre de Campo in Campaign	Miranda	Served as alférez, adjutant, captain, sargento mayor, maestre de campo, lt. governor and captain general
9-24-75	Maestre de Campo	Military Commander and Chief	Treviño	Lt. governor on five occasions, many times as maestre de campo of the kingdom, commander, chief and leader in campaign
7-1-76	Maestre de Campo	Military Commander and Chief	Treviño	
7-12-78	Maestre de Campo	Lt. Governor and Captain General	Otermín	
10-28-78	Maestre de Campo	Lt. Captain General in Campaign	Otermín	
11-26-78	Maestre de Campo	Encomendero		Served more than 28 years in New Mexico (ca. 1650) as alférez, captain, sargento mayor, maestre de campo, commander of troops, lt. governor and captain general in campaign
8-17-79	Maestre de Campo	Maestre de Campo in Campaign	Otermín	
11-9-81	Maestre de Campo	Lt. General of Cavalry	Otermín	Served His Majesty more than forty years (ca. 1641) as alférez, captain, sargento mayor, maestre de campo in campaigns, and lt. governor and captain general
10-13-83	Maestre de Campo	Certification of Services	Otermín	Served as alférez, captain, sargento mayor, maestre de campo, commander and chief of troops in campaign, lt. general of the kingdom, and alcalde ordinario of the Villa de Santa Fe
11-29-83	Maestre de Campo	Commander	Petriz de Cruzate	Served as a simple soldier, squadron leader, alférez, captain of cavalry, sargento mayor of the kingdom, maestre de campo, commander and chief, alcalde mayor and captain of war, and lt. governor under Otermín, and lt. governor and captain general under Villanueva

Date	Holding Rank	Commission/Title	Governor	Other titles mentioned and # of years in New Mexico
6-23-1684	Maestre de Campo	Certification of Service		
10-3-1684	Maestre de Campo	Certification of Services	Cabildo of Villa de Santa	Served His Majesty at his own expense since 1640, when he entered the kingdom; his father brought twelve families to New Mexico at his own cost. His posts include: title of alférez issued by Gov. Pacheco; captain of infantry issued by Gov. Argüello; captain and commander issued by Gov. Gúzman, lt. general of the kingdom issued by Gov. Ugarte; captain of cavalry and patent of hidalguía issued by Gov. Samaniego; maestre de campo and visitador general issued by Gov. Manso; captain of infantry, alcalde mayor and lt. captain general of the Río Abajo and Salinas jurisdictions issued by Gov. López de Mendizábal; visitador general of the kingdom, lt. captain general, and title of encomienda issued by Peñalosa; lt. governor and captain general, and two posts as visitador issued by Gov. Villanueva; maestre de campo, sargento mayor of the kingdom, and title of encomienda issued by Gov. Medrano; maestre de campo of the kingdom, lt. governor and captain general, and two titles of maestre de campo of campaigns issued by Gov. Miranda; two titles of captain and commander issued by Gov. Treviño; title of encomienda, four titles of lt. captain general, and title of encomienda issued by Gov. Otermín

4-24-1686	Maestre de Campo	Attested Copy of Certification	Two certifications issued by Gov. Ugarte; one certification issued by Gov. Samaniego; captain of infantry, and alcalde mayor and lt. captain general issued by Gov. López de Mendizábal; title of encomienda issued by Gov. Peñalosa; lt. governor and captain general of the Río Abajo, two titles of visitador, and lt. governor and captain general of the kingdom; maestre de campo of campaign; sargento mayor of the kingdom and title of encomienda issued by Gov. Medrano; maestre de campo of the kingdom, lt. governor and captain general of the kingdom, and two titles as maestre de campo of campaigns issued by Gov. Miranda; title of leader, commander and chief of campaign issued by Gov. Treviño; five titles as lt. captain general in campaign, and title of encomienda issued by Gov. Otermín; and a copy of a probanza and privileges issued by Gov. Martínez de Baeza

by governors of the period. They begin with alférez real and include captain of infantry, captain of cavalry, maestre de campo, and lieutenant governor. The records makes reference to military expeditions that Domínguez de Mendoza led against Apaches, Navajos, the Zuñi, and finally the rebellious Mansos in the El Paso del Río del Norte district. Apart from the fact that he would have been in only his teens and early twenties during that decade, we find significant internal evidence that the documents were forged at a much later date. The nature and purpose of the supposed forgeries have already been discussed in the preface to this study.[32]

The dubious character of this part of the documentary record leaves us in considerable doubt as to the young Domínguez de Mendoza's official activities during his first years or so in New Mexico. From later genuine documents, it appears likely that his actual rank in that early period was seldom, if ever, higher than alférez, or ensign, which is sometimes described as a sub-lieutenancy. In any case, the first episode of an exploratory or military nature involving Juan Domínguez de Mendoza and for which we possess supporting documentation is the expedition of don Diego de Guadalajara to Texas in 1654.

That enterprise had its origins in the work of an earlier party sent to the same area in 1650 by Governor Hernando de Ugarte y la Concha at the orders of the viceroy of New Spain.[33] It was headed by a pair of captains, Hernán Martín Serrano and Diego del Castillo, who commanded a small troop of about twenty-nine soldiers and an uncertain number of Indian auxiliaries.[34] From Santa Fe, they traveled southeast four hundred to five hundred miles, to the nation of the friendly Jumano Indians in south central Texas. On the Río de las Nueces, they found a Jumano encampment where they remained for six months. Much time was passed gathering shells from the river and burning them to recover freshwater pearls.

The little company also explored south and east, reaching the limits of the populous Caddoan-speaking Tejas. Upon the party's return to Santa Fe, a full report, along with a quantity of pearls, was delivered to the governor. Ugarte y la Concha, using Juan Domínguez de Mendoza as a messenger, sent both to the viceroy in Mexico City, who was so impressed that he ordered a follow-up expedition.[35]

That undertaking was organized by the new governor in Santa Fe, Juan de Samaniego y Jaca, in whose company Domínguez de Mendoza returned from Mexico City. In due course, Samaniego y Jaca appointed Sargento Mayor don Diego de Guadalajara, a native of Oaxaca, who owned a prosperous estancia downriver from the Pueblo of Isleta, as commander of the expedition in 1654, with the commission as lieutenant governor.[36] His force of thirty soldiers and two hundred Christian Indians marched approximately over the same route that the Martín Serrano–Castillo expedition had used four years earlier. Like his predecessors, Guadalajara encountered the Jumanos on the Nueces River, only now they complained of being hard-pressed by their enemies, the Cuitaos (possibly Tonkawas), who dwelled along their eastern flank. Guadalajara went into the camp on the river and promptly dispatched Captain Andrés López with a dozen soldiers to accompany a small army of Jumanos to seek out the Cuitaos.[37]

When the tribe was found, it made a hostile demonstration and quickly sent runners to summon its allies, the neighboring Escanjaques and Aijados. A fierce battle followed, lasting a full day. The Spaniards and the Jumanos emerged victorious, and López's men took back to their camp two hundred prisoners and bales of deerskins and buffalo hides. Now that warring tribes blocked any further advance eastward, Guadalajara cut short his stay and returned to Santa Fe with the prisoners and booty captured from the Cuitaos.

The principal details surrounding this expedition and the one that preceded it derived from a narrative report, known as the *Informe*, written by fray Alonso de Posada in March 1686 while he was in Mexico City. Posada specifically referred to Juan Domínguez de Mendoza as a participant in the expedition, and Posada twice mentioned that Domínguez de Mendoza was in Mexico City in 1686.[38] Jack D. Forbes indicates that Posada may have obtained his information about the thirty-year-old Guadalajara episode from Domínguez de Mendoza, who probably served in the capacity of an alférez.[39]

Be that as it may, Domínguez de Mendoza much later would produce a Certification of Services, allegedly issued to him by Governor Samaniego y Jaca at Santa Fe, January 12, 1653. In that document, the newly arrived governor speaks of Domínguez de Mendoza accompanying him on his trip from Mexico City, the New Mexican being there on messenger service, having brought to the viceroy the pearls and the report of the expedition to the Jumanos. That part appears to be true, but not what follows.[40]

According to Samaniego y Jaca, after reaching Santa Fe he sent Juan Domínguez de Mendoza at the head of a new expedition to obtain more pearls from the Río de la Nueces, during which he fought and defeated the Escanjaques and Aijados in a three-day battle. The Cuitaos are not mentioned. Thereafter, Domínguez de Mendoza marched back to Santa Fe, escorting sixteen hundred prisoners and 125 Christian Indians that he had liberated from captivity. All this service was performed at his own expense, as had been the 1650 expedition, which he also led and which resulted in his "new discovery" of the kingdom of Texas.[41]

In this forged document, Domínguez de Mendoza clearly usurped credit for leadership of the don Diego de Guadalajara expedition and, for good measure, that of the Martín Serrano–Castillo expedition as well. The dates in this contrived certification are badly askew, while details of his supposed fight with the Escanjaques and Aijados are considerably at odds with those given by Posada in his *Informe*. At this point, all we can accept is that Juan Domínguez de Mendoza was a member of the Guadalajara party, in a quite junior status, and the same thing may, or may not, have been true with regard to the Martín Serrano–Castillo venture. It should be noted that thirty years later, when he was preparing to embark upon a major expedition from El Paso del Río del Norte to the Jumanos on the Río de la Nueces, Domínguez de Mendoza cited his earlier experience with that tribe as one of his qualification for command. None of his contemporaries seem to have disputed him on that point.[42]

A Tempestuous Decade, 1659–1669

In July 1659, don Bernardo López de Mendizábal arrived in the Villa de Santa Fe to assume the governorship, replacing his predecessor, don Juan Manso de Contreras. López de Mendizábal quickly observed that New Mexico's foremost problem was posed by the Apaches, who waged unremitting warfare upon Spaniards and Pueblo Indians, for the purpose of seizing booty and taking Christian captives to be used or traded as slaves.

Within two weeks of taking office, the new governor sent out a reconnaissance party of ten Spaniards and thirty Pueblos under Captain Luis Martín Serrano to assess the situation. The officer soon returned with two Apache prisoners, who revealed under interrogation that their tribe was fully committed to continuation of its thievery and murders. This information, according to López de Mendizábal, led him to field a punitive expedition composed of forty mounted harquebusiers and eight hundred Christian Indians. Their orders were to inflict punishment upon the enemy Apaches wherever they could be found. Juan Domínguez de Mendoza received the governor's nod as leader of the undertaking.[43]

No campaign diary or itinerary has been located, but Governor López de Mendizábal afterward stated that "a brilliant victory" had been achieved. This he credited to Juan Domínguez de Mendoza, whose enthusiasm, courage, and leadership ability produced the desired result. As reward, he appointed him *alcalde mayor* over the jurisdictions of Sandia and Isleta and commissioned him lieutenant captain general in the Río Abajo, that is, military commander of the lower half of the province.[44]

A radically different picture of the purpose and effects of this military episode is furnished by fray Juan Ramírez, the Franciscan custos, headquartered at Santo Domingo Pueblo. Domínguez de Mendoza departed with his men on September 4, 1659, and four days later Ramírez composed a letter, endorsed by his fellow clerics, to be sent to authorities of the Inquisition and which contained a litany of charges against Bernardo López de Mendizábal.

One of the first complaints concerned the expedition then in the field. Although acknowledging that the Apaches posed a serious threat to the conventos and Pueblo people, the friar objected to López de Mendizábal's dispatching such a large body of troops to the interior, inasmuch as it left the settlements exposed to attack and possible destruction. Ramírez further declared that the army had gone forth precisely when crops were maturing, so that 840 cornfields faced ruin without anyone to harvest them. The loss would merely add to the food shortage in New Mexico, already critical.

The entire campaign, Ramírez charged, was a pretext for acquiring Apache captives, both men and women, that Governor López de Mendizábal could send south to the mines at San José del Parral in Nueva Vizcaya to be sold into slavery. The accusation of illegal slave trafficking by the governor, in fact, would be leveled against him repeatedly during his three years in office.[45]

In that interval, Juan Domínguez de Mendoza remained a staunch ally, and some would say a lackey, of the wily López de Mendizábal. Simple opportunism—a reaching for profit and power—seemingly prompted him to cast his fortunes with a man whose reckless behavior should have sounded a clear warning. Ambitiously, Domínguez de Mendoza sought favors from representatives of the royal Crown, namely, the governors, with whom he often shared a common political ideology. However, his partisanship in favor of the López de Mendizábal faction very nearly landed him in the clutches of the Inquisition, as actually happened with four other New Mexican supporters of the governor. Indeed, it was Governor López de Mendizábal's own fierce anticlericalism that eventually brought him to a prison cell of the Inquisition.

In the first decades of the seventeenth century, an evil tradition of rivalry and conflict developed between civil and religious authorities within New Mexico. Petty quarrels over jurisdictional issues grew into bitter feuds that split the fabric of New Mexican society into warring camps. In early 1642, shortly after leaving office, ex-governor Luis de Rosas was murdered in the night by a band of masked men. Although he had been guilty of brutally beating two clergymen, the Church did not appear to be directly implicated in his assassination. The Franciscan custos, however, refused permission for Rosas to be buried in consecrated ground, and most of the men involved in the murder were political supporters of the Franciscans.[46]

The scandalous episode forced a lull in the church–state conflict that lasted until López de Mendizábal arrived on the scene in 1659. His penchant for pomposity and determination to establish his authority over matters that the clergy considered to be within their domain at once led to a resurgence of the old animosities. For personal reasons, Juan Domínguez de Mendoza chose to side with the governor against the churchmen.

As a petty official in central New Spain, López de Mendizábal had demonstrated his disdain for the clergy. But upon rising to the lofty status of a governor in New Mexico, he discovered new ways to persecute those in the Church who might oppose his policies and conduct. One early bone of contention was his open encouragement of the *catzina* (kachina) dances performed by the Pueblo Indians, which were a central feature of the Native religion. Since the days of earliest settlement, the Franciscan friars labored, with little success, to stamp out these masked dances dedicated to rain-making and promotion of fertility. They considered them evidence of devil-worship and found the sexual gestures associated with the rituals to be particularly offensive.

Notwithstanding, Governor López de Mendizábal declared that he saw nothing diabolical in this. Rather, the catzina performance appeared quite harmless, not unlike the colorful folk dances that one observed in Spain. He said that as long as he was governor, the catzina dances could continue. He even ordered some of the Pueblo towns to resume the custom where it had been successfully halted by the friars.[47]

In November 1660, the governor paid an official visit to Isleta Pueblo, accompanied by a retinue that included Juan Domínguez de Mendoza. As it happened, Juan's brother Tomé was by chance in the village when the party arrived and afterward gave a formal deposition as to what occurred. Tomé Domínguez de Mendoza, unlike his sibling, was a staunch supporter of the proclerical faction, and his serious disagreements earlier with López de Mendizábal had led the governor to remove him from the office of *alcalde ordinario* of the Villa de Santa Fe.

Tomé Domínguez de Mendoza in his deposition would charge the governor with granting the Isletans permission to hold a catzina dance, which he himself attended along with his escort. Tomé protested the "superstitious" spectacle, among whose participants was one dancer in "an ugly costume, like a devil, with horns on the head and a bear skin . . . a horrible thing."[48] His remonstrance was ignored by the chief executive.

As his term progressed, López de Mendizábal became increasingly belligerent in his assaults upon the religious and in his mistreatment of those settlers like Tomé Domínguez de Mendoza who rallied to the defense of the Franciscans. He selected as his right hand a mestizo of dubious reputation, Captain Nicolás de Aguilar, for the express purpose of tyrannizing his Franciscan foes, believing that this individual could cause them the most harm. But the day of reckoning for New Mexico's governor was fast approaching.

Both the viceroy and officers of the Holy Office of the Inquisition at Mexico City received disturbing reports regarding the behavior of López de Mendizábal. The Franciscan order in late 1660 selected fray Alonso de Posada as the new custos for New Mexico, whereupon the Inquisition seized the opportunity to appoint him also as their special agent with broad powers to investigate affairs on the Upper Rio Grande. At the same time, the viceroy removed López de Mendizábal from office and named as replacement don Diego de Peñalosa y Briceño.

Father Posada arrived in New Mexico from the viceregal capital on April 29, 1661, and immediately orchestrated a massive investigation, taking depositions from friars and numerous residents. One of the first to testify was Tomé Domínguez de Mendoza, who presented lengthy statements regarding every aspect of the López de Mendizábal administration based on personal observations. Posada in addition directed the friars to collect and burn all the catzina masks they could find, as the best means to end the dances permanently. Some sixteen hundred masks consequently were destroyed, an act that must have traumatized the Pueblo Indians.[49]

Ultimately, Posada brought a series of charges against the ex-governor, among them heresy, practicing Judaism, suspicion of witchcraft, and illicit relations with Apache women servants, all religious crimes. Another accused the defendant of selling the office of lieutenant captain general to Juan Domínguez de Mendoza for three hundred pesos. At the beginning of October 1662, López de Mendizábal left Santa Fe under arrest and in chains, bound for trial before the tribunal of the Holy Office. Before his case could be completed, however, he died in the dungeons of the Inquisition on September 16, 1664.[50]

When López de Mendizábal was first arrested in New Mexico, four of his leading accomplices were also seized and enchained: Nicolás de Aguilar, Francisco Gómez Robledo, Diego Romero, and Cristóbal de Anaya Almazán. With the ex-governor and his wife, doña Teresa de Aguilera y Roche, who had also been arrested, they were transported down the Camino Real to face the tribunal of the Inquisition in Mexico.

Strangely, Juan Domínguez de Mendoza was not among them. Although implicated in testimony following the arrest of his brother-in-law, Cristóbal de Anaya Almazán, the most that the friars could come up with against Domínguez de Mendoza was a charge made by his *comadre*, doña Ana Moreno de Lara, who several years earlier had confided to fray Tomás de Alvarado about amorous advances toward her on the part of Domínguez de Mendoza. Alvarado revealed this information in May 1662 in an attempt to formulate a case against Domínguez de Mendoza for submission to the tribunal of the Inquisition, which also included complaints of disrespect for the clergy.[51]

Domínguez de Mendoza was not easily intimidated by the threat of arrest by the Inquisition. Upon hearing of the arrests of his fellow supporters of López de Mendizábal, Domínguez de Mendoza grabbed weapons and fled his house, declaring that should officials next come for him, he would resist to the death before being taken. Moreover, he pronounced the four already in custody to be cowards for not avoiding arrest.

Posada's secretary and notary, fray Salvador de Guerra, who reported on Domínguez de Mendoza's reaction, described him as "a man conspicuously inimical to the ecclesiastics who persecuted them by his writings, prevented them from administering the holy sacraments, and who beat the Indians in the churches . . . to prevent them from serving their spiritual pastors." Although Domínguez de Mendoza came under fire from other sources as well, he escaped indictment. The accusations were not substantial enough to bring about any formal charges of heresy against him. C. L. Sonnichsen has remarked, "Obviously the Inquisition could have finished Domínguez . . . , but it didn't, perhaps because he was next to indispensable in the harried province."[52] His military acumen, wealth, and social and political influence make that a plausible explanation.

In 1662, Juan Domínguez de Mendoza and his elder brother Francisco traveled down the Camino Real to Mexico City, bearing dispatches addressed to authorities of the Office of the Inquisition and royal officials of the Real Audiencia de Nueva España. Owing to delays, they did not reach the viceregal capital until late 1663. Shortly, the two were summoned to appear before the tribunal of the Inquisition and presented testimony regarding the recent tumultuous events in New Mexico. On June 20, 1663, Juan Domínguez de Mendoza declared he was thirty-four years of age and that he was staying in Mexico City on the Calle de Santa Catarina Martir in the house of a mestizo named Francisco. He affirmed that he was a *vecino* of the Río del Norte in the provinces of New Mexico in the jurisdiction of the Pueblo de la Isleta.[53]

Domínguez de Mendoza used the occasion to mount a vigorous defense of former governor don Bernardo López de Mendizábal, his recent benefactor who was then incarcerated, and at the same time he rebuked New Mexico's Franciscan friars for their behavior, thereby demonstrating his strong anticlerical bent. He reserved the bitterest words for his critic, the secretary fray Salvador de Guerra, whom he condemned for allegedly beating a Hopi Indian and then trampling him to death with a horse, and for living with various women in a state of concubinage.[54]

The Domínguez de Mendoza brothers made the long journey back to New Mexico, arriving there by early October 1663. At once Juan received an appointment as visitor-general of New Mexico by Governor don Diego de

Peñalosa y Briceño.⁵⁵ The governor also named him as *escudero* (stand-in or trustee) for the encomienda of Sargento Mayor Francisco Gómez Robledo, one of the four jailed associates of López de Mendizábal.⁵⁶ Peñalosa y Briceño, for reasons of his own, backdated the appointment by almost a year and a half to disguise the fact that he had been collecting the revenues of the encomienda for himself since that time.⁵⁷ The governor may have favored Dominguez de Mendoza in this instance, with the hope that it would appease one of his own sharpest critics. Peñalosa y Briceño, whose term was ending, now faced an investigation of his own corrupt administration.

The Spanish institution of the encomienda, introduced in New Mexico by founder Juan de Oñate early in the seventeenth century, was based on the Crown's power to collect tribute from the Indians, on the assumption that as vassals or wards of the government they owed a small annual payment symbolic of their status. Ordinarily, royal treasury officials received this revenue on behalf of the sovereign, but in some instances His Majesty entrusted or "commended" a parcel of Indians to an encomendero, who was allowed to collect the tribute for his own use.

The grant of encomienda carried with it the obligation on the part of the holder to answer the call for military service whenever needed. In New Mexico, the purpose of the grant of tribute, as Peñalosa y Briceño noted pointedly in his 1662 "Appointment as Escudero," was to provide the wages or stipend for the thirty-five designated encomenderos who enjoyed through assignment the tributes from the Pueblo Indians. The encomenderos formed, in effect, a small body of semiprofessional soldiers, serving as the core of the provincial militia.⁵⁸

Beyond their military commitment, encomienda holders were also required to look to the general welfare of their tributary Indians, including assisting them in any litigation that they might initiate. And further, encomenderos in New Mexico were required to establish formal citizenship in the Villa de Santa Fe, maintaining a residence there in addition to the one on their estancias. The purpose was to ensure a pool of competent candidates—men of stature and influence—who could run for the various municipal offices associated with the city council, or cabildo.⁵⁹

The prized grant of encomienda could be passed on to an heir, additionally for "two lives," meaning to a son and grandson, before it reverted to the Crown. If the new holder was a minor son who could not personally meet the military obligations and other duties, then the governor designated an escudero to fulfill them. The escudero received a percentage of the tribute as recompense, while the remainder collected from the Pueblo Indians went to the heir.⁶⁰

Juan Domínguez de Mendoza's appointment as escudero in 1662, on behalf of Francisco Gómez Robledo, was made owing to the imprisonment of the latter. After Gómez Robledo was acquitted by the Inquisition in 1664, his encomienda rights were restored. As an encomendero, Gómez Robledo held rights to the tributes of the following Pueblo communities in whole or in part: all of Tesuque, most of Pecos, half of Acoma, half of Sandia, half of Abó, half of Shongopavi (in Hopi territory), and two and a half parts of Taos. The fractional distribution of Pueblo tributaries to Spanish grantees was commonplace in New Mexico.[61] Fray Salvador de Guerra, reviewing the status of the trusteeship (September 22, 1662), reported that some leading men of the province held as many as ten different shares in encomiendas.[62]

Sometime during 1659–1661, Juan Domínguez de Mendoza was granted the encomienda of the pueblo of Jemez by Governor don Bernardo López de Mendizábal, formerly in the possession of the López de Ocanto family.[63] So far as is known, Domínguez de Mendoza was the first and only member of his family to be so favored, a seemingly strange circumstance given the many services to the Crown rendered by his father and older brothers. The chief explanation may lie in the fact that an encomienda only rarely became vacant and subject to reassignment. Vacancies occurred, for example, upon death of an encomendero who left no son as heir, or upon forfeiture by a holder who failed to meet his military obligation to the government. Juan González Bernal lost his one-third of the encomienda and tributes at Jumanas (or Humanas) pueblo (today's Gran Quivira) by neglecting to appear for an army muster at the Villa de Santa Fe in late 1668. That share was the one assigned to Juan Domínguez de Mendoza the following May 1 by Governor don Juan de Medrano.[64]

Domínguez de Mendoza, however, was not destined to enjoy the income from these sources for long. On September 3, 1670, the Siete Rios Apaches from southeastern New Mexico attacked Jumanos in force, slaying eleven persons, capturing thirty-one, and profaning, then destroying, the church with all of its contents. The entire pueblo was sacked. Governor Medrano, labeling the act an atrocity, bestowed the campaign title of maestre de campo on Domínguez de Mendoza and ordered him to undertake a retaliatory expedition. It met with considerable success but failed to prevent abandonment of Jumanos by 1671.[65]

Domínguez de Mendoza's third grant of encomienda, conferred upon him by Governor don Antonio de Otermín on November 26, 1678, was for an undisclosed share of the Pueblo of Isleta. It had belonged to Maestre de Campo Francisco de Valencia, who died without an heir. As happened with his Jumanos encomienda, Juan Domínguez de Mendoza lost the revenue from this grant very shortly. In the turmoil of the 1680 revolt, all tribute payments ceased, and the encomienda system was never reestablished in New Mexico.[66]

In addition to receiving the economic and social benefits as an encomendero, Juan Domínguez de Mendoza capitalized on important political connections, being elected as alcalde ordinario of the Villa de Santa Fe in January 1664.[67] Governor Peñalosa y Briceño also granted him the military rank of lieutenant captain general of the kingdom, as well as the political title of lieutenant governor, whose duty was to administer the Río Abajo jurisdiction, or the lower half of New Mexico. Among his duties of office, Domínguez de Mendoza monitored the security of that region and attended to judicial matters.

During March 1666, he and a small troop of eleven soldiers went on patrol, scouting for hostile Apaches in the vicinity of Acoma Pueblo. While there, two delegations of Indians from that pueblo approached him to denounce their resident priests, fray Nicolás de Freitas and fray Diego de Santander. They charged the pair with grave mistreatment, including flogging a fellow tribesman for assorted offenses.[68]

Domínguez de Mendoza decided that the accusations were serious enough to deserve further investigation, since it seemed to be a case worthy of review by the Inquisition. Hence, he went to Acoma to learn more from the people there, among them the caciques, or headmen. Afterward, he instructed the Indians not to obey the friars any longer. Subsequently, he submitted a formal report of the matter to both the governor and the custodian of the Franciscan order in New Mexico, who was fray Juan de Paz.

The two Acoma priests were outraged over the action taken against them by the lieutenant governor. They wasted no time in preparing a counter denunciation of Domínguez de Mendoza, depicting themselves as innocent victims of slander and attempting to draw into question his standing as a Catholic.

With a legal investigation and the collection of testimonies in full swing by May 1666, Freitas and Santander leveled serious charges of their own against Domínguez de Mendoza, accusing him of long-standing hostility toward the clergy and of encouraging the Pueblos in years past to perform their catzina dances. Father Nicolás de Freitas wrote that his behavior was so notorious that the public kept asking, "How is it that the Holy Office has not arrested Juan Domínguez?"[69]

The denunciation of Domínguez de Mendoza, upon being forwarded in 1667 to the Inquisition tribunal at Mexico City, was rejected, freeing him for the time being from the threat of formal charges and arrest. This drawn-out incident demonstrates that the lingering animosities from the López de Mendizábal–Peñalosa y Briceño era continued to negatively impact provincial life in New Mexico.

FIGURE 1   Acoma Pueblo looking east, ca. 1880–1890. Denver Public Library, Western History Collection, Ben Wittick (1845–1903), Z-1915.

Through the end of the 1660s, Juan Domínguez de Mendoza remained antagonistic toward the Franciscan friars. He continued to stir their ire with his disrespect for their authority, no doubt bolstered by his previous vindication stemming from charges filed with the Inquisition. Feeling powerless against him, the Franciscan leaders again sought recourse by means of the Inquisition. The next Franciscan commissary in New Mexico, fray Juan Bernal, collected testimony against Domínguez de Mendoza and sent his findings in a letter dated March 15, 1669, to the tribunal of the Inquisition in Mexico City.[70]

A response by Inquisition officials dated October 25, 1669, acknowledged receipt of the letter and chastised fray Juan Bernal for overstepping the bounds of his authority as commissary.[71] They informed Bernal that he inappropriately utilized inquisitional authority in dealing with an issue of "enmity and disrespect toward the religious," which was not an offense warranting review and investigation by the tribunal. Bernal was informed with scolding words that his actions were detrimental to the Office of the Inquisition. Once again, the Franciscans sought and failed to entangle Domínguez de Mendoza in a formal investigation by the Inquisition, hoping to damage his social and political standing in retribution for his outright and persistent disrespect for the religious. Instead, Domínguez de Mendoza continued to be a respected and trustworthy military leader favored by the governors of New Mexico, as well as a generous civic benefactor.

Domínguez de Mendoza's troubles with the friars did not hamper his sponsorship of the celebration of the royal oath and acclamation of the new king, Carlos II, which was publicly acknowledged in the Villa de Santa Fe on October 27, 1669. Upon the death of his father, Felipe IV, Carlos II acceded to the throne in 1665 at age four, with his mother, doña Mariana of Austria, as regent. Serving as alcalde of the Villa de Santa Fe in 1669, Domínguez de Mendoza paid "many ducats" to organize the royal fiestas in honor of Carlos II. As part of the celebration, he "brought out the boy who played the part of the king with all splendor in a triumphal car on the afternoon of the royal oath and the night of the masquerade."[72] Surrounded by the hardship and dangers of frontier life, and beleaguered by political strife, the citizens of New Mexico still managed to take simple pleasure in public festivities that lightened their spirits.

In Defense of the Kingdom, 1670–1678

Problems for New Mexico as a whole intensified in the years 1667 to 1672, as severe drought caused crop failures and famine. The adverse weather conditions also affected the food sources of the Apaches, leading them to increase the frequency and violence of their raids. Punitive expeditions sent forth to stem the tide were no more than marginally successful.

In early September 1670, Apaches from the mountains of Los Sietes Ríos, the modern-day Sacramento Mountains of southeast New Mexico, raided the Humanas Pueblo in the Salinas jurisdiction, ransacked the church, took as many as thirty-one captives, and left eleven people dead. Juan Domínguez de Mendoza accepted the appointment from Governor Juan de Medrano as maestre de campo of a force consisting of thirty Spanish soldiers and three hundred Christian Indians to chase after the marauders and rescue the captives.[73] In the end only six of the captives were rescued.

As Governor Medrano's term of office was ending in early summer 1671, he appointed Juan Domínguez de Mendoza to be "Sargento mayor of this kingdom and provinces," in response to an attack by Apaches on the incoming governor, don Juan de Miranda, and his retinue at the Paraje del Muerto in southern New Mexico. In the incident three people were killed and the mules of three wagons driven away. This appointment placed Domínguez de Mendoza as the third-highest regular military officer in New Mexico. Medrano noted that Domínguez de Mendoza had presented him with the documents in his service record that established him as a man of "merits and quality." [74]

Soon afterward, don Juan de Miranda reached the Villa de Santa Fe and replaced Medrano in the governor's chair. He promptly promoted Juan Domínguez de Mendoza in July 1671 to the superior rank of maestre de campo of the kingdom, that is, supreme commander of military forces, subject only to the governor. In the certificate of promotion, Governor Miranda summarized Domínguez de Mendoza's extensive military career and mentioned that he had been acting governor for an interval during the term (1665–1668) of Governor Fernando de Villanueva. His praise for the newly elevated maestre de campo can only be described as extravagant.[75] On August 5, 1671, Domínguez de Mendoza received an appointment as lieutenant governor and captain general of New Mexico, to act in the capacity as governor while Miranda was away from the Villa de Santa Fe leading a campaign against the Gila Apaches and Siete Rios Apache in southern New Mexico.[76]

That appears curious, to say the least, given Miranda's earlier experience as governor of New Mexico (1664–1665). During that first term, an anti-Miranda faction led by Tomé Domínguez de Mendoza filed grave charges against him, resulting in the governor's arrest, brief imprisonment at Santa Fe, and seizure of his property. Returning to Mexico City, Miranda appealed on the grounds of injustice and was exonerated. Subsequently, his property was returned and he accepted reappointment to the governorship of New Mexico.[77]

Even though he received final vindication, one would think that Miranda might harbor resentment against anyone bearing the Domínguez de Mendoza name. Perhaps, Juan, militarily speaking, really was indispensable, and so the governor, personal feelings aside, promoted him out of necessity. In that case, we could expect him to temper his encomiums.

The decade of the 1670s saw Juan Domínguez de Mendoza campaigning relentlessly against all of the Apache divisions, but none more so than the Apache de Nabajú, who by the following century would be known simply as the Navajo. These Indians then inhabited a rugged country in northwestern New Mexico, south of the San Juan River, or Río Grande as the Spaniards first called it. North of the river lay the beginning of the Ute homeland.

Between the canyons containing tributaries of the San Juan (Río Grande) rose steep-walled heights that the Spanish soldiers referred to as the Casa Fuerte, meaning "the stronghold" of the enemy. Ordinarily, the Navajo resided and farmed on the canyon floors, but in the event they were pursued by troops, in the wake of their own inroads against the pueblo communities and Spanish estancias, they could withdraw to the vast and highly defensible area of the

Casa Fuerte. The surrounding ranges were identified in contemporary Spanish sources as the Navajo Mountains.[78]

By his own claim, Domínguez de Mendoza in his younger days participated in two expeditions of reprisal into the heart of this isolated Navajo domain.[79] Thus, when it came time for him to coordinate a series of large-scale campaigns, beginning in 1675, he was well versed in the geography of those hostile precincts.

Governor don Juan Francisco Treviño (1675–1677) on September 24, 1675, dispatched Juan Domínguez de Mendoza with forty Spaniards and three hundred Pueblo Indian auxiliaries to the Navajo country below the San Juan River. He designated Zía Pueblo as the *plaza de armas*, or assembly and mustering point for the troops. The expedition in its sweep killed and captured numbers of the enemy, liberated Spanish and Pueblo captives, burned milpas (cornfields) and stored grain, and destroyed other possessions.[80]

Although Treviño asserted that his action led to a reduction in Navajo incursions, by the time his successor, don Antonio de Otermín, took office in 1677, hostilities resumed as fiercely as ever. Indeed, the new governor was profoundly dismayed to find the capital itself under assault, noting that Apaches de Nabajú had "committed many killings and robberies in it."[81]

Otermín, on July 12, 1678, provided for a new military expedition against the Navajos of the Casa Fuerte, placing Juan Domínguez de Mendoza in command, with the field rank of lieutenant captain general, leading a contingent of fifty soldiers and four hundred Pueblo Indians. This campaign, too, was launched from Zía, and like its predecessor inflicted "considerable destruction" on the raiders' camp.[82] Otermín specifically instructed Domínguez de Mendoza to "set out to the mountain range of the Piedra Alumbre and march through that territory, where I understand the main part of the said enemies gathered to commit robberies and damages in the jurisdiction of La Cañada, and, finding them, you will punish them."[83]

In addition, friendly overtures by two leaders of the Ute Indians led to an alliance in which Ute warriors would accompany Domínguez de Mendoza. Otermín provided specific instructions to treat these new allies "with all loving kindness so that they may give themselves more fully to intercourse and friendship with us." Lastly, Domínguez de Mendoza and his force were to attempt to locate the bones of Captain Alonso Fernández and Captain Juan de Herrera, who both died "at the hands of the said enemies."

There is no evidence that Domínguez de Mendoza found the remains of the two captains, which the governor had hoped to recover for ecclesiastical burial. However, Otermín commended Domínguez de Mendoza for his successful reprisal against the Navajo, lauding him as "a very honorable soldier and deserving that His Majesty and his royal ministers in his royal name may honor him, rewarding him in accordance with his services." He was credited with rescuing two captive women, destroying fields of corn, taking thirteen horses, and engaging the enemy in battle, resulting in thirty captives. The official discharge, dated August 23, 1678, indicated that the campaign lasted some five weeks.

Notwithstanding, a follow-up expedition became necessary later in the year, after a Navajo war party attacked Acoma Pueblo, apparently with the aim of destroying it. Governor Otermín was so incensed by their audacity that he initially proposed to head a pursuit of the offenders himself. But when he fell ill and was confined to bed, the task once again devolved upon Juan Domínguez de Mendoza, commanding fifty soldiers and four hundred Christian Indian allies. Meeting with another success, his discharge papers indicated that he had burned the settlement of the Indians and won many spoils.[84]

Finally, Domínguez de Mendoza served as co-commander of one last military effort to crush the Navajos of northwestern New Mexico. In August 1679 Otermín sent him to Zía with a large force on the now familiar route to the Casa Fuerte. In developing his strategy, the governor also ordered the secretary of government and war, Francisco Xavier, to lead a second body of troops from Taos, westward to San Juan, with the intention of catching the foe between double hammer blows. The specific outcome of the campaign is not shown in the records available, but no doubt enthusiastic claims of success, similar to those in the earlier venture, were made.[85]

In all of these campaigns against the Navajos, the Spanish armies suffered few casualties. Although their string of victories caused heavy damage to the Indians, they failed to deter depredations. Less than a year after Domínguez de Mendoza's last foray to the San Juan country, the Pueblo Revolt completely transformed the history of European–Indian relations in the region.

Catastrophe and Ruin, 1679–1682

In 1676, fray Francisco de Ayeta, head of the Franciscan order in New Mexico, successfully petitioned the Spanish king for new military and material aid, becoming, in the words of John L. Kessell, "an apt begger."[86] His request, intended to meet the Apache threat, resulted in approval by royal officials of fifty soldiers who were recruited in Mexico City, many of whom had been convicted of crimes and were sentenced to serve as paid soldiers on the frontier. The new reinforcements reached New Mexico in late 1677, by which time Apache assaults had caused partial or complete abandonment of six pueblos. In May 1679 Father Ayeta appealed for an additional fifty men. The Apaches, in fact, grew bolder and intensified attacks on Pueblo communities, conventos, churches, and Spanish estancias. If the situation continued unchecked, he warned, "a conflagration . . . might burn and lay waste" to the missionary program.[87]

Ayeta observed that the allied Apaches outnumbered the combined population of Pueblo Indians and Spanish citizens. As he informed His Majesty, New Mexico's Pueblos totaled seventeen thousand, of whom six thousand were warriors. The Spaniards, including people of mixed blood, could muster only 170 fighting men to protect their own settlements and to assist Pueblo communities. These men were so widely scattered across the province on isolated farms and ranches that it was impossible to unite even a small group of them with any celerity to pursue the raiders and retrieve stolen livestock and rescue captives. In addition to petitioning the royal Crown for the additional fifty soldiers, Ayeta urged the establishment of a presidio in the Villa de Santa Fe where these men would be stationed, signifying the need for a more formal and organized system of military defense.[88] The Crown never completely addressed this request before the course of New Mexico's history was irrevocably altered by the well-organized Pueblo Revolt of August 1680.

Father Ayeta certainly had knowledge of the sporadic flare-ups of violence that beset Pueblo–Spanish relations since the founding of New Mexico. However, his report fails to reveal the resentment felt by Pueblo Indians. At the same time, just as their animosity was reaching a new level of intensity in the later 1670s, the political influence of Pueblo leaders who favored cooperative relations with the Spaniards was waning, owing to strains on social, political, and economic relations. As to the sources of the Native resentment, like his fellow coreligionists, Ayeta seems to have possessed no more than a scant understanding.

Modern historians have examined at length the multiple causes that led to the downfall of the Spaniards in the Pueblo Revolt. Religious persecution by the Franciscan friars and government officials is usually offered as the primary reason for the uprising. But other factors contributed to the tragic event, such as drought, famine, tribute assessments, abuse of Native women, and forced labor. Juan Domínguez de Mendoza in 1681 heard firsthand from some of the Pueblo warriors that brutalities inflicted upon them by several Spanish officers, most prominently the secretary of government and war, Francisco Xavier, had prompted them to take up arms.[89]

The cataclysmic revolt broke forth on the feast of San Lorenzo, August 10, 1680. For once the Pueblos were united by common agreement, all but Isleta and the four southernmost villages of the Piros joining in the fury that swept the land. The vastly outnumbered settlers and the priests in their remote conventos suffered staggering casualties, the slain reaching 15 percent of New Mexico's total non-Indian population. That included twenty-one members of the clergy.[90]

In New Mexico's upper district, the Río Arriba, survivors from the stricken countryside streamed into the Villa de Santa Fe and joined local residents inside the *casas reales*, or government buildings. Governor don Antonio de Otermín strengthened his defenses as a huge Pueblo army arrived and laid siege to the capital. Downriver in the Río Abajo, Lt. Gov. Alonso García, who administered that district, gathered refugees together at Isleta Pueblo. Among them were Tomé and Juan Domínguez de Mendoza, who arrived with their immediate families, servants, and neighbors, driving herds of livestock salvaged from the disaster. Juan's stout residence, his Hacienda de Atrisco, had attracted those who managed to escape from the slaughter in the vicinity of Sandia Pueblo. But Juan quickly recognized that its defenses could not withstand a determined assault by the enemy. Therefore, he abandoned his estate and guided the people to Isleta. The Pueblo Indian warriors quickly moved in, looted his buildings, and then destroyed them.[91]

By August 14, four days after the revolt began, approximately fifteen hundred hungry and exhausted settlers assembled at Isleta. The majority were women and children, some barefoot and all traumatized by the tragedy. Lt. Gov. García called a council of the men-at-arms, together with seven surviving Franciscans, and explained the full gravity of their situation. Rumors from several friendly Pueblo Indians told of the deaths of Governor Otermín and the rest of the Spanish population of the Río Arriba. García sent messengers north with communications for the governor should he, in fact, still be alive. The failure of the messengers to get through to Otermín suggested that the governor and his followers had indeed perished.

At the lieutenant governor's council, the military officers unanimously agreed to leave Isleta and retreat southward out of New Mexico. At once the order was given, and the withdrawal of the pathetic multitude began. Ten days later, the fleeing cavalcade reached the Piro pueblo of Socorro, having traveled less than seventy miles.[92] From there the Spaniards marched another sixteen leagues down the Camino Real to the campsite of Fray Cristóbal, arriving by September 14. It was there that a priest and four soldiers bearing a message from Governor Otermín caught up with the southern division of refugees. This proved to be the first definitive news that the governor and some one thousand Río Arriba people had escaped from the siege of Santa Fe.

As was shortly learned, Otermín had abandoned the capital on August 21 and commenced a slow-moving exodus downriver. At Sandia Pueblo, a center of the outbreak in the Río Abajo, he found the population gone and the church profaned and partially burned. Just south of Sandia, a large body of Pueblo Indians fired upon the column with captured Spanish harquebuses. Otermín sent fifty soldiers against them, and the attackers fled. Their hostile actions so infuriated him that he ordered the pueblo set on fire. Throughout the valley, the advancing procession observed, in Otermín's words, "many haciendas on both sides of the river, all of which were sacked and destroyed." That would have included the house of Juan Domínguez de Mendoza.[93]

In the same vicinity, soldiers seized an Indian from whom it was learned that the Río Abajo survivors, accompanied by some Pueblos who remained loyal, had departed for El Paso. Cheered by that news, Otermín afterward dispatched his cleric with a fourteen-man escort to overtake García's division and instruct it to halt until the governor's contingent caught up.

That occurred on September 13, when for the first time all survivors of the revolt were united. At once, Otermín called a meeting of his officers and the leading civilians to determine whether the retreat should continue or whether a force should be mustered from their ranks and sent back upriver to challenge the enemy. Given the lack of supplies and the known strength of the enemy Pueblos, the decision went firmly in favor of continuing the march south. The two maestres de campo, Juan Domínguez de Mendoza and his brother Tomé, stood conspicuously with the majority.[94]

The governor's immediate destination was the small mission outpost of El Paso del Río del Norte, established in 1659 to minister to the local Manso Indians. Contact had already been made with fray Francisco de Ayeta, the Franciscan supply-master who had reached El Paso from Mexico City with a wagon train of provisions. There, he received news of the revolt, causing him to send a message north to those in command of the refugees that he was prepared to furnish all possible material aid for relief of the dispossessed New Mexicans.

Otermín with an escort hastened down the Camino Real and on September 18 met Father Ayeta and his supplies at the campground of La Salineta, east of the Rio Grande, about a dozen leagues above the Manso mission of Nuestra Señora de Guadalupe. A quantity of food was loaded on pack animals and sent speedily northward to the hungry people descending from upper New Mexico. Within a few days, they too reached La Salineta and camped for the next several weeks.

Governor Antonio de Otermín, normally an ineffectual and arrogant leader, had nevertheless in the midst of tragedy displayed true soldierly qualities and managed to make an orderly retreat from the Villa de Santa Fe to the safety of the El Paso country. Since it was necessary to arrive at a decision about the future of the displaced citizens, Otermín ordered a general muster to be conducted for the purpose of determining the exact number of persons who had come out of New Mexico with him, and the extent of their weapons, armor, and livestock salvaged from the defeat.

The results of the muster, completed by October 2, showed 1,946 individuals, of whom 155 men were able to bear arms. In addition, there were 317 Piros who had elected to march out with the Spaniards, plus a sprinkling of loyal Indians from Isleta, Jemez, and several other Pueblo communities. The figures revealed that a considerable number of people slipped away undetected during the march to Fray Cristóbal and had disappeared into Nueva Vizcaya, the frontier province bordering on the south. Knowing the importance of holding the citizens of New Mexico together, against the day when a reconquest could be launched, Otermín decreed that henceforth deserters would be shot. In spite of that intimidating threat, the slow leakage of population persisted during the twelve years of exile at El Paso.[95]

La Salineta, on a barren and chaparral-covered flat, was unsuitable for a long-term occupation. Hence, Governor Otermín soon established three town sites, roughly four miles apart on the Río Grande below El Paso and the Guadalupe mission. The farthest settlement downstream, the Real de San Lorenzo, became the residence of the governor, five priests, the leading New Mexico families and the cabildo of the Villa de Santa Fe.[96] Having lost their home seat in the New Mexican capital, the Santa Fe town councilors now reconvened to carry on their usual duties in exile. The cabildo would soon emerge as a power base for Juan Domínguez de Mendoza and his political machinations.

In the late September muster at La Salineta, the records include this entry:

> Maestre de Campo Juan Domínguez de Mendoza, married, appeared with full complement of personal arms and four additional firearms; a son capable of serving His Majesty, and another younger one; a little girl; thirty-two lean horses and eight mules, three orphan Spanish girls whom he was rearing in his house; and thirty-three servants, young and old. He was robbed by the enemy.[97]

Not mentioned in the summary were a quantity of personal possessions and some cattle that Domínguez de Mendoza probably succeeded in carrying away from his doomed estancia of Atrisco. The muster entry for Tomé Domínguez de Mendoza notes that the Pueblo Indian attackers killed thirty-eight of his relations, "being his daughters, grandchildren, sons-in-law, sisters, nephews, nieces, and sisters-in-law."[98] Four years later, Juan would claim that sixty-six of their kin had perished, while his friend and supporter fray Nicolás

López, in a letter to the viceregal secretary, inflated the figure again, saying that the family lost "more that seventy-six persons." López added that Juan's financial loss amounted to forty thousand pesos.[99]

Wherever the truth lay, this reality remained constant: the Domínguez de Mendoza family, like other patrician families of upper New Mexico, experienced the ruin of their fortunes and the slaughter of numerous kinsmen. Almost at once, however, Tomé Domínguez de Mendoza took the lead in enterprising ventures aimed at rebuilding personal wealth. He and his brother-in-law, don Pedro Durán y Chaves, for instance, used their status to gain a large share of the grain and cattle distributed by Father Ayeta to the refugees. This was done even though they owned cattle, horses, and sheep brought out of New Mexico, while others less fortunate had saved nothing.

Both Domínguez de Mendoza and Durán y Chaves, along with others of their clan, were soon engaging in trade with neighboring Nueva Vizcaya and Sonora. In fact, they were sending out livestock, wool, and textiles, locally made, while their poor fellow New Mexicans remained in miserable straits. Their conduct would eventually lead to charges of profiteering and result in a serious penalty.[100]

Soon after the refugees were placed in their new settlements, Father Ayeta departed with some urgency for Mexico City to put before the central government his testimony concerning the plight and desperate needs of the people of El Paso. When he returned in August 1681, his wagons bore a generous amount of foodstuffs, weapons, and tools. Moreover, Ayeta carried documents from the viceroy instructing Governor Otermín to undertake the reconquest as soon as possible, enlisting 150 soldiers for that purpose from the body of refugees, and the governor was told to establish a presidio in the environs of El Paso and garrison it with fifty salaried soldiers to be recruited outside that area.[101]

Governor Otermín, in the final week of October 1681, held a preliminary muster and enrollment of troops for the ordered reentry and reclaiming of New Mexico. To his dismay, he discovered just how many men had decamped with their families and fled to Nueva Vizcaya. Others, including high-ranking officers, remained in their homes but ignored the summons to duty, pleading serious infirmities. Prominent among the latter group were Tomé Domínguez de Mendoza and Pedro Durán y Chaves. The governor considered charging all the delinquents with treason to the king but thought better of it, since such drastic punishment would only sow greater discord in the much-diminished colony.

These realities did not augur well for the success of his undertaking. Indeed, in one of the last official documents written before his departure for the north, the governor slipped in a disclaimer, saying, "[T]he forces I have at present are not adequate for carrying out the . . . restoration and conquest of New Mexico. . . . I will nonetheless obey the specific orders of the king to do so."[102]

By November 4, Otermín had moved his entire force upriver from San Lorenzo to El Paso, where he distributed eighty-five carbines, furnished by the government, to soldiers lacking firearms. Then the army marched a dozen miles north to a campground called El Ancón de Fray García. Here, Otermín held a final review, formed squadrons, and named his second in command for this expedition. The final number showed 146 Spaniards and 112 Indian allies, primarily Mansos and Piros. The governor bitterly noted that his ranks included many undisciplined soldiers and boys without experience, owing to the failure of so many able veterans to answer his call.[103] Among other members of the expedition were fray Francisco de Ayeta, his secretary fray Nicolás López, and fray Antonio Guerra.

On November 7, while still encamped at El Ancón de Fray García, Otermín had his secretary of government and war, Francisco Xavier, prepare and witness a field commission naming Juan Domínguez de Mendoza as lieutenant general of the cavalry, which in effect placed him in authority, second only to the governor. The document certified that Domínguez de Mendoza "possessed the requisite experience, sufficiency, merits, quality and services to establish his capabilities in war and prove his zealotry in service to the king."[104] At the muster two days earlier, Domínguez de Mendoza declared twenty-two horses and three mules, all personal arms and cavalry equipment, and a servant to attend him during the campaign. Only the governor was taking more animals than he.[105]

For its size, the expedition traveled with considerable speed, by forced marches reaching the southernmost Piro pueblo of Senecú on November 26. It was found to be deserted and the church stripped and desecrated. The remaining three Piro villages encountered during the northward advance were in the same condition. Otermín ordered all of them burned.

With a stripped-down party of seventy soldiers, Governor Otermín made an all-night march and reached the Tiwa pueblo of Isleta just before dawn. At sunup some brief skirmishes took place before the Isletans surrendered, contending that they had mistaken the Spaniards for hostile Apaches. The pueblo as a whole had not participated in the revolt, although more than a hundred of its residents by now had fled on their own to join the Indian forces in the north. Governor Otermín decided to pause here with half the army while he sent Juan Domínguez de Mendoza and a sixty-man detachment on a lighting foray up the Rio Grande to test the sentiments and mettle of the

Pueblo Indians in the Río Abajo. The unsuccessful outcome of this mission, owing to brash actions by Otermín, would embroil Domínguez de Mendoza in a protracted controversy, becoming the first in a series of episodes that over the ensuing decade tarnished his reputation.[106]

At the beginning of the second week of December 1681, Juan Domínguez de Mendoza led his troop upriver in bitter winter weather. At the Tiwa pueblo of La Alameda, he found that its population had fled to the Sandia Mountains on the east, weeping as they left, according to a blind Indian woman who had been abandoned. The Spanish recovered metal religious objects that had come from the church of La Alameda, destroyed in the revolt. Then they continued their ascent of the river to the pueblos of Puaray and Sandia. Like La Alameda, both were deserted.

Domínguez de Mendoza now sent a message back to Otermín informing him that the storerooms of these three Tiwa villages were well stocked with corn and beans, and suggesting for that reason the governor move his base camp from Isleta northward to this area. He also explained his failure to obey orders that required him to set fire to those pueblos whose inhabitants had fled. As he put it, the Indians were more apt to return and negotiate for peace, seeing that their houses were still intact. He did, however, burn a large number of kachina masks, referring to them as "abominable figures."[107]

The Spanish force next pushed into the province of the Queres-speaking pueblos, visiting San Felipe, Santo Domingo, and Cochiti. Near the latter place, it was confronted by a mixed army of Indian warriors headed by war leader Alonso Catití.[108] Surprisingly, after Domínguez de Mendoza rebuked Catití and his fellow warriors for their rebellion and butcheries in 1680, they made strenuous overtures for peace. Evidently, to show good faith, the Indians removed the hide jackets they were wearing against the cold and presented them as gifts to the soldiers. If Domínguez de Mendoza can be believed, both sides broke down and wept for joy.

Domínguez de Mendoza had managed to create an opportunity for diplomatic negotiations intended to rectify the rift between the parties and restore peaceful relations. Talks continued while messengers were dispatched to neighboring pueblos. Then an Indian arrived from downriver bearing the unhappy news that Governor Otermín, following Domínguez de Mendoza's advice, was hurrying up from Isleta, but in doing so he burned the pueblos of La Alameda, Puaray, and Sandia. With that word, Domínguez de Mendoza's peace negotiations at Cochiti immediately collapsed.[109]

Recognizing that all was now lost, owing to Otermín's blunder, Juan Domínguez de Mendoza led his men south to the governor's new field camp two leagues from the still-smoldering ruins of Puaray. Now that his expedition of restoration and reconquest was reunited, Otermín convened a *junta de guerra* (war council) to consider his options and decide upon the next move. Formal depositions taken from officers and others almost uniformly agreed that since the Indians remained unrepentant, the horses were worn out, and no chance existed of subduing the enemy by force, the enterprise should be given up and a withdrawal made to El Paso.

That was Otermín's wish as well, his prophecy made at the outset that the expedition would fail having been fulfilled, although in part through his own ineptitude and vengeful actions. At Isleta he halted long enough to incorporate the remaining 385 native residents of that place into his retreating column. They were destined to be newly settled in the El Paso Valley, alongside the Piros and other Pueblo Indians who had joined the Spanish flight from New Mexico in 1680.[110]

The aborted expedition of reconquest was not yet home before the bitter and petulant governor dispatched a wordy report to Mexico City, apprising the viceroy in self-serving terms of the reasons for his failure. Among them was his discovery that the Indians, far from softening their obstinacy, remained secure in "their natural inclination toward obscenities, idolatry, and liberty." Other reasons included the severity of the weather, causing Otermín constant headaches; shortage of supplies, especially armaments and horses; and importantly, the refusal of Lt. Gen. Juan Domínguez de Mendoza to obey certain orders, and dereliction of duty at the Cochiti conference where Domínguez de Mendoza neglected to disarm and arrest the attending Pueblo leaders. These charges would continue to haunt Domínguez de Mendoza for several years.[111]

In the wake of those events, Governor Otermín had to face two unpleasant realities. First was the clear evidence that New Mexico would not be recovered from the apostate Pueblo Indians anytime soon. That meant the refugee camps in the El Paso area, until now considered temporary, must be transformed into permanent settlements. The second hard reality concerned the growing restlessness of the local Manso Indians and the nearby Sumas. They and other tribes across northern New Spain had been inspired by the achievement of the Pueblo Indians and seemed to be awaiting their moment to openly resist Spanish rule. Further, the nomad Apaches of southern New Mexico were taking advantage of the suddenly expanded population center of El Paso, to step up their plunder raids in that quarter.

With all of these problems at hand, Governor Otermín yet found time to pursue Tomé Domínguez de Mendoza and his brother-in-law, don Pedro Durán y Chaves, for sowing discord among the settlers. In the fall of 1681, both men declined an order to enlist in the pending restoration and reconquest of New Mexico, pleading poverty and assorted physical ailments resulting from old wounds and advanced age. The poverty excuse rang especially hollow, owing to their reputations for wide commercial dealings and sharp business practices.

Although the specifics are unknown, Otermín reported briefly to the viceroy on October 27, 1682, "In the interest of good government, don Pedro Durán y Chaves and Tomé Domínguez de Mendoza have been exiled along with their immediate kin." Elsewhere the place of exile is mentioned as the valley of the Sacramento River, a few miles north of today's city of Chihuahua.[112]

Juan Domínguez de Mendoza was having his own headaches, mainly growing out of the blame that Otermín laid on him for the failure of the expedition to restore New Mexico. The viceregal *fiscal*, or royal attorney in Mexico City, had begun building a case against him centered on his unwillingness to arrest Pueblo leaders when they were in his power at Cochiti. Domínguez de Mendoza probably learned early that the judicial inquiry was in progress. He would make a formal rebuttal to the main charge and lesser ones while in Mexico City three years later.[113]

When Governor Otermín arrived back in El Paso from the north, he found the refugee colony torn by "discords, hatreds, and ill will," much of it born of petty rivalries but also produced by food shortages and fears of Indian attack. A large measure of the animosity was directed toward him, adding to the unbearable stress he had endured since the outbreak of the Pueblo Revolt. In late March 1682, the venerable Father Ayeta, himself ill and crippled, was preparing to depart for Mexico City. Otermín in despair pleaded with him, saying: "For the love of God and St. Anthony as soon as you arrive in Mexico [City], do everything you possibly can to get me out of here."[114]

Another year would pass, however, before Otermín would be relieved and his successor would reach the El Paso Valley. That successor was the very able don Domingo Jironza Petríz de Cruzate, a military officer from Spain who had been in the New World thirty-six months before receiving appointment as the New Mexico governor for a three-year term.

Juan Domínguez de Mendoza may have felt some disappointment at not being offered the office, which he greatly coveted. But given his past and current legal difficulties, and the fact that no New Mexican family had ever seen one of its own elevated by royal appointment to the governorship, he could not have realistically expected to receive that appointment from the viceroy. Still, he remained watchful for an opportunity to serve the Crown in a capacity that might increase his chances for preferment at some future date.

Misfortune Turns to Opportunity, 1683–1689

Governor don Antonio de Otermín, broken in health, surrendered his office on August 28, 1683. The following day, Jironza Petríz de Cruzate, newly arrived from Mexico City, stepped into his shoes as governor. Just a few weeks earlier, a band of a dozen Jumano Indians from La Junta (the junction of the Rio Grande and the Conchos River southeast of El Paso) arrived and appeared before Governor Otermín requesting that missionaries be sent to their settlements and Spanish military assistance provided to relieve a growing Apache threat. Otermín made no promises, preferring to leave the handling of their matter to his successor.[115]

The Jumano Indians returned in October to be greeted warmly by Governor Jironza Petríz de Cruzate and Father Nicolás López, the latter having served as Father Ayeta's secretary during the 1681–1682 reconquest attempt, and who had recently been promoted to the office of vice-custos. Heading the Jumano delegation on this occasion was one of the prominent leaders, known to the Spaniards as Juan Sabeata. His words were translated by Hernán Martín Serrano, the aging soldier who in 1650 co-commanded the small expedition from Santa Fe to the Jumano country in west Texas. During six months with the Indians, collecting freshwater pearls, Martín Serrano had apparently learned the Jumano language.

Sabeata painted a rosy picture of his fellow tribesmen eagerly awaiting Christian baptism and spoke of their need for the Spaniards to defend them from Apache enemies. He also tossed in reference to the populous nation of the Tejas Indians, who lived in an easterly direction beyond the Jumanos and were as yet poorly known to the Spanish government.[116]

Jironza Petríz de Cruzate was sympathetic to Sabeata's blandishments but initially was unprepared to take action, owing to the scarcity of men, arms, and supplies available to him in poverty-stricken El Paso. All signs indicate that Father López intervened and persuaded the governor to field a small expedition to visit La Junta for missionary purposes, then to continue on into central Texas to contact the substantial Jumano population known to reside there.

In acceding to the wishes of the padre, Jironza Petríz de Cruzate surprisingly named Juan Domínguez de Mendoza to take the helm as commander of the military escort. The governor had brought from Mexico City instructions to investigate the role of Domínguez de Mendoza in the discredited military operation in upper New Mexico. On the basis of Otermín's accusations against his second-in-command, the viceroy's advisers had concluded that Domínguez de Mendoza was probably guilty of serious crimes.

In the course of the reconquest, Father López had taken the side of Domínguez de Mendoza in opposition to Governor Otermín and Father Ayeta. By the time that pathetic affair had ended, López had become Domínguez de Mendoza's ardent partisan, remaining so, and even representing at a later time his interests at the viceregal court in Mexico City. In the Jumano expedition to Texas, the two men's private interests conveniently merged. The churchman López was a fierce and impassioned advocate of expanding Spain's missionary program, the more so after the stunning loss of New Mexico and the martyrdom of the majority of its clergy. Juan Sabeata's entreaties stirred in him a new energy and produced a gilded vision of another realm to be claimed for the Church in the wilderness of Texas.

Juan Domínguez de Mendoza, a visionary in his own right as well as an opportunist, hungered for some achievement in the area of public service that could help restore his blemished star in the eyes of the viceroy and the king. Exploration of western Texas and conversion of the Jumanos, accomplished in conjunction with his good friend Father López, seemed to fit his needs perfectly.

The wonder is, at first glance, that Governor Jironza Petríz de Cruzate selected Domínguez de Mendoza, with all of his drawbacks, for the leadership of this potentially significant venture. But as happened so often in Domínguez de Mendoza's career, his status, relative wealth, and proven military abilities seemed to override his manifold defects, so that the governor now approved him for the task at hand. As one historian suggests, this appointment could also have been a skillful move on the governor's part to remove temporarily a known troublemaker from the ranks of El Paso's contentious residents.[117]

In his eagerness to answer Sabeata's call for missionaries, Father López initially proposed to go at once, accompanied only by two Franciscans, fray Juan de Zavaleta and fray Antonio Acevedo. Governor Jironza Petríz de Cruzate would not hear of that, insisting that for their protection they should have an armed escort. Therefore, on November 13, 1683, the governor issued a proclamation calling for volunteers. According to Domínguez de Mendoza's later statement, twenty men responded, among them his own sons, Baltasar and Juan, and his son-in-law Diego Lucero de Godoy.[118]

Several years later, giving a written account of his merits to royal officials, Jironza Petríz de Cruzate specifically noted that the expedition was funded at his own cost with Maestre de Campo Juan Domínguez de Mendoza serving as *capitán, cabo y caudillo* in command of thirty men, "for the discovery of the Jumano Indians and to battle the Apache nation," according to a document of certification signed by officials of the cabildo of Santa Fe.[119] It was on November 29, 1683, that the governor bestowed upon Juan Domínguez de Mendoza the commission as commander of the expedition to Texas. In that document, Jironza Petríz de Cruzate enumerated many of the appointee's past services to the Crown, by way of qualifying him for this weighty assignment, and in so doing he referred to the Domínguez de Mendoza "titles, patents and certification which he presented before me."[120]

At the same time, Jironza Petríz de Cruzate issued a set of instructions "to be observed by Maestre de Campo Juan Domínguez de Mendoza . . . [who is] going to the new discovery of the Jumano nation and all of the other nations friendly to them." In it, he directed that should Domínguez de Mendoza die during the course of the expedition, then Sargento Mayor Diego Lucero de Godoy, the son-in-law of Domínguez de Mendoza, should assume command, and in the event of his death Captain Felipe Romero must take charge.[121]

The Jumano *entrada* was not the only expedition organized and financed by Jironza Petríz de Cruzate during November 1683. With the increasing threat of Apache hostilities pressing in and around the communities of the New Mexican exiles in the El Paso region, the governor called up able-bodied men with arms, and veteran leaders, forming two additional groups to combat the Apache.[122] One was a reconnaissance campaign that left El Paso on November 14 under the command of Captain Salvador Olguín with orders to proceed as far as the Paraje de las Barrancas, located between the pueblo of Socorro and Isleta Pueblo along the Rio Grande, to determine the current intentions of the "apostate Indians" and to chastise hostile Apaches in the area.

The governor assigned command of the other expedition to Captain Antonio Domínguez de Mendoza, a nephew of the maestre de campo, being a son of Francisco Domínguez de Mendoza. This armed group was instructed to track the "enemy Apache" and also left El Paso in November, eventually encountering Apaches at a place called Cerro Hueco, where a battle occurred with victory being claimed by the Spaniards. During the time these two expeditions were in the field, arrangements were still being made for the Jumano entrada.

The three impatient missionaries—fray Nicolás López, fray Antonio Acevedo, and fray Juan de Zavaleta—departed for La Junta on December 1, while their escort was still forming at the settlement of San Lorenzo twelve leagues below El Paso. There, Juan Domínguez de Mendoza had built a new home for his family and now was using it as headquarters in making preparations to launch the expedition to Texas. The country from that point down to La Junta was inhabited by Suma Indians, culturally akin to the Mansos, and since they were partially Christianized, the road followed by the three clergymen was considered safe.[123] The Franciscan trio planned to use the time until the main expedition caught up with them to commence proselytizing among the assorted peoples residing in the La Junta district. On their short trip they were accompanied only by Juan Sabeata and several other Jumano leaders.[124]

After some delay, the military escort set forth on December 15, 1683, the date of the first entry in the Domínguez de Mendoza journal, whose rigorous keeping had been required by Jironza Petríz de Cruzate's instructions. At the end of that day the party camped five leagues from San Lorenzo, at the abandoned adobe house of Juan Domínguez de Mendoza's brother Tomé.[125]

Not until December 29 did the escort arrive at the junction of the Rio Grande and Conchos, where Domínguez de Mendoza found the padres already at work converting and baptizing the Indians. These were largely Julimes, Uto-Aztecan speakers and farmers, whose settlements stretched from some distance up the banks of the Conchos River. In addition, the Spaniards saw enclaves of Jumanos, who were economically wedded to hunting and long-distance trading. These were the two predominant Native groups among the "seven nations" Domínguez de Mendoza mentioned at a later date as dwelling in the vicinity of La Junta de los Rios.[126] Two or more crude mission chapels had already been raised in the area, so that when the Texas expedition resumed its march toward the central range of the Jumanos on December 31, Father Acevedo stayed behind to minister to this scattered flock.

Maestre de Campo Juan Domínguez de Mendoza's entrada or penetration into the heart of Texas with the remaining pair of missionaries was destined to extend over the succeeding six months. On January 13, 1684, led by Juan Sabeata, they reached the Rio Salado, or Pecos River, northeast of today's Fort Stockton, Texas. From that point the Spaniards descended southward to the river ford at Horsehead Crossing, passing along the way a people named Hediondos, believed by Forbes to be a subgroup of the Jumanos.[127]

Further, during this stage of the trip, the party suffered a small mutiny. Domínguez de Mendoza recorded only that several malcontents clamoring to abort the expedition and return to La Junta stirred up dissension in the ranks and among the Indians. The two ringleaders assailed him with swords, and after fending off the attack, he ordered both of them shot. But following an appeal from Fathers Lopez and Zavaleta, their lives were spared. As time would show, however, the matter was far from closed.[128]

After fording the Pecos River, the expedition headed northeast, reaching the headwaters of the Río de las Nueces (River of the Nuts) on the last day of January. That stream took its name from pecan groves that flourished on its banks. Most scholars now identify it as the Middle Concho River.[129]

The men then advanced slowly down this river to its confluence with the main Concho, called the Río de las Perlas, hunting buffalo much of the way. The meat went to feed a horde of Indians from assorted tribes, most of them unidentifiable, which followed in the wake of the small Spanish cavalcade, but Domínguez de Mendoza seems also to have been collecting hides for trade purposes. From the Pecos River onward, Apaches had been harrying the party, their interest lying principally in the theft of horses. Joining in the attacks were Salineros, far-ranging raiders from Nueva Vizcaya.

At a campsite designated Desamparados on February 28, a group of defectors numbering nine men deserted and fled toward home mounted on the best horses. They were joined by some of "the friendly infidels," whose departures led to ill feeling among the Indians remaining. Afterward, charges of misconduct would be brought against Domínguez de Mendoza in connection with this incident, suggesting that his own failure of duty provoked the rebellion of the soldiers.[130]

After more travel, the party came on March 16 to a larger river, which was given the name San Clemente. Domínguez de Mendoza wrote admiringly of the nut and fruit trees lining its banks and the abundance of animals and birds. Moreover, he reported that six days' journey downstream shells could be found, "in many of which there are pearls." Apparently, this information was communicated by the Indians. All evidence points to the San Clemente being the Colorado River of Texas, the Spaniards striking it not far above the mouth of the Concho, its tributary. Here the expedition remained encamped from mid-March until the first of May, building during that interval a fortified tower of two rooms, in one of which religious services were conducted.

The Caddoan confederacy of the Tejas Indians that sprawled across east Texas had sent envoys promising that their representatives would "come to meet us," recorded Domínguez de Mendoza. But none appeared. So, using that and expanding Apache attacks as excuses, he decided to take his diminished band of soldiers back to El Paso.[131]

Before leaving, Juan Domínguez de Mendoza, promised the Indians of the region that he would return within a year to reestablish a Spanish presence. They had grown disenchanted, however, in view of his poor performance in dealing with Apaches, so by the time the maestre de campo and his men departed, the Native people had largely abandoned them. The retreating Spaniards swung south of their outbound route, and on May 22 they reached the Pecos River. June 6 found them once more on the Rio Grande at La Junta. In their absence, Father Acevedo had built a proper church and at the same time baptized fifteen hundred Indians. That heartening development, nevertheless, was overshadowed by other jolting news.[132]

Domínguez de Mendoza now learned that the Suma nation together with others had risen in revolt and was lying in wait along the Rio Grande to make war upon him as he climbed the road leading to El Paso. Furthermore, the river was at flood stage, rendering travel upriver even more precarious. Consequently, after consulting his soldiers, he determined to take a long, round-about route up the Conchos River to the mouth of the Río Sacramento, then follow that stream as it bowed westward, and finally cross the north–south Camino Real above the future Chihuahua City.

In the final week of June 1684, the haggard expedition arrived at the new house of Domínguez de Mendoza's father-in-law, the exiled don Pedro Durán y Chaves, located presumably on or near the Camino Real. After a week's layover to pasture the exhausted horses, the march resumed on July 2 and extended eight leagues up the Camino Real to the settlement of Los Suaces, a stopping point well known to travelers.

Here, Maestre de Campo Juan Domínguez de Mendoza for six days enjoyed the hospitality of his brother's new home. Tomé Domínguez de Mendoza, like Durán y Chaves, had made the best he could of his exile from El Paso. At this place, time was spent acquiring supplies and again pasturing the horses. Thus restrengthened, the expedition easily reached El Paso in ten days, arriving on July 18, 1684, without further inconveniences.[133]

One additional document of record was composed by Domínguez de Mendoza five days later, at the behest of Father López. It was a laudatory summary of the work and accomplishments of the three Franciscans during the life of the expedition. Plainly, López intended to use the statements of Domínguez de Mendoza in buttressing his future petitions aimed at winning government support for a return to Texas.[134]

In reality the months-long jaunt to the Río San Clemente produced little of substance. Its announced purpose as originally framed by Governor Jironza Petríz de Cruzate had been to gain knowledge of Indians outside the pale of Spain who, according to numerous reports, were ripe for conversion to Christianity.[135]

The Tejas of east Texas represented the grand prize in such an endeavor, and yet Domínguez de Mendoza and López were unable to make any meaningful contact with those people. Domínguez de Mendoza attributed the failure to a shortage of supplies and, more significantly, to the barrier imposed by hostile Apaches. Even the modest success registered by the missionaries at La Junta de los Ríos soon dissolved. The spirit of revolt among the Sumas spread to the Indians there and would have resulted in the martyrdom of Fathers Zavaleta and Acevedo had not some of the new Christians remained loyal. They spirited away the two priests, carrying their vestments and sacred altar vessels, up the Conchos River to the distant town of San José del Parral and safety.[136]

Juan Domínguez de Mendoza and fray Nicolás López upon their arrival in El Paso found conditions in the area wretched. The uprising of the Sumas and Mansos had spread to other desert tribes all across New Spain's frontier from Sonora to Coahuila. In April 1684, the mission at Los Janos in Nueva Vizcaya was sacked and the missionary killed. Governor Jironza Petríz de Cruzate responded by organizing a troop of thirty soldiers that fought the hostile Indians at the Peñol of Los Janos.[137] The success of the Pueblo Revolt and the inability of the Spaniards to suppress it had inspired and now sustained a more general conflagration, one that meager Spanish resources at first seemed unable to control.

The Santa Fe cabildo in exile, speaking on behalf of the ill-fed and ill-clad citizenry, submitted a petition to Governor Jironza Petríz de Cruzate suggesting that since the El Paso Valley had become uninhabitable, he should grant permission for its abandonment. This was just the latest in a series of such requests, and as earlier, the governor rejected it. He was fully aware that his superiors regarded El Paso as a key bastion in defending the turbulent frontier and as the launching platform for the future restoration of upper New Mexico.

On September 19, 1684, Farther López called all the missionaries to a conference at Senecú, downriver from El Paso, to address the problem of the current revolt and the acute discontent of the settlers. He proposed the election of a clerical representative who could visit Mexico City, explain the dire needs of the El Paso colony, and implore civil and religious officials for material aid. Not unexpectedly, López won unanimous approval to assume that task himself. Shortly after this meeting, he departed for the viceregal capital.[138]

Maestre de Campo Juan Domínguez de Mendoza, in the months that followed, worked to build a cadre of supporters in an effort to strengthen his hand in local affairs. In particular, he sought to discredit Jironza Petríz de Cruzate, partly because Domínguez de Mendoza wanted the governorship for himself, but also because the governor had sent damaging reports about him to the viceroy's prosecuting attorney in Mexico City.[139]

Domínguez de Mendoza, to advance his own ambitions, came to dominate the cabildo, aided by his Durán y Chaves in-laws. That municipal body on September 7, 1685, composed a secret letter to Mexico City charging Governor Jironza Petríz de Cruzate with dishonorable conduct and offering a litany of accusations against him. Fray Nicolás López, who was by now in the viceregal capital, had sent a message to members of the cabildo urging them to denounce their governor, and this indictment of him had followed. The antigovernor campaign being waged by López was aimed at blocking his reappointment to office, when his current term ended a year hence. The New Mexican missionary at the same time was lobbying in high government circles to have Domínguez de Mendoza become Jironza Petríz de Cruzate's successor.[140]

Once the cabildo had drawn up its formal denunciation of the governor, it faced the problem of getting the document out of El Paso, inasmuch as the governor had forbidden anyone to leave the valley without his express authorization. One of the council's own members, Lázaro de Misquía, was selected to depart by stealth and deliver the list of accusations into the hands of the viceroy and his advisers. Juan Domínguez de Mendoza chose to accompany him as head of a four-man escort that included his son Baltasar and son-in-law Captain Diego Lucero de Godoy. At the viceregal court, Domínguez de Mendoza planned to argue personally for his elevation to New Mexico's governorship. Before sunrise on September 27, 1685, the little party slipped away, beginning the long journey to Mexico City.

At once, Governor Jironza Petríz de Cruzate learned of the illegal leave-taking. He wasted no time in initiating criminal proceedings and using them as a pretext to make Domínguez de Mendoza's long record of misconduct its focus. Therein, the governor at a trial in absentia cited Maestre de Campo Juan Domínguez de Mendoza as the chief defendant. His intention was to bring his political foe into such disfavor that Domínguez de Mendoza could stand no chance in winning the New Mexico office of governor.[141]

The records of the eight-day trial, extending to October 6, 1685, include testimony of more than a dozen witnesses who described Domínguez de Mendoza's serious offenses beginning well before the Pueblo Revolt. He received blame for the failure of the 1681–1682 attempted restoration of New Mexico. And his mistreatment of his own men as well as the Natives encountered during the Jumano expedition alienated both, thereby forcing the party's return before achieving one of its main objectives, the discovery of the kingdom of the Tejas Indians.

The animosity shown by most of the witnesses toward Domínguez de Mendoza was fierce. If they were to be believed, the man was widely hated and feared by Spanish citizens and Indians alike and was "worse than the devil." Further, he had bragged that upon gaining the governorship, with the aid of Father López, he would promptly hang the nine deserters from his recent Texas expedition. As a result of these proceedings, historian Vina Walz observed, "Juan Domínguez emerged, fairly or unfairly, as the arch criminal without a rag of reputation left."[142]

When Father López reached Mexico City in the first half of 1686, soon to be followed by Domínguez de Mendoza, he used his political skills and the influence of the Franciscan order to further his aspirations for the speedy reclaiming of New Mexico and the opening of a new missionary field among the Jumano Indians. In the previous year, the king of Spain had instructed his viceroy at Mexico City to assemble a report describing the nature of the land and the possibilities for improving communications within the frontier provinces on the viceroyalty's northern rim. In part the royal mandate was in response to the 1684 encroachment of a small French colony on the Texas Gulf Coast, led by explorer René Robert Cavalier, Sieur de la Salle.[143]

The viceroy selected fray Alonso de Posada to compile the report for His Majesty, because from long service among the Pueblo Indians and a term as custodian of the Franciscan order in New Mexico, 1661–1665, Posada was well qualified for the work.[144] Father Nicolás López also prepared a similar memorial with its own map, as part of the supplementary documentation for Posada's work. In a covering letter, he called attention to the many nations of Indians he had visited in Texas in 1683–1684 who "were asking for the water of baptism." By such a reference, he paved the way for his future appeals to gain royal approval for the establishment of permanent missions among the Jumanos.[145]

Juan Domínguez de Mendoza, now in Mexico City, also submitted a memorial to the king, no doubt at the urging of his friend and ally Father Nicolás López. It largely focused on his own grandiose plans for the settlement of Texas. In it, he begged for two hundred armed men, whom he proposed to lead back to the Río de las Nueces in Texas, and for them to build two fortified presidios. The soldiers could be fed from the herds of buffalo and deer abounding in the area, and the Indians would flock to settle nearby, recognizing that he was keeping his earlier pact with them to return. Domínguez de Mendoza also promised to make a search for the elusive French intruders. The self-serving tone of this particular memorial could not have escaped the notice of those Spanish officials who chanced to read it.[146]

Such was the case, as well, with a second memorial of his, presented like the first one to the viceroy, on November 18, 1685. This document summarized briefly the history of the recent Jumano expedition and extolled Domínguez de Mendoza's accomplishments during the course of that venture. Moreover, it presented anew his side of the 1681 entrada to pacify New Mexico and again laid blame on the shoulders of Governor don Antonio de Otermín for its miscarriage.[147]

Writing to the viceroy several months earlier, in June 1685, fray Nicolás López described the sincere desire of numerous Indians to become Christians and vassals of the Spanish Crown.[148] He appealed to the viceroy for assistance in carrying out missionary work to bring these Indians within the fold of the Church. In addition, he mentioned that these friendly Indians were willing to make war against the hostile tribes that threatened the settlements at San José del Parral in Nueva Vizcaya. López lamented the poor conditions at El Paso and appealed for aid to the settlers, also suggesting the relocation of the remnants of the New Mexico settlers to Texas, since there appeared to be no hope of regaining New Mexico.

This petition was referred to the fiscal in Mexico City, don Pedro de la Bastida, who gave a lengthy opinion dated July 27, 1685, in which he opposed moving the settlers and expressed doubt concerning the sincerity of the messages of peace received from the apostate Pueblos. He stated that the aid that was sent over the course of the past few years had cost the treasury a considerable sum and that the expense had been "without any fruit." Although he was willing to recommend additional aid to the extent of four or five thousand pesos to assist the settlers at El Paso, he opposed any major expenditure until a satisfactory person was sent to govern the province and investigate the general situation. Bastida stressed that no additional friars should be sent at the present time. Curiously, the entrada of Domínguez de Mendoza and López to the east received only passing mention, and it was obvious that the fiscal was not in any way impressed by Lopez's reports concerning that journey. On August 3, 1685, the junta general voted to approve the fiscal's opinion.

Angered by the dismissal of the fiscal and the junta general regarding the initial missionary work in Texas and the prospect of bringing many souls to the Catholic faith, López appealed directly to royal officials of the Council of the Indies and to the king.[149] Writing to the king in April 1686, he made a request for twenty friars and for "one hundred men from the prisons" along with three hundred head of cattle and two hundred horses.[150] López again proposed moving the remnants of the New Mexico settlers to Texas because of the deplorable conditions at El Paso. Already more than two hundred men had left El Paso for other territories to the south. In his opinion the abundance of the lands of Texas would sustain the settlers better than the meager fruits of the region around El Paso, and thus the cost for sustaining the settlers would be very minimal compared to remaining there. López even sought aid by requesting provisions from his two brothers, both miners at the Minas del Rosario, to facilitate the move, and he mentioned he would have two presidios built in Texas. To his disappointment, nothing came from the appeals of fray Nicolás López.

In connection with the preparations of the memorials of Juan Domínguez de Mendoza, the aspiring military leader took pains to bring his service record up to date and have it properly certified. He had actually begun that process a year earlier while still in El Paso. There, on October 3, 1684, he obtained from the Santa Fe cabildo a certification of the body of documents in his possession that pertained to his past services.[151]

Another formality was observed five days later when the cabildo issued a certified statement as to the personal appearance of Domínguez de Mendoza and his two sons, Baltasar and Juan, including specific physical marks that could serve to confirm the identity of each individual.[152] The rare description of Juan Domínguez de Mendoza's appearance at age fifty-seven reveals that he was considered a tall man of good stature in comparison to his peers, but not excessively tall, with black hair going gray, and was acknowledged as being "of goodly countenance." Also cited were several notable physical features that served as evidence of the risks of his profession, including the disfiguration of his left hand.

> He has three wounds, all on the left side. The first is in a shoulder blade, which was broken at the Peñol de Acoma, and as a result he has a withered shoulder. The second is in his left hand, the whole span of the said hand being cleft. The third is above the knee on the said left side, across the thigh, and he has another wound on the right side of his head.[153]

Once in Mexico City, Domínguez de Mendoza petitioned a municipal magistrate to recertify the original document of attestation he had secured from the Santa Fe cabildo and had carried out along with his other papers upon fleeing El Paso.[154] Now with both himself and his ally Father López reunited in the viceregal capital, they redoubled efforts in the hope of achieving that common aim: convincing royal officials to support their calls for the Spanish occupation of the country of the Jumano and Tejas Indians. López had been elevated from vice-custodian to the office of custodian of New Mexico by the council of Franciscans at provincial headquarters in Mexico City. At the very least, his advancement ought to have given him a stronger voice in petitioning the viceroy and king.[155]

For his part, Juan Domínguez de Mendoza wasted no time in asking the viceroy during November 1685 to grant him the governorship of New Mexico, presenting as evidence of his merits the personal service record that he had carefully compiled over the years. That extensive collection of documents offered proof of his distinguished career in New Mexico, serving the Crown and Church, while holding high military and political offices. It alone, Domínguez de Mendoza seemed to believe, should guarantee him the governor's chair. Within a few months, however, his aspirations received a severe blow. In February 1686, it was revealed that the viceroy had passed over Domínguez de Mendoza and selected a former presidial soldier at El Paso, now a resident of Mexico City, don Pedro Reneros de Posada, to succeed Jironza Petríz de Cruzate as governor of New Mexico. Evidently, Reneros de Posada, a virtual unknown, had been able to muster influence in high places.[156]

Subsequently, Father López in a letter to the royal secretary at Madrid, don Antonio Ortiz de Otalora, stated with a hint of bitterness that Juan

Domínguez de Mendoza was denied the New Mexico governorship by the viceroy and his advisers, who instead "gave it to a person [Reneros de Posada] entirely incompetent for the business." Additionally, the priest noted that Domínguez de Mendoza, although he had not been appointed governor, still believed that owing to his experience and knowledge, he was best qualified to lead an expedition into Texas "to force out the French who may now be settled there." López by way of extending a personal recommendation referred to the advantages that would come to the king by accepting Domínguez de Mendoza's proffered services, since he was the only one fit for leading such a military expedition.[157]

Juan Domínguez de Mendoza by now concluded that he was unlikely to gain preferment for any government office at the hands of the viceroy. That belief led fray Nicolás López to declare, "The general [Domínguez de Mendoza] has desired to take ship and place himself at the feet of His Majesty to inform him concerning all these [Indian] kingdoms and provinces."[158]

The record of Domínguez de Mendoza's trial in absentia conducted at El Paso by Governor Jironza Petríz de Cruzate had been forwarded to the viceroy for judgment. Besides the main charge that he had abandoned his post at El Paso without license of the governor, Juan Domínguez de Mendoza was also accused of circulating false rumors that he had been appointed governor, causing "horror and discontent" among the citizenry; also that on the Jumano expedition he had failed to behave with prudence and zeal; and finally, reaching back to accusations made in 1681–1682, that in the campaign of upper New Mexico he had disobeyed orders of Governor Otermín, thereby causing the failure of the expedition.

Owing to the sluggish functioning of the ponderous colonial bureaucracy, Viceroy Conde de la Monclova did not render a verdict in the case until April 30, 1687. After considering testimony given by Juan Domínguez de Mendoza and his two sons, the viceroy dismissed the charges, except for the one that dealt with the illegal flight from El Paso. In that instance, he found all members of the Domínguez de Mendoza party guilty as charged. The only penalty assigned, however, was payment of court costs. The ruling came close to a complete exoneration.[159]

Although having been acquitted of charges that he had failed in his duty and disobeyed Governor Otermín, Domínguez de Mendoza continued to worry that "his good name and reputation" were tarnished by the ill-founded accusations. So, not long after the legal settlement of his case, he sought and obtained a detailed statement from fray Antonio Guerra, one of the priests who had accompanied him in all the operations that occurred in New Mexico during 1681–1682. Father Guerra, at present serving in the El Paso district, delivered a firm testimonial in support of Domínguez de Mendoza. It was added to the now bulging portfolio of service documents that Domínguez de Mendoza would attempt to present to the king at court in Madrid, nearly six years later.[160]

Any hope that Domínguez de Mendoza and López may have originally held that they could obtain approval to lead a follow-up expedition back into Texas had long since evaporated. The fiscal and the viceroy decided that until the Pueblo Indians of New Mexico were restored to Spain and its church, no more resources should be directed to the exploration of west Texas. Therefore, Domínguez de Mendoza with his sons settled into life at the capital, quite possibly in reduced circumstances. Yet he remained connected to persons of standing, including among his friends powerful men at the viceregal court.[161]

If Maestre de Campo Juan Domínguez de Mendoza entertained any lingering expectations that he might yet be considered for the New Mexico governorship, they were dashed in early 1688 upon learning that don Domingo Jironza Petríz de Cruzate was reappointed to a second term, replacing Governor Reneros de Posada, who had proven inept. Shortly afterward, Domínguez de Mendoza requested permission for his wife and family to leave El Paso and join him in Mexico City. He had been absent from them since fleeing El Paso Valley almost four years earlier.

The petitioner declared that his wife, doña Isabel Durán y Chaves, fell grievously ill and needed long-term care, which she could not receive at home, because the frontier settlement lacked a doctor and a pharmacy. Also, she was eager to rejoin her husband and to be accompanied on the journey south by other members of her household. The viceroy granted the appeal with certain reservations.

The eldest son of the family, Baltasar Domínguez de Mendoza, was sent north to bring back his mother and others. On March 1, 1689, Baltasar faced the restored governor, Jironza Petríz de Cruzate, at El Paso, probably with some awkwardness given the circumstances in which he, his younger brother, and father had deserted the governor's jurisdiction in 1685. But an official order of the viceroy could not be ignored. Hence, Jironza Petríz de Cruzate issued a travel license for doña Isabel and her party, including a married daughter and several Indian girls she raised in her houshold.[162]

An Untimely and Unfitting Demise, 1690–1701

During the following three years, Juan Domínguez de Mendoza and his reunited family must have basked in the relative comfort of the viceregal capital of New Spain, then the most cosmopolitan city in the New World. Quite likely, supported by a social network of extended family, friends, and political allies, he was accumulating financial resources for his long-desired trip to Spain and the royal court. By 1690, he would have learned that the high-ranking Spaniard don Diego de Vargas Zapata y Luján had purchased the governorship of New Mexico for "a pecuniary contribution of 2,500 pesos to the royal treasury." In chronic need of funds, the government resorted to selling offices of both high and low station.[163]

Through connections he retained with people in El Paso, Juan Domínguez de Mendoza must have received word in early 1693 regarding the restoration of New Mexico led by Vargas Zapata y Luján. Notwithstanding, he remained undeterred in his efforts to present his case in Madrid for the governorship of New Mexico. Finally, in June 1693, he petitioned the new viceroy Conde de Galves for permission "to go to the kingdom of Castile on urgent business which absolutely requires [my] personal attention." The viceroy readily consented and issued him the appropriate travel license on June 12. By coincidence, that same month New Spain's renowned author, scholar, and mathematician don Carlos de Sigüenza y Góngora wrote a slim pamphlet, *El Mercurio Volante*, describing in print for the first time the expedition of don Diego de Vargas Zapata y Luján into upper New Mexico the previous year, 1692. That event marked the beginning of the restoration of the Pueblo Indians under Spanish rule. With it, Vargas earned the glory coveted by all status-conscious Spaniards.[164]

Maestre de Campo Juan Domínguez de Mendoza, since the great revolt of 1680, had attempted repeatedly to position himself to become New Mexico's savior and win the accolades now being showered upon Governor Vargas. But every one of his plans to achieve that end misfired. Upon receipt of his viceregal license, he bade good-bye to his family and, taking son Baltasar, he traveled the Camino Real over the mountains to Veracruz on the Gulf Coast, where a fleet was waiting. Father and son boarded one of the ships and soon sailed for Spain.[165]

Ill fate still dogged Juan Domínguez de Mendoza's footsteps. Nearing his destination, his vessel was shipwrecked off the Spanish mainland. Juan and Baltasar were rescued, while losing all their baggage, which included, in Baltasar's words, "the residue of their fortune." Only the file containing the precious service record was saved. Once on dry land, the pair made their way to Madrid. In the city's general hospital, Juan Domínguez de Mendoza obtained shelter, "for lack of [other] means," and immediately after admission he died. Injuries or stresses resulting from the shipwreck apparently led to his sudden death, most likely sometime around October or November 1693.[166] No record with any specific details of his illness or his passing has yet been uncovered.

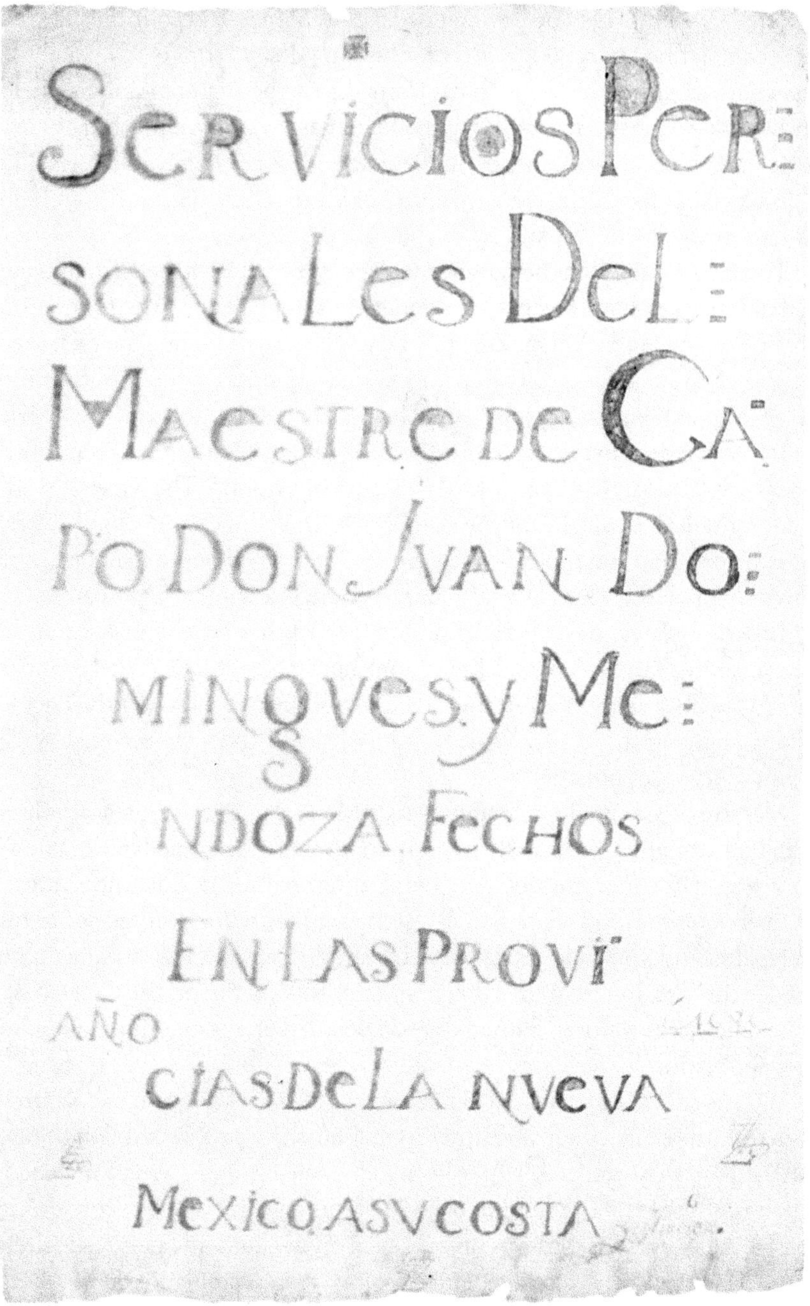

FIGURE 2. Cover sheet for the Juan Domínguez de Mendoza documents. Personal services of the Maestre de Campo Don Juan Domingues y Mendoza. Done in the provinces of Nueva Mexico at his own cost.

This end was by no means the honorable death he most likely envisioned for himself as a soldier of the Crown. It was seemingly an unfitting demise for a remarkable man with a distinguished and lengthy military career, who faced death constantly in campaigns against hostile Indians in the far reaches of Spain's empire. News of his unfortunate death would have taken as long as six to nine months to reach New Mexico. Although no record of his burial has been located, he was likely laid to rest in Madrid, a half a world away from family and friends, with his son Baltasar as the sole family witness to his passing.

Baltasar Domínguez de Mendoza remained in Madrid for a year, following up on his late father's mission. Indeed, it would be surprising if Juan Domínguez de Mendoza with his dying words had not exacted a sworn promise from his son to uphold the family honor and pursue the rewards for past services that a generous monarch ought to recognize.

Baltasar submitted a petition directly to King Carlos II, accompanied by his father's service record, in which he asked that he himself be appointed governor of New Mexico or alcalde mayor of Sonora. For legal reasons, the petition was denied by the Council of the Indies, the royal advisory body to which the Crown had referred the matter. The same result occurred when Baltasar next asked for a more modest political office in Nueva Galicia, northwest of Mexico City. Finally, in desperation, he sought from the king membership in one of the three prestigious military orders for himself and his brother Juan, as a token of royal gratitude for their devotion to His Majesty's interests in New Mexico. On a technicality, that too was denied him.[167]

Now destitute, Baltasar managed to wring two small favors from the parsimonious Crown. One was free passage on a ship to New Spain, granted in a license signed by the king on May 26, 1695, with departure from the port of Cádiz in July 1695. The other was a royal *cédula* for the viceroy in Mexico City, directing him to find some sort of employment for Baltasar "in consideration of the fact that don Juan Domínguez de Mendoza served me for more than forty years in the wars of New Mexico . . ."[168]

Baltasar Domínguez de Mendoza returned safely to Mexico City, where he married and continued to reside. He apparently maintained contact with relatives and associates in New Mexico and was probably kept apprised of various developments there. This is evidenced by the fact that on August 28, 1699, the cabildo of the Villa de Santa Fe unanimously assigned full power of attorney to "don Baltasar Domínguez de Mendoza, a citizen of Mexico City," so that he could press a lawsuit brought by the Santa Fe cabildo against former governor don Diego de Vargas. Baltasar was enlisted to represent the interests of the cabildo and citizens of New Mexico in obtaining a judgment in the matter of "losses and damages" alleged to have been caused by Vargas in the "failure to fulfill his duty."[169]

Spurred on by vengeful Governor don Pedro Rodríguez Cubero, the cabildo and various outspoken citizens of New Mexico aggressively sought to discredit Vargas by focusing on a number of irregularities in the handling of royal finances during his governorship. By mid-May 1700, Baltasar transferred the power of attorney to don Fernando de Gálvez, a registered procurator of the royal Audiencia, a man well trained in the legal machinations of government in New Spain.[170]

At that point the trail of available documentation comes to an end. One additional document dealing with Juan Domínguez de Mendoza's younger son, Juan, is a letter of recommendation written by New Mexico governor Pedro Rodríguez Cubero in 1701, addressed to the king. It certified that this younger Juan Domínguez de Mendoza had acquitted himself admirably in a military expedition to the Hopi country in western New Mexico. A government functionary in Madrid deposited the letter in the personal service record of the elder Juan Domínguez de Mendoza. It was the final entry for that much-traveled file.[171]

Notes

1. Mexico, Distrito Federal, Mexico City, Asunción Church (Catedral), Bautismos, 1627–1639, LDS Microfilm #0035170. Credit goes to Gina Hacker for locating the baptismal record of Juan Domínguez de Mendoza. The record reads: "*en Treinta de mayo de seiscientos y veinte y siete con Licensia del L[icencia]do Diego de Estrada Cura Semen[ar]o Baptiso a Ju[a]n hijo de Tome Dominguez y de Helena de la Cruz fueron Padrinos Hernan Bazquez y M[ari]a de Villegas su mujer, Diego de Estrada (rubric), Francisco Gomez (rubric).*" By his own account, Juan Domínguez de Mendoza declared he was thirty-three years old, on October 29, 1661, and on October 31, 1664, he declared he was thirty-five years old, more or less. Both accounts inaccurately indicate he was born circa 1628–1629. Archivo General de la Nación, México (AGN), Real Audiencia, Concurso de Peñalosa, Vol. 1, leg. 1, no. 2, f. 220v/367v, Testimony of Capitán Juan Domínguez de Mendoza, October 29, 1661, Villa de Santa Fe; and AGN, Tierras, vol. 3268, ff. 409r–409v, Testimony of Capitán Juan Domínguez de Mendoza, October 31, 1664, Villa de Santa Fe.

2. AGN, Inquicisión, vol. 304, exp. 26, f. 180r, Escrito de fray Estéban de Perea, March 4, 1633, Convento del Pueblo de Cuarác.

3. Doc. 1, infra, Proof of Lineage of Elena de la Cruz, 1625; and "Domínguez de Mendoza," unpublished manuscript by Patsy Mendoza Castro de Ludwig, in possession of the editors. The paternal grandfather of Elena de la Cruz was Francisco de Mendoza, the source of the Mendoza surname used by Juan Domínguez de Mendoza and his siblings.

4. Fray Angélico Chávez, *Origins of New Mexico Families in the Spanish Colonial Period* (rev. ed.; Santa Fe: Museum of New Mexico Press, 1992), 25.

5. Lansing B. Bloom, ed., "Fray Esteban de Perea's Relación," *New Mexico Historical Review* 8 (July 1933): 215, 221. The accounts of the Mexico City treasury officers give detailed lists and prices of purchases made at that time. Archivo General de Indias (AGI), Sevilla, Contaduría, 728, Caja de México. Cuentas de los oficiales reales de México, 1626–1628, and AGI, Contaduría, 729, Cuentas de los oficiales reales de México, 1628–1630; photostat copies located at the Southwest Research Center, University of New Mexico. From an early date, wholesalers of Mexico City supplied goods to local merchants and to churchmen throughout the period of the viceroyalty. Louise Schell Hoberman, *Mexico's Merchant Elite, 1590–1660* (Durham, NC: Duke University Press, 1991), 78–79.

6. AGN, Inquisición, vol. 304, f. 180r, Escrito de fray Estéban de Perea al Santo Oficio, October 3, 1632.

7. Domínguez reached Mexico City by June 21, 1634. See Scholes Collection, Center for Southwest Research, University of New Mexico, Personal Notes from AGN, Inquisición, vol. 372, exp. 16 y 19, Información contra Gaspar Pérez, Armero, flamenco, por palabras mal sonatas, 1632; and AGN, Inquisición, vol. 380, exp. 2, f. 250r, Testimony of Tomé Domínguez, vecino de la Ciudad de México, May 26, 1633, Convento de la Concepción de Cuarác.

8. Papers in the legal cases involving Tomé Domínguez, AGN, Bulas de la Santa Cruzada, vol. 2, exp. 1, ff. 1r–5r, Litigio promovido por Miguel de Urquiola albacea del difunto Pedro de Ibarra contra Thomé Domínguez por una deuda, 1634, Ciudad de México.

9. Biblioteca Nacional de México, leg. 1, no. 7, f. 482, Settlement of the Estate of Francisco Gómez de Torres; photostat copy located at the Southwest Research Center, University of New Mexico.

10. Spanish Archives of New Mexico (SANM), State Records Center and Archives (SRCA), Santa Fe, Series II, no. 2: Commission of Thomé Domínguez, Pueblo de Socorro, December 15, 1636.

11. AGN, Real Hacienda, Bulas de la Santa Cruzada, vol. 2, exp. 4, ff. 13r–92r, Hernando Delgado, cirujano, promueve un litigio en contra de Thomé Domínguez, principal, y Tomás de Sein, fiador, por una deuda, 1634, Ciudad de México.

12. Doc. 9, infra, Title of Maestre de Campo, Santa Fe, October 15, 1658; and Doc. 64, infra, Résumé of papers presented by Baltasar Domínguez de Mendoza, Madrid, August 19, 1694.

13. AGN, Inquisición, vol. 593, exp. 1, f. 232r, Testimony of fray Tomás de Alvarado, April 5, 1662, Convento del San Francisco de Sandia.

14. Charles Wilson Hackett, ed., *Historical Documents Relating to New Mexico, Nueva Vizcaya, and Approaches Thereto, to 1773* (Washington, D.C.: Carnegie Institute of Washington, 1923–1937), 3:119.

15. Ibid.

16. Ibid., 3:119–20.

17. AGN, Inquisición, vol. 596, exp. 1, f. 6r, Testimony of Capitán Tomé Domínguez de Mendoza, May 21, 1661, Convento de San Antonio de Isleta. The estancia was originally located west of the Rio Grande, but the river later changed its course so that the site is now on the east side.

18. Chávez, *Origins of New Mexico Families*, 24–25; and AGN, Inquisición, vol. 582, exp. 2, Proceso contra Cristóbal de Anaya Almazán, 1660–1666. In the Scholes Collection, in the file labeled "Tomé Domínguez, the Elder," there is a note taken from AGN, Inquisición, vol. 593, indicating that Tomé *el Viejo* died prior to May 17, 1661, being about seventy years of age. In the documents of the Proceso contra Cristóbal de Anaya Almazán, just cited, mention is made that doña Juana de la Cruz, a sister of Elena de la Cruz, and Tomé's sister-in-law, was living on the estancia in 1658.

19. Doc. 46, infra, Certification of Documents Showing Services of Maestre de Campo Don Juan Domínguez de Mendoza, El Paso, October 3, 1684; and Charles Wilson Hackett and Charmion Clair Shelby, eds. and trans., *Revolt of the Pueblo Indians of New Mexico and Otermín's Attempted Reconquest* (Albuquerque: University of New Mexico Press, 1942), 1:cxli. Hackett affirms that the pueblo of Alameda at this time was west of the river. Hackett and Shelby, *Revolt of the Pueblo Indians*, 1:cxliv.

20. France V. Scholes, *Troublous Times in New Mexico, 1659–1670*, Publications in History, no. 9 (Albuquerque: University of New Mexico Press, 1942), 1:40. On the subject of instability in the Spanish family, see James Casey, *Early Modern Spain: A Social History* (London: Routledge, 1999), 193–99.

21. Gloria M. Valencia y Valdez, José Antonio Esquibel, Robert D. Martínez, and Francisco Sisneros, eds., *Aquí se comienza: A Genealogical History of the Founding Families of La Villa de San Felipe de Albuquerque* (Albuquerque: New Mexico Genealogical Society, 2007), 185.

22. Ibid., 181 and 184.

23. Chávez, *Chávez*, 25.

24. Hackett and Shelby, *Revolt of the Pueblo Indians*, 2:67; Chávez, *Origins of New Mexico Families*, 60. See Domínguez de Mendoza Genealogy Chart 2, infra.

25. Chávez, *Chávez*, 28; and Doc. 47, infra, Certification of Documents. . . . Juan Domínguez de Mendoza, El Paso, October 3, 1684. Also see letter of Governor Otermín, September 14, 1680, in Ralph Emerson Twitchell, *The Spanish Archives of New Mexico* (Cedar Rapids, IA: Torch Press, 1914), 2:33.

26. John L. Kessell and Rick Hendricks, eds. and trans., *By Force of Arms: The Journals of Don Diego de Vargas, 1691–1693* (Albuquerque: University of New Mexico Press, 1992), 18.

27. Doc. 36, infra, Instruction as Lieutenant Captain General, Santa Fe, October 28, 1678. For a comment on the poor quality of temporary militia forces

generally, see Christon I. Archer, *The Army in Bourbon Mexico, 1760–1810* (Albuquerque: University of New Mexico Press, 1977), 8. On the scarcity of regular royal troops in the viceroyalty up to the end of the mid-eighteenth century, see María del Carmen Velázquez, *El estado de guerra en Nueva España, 1760–1808* (Mexico: El Colégio de México, 1950), 90–91.

28. Doc. 42, infra, Commission as Commander of the Expedition to Texas, El Paso, November 29, 1683.

29. Ibid.

30. Doc. 2, infra, Commission as Alférez Real, Santa Fe, October 12, 1643; and Doc. 60, infra, Résumé of papers presented by Baltasar Domínguez de Mendoza, Madrid, August 19, 1694. It should be noted that a staff officer might be commissioned as a campaign officer at a higher or lower rank than his staff rank. Thus, during a campaign, he simultaneously held two ranks.

31. Juan Domínguez de Mendoza's lobbying for the New Mexico governorship will be described below. See table 1, infra, for his sequence of appointments.

32. Doc. 2, infra, Commission as Alférez Real, Santa Fe, October 12, 1643; and Doc. 7, Certification of Services, Santa Fe, January 12, 1653. In addition, consult Jack D. Forbes, *Apache, Navaho, and Spaniard* (Norman: University of Oklahoma Press, 1960), 143–45.

33. AGI, Indiferente, 120, N. 44, f. 1v, Relación de méritos y servicios de Diego de Guadalajara Bernardo de Quirós, Teniente de Gobernador de Nueva Vizcaya, 1664. See Supp. Doc. 4, infra.

34. The number of soldiers is given by Cristóbal de Anaya Almazán as found in AGN, Inquisición, vol. 582, exp. 2, f. 312r, Proceso y causa criminal contra Cristóbal de Anaya Almazán, 1661.

35. Nancy Parrott Hickerson, *The Jumanos, Hunters and Traders of the South Plains* (Austin: University of Texas Press, 1994), 110–11. Doc. 8, infra, Certification of Services, Santa Fe, September 13, 1653.

36. Chávez, *Origins of New Mexico Families*, 42; AGI, Indiferente, 120, N. 44, f. 1v, Relación de méritos y servicios de Diego de Guadalajara Bernardo de Quirós, Teniente de Gobernador de Nueva Vizcaya, 1664. See Supp. Doc. 4, infra.

37. Hickerson, *Jumanos*, 112–14. For conflicting views over the linguistic identity of the Jumanos, see Carroll L. Riley, *The Kachina and the Cross: Indians and Spaniards in the Early Southwest* (Salt Lake City: University of Utah Press, 1999), 272; and Bill Lockhart, "Protohistoric Confusion: A Cultural Comparison of the Manso, Suma, and Jumano Indians of the Paso del Norte Region," *Journal of the Southwest* 39 (Spring 1997): 113–49.

38. AGI, Estado, 43, N. 1, ff. 9v and 27v, Descubrimiento y situación de Quivira y Teguayo, Alonso de Posada, March 14, 1686 (Mexico).

39. The *Informe* was transcribed and published in Spanish by Cesáreo Fernández Duro, *Don Diego de Peñalosa y su descubrimiento del reino de Quivira* (Madrid:

Imprenta y Fundación de Manuel Tello, 1882), 53–67. An English translation is provided by Alfred Barnaby Thomas, ed., *Alonso de Posada Report, 1686* (Pensacola, FL: Presidio Bay Press, 1982). Also see Forbes, *Apache, Navaho, and Spaniard*, 146.

40. In Doc. 8, infra, Certification of Services, Santa Fe, September 13, 1653, ex-Governor Hernando de Ugarte y la Concha acknowledges that he sent Juan Domínguez de Mendoza to Mexico City with "dispatches concerning the discovery of pearls." Scholes identifies this as a genuine document. That Domínguez de Mendoza was selected as courier to the viceroy also supports that he did participate in the Jumano expedition.

41. Doc. 7, infra, Certification of Services, Santa Fe, January 12, 1653. Not unexpectedly, this document contains lavish praise of Domínguez de Mendoza's conduct.

42. The itinerary of Domínguez de Mendoza's 1683–1684 Jumano expedition appears in Doc. 45, infra, Journal of the Expedition to Texas, 1683–1684.

43. Doc. 10, infra, Commission as Captain of Mounted Harquebusiers, Santa Fe, August 30, 1659.

44. Doc. 11, infra, Appointment as Alcalde Mayor and . . . Lieutenant Captain General in the Río Abajo, Santa Fe, November 19, 1659.

45. The Ramírez letter dated September 8, 1659, is translated in Hackett, *Historical Documents*, 3:186–93. On slavery, see Forbes, *Apache, Navaho, and Spaniard*, 149.

46. France V. Scholes, "Church and State in New Mexico, 1610–1650," *New Mexico Historical Review* 11 (October 1936): 340.

47. Hackett, *Historical Documents*, 3:186.

48. Ibid., 3:177–78.

49. Scholes, *Troublous Times*, 97–98. Fray Alonso de Posada took the habit of the Order of San Francisco on October 20, 1646, in Mexico City at age twenty. He was a native of Congosto in the Reino de León, Spain, being a son of Licenciado Alonso de Llanos y Posada and María González. Libro de entradas y profesiones de novicios de este convento de Padre San Francisco de México 1562–1680, Bancroft Library, Mexican Manuscripts 216–18, f. 118v, entry #1077.

50. Hackett, *Historical Documents*, 3:210; and Scholes, *Troublous Times*, 117, 157.

51. AGN, Inquisición, vol. 586, exp. 1, f. 172v, Testimony of doña Ana Moreno, May 7, 1662, Convento de San Francisco de Sandia; and Chávez, *Origins of New Mexico Families*, 10.

52. C. L. Sonnichsen, *Pass of the North: Four Centuries on the Rio Grande* (El Paso: Texas Western Press, 1968, 1980), 1:41; and Hackett, *Historical Documents*, 3:138–39.

53. AGN, Inquisición, vol. 507, f. 19r, Declaration of Juan Domínguez de Mendoza contra don Diego de Peñalosa y Briceño, May 20, 1662, Ciudad de México.

54. Hackett, *Historical Documents*, 3:234. A brief summary of Domínguez de Mendoza's testimony is given here.

55. See Doc. 13, infra, Title of Lieutenant Captain General and Visitador General, October 6, 1663.

56. Doc. 12, infra, Appointment as Escudero of the Encomienda of Sargento Mayor Francisco Gómez Robledo, Santa Fe, May 7, 1662; and Scholes, *Troublous Times*, 133, 215.

57. Hackett, *Historical Documents*, 3:251.

58. Doc. 12, infra, Appointment as Escudero, Santa Fe, May, 1662; and Scholes, *Troublous Times*, 130. For background on the encomienda institution, consult these standard sources: Lesley Byrd Simpson, *The Encomienda in New Spain* (Berkeley: University of California Press, 1982); Silvio A. Závala, *La Encomienda indiana* (Mexico: Editorial Porrua, 1973). For an overview in New Mexico, see David H. Snow, "A Note on Encomienda Economics in Seventeenth-Century New Mexico," in Marta Weigle, with Samuel Larcombe and Claudia Larcombe, *Hispanic Arts and Ethnohistory in the Southwest* (Santa Fe, NM: Ancient City Press, 1983), 347–57. For a detailed study of one encomendero clan of New Mexico, see José Antonio Esquibel, "The Romero Family of Seventeenth-Century New Mexico," Part I and Part II, in *Herencia* 11 (January 2003): 1:1–30, and (July 2003): 3:2–20.

59. France V. Scholes, "Civil Government and Society in New Mexico in the Seventeenth Century," *New Mexico Historical Review* 10 (April 1935): 102.

60. On the use of *escuderos* as a legal term, see Rafael Altamira y Crevea, *Diccionario castellano de palabras jurídicas y técnicas* (Mexico: Instituto Panamericano de Geografía e História, 1951), 142–43. For a succinct statement on the nature of the institution, see Robert Himmerich y Valencia, *The Encomenderos of New Spain, 1521–1555* (Austin: University of Texas Press, 1991), 9–17.

61. Scholes, *Troublous Times*, 194. Závala, *La Encomienda indiana*, 193; Snow, "Encomienda Economics," *Hispanic Arts*, 354; and Esquibel, "Romero Family of Seventeenth-Century New Mexico," Part 2, *Herencia* (January 2003): 16–17.

62. Hackett, *Historical Documents*, 3:250; and Závala, *La Encomienda indiana*, 655.

63. AGN, Tierras, vol. 3268, f. 109v, Response of Governor don Bernardo López de Mendizábal to accusation of Domingo López de Ocanto, October 1661.

64. Doc. 20, infra, Title of Encomienda, Santa Fe, May 1, 1669. Almost all original title documents of encomienda for New Mexico were destroyed during the revolt of 1680. Thus, Domínguez de Mendoza's two titles and his appointment as escudero, preserved in his service record, have exceptional value for the historian attempting to understand how the trusteeship functioned in New Mexico. For comparative purposes, a translation of a title of encomienda with a facsimile of the original document granted by Governor Francisco de Montejo of Yucatán is provided in Simpson, *Encomienda in New Spain*, 203–4.

65. Doc. 22, infra, Commission as Maestre de Campo, Santa Fe, September, 11, 1670; and James E. Ivey, *In the Midst of Loneliness: The Architectural History of the Salinas Missions* (Santa Fe, NM: National Park Service, 1988), 230.

66. Doc. 54, infra, Copy of the Sentence Pronounced in the Proceedings against Maestre de Campo Juan Domínguez de Mendoza, Mexico, April 30, 1687.

67. Doc. 14, infra, Decree of Governor Peñalosa, Santa Fe, January 7, 1664.

68. AGN, Inquisición, vol. 610, exp. 7, ff. 67r–71, Denunciaciones contra Juan Domínguez de Mendoza, 1666–1667.

69. The details of this contentious episode appear in Scholes, *Troublous Times*, 247–48.

70. AGN, Inquisición, vol. 590, exp. 3, ff. 513v–514r, El Tribunal al comisario del Nuevo México, Fray Juan Bernal, October 25, 1669, Mexico City. Fray Juan Bernal took the habit of the Order of San Francisco at age fifteen and four months, on February 12, 1648, in Mexico City. A native of Mexico City, he was a son of Bartolomé Bernal (native of San Lucar, Spain) and doña Beatris de la Barrera (native of Sevilla, Spain). See Libro deentradas y profesiones, f. 120, entry #1099.

71. AGN, Inquisición, vol. 590, exp. 3, f. 513v–514r, El Tribunal al comisario del Nuevo México, Fray Juan Bernal, October 25, 1669, Mexico City.

72. Doc. 26, infra, Certification of Services, Santa Fe, January 26, 1672.

73. Doc. 22, infra, Commission as Maestre de Campo in Campaign, Santa Fe, September 11, 1670.

74. Doc. 23, infra, Commission as Sargento Mayor of the Kingdom, Santa Fe, June 27, 1671.

75. Doc. 24, infra, Commission as Maestre de Campo General of the Kingdom, Santa Fe, July 27, 1671.

76. Doc. 25, infra, Appointment as Lieutenant of the Governor and Captain General, Santa Fe, August 5, 1671.

77. Scholes, *Troublous Times*, 219–20.

78. Frank D. Reeves, "Early Navajo Geography," *New Mexico Historical Review* 31 (October 1956): 295–96; and Frank E. Wozniak, "The Location of the Navajo Homeland in the Seventeenth Century: An Appraisal of the Spanish Colonial Records," in *Current Research on the Late Prehistory and Early History of New Mexico*, ed. Bradley J. Vierra and Clara Gualtieri (Albuquerque: New Mexico Archaeological Council, 1992), 328–31. See also Rick Hendricks and John P. Wilson, eds. and trans., *The Navajos in 1705: Roque Madrid's Campaign Journal* (Albuquerque: University of New Mexico Press, 1996), 68.

79. Doc. 24, infra, Commission as Maestre de Campo General of the Kingdom, Santa Fe, July 27, 1671.

80. Doc. 31, infra, Commission as Military Commander and Chief, Santa Fe, September 24, 1675.

81. Doc. 33, infra, Commission as Lieutenant Captain General in Campaign, Santa Fe, July 12, 1678.

82. Ibid.; Wozniak, "Navajo Homeland," 331.

83. Doc. 34, infra, Instruction as Lieutenant Captain General, Santa Fe, July 12, 1678 (quotations from succeeding paragraphs herein).

84. Doc. 35, infra, Commission as Lieutenant Captain General in Campaign, Santa Fe, October 28, 1678; and Doc. 34, infra, Instruction as Lieutenant Captain General, Santa Fe, July 12, 1678.

85. Doc. 38, infra, Commission as Maestre de Campo in Campaign, Santa Fe, August 17, 1679.

86. John L. Kessell, *Spain in the Southwest* (Norman: University of Oklahoma Press, 2002), 119. Fray Francisco de Ayeta was born circa 1640 in Pamplona, Spain, being a son of Juan de Ayeta (a native of Pamplona) and Graciosa de Oscos (a native of Pamplona). Ayeta took the habit of the Order of San Francisco in Mexico City on November 26, 1659. At some point he traveled to Spain, and in April 1673 he sought license to return to Mexico City. At that time he was described as being thirty-four years of age and a *predicador* of the Santa Provincia del Santo Evangelio de México. License was granted in June 1673 in Madrid, and Ayeta made his way to Cádiz, where in July 1673 he boarded a ship named *Santa Teresa de Jesús*, under the command of Miguel de Estanba. Libro de entradas y profesiones, f. 154r; and AGI, Contratación, 5439, N. 115, 2ff, Expediente de información y licencia de pasajero a Indias de fray Francisco de Ayeta, franciscano, predicador, a Nueva España, July 7, 1673.

87. Petition of fray Francisco de Ayeta, Mexico, May 10, 1679, in Hackett, *Historical Documents*, 3:296–99.

88. Hackett, *Historical Documents*, 298–99.

89. David J. Weber, ed., *What Caused the Pueblo Revolt of 1680?* (Boston: Bedford/St. Martin, 1999), 10–13; Marc Simmons, "The Pueblo Revolt: Why Did It Happen?" *El Palacio* 86 (Winter 1980–1981), 11–15; Robert W. Preucel, "Writing the Pueblo Revolt," in *Archaeologies of the Pueblo Revolt*, ed. Preucel (Albuquerque: University of New Mexico Press, 2002), 4–7; and Hackett and Shelby, *Revolt of the Pueblo Indians*, 2:262.

90. Kessell, *Spain in the Southwest*, 123.

91. See note 20, supra. See also Paul Kramer, "The Dynamic Ethnicity of the People of Spanish Colonial New Mexico," in *Transforming Images: New Mexican Santos In-Between Worlds*, ed. Claire Farago and Donna Pierce (University Park: Pennsylvania State University Press, 2006), 87.

92. Hackett and Shelby, *Revolt of the Pueblo Indians*, 1:lxvii–lxxi; and Andrew L. Knaut, *The Pueblo Revolt of 1680* (Norman: University of Oklahoma Press, 1995), 9–12.

93. "Otermín's March," August 26, 1680, in Hackett and Shelby, *Revolt of the Pueblo Indians*, 1:26–27; and Elinore M. Barrett, *Conquest and Catastrophe* (Albuquerque: University of New Mexico Press, 2002), 92–93. Some reports show that Juan Domínguez de Mendoza escaped with ten family members and thirty-three servants. Kramer, "Dynamic Ethnicity," 87.

94. "Opinions of Council," Fray Cristóbal campground, September 14, 1680, in Hackett and Shelby, *Revolt of the Pueblo Indians*, 1:116–17.

95. "Muster and Review," La Salineta campground, September 29, 1680, in Hackett and Shelby, *Revolt of the Pueblo Indians*, 1:134–53; and Kessell, *Spain in the Southwest*, 150–51.

96. Vina Walz, "History of the El Paso Area, 1680–1692" (PhD diss., University of New Mexico, Albuquerque, 1951), 35–36.

97. "Muster and Review," La Salineta campground, September 29, 1680, in Hackett and Shelby, *Revolt of the Pueblo Indians*, 1:138.

98. Hackett and Shelby, *Revolt of the Pueblo Indians*, 1:138.

99. Doc. 50, infra, Memorial of Juan Domínguez de Mendoza, Mexico, November 18, 1685. Fray Nicolás to Secretary Antonio Ortiz de Otalora, Mexico, in Hackett, *Historical Documents*, 3:363–64.

100. "Interrogatory: Investigations," San Lorenzo, October 20, 1681, in Hackett and Shelby, *Revolt of the Pueblo Indians*, 1:163–73.

101. France V. Scholes, "Royal Treasury Records, Relating to the Province of New Mexico, 1596–1683," *New Mexico Historical Review* 50 (April 1975): 151.

102. "Muster Roll," El Ancón de Fray García, November 7–10, 1681, in Hackett and Shelby, *Revolt of the Pueblo Indians*, 2:192. Notwithstanding the governor's pessimism, the Spaniards held out hope that the Pueblo Indians might have come to their senses and "would flock to them to be pardoned." That unrealistic expectation was soon abandoned. Riley, *Kachina and the Cross*, 228.

103. Hackett and Shelby, *Revolt of the Pueblo Indians*, 2:190–91; and Forbes, *Apache, Navaho, and Spaniard*, 187.

104. Doc. 39, infra, Commission as Lieutenant General of the Calvary, El Ancón de fray García, November 9, 1681.

105. "Muster Roll," El Ancón de fray García, November 7–10, 1681, in Hackett and Shelby, *Revolt of the Pueblo Indians*, 2:192.

106. Otermín's detailed instructions and orders to Domínguez de Mendoza appear in translation in Hackett and Shelby, *Revolt of the Pueblo Indians*, 2:215–17.

107. Juan Domínguez de Mendoza to Antonio de Otermín, Sandia, December 10, 1681, in Hackett and Shelby, *Revolt of the Pueblo Indians*, 2:225.

108. Alonso Catití was referred to as a brother of Captain Pedro Márquez, indicating that he was at least part Spanish, but his loyalties lay with his Pueblo kin. Chávez, *Origins of New Mexico Families*, 70.

109. Doc. 50, infra, Memorial of Juan Domínguez de Mendoza, Mexico, November 18, 1685; also, Riley, *Kachina and the Cross*, 228–29.

110. Knaut, *Pueblo Revolt*, 173–74.

111. Antonio de Otermín to Viceroy, El Estero Largo, February 11, 1682, and Reply of the Fiscal, don Martín de Solís Miranda, Mexico, June 25, 1682, in Hackett and Shelby, *Revolt of the Pueblo Indians*, 2:370–403. For Domínguez de Mendoza's own lengthy declaration containing justification for his actions, see Hackett and Shelby, *Revolt of the Pueblo Indians*, 2:257–66.

112. Walz, "History of the El Paso Area," 101. Fray Angélico Chávez was seemingly in error when he stated that Pedro Durán y Chaves and Tomé Domínguez de Mendoza "managed to get permission" to leave El Paso for the south in 1684. See Chávez, *Chávez*, 51.

113. Doc. 50, infra, Memorial of Juan Domínguez de Mendoza, Mexico, November 18, 1685.

114. Sonnichsen, *Pass of the North*, 46.

115. Hickerson, *Jumanos*, 127.

116. Doc. 41, infra, Statement of Juan Sabeata before Governor Jironza Petríz de Cruzate, El Paso, October 20, 1683.

117. Walz, "History of the El Paso Area," 129.

118. Fray Silvestre de Escalante, "Extracto de Noticias, 1777," Biblioteca Nacional, México, vols. 19/397 and 20/428.1, leg. 3, no. 1. There is some indication that the escort may have actually totaled as many as twenty-six. If so, Domínguez de Mendoza's sons were probably not counted as part of the original muster of twenty. See Brian Imhoff, ed., *The Diary of Juan Domínguez de Mendoza's Expedition into Texas (1683–1684)* (Dallas, TX: William P. Clement Center for Southwest Studies, 2002), 12 n. 6.

119. AGI, Indiferente, vol. 133, N. 58, f. 2r, Relación de méritos y servicios de Domingo Gironza Petris de Cruzati, Gobernador y Capitán General de Nuevo México, 1693.

120. Doc. 42, infra, Commission as Commander of the Expedition to Texas, El Paso, November 29, 1683.

121. Doc. 43, infra, Instruction for the Expedition to Texas, El Paso, November 29, 1683.

122. AGI, Indiferente, vol. 133, N. 58, f. 2r, Relación de méritos y servicios de Domingo Gironza Petris de Cruzati, Gobernador y Capitán General de Nuevo México, 1693.

123. Walz, "History of the El Paso Area," 132.

124. Sonnichsen, *Pass of the North*, 53. For cultural affiliations of the Sumas and Mansos, see Lockhart, "Protohistorical Confusions," 115–20.

125. Doc. 45, infra, Journal of the Expedition to Texas, 1683–1684. The end of the first entry indicates that "the reverend fathers went on ahead with Sabaeta," from the campsite at the house of Tomé Domínguez de Mendoza. This information conflicts with other evidence that the padres had left for La Junta much earlier. The puzzling statement does not appear in the Herbert E. Bolton translation, *Spanish Exploration in the Southwest, 1542–1706* (New York: Barnes and Noble, 1916), 320, or in the Imhoff transcription, *The Diary of Juan Domínguez de Mendoza's Expedition into Texas*, 12 n. 6. On various versions of the journal, see Doc. 46, infra, n. 1.

126. Howard G. Applegate and C. Wayne Hanselka, *La Junta de los Rios del Norte y Conchos* (El Paso: Texas Western Press, 1974), 15–16.

127. Forbes, *Apache, Navaho, and Spaniard*, 197; and Doc. 45, infra, Journal of the Expedition to Texas, 1683–1684.

128. Doc. 45, infra, Journal of the Expedition to Texas, 1683–1684.

129. Domínguez de Mendoza's exact route through west Texas has been the subject of much academic debate. For a summary of the most prominent theories, consult Robert S. Weddle, "Juan Domínguez de Mendoza," in *The New Handbook of Texas* (Austin, TX: Texas Historical Association, 1996), 2:673.

130. Doc. 45, infra, Journal of the Expedition to Texas, 1683–1684. Imhoff, *Diary of Juan Domínguez de Mendoza's Expedition into Texas*, attempts to identify several of the conspirators, who are otherwise unnamed in the documents. One apparently was Felipe Romero, the third-ranking officer in command of the expedition.

131. Doc. 45, infra, Journal of the Expedition to Texas, 1683–1684.

132. Forbes, *Apache, Navaho, and Spaniard*, 198. The official journal gives June 6 as the date of arrival at La Junta, whereas Domínguez de Mendoza's certification (Doc. 44, infra, Certification, June 23, 1684) at the expedition's close provides the date of June 4.

133. Doc. 45, infra, Journal of the Expedition to Texas, 1683–1684.

134. Doc. 44, infra, Certification, June 23, 1684.

135. Doc. 42, infra, Commission as Commander of the Expedition to Texas, El Paso, November 29, 1683; and Doc. 43, infra, Instruction for the Expedition to Texas, El Paso, November 29, 1683.

136. Carlos Eduardo Castañeda, *Our Catholic Heritage in Texas* (Austin, TX: Von-Boeckmann, 1936–1958), 1:274–75.

137. Supp. Doc. 11, infra, Account of the Services of Don Domingo Jironza Petríz de Cruzate, January 12, 1693.

138. Walz, "History of the El Paso Area," 164–65, 168.

139. Doc. 48, infra, Excerpt from a Letter of Governor Jironza Petríz de Cruzate to the Viceroy, El Paso, August 26, 1685.

140. Sonnichsen, *Pass of the North*, 57–58; and Walz, "History of the El Paso Area," 198–99.

141. Walz, "History of the El Paso Area," 202.

142. Doc. 51, infra, Criminal Case against Maestre de Campo Juan Domínguez de Mendoza and Others Who Fled with Him, Guadalupe del Paso, September 28–October 6, 1685.

143. Donald E. Chipman and Harriet Denise Joseph, *Spanish Texas 1519–1821* (Austin: University of Texas Press, 1992), 70; On the French intrusion led by La Salle, see Robert S. Weddle, *The French Thorn, Rival Explorers in the Spanish Sea, 1682–1762* (College Station: Texas A & M University Press, 1991), 26–39.

144. Thomas, *Alonso de Posada Report, 1686*, 2.

145. The López cover letter appears in Hackett, *Historical Documents*, 3:259–60. See Supp. Doc. 10, infra, Memorial of fray Nicolás López to His Majesty, Mexico

City, April 24, 1686. López's report was also printed in Fernández Duro, *Don Diego de Peñalosa*, 68–74. The map forming part of his original submissions has not yet come to light.

146. Doc. 49, infra, First Memorial of Juan Domínguez de Mendoza to the Viceroy, Mexico City, November 18, 1685.

147. Doc. 50, infra, Second Domínguez de Mendoza Memorial [Mexico City], November 18, 1685. For reference to this pair of memorials, see Imhoff, *The Diary of Juan Domínguez de Mendoza's Expedition into Texas*, 15, 181–82.

148. Supp. Doc. 8, infra, Excerpt from a Petition of fray Nicolás López to the Viceroy, Mexico City, June 7, 1685.

149. Supp. Doc. 9, infra, Letter of fray Nicolás López to the Secretary of the Council of the Indies, don Antonio Ortiz de Otalora, Mexico City, April 24, 1686.

150. Supp. Doc. 10, infra, Memorial of fray Nicolás López to His Majesty, Mexico City, April 24, 1686.

151. Doc. 46, infra, Certification of Documents Showing the Services of the Maestre de Campo Don Juan Domínguez de Mendoza, El Paso, October 3, 1684. See the forward by Scholes concerning the appearance of forgery of this document. According to Scholes, the authentic certification is in the attested copy of the cabildo of Santa Fe's certification found in Doc. 52, infra, Attested Copy . . . by the Cabildo of Santa Fe Certifying the Titles of Offices of Juan Domínguez de Mendoza, Mexico City, April 23–24, 1686. A variant of the certification is translated in Hackett, *Historical Documents*, 3:357–58.

152. Doc. 47, infra, Certification of the Personal Appearance and Services of Maestre de Campo Don Juan Domínguez de Mendoza and His Two Sons, El Paso, October 8, 1684.

153. Doc. 52, infra, Attested Copy . . . by the Cabildo of Santa Fe Certifying the Titles of Offices of Juan Domínguez de Mendoza, Mexico City, April 23–24, 1686.

154. Ibid.

155. Supp. Doc. 8 infra, Excerpt from a Petition of fray Nicolás López to the Viceroy, Mexico, June 7, 1685; and Doc. 53, infra, Petition of fray Nicolás López to the Viceroy, Mexico City, March 26, 1686.

156. Supp. Doc. 9, infra, Letter of fray Nicolás López to the Secretary of the Council of the Indies, don Antonio Ortiz de Otalora, Mexico City, April 24, 1686; Hackett, *Historical Documents*, 3:363; and Kessell and Hendricks, *By Force of Arms*, 24.

157. Supp. Doc. 9, infra, Letter of fray Nicolás López to the Secretary of the Council of the Indies, don Antonio Ortiz de Otalora, Mexico City, April 24, 1686.

158. Hackett, *Historical Documents*, 3:364.

159. Doc. 54, infra, Copy of the Sentence Pronounced in the Proceedings against Maestre de Campo Juan Domínguez de Mendoza, Mexico City, April 30, 1687.

160. Doc. 55, infra, Testimony concerning the Conduct of Juan Domínguez de Mendoza during the Expedition of 1681–82 [El Paso del Norte], May 19–June 12, 1687.

161. Sonnichsen, *Pass of the North*, 62.

162. Doc. 56, infra, Permission for Maestre de Campo Juan Domínguez de Mendoza to bring his wife and family from El Paso del Río del Norte, Mexico City, July 23, 1688; and Doc. 57, infra, Decree of Governor Domingo Jironza Petríz de Cruzate, El Paso, March 1, 1689.

163. John L. Kessell, ed., *Remote Beyond Compare* (Albuquerque: University of New Mexico Press, 1989), 42–43, 51.

164. Irving Albert Leonard, trans. and ed., *The Mercurio Volante of Don Carlos de Sigüenza y Góngora* (Los Angeles: Quivira Society, 1932), 43–44; and D. A. Brading, *Patriots and the Liberal State, 1492–1867* (New York: Cambridge University Press, 1991), 367.

165. Doc. 59, infra, License for Maestre de Campo Juan Domínguez de Mendoza to Go to Spain, Mexico City, June 12, 1693.

166. Doc. 61, infra, Report of the Council of the Indies concerning Petitions Made by Baltasar Domínguez de Mendoza, Madrid, October 1, 1694.

167. Doc. 62, infra, Summary of the Petition of Baltasar Domínguez de Mendoza to the Crown [Madrid], 1694; Doc. 61, infra, Report of the Council of the Indies, Madrid, October 1, 1694; and Doc. 63, infra, Petition Asking for Admission to One of the Military Orders, Madrid, March 1695.

168. Doc. 65, infra, Papers concerning the Return of Baltasar Domínguez de Mendoza to New Spain, Madrid, May 26–July 8, 1695.

169. John L. Kessell, Rick Hendricks, Meredith D. Dodge, and Larry D. Miller, eds., *That Disturbances Cease: The Journals of Don Diego de Vargas, New Mexico, 1696–1700* (Albuquerque: University of New Mexico Press, 2000), 260.

170. Ibid.

171. Doc. 67, infra, Certification of Services of Don Juan Domínguez de Mendoza, the Younger, Santa Fe, September, 18, 1701.

PART ONE

Military Service Records of Juan Domínguez de Mendoza and Related Documents

Translations by Eleanor B. Adams

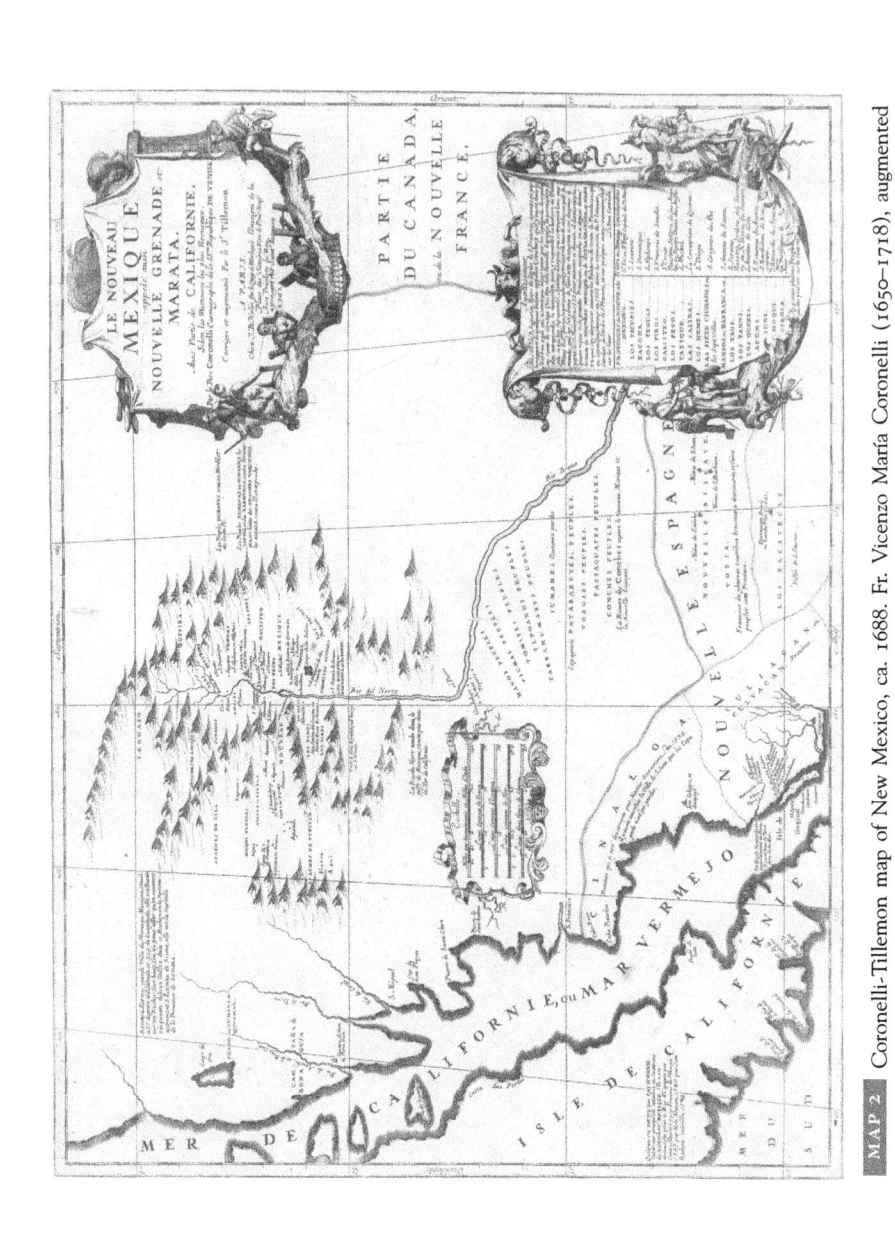

MAP 2. Coronelli-Tillemon map of New Mexico, ca. 1688. Fr. Vicenzo María Coronelli (1650–1718), augmented by Jean Nicolás du Tralage, Sieur de Tillemon (d. 1699), and published by Jean Baptiste Nolin (1648–1708), *Le Nouveau Mexique appele aussi Nouvelle Grenade et Marata; Avec partie de Californie*, ca. 1688, Paris. Library of Congress, Geography and Map Division, Washington, D.C.

Document 1

Proof of Lineage of Elena de la Cruz

Mother of Juan Domínguez de Mendoza

1625[1]

[Summary][2]

On August 8, 1625, Tomé Domínguez, "merchant [and] citizen of the City of Mexico," and his wife, Elena de la Cruz, gave power of attorney to Francisco Franco authorizing him to go to Vera Cruz to obtain legal proof of the lineage of the said Elena de la Cruz. In Vera Cruz, August 30–September 10, a formal inquiry was made in the usual form. Six witnesses were examined who testified: (1) that Elena de la Cruz was the daughter of Benito París and Leonor Francisca, deceased citizens of Vera Cruz; (2) that her paternal grandparents were Juan Gonzáles and Isabel Gallega, former residents of Vera Cruz; (3) that her maternal grandparents were Francisco de Mendoza and Leonor de Grimaldos, citizens of Puerto de Santa María in Spain; and (4) that the said parents and grandparents were "old Christians," unstained by any mixture of blood with Moors, Jews, *conversos*, or persons who had been tried and punished by the Holy Office of the Inquisition.[3]

Notes

1. Biblioteca Nacional de España, Madrid (BNE), MSS 19258, photos 106–12. The original *probanza* consists of eight unnumbered leaves. All the essential facts are given in this summary.

2. See part 3 of this book, "In Service to the Crown: The Family of Juan Domínguez de Mendoza," for details extracted from this proof-of-lineage document. (E & S)

3. The name of the maternal grandfather helps explain the fact that Elena de la Cruz was also known as Elena Ramírez de Mendoza. In testimony before the tribunal of the Holy Office, April 27, 1663, Cristóbal de Anaya Almazán testified his wife was Leonor Ramírez de Mendoza, daughter of Tomé Domínguez and Elena Ramírez de Mendoza. Archivo General de la Nación, México (AGN), Inquisición, vol. 582, exp. 2, Proceso y causa criminal contra Christobal de Anaya,

por proposiciones hereticas. Elena Ramírez de Mendoza had a sister named Juana de la Cruz y Mendoza who was in the service of don Dionisio de Peñalosa y Briceño, Governor of New Mexico, 1661–1664, and her son, Luís de Ulloa, was a page in Peñalosa y Briceño's service. Chávez, *Origins of New Mexico Families*, 24–25. (E & S)

Document 2

Commission as Alférez Real
Santa Fe, October 12, 1643[1]

Captain Alonso Pacheco de Heredia,[2] governor, chief magistrate, and captain general of these provinces of New Mexico and the others adjacent to them for the king, our lord, etc.[3]

Because of the person, quality and merits of Alférez don Juan Domínguez de Mendoza, I have complete confidence that he is a faithful, diligent, and honorable soldier. He has serviced His Majesty in these provinces more than three years with his arms and horses at his own expense, taking part, with great personal expense and hardship, in many expeditions which have been the most important which have offered themselves in this pacification during the said time, as is proved by his attestations and certifications, to which I refer.[4] In all the military operations which have taken place he has conducted himself as an honorable and outstanding soldier. Therefore, in consideration of this and his merits, I have decided to name and appoint the said Alférez don Juan Domínguez de Mendoza as alférez of the royal standard. As such alférez real of this conquest and pacification he may raise the said royal standard on all occasions which may arise in the service of His Majesty, and enjoy the preeminences, places, due honors, and plenary authority exercised by the alféreces reales of the royal armies; provided that first, before using the office, he shall make oath and homage in my hands according to the fuero [body of privileges] of the hidalgos of Castile to guard the said royal standard and not to lower it before any prince of the world except to His Majesty and me in his name, or my successor, and to die rather than do the contrary, and to fulfill the orders that I and the higher officials of the army may give him; and for all of this I give him power and authority as I hold it from the king, our lord. Therefore, I order you [the secretary of government and war] to issue his title of alférez real in due form, signed by my hand and sealed with the seal of my arms, and countersigned by the undersigned secretary.

Done in this villa of Santa Fe of New Mexico on the twelfth day of the month of October, 1643. (Seal) Alonso Pacheco de Heredia (rubric). By order of the governor and captain general, Lorenzo Librán, secretary of government and war (rubric).

In the villa of Santa Fe of New Mexico, on the fifteenth day of the month of October of the year 1643, before Captain Alonso Pacheco de Heredia, governor, chief magistrate, and captain general of these provinces of New Mexico for the king, our lord, and in the presence of me, the secretary mentioned below, and of the witnesses named below, the Alférez don Juan Domínguez de Mendoza, to whose identity I certify, appeared and produced the aforesaid title of alférez real, petitioning the governor to administer the oath and ceremony which he is therein ordered to make in order to use and exercise the said office; whereupon the said governor admitted him to office. And the said alférez real, joining hands with the governor, swore in due form according to the fuero of the hidalgos of Castile and made homage, promising to guard the royal standard which is given into his keeping and to defend it and not to hand it over in peace or in war to the enemy or to any prince of the world, nor to lower it except to the king, our lord, to the governor in his name, and to those who may succeed him in the said office, and to die for it rather than to do anything else. And thus he promised and swore, Captain Simón Pérez de Bustillo, Alférez Miguel de Hinojos, and Alonso Rodríguez Varela being witnesses.[5] And he signed it together with the governor.

Done ut supra. Don Juan Domínguez y Mendoza (rubric). Alonso Pacheco de Heredia (rubric). By order of the governor and captain general, Lorenzo Librán, secretary of government and war (rubric).[6]

His lordship appointed Don Juan Domínguez y Mendoza as alférez real.

Notes

1. BNE, Madrid, MSS 19258, photos 12–14.

2. Alonso Pacheco de Heredia served as governor of New Mexico from the autumn of 1642 to December 5, 1644. Dates for the terms of office of provincial governors given in the notes to this series of documents are based in most cases on the records of salary payments in Archivo de la Indias, Sevilla (AGI), Sección

de Contaduría. These materials have been made available by the research of Professor L. B. Bloom. Salary, which amounted to two thousand pesos annually, was paid from the date on which a governor left Mexico City on his journey to New Mexico to the date on which he relinquished office to his successor in Santa Fe. Thus, the total payments included a considerable sum for travel time. The dates given in these notes, however, are for the actual terms of service in New Mexico. In cases where the records of salary payments are lacking, other sources have been used. Unfortunately, the latter rarely record the exact date of a change of governors. Consequently, it is not possible to give the month and day in all cases. France V. Scholes, "Royal Treasury Records Relating to the Province of New Mexico, 1596–1683," *New Mexico Historical Review* 50 (April 1975): 19–21. (E & S)

3. This is one of the Group A documents of the fraudulent/reconstruction series, as discussed in the preface. It places the beginning of Domínguez de Mendoza's services in New Mexico in 1640 or earlier, whereas Domínguez de Mendoza's own statements indicate he first came to New Mexico with Governor Pacheco de Heredia in 1642. In 1643, the date of the document, Domínguez de Mendoza was sixteen years old. Although it is possible that the governor would have named such a young and relatively inexperienced person to the permanent post of alférez real in the local militia, there is reason to believe that Domínguez de Mendoza did not receive the rank. Doc. 24 (July 27, 1671), which is authentic, contains no reference to the appointment as alférez real by Pacheco de Heredia. It does record, however, that in the time of Governor don Fernando de Argüello Carvajal, Domínguez de Mendoza served as alférez in campaign. This statement rings true. Argüello Carvajal was governor from December 6, 1644, to May 4, 1647. By that time Domínguez de Mendoza was older and more experienced in local frontier warfare. It should be noted, moreover, that Doc. 24 (July 27, 1671) refers to him as a campaign alférez, a temporary rank, and not as alférez real. Likewise, Doc. 8 (September 13, 1653), Doc. 15 (June 25, 1665), Doc. 20 (May 1, 1669), and Doc. 22 (September 11, 1670), which are also authentic, refer to him merely as alférez, not as alférez real. Further evidence of forgery is found in the fact that the appointment is not mentioned in the copy of the authentic certification of Domínguez de Mendoza's services executed by the cabildo of Santa Fe on October 3, 1684—Doc. 52 (April 23–24, 1686)—but is listed in the fraudulent certification of the same date in Doc. 46 (October 3, 1684). Finally, the fact that the handwriting of this appointment and all of the Group A documents appears to be that of Baltasar Domínguez de Mendoza also strengthens the forgery thesis for this document.

4. New Mexico was regarded as an arena of conquest and pacification long after the Oñate period.

5. Captain Simón Pérez de Bustillo was about sixty-seven years old in 1643, having come to New Mexico as a soldier in 1598 with his parents and siblings.

He was a son of Juan Pérez de Bustillo and María de la Cruz. By the marriages of his sisters he was related to the Hinojos and Varela families. Alférez Miguel de Hinojos was a nephew of Captain Simón Pérez de Bustillo, and a son of Hernando de Hinojos (who came to New Mexico as a soldier in 1598) and Beatriz Pérez de Bustillo. Alonso Rodríguez Varela may very well be the same person known as Alonso Varela, the younger, who was a public scribe in New Mexico in 1642 and was a son of Alonso Varela, the elder, and Catalina Pérez de Bustillo. Chávez, *Origins of New Mexico Families*, 48, 87, and 110–11. (E & S)

6. There is a record of banns of matrimony from the Catedral de México, Mexico City, dated August 6, 1631, for Lorenzo Librán, son of Juan Librán and Leonor de los Santos, and his prospective bride, Ana de León, daughter of Juan López de Torrez and María de León. Información Matrimonial, Asunción, 1620–1648, LDS #0035267. (E & S)

Document 3

Commission as Captain of Infantry

Santa Fe, December 7, 1644[1]

Captain don Francisco de Argüello Carvajal,[2] governor and captain general of the kingdom and provinces of New Mexico for the king, our lord, etc.[3]

Inasmuch as it is necessary for the service of the king, our lord, and for the good government to have a guard and royal standard for a certain period in these *Casas Reales*, I have made a general list of all the people of this villa and provinces, and in order that it may be done in a satisfactory manner and in military style, it is necessary to appoint a captain of infantry to command and govern the said guard, who should be a person of satisfaction, courage, quality, ability, and trust for such a post.

The aforesaid qualities and many others concur in the person of Captain don Juan Domínguez y Mendoza, in consideration of how much and how well he has served his majesty in these provinces for more than ten years past, entering them in the year 1640, bringing two men at his own expense for service of the king, our lord, in this new kingdom and provinces. Subsequently he left here for New Spain for some supplies of clothing and other things of which were in great need. He returned with this in the year 1642, bringing at his own expense three men for the aid and settlement of the said kingdom. At that time the province of Zuñi was in revolt, for the natives had rebelled and fortified themselves in the Peñol de Caquima.

And on account of the satisfaction which has been received from the said captain, General Alonso Pacheco, who governed these provinces, appointed him captain and commander of the armed forces which went to the said province and fortress, where he distinguished himself with great valor and courage in the ensuing encounters with the enemies and rebellious factions, governing the force which he took under his command with great sufficiency and mature counsel, coming out of it all with most brilliant and praiseworthy fame, leaving the sowings of the said rebels destroyed, as a result of which they were reduced to the royal obedience within a short time.[4] In addition, on three other occasions he went to New Spain.

When he returned to these said provinces the first time, he brought at his own cost and expense four soldiers, and on the second [occasion] he brought another four [soldiers] in the same manner, and on the third and last [occasion], which was in the year 1646 [sic], he likewise brought at his own cost a settler with his wife and eight children, four of them grown boys who afterwards began to serve His Majesty. In all that he has done, as can be seen, [he has performed] services that are very great to the king, our lord, which are very important in this Tierra Nueva [for its] growth and population, and from which, as stated, spring all [his] efforts, at great cost to his property and person.[5] With his arms and horses he went out to pacify Christian Indians that disregarded the obedience to His Majesty as [occurred] in particular when he castigated and pacified the Picurís nation.[6] In everything that he has performed, he has responded as a valorous and honored soldier, as well as on many other occasions in which he conducted castigations of enemies, likewise all at a very large expense. From the titles and certifications that he has presented before me, attentive to which, and to the satisfaction I have of his person, in the name of His Majesty, I elect and appoint the said Captain Juan Domínguez de Mendoza as Captain of Infantry of all the people, captains and soldiers, who are enlisted for the said protection, and as such, to use and direct the said office in all the cases and things connected to and concerning him. According to, and as is required to make use of the said title and to wear the insignia according to custom, I grant commission and royal authority in sufficient form, according to that which I have from the king, our lord. And, I order the maestre de campo and the sargento mayor of this kingdom to have honor and respect toward the said, as captain of the said defense and of the other official captains and soldiers of this said kingdom, and being enlisted for this cause they will recognize, respect and obey him as their captain, defending and complying [with] the words of this document under penalties that are imposed on them, which is the will of

His Majesty, and of mine, in his royal name, enjoying, as given to enjoy, all the honors, preeminence, exceptions, graces, privileges, and liberties, which by reason of the said office should be granted him for life and on account of the services of the aforesaid [Juan Domínguez de Mendoza] being so positive and his serving in said military position at his own expense and cost, which speaks for itself, [and he] ought not to owe anything to the *derecho del onorato*, neither to the *media anata*, with regard to which I send you the present dispatch signed by my hand and sealed with the seal of my arms and countersigned below by the secretary, which is dated in the Villa de Santa Fe of New Mexico, seventh day of the month of December 1644.[7]

Notes

1. BNE, Madrid, MSS 19258, photos 15–16.

2. Don Fernando de Argüello Carvajal served as governor of the presidio of Sinaloa for several years prior to his appointment as governor of New Mexico. His term of office in New Mexico extended from December 6, 1644 to May 4, 1647. AGI, Contaduría, leg. 742, Caja de México, Cuentas de los oficiales reales de México, 1648–1650.

3. This is one of the Group B documents that are called into question about their authenticity, as mentioned in the preface. With regard to this document several points may be noted. It states that Domínguez de Mendoza "has served His Majesty in these provinces for more than ten years past, coming to them, as he did, in the year 1640," etc. The date of the document, however, is December 7, 1644, or only four years after the stated date of arrival. However, this inconsistency can be explained by considering that perhaps Juan Domínguez de Mendoza came to New Mexico in the company of his father around 1633–1634, returned to Mexico City with his father, and then entered the kingdom as a resident with his father sometime between 1636 and 1640. Second, the statements concerning the various journeys made by Domínguez de Mendoza, beginning in the year 1640 and extending over a period of years thereafter, deserve discussion. Although we have no positive proof that Domínguez de Mendoza accompanied his father to New Mexico in 1640, it is possible that he may have done so. The most reliable evidence we have indicates that the time that he "entered" New Mexico was 1642, or possibly early 1643 (see the Introduction to this book). The present document records a trip in 1642, which may have been the first or second one Domínguez de Mendoza made. The document then goes on to state that subsequently he made three more trips to New Spain and back, the last one being in 1646. It is obviously impossible, however, to record an event of 1646 in a document dated 1644. If the document is an authentic original, then, in order to explain the discrepancy the last trip was made in 1644. It is possible that the scribe, in dating the document, carelessly wrote "*quarenta y cuatro*," instead

of "*quarenta y seis.*" But if the date of the document should be 1646, then we might expect that the scribe, in recording Domínguez de Mendoza's last trip, would have written "*este año de seiscientos y quarenta y seis,*" not "*el año,*" etc. If we resort to the second alternative and date the last trip in 1644, we encounter other difficulties. Assuming Domínguez de Mendoza came in 1642, the date of arrival was not earlier than October or November of that year. This means that the three round trips were made within a space of a little more than two years at the most. This would have been possible, provided Domínguez de Mendoza had spent almost all of his time in journeying back and forth. But in such a case, when would he have had time to take part in the various military expeditions and reprisals mentioned in this document and the preceding one? Moreover, Domínguez de Mendoza was still a youth, and the account of all his doing, including the enlistment of colonists at his own expense, constitutes an extraordinary record of activity for a person still in his teens; in short, we encounter so many problems that serious doubt is created concerning the authenticity of the document and the truthfulness of the events it records. Third, it is possible that Governor Alonso Pacheco de Heredia sent the expedition to Zuñi sometime during his term of office (1642–1644), and Domínguez de Mendoza may have taken part in it. Assuming the expedition occurred in 1643 or 1644, Domínguez de Mendoza would have been sixteen or seventeen years old, and it is difficult to believe that the governor would have named as commander of the expedition such a young man, and a newcomer in the province, when older and more experienced soldiers were available. Furthermore, the document is dated December 7, 1644, the day after Governor Argüello Carvajal took office. Although the governor's decision to create a company of infantry to serve as guard in Santa Fe might have been made so soon after he took office, it seems unlikely that he would have acted in such haste. And it is also doubtful that he would have named a youth of seventeen as a company commander. Also, Doc. 24 (July 27, 1671) records that Domínguez de Mendoza served as a campaign alférez in the time of Argüello Carvajal but does not record any appointment as captain. Likewise, the reference to Domínguez de Mendoza as an alférez in Doc. 8 (September 13, 1653) and Doc. 11 (November 19, 1659) also creates doubt concerning an appointment to higher rank at an earlier date. Additionally, the present document is listed in the fraudulent certification of the cabildo of Santa Fe, dated October 3, 1684, and found in Doc. 46, infra, but is not mentioned in the copy of the authentic certification of the same date in Doc. 52 (April 23–24, 1686). Finally, the document employs the "y" form of the family name, instead of the "de" form found in the authentic titles. In view of all the foregoing, we may conclude that the document is probably a forgery or a clumsy reconstruction drawn up at a later date.

4. In 1632, the Zuñi Indians killed fray Francisco Letrado in the pueblo of Hawikuh. Abandoning their pueblos, they withdrew to the Peñol de Caquima

on Corn Mountain. A punitive expedition was sent against them, but they were not pacified. The Indians continued to occupy the mesa stronghold until 1635, when they began to reoccupy their pueblos. The custodian, fray Cristóbal de Quirós, was anxious to resume missionary work among them, and in September 1636 he petitioned Governor Martínez de Baeza for a military escort for the friars he desired to send out. But the governor resented the manner in which the custodian's request was made, and he refused the escort. Some sort of expedition to Zuñi may have been made in 1636, but there is no evidence that the missions were reestablished. F. W. Hodge, *History of Hawikuh* (Los Angeles: Southwest Museum, 1937), 91–95; France V. Scholes, *Church and State in New Mexico, 1610–1650* (Albuquerque: University of New Mexico Press, 1937), 107–9. It was Bandelier's conclusion that the resumption of missionary work did not occur until after 1642. He cited the disorders that occurred subsequent to 1636 and culminated in the murder of Governor Rosas in 1642: "All this contributed to check attempts in the direction of Zuñi." Adolph F. Bandelier, "Documentary History of the Zuñi Tribe," in *Journal of American Ethnology and Archaeology* (Boston: Houghton, Mifflin, 1892), 3:101–2. I am in entire agreement with Bandelier's conclusion. The bitter controversies and the tragic events that characterized the administration in the missionary program undoubtedly prevented any attempt to reestablish the Zuñi missions until after the arrival of Governor Pacheco de Heredia in 1642. Although the documents of the Pacheco de Heredia period do not record a punitive expedition to Zuñi, it is possible that the governor made such an expedition as part of his general program and restoring order.

5. Tierra Nueva, New Land, was a term that was often applied to New Mexico in the sixteenth and seventeenth centuries.

6. There are not any documentary data to confirm this reference to a reprisal against the Picurís Indians, which would have occurred during the term of Governor Pacheco de Heredia. In 1681, Juan Domínguez de Mendoza testified that in the time of Governor Argüello Carvajal "twenty-nine Jemez Indians were hanged as traitors and confederates of the Apaches," and he also mentioned the punishment of Indians of the pueblos of Isleta, Alameda, San Felipe, Cochiti and Jemez, who were involved in a conspiracy in the time of Governor Ugarte de la Concha. See Hackett and Shelby, *Pueblo Revolt*, 2:266. No mention was made, however, of any movement, then or later, in which the pueblo of Picurís took part. But in view of the fact that Doc. 3 (December 7, 1644) above may be fraudulent, it does not provide a basis for reliable conclusions without any supporting evidence.

7. The media anata was a government tax on half of the first year's salary of an appointed official, which was instituted in 1631 to replace the *meseda*, or tax amounting to a month's salary levied on secular positions in Spain and the Indies.

Document 4

Title of Captain and Commander
Santa Fe, April 14, 1646[1]

Captain don Luis de Guzmán y Figueroa, governor and captain general of the kingdom and provinces of New Mexico for the king our lord, etc.[2]

Inasmuch as the hostile Apache tribe called del Acho, of the eastern mountains toward Taos and Picurís, have committed and continually commit great robberies and killings in the pueblo of Taos and in Picurís, and in all the others where they have been able to do so, sentence of death has been passed against them and the rest of the nation of Apache enemies by my predecessors and confirmed by me.[3] All the said Christian Indians of the said pueblos are exhausted and discouraged by the said killings and robberies which the Apaches of the said tribe have committed and commit.
The said Christians have asked me for aid during these last few days; and especially yesterday, the thirteenth of this present month, two Indians, natives of the pueblo of los Pecos, called Cristóbal Chepira, war captain, and Francisco Macha, arrived at these casas reales in all haste at the hour of midnight; and in the presence of Captain Juan Griego, interpreter general, and through his interpretation, they said that they came with great urgency to ask his lordship to succor and aid them as Christians, which they were.[4] The governor, don Pedro Meju, and captains of the said pueblo had sent them for this purpose, because yesterday, the said day, a great number of the said Apache enemies, whom they call "del Acho," arrived in sight of the pueblo in warlike array. For this reason the natives of the said pueblo are in confusion and stringency, not knowing what their design may be, and they fear a great betrayal like those committed so many times in numerous Christian pueblos. Therefore, they came to ask his lordship for help and favor against the above-mentioned [Apaches] because they are common and known enemies; and [they said] that haste was important.[5]

In view of the foregoing, and because I realize how important it is for the service of His Majesty and the peace and preservation of these provinces, [it is necessary] to give help to the said Christian natives and to wage war on the aforementioned enemies. [The enemies] are those who do most harm and who have committed the most killings and robberies in the Christian pueblos of Taos and Picurís, and there is no doubt they will continue and destroy them unless an exemplary punishment is inflicted and unless they are destroyed by fire and blood. Consequently, in accordance with the said sentence which has been pronounced against them by my predecessors, and confirmed by me, I deem it well and a particular service to the king, our lord, [to wage war against them] because this kingdom needs to finish and destroy a nation so inimical to our Holy Catholic Faith and one which harasses this land of newly converted Christian nations.

Therefore, I have organized a troop of soldiers to carry out an action of such great importance; and it is necessary to appoint a person of all satisfaction, valor, experience, and sufficiency in the affairs of war to rule and command them in military force and achieve the service of His Majesty. Because these and all the other desirable qualities concur in the person of Maestre de Campo don Juan Domínguez de Mendoza, to whom this said action can be entrusted, I therefore, in the name of the king, our lord, appoint and name him captain and commander of all the military force, both Spaniards and natives, who are going for the said purpose. And, I order all of them to hold and consider him as their captain and commander, to keep and fulfill the orders he may give them under the penalties he may impose upon them, which he will execute on the transgressors [and] disobedient, for such is the will of His Majesty and mine in his royal name.

In order to get good results in the above-mentioned matter, let the said maestre de campo set forth today in all haste and with due care and secrecy by the most direct route to the pueblo of Pecos. When he arrives, he will find out and see where the said enemies are and obtain information from Pedro Meju, chief captain of the said pueblo. If the said enemies are there or in another place known to him, and he finds them, he will wage war by fire and blood until they are destroyed and finished. If he does not find them there, he will pursue them until he overtakes them, and there he will bring about the destruction of them all, as has been said, and in such manner that so great a service to His Majesty and the public good of this kingdom and reputation of the Spanish nation maybe attained. For all that may occur in the said military action I give the said commander plenary authority to act as one who is present at the scene of action and to whose person so important an undertaking is entrusted. For all this I ordered the present writing issued to him, signed by my name and sealed with the seal of my arms, and countersigned by the undersigned secretary.

Done in the Villa of Santa Fe of New Mexico on April 14 of the year 1646. (Seal) Don Luis de Guzmán y Figueroa (rubric). By order of his lordship, Francisco de Anaya Almazán,[6] secretary of war and government (rubric).

Notes

1. BNE, Madrid, MSS 19258, photos 17–18.

2. Luis de Guzmán y Figueroa was appointed governor of New Mexico by the viceroy of New Spain, don García Sarmiento de Sotomayor, Conde de Salvatierra, on June 18, 1646. AGI, Contaduría, leg. 740, Caja de México, Cuentas de los oficiales reales de México, 1646–1648. In as much as the record of his final salary payment is not available in the treasury accounts, it is impossible to fix the exact date on which his term of office ended. His successor, Hernando de Ugarte y la Concha, arrived in 1649, probably in the spring of that year.

3. The Achos are mentioned in the diary of Juan de Ulibarrí's expedition to Cuartelejo in 1706. Ulibarrí encountered some of them near the Río de Santa María Magdalena (probably the present Cimarron Creek) about forty miles east of Taos. They are sometimes identified as Jicarilla Apache but more likely were a western branch of the Lipan Apaches. Alfred Barnaby Thomas, *After Coronado* (Norman: University of Oklahoma Press, 1935), 17, 63. (E & S)

4. Captain Juan Griego was born around 1605, describing himself as a native of Santa Fe, age fifty-six, in a statement given in 1661; AGN, Inquisición, vol. 593, exp. 1, f. 201v, Testimony of Capitán Juan Griego, November 1, 1661, Villa de Santa Fe. He was a son of Juan Griego and Pascuala Bernal, original settlers who had come to New Mexico with don Juan de Oñate in 1598. Chávez, *Origins of New Mexico Families*, 41. As a witness in the investigation of Governor Bernardo López de Mendizábal by the Inquisition, Captain Juan Griego identified himself as a mestizo, being of mixed Spanish and Indian heritage. In July 1662, Governor López de Mendizábal had in his possession two sets of official papers of merits of Captain Juan Griego, one of which probably related to his father, also named Captain Juan Griego. The first set consisted of twenty-seven pages, and the second set of forty-four pages. The length of these papers is an indication of the long and active duty that Captain Juan Griego and his father provided during their lives. AGN, Inquisición, vol. 587, p. 387 (bound typescript, Center for Southwest Research, University of New Mexico), Nombre de testigos y sus qualificaciónes, 1662; AGN, Real Audiencia, Concurso de Peñalosa, vol. 1, leg. 1, no. 1, f. 37v, List of Papers of Merits and Services of New Mexico Vecinos, July 17, 1662, Villa de Santa Fe; see Supp. Doc. 3, infra. (E & S)

5. This is one of the Group B documents that are called into question about their authenticity, as mentioned in the preface. It is dated April 14, 1646, more than two months before Guzmán y Figueroa was appointed governor and more than a year before he took office in Santa Fe as successor to Governor Argüello Carvajal. This fact would prove its spurious character, unless we assume that the scribe carelessly made an error in dating it. But if such an error was made, and if the month and day are correct, the year could not have been earlier than 1648. Evident inconsistency is also found in the fact that Domínguez de Mendoza

is referred to as maestre de campo, whereas Doc. 8 (September 13, 1653) and Doc. 11 (November 19, 1659), which are authentic, refer to him as an alférez. In the authentic titles of offices, the earliest record of a military appointment is found in Doc. 10 (August 30, 1659). The present document is not listed in the copy of the certification of the cabildo of Santa Fe dated October 3, 1684, in Doc. 52 (April 23–24, 1686) but is mentioned in the fraudulent certification of the same date in Doc. 46 (October 3, 1684). Doc. 24 (July 27, 1671) records that in the time of Governor Guzmán y Figueroa the young Domínguez de Mendoza served in a campaign against the Navajos, but it doesn't mention an expedition against the Apaches del Acho.

6. Francisco de Anaya Almazán was a native of Mexico City whose parents came from Salamanca, Spain. In New Mexico he married Juana López de Villafuerte, a daughter of Francisco López Paredes, or Pareja (a native of Jérez de los Caballeros and a soldier of New Mexico) and María de Villafuerte (a Mexican Indian woman from the Pueblo of Cuatitlán in the Valley of Mexico). A son of Francisco de Anaya Almazán named Cristóbal de Anaya Almazán married doña Leonor Ramírez de Mendoza, a sister of Juan Domínguez de Mendoza. Chávez, *Origins of New Mexico Families*, 3–4; AGN, Inquisición, vol. 356, exp. 133, f. 310r, Declaration of María de Villafuerte, May 9, 1626, Villa de Santa Fe; and AGN, Inquisición, vol. 582, f. 309r–312v, Declaration of Cristóbal de Anaya Almazán, April 26, 1663, Ciudad de México. (E & S)

Document 5

Appointment as Lieutenant Governor and Captain General

Santa Fe, April 15, 1650[1]

Captain Hernando de Ugarte y la Concha,[2] governor, *justicia mayor* [chief magistrate] and captain general of these provinces of New Mexico and the others adjacent to it, and judge general of *bienes de difuntos* [property of deceased persons] for the king, our lord.[3]

For the service of His Majesty and fulfillment of His Majesty's orders, it is necessary that a journey of inspection of all the pueblos of the Río Abajo as far as that of Senecú be made. For this purpose I must go in person, and in order that during my absence and while I am occupied with other business I may not be needed to attend the matters which come up in this villa and government, it is necessary to name a satisfactory person as my lieutenant governor, justicia mayor, and captain general. I have a good observation and extensive knowledge concerning Captain don Juan Domínguez y Mendoza, inasmuch as the aforesaid has served His Majesty in this conquest and pacification for more than ten years and has held, used, and exercised the highest offices existing in this government, both in peace and in war, and my predecessors have entrusted to him the affairs and commissions of greatest importance which have offered themselves in this government, for all of which he has given a good and praiseworthy accounting. In consideration of these services and many others which the said Captain don Juan Domínguez y Mendoza has rendered his majesty in these said provinces, and because I hope he will continue to serve with the same results, I, therefore, for the present, name, elect, and appoint the said Captain don Juan Domínguez y Mendoza as my lieutenant general, in order that he may use this office and act in my place. He may have jurisdiction over all civil and original matters, both those relating to Spaniards as well as to natives, both those of government and those of peace and war, because of all of it I give him commission and sufficient power and plenary authority as I hold it from the king, our lord. I order all the higher officials, captains, and soldiers, men of peace and war, and natives, to hold, consider, respect, and receive the said Captain don Juan Domínguez y Mendoza as such my lieutenant governor and captain general, and to observe and fulfill his orders and commands as if they were ordered and commanded by me, because I now pronounce him received. For this proposal I ordered this title and appointment issued to him in due form, signed by my hand and sealed with the seal of my arms, and countersigned by the undersigned secretary.

Done in the Villa of Santa Fe of New Mexico on the fifteenth of April of the year 1650. (Seal) Hernando de Ugarte y la Concha (rubric). By order of his lordship, Francisco de Anaya Almazán, secretary of war and government.

Notes

1. BNE, Madrid, MSS 19258 photos 19–20.
2. Don Hernando de Ugarte y la Concha was appointed governor of New Mexico in the summer of 1648. He set out from Mexico City on November 17 of that year and probably took office in the Villa de Santa Fe in the spring of 1649 (documentary evidence for the exact date not available). His term ended in April 1653. AGI, Contaduría, leg. 742 and 748, Caja de México, Cuentas de los oficiales reales de México, 1646–1648 and 1654–1658, respectively. The most reliable data for the terms of office of the seventeenth-century governors of New Mexico are the records of those salary payments found in the treasury accounts (Sección de Contaduría) in the Archivo General de Indias, Sevilla. The annual salary was two thousand silver pesos. Salary was paid from the date on which a

governor left Mexico City on his journey to New Mexico to the date on which he relinquished office to his successor in Santa Fe. In certain cases the treasury records of the salary payments are incomplete, and consequently we do not have exact information concerning the actual terms of office of all the governors. See France V. Scholes, "Royal Treasury Records Relating to the Province of New Mexico, 1596–1683," in *New Mexico Historical Review* 50 (April 1975): 20.

3. This is one of the Group B documents that are called into question about their authenticity, as mentioned here in the preface. In 1650 Domínguez de Mendoza was almost twenty-three years old, and it is doubtful that he could already have held the "highest offices," so that Ugarte y la Concha would have named him lieutenant governor. If he actually served as lieutenant governor under Ugarte y la Concha, the fact would probably have been noted in the authentic certification and services issued by Ugarte y la Concha in 1653, Doc. 8 (September 13, 1653). This certification mentions various services, some of which are confirmed by Doc. 24 (July 27, 1671), but there is no mention of an appointment to office. Moreover, in the certification and in Doc. 6 (November 10, 1652), Domínguez de Mendoza is referred to as an alférez, a low rank for a man who had supposedly held the highest offices and had served as lieutenant governor. As further evidence that the document is not authentic, it may be noted that it is not mentioned in the copy of the attested certification of the cabildo of Santa Fe, October 3, 1684, in Doc. 52 (April 23–24, 1686) but is in the fraudulent certificate of the same date in Doc. 46 (October 3, 1684).

Document 6

Commission as Captain of Cavalry

Santa Fe, November 10, 1652[1]

Captain and Sargento Mayor don Juan de Samaniego y Jaca,[2] Knight of the Order of St. John, governor, chief magistrate and captain general of the kingdom and provinces of New Mexico for the king, our lord, etc.[3]

With regard to the quality and merits of Alférez don Juan Domínguez y Mendoza, I am entirely satisfied that he is a faithful, diligent, and honorable soldier, who has served His Majesty in these provinces for more than ten years with his arms and horses at his own expense, making, at extreme cost to his fortune and personal hardship, many expeditions which have been the most important that have occurred in this conquest and pacification, as is proved by his attestations and certifications, to which I refer. In the disturbances and uprisings made in this jurisdiction by the natives of the province of Emes [Jemez] and Picurís, who denied obedience to His Majesty and rebelled,[4] he accompanied the royal standard and my person for the said pacification, performing the offices of alférez real, which the said Alférez Real don Juan Domínguez y Mendoza was at that time, and in the said pacification he fulfilled his obligations and performed all the things entrusted to him, giving a good and praiseworthy account of himself in all that was assigned to him by me. In all military actions that took place in this pacification and on other occasions he has behaved as an honorable and outstanding soldier. In addition, during an uprising or insurrection which occurred in this province in disservice of His Majesty, the said alférez, as an honorable and faithful soldier, valorously opposed the said mutineers, and in the encounter with the aforesaid [mutineers], who were angry with those who remained faithful and loyal to the service of His Majesty, he received a wound through the nostril.[5] Nevertheless, the said Alférez don Juan Domínguez y Mendoza has always continued to accompany the royal standard of His Majesty and to defend the ministers and justices of the king, our lord. In view of the above and in consideration of his merits, I have decided to appoint and name the said Alférez don Juan Domínguez y Mendoza captain of cavalry in the maintenance, conquest, and pacification of this government. As such captain he may lead and recruit men, and raise the standard for his said company, which he may have under his hand and military command for the service of His Majesty wherever he may be ordered by me. He may command the said company with the preeminences, places, honors, and plenary authority with which the other captains of the royal armies of His Majesty exercise, for I give him power and authority for all this as I hold it from the king, our lord.

For this and for the said purpose I order the higher officials and other people to hold, consider, and receive you as such captain of cavalry, because I now pronounce you received. Therefore I ordered this title and appointment of captain issued to you in due form, signed by my hand and sealed with the seal of my arms, and countersigned by the undersigned secretary.

Done in this Villa of Santa Fe of New Mexico on the tenth day of the month of November 1652. (Seal) Don Juan de Samaniego y Jaca (rubric). By order of his lordship, Juan de la Escallada y Castillo, secretary of government and war (rubric).[6]

Notes

1. BNE, Madrid, MSS 19258, photos 22–23.
2. Juan de Samaniego y Jaca was appointed governor of New Mexico in 1652. On June 10 of that year the viceroy issued an order authorizing two years' salary

in advance, which was paid to Samaniego on June 20. He left Mexico City on November 16, 1652, and took office in Santa Fe as successor to Governor Ugarte y la Concha on April 24, 1653. AGI, Contaduría, 747 and 750, Caja de México, Cuentas de los oficiales reales de México, 1652–1653 and 1656–1658, respectively. A native of Estella in the kingdom of Navarra and a son of Lorenzo de Samaniego y Jaca and Catalina Díez de Ulzurrun y Roncal, Juan de Samaniego received the military habit of Caballero de la Orden de San Juan de Jerusalén in 1637. Leopoldo Martínez Cosio incorrectly lists don Juan de Samaniego as a Caballero de Santiago and not as a Caballero de San Juan de Jerusalén, apparently confusing don Juan with his brother don Lorenzo de Samaniego y Jaca, who was a Caballero de Santiago (1638). Archivo Histórico Nacional, Órdenes Militares, San Juan de Jerusalén, exp. 25285, Pruebas de Juan de Samaniego Díez de Ulzurrun Jaca y Roncal, 1637; Archivo Histórico Nacional, Órdenes Militares, Santiago, exp. 7503, Pruebas de Lorenzo de Samaniego Jaca y Díez de Ulzurrun, 1638; and Leopoldo Martínez Cosio, *Los caballeros de las ordenes militares en México* (Mexico: Editorial Santiago, 1946), 327. (E & S)

3. This is one of the Group A documents that are called into question about their authenticity, as mentioned in the preface. The document is dated November 10, 1652, six days before Samaniego y Jaca left Mexico City on his journey to New Mexico, and more than five months before he took office in Santa Fe. It is listed in Doc. 46 (October 3, 1684), the fraudulent certification of the cabildo in 1684, but not in the copy of the genuine attested certification presented in Doc 52 (April 23–24, 1686). Doc 24 (July 27, 1672) refers to Domínguez de Mendoza's service during the time of Samaniego y Jaca, but does not mention an appointment as captain of cavalry. Moreover, it may be noted that the commission refers to Domínguez de Mendoza as alférez real, the rank supposedly conferred upon him by Governor Pacheco de Heredia; see Doc. 2 (October 12, 1643). But according to Doc. 4 (April 14, 1646), he held the rank of maestre de campo in 1646, and we find that he was appointed lieutenant governor and captain general according to the information in Doc. 5 (April 15, 1650).

4. In 1681 Juan Domínguez de Mendoza testified that the Indians of Jemez were involved in plots during the administration of governors Argüello Carvajal and Ugarte y la Concha but did not mention any "disturbances" in the title of Samaniego y Jaca. Hackett and Shelby, *Revolt of the Pueblo Indians*, 2:266. We have no record of any trouble involving the Indians of Picurís.

5. The only incidents of which we have record that could be regarded as an insurrection or a mutiny are those which occurred in 1640–1642, during and after the governorship of Luis de Rosas, see Scholes, *Church and State*, chs. 5–7. Domínguez de Mendoza arrived in 1642 with Governor Pacheco y Heredia, who had instructions to investigate events of the preceding years and eventually

executed certain soldiers said to have been implicated in the murder of Governor Rosas. But the contemporary documents, which are incomplete, to be sure, do not record any disturbances during Pacheco y Heredia's governorship that could be described as a mutiny. For Domínguez de Mendoza's services at the time we have no information except that contained in the fraudulent or reconstructed documents of the Servicios Personales papers.

6. This document is among the earliest accounts of Juan de la Escallada y Castillo in New Mexico. As a soldier, he escorted the wagon trains in 1652 and 1658. He was married in New Mexico with Ynéz Lucero González and had two known daughters, who married Peralta brothers. Chávez, *Origins of New Mexico Families*, 29. (E & S)

Document 7

Certification of Services

Santa Fe, January 12, 1653[1]

Captain don Juan de Samaniego y Jaca, Knight of the Order of St. John, governor, chief magistrate and captain general of these provinces of New Mexico and the others adjacent to it for the king, our lord, etc.

I certify to the king, our lord, and to his Royal Council of the Indies, and to the viceroys and other ministers of His Majesty who may see this, that in the year 1651, when I came here to govern this kingdom, Captain don Juan Domínguez y Mendoza accompanied me from New Spain. He had gone there to take the viceroy the dispatches concerning the new discovery he had made of the pearls and kingdom of Quivira and Texas, which he had undertaken at his own expense, as well as the said journey to Mexico City. During the period of my government he has served His Majesty in these provinces at his own cost and expense, going by my order on the expedition of the pearls, during which he carried out and fulfilled with great punctiliousness my commands and the instruction which was given to him by my order. He commanded the people whom he took with great sagacity, valor, and courage in the rude war and battle which was waged with the Escanjaques and Ayjados Indians, which lasted three days, killing a large number of them, taking prisoner more than 1600 persons, their wives and children, and rescuing from them 125 persons, Christian men, women, and children, whom the said enemies held captive for some time, as has been said.[2] He gave me a good and praiseworthy accounting of this, as he also did in the expedition he made by my order to the Sierra Blanca to wage war on the common enemies of our Holy Catholic Faith, the

Apache nation, for having profaned and robbed the holy temple of Jumanos, rescuing out of their power twenty-seven women and children whom they were holding captive, together with all the rest that had been carried off, and leaving them well punished, he returned, having gained great reputation among his friends and enemies.[3]

And then, the following year, in an extremely severe season of snows, he set forth by my order to wage war on the said Apaches of the ranges of the Navajo and Casa Fuerte who had made an ambush in the province of the Christian Indians of the Jemez nation, killing nineteen of them and carrying off thirty-five captives with excessive boldness and daring.[4] When the said captain reached the said jurisdictions he waged war on them, he captured 211 of their women and children, and took from them the Christian women who had been carried off, together with five more whom they had captured a year before, including a Spanish woman called Regina de Peralta.[5] As a result the said enemies came to ask for peace, which was granted generally, and which they observe and keep today.

And immediately, by my order, the said Captain don Juan Domínguez y Mendoza was sent to the pacification of the province of the Mansos because they had wanted to kill the friars, their ministers, who asked me for aid, for which purpose I sent the said captain.[6] And leaving them pacified and punished, hanging two who were leaders of the revolt, he returned, having done all the above said at his own cost and expense.

Therefore, I find him worthy of all the favors which His Majesty and the viceroys and governors of this kingdom may be pleased to grant him. At his petition I ordered the present writing issued to him, signed by my hand and sealed with the seal of my arms, and countersigned by the undersigned, my secretary of war.

Done in this Villa of Santa Fe of New Mexico on the twelfth day of the month of January of the year 1653. (Seal) Don Juan de Samaniego y Jaca (rubric). By order of his lordship, Juan de la Escallada y Castillo, secretary of government and war (rubric).

Notes

1. BNE, Madrid, MSS 19258 photos 24–25.
2. The Escanjaques, or Escanxaques, and the Ayjidos Indians are unidentified tribes of Central Texas, known from the early 1600s. (E & S)

3. Humanas is the site known today as Gran Quivira in New Mexico. (E & S)

4. The mountain ranges of Navajo and Casafuerte were in northwest New Mexico, in the area south of the modern-day San Juan River, referred to as the Río Grande in seventeenth-century records. Hendricks and Wilson identify Casa Fuerte and a ridge line with a steep eastern side extending south from present-day Dulce, New Mexico, about twenty-five miles until it joins with another mountain range. Rick Hendricks and John P. Wilson, eds. and trans., *The Navajos of 1705: Roque Madrid's Campaign Journal* (Albuquerque: University of New Mexico Press, 1996), 68. (E & S)

5. This Regina de Peralta may be the same woman who was the wife of Cristóbal de Apodaca. This couple survived the Pueblo Indian Revolt and passed muster with two children in 1680. Chávez, *Origins of New Mexico Families*, 86. (E & S)

6. The Mansos, whose linguistic affiliation remains uncertain, were living along the Río Grande at El Paso del Río del Norte and northward into New Mexico when don Juan de Oñate's colonizing expedition passed through the area in 1598. In 1659 the mission of Nuestra Señora de Guadalupe was established for them on the site of today's Ciudad Juárez, Chihuahua. Patrick H. Beckett and Terry L. Corbett, "Indian Diversity in Southern New Mexico, 1581–1988," in Bradley J. Vierra, ed., *Current Research on the Late Prehistory and Early History of New Mexico* (Albuquerque: New Mexico Archaeological Council, 1992), 3–9. (E & S)

Document 8

Certification of Services
Santa Fe, September 13, 1653[1]

General Hernando de Ugarte y la Concha, former governor and captain [general] of the kingdom and provinces of New Mexico for the king, our lord, etc.

I certify to his Royal and Catholic Majesty, and to all the viceroys, governors, presidents, and *oidores* of all his kingdoms and dominions, that during all the period of my government I have seen Alférez Juan Domínguez serve His Majesty in these provinces at his own expense, very well provided with arms and horses, in all the expeditions, reprisals, pacifications, and wars which have taken place in the royal service during the said time; especially in the expeditions which have been made against the common enemy, the Apache nation, and in the wars against them. Because of the way they have been harried and as a result of the last two wars waged against them, in which the above-mentioned Alférez Juan Domínguez took part, one being at the time of their sowings and the other in the rigor of winter with great hardship, the said enemies have come to ask for peace and to render obedience. They have observed it for a year and are observing it at the present time without daring to do any harm, fearful and with grave terror and dread of the great valor of the Spaniards, who overran their lands in the rigor of winter and ascended the ruggedness of their mesas and waged so great a war against them as has never been seen in this kingdom.[2] In this service the said alférez displayed his valor to great advantage, striving for the reputation of the Spaniards with the enemies as a brave soldier. From this encounter and from all the others at which he has been present he has come out with praiseworthy fame, being withal very punctilious and obedient to the orders of his superiors, as I have usually found him during my government, with regard to what has offered itself in the service of His Majesty; and especially in going as he did by my order to Mexico City when I sent the dispatches concerning the discovery of pearls to the most excellent lord viceroy.[3] And he did it all with great care at his own expense.

For the reasons here expressed and related, and because he has employed himself in the service of His Majesty in this kingdom continuously over a period of more than ten years, I find and judge him worthy and deserving of all the honor and favor that His Majesty may be pleased to show him, in whose royal name and by petition of the aforesaid, I issued the present writing, signed by my name and sealed with the seal of my arms.

Done in the Villa of Santa Fe of New Mexico on September 13 of the year 1653. (Seal) Hernando de Ugarte y la Concha (rubric).

Notes

1. BNE, Madrid, MSS 19258, photo 21.
2. These statements probably refer to campaigns against the Navajo.
3. Reference is made here to Domínguez de Mendoza's journey to Mexico City in 1650–1651 to report to the viceroy concerning an expedition to central Texas during which freshwater pearls were found.

Document 9

Title of Maestre de Campo
Santa Fe, October 15, 1658[1]

Captain don Juan Manso de Contreras, governor, justicia mayor and captain general of these provinces of New Mexico and the others adjacent to it, and *juez general de bienes de difuntos* [superior probate judge] for the king, our lord, etc.[2]

Today, the ninth of the present month of October of the year 1658, I received a letter from Captain Bartolomé de Cisneros, alcalde mayor [administrative magistrate] and military captain of the provinces of Zuñi and Moqui, in which he informs me that at dawn on the seventh day of the said month of October a powerful army of Apaches, the common enemies of our Holy Catholic Faith, came, and these enemies treacherously and atrociously killed the reverend padre predicador fray Pedro de Ayala, in the pueblo of Hawikuh, capital of that province.[3] They also killed more than two hundred Christian persons and profaned the holy temple and sacred vessels and other ornaments, and sacked the convent and pueblo, capturing more than two thousand persons, men, women, and children, burning the said temple and convent and pueblo with excessive insolence and shamelessness, carrying off the herds of livestock and horses. These enemies said that at the crescent moon they would return to harry the entire said province.

In order that such atrocities and audacities might not go unpunished, I thought it well, in conformity with what His Majesty orders me, to summon to a council of war the cabildo of the Villa of Santa Fe, capital of these said provinces, and also the maestre de campo general of the kingdom, the sargento mayor, and other captains, active and retired, encomenderos, and other citizens of the kingdom, in order to reach the best agreement in the service of His Majesty. All of those, unanimously and of one accord, were of the opinion that an army of one hundred men should be formed, harquebusiers with horses completely equipped with armor of flanks, breast- and headpiece, in order that the said horses might not be killed. The said one hundred men are also to go well armed for the said purpose, together with four thousand Christian Indians armed with bow and arrow, to be chosen from the most bellicose and warlike of the kingdom, in order that a severe and exemplary punishment may be achieved and inflicted, taking from the powers of the said enemies what they have carried off from the holy temple and also the Christian people they seized and any others captured on other occasions. And they feel this in their consciences and as vassals of His Majesty, in addition to the rest which is shown by the [records of] the said council of war which took place on the tenth of the said month of October, to which I refer.

And inasmuch as it befits the service of God our lord and the Royal and Catholic Majesty, and peace and conservation of this kingdom, in accordance with this council of war and because this barbarous and treacherous nation is under sentence of death imposed by all my predecessors and confirmed by me, I order that for the sixteenth day of this present month of October the said one hundred men shall be enrolled and well equipped with arms and horses, and also the Indian force, in the *plaza de armas* which I have decided upon, which is the pueblo of San Juan de los Caballeros of the province of the Teguas [Tewas]. Therefore, it is fitting and necessary to name a leader to command and govern them in proper form and military discipline such as the case requires, and who shall be of every quality, Christianity, knowledge, conscience, and valor and experience, capable in military policy. These and many other praiseworthy and good qualities are found and concur in the person of the present maestre de campo and visitador general of this kingdom, don Juan Domínguez de Mendoza, in consideration of the many pleasing services which he has been doing His Majesty at great personal expense and danger to his life for twenty years during which he has served His Majesty at his own expense and cost, continuously furnishing a large number of soldiers with all arms and horses, in addition to victuals, very great and outstanding services which he has continually rendered His Majesty. And the service he is rendering His Majesty at present is very worthy and memorable since for the present occasion, which is one of the most arduous and grave which has happened in this kingdom, in addition to serving in person, at his own cost and expense he equipped fifty men with two hundred horses and the other supplies necessary. And in view of the many other relevant services which he has rendered His Majesty, as is shown by his titles and certifications from my predecessors, to which I refer, and also because he is the legitimate son of General don Bartolomé [sic] Domínguez, who was one of the first conquerors and settlers of this kingdom, bringing to it thirty families at his own expense, a very considerable service which he did His Majesty. In his royal name, I name, elect, and appoint the said Maestre de Campo don Juan Domínguez de Mendoza maestre de campo, governor, commander, and chief with all my authority accordingly as I hold it from the king, our lord, for such is his will and mine in his royal name. And I order all the military force, both Spaniards and natives, to hold and consider him as their maestre de campo, governor and commander, and chief, to guard and fulfill the orders he may give them under the penalties which he may impose upon them, which he will execute on the transgressors and disobedient, for such is the will of His Majesty and mine in his royal name.

And in order to achieve success in the aforesaid, let the said maestre de campo set out today on this date with all haste and secrecy, and when he has arrived, he will ascertain and see where the said enemies are; and in the place where he finds them, whether it is in the said jurisdiction or outside of them, he will wage war on them by fire and blood until they are destroyed and finished, not sparing any of this barbarous nation except the innocent children, in order that so great a service to His Majesty and the public good of this kingdom and reputation of this Spanish nation may be obtained. And for all that may offer itself on the said occasion, I give him, the said Maestre de Campo don Juan Domínguez de Mendoza, plenary authority to act as one is present at the scene of action and to whose person so important a function as the service of both Majesties and public good of this kingdom is entrusted. For all of this I order the present writing to him, signed by my hand and sealed with the seal of my arms, and counter-sealed by the undersigned secretary.

Done in this Villa of Santa Fe of New Mexico on the fifteenth day of the said month of October of 1658, with the declaration that it goes on ordinary white paper because the stamped paper is not current in these parts. (Seal) Juan Manso (rubric). By order of his lordship, Juan Lucero de Godoy, secretary of war and government (rubric).[4]

Notes

1. BNE, Madrid, MSS 19258, photos 26–28.
2. For a brief biography of Governor Juan Manso de Contreras, see Rick Hendricks and Gerald Mandell, "Juan Manso, Frontier Entrepreneur," *New Mexico Historical Review* 75 (2000): 339–67.
3. Fray Pedro de Ávila y Ayala, missionary at the Zuñi pueblo of Hawikuh, was slain by Apaches in his convento on October 7, 1672. A native of Campeche in Yucatán, he was sent by his Franciscan superiors to New Mexico in 1671. Juan de Durán Miranda was governor of New Mexico (1671–1675) at the time of Ayala's death, not Governor Juan Manso de Contreras (1656–1659). See Frederick Webb Hodge, *History of Hawikuh, New Mexico, One of the So-Called Cities of Cibola* (Los Angeles: Ward Ritchie Press, 1937), 99, 126. Also, Forbes, *Apache,*

Navaho, and Spaniard, states, "The whole affair of 1658 seems to be pure fiction . . . as the document appears to be a forgery" (150). Actually, some of the details are accurate, the day and month of fray Pedro's martyrdom, for instance. The fabrications all point toward the same end—the enhancement of Juan Domínguez de Mendoza's record or services on behalf of the Crown. (E & S)

4. Juan Lucero de Godoy, a son of Pedro Lucero de Godoy and Petronila de Zamora, was born around 1624–1625 in the Villa de Santa Fe and began to serve as a soldier at age seventeen in 1641. He had a lengthy career in service to the king, declaring in 1693 that he had served for fifty-two years. Juan Lucero de Godoy first married doña Luisa Romero, daughter of Matías Romero and doña Isabel de Pedraza, in Santa Fe on April 8, 1641, and then married doña Juana de Carvajal. The ceremony for his first marriage took place in the palacio of the Villa de Santa Fe. In 1662, Juan Lucero de Godoy was still secretary of government when he and his sister, Catalina de Zamora, gave testimony before Inquisition officials in the case against Governor López de Mendizábal. Both declared they were *castizo*, whereas their father declared he was *español*, indicating that their mother was part Indian. Chávez, *Origins of New Mexico Families*, 60. AGN, Inquisición, vol. 593, f. 192v, Ratification of the testimony of Juan Lucero de Godoy, November 1, 1661, Villa de Santa Fe; AGN, Inquisición, vol. 629, exp. 2, ff. 118v–119r, Testimony of Sargento Mayor Juan Lucero de Godoy, age 50, May 27, 1675, Villa de Santa Fe; and AGN, Inquisición, vol. 586, exp.1, f. 82r, Audiencia de Diego Romero, July 7, 1663, Ciudad de México; and AGN, Inquisición, vol. 587, pp. 386–87, bound typescript, Center for Southwest Research, University of New Mexico. (E & S)

Document 10

Commission as Captain of Mounted Harquebusiers
Santa Fe, August 30, 1659[1]

Captain don Bernardo López de Mendizábal, governor and captain general of the kingdom and provinces of New Mexico for the king, our lord, etc.[2]

It is necessary to punish the hostile Indians of the Apache nation, destroy their power, and lay waste their sowings, in order that they may not have occasion to commit greater assaults than those they have made since I arrived to govern this kingdom, which I found greatly harassed by the said enemies on account of the booty they have carried off and because they have killed many Christian natives and taken others as slaves. At the beginning of my government the said enemies failed to come to reaffirm peace as they have done in the time of my predecessors, although such peaceful relations have been assumed in order to assure in this way the citizens and natives of this kingdom. Fearing that this dissimulation might occasion greater harm, at the first of this month I sent Captain Luis Martínez in command of the ten mounted Spanish harquebusiers and thirty Christian Indians in order that he might reconnoiter the state of the said enemies and their designs.[3] In this endeavor he seized two of them of their nation, whom he brought to me. Having been amply informed that all those of their nation are eager to make great attacks and to continue their robberies and killings, in order to prevent such grave difficulties, I have recruited eight hundred Christian Indians and a company of forty mounted Spanish harquebusiers so that all possible punishment may be inflicted on the said enemies. In order that such an action may have complete success, it is necessary to name a captain of the said company, as well as of the Christian Indians, a person of entire satisfaction, valor, practice, and experience.

Because these and many other qualities concur in you, Alférez don Juan Domínguez de Mendoza, and in consideration of your services, and quality, and of the fact that you are the legitimate son of Captain Tomé Domínguez, who has also served His Majesty many years in this kingdom and has held the best posts, both of justice and of war, and has held many times the office of lieutenant of the governor and captain general for some of my predecessors; and because you have served His Majesty with outstanding valor and diligence since you have had the use of reason, as is proved by your certifications and papers, and hoping that henceforth you will continue to do so; in his royal name I appoint and name you captain of the said Spanish company of mounted harquebusiers and of those of the said Christians, in order that you may command and govern them in good military discipline in all that may be entrusted you. I order the maestre de campo, leader of the said detachment of this kingdom to hold and consider you as such captain of mounted harquebusiers; and I command the inferior officers and soldiers of your company to respect, honor and obey and observe your order and commands under the penalties you may impose upon them, which you will execute upon the transgressors and disobedient, because I give you power and authority as I hold it from the king, our lord, to use and exercise the said duty and office of captain of mounted harquebusiers and to wear the usual insignia. In order that all the honors, privileges, liberties, and exemptions which are due the captains of mounted harquebusiers of the royal armies may be observed with you, and so that it may be of record, I order the present writing issued to you, signed by my name and sealed with the seal of my arms, and counter-signed by my undersigned secretary, who will record this commission in the general books of this government.

Done in this Villa of Santa Fe, capital of the provinces of New Mexico, on August 30, 1659. (Seal) Don Bernardo López de Mendizábal (rubric). By order of his lordship the governor and captain general, Miguel de Noriega (rubric), secretary of war and government.[4]

Notes

1. BNE, Madrid, MSS 19258, photo 30.
2. Don Bernardo López de Mendizábal served as governor of New Mexico from July 11, 1659 to mid-August 1661. For an account of his career and his term of office, see France V. Scholes, "Troublous Times in New Mexico, 1659–1670," *New Mexico Historical Review* (Albuquerque: University of New Mexico Press), 1937 to 1941, and afterward issued as a separate monograph (Albuquerque: University of New Mexico Press, 1942). Don Bernardo López de Mendizábal was a son of Capitán don Cristóbal López de Mendizábal and doña Leonor de Pastrana (buried April 27, 1666, in the Church of Santa Catalina de Sena below the altar of Las Once Mil Virgines), residents of Mexico City. Doña Leonor de Pastrana was a granddaughter of Juan Núñez de León, who had been tried by the Inquisition for secretly practicing Judaism and made to give a public auto-de-fé on April 20, 1603, in Mexico City. Don Cristóbal López de Mendizábal and doña Leonor de Pastrana were also the parents don Gregorio López de Mendizábal, deceased by April 1663, Licenciado don Juan López de Mendizábal, don Cristóbal López de Mendizábal, deceased by April 1663, and doña Gertrudis López de Mendizábal, wife of Capitán don Juan de Andrada Moctezuma, and a resident of Mexico City. Don Bernardo died on August 23, 1663, while still under investigation by the Office of the Inquisition. AGN, Inquisición, vol. 594, exp. 1, f. 2r–4v, Primer Audiencia de Don Bernardo López de Mendizábal, April 28, 1663, Mexico City; AGN, Real Audiencia, Concurso de Peñalosa, vol. 3, leg. 1, no. 10, f. 64r/68r, Petition of Juan Félis de Galvés in the name of Capitán don Juan Andrada Moctezuma and doña Gertrudis López de Mendizábal, n.d., Mexico City. (E & S)
3. This Captain Luis Martínez appears to be the same person known as Captain Luis Martín Serrano, a longtime resident of La Cañada, located about twenty miles north of Santa Fe. His father, Hernán Martín Serrano, came to New Mexico as a soldier with don Juan de Oñate in 1598. Luís Martín Serrano died sometime between October 29 and November 30, 1661, when a reference was made to his widow, Catalina de Salazar. AGN, Real Audiencia, Tierras, vol. 3268, ff. 143r–144v, Testimony of Catalina de Salazar, November 1661, Villa de Santa Fe; and Chávez, *Origins of New Mexico Families*, 71–72. (E & S)

4. Miguel de Noriega, born circa 1626, came to New Mexico in 1659 as the secretary of Governor don Bernardo López de Mendizábal. A native of Villa de San Vicente de la Varguera in the Montañas de Burgos, Spain, Noriega was a vecino of Mexico City, with a residence next to the church of Señor San José de Gracia (AGN, Inquisición, vol. 596, f. 43v, Testimony of Capitán Miguel de Noriega, April 17, 1663, Ciudad de México). On October 23, 1661, Captain Miguel de Noriega was a witness on behalf of Juan Domínguez de Mendoza (AGN, Real Audiencia, Concurso de Peñalosa, vol. 1, leg. 1, no. 3, f. 246r/387r, Witnesses on behalf of Juan Domínguez de Mendoza, October 23, 1661, Villa de Santa Fe). After Governor López de Mendizábal and his wife, doña Teresa de Aguilera y Rocha, were arrested by the officials of the Inquisition in 1662, Noriega was assigned to guard doña Teresa on the trip from New Mexico to Mexico City. (E & S)

Document 11

Appointment as Alcalde Mayor of the Jurisdictions of Sandia and Isleta and as Lieutenant Captain General in the Río Abajo

Santa Fe, November 19, 1659[1]

Captain don Bernardo López de Mendizábal, governor and captain general of the kingdom of New Mexico for the king, our lord, etc.

Whereas the administration of the royal justice and good government, for which it is necessary to provide, has been exercised by Captain Alonso García[2] in the jurisdiction of Sandía, and in that of Isleta by Sargento Mayor Tomé Domínguez de Mendoza,[3] alcalde mayor of [the said jurisdiction] and lieutenant general of the Río Abajo; [and whereas] they must cease to exercise the said offices because they must stand residencia for the time they have served; in order to continue the said administration in matters of justice as well as in those of war, it is therefore necessary to name a person of all experience, valor, and satisfaction so that with good order and accord he may defend the frontiers of all the Río Abajo and the Salinas [districts], aiding the Christian natives and protecting them against their enemies, waging against the [said enemies] all the war and punishment possible for the many killings and robberies they are so continually committing.

Captain Juan Domínguez de Mendoza has these qualities because of his merits and the services which he has rendered His Majesty in this kingdom ever since he has had the use of reason. He has taken part in many campaigns and reprisals against the infidel enemies of our Holy Catholic Faith with outstanding courage and valor, holding at various times the offices of alférez, commander, and captain of Spanish infantry. In such capacity, as soon as I reached this kingdom, he went out on campaign by my appointment with more than eight hundred men, Spaniards and Christian Indians, to reduce the forces of the said enemies and destroy their milpas [fields] and sowings, inflicting upon them the greatest reprisal possible. On this occasion the said captain conducted himself with great valor, commanding and encouraging his soldiers in such a way that as a result of good leadership and courage a brilliant victory was obtained against the aforesaid enemies. His father, Captain Tomé Domínguez the elder, has often served His Majesty in this kingdom on all occasions of peace and war which have occurred, procuring the greatest defense and increase of these said provinces. At his own cost and expense he brought to them ten families who are here today with their wives and children and he has held the civil offices of alcalde ordinario in this said villa and of lieutenant of the governor and captain general many times with the approval of my predecessors . . . [illegible] . . . as is shown by his certifications and papers presented before me.

In consideration of the foregoing, in the name of His Majesty, I name and appoint the said Captain Juan Domínguez de Mendoza alcalde mayor of the jurisdiction of Sandia and pueblo of Isleta as far south as the house of Sargento Mayor Tomé Domínguez, his brother.[4] [I also appoint him] my lieutenant captain general in order that as such he may exercise the said office in matters relating to war in the said jurisdiction of Sandia as well as those of Cochiti, Jemez, and Isleta, and also as far as the pueblo of Senecú, and in the jurisdiction of Las Salinas, by virtue of which he may freely pursue the said enemies, making the necessary reprisals.[5] For the said purpose I order all the citizens, both Spaniards and Indians, and all others of any status whatsoever, to give him all the favor and aid necessary, observing and fulfilling his orders as if they were mine. And I order the said captain to seek the alleviation and defense of the Christian natives and [promote] their teaching and indoctrination with particular care and vigilance, in order that they may receive it in a manner conducive to the service of both Majesties and in order that they may not commit the sin of idolatry but be taught and instructed in the matters and mysteries of our Holy Catholic Faith. To use and exercise the said offices of alcalde mayor of Sandia and Isleta, and of my lieutenant captain general in the jurisdictions of the Río Abajo and frontiers mentioned, I give him as complete power and authority as I hold from the king, our lord, in whose royal name I order the citizens, Spanish and native, governors, alcaldes, and captains, and any others there may be in said jurisdictions, to hold and consider the said Captain Juan Domínguez de Mendoza as alcalde mayor and my lieutenant captain general, each one as may concern him according to the form expressed, observing his orders and commands under the penalties he may impose, which he will execute on the disobedient. And he may enjoy all the honors, exemptions, privileges and liberties which are due him by virtue of the said office; and in order that he may wear the usual insignia for all the aforesaid, I give him power and commission as is required by law. And so that it be on record, I ordered the present writing issued to him, signed by my name and sealed with the seal of my arms, and countersigned by my undersigned secretary.

Done in Santa Fe on November 19 of the year 1659. (Seal) Don Bernardo López de Mendizábal (rubric). By order of his lordship the Governor and Captain General, Miguel de Noriega, secretary of government and war (rubric).

Notes

1. BNE, Madrid, MSS 19258, photo 29.

2. Captain Alonso García was a native of Zacatecas, born circa 1627–1628, residing in 1660 at his Estancia de San Antonio, located twenty leagues south of Santa Fe in the Río Abajo region. AGN, Inquisición, vol. 587, exp. 1, f. 56r, Testimony of Alonso García, January 15, 1661, Ciudad de México. He married Teresa Varela, a descendant of one of the soldiers of Oñate's 1598 colonizing expedition to New Mexico. Their daughter Juana García de Noriega married Antonio Domínguez de Mendoza, a son of Francisco Domínguez de Mendoza and Juana de Rueda, and a nephew of Juan Domínguez de Mendoza. Chávez, *Origins of New Mexico Families*, 26, 33–34. In April 1668, Capitán Alonso García was described by Captain Francisco de Ortega as a mestizo holding the appointment as *alcalde mayor y capitán a guerra* of the jurisdiction of Sandia. AGN, Inquisición, vol. 608, f. 392v, Testimony of Capitán Francisco de Ortega, April 5, 1668, Convento de San Antonio de Isleta. (E & S)

3. Tomé Domínguez de Mendoza, born in February 1623, in Mexico City, and the namesake of his father, Tomé Domínguez, was a brother of Juan Domínguez de Mendoza. Tomé Domínguez de Mendoza established his estancia below the pueblo of Isleta and was married to Catalina López Mederos. Chávez, *Origins of New Mexico Families*, 25. See part 3 of this volume for additional historical information about Tomé Domínguez de Mendoza. (E & S)

4. The estancia of Tomé Domínguez de Mendoza was four leagues below Isleta. The village of Tomé is located on the property once belonging to Tomé

Domínguez de Mendoza and which was abandoned by him and his family in August 1680.

5. The Salinas district was located on the east side of the Manzano Mountains in the Estancia Basin and included the southern Tiwa and Tompiro Pueblo Indians. The three northern communities were the Tiwa pueblos of Chilili, Tajique, and Quarai, and the six southern communities were the Piro settlements as far south as the pueblo of Las Humanas, today known as Gran Quivira, and part of the Salinas National Monument. (E & S)

Document 12

Appointment as Escudero of the Encomienda of Sargento Mayor Francisco Gómez Robledo

Santa Fe, May 7, 1662[1]

Captain and Sargento Mayor don Diego Dionisio de Peñalosa Briceño y Verdugo, encomendero in the kingdom of Peru, provincial alcalde of the Santa Hermandad of the city of La Paz and five provinces in its district, governor and captain general in these [provinces] of New Mexico for His Majesty, etc.[2]

The king, our lord (God keep him many years), has specified the number of thirty-five encomenderos, who, enjoying the tributes of the pueblos as wages, stipend, or pay, shall serve as soldiers in the continual war against infidels for the defense of what has been conquered and settled, serving with their arms and horses in person, or sending their escuderos if they have a legitimate impediment or permission from the prince or the governor who represents him. At the present time, the Holy Office of the Inquisition of Mexico City has ordered Sargento Mayor Francisco Gómez Robledo, one of the said encomenderos, to be taken prisoner.[3] To fulfill the obligation of my office with regard to good military government, and in order that the frontiers and open areas, pacified and unpacified,[4] may be protected against continual invasion; for the present, in consideration of the merits and services and good qualities of Captain don Juan Domínguez de Mendoza, I name and appoint him in place of the said sargento mayor in order that he may fulfill for him all the obligations and duties which the holder was obliged to perform by virtue of the office of encomendero. For his work and occupation and in order that he may maintain arms and horses, which he must keep ready and preserved, I assign to him half the tributes belonging to the said Francisco Gómez, reserving the other half for the maintenance of the latter while his imprisonment lasts, or until something else is ordered and commanded by the supreme government of these kingdoms and in the royal audiencia, to which tribunals I have reported, as well as to the Holy Office of the Inquisition.[5]

In order that he may attend to this with due care during the interim, he shall make oath of fidelity with the usual solemnity, and shall enjoy in the same way as the encomendero himself all the honors favors, preeminences, exemptions, and liberties which are conceded to him in their entirety by virtue of the said appointment. I order the alcaldes mayores to have half of the said tributes brought to him; and the Indians are charged to recognize him as such, with the declaration that they must not give him any personal service nor commute the two pesos of tribute into such [services] on account of the grave inconvenience which results from this abuse because it is a transgression of what has been ordered and determined by repeated royal cédula.

Done in the Villa of Santa Fe on May 7 of the year 1662. (Seal) Don Diego de Peñalosa Briceño (rubric). By order of the governor and captain general, Juan Lucero de Godoy, secretary of government and war (rubric).

Title of escudería of the encomienda of Sargento Mayor Francisco Gómez Robledo.

Notes

1. BNE, Madrid, MSS 19258, photos 31–32.
2. Don Diego Dionisio de Peñalosa Briceño y Verdugo served as governor of New Mexico from mid-August 1661 to about February 1, 1664. For a discussion of his career, see Scholes, *Troublous Times in New Mexico*, chs. 5, 6, 9–11.
3. Francisco Gómez Robledo, born circa 1628, was a native of New Mexico and a son of Francisco Gómez and Ana Robledo. On May 4, 1662, his possessions were embargoed, and a record documenting his possessions was written at the corner of the plaza in Santa Fe. At this time, Gómez Robledo held titles of encomienda for the pueblos of Pecos, Tesuque, half of Acoma, half of Sandia, half of Abó, half of Xenogpauy (Hopi village of Shungópavi), and two and a half parts of Taos. His property consisted of a grant of an estancia in the Arroyo de Tesuque, another estancia named Barrancas, two grants of estancia near the pueblo of San Juan one of which was one league north of the pueblo and unoccupied, another called the Estancia del Yunque, and another in Taos. Among his personal papers he had fourteen appointments as *capitán y cabo*, two "*provisiónes real*" as sargento mayor, one

title (*titulo*) of fiscal, another *provisión real de cabo*, one "*merced de alférez real*," and two titles and one *merced* as *teniente de gobernador y capitán general*. His house in Santa Fe consisted of a living room or hall (*sala*), three rooms (*aposentos*), and a patio with an orchard or garden (*guerta*) in the back. Chávez, *Origins of New Mexico Families*, 36; AGN, Real Audiencia, Concurso de Peñalosa, vol. 2, leg. 1, no. 6, ff. 3r–3v/248r–248v, Inventory of the property of Sargento Mayor Francisco Gómez Robledo, May 4, 1662, Convento de Nuestra Señora de la Villa de Santa Fe; and AGN, Real Audiencia, Concurso de Peñalosa, vol. 2, leg. 1, no. 6, ff. 34r/279r, Inventory of the property of Sargento Mayor Francisco Gómez Robledo, May 4, 1662, Convento de Nuestra Señora de la Villa de Santa Fe. (E & S)

4. The manuscript reads, "*las fronteras y campañas enemigas y nuestras.*"

5. Early in May 1662, fray Alonso de Posada, acting on orders from the Holy Office of the Inquisition, arrested Francisco Gómez Robledo, Diego Romero, Cristóbal de Anaya Almazán, and Nicolás de Aguilar. The first two were encomenderos, and Anaya Almazán succeeded to his father's encomienda soon after his arrest. Having been instructed to embargo the property of the prisoners pending trial by the Holy Office, Posada sought to impose jurisdiction with regard to their encomienda revenues. This action was opposed by Governor Peñalosa, who insisted that inasmuch as the encomiendas were royal favors (*mercedes*) granted to provide for the maintenance of a minimum number of soldier-citizens (thirty-five, as stated in the document above), it was necessary from a military standpoint to appoint temporary substitutes (escuderos) to serve in place of Gómez Robledo, Romero, and Anaya Almazán, at least until special instructions were received from Mexico City. For the encomiendas of Gómez Robledo and Romero he named as escuderos two persons who were members of his personal entourage, and assigned them half of the encomienda revenues in each case for their services. Posada alleged that this action was merely a subterfuge to enable Peñalosa to collect the tribute for himself, and that formal titles of *escudería* were never issued to the persons appointed. This was evidently true, for in late 1663, when Peñalosa was preparing to leave New Mexico he issued titles of escudería for the encomiendas of Romero and Gómez Robledo to Cristóbal Durán y Chaves and Juan Domínguez de Mendoza, respectively. The documents were antedated to May 4 and May 7, 1662. See Scholes, *Troublous Times in New Mexico*, 129–33. Gómez Robledo was acquitted by the Holy Office on October 23, 1664, and after his return to New Mexico apparently resumed full control of his encomiendas. Peñalosa's action of granting title of escudero of the encomiendas of Francisco Gómez Robledo to Juan Domínguez de Mendoza is mentioned in a statement given to the Inquisition by fray Nicolás de Villar, see AGN, Inquisición, vol. 507, f. 676, witness #23, *capitulo* 21 (bound typescript, Center for Southwest Research, University of New Mexico). Peñalosa had been illegally taking the encomienda tributes for himself, and thus the backdating of the title of encomienda was an attempt to cover his tracks. (E & S)

Document 13

Title of Lieutenant Captain General and Visitador General
October 6, 1663[1]

Captain and Sargento Mayor don Diego Peñalosa Briceño y Verdugo, encomendero in the kingdoms of Peru, *alcalde provincial* of the Santa Hermandad of the City of La Paz and five provinces in its district, governor and captain general in these [provinces] of New Mexico for the king, our lord, etc.

Inasmuch as I am ill and unable to mount horseback because of my many indispositions, it is necessary for me to name a visitor general of the kingdom who shall act as my lieutenant captain general, in order that, representing my person, he may make the *visita* in all the provinces and pueblos of this kingdom and those which pertain to this government, and so that in case of war my person may not be necessary in all the matters that may come up, both in civil and in military affairs. Such a person, as is fitting in the service of the king, our lord, must be of quality, Christianity, knowledge and conscience, valor, and experience in civil and military affairs.

These and many other [qualities] concur in the person of Maestre de Campo don Juan Domínguez de Mendoza, senior alcalde ordinario of this Villa of Santa Fe, in consideration of the many services he has rendered his Majesty during twenty-five years he has served, from ordinary soldier to sargento and alférez, captain of infantry, many times sargento mayor of the kingdom, occupying the post of maestre de campo of the kingdom and that of maestre de campo of campaign three times, as well as that of military commander and chief in active wars; and because he has occupied many times the offices of lieutenant governor and captain general and visitor of the kingdom for my predecessors, and has exercised all posts of the republic, giving a very good and praiseworthy account of himself, as is proved by his titles and certifications which he has presented in my presence. It is evident from them that he has served His Majesty at his own cost and expense, and in addition to his personal expenses he has been and is accoutering a large number of soldiers, giving them the necessary horses and other supplies for the expedition and escorts and other forays which have been necessary to prevent encroachment by the enemy. The aforesaid is the legitimate son of General don Bartolomé [sic] Domínguez, who was one of the first conquerors and settlers.[2] Therefore, in consideration of this I have thought it well to appoint and name him my lieutenant captain general and visitador general of the kingdom in the name of the Royal and Catholic Majesty of the king, our lord, for such is his will and mine in his royal name. And I order the maestre de campo and the sargento mayor and other captains, active and retired, and other citizens, Spaniards as well as natives, to hold and consider him as my lieutenant general and visitador general under the penalties he may impose upon them, which he may exercise on the rebellious and disobedient and transgressors. And in order that he may do so, I give him power and plenary authority accordingly and as I hold it from the king, our lord, for such is his will and mine in his royal name. And he shall enjoy all the honors, liberties, and dignities in the same way as all the lieutenant captains general of the armies and forces of His Majesty enjoy them, well and completely without any omission. For the purpose I ordered the present writing issued to him, signed by my hand and sealed with the seal of my arms, and countersigned by the undersigned secretary of war and government; with the declaration that it goes on white paper, because the stamped paper is not current in this kingdom.

Done on October 6 of the year 1663. (Seal) Don Diego de Peñalosa Briceño (rubric). By order of the governor and captain general, Juan Lucero de Godoy, secretary of government and war (rubric).

Notes

1. BNE, Madrid, MSS 19258, photos 33–34.

2. For some unexplained reason, Tomé Domínguez, the father of Juan Domínguez de Mendoza, is referred to as Bartolomé Domínguez. This same error appears in a document dated August 19, 1694, Madrid, but the reference to Bartolomé Domínguez is crossed out, indicating the need for deleting that reference; see AGI, Indiferente, 133, N. 142, Relación de méritos y servicios de Baltasar Domínguez de Mendoza, teniente de capitán general y visitador de Nuevo México, August 19, 1694. A copy of this same document is also preserved in the Domínguez de Mendoza Servicios Personales and is found in Doc. 60, infra, Résumé of Papers Presented by Baltasar Domínguez de Mendoza, Madrid, August 19, 1694. Tomé is the Portuguese variation of the name Tomás (Thomas) and is not a variation of the name Bartolomé. The earliest documented evidence of the Domínguez family's association with New Mexico is found in an Inquisition document written in New Mexico in 1633 by fray Estéban de Perea that makes reference to a lawsuit of 1632 against Tomé Domínguez, a wine merchant of Mexico City who sold his goods on the Calle de Tacuba. Whether that date is early enough to qualify him as "a first conqueror and settler" is open to question. AGN, Inquisición, vol. 304, exp. 27, ff, 197r 197v, Testificación contra Juan de la Cruz y su mujer [Beatriz de los Ángeles] por supersticiosos, 1631. (E & S)

Document 14

Decree of Governor Peñalosa
Santa Fe, January 7, 1664[1]

The governor and captain general, etc.

I order Captain Juan Domínguez de Mendoza, alcalde ordinario of the Villa de Santa Fe, my lieutenant captain general and visitador of all the provinces and pueblos of New Mexico, to go to the estancias of Captains Andrés Hurtado,[2] Cristóbal Baca,[3] and Juan Luís,[4] and to notify each one of them to appear before me in this villa within the third day after the notification under penalty of one hundred pesos, one half to be applied for the *cámara* [government administration] of His Majesty and the other for expenses of war, to be collected at once without any supplication or appeal. I will consider them to have incurred and to have been condemned to this [penalty] if they do the contrary.

Done in the Villa of Santa Fe on the seventh day of January of the year 1664. Don Diego de Peñalosa Briceño (rubric). By order of the governor and captain general, Juan Lucero de Godoy (rubric), secretary of government and war.

In the estancias of San Nicolás on the ninth day of the month of January of the year 1664, Captain don Juan Domínguez de Mendoza, alcalde ordinario of the Villa of Santa Fe and its district, lieutenant general of the Río Abajo, [and] visitador general of the whole kingdom, notified the above decree to Captain Juan Luís and Captain Andrés Hurtado. They said they heard and obeyed it as emanating from their governor and captain general and that God giving them life and health, they will be in the villa within the appointed time. And they signed it in my presence on January 9. Before me as *juez receptor*, don Juan Domínguez de Mendoza (rubric).[5] Juan Luís (rubric). Andrés Hurtado (rubric).

Notes

1. BNE, Madrid, MSS 19258, photos 35–36.
2. The earliest account of Andrés Hurtado in New Mexico is from the year 1661, when he held the position of "*capitán de caballos actual*," according to his own account in which he declared he was a native of Zacatecas and gave

his age as thirty-three, indicating he was born circa 1628; AGN, Inquisición, vol. 593, f. 169v, Testimony of Andrés Hurtado, September 29, 1661, Villa de Santa Fe. In New Mexico he married doña Bernardina de Salas y Orozco Trujillo, a daughter of Diego de Trujillo. Three of the daughters of Andrés Hurtado and doña Bernardina were known by the surname of Salazar. Among the residents of Zacatecas in the early 1600s were Pedro Hurtado and Catalina de Salazar, who married on July 17, 1617, in the church of Nuestra Señora de Zacatecas, and who may have been the parents of Andrés Hurtado. Chávez, *Origins of New Mexico Families*, 49; and Mexico, Zacatecas, Sagrario, Matrimonios (1606–1619), LDS microfilm #977702. (E & S)

3. Cristóbal Baca was a native of New Mexico who married doña Ana Moreno de Lara, daughter of Diego de Trujillo and Catalina Vásquez. Ana Moreno de Lara was an aunt of doña Bernardina de Salas y Orozco Trujillo, the wife of Andrés Hurtado. Cristóbal Baca and doña Ana Moreno de Lara were compadres of Juan Domínguez de Mendoza, indicating they were godparents of each other's children. In 1662, doña Ana told fray Tomás Alvarado that Juan Domínguez de Mendoza had made amorous advances toward her. There is no known record that her allegation was investigated. Chávez, *Origins of New Mexico Families*, 10; and AGN, Inquisición, vol. 593, f. 308; and AGN, Inquisición, vol. 586, ff. 173r–173v, Ratification of testimony of doña Ana Moreno de Lara, age twenty-five, May 31, 1662, Convento de San Francisco de Sandia. (E & S)

4. Juan Luís, also known as Juan Luís Luján, was a native of Santa Fe, New Mexico, who was born circa 1615 and whose wife was a member of the Baca family. He was still living as of 1685 and gave testimony that year in the criminal case against Juan Domínguez de Mendoza (see Doc. 51, infra, Criminal Case against Maestre de Campo Juan Domínguez de Mendoza and Others Who Fled with Him, Guadalupe del Paso, September 28–October 6, 1685). (E & S)

5. A juez receptor was a delegated judge whose duty was to receive the submission of parties to the law. For an example of these duties, see Doc. 15, infra, Appointment as Lieutenant of the Governor and Captain General in the Jurisdictions of the Río Abajo, Santa Fe, June 25, 1665. (E & S)

Document 15

Appointment as Lieutenant of the Governor and Captain General in the Jurisdictions of the Río Abajo

Santa Fe, June 25, 1665[1]

Captain and Sargento Mayor don Fernando de Villanueva, governor and captain general of these provinces of New Mexico for His Majesty, etc.[2]

Inasmuch as the administration of royal justice of the Río Abajo, from the pueblo of La Cienega, the Queres, and Jemez, to the pueblo of Senecú should have someone to administer justice to them in my name and as my representative, it is necessary to appoint a person as my lieutenant general. This person must be of entire satisfaction, valor, experience, sufficiency, merits, and quality such as the case requires, so that he may have jurisdiction in all the cases and matters pertaining to and concerning the office which may present themselves, observing the law in everything, acting as juez receptor, hearing the parties with equality, and granting the appeals they may make to me when this is allowed by law; always seeking the greater service of both Majesties and the conservation and achievement of the teaching of the evangelical law among the natives so that they will obey their spiritual ministers with the veneration and respect which they owe them.

The person of General don Juan Domínguez de Mendoza is very suitable and fitting for the said purpose because the above-mentioned qualities concur in him together with many other praiseworthy services and procedures. For this reason my predecessors have kept him occupied in the posts of alférez, captain, visitador general, and lieutenant governor in the said jurisdiction; and in the government of this villa he has exercised the authority of *alcalde ordinario de primer voto*. As a result of these experiences he has attained great maturity of judgment. In addition, he has inflicted punishments on the infidel Apache enemies, confounding their pride and barbarous procedure, both as commander and subordinate. Therefore, I judge him worthy of all honor, and his merits deserving of reward in remuneration of his many services.

In the name of the king, our lord, I appoint him my lieutenant governor and captain general of the said jurisdictions, and I order the alcaldes mayores, citizens, and natives of all the said *cordillera* [string of towns] to hold, consider, and obey him as such, observing and fulfilling the orders and summonses which he may make in the service of both Majesties, executing them without delay.[3] And in serious and difficult cases, concerning which there may be some doubt, he will notify me, keeping the parties prisoner and holding their goods, real or personal. For all of this and what pertains to and concerns it, and in order that he may bear the usual insignia and enjoy the honors, exemptions, and liberties which are due him, I give him full power in due form, as well as to punish the rebellious and transgressors, for such is the will of His Majesty and mine in his royal name. Therefore

I ordered the present writing issued to him, signed by my name and sealed with the seal of my arms, and countersigned by the undersigned secretary of war and government.

Done in the Villa of Santa Fe of New Mexico on the twenty-fifth day of the month of June of the year 1665. (Seal) Fernando de Villanueva (rubric). By order of the governor and captain general, Francisco Xavier, secretary of government and war (rubric).

Notes

1. BNE, Madrid, MSS 19258, photos 37–38.
2. Don Fernando de Villanueva was appointed governor of New Mexico by the viceroy Marqués de Mancera, on January 14, 1665. He took office in Santa Fe on June 22, 1665, and served until November 29, 1668. AGI, Contaduría, legs. 757, 759, 763A, Caja de México. Cuentas de los oficiales reales de México, 1664–1666, 1667–1668, and 1669–1671, respectively; and AGI, Indiferente, 123, N. 59, Relación de méritos y servicios de Fernando Villanueva, Gobernador y Capitán General de Nuevo México, 1671. For a record of his merits and services, see Supp. Doc. 4, infra, Account of the Services of Don Fernando de Villanueva, Governor and Captain General of the Provinces of New Mexico by Appointment of the Marqués de Mancera, Viceroy of New Spain, October 30, 1671. (E & S)
3. The word *cordillera* means "the relay list" that bears the names of the various districts within New Mexico and here refers back to the word "jurisdictions," used earlier in the sentence. Regarding the function of the *cordillera* in circulating official decrees among provincial alcaldes mayores, consult Marc Simmons, *Spanish Government in New Mexico* (Albuquerque: University of New Mexico Press, 1990), 186. (E & S)

Document 16

Appointment as Visitador of the Mission Supply Caravan

Santa Fe, October 16, 1665[1]

Captain and Sargento Mayor don Fernando de Villanueva, governor and captain general of these provinces of New Mexico for His Majesty, etc.

Inasmuch as at the general time the royal supply train, of which General Juan Manso is in charge as its contractor, is about to leave this kingdom, and because, as is the custom, it is to be inspected in order that no prohibited thing or contraband may leave in it without permission and declaration; and because continually many servants of the citizens are wont to flee, merely for their own pleasure, leaving their masters, wives, and children; and on account of other things which might arise and originate during the departure of the said wagons until they leave the settled area, quarrels as well as any other incident that may occur; and in order to avoid them and so that all may be done with justice, it is most necessary to appoint a person of entire satisfaction and trust, experienced in law, of loyalty, quality, merits, and praiseworthy methods of procedure such as the case requires, in order that he may go as visitador with all my authority and representing my person.[2]

In consideration of the fact that the aforesaid qualities and many other important ones concur in the person of General don Juan Domínguez de Mendoza, my lieutenant in all the jurisdictions of the Río Abajo, Queres, and Jemez, for the present, and in the name of the royal and Catholic Majesty of the king, our lord, I elect, appoint, and name him as such visitador with all my authority and plenary power in due form imposed by law, in order that in the regions and places which may seem best to him and may be necessary he may undertake the said inspection and all proceedings which offer themselves, acting as juez receptor. And I order all the persons who go and assist in the said wagons to respect, esteem, and obey him as such, and to respond to his summonses and orders in what pertains to him by virtue of the said office, for such is the royal will and mine in his royal name. Therefore I ordered the present writing issued to him, signed by my name and sealed with the seal of my arms, and countersigned by the undersigned secretary of government and war.

Done in the Villa of Santa Fe on the sixteenth day of the month of October of the year 1665. (Seal) Fernando de Villanueva (rubric). By order of the government and captain general, Francisco Xavier (rubric), secretary of government and war.

Notes

1. BNE, Madrid, MSS 19258, photos 39–40.
2. Don Juan Manso, ex-governor of New Mexico, became a contractor (*asentista*) of the mission supply caravan in 1664, with a contract for nine years. For additional data concerning the supply caravans, see France V. Scholes, "The Supply Service of the New Mexican Missions in the Seventeenth Century," *New Mexico Historical Review* 5 (1930): 93–115, 186–210, 386–404. For details of the

commercial dealings and estate of don Juan Manso at the time of his death, see Rick Hendricks and Gerald J. Mandell, "Juan Manso, Frontier Entrepreneur", *New Mexico Historical Review* 75, no. 3 (2000): 339–65.

Document 17

Appointment as Visitador of the Trading Caravan
Santa Fe, December 16, 1666[1]

Captain and Sargento Mayor don Fernando de Villanueva, governor and captain general of these provinces of New Mexico, etc.

Captain Cristóbal de Anaya,[2] citizen of these provinces, provincial judge of the Santa Hermandad,[3] has informed me [of his intention] to leave these provinces with a train of eight wagons for the Real y Minas de San José del Parral with merchandise and products of this country, and has asked my permission to do so; and, in addition, has asked permission to take an escort to be paid out of the property to which he refers, consisting of the said products and of cattle and sheep. And because he says that he has appointed and paid Captain Diego González Lobón,[4] Pedro de Montoya,[5] and Luis de Carvajal,[6] who, he states, go willingly and with pay, and in addition, twenty-four or twenty-six Indians with bow and arrow, who, he says, go willingly and with pay, as well as other things which are expressed at greater length in the license which I have granted him, he shall make declaration of the same before General don Juan Domínguez de Mendoza, lieutenant general of the Río Abajo, to whom I give my commission to make him show the said license and to go to the pueblo of Senecú and inspect the said wagon train and the other things mentioned in the said license. He shall not consent to departure of any man, Spaniard or Indian, besides those contained in the said license, and he shall return the rest or seize them, not allowing them to go on, nor shall he consent that more cattle or sheep leave, nor any other things in addition to what the license contains, for I so order and command him as befits the good administration of royal justice and ordinance of this kingdom. After recording the action he may take at the foot of this commission, he shall remit same to the archive of this government.

Done in Santa Fe of New Mexico on December 16 of the year 1666. Fernando de Villanueva (rubric). By order of the governor and captain general, Juan Lucero de Godoy, secretary of government and war (rubric).

Auto de visita

In the pueblo of Senecú on the twenty-fifth day of the month of January of the year 1667, general don Juan Domínguez de Mendoza, lieutenant of the governor and captain general, said that by virtue of the above commission, inasmuch as he is ordered by it to make the inspection of the wagons which Captain Cristóbal de Anaya is taking to San José del Parral and it is the will of the governor and captain general that nothing contraband nor any person leave this kingdom without permission, he ordered the said Captain Cristóbal de Anaya to show him the license granted to him by the said governor and captain general. He, being present, declared all he is taking and showed the license signed by the said governor and captain general. And the said lieutenant, having seen it, ordered all the Spaniards and Indians mentioned in it to appear before him and asked them whether they were going of their own free will. They replied that they were and that they were going with the said Cristóbal de Anaya to help him since they are being paid and are content with their work. He also made the inspection of the said wagons, entering them with me and two witnesses, who were Estéban de Gracia[7] and Domingo Martín,[8] and no forbidden thing or contraband was found in them. Whereupon, having registered the Apache captives,[9] he allowed [the caravan] to proceed, accordingly and as is contained in the license. And he ordered this set down in the form of an *auto* to be remitted, together with the said commission, to the governmental archive. Thus he provided, ordered, and signed in the presence of me, the said secretary, to which I certify. Juan Domínguez de Mendoza (rubric). In my presence, Juan Lucero de Godoy, secretary of government and war (rubric).

Notes

1. BNE, Madrid, MSS 19258, photos 41–43.

2. Cristóbal de Anaya Almazán was a native of New Mexico, born circa 1626–1629. He was married to a sister of Juan Domínguez de Mendoza. Cristóbal had bought his Estancia de San Antonio from his father-in-law, Tomé Domínguez, and the property contained "*tierras de labor y asequia*," irrigated farm land. The house on this property, located in the area of modern-day Algodones along the Rio Grande just north of Sandia Pueblo, consisted of a living room or hall (sala), two rooms (aposentos), one kitchen (*cosina*), one room (aposento) outside of the house with doors and windows made of timber with metal locks. Chávez, *Origins of New Mexico Families*, 4; AGN, Real Audiencia, Concurso de Peñalosa, vol. 3, leg. 1, no. 22, Embargo of the Property of Captain Cristóbal de Anaya Almazán, May 25, 1662, Estancia de San Antonio, 44ff. (E & S)

3. The Santa Hermandad was a royal police force with judicial powers, organized by Queen doña Isabel of Castilla y León in 1476 and transferred to New Spain in 1552. Colin M. MacLachlan, *Criminal Justice in Eighteenth Century Mexico* (Berkeley: University of California Press, 1974), 10–11. (E & S)

4. Captain Diego González Lobón, a vecino of the Villa de Santa Fe, was a son of Domingo González and Magdalena de Carvajal and was very likely a native of New Mexico; see Chávez, *Origins of New Mexico Families*, 38–39. He and his wife, Margarita Pérez, held many grievances against Governor don Bernardo López de Mendizábal, complaining of his tyranny. AGN, Real Audiencia, Tierras, vol. 3268, exp. 1–01, leg. 2, no. 32, f. 43, Testimony of Capitán Diego González Lobón, October 18, 1641, Villa de Santa Fe. Diego González Lobón submitted his papers of merits and services presented to Governor López de Mendizábal in July 1659 in hopes of receiving some position in his administration. These papers were in the possession of López de Mendizábal as recorded in AGN, Real Audiencia, Concurso de Peñalosa, vol. 1, leg. 1, no. 1, f. 37v, List of Papers of Merits and Services of New Mexico Vecinos, July 17, 1662; see Supp. Doc. 3, infra. (E & S)

5. There was an elder Pedro de Montoya and a younger one of the same name who were not related to one another. The Pedro de Montoya mentioned in this record appears to be the younger one, born circa 1638, who was a relative of the González Lóbon–Vitoria Carvajal family. This Pedro de Montoya was a vecino of the Villa de Santa Fe, who was referred to as a *cuñado* of Sargento Mayor Diego del Castillo in January 1663, AGN, Tierras, vol. 3268, exp. 1–02, f. 296v–297v, Testimony of Pedro de Montoya, January 9, 1663, Villa de Santa Fe. Montoya was also mentioned as being the nephew of Antonia González de Vitoria, a sister of Captain Diego González Lobón. She and Montoya were regarded as enemies of Governor López de Mendizábal and his wife, doña Teresa de la Roche y Aguilera. AGN, Inquisición, vol. 596, exp. 1, f. 157r, Testimony of doña Teresa de Aguilera y Roche, 1663, Ciudad de México. (E & S)

6. Luis de Carvajal was most likely a member of the family founded in New Mexico by Juan de Vitoria Carvajal, and thus very likely a relative of Captain Diego González Lobón and Pedro de Montoya. Lack of documentation prevents the identification of his parents and origins. He is likely the same person of this name who had a hacienda along the Rio Grande that was passed by the refugees of the Pueblo Indian Revolt in 1680. Chávez, *Origins of New Mexico Families*, 15. (E & S)

7. Estéban de Gracia, also known as Estéban López de Gracia, was later among the survivors of the Pueblo Indian Revolt of 1680. He was apparently a member of the López de Gracia family of the Isleta and Salinas jurisdictions. Chávez, *Origins of New Mexico Families*, 55–56. (E & S)

8. Domingo Martín, also known as Domingo Martín Serrano, was a member of the Martín Serrano clan of La Cañada jurisdiction in New Mexico, where his

descendants resettled after 1693. He was married to Josefa de Herrera. Chávez, *Origins of New Mexico Families*, 73. (E & S)

9. The Spanish reads "*piezas de Apaches.*" These were Apaches captured during "just war" of reprisal. Their legal status was that of involuntary laborers assigned by formal legal process to vecinos who were obligated to teach Christian ways and doctrine to them. For all practical purposes, however, they were slaves. They were freely bought and sold, and as this document indicates, numbers of them were sent to New Spain to be sold as household servants or as laborers in mines and on cattle ranches. Provincial governors occasionally sent young Apache boys and girls to their friends in the viceregal capital. In the 1660s and 1670s the authorities in New Spain made an effort to prohibit this form of involuntary service.

Document 18

Appointment as Lieutenant of the Governor and Captain General
Santa Fe, February 10, 1667[1]

Captain and Sargento Mayor don Fernando de Villanueva, governor and captain general of these provinces of New Mexico for the king, our lord, etc.

Captain Andrés de Gracia of El Paso del Río del Norte of this jurisdiction wrote letters asking for aid because the Manso nation was in revolt, as a result of which the friars of that conversion were in danger.[2] With regard to these letters, councils of the captains, cabildo, and retired officials were held and edicts [were pronounced] in which the said Paso del Río del Norte was declared to be of this jurisdiction.[3] And in accordance with the said council I issued an order that Maestre de Campo Tomé Domínguez de Mendoza should go forth with twenty-five men, with powder and munitions, to help the said friars and make the said conversion safe and peaceful, and [to execute] the rest contained in the edicts. In the second dispatch from the said Captain Andrés de Gracia, he states that the said aid is unnecessary and the [men] should halt and turn back because he has hanged two Indians, abettors of the uprising. [He has done this] without remitting autos or knowing how to prepare them. By these letters he shows that he made himself judge without jurisdiction or authority from me.

In addition, the Indians of the *ranchería* of El Chilmo and Capitán Chiquito were in revolt and attacked the highways, although they had been friendly and at peace.[4] Councils were also held concerning this, and an order was

FIGURE 3. Report on military and administrative affairs by New Mexico Governor Fernando de Villanueva, which contains the appointment of Juan Domínguez de Mendoza as lieutenant governor and captain general. February 10, 1667.

issued to the alcalde mayor of Senecú, Juan García,[5] to go in peace to the said rancherías and summon and bring the said captains to me in order to learn the reason for their unrest so that they might be calmed and the roads made safe for the peace and tranquility of this kingdom. When the said alcalde mayor of Senecú, Juan García, went to the said rancherías and dwellings of the aforementioned [captains], he found them abandoned, for they had fled.

Therefore, I issued an edict covering both matters to the effect that when the active wars which were then going on in this *Custodia* and these provinces were quieted, I would go down in person to tranquilize the said Mansos and Apaches del Chilmo and Paso del Río del Norte and [to attend to] matters pertaining to the services of His Majesty. And our Lord God has been pleased to bring the Apache nation to recognition of their errors by means of the punishments inflicted upon them, which caused them to come to sue for peace, which was granted and given to all of them generally except to El Chilmo and Capitán Chiquito, who have not come. For this reason I am going in person for the said purpose of making the roads safe and pacifying the said Mansos and all else under the royal jurisdiction of this kingdom. Because it is a distance of 130 leagues from this villa to the said Paso del Río del Norte, and since I do not know whether for the said royal jurisdiction I shall go farther on, it is necessary to appoint a lieutenant general and magistrate in these provinces to take my place in the interval in the matters which may arise, and in order that the kingdom and provinces and their vassals may have justice to govern, defend, and aid them, it is necessary to appoint a person in my name for this purpose, who may administer both in peace and in war and shall be of the parts, services, and quality required.

And because of those that concur in General don Juan Domínguez de Mendoza, and because of the services he has rendered His Majesty and my confidence that he will continue the same, I name the said General Juan Domínguez de Mendoza as my lieutenant governor and captain general of these provinces in the name of His Majesty, giving him authority for it according as I hold it from the king, our lord. I order and command him to maintain all these provinces and vassals in peace, and to hear them and preserve justice. He will not start wars on his side against the said Apache enemies, to whom I have granted peace generally. Rather, he will conserve them in good friendship as far as possible. And in all he will act as a faithful Christian, Catholic, Apostolic, and Roman, seeking the greatest service of both Majesties; and he will defend the royal jurisdiction. Therefore, I order the cabildo of this Villa of Santa Fe and all the other citizens, residents, and inhabitants of these said provinces and this kingdom, both Spaniards and natives, to hold and consider the said General don Juan Domínguez de Mendoza as such lieutenant governor and captain general of the whole [kingdom], and to obey and respect him under the penalties he may impose upon them and His Majesty has determined for those who do the contrary, to which I pronounce them liable and condemned, for such is the will of His Majesty and mine in his royal name. Therefore I ordered this title issued to him, signed by my hand and sealed with the seal of my arms, and countersigned by the undersigned secretary of government and war.

Granted in the Villa of Santa Fe on February 10, of the year 1667. (Seal) Fernando de Villanueva (rubric). By order of the governor and captain general, Juan Lucero de Godoy (rubric), secretary of government and war.

In the Villa of Santa Fe of New Mexico on the fifth day of April of the year 1667, the lieutenant general presented himself before the cabildo with the above title which was read *de verbo ad verbum*. And, having heard it, he said that he obeyed it and he placed it upon his head as an order of the governor and captain general. And by virtue of this [the members of the cabildo] took it in their hands and placed it upon their heads and they signed it in my presence, the present notary of the cabildo to which I certify. Andrés López Sambrano (rubric).[6] Bartolomé Gómez Robledo (rubric).[7] Domingo López de Ocanto (rubric).[8] Alonso García (rubric). Francisco Ximénez (rubric).[9] Francisco de Anaya Almazán (rubric). In my presence, Fernando de Ynojos, notary of the cabildo (rubric).[10]

Title of lieutenant of the governor and captain general in all these provinces of New Mexico in the person of General Juan Domínguez de Mendoza.

Notes

1. BNE, Madrid, MSS 19258, photos 44–47.
2. Andrés López de Gracia, born circa 1616, was a native of Puebla de los Ángeles in New Spain, and a son of Bentura [López de Gracia]. In 1646 he was one of fourteen soldiers hired as part of the escort for the supply wagons of the Franciscan friars heading to New Mexico from Mexico City. He was described as "tall, slim, swarthy . . . a scar on the left side of his forehead near the hairline." See Joseph P. Sánchez, *Between Two Rivers: The Atrisco Land Grant in Albuquerque History, 1692–1968* (Norman: University of Oklahoma, 2008), 191n7, citing AGN, Hacienda, 472, Lista de los soldados que van a la Nueva México, 1646.

Andrés López de Gracia, a resident of the jurisdiction of Isleta in 1638, became the first alcalde mayor of the settlement of El Paso del Río del Norte, in 1661. His house was described in September 1661 as being "*en la toma del Río del Norte entre los Mansos y Sumas.*" AGN, Inquisición, vol. 593, f. 158r, Testimony of Capitán Diego de Trujillo, September 26, 1661, Villa de Santa Fe. André López de Gracia had four sisters: 1) Sebastiana López de Gracia, wife of Diego González de Apodaca, who lived on an estancia located one league from the pueblo of Quarac; 2) Isabel López de Gracia, wife of Pedro Cedillo Rico de Rojas; 3) Lucía López de Gracia, wife of José Nieto and resident of the Salinas jurisdiction; and 4) María López Millán, born circa 1613 and wife of Francisco de Valencia, who resided on an estancia one league south of the pueblo of Isleta in the general area of the modern-day town of Valencia. José Antonio Esquibel, "López de Gracia: Clarifying Familial Relations," *Nuestra Raíces* 6, no. 3 (Fall 1994): 92–98; AGN, Inquisición, vol. 507, f. 300r, Testimony of Maestre de Campo Francisco de Valencia, April 10, 1665, Villa de Santa Fe; AGN, Inquisición, vol. 507, f. 307v, Testimony of José Nieto, September 28, 1665, Villa de Santa Fe; AGN, Inquisición, vol. 593, ff. 120r, Testimony of María López de Millán, May 24, 1661, Convento de Isleta; and AGN, Inquisición, vol. 608, f. 441r, Testimony of Lucía López de Gracia, March 4, 1668, Convento de Cuarác. Chávez, *Origins of New Mexico Families*, 55–56. (E & S)

3. Both of the governors of New Mexico and the adjoining kingdom of Nueva Vizcaya claimed jurisdiction over the El Paso del Norte district. The edicts referred to here represent an early attempt to resolve this controversy. Four years earlier, on December 26, 1662, Tomé Domínguez de Mendoza, Teniente de Capitán General y Tesorero de la Santa Cruzada, made reference in a testimony to "the *paraje* of Guadalupe del Paso del Río del Norte, which is in the jurisdiction of Nueva Vizcaya." Apparently, as a government official he considered El Paso to be within the jurisdiction of Nueva Vizcaya. AGN, Real Audiencia, Concurso de Peñalosa, vol. 2, leg. 1, no. 8, f. 9r/391r, Testimony of Maestre de Campo Tomé Domínguez de Mendoza, December 26, 1662, Villa de Santa Fe. (E & S)

4. The Manso Indian ranchería of Capitán Chiquito was located on the Rio Grande above El Paso del Norte. The Spanish word *capitán* was roughly equivalent to the English word *chief*. Mansos living in the Mesilla Valley under the leadership of Captain Chiquito remained unconverted and participated in the Manso rebellion of 1684. Patrick H. Beckett and Terry L. Corbett, "Indian Cultural Diversity in Southern New Mexico, A.D. 1581–1988," in *Current Research on the Late Prehistory and Early History of New Mexico*, ed., Bradley J. Vierra (Albuquerque: New Mexico Archaeological Council, 1992), 3–9. (E & S)

5. Juan García Holgado was a longtime resident of the Río Abajo region of New Mexico, living for a while in the jurisdiction of Isleta (1638) and then being alcalde of the pueblo of Alameda (1650). He was a son of Alvaro García Holgado, a soldier, and Juana de los Reyes. See Chávez, *Origins of New Mexico*

Families, 33–34. In 1638, Juan García Holgado declared he was twenty-six years of age (b. ca. 1612) and a vecino of the jurisdiction of San Antonio de Isleta. AGN, Inquisición, vol. 385, exp. 15, f. 4r, Testimony of Juan García Holgado, August 6, 1638, Convento de San Francisco de Sandia. (E & S)

6. Andrés López Sambrano was a native of San Miguel in Culiacán and was born circa 1618–1622. When he testified in 1662 before the officials of the Inquisition in the case against Governor López de Mendizábal he identified himself as being castizo, indicating that one of his parents was of mixed European and Indian ethnicity. López Sambrano married Ana María de Anaya (aka Ana de Almazán), also castiza and a daughter of Francisco de Anaya Almazán and Juana López de Villafuerte. Chávez, *Origins of New Mexico Families*, 58, 66; AGN, Inquisición, vol. 598, exp. 7, f. 117r, Testimony of Capitán Andrés López Sambrano, March 3, 1662, Villa de Santa Fe. (E & S)

7. Bartolomé Gómez Robledo, a native of New Mexico born circa 1639–1640, was a member of one of the more prominent families of seventeenth-century New Mexico. He was a son of Francisco Gómez, originally from Portugal, and doña Ana Robledo. Bartolomé occupied a number of high civil positions, including regent and high sheriff in Santa Fe. Chávez, *Origins of New Mexico Families*, 35–36. (E & S)

8. In October 1661, Domingo López de Ocanto, a vecino of the Villa de Santa Fe, identified himself as a son of Capitán Juan López de Ocanto, apparently deceased, and mentioned his "poor mother" and an unmarried sister in his care. AGN, Real Audiencia, Tierras, vol. 3268, f. 110r, Testimony of Domingo López de Ocanto, October 18, 1661, Villa de Santa Fe. In this same year, Domingo held the post of clerk of the town council of Santa Fe in 1661 and was encomendero of the pueblos of Nambé and Jemez, a position he inherited from his father. Chávez, *Origins of New Mexico Families*, 57. In 1662, he declared he was a native and vecino of the Villa de Santa Fe, age twenty-five (b. ca. 1637) and married to Juana de Mondragón. AGN, Inquisición, vol. 598, f. 119r, Testimony of Domingo López de Ocanto, April 4, 1662, Convento de San Francisco de Sandia. In 1663, a reference was made in regard to Ines de Zamora and her son, "Domingo López," as relatives of the Lucero de Godoy family. AGN, Inquisición, vol. 596, 155v–156r, Testimony of doña Teresa de Aguilera y Roche, 1663, Mexico City. Ines's sister, Petronila de Zamora, was the first wife of Pedro Lucero de Godoy. Chávez, *Origins of New Mexico Families*, 59. Domingo's parents, Juan López de Ocanto and Ines de Zamora, were married in the church of the Villa de Santa Fe on February 19, 1634, with Capitán Alonso Martín Barba and his wife, Francisca de Herrera Abrego, as sponsors. AGN, Inquisición, vol. 380, exp. 2, f. 242v, Testimony of Capitán Alonso Martín Barba. Juan López de Ocanto was a native of Cartagena de Levante, Spain, and Ines de Zamora was a daughter of Alférez Diego de Montoya and Ana Martín Barba. The official witnesses to the marriage were Governor Francisco de la Mora Ceballos, his lieutenant, Alonso Varela, and

Sargento Mayor Francisco Gómez; the notary for the prenuptial investigation was Diego de la Serna. AGN, Inquisición, vol. 380, exp. 2, f. 256r, Certification of the Marriage of Juan López and Inez de Zamora. (E & S)

9. Very little is known about Francisco Jiménez. He was apparently a relative of Felipa Jiménez García (also known as Felipa de Ortega), the wife of Diego González Bernal. Chávez, *Origins of New Mexico Families*, 40, 50; and AGN, Inquisición, vol. 593, p. 291–92 (bound transcription, Center for Southwest Research, University of New Mexico, Testimony of Diego González Bernal, March 8, 1662, Villa de Santa Fe). (E & S)

10. Hernando de Hinojos may have been a son or grandson of Captain Hernando de Hinojos, who accompanied the colonizing expedition of New Mexico led by don Juan de Oñate in 1598. In 1661, Miguel de Hinojos, an encomendero and son of Captain Hernando de Hinojos, mentioned he had a brother whom he did not identify by name. Chávez, *Origins of New Mexico Families*, 48. (E & S)

Document 19

Edict Concerning a Council of War and Petition for Horses and Provisions for a Campaign against the Apaches

Santa Fe and Santo Domingo, February 18–26, 1668[1]

In the Villa of Santa Fe of New Mexico on the eighteenth day of the month of February of the year 1668, Captain and Sargento Mayor don Fernando de Villanueva, governor and captain general of these provinces of New Mexico for His Majesty.

I state that I have seen two letters which I received this very day, one from Vicente Cisneros and the other from the lieutenant [of the governor and captain general of the Río Abajo].[2] They describe the pertinacity of the Apache enemy in robbing, killing and laying siege to the houses, as they did to Vicente Cisneros's house and now recently to that of Captain Felipe Romero, as is evident from the said letters and many others which have been received.[3] They entered the houses themselves and robbed [everything], even the bed linen, and killed six Christian Indians who were defending the said house; not to mention the horses and cows they have carried off and the Spaniards and natives they have killed, although they have been given no reason to do so, but rather had been granted the peace which this kingdom was enjoying when I left [the province],[4] publicly and with council of war. In order to defend these provinces of the king, our lord, and his vassals and Christian natives, seeking the best means to the service of both

Majesties and defense of Christianity, I order a council of war to be held with the alcaldes ordinarios, procurador general and officials of war and retired officials, so that they may give their opinion and the most suitable method of defense may be sought. Inasmuch as Maestre de Campo Tomé Domínguez de Mendoza, although he has seen the wars so incessant in this kingdom, has not come to this villa for more than seven months, I order the sargento mayor of the kingdom, who is Bartolomé Romero[5] at present, to have the above-mentioned persons summoned. When they have assembled, the said letters and this edict are to be read to them; and after conferring on the matter, they are to give their votes and opinions in the form most keeping with the greatest service to both Majesties, for thus it befits his royal service, defense and conservation of these provinces, in order that I may decide the course of action which will result in the greatest service. Thus I ordered and signed. Don Fernando de Villanueva. By order of the governor and captain general, Juan Lucero de Godoy, secretary of government and war.

Council of War

In the said Villa of Santa Fe of New Mexico on the said eighteenth day of February of the year 1668, in fulfillment of the above edict, the said sargento mayor and the alcaldes ordinarios, procurador general and alférez real, and the others whose signatures appear below met in these casas reales. And I, the present secretary, read the edict of the governor and captain general and the letters to which it refers. Having heard and understood them, they deliberated the case at length; and unanimously and of one accord said that this kingdom today is in deplorable state which is publicly known because of the scarcity of sustenance. And [they said] that in order to put into effect as efficacious a remedy as the daring of the said enemies demands because of the flagrant killings and robberies and the obstinacy and rebelliousness which they show today, in revenge for the killings in cold blood committed against [Spaniards and natives] it is now necessary to make a good expedition against the said enemy, with the strongest possible force. For this purpose, because of the lack of provisions already mentioned and the weakness of the horses, let the governor and captain general be pleased to make a formal demand to the reverend father custodian in order that his fathership, as so loyal a vassal of His Majesty, may issue his patent to the effect that fifty or sixty men may be succored by the convents of his custody with all the provisions sufficient for a two months' campaign and also with such horses as the convents may have in good condition; and accordingly let the pueblos where there are any [provisions] succor the friendly Indians who go on the said expedition. And meanwhile let the household and family of Captain Felipe Romero be ordered to retire to the pueblo of Sevilleta, and Captain Xirón [Jirón] to that of Socorro,[6] taking precautions to safeguard the other houses which may be defenseless so as to prevent in this way the said enemy from becoming more daring, for greater and more deplorable ravages have been seen as a result of lesser incidents. This is what they feel can be done in view of the lack [of provisions] referred to. And the governor and captain general, as so great a servant of His Majesty, will make the most suitable provision in the service of both Majesties and defense of this Christian community. And they signed it with their names. Bartolomé Romero. Pedro [Lucero] de Godoy.[7] Francisco de Madrid.[8] Juan Ximénez.[9] Francisco de Ynostrossa (Hinostrosa). Francisco Gómez Robledo. Andrés López Zambrano [Sambrano]. Juan Griego, Lorenzo de Madrid.[10] José Nieto.[11] Francisco García.[12]

In my presence, Juan Lucero de Godoy, secretary of government and war.

Edict of the Governor

In the Villa of Santa Fe on the said day, month and year, Governor and Captain General don Fernando de Villanueva, having seen the decision of the council of war, state that he is in agreement with its contents because it was made by experienced soldiers and servants of His Majesty. The originals of these proceedings are to be remitted to the reverend father custodian fray Juan Talabán.[13] On behalf of the king, our lord, the said governor exhorts and requires, and on his own behalf, begs and charges [the said custodian] to be pleased, as so great a vassal of His Majesty and so great a minister in this custody and provinces, whose holy zeal is so well known, to consider the great need and precise obligation to defend this Christian community, because the circumstances are public knowledge and prompt action is required in order to protect the lives of everyone, and to order the convents of Jemez, Isleta, Zía, Socorro and Senecú, Acoma, and others which his fathership thinks may be able to do so, to furnish the number of *fanegas* [of grain] they are able to give. And his reverend fathership will mention in his pious reply the quantities he may be kind enough to grant, so that on this basis the said governor may be able to come to a decision concerning the action proposed in the service of both Majesties. The secretary of government and war is to go to the convent of Santo Domingo and make the said edicts known to him. Thus he ordered and signed. Don Fernando de Villanueva. In my presence, Juan Lucero de Godoy, secretary of government and war.

Reply of the Father Custodian

In the convent of Santo Domingo on the twentieth day of the month of February of the year 1668, I, the present secretary of government and war, by order of the governor and captain general read and made known to the very reverend father preacher fray Juan Talabán, custodian and ecclesiastical judge in these provinces, the above edicts and proceedings of the council of war. Having heard them, his reverend fathership said that he heeds them and that it is manifest to this whole kingdom that last year, 1667, it pleased God, our Lord, to inflict upon all this land not only the plague of locusts which cut down fields, but also the scourge of sterility, which affected the convents, some wholly, and others in large part. For this reason many ministers are suffering such extreme necessity this year that it has obliged the said reverend father, our custodian, to aid some convents with grain he has taken from others, in order to avoid failure to fulfill the ministry of the holy sacraments. In addition, having compassion on the extreme need which the cabildo of the Villa of Santa Fe represented to him by letter as being suffered in the said government, he found himself obliged to take some fanegas of maize with which to succor them from the convent of Santo Domingo. The father *definitor* and guardian of Pecos, fray Diego Enríquez, did likewise. And, no less moved to compassion because he saw that the natives of the said pueblo of Santo Domingo were dying of hunger and that many families were determined to leave the said pueblo to seek the remedy and relief from their hardship in lands frequented by the Apache enemy, he decided to give food daily to all the natives of the said pueblo, as is actually being done. They would have perished if they had not found paternal support in his reverend fathership. But nevertheless, mindful of the greatest service to both Majesties, welfare and benefit of this realm of the king, our lord, he will make an effort to provide what is necessary for the expedition planned by his lordship in this respect. As for the horses mentioned in the said edicts, he stated that inasmuch as the friars who assist in this holy custody are employed in ministering the holy sacraments both to the Spanish citizens and to the natives, they use [the horses] and they are absolutely necessary for this purpose, for without [horses] it would be impossible to attend to [this duty] because of the danger of encountering the enemy, the distances from one mission to another, and the nature of the land. Moreover, on account of the hostility of the Apaches, [some of] the said [missions] are being closed.[14] The friars do not breed the said horses but acquire them by soliciting alms. Therefore he must consult the nearest friar-ministers, mindful of the haste the matter requires, so that the most suitable disposition may be made in accordance with their opinion and vote. And [he asks] that the secretary of government and war give him a copy of all the edicts and of this reply in legal form in order that the fathers may see his lordship's motives for making such provisions, and he will notify the [governor] of the results of the consultation as soon as possible. He gave this as his reply and signed it before me, the said secretary of government and war. Fray Juan Talabán, custodian. In my presence, Juan Lucero de Godoy, secretary of government and war.

[The certificate of the copy follows here]

Edict

In this convent of Santo Domingo on the twenty-second day of the month of February of the year 1668, our reverend father preacher fray Juan de Talabán, custodian and ecclesiastical judge of these provinces of New Mexico, said that on the twentieth day of this present month and year, the secretary of government and war, Juan Lucero de Godoy, came to this convent by order and command of the Sargento Mayor don Fernando de Villanueva, governor and captain general of this kingdom, to make known the originals of the edicts of which a literal copy appears above. Having replied as appears in them, he commanded and ordered the fathers definitors fray Tomás de Alvarado and fray Diego Enríquez to meet in this said convent. And because the other fathers definitors, who are at present our reverend fathers fray Antonio de Ybargaray,[15] fray Francisco de Salazar,[16] and father fray Juan de Plasencia, and very far away and cannot be summoned, he appointed and named as *discretos* for the said council and determination the father preachers and guardians fray Nicolás de Cuéllar, fray Nicolás Enríquez,[17] fray Nicolás de Freitas,[18] and fray Salvador de Guerra, definitor habitual. The said edicts were made known to them so that having seen them, and keeping in mind the welfare and the good of the poor natives and the citizens of this kingdom, and the prevention of greater harm to this Christian community, they may come to a decision in accordance with what they may consider most advantages to the service of both Majesties. This he provided, ordered, and signed. Done ut supra. Fray Juan de Talabán, custodian (rubric). By order of our reverend father custodian, fray Salvador de Guerra, secretary (rubric).

Decision of the Council

In this convent of Santo Domingo on the twenty-third day of the month of February of the year 1668, our reverend father custodian fray Juan de Talabán, ecclesiastical judge, and the reverend fathers definitors and discretos assembled and convened for the determination of what Sargento Mayor don Fernando de Villanueva, governor and captain general of these provinces of New Mexico, saw fit to make known to his fathership, having seen the copy of the edicts and proceedings of the council of war, each one separately and all *in solidum* said that although the need of the convents and pueblos is so great that it has obliged his fathership to issue his letters and patents ordering the friars, with their usual charity, to give food to the natives at the sound of the bell in all the pueblos of this custody according to the resources of the said conventos, they nevertheless had decided that the said expedition should be aided with some food supplies. With regard to horses, since it is not a matter they can decide, let the friars use their discretion in giving such aid. And let protestations be made, as by this writing they do solemnly protest once, twice, and three times, and as many as they legally must and can, that the said aid is given for the defense of the Christian community and the holy temples and that it is no means the intention of this *definitorio* that effusion of blood or deaths of the said Apache enemies should ensue, because it is done only to avoid greater damage. And let the governor be required, as by this writing he is required, not [to allow] the said charitable succor [granted] because of the extreme necessity prevailing this year to make a precedent, because His Majesty (God keep him) has encomenderos for the defense of these provinces, whom he supports out of his royal patrimony so that they may conserve it in peace and war. In addition, let the governor and captain general give bond for any horses or mules the friars may lend, and obligate himself to make satisfaction for those which die, are lost, or are killed by the enemy, because they are absolutely necessary for the administration and exercise of the Holy Sacraments. And let our reverend father custodian help with fifty fanegas of provisions, [the amount to be given by each] convent to be regulated as he sees fit. And this decision and protest is to be made known to his lordship in due form. This is what they determined and they signed with the said father, our custodian. Done ut supra. Fray Juan de Talabán, custodian (rubric). Fray Diego Enríquez, definitor (rubric). Fray Francisco Gómez de la Cadena, discreto (rubric). Fray Nicolás de Villar, discreto (rubric).[19] Fray Nicolás Enríquez, discreto (rubric). Fray Nicolás de Freitas, discreto (rubric). Fray Salvador de Guerra, definitor habitual (rubric). Fray Tomás de Alvarado, definitor (rubric).[20]

Edict

In this convent of Santo Domingo, on the said day, February 23 of the year 1668, our reverend father custodian fray Juan de Talabán, ecclesiastical judge, said that he agreed and concurred with the decision of the reverend fathers of the definitorio. He orders and commands the father preacher and guardian of the villa of Santa Fe, fray Francisco Gómez de la Cadena, to take charge of these edicts and to go to the casas reales of the said villa; and, having kissed the hand of Governor Captain General don Fernando de Villanueva, he is to make the said edicts and decision known to his lordship. He is to put his lordship's reply at the foot of this edict in legal form so that when his lordship decides upon the date, letters and patent may be issued to the effect that the convents which will be designated shall give and hand over the provisions allotted from each of them up to the number of fifty fanegas. Thus he provided, ordered, and signed. Done ut supra. Fray Juan de Talabán, custodian (rubric). By order of our reverend father custodian, fray Salvador de Guerra, secretary (rubric).

Requerimiento

In the Villa of Santa Fe on the twenty-fourth day of the month of February of this year of 1668, I, fray Francisco Gómez de la Cadena, preacher, guardian of the convent of the said villa, and discreto appointed by our reverend father fray Juan de Talabán, custodian and ecclesiastical judge, came to these casas reales of the said villa by order of the said reverend father our custodian, fray Juan de Talabán. And I made known to Sargento Mayor don Fernando de Villanueva, governor and captain general of all this kingdom, the decision of the reverend defintiorio of this custody with regard to the petition which his lordship made to our reverend father custodian for aid in provisions and horses. He said that he hears and sees the offer made after mature consideration by the reverend father custodian and the reverend definitorio with their provident zeal and charity, so urgent because of the pressure which the enemy is exerting with invasions, killings, and robberies. And in the name of His Majesty, (God keep him) he expresses his gratitude and thanks to them for it as captain general, and he accepts the offer of fifty fanegas of provisions. With regard to giving bond for the horses they offer, his lordship does not consider himself qualified to do so nor is there any reason why he should put up bond for them since the defense is general, both for convents and friars and for the rest of this Christian community. It is not an expedition or war started by his lordship, but for general defense as he has said. [He asks] the reverend father fray Francisco Gómez de la Cadena to allow him to make a copy of these edicts so that he may summon a council of the captains, cabildo, and military commanders to consider them; and he will inform his reverend fathership of the outcome. And always with due thanks. He gave this as his reply and signed it. Fernando de Villanueva (rubric). Fray Francisco Gómez de la Cadena (rubric).

Letter of the Father Guardian of the Villa

My Reverend Father and Sir:

As soon as I reached this your convent of the villa, I executed your command, and insofar as it concerned me I was silent and submissive. They reply was very good. By it the governor ordered a council of war to be summoned, and they all said it was not sufficient provision. They must want to leave the convents without anything. Thus the expedition may be abandoned. I have told his lordship that the custody for its part is doing all it can. I trust that your lordship enjoys entire good health, and I remain as ever yours obediently.

Because Alonso García is a person of trust, I remit these papers by him. Your lordship will advise me of their receipt, and, doing me honor, will commend me to my father guardian, father fray Juan de la Chica. I kiss the hand of your lordship whom God keep as I desire. Villa, [of Santa Fe], February 26 of the year 1668.

Notes

1. Biblioteca Nacional de México, leg. 1, doc. 29.

2. In 1661 Vicente Cisneros was referred to as a mestizo of the Acoma parish. He and his brother Bartolomé Cisneros were residing in the Zuñi jurisdiction in 1662. Apparently, Vicente Cisneros returned to the Río Abajo jurisdiction by 1668. AGN, Inquisición, vol. 593, ff. 56r and 158v, Testimonies of Captain Diego de Trujillo, September 26, 1661, Villa de Santa Fe; Chávez, *Origins of New Mexico Families*, 104. (E & S)

3. In 1661 Felipe Romero resided with his wife doña Jacinta de Guadalajara y Quiros at their estancia of San Antonio de Sevilleta, near the pueblo of Alamillo. This is apparently the same location that was raided by Apaches as described in this document. Testimony given in 1662 by doña Catalina de Zamora, wife of Sargento Mayor Diego Romero, identified doña Jacinta de Guadalajara as a daughter-in-law of doña Isabel de Pedraza, and thus Felipe Romero was a son of Matías Romero and doña Isabel de Pedraza, and a grandson of Bartolomé Romero and doña Lucía López Robledo. AGN, Inquisición, vol. 593, ff. 223v–224v, Testimony of Catalina de Zamora, March 9, 1662, Villa de Santa Fe; Chávez, *Origins of New Mexico Families*, 95, 97. (E & S)

4. See Doc. 18 (February 10, 1667). (E & S)

5. Bartolomé Romero was alcalde of Santa Fe in 1661, and the husband of Josefa de Archuleta. He was a first cousin of Felipe Romero and a son of Bartolomé Romero and doña María del Moral, a daughter of Captain Francisco Pérez Granillo. Chávez, *Origins of New Mexico Families*, 96–97; AGN, Inquisición, vol. 586,

exp. 1, ff. 70v–72v, Audiencia primera del Capitán Diego Romero, May 1663, Mexico City; and José Antonio Esquibel, "The Romero Family of Seventeenth-Century New Mexico," parts I and II, in *Herencia* 11 (January 2003): 1:1–30, and July 2003. (E & S)

6. The Captain Xirón mentioned here appears to be Captain José Telles Jirón, born circa 1631 and originally from Cuyoacán in New Spain. He was an encomendero of the pueblos of San Felipe and Cochiti in 1661 and a resident of the jurisdiction of Senecú in 1667. His wife, Catalina Romero, was a sister of Felipe Romero (see n. 3 above). Chávez, *Origins of New Mexico Families*, 106; and AGN, Inquisición, vol. 586, exp. 1, f. 71v, Primer audiencia del Capitán Diego Romero, May 1663, Mexico City. José Telles Jirón came to New Mexico in 1649 as a soldier paid by the royal treasury to accompany incoming governor don Hernando Ugarte y la Concha (1649–1653). He served the governor at the casas reales in Santa Fe and was one of eight soldiers who came with the governor that remained in New Mexico. Kessell and Hendricks, *By Force of Arms*, 140. Telles Jirón, born circa 1631, was a native of Los Altos de San Jacinto in the region of Cuyoacán in New Spain. AGN, Inquisición, vol. 608, exp. 6, f. 424r, Testimony of Captain José Telles Jirón, April 19, 1667, Convento de la Asumpción de Nuestra Señora del Socorro; and Chávez, *Origins of New Mexico Families*, 106. On October 16, 1661, he was in the Villa de Santa Fe providing testimony for the Inquisition's investigation of Governor don Bernardo López de Mendizábal. Telles Jirón complained that López de Mendizábal revoked his possession of two grants of encomienda. He explained that during the governorship of don Juan Manso (1656–1659) he was granted the encomiendas of the pueblos of San Felipe and Cochiti, which were parts of the "those of some of the Jemez Indians." AGN, Tierras, vol. 3268, exp. 1–01, ff. 129–30, Testimony of Ayudante José Telles Jirón, October 16, 1661, Villa de Santa Fe. José Telles Jirón, his wife, Catalina Romero, and their children survived the August 1680 Pueblo Indian uprising and became residents of El Paso del Río del Norte. This couple was still living in 1693, when they confirmed their intent to participate in the resettlement of New Mexico under the leadership of Governor don Diego de Vargas. John L. Kessell, Rick Hendricks, and Meredith D. Dodge, *To the Royal Crown Restored*, 39. (E & S)

7. Pedro Lucero de Godoy was a native of Mexico City born in 1599. He held the rank of maestre de campo in 1662 and 1663. He was first married to Petronila de Zamora, by whom he had Juan Lucero de Godoy, the secretary of government and war, and doña Catalina de Zamora, the wife of Diego Romero. Widowed of his first wife, Pedro Lucero de Godoy married doña Francisca Gómez Robledo in a ceremony that took place at the palacio of the Villa de Santa Fe on April 8, 1641, and included the marriage of his son to Luisa Romero and his daughter to Diego Pérez Romero. Pedro's brother, Licenciado Diego Lucero, was a priest who resided next to the church of Santa Catalina de Martir in Mexico City in 1674. Chávez, *Origins of New Mexico Families*, 59–60; José Antonio Esquibel,

"'Esta Gran Familia': The Genealogy of the Lucero de Godoy Family of Mexico City," *El Farolito* 6, no. 3 (Fall 2003): 5–21; AGN, Inquisición, vol. 629, exp. 2, f. 95r, Testimony of Cristóbal de Rivera, May 9, 1674, Mexico City; AGN, Inquisición, vol. 629, exp. 2, ff. 98r–99r, Testimony of *Bachiller* Diego Lucero de Godoy, June 14, 1675, Mexico City; AGN, Inquisición, vol. 629, exp. 2, f. 118r, Certificación del casamiento de Diego Romero y Catalina de Zamora, May 27, 1675, Villa de Santa Fe; and AGN, Inquisición, vol. 586, exp. 1, f. 82v, Primer audiencia del Capitán Diego Romero, May 1663, Mexico City. (E & S)

8. In 1662 Francisco de Madrid, born circa 1613–1615, held the rank of sargento mayor of the kingdom of New Mexico, held the position of captain of the horses of encomenderos, was appointed as *comisario de la cavallería* (government horse herd), and twice held the post of alcalde ordinario of the Villa de Santa Fe. In testimony he gave before officials of the Inquisition in the case against Governor López de Mendizábal, he declared he was castizo, meaning one of his parents was español and the other was of mixed español-Indian (mestizo/mestiza) background. Francisco de Madrid first married Sebastiana Ruiz, a daughter of Juan Ruiz Cáceres. Widowed of his first wife, he married María de Albizu, a mestiza and a daughter of Maestre de Campo Tomás de Albizu, and the widow of Cristóbal Enríquez, who was executed in 1643 for his role in the murder of Governor Luis de Rosas. AGN, Inquisición, vol. 587, f. 201v, Names of witnesses in the order in which they appear, 1662, New Mexico; AGN, Inquisición, vol. 593, ff. 154r–156v, Testimony of Sargento Mayor Francisco de Madrid, September 6, 1661, Villa de Santa Fe; AGN, Real Audiencia, Concurso de Peñalosa, vol. 1, leg. 1, no. 2, Testimony of Capitán Juan Domínguez de Mendoza, October 23, 1663, Villa de Santa Fe; Chávez, *Origins of New Mexico Families*, 28, 66, and José Antonio Esquibel, "Francisco de Madrid II: New Genealogical and Historical Information from Seventeenth-Century Inquisition Records," *El Farolito* 4, no. 3 (Fall 2001): 11–14; and José Antonio Esquibel, "Founders of the Villa de Santa Fe: Francisco de Madrid, Part 1" *El Farolito* 12, no. 1 (Spring 2009): 5–18. (E & S)

9. Very little is known about Juan Jiménez except that he married Catalina Durán. Chávez, *Origins of New Mexico Families*, 50. (E & S)

10. Lorenzo de Madrid, born circa 1633, was a son of Francisco de Madrid (born circa 1594) and, most likely, Maria de la Vega Márquez. He first married doña Antonia Ortiz, by whom he had four known sons, and then married Ana de Anaya Almazán, the widow of Andrés López Sambrano. AGN, Inquisición, vol. 586, Primer audiencia de Diego Romero, May 1663, Mexico City; AGN, Inquisición, vol. 1551, exp. 28, f. 379r, Testimony of Francisco Gómez Robledo, October 21, 1682, Real de San Lorenzo; Chávez, *Origins of New Mexico Families*, 66; and Esquibel, "Founders of the Villa de Santa Fe: Francisco de Madrid, Part 1," 13. (E & S)

11. José Nieto, a native of Santa Fe born circa 1616–1620, and his wife Lucía López de Gracia, born circa 1620, were residents of the jurisdiction of Salinas

in the 1660s. In 1667 and 1668, Nieto held the position of alcalde mayor of the jurisdiction of Las Salinas. Nieto, his wife, two daughters, and four nieces and nephews were killed in their home in the Galisteo area during the Pueblo Revolt of 1680. AGN, Inquisición, vol. 608, f. 431r, Testimony of Lucía López de Gracia, 1667, Convento del Pueblo Cuarác; AGN, Inquisición, vol. 608, f. 435r, Testimony of Capitán José Nieto, March 4, 1668, Convento del Pueblo de Cuarác; AGN, Inquisición, vol. 608, f. 441r, Testimony of Lucía López de Gracia, March 4, 1668, Convento del Pueblo de Cuarác; Chávez, *Origins of New Mexico Families*, 80–81. (E & S)

12. Captain Francisco García, born circa 1608 at San Gabriel del Yunque, was a brother-in-law of José Nieto and a weaver by trade. In the 1660s he was a resident of the Río Abajo area, specifically in the jurisdictions of Isleta and Las Salinas. At some point he served in the post as Protector de los Indios, a position that advocated for and represented Christian Indians when they brought forth legal complaints and lawsuits. AGN, Inquisición, vol. 507, f. 305v, Testimony of Captain Francisco García, September 28, 1665, Villa de Santa Fe; Chávez, *Origins of New Mexico Families*, 33. (E & S)

13. Fray Juan Francisco Talabán took the habit of the Orden de San Francisco in Mexico City on January 20, 1649. He was a native of Sevilla, Spain, and a son of Juan García Talabán, a native of the Villa de Plasencia in Castilla, and María de los Ángeles Yojeda, a native of Sevilla. Bancroft Library, Mexican Manuscripts, 216–18, Libro de contradas y profesiones de novicios de este convento de Padre San Francisco de México 1562–1680, f. 124v, entry #1115. He was killed at the Convento de Santo Domingo on August 10, 1680, during the uprising of the Pueblo Indians. Fray Agustín de Vetancurt, *Menológio franciscano de varones mas señalados que con sus vidas ejemplares, religiosa, ciencia, predicación evangélica, en su vida y muerte ilustraron la Provincia del Santo Evangélico de México*, vol. 4, 275, Biblioteca Histórica de la Iberia, vol. 10 (Mexico: Imprenta de I. Escalante, 1871). (E & S)

14. The Spanish is very obscure here, but this seems a reasonable interpretation.

15. Fray Antonio de Ybargaray took the habit of the Orden de San Francisco in Mexico City on January 17, 1629, at the age of twenty-two (b. ca. 1607). He was a native of the Villa de Bilboa in the Basque Province of Vizcaya and a son of Juan de Ybargaray and Elvira de Ichipis. Bancroft Library, Mexican Manuscripts, 216–18, Libro de contradas y profesiones de novicios de este convento de Padre San Francisco de México 1562–1680, f. 17v, entry #840. (E & S)

16. Fray Francisco de Salazar was a native of the Villa de Arsiniega in the Basque Province of Vizcaya and a son of Pedro de Santa Zobo.^{ma} [?] and Ana de Allende. He took the habit of the Orden de San Francisco in Mexico City at the age of twenty-two on January 17, 1629 (b. ca. 1607). Bancroft Library, Mexican Manuscripts, 216–18, Libro de contradas y profesiones de novicios de este convento de Padre San Francisco de México 1562–1680, f. 17v, entry #839. (E & S)

17. Fray Nicolás Enríquez was a native of Jalisco, Nueva Galicia. In October 1663, Enríquez referred to himself as apostolic definitor and the elder Franciscan priest in New Mexico. He was residing at the Convento de la Inmaculada Concepción in the Villa de Santa Fe in May 1664. Hackett, *Historical Documents*, 3:240 and 245.

18. Fray Nicolás Freitas took the habit of the Orden de San Francisco in Mexico City on June 4, 1650, at the age of sixteen (b. ca. 1634). He was a native of Mexico City and a son of Juan de Freitas (also recorded as Fleytas), a native of the Canary Islands, and Gerónima de Rueda, a native of Mexico City. Bancroft Library, Mexican Manuscripts 216–18, Libro de contradas y profesiones de novicios de este convento de Padre San Francisco de México 1562–1680, f. 1131v, entry #1142. He came to New Mexico in December 1658 in the company of Governor don Bernardo López de Mendizábal along with as many as eighteen other friars. Hackett, *Historical Documents*, 3:157. (E & S)

19. Fray Nicolás de Villar was a native of the City of Guadiana (Durango) in Nueva Vizcaya and gave his age as forty-four in 1661 (b. ca. 1617). AGN, Inquisición, vol. 593, f. 162r, Testimony of Fray Nicolás de Villar, September 27, 1661, Convento de la Inmaculada Concepción, Villa de Santa Fe. (E & S)

20. Fray Tomás de Alvarado was a native of La Fuente del Maestre in Estremadura, Spain, and gave his age as sixty in 1662 (b. ca. 1602). AGN, Inquisición, vol. 598, exp. 8, f. 123r, Testimony of Fray Tomás de Alvarado, April 5, 1662, Convento de San Francisco del Pueblo de Sandia. (E & S)

Document 20

Title of Encomienda

Santa Fe, May 1, 1669[1]

Captain don Juan de Medrano Messía, governor and captain general of the kingdom and provinces of New Mexico for the king, our lord, and judge-general of bienes de difuntos in these [provinces].[2]

At present one-third of the encomienda and tributes of the pueblo of Humanas of the Tunpira [Tompiro] nation is vacant.[3] These [tributes] were formerly collected by Alférez Juan González Bernal,[4] now deceased, and it appears that as a result of the death of the aforesaid, his son, Juan González,[5] collected them. By my order a proclamation was published concerning a council of war held on December 2 of the past year [1668] because these provinces were at war and the Apache enemies had overrun them, killing

Spaniards and Christians, stealing herds of horses and droves of mules; and by this [proclamation], for the remedy of this situation and in order to go forth from different directions to punish the enemy, all the encomenderos were ordered to pass general muster before me with their arms and horses within twelve days, with the warning that if any of the said encomenderos or the escuderos appointed did not appear at the said muster, their said encomiendas would be pronounced vacant. The said muster took place in this Villa of Santa Fe on December 16, and a second muster was held on January 7 in the pueblo of Isleta. At neither of them did any person appear legally to represent or to pass muster as escudero for the said Juan González, nor did the aforesaid do so, having violated the edict and failed to fulfill it. And since no person is serving for the said encomienda as His Majesty orders, and especially at a time when this kingdom is so afflicted and attacked by the Apache Indians, and because it is necessary to have soldiers [to rally] to its defense at the sound of the war drum, the said part of the encomienda of the pueblo of Humanas and others was pronounced vacant.

In consideration of this it is necessary to confer the said encomienda and tributes on a person of the satisfaction, legal qualifications, merits, and services which are required for the services of His Majesty. Because these and other [qualities] concur in Captain Juan Domínguez de Mendoza, in consideration of the fact that he has served His Majesty in these provinces more than twenty-five years, acting as soldier, alférez, captain, and lieutenant general of these provinces, and alcalde ordinario of this villa, and has gone forth as commander on different occasions to punish the Apache enemies of these provinces; and in consideration of the fact that he serves in them at his own expense with arms and horses, in the name of His Majesty and in view of the above, I grant to the said Captain don Juan Domínguez de Mendoza the part of the encomienda and tributes of the pueblo of Humanas, which is one-third of the said pueblo, in place of salary, and in perpetuity for the three lives which His Majesty concedes, in order that he may enjoy and possess the said tributes which the said natives were paying, under the obligation the encomenderos of these provinces have and also to aid and defend the natives of his said encomienda, seeing to it that they are well instructed in the matters of our Holy Catholic Faith and well treated in deed and word, defending them from their enemies in all their litigations and affairs, procuring their greatest increase, utility, and alleviation. And I order and command all the natives who now are and henceforth may be of the said part of the pueblo of Humanas to consider him as their encomendero and to pay him the tribute which they were paying to the said Juan

González Bernal and which they must pay His Majesty as his vassals which consists of a cotton *manta* and a fanega of maize per household per year, and no more; conceding as I concede to the said Captain don Juan Domínguez [de Mendoza] all the favors, honors, and concessions that are granted to him by reason of being encomendero of these provinces, because for one and the other I ordered the present writing issued to him, signed by my name and sealed with the seal of my arms, and countersigned by the secretary of government and war.[6]

Done in the Villa of Santa Fe of New Mexico on the first day of the month of May of the year 1669. Juan Medrano Messía (rubric). (Seal) By order of the governor and captain general, Francisco del Castillo Betancur (rubric), secretary of government and war.

Notes

1. BNE, Madrid, MSS 19258, photos 55–57.

2. Juan Rodríguez de Medrano Messía served as governor of New Mexico from November 30, 1668, to July 20, 1671. AGI, Contaduría, legs. 759 and 767, Caja de México. Cuentas de los oficiales reales de México, 1667–1668 and 1675–1676, respectively; photostat copy located at the Southwest Research Center, University of New Mexico.

3. The pueblo of Las Humanas, site of the Convento de San Buenaventura, was located in Las Salinas district on the east side of the Manzano Mountains. Today its ruins bear the name of Gran Quivira.

4. Juan González Bernal was a native of New Mexico, a son of Sebastián González (a native of Portugal) and Isabel Bernal (a daughter of Juan Griego and Pascuala Bernal, original settlers who came with Oñate in 1598). He married Apolonia (Polonia) Varela, born circa 1623. She first married Julián de Escarramád. Widowed of her first husband, she married Juan Bautista de Zaragoza around 1640 against her will and under duress by Governor Luis de Rosas. As a resident of the Villa de Santa Fe in September 1640, Apolonia Varela petitioned to have her marriage annulled on grounds that no license to marry was ever granted by church authorities and testified that she was forced by Rosas to marry Zaragosa. She was placed in the home of Alférez Real Andrés López de Gracia until a decision was reached. The marriage was annulled on July 3, 1641. She subsequently married Juan González Bernal, and outlived him by many years. She was still alive in January 1693, when she was enumerated in the household of her son, Sebastián González, and gave her age as seventy, making her one of the oldest citizens of New Mexico at that time. She was willing to accompany her son for the purpose of resettling the Villa de Santa Fe. Apolonia Varela was a resident of Santa Fe as late as May 1697. Chávez, *Origins of New Mexico*

Families, 40, 189, 359, and 360; AGN, Inquisición, vol. 425, exp 23, f. 633r–636r, Acusasción presentada por Apolonia Varela, 1641; Kessell, Hendricks, Dodge, *To the Royal Crown Restored*, 54; John L. Kessell, Rick Hendricks, Meredith D. Dodge, Larry D. Miller, and Richard Flint, eds. *Blood on the Boulders: The Journals of Don Diego de Vargas, New Mexico, 1694–97*, Book 2 (Albuquerque: University of New Mexico Press, 1998), 1143. (E & S)

5. Juan González appears to have also been known as Juan González Bas, who was married to Nicolasa Zaldívar Jorge. Very little is known about this man, except that he had a son named Juan González Bas, who settled in the Río Abajo area after 1693. This son held many civil and military positions of prominence, including alcalde mayor of Albuquerque. Chávez, *Origins of New Mexico Families*, 189. (E & S)

6. In seventeenth-century New Mexico, *manta* referred to rough cotton cloth woven by Pueblo Indians and used by them and settlers as garments and bedding. Individual mantas, or squared pieces, were a common article of tribute under the encomienda system in New Mexico. (E & S)

Document 21

Documents Concerning Provisions and Livestock Given by the Conventos for an Expedition against the Apaches

June 16–July 4, 1669[1]

[To] Very Reverend Father Preacher Fray Juan de Talabán, custodian and ecclesiastical judge of these provinces. June 16, 1669.

Today, Sunday, which is the sixteenth of the present month, at about the hour of the Angelus, I received two letters, one from the reverend father definitor fray Fernando de Monroy, and the other from Captain Francisco Xavier.[2] Both inform me that a great ambuscade of Apache enemies hurled themselves on the pueblo of Acoma and killed twelve persons of the said pueblo, carried off two women alive, eight hundred head of *ganado menor*, sixty head of cattle, and all the horses there were in the pueblo.[3] After the said Francisco Xavier had left the [pueblo], the father definitor, as is shown by a paper of his, asked him for aid; and, having gone out to encounter the enemies, they fought valorously, and nevertheless the [enemy] killed Captain don Cristóbal de Chaves.[4] The father definitor informs me that the province is lost and that the neighboring ones should be aided and defended because the Apaches are very audacious. Captain Francisco

Xavier tells me the same and that unless reprisal is made and the milpas of these rapacious enemies cut down, they will undoubtedly destroy this kingdom, for thus the said Apaches proclaim at the top of their voices and in the Spanish language. And the [Apaches] and the Salineros have congregated with those of Casa Fuerte.[5] They also wounded four soldiers and many horses.

I have decided to do what is possible to remedy the situation and to be in the pueblo of San Diego de Jemez on the second of the coming month of July, and I have designated it as the plaza de armas from which I shall set out with fifty soldiers and six hundred Christian Indians.

The land is so impoverished as a result of such great famines and misfortunes, as your fathership knows, and it is necessary that this force have food. In the name of His Majesty I am notifying your very reverend fathership in order that you may give permission to the fathers, preachers, and guardians who might have any provisions to relieve such urgent need with them and with some head of cattle and livestock. This should be ready in the pueblo of Jemez for the second day of July, for, if there were any supplies in the kingdom, my soul, which belongs to God, is the only thing I would not give to buy them. There are none, as your very reverend fathership knows. Therefore, I give you this information and I am certain that as a faithful and loyal vassal of His Majesty you will assist on an occasion of such great urgency. In [reply to] another letter which I wrote to your very reverend fathership in April with regard to making an expedition to punish the enemy, in which I asked for the same supplies, you suggested that there were some in the pueblo of Jemez and in that of Pecos, and that I should take them. I live in such great anxiety that if your very reverend fathership were not aware [of the situation], it would be useless [to try to remedy it]. I am also taking thirty head of cattle from Maestre de Campo Francisco de Valencia and from Maestre de Campo Tomé Domínguez [de Mendoza] and from Captain Alonso García, who are those who have herds.

Let your very reverend fathership appoint the friar whom he considers most suitable and appropriate to go as chaplain and accompany me on this expedition. And he also is to be in the pueblo on the second day of July. I trust that your very reverend fathership will act in every way in accordance with your great obligations, apprising me of the receipt of this letter. God keep your very reverend fathership. Santa Fe, today, June 16 of the year 1669. Your servant kisses the hand of your very reverend fathership.

Juan de Medrano Messía (rubric).
[To] Don Juan de Medrano Messía, governor and captain
general of these provinces.

Yesterday, the seventeenth of this month, after the Angelus, I received a letter from your lordship, dated the sixteenth of the same, in which you inform me of the calamitous event, ambuscade, and the death of Cristóbal de Chaves, and of the strength of the enemy, whose arrows doubly wound my heart, both because I am aware of their audacity and because I find every day that the ministration of these converted should become nearer to impossible as a result of the robberies they have committed in the convents of [the Río] Abajo, and now in that of Acoma. And I feel not only this harm done by the enemy, but also that which the friendly and domesticated Indians have committed in the poor convents, stealing and killing herds, the extremes of kindness and supreme charity which this *custodia* has shown them having been insufficient [to deter] them. The herds are kept for the sole purpose of maintaining these ministers and to obtain what adornment is possible for these temples, for no one succors them and God alone supports them. This custodia has spent most of what little it has in sustaining the natives, and it has been necessary to give succor to the convents of Senecú and Socorro, and now to that of Acoma. And the convents of Nambé, [San] Ildefonso, and San Juan are in such desperate straits that it is absolutely necessary for me to help them as best I can so that those souls may not lack ministers. Although this is so, and it is obligatory to alleviate such urgent want, and although the cattle which this custodia has are so insufficient in number for such great consumption, and there is no hope of relief since the Order of St. Francis has no door to which to go in the hope of receiving alms; nevertheless, considering only the straits and extremity which your lordship makes known to me, and that the war is defensive, the measure to be employed being the destruction of grain fields of the enemy, with the sole intention of cooperating in what is just, remaining aloof from every other aid foreign to what I owe to my state, [acting] in accordance with what has been decided by the sacred councils, sanctions, canons, and determinations of the Holy Church, of which I make protestations in the form in which I must and can in the safety of my own conscience and that of my subjects, I say that the most I can do is to succor the expedition with 160 ewes, 40 sheep, and 24 head of cattle, which amounts in all to the number of the 224 head of livestock. With regard to the supply of grain, I say that the famine had affected this custodia no less than the rest of the kingdom because it has continued for two years and something more, and the ministers have been giving sustenance to all the Indians at the sound of the bell, as well as giving them seed to sow in order to remedy in this way the total ruin threatened by such great need. If they had not done so, no Indians would be alive now, since, as is shown by the books and dispositions of the convents, the consumption in this way has been great. I have seen that the friars have done this charity to the Indians in person, and I myself have done so. Moreover, since your lordship entered this unhappy kingdom in the month of November of the past year and found the scarcity of food, this custodia has relieved it insofar as it has been able to do so, taking from the convents of Santo Domingo, Jemez, Pecos, Taos, Picurís, Socorro, and Senecú the wheat and maize they have been able [to give]. As a result, all of them have so little today that it is insufficient for their needs. Although I said in the month of April that the convent of Jemez had some provisions, today it needs them, because father fray Tomás de Alvarado gave succor of wheat and maize from there to your lordship during Holy Week of this year. And on a second occasion father definitor Trujillo, guardian of the same convent, gave wheat and maize to your lordship. And the convents of Galisteo, Sandia, and Sía [Zía] have been aided from there, and at present it is giving food to the Indians, who are dying without human means of remedy. The conclusion to be drawn from what has been said is that there is no recourse whatsoever there. I find that only from Pecos can twenty fanegas of wheat be given, and this means taking their own sustenance from them. All of which I did with a very good will so that God and His Church and His Majesty and his lands may be defended. Without its serving as a precedent for another occasion, if it please your lordship, you may send to Pecos for the wheat because if it is entrusted to the Indians, they will steal it.

Your lordship will find the friar whom your lordship tells me to appoint as chaplain in Jemez, as you suggest in your letter to me. God keep your lordship many years. Sandia, June 18 of the year 1669. Your servant and chaplain kisses the hand of your lordship. Fray Juan de Talabán (rubric).

Very Reverend Father Preacher Fray Juan de Talabán, custodian and ecclesiastical judge of these provinces.

It is necessary for me to reply to your letter in accordance with what your reverend fathership writes me. By it and the experience I have had of your procedure, I am certain and sure that the calamities sadden you, both the robberies and killings of soldiers and Christian Indians which the Apache enemies have committed, and the general disaster of the famine which has provoked the Christian Indians to ruin the convents by killing their herds and animals; ignorant people, for I know with what love and charity their hunger has been relieved in all the convents with what there has been and is in them. I am also aware that because of the robberies of cattle which the Apaches have committed in Socorro and Senecú, your very reverend fathership has succored these convents as well as that of Nambé and those of San Ildefonso and San Juan in order to sustain the ministers who assist in them, and that what the convents have is very little in proportion to such great expense. And because of the poverty of these provinces it is certain that the friars of my father St. Francis will not find alms. God knows I would rejoice to have much to give them.

Your very reverend fathership says in your letter that only considering the straits and extremity I describe to you, and that the war is defensive, the means I intend to use being the destruction of the grain fields of the Apache enemies, without other intent, you will cooperate in what is just, holding yourself aloof from every other aim and aberrant intention and [acting] only in accordance with what your very reverend fathership owes to your state and with what has been determined by the sacred councils, canons, and decisions of the Holy Church; and that in the form in which you must and can your very reverend fathership makes protestation of them with safe conscience for yourself and your subjects. [And you say] that the most you can do to aid the expedition is to give 160 ewes, 40 sheep, and 24 head of cattle. All this amounts to 224 head of livestock and twenty fanegas of wheat, for which, in the name of His Majesty, I give thanks to your very reverend fathership who acts in every way as his faithful vassal and as a virtuous pastor and a charitable and benevolent father.

For my part, I will live so grateful for such an action that I will put it as a blazon on the doors of my house, not forgetting the succor of provisions this holy custodia has given in such necessity for the sake of His Majesty (God keep him) and me as his governor and captain general of these provinces, and the soldiers and natives who go with me on this expedition to cut down the sowings of the Apache enemies and punish them wherever I find them. In no way does cooperation in this expedition lay a burden on the conscience of your very reverend fathership nor on that of any of your subjects. I also have a clear conscience, and my men do, because my sole purpose in going forth to carry out [the expedition] is the service of God, our Lord, for the defense of this kingdom, without other interest than defending it and preventing its holy temples, churches, and priests from being vituperated and outraged by such barbarous enemies. Moreover, the reverend father definitor fray Fernando de Monroy writes that by a miracle the ambuscade which attacked the pueblo of Acoma did not enter it and destroy the church although the livestock was carried off. My intention in [making] this expedition, as I have said, is to see whether I can remedy the situation so that these voracious enemies will cease to afflict this wretched land, for as long as they are [quiet] and leave us alone, I will never seek out nor disturb them for any private ends.

I beg your very reverend fathership to be good enough to order that the livestock be ready in Jemez for the second day of July, and I will send to Pecos for twenty fanegas of wheat. Let me know about your health. And in the said pueblo of Jemez, as plaza de armas, I will certify to the succor which your very reverend fathership and this holy custodia have given to aid us in the service of God, without its serving as a precedent hereafter.

God keep your very reverend fathership many years. Santa Fe, June 19, 1669, June 19 of the year 1669. Your obedient servant kisses the hand of your very reverend fathership. Juan de Medrano Messía (rubric).

Captain don Juan de Medrano Messía, governor and captain general of this kingdom and provinces of New Mexico for His Majesty.

I certify that because of the great need and famine there is in this kingdom, and [the need to make] reprisal against the Apache Indians, common enemies, who during the seven months I have been governing have killed six Spanish soldiers and 373 Christian Indians, stolen more than two thousand horses, mares, and mules, and more than two thousand head of ganado menor, the property of the convents of this holy custodia and of the citizens and inhabitants of these provinces, keeping these [provinces] so ravaged and destroyed, that it is a miracle anyone remains in them. In order to remedy the situation as far as possible I decided that an expedition consisting of fifty Spanish soldiers and six hundred Christian Indians should be made to the lands of the said Apaches to punish them and cut down their sowings. And in order to be able to carry it out in spite of the lack of provisions, so great that the Christian Indians are dying of hunger on the roads, feeding on hides, herbs of the field, and vermin, while the Spaniards and other civilized people sustain themselves only with little meat and milk; and in view of the great lack of resources to make it possible to go forth to inflict said punishment, I wrote a letter to the very reverend father preacher, fray Juan de Talabán, custodian and ecclesiastical judge of these provinces, so that aid might be given by the convents of this holy custodia with some provisions and meat for the sustenance of the fifty Spanish soldiers and six hundred Christian Indians.

Then, well-armed and in accordance with military usage, they passed muster in this pueblo of San Diego de Jemez where, by order of the very reverend father custodian, the Reverend Father Joseph Trujillo, definitor of this holy custodia and guardian of the said pueblo, handed over to me twenty fanegas of biscuit, two hundred head of ganado menor and twenty-four head of cattle, amounting in all to 224 head. All this was handed over to Maestre de Campo Francisco de Madrid, whom I have appointed head and commander of the expedition, reprisal, and destruction which it has been possible to undertake as a result of this succor. The said reverend father custodian and the other friars of this holy custodia have only given it so that the lands of the enemy may be laid to waste and with no intention of cooperating in effusion of blood, but solely to reduce the strength of the enemy so that they may not do so much damage. I consider it a pious, charitable work. And making it possible by means of said aid for these fifty soldiers and six hundred Indians to set out is a very special service, worthy and deserving of high estimation, in which I hold it. In the name of His Majesty I give thanks to the very reverend father custodian, fray Juan de Talabán, and the reverend fathers definitors and other fathers preachers and guardians of this holy custodia. And in order that it may be on record, I issued the present writing signed by my name and countersigned by the secretary of government and war.

Done in the pueblo of San Diego de Jemez on the fourth day of the month of July of the year 1669. Juan de Medrano Messía (rubric). In my presence, Francisco del Castillo Betancur, secretary of government and was (rubric).

Notes

1. Biblioteca Nacional de México, leg. 1, no. 32.
2. *Ganado menor* is the general term for small livestock such as sheep and goats. *Ganado mayor* is the term for large livestock such as cattle and horses.
3. Francisco Xavier, born circa 1628, came to New Mexico in the company of Governor don Bernardo López de Mendizábal in 1659. By 1663 he was married to Graciana Griego, a daughter of Juan Griego, the younger, and Juana de la Cruz. Graciana's maternal grandmother, Beatriz de los Ángeles, was a Mexican Indian who was denounced to the Inquisition during the late 1620s and early 1630s for making potions and casting spells against others. Francisco Xavier occupied

the position of secretary of government and war under Governor don Antonio de Otermín at the time of the Pueblo Revolt in August 1680. In fact, Pueblo Indians later explained that their complaints about the abuse of power by Xavier went unheeded by Governor Otermín, and this was one of the reasons they gave for the revolt. See Doc. 55, May 19–June 12, 1687; and Chávez, *Origins of New Mexico Families*, 113. (E & S)

4. Cristóbal de Chaves (Durán y Chaves) was married sometime between March 1664 and October 1665 to Catalina Domínguez de Mendoza, a daughter of Tomé Domínguez de Mendoza and Catalina López Mederos and a niece of Juan Domínguez de Mendoza. In 1663 and 1664 Chaves was a resident of the Sandia jurisdiction. Chávez, *Origins of New Mexico Families*, 21. On March 9, 1664, Captain Cristóbal Durán y Chaves appeared at the Convento de San Francisco de Sandía, where his testimony against Governor don Diego de Peñalosa was recorded. Durán y Chaves stated he was a native of New Mexico, single, and age twenty-four (b. ca. 1640). In October 1665, he ratified his testimony and declared he was twenty-five years of age, a vecino of the jurisdiction of Sandia, and married to doña Catalina Domínguez de Mendoza. AGN, Inquisición, vol. 507, ff. 231r–233r, Testimony of Captain Cristóbal Durán y Chaves, March 9, 1664, Convento de San Francisco de Sandia, and f. 233v, Ratification of the testimony of Captain Cristóbal Durán y Chaves, October 16, 1665, Convento de San Francisco de Sandia. (E & S)

5. This band of Apaches Salineros occupied the mountain ranges of the area of Zuñi in western New Mexico, see Doc. 24 (July 27, 1671). They were most likely named for making their camps in the Zuñi Salt Lake area. As noted in the document above, this band of Apaches Salineros were known to have combined forces with the Navajos of Casa Fuerte in northwestern New Mexico. For other references to this band of Apaches, see Kessell and Hendricks, eds., *To the Royal Crown Restored*, 552 and 560. (E & S)

Document 22

Commission as Maestre de Campo in Campaign

Santa Fe, September 11, 1670[1]

Captain don Juan Rodríguez de Medrano Messía, governor and captain general of these provinces of New Mexico for His Majesty, and *juez general de bienes de difuntos* [superior probate judge] in these [provinces], etc.

By my order, reprisal and just war is to be made against the Apache enemies of the cordilleras [mountains] of the Siete Ríos and their environs in the jurisdiction of Las Salinas, because on the third of this month they launched a great ambuscade on the pueblo of Humanas, took possession of it, and killed eleven persons, carrying off thirty-one captives, destroying the holy temple, profaning it, and smashing the images of the saints, dragging and destroying the vestments, and committing many other atrocities. In order that the punishment for such daring, insolence, and shamelessness may be put into effect, I have named the pueblo of Abó as plaza de armas, from which thirty Spanish soldiers and three hundred Christian Indians are to set forth, armed for war according to the custom of the country. With these I have formed a *tercio* [regiment] with a company of Spanish infantry.[2] And it is necessary to appoint a maestre de campo of campaign to command and govern them both in the field and otherwise, and he should be a person of the parts, practice, and experience which is required in matters of war, of knowledge, sufficiency, and conscience, in order that he may march with the said tercio for the said undertaking and reprisal.

Because these and many other [qualities] concur in the person of Captain don Juan Domínguez de Mendoza and in consideration of his quality, merits, and personal services which he has rendered His Majesty in these provinces for more than twenty years, occupying the posts of soldier, sargento, alférez, and captain of infantry, going forth on many occasions as commander and chief of different troops of soldiers to punish the enemy, giving in all a very good account of himself, I have thought it well to appoint and name him, as for the present I so appoint and name him in the name of His Majesty, maestre de campo of the said tercio which has been formed, in order that he may serve with it in the field and otherwise on this undertaking and expedition.

I order and command the sargento mayor, captain of infantry, adjutant, alférez, and other officials of the said company and all the soldiers of the said tercio and the governors of the Christian Indians and their captains, and all the persons who may march with [the expedition] to hold, consider, revere, respect, and obey the said Captain don Juan Domínguez de Mendoza as such their maestre de campo in the field and otherwise, fulfilling and observing all the orders which he may give them in writing and orally, under the penalties which he may impose upon them in the name of His Majesty which he will execute on the rebellious and disobedient briefly and summarily according to the usage of war. And because he has served His Majesty in this kingdom longer than twenty years, as has been said, I relieve him of the tax of the media anata so that without paying it he may enjoy the honors pertaining to the post of maestre de campo of the tercio in campaign to which he has been appointed, and all the honors, exemptions, preeminences, immunities, privileges, and liberties which by virtue of the said office of maestre de campo pertain and belong to him, without there being anything lacking, because for all the above I give him power and authority as is required by law, and in adequate form and military order, for thus it befits the service of His Majesty, in whose royal name he may bear the usual insignia.[3] In order that it may be on record, I ordered the present title issued to him, signed by my name and sealed with the seal of my arms, and countersigned by the secretary of government and war.

Done in the Villa of Santa Fe of New Mexico on the eleventh day of the month of September of the year 1670. (Seal) Juan de Medrano Messía (rubric). By order of the governor and captain general, Antonio González (rubric), secretary of government and war.[4]

Captain don Juan Rodríguez de Medrano Messía, governor and captain general of these provinces of New Mexico for His Majesty.

[Certification of an Earlier Campaign]

I certify that Maestre de Campo don Juan Domínguez de Mendoza mentioned in this title went on the campaign and acted in it as a good soldier with all reputation and credit, fighting with the enemy and killing thirteen Indian vagabonds, and freeing six Christian Indians whom the said Apaches had carried off when they sacked the pueblo of Humanas. And since he had been present at the said campaign and had returned from it, he asked me for discharge from the said post, and for having performed his duty I gave him the present discharge and signed it with my name in order that it may be of record.

Done in the Villa of Santa Fe of New Mexico on the fifth day of the month of June of the year 1670. Juan de Medrano Messía (rubric). By order of the governor and captain general, Antonio González (rubric), secretary of government and war.

Notes

1. BNE, Madrid, MSS 19258, photos 50–52.
2. The phrase used in the original text is "*tercio y pie de ejercito con . . .*"

3. A media anata represented half of the first year's salary of a newly appointed official, which was collected by the government as a tax.

4. Antonio González, also known as Antonio González Bernal, was a native of Santa Fe and a brother to the encomendero Juan González Bernal. He served as secretary of the cabildo of the Villa de Santa Fe in 1661. In this same year he held the post of *protector de indios*, representing the legal rights of the Indians of New Mexico. Chávez, *Origins of New Mexico Families*, 40. AGN, Tierras, vol. 3268, f. 208r ff, Petition of Antonio González, Escribano y Protector y Defense de los Indios, October 1661, Villa de Santa Fe. In 1664, Alférez Antonio González gave his age as thirty (b. ca. 1634) and his birthplace as the Villa de Santa Fe. AGN, Inquicisión, vol. 507, exp. 1, f. 227r, Testimony of Antonio González, escribano del cabildo, February 22, 1664, Villa de Santa Fe. (E & S)

Document 23

Commission as Sargento Mayor of the Kingdom

Santa Fe, June 27, 1671[1]

Captain don Juan Rodríguez de Medrano Messía, governor and captain general of these provinces of New Mexico for His Majesty, and juez general de bienes de difuntos [superior probate judge] in these [provinces], etc.

Inasmuch as I have retired Sargento Mayor Antonio González from the post of sargento mayor of the kingdom, which he held, it is necessary to appoint another person in his place to serve the said post, who should have the qualities required in military affairs. Moreover, [the province] is alive with and destroyed by the infidel Apache, enemies of our Holy Catholic Faith, [especially] those of the cordilleras [mountains] of Gila and Siete Ríos. General don Juan de Miranda, who is on his way to these provinces as governor and captain general, informs me by letter that on the twenty-fourth day of this month when he stopped with three wagons and two friars in the Paraje del Muerto, [which is] on the royal road to New Spain, he was ambushed by the said Apaches, who killed four persons and carried off the drove of mules belonging to His Majesty. The said governor asks me to help him, carrying aloft the royal standard. [For such an occasion] it is necessary that there be a sargento mayor to give the military order and that he be a soldier of experience, as has been said.

On account of the good qualities which concur in the person of Maestre de Campo don Juan Domínguez de Mendoza, in consideration of his merits and quality and the fact he has served his majesty for twenty-six years in these provinces in active ways, as is shown at greater length in the papers concerning his services which he has presented before me, in the name of His Majesty I appoint and name him sargento mayor of this kingdom and provinces. In order that as such he may hold, use, and exercise the said post in all the matters and cases concerning it and those pertaining to war, I order and command all the soldiers, sargentos, alférez, and captains of this kingdom, observing and fulfilling all the orders with regard to war that he may give them in writing or orally, and under the penalties which on behalf of His Majesty, or me, he may impose on them, which he will execute on the rebellious and disobedient according to the usage of war, briefly and summarily, prescinding judicial inquiry. I order and command the maestre de campo of this kingdom to hold and consider him as such sargento mayor, and the said sargento mayor is to keep, fulfill, observe, and execute the orders the said *maestre de campo* of the kingdom may give him in what pertains to His Majesty's services. In order that he may use and exercise the said office to which he is appointed, I give him power and authority as sufficient as is required in law and military order, conceding to him, as I do concede to him in the name of His Majesty, all honors, favors, privileges, and liberties which all the other sargento mayor of the tercios, active armies, strongholds, castles, and other frontiers enjoy, and they are granted to him according to the royal ordinances and mandates in accordance with the will of His Majesty, although he is not to obtain any salary whatsoever by virtue of the said post of sargento mayor, because His Majesty has not assigned it in these provinces. And in order that he may bear the usual insignia and in order that it may be of record, I order the present title issued to him, signed by my name and sealed with the seal of my arms, and countersigned by the present secretary of government and war.

Done in the Villa of Santa Fe of New Mexico on the twenty-seventh day of the month of June of the year 1671. (Seal) Juan de Medrano Messía (rubric), By order of the governor and captain general, Antonio González (rubric).

Notes

1. BNE, Madrid, MSS 19258, photos 53–54.

Document 24

Commission as Maestre de Campo General of the Kingdom
Santa Fe, July 27, 1671[1]

Captain don Juan de Miranda, *regidor perpetuo* of the Concejo de Tineo in the principality of Asturias, governor and captain general of these provinces of New Mexico for His Majesty, etc.[2]

As a result of the unremitting wars which the Apache nation, common enemies of our Holy Catholic Faith, continually wage in all this kingdom and its districts and environs, going forth from ambush to [attack] the royal roads and paths, Christian pueblos, and estancias of the Spanish citizens, there is nothing in all these provinces secure from their treasons and artfulness. They atrociously kill Spaniards and natives, profanely destroy the holy temples and sacred things, at which they have scoffed, making a mock of them with excessive insolence and shamelessness; and they steal the herds of horses and livestock belonging to the citizens and natives of these provinces. For the remedy of this and in consideration of what His Majesty orders in the defense, security, and aid of these provinces and their inhabitants, it is necessary that there be a number of military officials to execute and transmit in settlements, on campaigns, and other places the military orders which are necessary and emanate from me in the service of His Majesty. For execution of this, it is necessary to appoint a person as maestre de campo general of all this kingdom and its territories and that such a person have the necessary qualities of experience and sufficiency, loyalty, rank, merits, and services, and ability in military and civil matters.

These and many other qualities are found and concur in the person of General don Juan Domínguez de Mendoza, who has rendered personal service to His Majesty during thirty years in this place, being present in the campaigns and cruel wars of this kingdom. He occupied the post of alférez in campaign during the government of General don Fernando de Argüello, of which he gave a good account, fighting with the enemy. During the government of General don Luis de Guzmán y Figueroa he continued in the royal service in the campaigns of the Río Grande, Navajo, and Casa Fuerte, where he went at his own expense, and in the actions fought at dawn and other encounters he distinguished his person as an honorable soldier. Continuing this [service] during the government of general Hernando de Ugarte y la Concha, when there was a conspiracy between Christian

Indians and enemies, he was present at the punishment of the [Indians of the] jurisdiction of Casa Fuerte, Navajo and Matanassa, where heavy punishments were inflicted until treason and confederation of the Christian Indians and the Apaches were discovered, being present at the execution of those who were hanged in different jurisdictions.[3] During the government of General don Juan de Samaniego he went on the expedition to the east, the said maestre de campo being one of those who took part in the war of the Cutoas, which lasted a whole day, in which more than five hundred souls were captured and killed, during which he won great reputation with friends and enemies. He also assisted personally in other punitive expeditions and just wars that were waged during that time. He also took part in those that were undertaken during the government of General don Juan Manso, the punishment which was inflicted on Salineros Indians of the Zuñi range being of great importance. For these services General don Bernardo [López] de Mendizábal, when he arrived in the province, appointed him captain of the military force which went forth to the campaign of the Río Grande, where severe punishment was again meted out to the Apache enemies, many of whom were captured and killed.[4] And he appointed him lieutenant general of the jurisdictions and territories of the Río Abajo and Salinas, and commander and chief of different expeditions, which he carried through with valor. During the government of don Diego de Peñalosa he exercised the said post of lieutenant general, not counting other orders which he (Peñalosa) committed to him for execution. Also, on the [first] occasion that I was governor and captain general, he attended to my orders and commands, and he was alcalde ordinario of this villa. And upon entering the province, don Fernando de Villanueva continued him in the office of lieutenant general inspector (visitador) of the royal supply train, and commander of several campaigns. During the government of General don Juan de Medrano, the governor employed him in the posts of maestre de campo de campaña in the active war waged against the Indians of Siete Ríos who profaned the holy temple of Humanas. And afterward he made him sargento mayor of the whole kingdom and issued a grant of encomienda to him.

In consideration of the above, and of the fact that he has governed this kingdom in the absence of General don Fernando de Villanueva, as a reward for his services and in the name of His Majesty, I now name, appoint, nominate, and institute the said General don Juan Domínguez de Mendoza as maestre de campo of all the kingdom and its campaigns, in order that as such he may use and exercise the said office, observing my orders and executing them, and distributing them inviolably, as well as giving those which pertain to him and may be necessary in military style and discipline in plazas, campaigns, and in sight of the enemy, which are to be obeyed and executed. I order the sargento mayor of the whole kingdom, the maestres de campo, and sargentos mayores of campaign, military commanders and chiefs, captains of infantry and cavalry, alféreces, adjutants, and sargentos, encomenderos, and soldiers of all this kingdom to hold, consider, esteem, and respect him as such maestre de campo, and to observe and fulfill his orders and commands under the penalties imposed by law, which he will execute briefly and summarily on the disobedient and transgressors. For all of this and in order that he may bear the usual insignia and enjoy the honors, privileges, exemptions, preeminences, and liberties which are due him by reason of the said office and as all the other maestres de campo of the armies, forces and garrisons of His Majesty do and should enjoy them, I give him power and plenary authority insofar as I am able to do so and His Majesty grants me authority, ordering the present writing issued to him, signed by my name and sealed with the seal of my arms, and countersigned by the undersigned secretary of war and government.

Done in the Villa of Santa Fe on the twenty-seventh day of the month of July of the year 1671. (Seal) Don Juan de Miranda (rubric). By order of the governor and captain general, Francisco Xavier, secretary of government and war (rubric).

Notes

1. BNE, Madrid, MSS 19258, photos 62–66.
2. Don Juan de Miranda served twice as governor of New Mexico in the seventeenth century. He was appointed in 1663 for a three-year term as governor by viceroy Conde Baños, and took office in Santa Fe in the spring of 1664. For reasons that are not entirely clear, he was removed from office and was succeeded as governor by Villanueva on June 22, 1665. Returning to Mexico City, Miranda apparently gave a satisfactory account of his actions, and he was re-appointed governor, to succeed Governor Rodríguez de Medrano Messía. Miranda's second term extended from July 21, 1671, to March 10, 1675. AGI, Contaduría, legs. 754, 755, 760, 763A, 767, and 768, Caja de México, Cuentas de los oficiales reales de México, 1661–1663, 1663–1664, 1668, 1669–1671, 1675–1676, and 1676–1678, respectively; photostat copy located at the Southwest Research Center, University of New Mexico. See also Scholes, *Troublous Times in New Mexico*, 219–21.

Don Juan de Miranda, a native of the Consejo de Tineo, Asturias, in the realm of León, was a natural son of don Juan de Miranda and Isabel de Areces, both single and not married to each other. He claimed that his parents and his paternal grandparents, don Juan de Miranda and Isabel Fernández de Areces, were well-known hidalgos. In early 1660, don Juan de Miranda sought passage to New Spain, receiving license from the king on February 26, 1660. At this date he already held the post as *regidor perpetuo* of the Conjeso de Tineo. In March 1660, he was in Madrid, where he brought forward three witnesses on his behalf as part of the process for preparing to travel to the Americas. The witnesses confirmed his parentage and nobility as a hidalgo. These witnesses were: Juan González, age forty, a vecino and native of the Consejo de Tineo, a resident of the royal court, living in the house of don Alonso Sáenz de los Herreros on the Calles de las Aguas; and Licenciado don Francisco Castillón or Castrellón, a vecino and native of the City of Oviedo and a cleric of minor orders residing in Madrid. AGI, Contratación, 5432, N. 2, R.11, Expediente de información y licencia de pasajero a indias de Juan de Miranda, Regidor perpetuo del Consejo de Tineo, April 17, 1660. (E & S)

3. This is an area south and east of the present-day San Juan River in northwest New Mexico.

4. During the seventeenth century, the Navajo were regarded by the Spaniards as a band of the Apache and were sometimes described as Apaches Navajos, or simply Apaches of Río Grande and Casa Fuerte, by which was meant the Navajo. (E & S)

Document 25

Appointment as Lieutenant of the Governor and Captain General

Santa Fe, August 2, 1671[1]

Captain don Juan de Miranda, regidor perpetuo of the Concejo de Tineo in the principality of Asturias, governor and captain general of these provinces of New Mexico for His Majesty, etc.

Yesterday, which was the first day of August of this present year, I received a message from Lieutenant General Tomé Domínguez de Mendoza and from Sargento Mayor Juan Lucero de Godoy, alcalde mayor of the district of Senecú, and another from Father Preacher fray Nicolás Hurtado, in which they inform me that on the twenty-seventh day of the said month in the middle of the day a group of mounted enemies belonging to the Apache tribe of the cordilleras of Gila and Siete Ríos, captained by El Chilmo and other treacherous partisans of his, hurled themselves upon the livestock of the pueblo [of Senecú] and, with excessive daring and shamelessness, carried off a number of cows.[2] When Salvador Olguín went out to overtake them with the soldiers of the guard and natives who were in the garrison (*guarnación*) of the said pueblo, the Apaches had prepared an ambuscade with a large number of men so that it was impossible to take the livestock from them. Indeed, they wounded the said Alférez Salvador Durán [*sic*; Olguín] and killed one Christian Indian and wounded seven.[3] They keep the settled Christians intimidated and the royal roads which go from this kingdom to that of New Spain cut off so that there is nothing secure, committing many thefts and systematic robberies against citizens and travelers. Moreover, when I entered [the kingdom], they killed four persons and robbed me of the animals belonging to His Majesty and to me which I was bringing, placing me in manifest danger of my life and loss of the royal standard, effronteries which demand severe punishment. Therefore, I have determined to go forth in person to the campaign with a detachment of armed force in search of the said enemy in order to punish them and check their pride, as is most fitting for the service of God, our Lord, and His Majesty.

In order that during my absence from this villa and its districts there may be a person in my place to represent me, with full authority as I hold it from the king, our lord, to administer justice in civil and military matters, affirming or prohibiting whatever I could [affirm or prohibit] if I were present, it is necessary to appoint a lieutenant of the governor and captain general in whom the qualities of experience and sufficiency, merits, quality, and services concur. Since those of General don Juan Domínguez de Mendoza, present maestre de campo of this kingdom, are so well known, I have thought it well to appoint and name him, as I do for the present appoint and name him, as such, in order that he may administer justice and war, attending to the affairs which may offer themselves, giving me notice of everything, acting as one who is present. I order the cabildo of this villa and the ministers of justice and war, encomenderos, citizens, residents, and inhabitants of this villa and the other jurisdictions to hold, consider, esteem, and obey him as such my lieutenant governor and captain general, to respond to his summons and orders, observing those he may give them inviolably under the penalties imposed by law, which he will execute on the rebellious and transgressors, for such is the royal will and mine in his royal name. For the aforesaid and in order that he may bear the usual insignia and enjoy the honors, exemptions and liberties that are due him by reason of the said office, I ordered the present writing issued to him, signed by my name and sealed with the seal of my arms, and countersigned by the undersigned secretary of war and government.

Done in the Villa of Santa Fe on the second day of the month of August of the year 1671. (Seal) Juan de Miranda (rubric). By order of the governor and captain general. Francisco Xavier, Secretary of government and war (rubric).

Notes

1. BNE, Madrid, MSS 19258, photos 67–69.
2. The manuscript reads as if the date was August 27, but the scribe obviously meant July 27.
3. Salvador Olguín was a native of New Mexico, born circa 1637, and a son of Cristóbal Holguín and Melchora de Carvajal. He survived the wound described in this document, and with his wife, nine children, and ten servants, he also survived the Pueblo Indian Revolt of August 1680. In the document above, Salvador Olguín is apparently misnamed as Salvador Durán. There was a contemporary named Salvador Durán who was also a soldier, who was born sometime around 1640–1650 in New Mexico. Chávez, *Origins of New Mexico Families*, 28, 82. (E & S)

Document 26

Certification of Services
Santa Fe, January 26, 1672[1]

Captain don Juan Rodríguez de Medrano Messía, governor and captain general of these provinces of New Mexico and the others adjacent to it, and judge general of bienes de difuntos for the king our lord, etc.[2]

I certify to the king our lord in his royal Council of the Indies, to the most excellent lord viceroy and the royal tribunal of New Spain, who may see the present writing, that I know Maestre de Campo don Juan Domínguez y Mendoza, citizen of this villa and encomendero in these provinces, and I have seen him serve His Majesty more than three years, exercising the post of maestre de campo of this kingdom in an entirely satisfactory manner. As is proved by his papers which he presented to me, [he is] a hidalgo, well known, outstanding, and honored, and he proves by the said papers that he has served His Majesty in these provinces more than thirty-six years at his own cost and expense, and during the said time he has occupied all the posts of militia and republic which there are in this kingdom, as is shown by the said papers, and I consider them the most brilliant services of this kingdom. He is one of its first settlers, bringing to it for this purpose a number of families at his own expense, as is shown by said papers, which proves the many expenditures he has made in the royal services of His Majesty. His family is among the most important of this kingdom, and he has two sons who are now serving His Majesty as soldiers. The oldest is called Captain don Baltasar Domínguez y Mendoza, and the second, don Juan Domínguez de Mendoza.

In the royal oath and acclamation of the king, our lord, don Carlos II, which was made in this villa on the twenty-seventh day of October of the past year of '69, in which the said maestre de campo participated as alcalde ordinario of this villa, he excelled with all brilliancy in the royal fiestas. The aforesaid directed [these fiestas] and paid the expenses, on which he expended many ducats, for they were held according to the custom in similar fiestas and functions, and the said maestre de campo don Juan Domínguez y Mendoza brought out the boy who played the part of the king with all splendor in a triumphal car on the afternoon of the royal oath and the night of the masquerade. In all that pertained to him in this function the said maestre de campo, and his son don Baltasar as well, performed the obligations of their blood as faithful and loyal vassals of His Majesty.

I find the said Maestre de Campo don Juan Domínguez y Mendoza most worthy and deserving of all the favors His Majesty and the lords viceroy of New Spain and lords governor of this kingdom may be pleased to do him, for he will give a good account of himself as he has always done. And in order that it may be on record, I granted the present writing at the petition of the said Maestre de Campo don Juan Domínguez y Mendoza.

Done in the Villa de Santa Fe of New Mexico. Countersigned by the undersigned secretary on the twenty-sixth day of the month of January of 1672. Signed by my name and sealed with the seal of my arms. (Seal) Juan de Medrano Messía (rubric). By order of the governor and captain general, Antonio González, secretary of government and war (rubric).

Notes

1. BNE, Madrid, MSS 19258, photos 48–49.
2. This is one of the Group B documents of the fraudulent series. It is listed in Doc. 46, also believed to be forged, but not in the copy of the cabildo's certification in Doc. 52. Medrano was no longer governor of New Mexico on January 26, 1672, for his term of office ended on July 20, 1671. The family name is written Domínguez y Mendoza, instead of Domínguez de Mendoza, the form used in the

genuine titles. The statement that Juan Domínguez de Mendoza had served "more than thirty-six years" would date the beginning of his services in 1635, or thereabouts, whereas other references in the Servicios Personales records give a range of his service beginning somewhere around 1634–1645. Domínguez de Mendoza's son, Baltasar, is referred to as *captain*. According to a muster roll of 1681 (Hackett and Shelby, *Pueblo Revolt*, 2: 67), Baltasar was then only fourteen years of age. This would place his age at four or five in the year 1672, when the present document says he was a captain. Doc. 47 (October 8, 1684) records that he was twenty-five in 1684, but this document is apparently a forgery. But assuming he was twenty-five in 1684, he would have been only thirteen years old in 1672, the alleged date of the present document, so that statement that he was already a captain would be suspect. Moreover, even the suspect titles of don Baltasar, Docs. 27 (December 27, 1672) and 29 (October 20, 1674) record that he received the rank of captain only in 1674. At that time he would have been either fifteen or seven years old, depending on the age we accept as true, and in either case he would have been too young to have had a commission as captain. Likewise, the statement in the present document that Juan Domínguez de Mendoza, the younger, was already serving as a soldier is undoubtedly false. According to Doc. 47 (October 8, 1684), he was twenty years old in 1684. Even if we assume that this is correct, he would have been only seven years old in 1671. If he was five years younger than Baltasar, as Doc. 47 states, and if Baltasar was born in 1667, as the muster roll of 1681 indicates, then Juan, the younger, had been born when the present document was supposedly drawn up. That this was probably true is confirmed by a statement in a muster roll of 1680 that Juan Domínguez de Mendoza, the elder, had a capable son of military service (Baltasar) and "another younger one" (Hackett and Shelby, *Pueblo Revolt*, 1:138). On the basis of the foregoing, there would seem to be no doubt that the document was forged at some later date. The account of the festival celebrating the oath of allegiance to Carlos II may well refer to an actual incident, although inasmuch as Carlos II succeeded to the throne in 1665, it is not immediately clear why the celebration may have taken place four years later in 1669 in the Villa de Santa Fe.

Document 27

*Commission as Alférez Real Granted to
Don Baltasar Domínguez de Mendoza*

Santa Fe, December 27, 1672[1]

General Juan de Miranda, regidor perpetuo of the Consejo de Tineo in the principality of Asturias, former and present governor and captain general of this kingdom and provinces of New Mexico for the king, our lord, etc.

For the guard and custody of the royal standard and in order that there may be a person to raise it before me on campaign and in settled areas[2] on occasions that may offer themselves in the royal service, it is most necessary to appoint as alférez real of this kingdom a person of every quality, valor, loyalty, merits, services, and praiseworthy actions, such as the case requires. In consideration of these of don Baltasar Domínguez y Mendoza, soldier who has served and serves his Majesty in the continual wars against the infidel nation of Apache enemies, and in consideration of the many merits and services of the present maestre de campo of this kingdom, don Juan Domínguez y Mendoza, his father, who has served his Majesty more than thirty years, occupying the most important posts and places of militia and war to satisfaction of my predecessors; and because, in imitation of his said father, the said don Baltasar will sacrifice himself in the royal services of his Majesty, in his royal name I elect, name, and appoint the aforesaid as such alférez real of the whole kingdom. And, being present, he swore to die in defense of the [royal standard] and to guard it until he loses his life or accounts for it, handing it over to me in my hands. And I order the maestre de campo, sargento mayor of the kingdom and [sargentos mayores] of campaign, and the captains of infantry and cavalry, alférez, and other officials of war, active and retired, and the encomenderos and soldiers, to hold, consider, esteem, and obey him as such, and to observe and fulfill his orders and commands under penalties imposed by law. For all this, and in order that he may bear this usual insignia and enjoy well and completely the honors, favors, privileges, exemptions, and liberties which are due him, such as the other alféreces reales of the armies and forces of His Majesty enjoy, I give him power and authority, ordering that [this writing] be issued to him, signed by my hand and sealed with the seal of my arms, and countersigned by the undersigned secretary of war and government.

Done in the Villa of Santa Fe on the twenty-seventh day of December of the year 1672. (Seal) Don Juan de Miranda (rubric). By order of his lordship, Francisco Xavier, secretary of government and war (rubric).

Notes

1. BNE, Madrid, MSS 19258, photos 72–73.
2. The text reads "*en campaña y poblado.*"

Document 28

Commission as Maestre de Campo in Campaign
San Juan de los Caballeros, July 15, 1673[1]

General don Juan de Miranda, regidor perpetuo of the Consejo de Tineo in the principality of Asturias. Former and present governor and captain general of the kingdom and provinces of New Mexico for the king, our lord, etc.

Reprisal and just war is now to be made by my order against the common enemies, the Apache nation, irreducible and perverse, treacherous and traitorous, for the very grave harm they have done and continually do in the kingdom. Their boldness and insolence has extended so far that they have burned churches and pueblos, profaning the holy temples, robbing and destroying and making a wreck of sacred things, capturing and killing the settled Christians in an atrocious manner, stealing the herds of horses and livestock, going so far as to have killed the friars minister of the pueblo of Aguico [Hawikuh] in the province of Zuñi, and making assemblies and invocations for this purpose.[2] Not counting the aforesaid transgressions, they are deserving of severe punishment in the jurisdictions of the Río Grande, Casa Fuerte Navajo, and all the other jurisdictions and territories where it is necessary, and of being hunted down in order that they may be carried off by blood and fire and their grain, milpas, and food supplies destroyed and taken from them.

For this disposition and purpose I have created a detachment and active army of forty Spanish soldiers, harquebusiers, and three hundred of the settled Christian Indians arrived with bows and arrows according to the usage of the country under [the command of] Captain and Sargento Mayor Pedro de Leiva, my lieutenant governor and captain general.[3] And it is necessary to appoint the commanders required for the good execution of the military orders, punishments, and assaults which are to be are in the service of both majesties and the general welfare is heard [?] and defense of the Holy Gospel and the honor of His Majesty. It is [also] necessary to name a person or maestre de campo of all the military force and campaign and that such a person possesses the required experience, sufficiency, merits, quality, loyalty, and services, and be capable in matters of war.

These and many other good qualities are found and concur in the person of Maestre de Campo don Juan Domínguez de Mendoza, a soldier of valor and great experience who has served His Majesty in this kingdom more than thirty years, very well equipped with all arms and horses at his cost and expense. He has been present at the most important reprisals and just wars against said enemies of our Holy Faith which have occurred in this kingdom in which he has distinguished his person to very great advantage, winning satisfaction among friends and enemies, both as commander and as subordinate in campaigns, escorts, and in combat against the common enemy. On account of his actions my predecessors have employed him in the posts of alférez, captain of infantry and cavalry, sargento mayor, and maestro de campo of this kingdom, lieutenant governor and captain general; and in my past term of office and the present one I have employed him in posts of war, and as maestre de campo of the kingdom and my lieutenant in the villa [of Santa Fe] in my absence, not counting the civil posts he has exercised, occupying that of alcalde ordinario, in all accord he has given a favorable account of himself.

The remuneration [record] of which and because the present occasion is so greatly in the service of both Majesties, defense of the Holy Gospel, and benefit of all the kingdom, [and] in consideration of the fact that I have confidence that he will continue to [serve] as before, I now appoint, name, and elect the aforesaid Maestre de Campo don Juan Domínguez de Mendoza, in the name of his Majesty, as such maestre de campo of the army, in order that he may use the said office and issue and transmit the orders which may be necessary and pertain to him, necessary under law, which I order the sargento mayor, captain, alférez, active and retired commanders, encomenderos, ordinary soldiers, and natives to obey, fulfill, and execute under the penalties conferred by law, which he would execute on the transgressors and disobedient, persistent in the royal will and in the royal name. For all this and in order that he may enjoy the favors, privileges, exemptions, liberties, preeminences, and prerogatives which are due him and in the armies, armadas, forces, plazas, castles, and fortresses of His Majesty enjoy them; and in order that he and Lieutenant Governor Pedro de Leiba may go in unity and agreement, doing their best in the service of His Majesty, since they go for one purpose; and with this declaration that the aforesaid owes nothing for the taxes of *onorato* and media anata for the positions and posts he has occupied, serving at his own expense more than thirty years in active warfare. I order the present writing issued to him signed by my name and sealed with the seal of my arms, and countersigned by the undersigned secretary of war and government.

Done in this pueblo and plaza de armas of San Juan de los Caballeros on the fifteenth day of the month of July of the year 1673. (Seal) Don Juan de Miranda (rubric). By order of the governor and captain general, Francisco Xavier (rubric), secretary of government and war.

Notes

1. BNE, Madrid, MSS 19258, photos 58–59.
2. This may be a reference to the killing of fray Pedro de Ávila y Ayala at Hawikuh in late 1672 by Apache raiders. Frederick W. Hodge, *History of Hawikuh*, 94–99.
3. Pedro de Leyva was born circa 1614–1619 in El Valle de San Bartolomé, Nueva Vizcaya. He was a son of Sargento Mayor Cristóbal de Nevares, a resident of Santiago Papasquiaro in Nueva Vizcaya, where he and his wife, Ana Martínez, died in an Indian attack in August 1671. Pedro de Leyva was a resident of New Mexico as early as 1637 and was in Santa Fe in February 1639 when he and Francisco de Valencia stood as witnesses for an official decree. The fact that he was captain and lieutenant governor for the Salinas Pueblo district and later held the rank of maestre de campo (field commander) suggests he probably came to New Mexico as a soldier-citizen of the frontier. He was married by 1650 to Catalina García. Chávez, *Origins of New Mexico Families*, 53; Hackett, *Historical Documents*, 3:53. (E & S)

In 1660, Pedro de Leyva was a resident of the jurisdiction of Tajique, today located in Torrance County, New Mexico. Under Governor don Bernardo López de Mendizábal (1659–1661), he was alcalde mayor of the Humanas region, located on the eastern side of the Manzano Mountains and toward the south. López de Mendizábal removed Leyva from this office in September 1661, because Leyva was favorably disposed to the affairs of the Church. In December 1677, Leyva was serving as a member of the cabildo of the Villa de Santa Fe, and in the following year he was residing at El Paso del Río del Norte, where he held the post of maestre de campo general of the Río del Norte jurisdiction. He was still serving in this post when the Pueblo Indians attacked and killed his wife and three children at their home in Galisteo in early August 1680. Hackett, *Historical Documents*, 2:161, 163, 181, 205, 288, 291, 296. (E & S)

Pedro de Leyva had one known sister, who was a resident of Parral prior to 1661, and three known brothers: Cristóbal de Nevares Heredia, captain of the presidio of Cerro Gordo in Nueva Vizcaya in 1661, who later held the rank of general; Alférez Juan de Nevares Heredia, a resident of Santiago Papasquiaro in 1659; Alférez Nicolás de Nevares, who married his first cousin, Josefa Leyva, on March 7, 1666, Santiago Papasquiaro, Nueva Vizcaya, and who died in 1667 at his hacienda in the area of the Pueblo de San Nicolás near Santiago Papasquiaro. AGN, Real Audiencia, Concurso de Peñalosa, vol. 1, no. 2, ff. 213v/360v,

Testimony of Capitán Juan González Lobón, October 29, 1661, Villa de Santa Fe; Mexico, Durango, Church of Santiago Papasquiaro, Marriages, LDS microfilm #0654993; José Antonio Esquibel, "The Leyva–Nevares Heredia Extended Family of Nueva Vizcaya, 1659–1710," in *El Farolito* 3, no. 3(Fall 2000): 5–15; vol. 3, no. 4 (2000): 21–26; and vol. 4, no. 1 (2001): 17–21. (E & S)

Document 29

Commission as Captain of Cavalry Granted to Don Baltasar Domínguez de Mendoza

Santa Fe, October 20, 1674[1]

General don Juan de Miranda, regidor perpetuo of the Consejo de Tineo in the principality of Asturias, former and present governor and captain general of this kingdom and provinces of New Mexico for His Majesty, etc.

In obedience to what His Majesty commands me with regard to calming, pacifying, and tranquilizing these provinces of New Mexico, it is necessary to provide an armed force sufficient both for the enemy frontiers and for the already conquered and settled [area]. Therefore, I have decided to have a number of captains of militia who are to be persons of particular experience in matters of war. Because these and other good parts concur in Alférez Real don Baltasar Domínguez y Mendoza, and in consideration of his merits and services and those of the present maestre de campo of these provinces, don Juan Domínguez y Mendoza, his father, and hoping that henceforth he will continue to serve, I have thought it well to appoint and name him, as for the present I do appoint him captain of cavalry of one of the standing companies[2] in these provinces. As such he will raise the standard and will have clarions sounded, bearing the usual insignia, using and exercising the said office in all the affairs and matters pertaining to and concerning it, correcting and punishing the soldiers of his company for the excesses they may commit, briefly and summarily according to the usage of war, prescinding judicial inquiry. I order them to hold, consider, respect, and obey him as their captain, observing and fulfilling the orders he may give them in the terms and under the penalties he may impose upon them, because in order that he may execute those in rebellion and disobedient and enjoy the honors, favors, preeminences, exceptions, liberties, and prerogatives that by reason of the said office are due and belong to him, fully and completely without there being anything lacking, according to and in the way they are kept and must be observed with regard to the other captains of the armies and forces of His Majesty, I give him power and authority as is required by law for a period dependent on the will of His Majesty and mine in his royal name, for which I ordered this commission issued to him, signed by my hand and sealed with the seal of my arms, countersigned by the undersigned secretary of war and government.

Done in the Villa of Santa Fe on the twentieth day of the month of October of the year 1674. (Seal) Don Juan de Miranda (rubric). By order of his lordship, Francisco Xavier, secretary of government and war (rubric).

Notes
1. BNE, Madrid, MSS 19258, photos 70–71.
2. The text reads "*companías del número.*"

Document 30

Commission as Maestre de Campo in a Campaign against the Faraon Apaches

Pecos, January 5, 1675[1]

General don Juan de Miranda, regidor perpetuo of the Consejo de Tineo in the principality of Asturias, former and present governor and captain general of the kingdom of New Mexico for the king, our lord, etc.

I had arranged [to go] in person with a detachment and active army [*pie de ejercito*] of forty-four Spanish soldiers [to serve as] harquebusiers and two hundred fifty Indians [armed] with bows and arrows, to make reprisal and just war against the Apache nation called Faraones, Indian enemies of our Holy Faith, and the other nations allied with them, waging war against all of them by blood and fire as traitors, treacherous thieves, breakers of the public peace, public menaces to the pueblos, temples, and highways.[2] Therefore I designated this pueblo of Pecos as plaza de armas from which [we were] to set forth to wage war upon them by blood and fire. Here, for many reasons, I have now decided to appoint a person of all satisfaction and credit as lieutenant captain general to take my place during the campaign, as well as the necessary military commanders [of lesser rank]. And in order to fill out the number of the [latter], it is necessary to appoint as maestre de campo of the army a person of all nobility, loyalty, merits, sufficiency, and experience, a soldier of valor and reputation, capable and well informed in military matters.

These and many other good qualities are found and concur in the person of Maestre de Campo don Juan Domínguez de Mendoza. I am well satisfied with him because of the services in which he has employed himself, having served His Majesty from the time he has had the use of reason and having been present at many reprisals and just wars, including the most important ones that have taken place, in which he has distinguished himself as a very brave soldier, winning credit and reputation among friends and enemies, and always at his own expense. Because of his actions my predecessors and I, during the two terms of my office I have served, have employed him in many posts and positions, and he has exercised those of alférez, adjutant, captain, sargento mayor, maestre de campo, lieutenant governor and captain general, not counting other commissions and public offices, of which he has given good and praiseworthy account, all of which is shown by his titles and documents, to which I refer. In reward and remuneration for his services, which are public and well known, and because on the present occasion, in order that the greatest services to His Majesty may be attained, it is important that he be present, assisting Maestre de Campo Francisco Gómez Robledo, my lieutenant captain general in this campaign, I now name, appoint, and nominate the aforesaid in the name of the king, for the present, as maestre de campo of the said army. And I order that he be received as such by the commander-in-chief and other subordinate military commanders. And the retired officers [*reformados*], soldiers, and all the Indians enlisted, and the others who are on active duty on the present occasion shall hold, consider, esteem, and obey him as their maestre de campo, and they shall observe, fulfill, and execute on the transgressors and disobedient, acting in a manner to justify my confidence in him and maintaining all vigilance in military operations in order that an exemplary punishment may be inflicted upon these irreducible barbarians.

For all of this and what pertains to and depends from it, and in order that he may enjoy the favors, exemptions, privileges, and liberties which are due him and belong to him, as to other maestres de campo of the armies, posts, and forces of His Majesty, and in order that he may wear the usual insignia,

I give him power and authority in sufficient legal form, ordering the present writing issued to him with the declaration that he owes nothing to the taxes of onorato and media anata. And so that it may always be of record and well known to the whole army, Spaniards and natives, I ordered it issued to him, signed by my name and sealed with the seal of my arms, and countersigned by the undersigned secretary of war and government.

Done in this pueblo and plaza de armas of Pecos on the fifth day of the month of January of the year 1675. (Seal) Don Juan de Miranda (rubric). By order of the governor and captain general, Francisco Xavier, secretary of war and government (rubric).

Notes

1. BNE, Madrid, MSS 19258, photos 60–61.

2. This is the earliest reference to the Faraon Apache, who were found in northeastern New Mexico and in the northern part of the Texas Panhandle. "This tribe, no longer known by name, seems to have formed the southern division of the Querechos of Coronado (1541), the Vaqueros of Benavides (1630) and other seventeenth century writers, and part at least of the Llaneros of more recent times." Frederick Webb Hodge, *Handbook of American Indians*, Washington, 1907–10, I:453. Governor Diego de Vargas mentioned them in his campaign journal of 1692 as being in alliance with Indians of Pecos and other tribes. José Manuel Espinosa, *First Expedition of Vargas into New Mexico, 1692*, Albuquerque, 1940: 110; Kessell and Hendricks, *By Force of Arms*, 188, 222n96, 409, 454, and 553. In the early eighteenth century, the Faraones carried on trade with the pueblo of Pecos and at intervals raided the New Mexico frontier from Taos to Albuquerque. Expeditions were made against them by Governor Pedro Rodríguez Cubero in 1702, by Governor Vargas in 1704, by Governor Juan Ignacio Flores Mogollón in 1712, and in 1714 by Governor Antonio Valverde Cosío. During the 1704 campaign, Governor Vargas died while chasing the Faraones Indians along the eastern slope of the Sandia range. In 1715 Governor Flores Mogollón held councils of war to plan a new expedition, and the need for action was emphasized by a raid by the Faraones on Picurís in July of that year. In September, Juan Páez Hurtado took a detachment of Spaniards and friendly Indians southeastward from Picurís to the Canadian River, and thence eastward into Texas, but he was unable to contact the enemy. Alfred Barnaby Thomas, *After Coronado: Spanish Exploration Northeast of New Mexico, 1696–1727* (Norman: University of Oklahoma Press, 1935), 22–26, 80–98, passim.

Document 31

Commission as Military Commander and Chief
Santa Fe, September 24, 1675[1]

Don Juan Francisco Treviño, chief usher of the royal person and household of His Majesty in his kingdom of Navarre, captain of Spanish infantry in the state of Flanders, governor and captain general of the kingdom and provinces of New Mexico for His Majesty, etc.[2]

Because of the atrocities, treacheries, and robberies which the hostile Apache nation has committed and continually commits, I have enlisted a force of armed men, consisting of forty harquebusiers and three hundred [Indians armed] with bows and arrows, in order to inflict punishment and just war on them and curb their daring. On the thirtieth of the present month [this force will assemble] in the pueblo of Zía, which I have chosen as plaza de armas, in order that they may go out in good order and military discipline to the mountain ranges of Navajo, Casa Fuerte, and other places necessary so that the said punishment may be put into effect and carried through and the daring [of the Indians] checked.[3] For the execution of this it is necessary that the said detachment and active army go under the command of a person in whom concur the qualities of practice and experience required in military affairs.

In consideration of the merits, quality, personal services, practice, and experience of Maestre de Campo don Juan Domínguez de Mendoza, of which I have knowledge; and because my predecessors, taking into account the manner in which he has served his majesty in many wars and punitive expeditions against the barbarous Apaches, have placed in his charge many military operations and reprisals, which he has executed with all resolution acting as commander and chief, leader of campaign, and performing other duties entrusted to him; therefore, in view of the great importance of the present occasion and because I am well satisfied with him as leader, commander, and chief for the abovesaid with all plenary authority in order that he may act in everything in the service of His Majesty as one who will have the matter at hand. And I order the maestre de campo, sargento mayor, captain, alférez, and other soldiers, and the retired commanders and those who may be created in the said campaign, to hold, consider, esteem, respect, and obey his orders and commands as emanating from me and without any

FIGURE 4 Pueblo of Zuni looking southeast, ca. 1879. Denver Public Library, Western History Collection, John K. Hillers (1843–1925), X-30318.

limitation, by the authority which I grant him in the royal name of the king, our lord. And in order that he may successfully execute [his commission], I give him plenary power in all form, so that he may punish the disobedient. For this purpose, and in order that he may enjoy well and completely the honors, privileges, exceptions, and liberties which are due him and bear the usual insignia, I ordered the present writing issued to him, signed by my name, sealed with the seal of my arms, and countersigned by the undersigned secretary of war and government.

Done in the Villa of Santa Fe on the twenty-fourth day of the month of September, 1675. (Seal) Don Juan Francisco Treviño (rubric). By order of his lordship, Luis de Quintana, secretary of war and government. (rubric)

Don Juan Francisco Treviño, chief usher of the royal person and household of His Majesty in his kingdom of Navarra, captain of Spanish infantry in the state of Flanders, governor and captain general of the provinces and kingdom of New Mexico for His Majesty, etc.

I certify to his royal and Catholic Majesty and to all his tribunals and royal justices where the present writing may be seen that Maestre de Campo don Juan Domínguez de Mendoza, citizen of these provinces, mentioned in this writing, has served His Majesty during the period of my government [doing] the things which I have ordered him to do in the royal service with my great approbation, for he has attended to them with all punctiliousness as a loyal vassal of His Majesty. And very especially he displayed his valor and zeal for the royal service on the occasion, shortly after I had taken possession of my office, when I sent him, as is shown by the title, to make a punitive expedition and just war on the Apache nation of the mountain ranges toward the west, common enemies of our Holy Faith, who had perpetuated grave atrocities of killings, treacheries, depredations of sacred houses of divine worship and of the herds of the kingdom. Having enlisted a detachment and active army (pie de ejercito), he went forth and inflicted punishment on the said Indians, killing fifteen of them, rescuing from captivity six Christian Indians and a girl, daughter of a Spanish citizen. And he captured thirty-five persons of said enemies, burning large quantities of their maize and other supplies, so great a service to His Majesty that as a result the forces with which they made their assemblies and convictions for the ambuscades which they committed against the settled Christians were reduced. He has always been prepared, ready, and accounted with all arms and horses, not only assisting in person at all matters in the service of His Majesty and defense of this kingdom, but also supplying at his own expense horses, arms, and food for all the soldiers who went as escorts to the defense of the pueblos. And the afore-named has occupied the most honorable posts and those of greatest qualifications of this kingdom, both military and civil, for he has served as lieutenant of the governor and captain general of this kingdom on five occasions during the government of my predecessors, and also as many times as maestre de campo of the kingdom, and as commander, chief, and leader in campaign by my appointment on the occasion described, and others in which my predecessors have occupied him. He has given a good account and as complete satisfaction as can be desired in all these. Therefore, I consider him very deserving of remuneration for his services by His Majesty (God keep him) and by the governors in his name. And at his petition I ordered the present writing issued to him, signed by my name and sealed by the seal of my arms.

Issued in the Villa of Santa Fe of New Mexico on the tenth day of the month of August of the year 1677. Don Juan Francisco Treviño (rubric).

Notes

1. BNE, Madrid, MSS 19258, photos 77–81.
2. Don Juan Francisco Treviño served as governor of New Mexico from March 11, 1675, to November 29, 1677. AGI, Contaduría, legs. 766, 767, 768, Caja de México. Cuentas de los oficiales reales de México, 1674–1675, 1675–1676, and 1676–1678, respectively; photostat copy located at the Southwest Research Center, University of New Mexico.
3. In the photograph of this document certain phrases are illegible, because of the failure of the photographer to use care in smoothing out a fold in the manuscript. The words in brackets undoubtedly give the sense of the words that cannot be read.

Document 32

Commission as Military Commander and Chief
Estancia de San Antonio, July 1, 1676[1]

Maestre de Campo Tomé Domínguez de Mendoza, lieutenant of the governor and captain general of these provinces of New Mexico by commission of Captain Juan Francisco Treviño, governor and captain general of the aforesaid provinces for the king, our lord, etc.

The governor and captain general has been advised by repeated messages that the infidel Apache enemies are near the pueblos of Nuestra Señora del Socorro and San Antonio de Senecú, whence on different occasions they hurl themselves in attacks upon the said pueblos and carry off all the herds of sheep, cattle, and horses they can. In order to stop such depredations and so that the said enemies may be punished, the said governor and captain general has decided that a troop of Spaniards, together with another of Christian Indian archers, shall go forth with a chief and commander to rule and govern them and lead them under military discipline. For this purpose the said governor and captain general sent me a letter in the form of an order, its date on the eighteenth day of the month of June of this present year of 1676, in order that I, as his lieutenant, might organize and dispatch the aforesaid armed force and also appoint and name a commander.

By virtue of this and in the name of the king, our lord, and of the governor in his royal name, I approach and name as such commander and chief Maestre de Campo don Juan Domínguez de Mendoza in consideration of his many and great services and because he has gone out to the campaign many other times, commanding and governing an active army (pie de ejercito), as he did in the past year and on many occasions, having given a very good and praiseworthy account of himself. And in consideration of the fact that he will continue in the royal service, I have thought it well to appoint him as such commander and chief and to order all the Spaniards and Indians who are going and may go to the said *entrada* and punishment to hold and consider, esteem and respect the said Maestre de Campo don Juan Domínguez de Mendoza to take the muster roll of all the force, both Spaniards and natives, who are enrolled for the said war and punitive expedition, when he reaches the pueblo of Nuestra Señora del Socorro, and to march with all of them to the places where he has heard that the enemy may be. When the campaign has started, he will do and act as is most fitting in the service of both Majesties, divine and human, achieving in all [ways] the exemplary punishment of the enemy, acting in everything with due accord and valor as he has always done on other occasions. He is to follow the mountain ranges of the Sierra de la Magdalena and Sierra de los Ladrones, and he will conduct the campaign as one who is present at the scene of action, disposing, ordering, and doing what is most fitting. For all of the foregoing I give and grant him sufficient power and authority insofar as I can according to law, and he shall give me an adequate report and relation of everything to forward to the governor and captain general so that he may dispose and command as is most fitting.

I signed it with my name today, July 1 of this present year of 1676. In this estancia de San Antonio, etc. Thomé [Tomé] Domínguez de Mendoza (rubric).

Notes

1. BNE, Madrid, MSS 19258, photos 74–76.
2. Elder brother of Juan Domínguez de Mendoza. This commission was issued at the estancia of Tomé Domínguez de Mendoza, four leagues south of Isleta.

Document 33

Commission as Lieutenant Captain General in Campaign
Santa Fe, July 12, 1678[1]

Don Antonio de Otermín, governor and captain general of the kingdom and provinces of New Mexico for the king, our lord, etc.[2]

The hostile infidel Apache nation, irreducible and perverse common enemies of our Holy faith who surround this kingdom on all sides, are continually committing grave crimes such as atrocious killings in the fields and settlements and thefts of herds of horses and all kinds of livestock. As is obvious from their treacherous artifices, they aim at the complete destruction of [this kingdom], for their daring and barbarous designs have reached such a peak that they have laid waste the holy temples, stolen their images and sacred things, even setting fire to them, and have killed the ministers and Spanish soldiers, without reserving from their anger even innocent babes. [These are] terrible crimes which demand severe punishment in order that the pride and insolence of the aforesaid may be checked, because they are so numerous that there is no security from them, not even in the Villa of Santa Fe, which is the capital of this kingdom, for they have committed many killings and robberies in it, as happened yesterday, the eleventh of this month, when three horses were carried off from this villa in broad daylight.

In order to inflict punishment and just war on the said enemies. I have created a detachment and active army of fifty Spanish soldiers [to serve as] mounted harquebusiers, and four hundred Christian Indians, in order that they may go marching in all order and military discipline to the mountain ranges of the west along the trails from the pueblo of Zía, where they are to pass muster before me, because I have designated it as plaza de armas. And following the track, they will go inflicting punishment on the said enemies, carrying it to due execution in fact and destroying all the grain fields of those who may be found in the jurisdiction of Casa Fuerte, Navajo, Río Grande,[3] and all the other districts until an exemplary reprisal is accomplished; and they will try their utmost to take from them and restore the chalice, patens, and sacred vestments which have been carried off, as well as three Spanish women and all the Christian captives who have been taken from different pueblos.

In order that the said force may have a chief to command and govern them, who will execute with their aid all the things here expressed and those which may befit the service of God, our Lord, and His Majesty in the defense of this kingdom, it is necessary to appoint a person of the requisite qualities and experience, practical knowledge, sufficiency, merits, quality, and services, capable in matters of war, so that in my place and as if I were present, he may act as lieutenant general in campaign, executing, ordering, and regulating all that may be for the service of both Majesties without any limitation. For the said purpose you, Maestre de Campo don Juan Domínguez de Mendoza, are a fitting choice, and I am well satisfied that you will act with all prudence and reputation, as you have done on all occasions which have occurred in the royal service in which my predecessors have occupied you, both in offices of justice and in those of war, of which you have given a good account. The present occasion is an important one, and I have confidence that you will carry it out, executing what I order until it is accomplished. And, having done so and left things in good order, you will set out to the mountain range of the Piedra Alumbre[4] and march through that territory, where I understand the main part of the said enemies gathered to commit robberies and damages in the jurisdiction of La Cañada, and, finding them, you will punish them. And in the same way you will undertake to find the bones of Captains Alonso Fernández and Juan de Herrera, who died at the hands of the said enemies, and you will bring them to a settled part where they may be given ecclesiastical burial.

I order all the Spanish soldiers, officers, and retired [officers], and all the Christian natives who are enlisted for the said journey, to hold, consider, esteem, and obey you as such, and to observe, fulfill, and execute your orders and commands as if they were given by me if I were present, under penalties imposed by law, which you will execute at once on the disobedient and transgressors. And you will observe in everything the instruction which given you with this, fulfilling it and executing its contents, noting that because some cases may offer themselves which cannot be foreseen now, you will act in everything as one who is present at the scene of action and in such a way that you may enjoy the favors, exemptions, and liberties which are due you by reason of the said office, and in order that you may bear the usual insignia, I give you sufficient power as is required by law and is necessary, for such is the royal will and mine in his royal name. Therefore I ordered the present writing issued to you, signed by my name and sealed with the seal of my arms, and countersigned by the undersigned secretary of war and government.

Done in this Villa of Santa Fe on the twelfth day of the month of July of the year 1678. (Seal) Don Antonio de Otermín (rubric). By order of the governor and captain general, Francisco Xavier, secretary of war and government (rubric).

Don Antonio de Otermín, governor and captain general of the kingdom and provinces of New Mexico for the king, our lord.

In consideration of don Juan Domínguez de Mendoza has fulfilled and executed the order given him by me appointing him my lieutenant captain general in campaign as [is evident from]⁵ this patent and instruction, and has executed punishment on the infidel enemies, killing them in active war, capturing fifty persons, their wives and children, and taking from the said enemies two captive women, inflicting considerable destruction of their milpas of maize and other grains, and seizing from them thirteen horses and many other spoils, all of which he performed with all resolution, valor, and care as he has done on other occasions which have arisen in the royal service, he asked me for his honorable discharge for having accomplished what he was ordered in military style, having left the enemy terrified and their property destroyed. On account of these services I certify to the royal ministers of His Majesty by whom the present writing may be seen that the aforesaid is a very honorable soldier and deserving that His Majesty and his royal ministers in his royal name may honor him, rewarding him in accordance with his services. And at his petition and in order that it may be of record, I issued the present certification and discharge in this Villa of Santa Fe on the twenty-third day of August of the year 1678. Signed by my name and sealed with the seal of my arms, and countersigned by the secretary of war and government. (Seal) Don Antonio de Otermín (rubric). By order of his lordship, Francisco Xavier, secretary of war and government (rubric).

Notes

1. BNE, Madrid, MSS 19258, photos 139–141.

2. Antonio de Otermín served as governor of New Mexico from November 30, 1677, to August 26, 1683. He served as governor of Sinaloa in 1672. AGN, Real Hacienda, Archivo Histórico de Hacienda, vol. 474, exp. 78, Fianzas, Antonio de Otermín, Gobernador y Capitán General del Presidio de Sinaloa, 1672.

3. Today known as the San Juan River.

4. In Bernardo Miera y Pacheco's map of 1779, reproduced in Alfred Barnaby Thomas, *Forgotten Frontiers*, the words *Valle de Pierda Alumbre* are written in between the Río Chama and the Cerro de los Pedernales. Thus, it appears that the area referred to in the text was the region of the Chama above Abiquiú. According to the present document and the one that follows, Domínguez de Mendoza was to go from Zía to the Navajo strongholds situated to the north and northwest toward the San Juan River and inflict reprisals. Then, on the return route, he was to come back through the upper Chama area and make war on the Indians of that district who had been carrying out raids in the jurisdiction of La Cañada, which comprised the Tewa pueblos and Spanish estancias along the Río del Norte (modern Rio Grande) and its tributaries north of Santa Fe.

5. A fold in the manuscript here or bad photography makes this phrase incomplete, and thus a probable phrase appears in brackets.

Document 34

Instruction as Lieutenant Captain General
Santa Fe, July 12, 1678[1]

Don Antonio de Otermín, governor and captain general of the kingdom and provinces of New Mexico for His Majesty.

To you, Maestre de Campo don Juan Domínguez de Mendoza, whom I have appointed as my lieutenant captain general in campaign, in order that you may observe and execute the following instruction in its entirety:

When all the enlisted force under your command has assembled in the plaza de armas of the pueblo of Zía, you will march out with your army in proper order and military discipline, sending spies ahead to acquaint themselves with the country and see whether any enemies or enemy may be found and captured so that you may examine him to learn where the [enemies] are and all their designs, in order that such information may enable you to make the best plan to ensure success.

From the most experienced Indians and best guides you will inform yourself of the route you must take, always trying to go concealed in such a way that the [enemy] may not see you and retire. And if it may seem best to you for this purpose to keep your force lying in ambush by day and to march at night, you will do so with vigilance, trying to discover [the whereabouts] of the enemy by the smoke or fire which they make in their settlements. Having discovered them, you will fall upon them, waging war against them with all resolution, destroying their sowings and all the grain they may have sown. [You will] exercise extreme care in learning and inquiring where the holy chalices and sacred things, and captives who have been carried off from the Christian settlements, are, in order that, having found out, you may take possession of the said objects and bring them to me with all veneration so that they may be returned to the churches where they belong; and the Christians are to be returned to their pueblos and set at liberty.

You will march to the mountain ranges of Casa Fuerte, Navajo, Río Grande, and their districts, always with the necessary vigilance, keeping our force always on the watch, inflicting punishment and destruction, and not permitting anyone to separate himself from you by day, inasmuch as experience has shown that however short a distance they may go from the column, [the enemies] have killed them without its being possible to prevent it. You will see that all care is taken to set watches over the camp and horses on account of the assaults the said enemies make by night, which cause the horses to stampede. The [enemies] are wont to shoot many of the Christian force with arrows, and on other occasions it has been impossible to remedy this as a result of the negligence, since the commanders have permitted youths of little experience to keep watch in place of those appointed to do so. Therefore I order you to not permit this except in case of absolute necessity.

If you should capture any women or children in the assaults you may make, you will place them under good guard and watch by day and by night, not permitting the Indians, as irresponsible persons, to commit any excesses with the women. And you will punish severely anyone who does so, seeing to it that none of the captives flee.

If any Indians should come out from the mesas and high places to speak to you, trying with their usual lies to prevent the reprisal you are to inflict upon them, you will give them to understand that it is done because of their crime, and you will prosecute it with more lively desires, explaining that they are to be punished until they are destroyed for being so obstinate and perverse.

You will administer whatever disciplinary measures you may find advisable and necessary with all resolution and prudence, not permitting anyone to maltreat or vex the Christian Indians; rather they are to be treated with love and as vassals of His Majesty.

Two infidel Indians of the Yuta [Ute] nation, together with many others of their nation who have entered the pueblo of Taos in peace, have united themselves in friendship and communication with us, and I have admitted them to the sure protection of His Majesty. And because they are gratified by the friendly intercourse and courteous treatment [they have received] and because I made one of them captain of his nation to see whether they can be reduced to the yoke of the Holy Gospel, they have come to go on this campaign. Therefore, in hope that it will be possible to reduce them to our Holy Faith, you will exercise great care in seeing to it that you and all the Spaniards and Christian Indians are attentive and friendly and treat them with all loving kindness so that they may give themselves more fully to intercourse and friendship with us.

When you have carried out the punishments and reprisals which you are to inflict, you will set out with extreme caution on the return march by way of the mountain ranges of the Piedra Alumbre where a number of enemies assemble to commit killings and robberies. You will reconnoiter and clear that territory; and you will search for the bones of Captains Alonso Fernández and Juan de Herrera, who died by the hand of the said enemies, and you will bring them to a settled place so that they may be buried in consecrated ground. And because some cases may present themselves which cannot be foreseen now, I charge and order you to act in everything as one who is at the scene of action. And on your return you will inform me about everything you have dome, dispatching messengers from a safe place.

You will execute this as ordered, and for the fulfillment of the same I ordered [this instruction] issued to you, signed by my name and attested by the secretary.

Issued in the villa of Santa Fe on July 12 of the year 1678. Don Antonio de Otermín (rubric). By order of his lordship, Francisco Xavier, secretary of war and government (rubric).

In the villa of Santa Fe of New Mexico on the twenty-third day of the month of August of the year 1678, before don Antonio de Otermín, governor and captain general of this kingdom for His Majesty, Maestre de Campo don Juan Domínguez de Mendoza, lieutenant captain general appointed by me for this campaign, presented this instruction together with the commission which was given him to carry it out and to punish and wage just war against the Apache enemies.[2] He asked for certification that he had executed all the orders he received with all prudence, valor, and resolution, and asked for his honorable discharge, which was given him. And so it may be of record, his lordship signed it in my presence as secretary of government and war. Don Antonio de Otermín (rubric). By order of his lordship, Francisco Xavier, secretary of government and war (rubric).

Notes

1. BNE, Madrid, MSS 19258, photos 134–136.
2. See Doc. 33, supra, Commission as Lieutenant Captain General in Campaign, Santa Fe, July 12, 1678.

Document 35

Commission as Lieutenant Captain General in Campaign
Santa Fe, October 28, 1678[1]

Don Antonio de Otermín, governor and captain general of the kingdom and provinces of New Mexico for His Majesty, etc.

I have created a detachment and active army of fifty soldiers [to serve as] mounted harquebusiers, and four hundred Christian Indians [armed] with bows and arrows, both of which were enlisted to accompany me to inflict punishment and just war on the infidel enemy Indians, the Apache nation of the mountain ranges of the west.[2] In order to restrain their insolence, their crimes and atrocities have been punished in the general destruction inflicted upon them by my order, which resulted in the death of some of them and the capture of others. Nevertheless, adding crimes, they lay in ambush at the Peñol de San Esteban de Acoma where they destroyed some sowing, killed an Indian, and attempted to destroy the said pueblo and stronghold. They have committed other ravages in other jurisdictions, atrociously killing the settled Indians on the roads and trails; and their audacity and shamelessness have extended so far that they carried off seven animals from this villa, there being nothing safe from the said enemies. All these crimes demand severe punishment, and for this reason, seeking the greatest services of God, our Lord, and of His Majesty, I arranged to go forth in person to execute the necessary reprisals; but I am ill in bed and the time appointed for the said enrollment is drawing near. Therefore, in order that so important a thing may be carried into effect, it is fitting to appoint a person in my place as my lieutenant captain general in campaign with all plenary authority to march from the plaza de armas of the pueblo of Zía in good order and military discipline to the said mountain ranges of the west of Casa Fuerte Navajo, *peñoles*, and other places which may seem necessary to him, attacking the said enemies with great destruction and burning all their grain supply which may be found.

Because you, Maestre de Campo don Juan Domínguez de Mendoza, are well qualified for the said purpose and because I am satisfied that you will act with resolution and determination, maintaining good relations among the people who follow you so that, united and content, they may better employ themselves in the services of both Majesties; and in order that you may execute and arrange all that is necessary as if I were present, I give you as sufficient power and authority as is required by law and is necessary. And I order the other military commanders, retired [commanders], and encomenderos, and the Christian natives to hold, consider, esteem, and obey you as such my lieutenant captain general in campaign, and to observe, fulfill, and execute the orders which you may give them in the service of His Majesty under penalties imposed by law, for such is the will of His Majesty and mine in his royal name. You will carry out in its entirety the instruction which is given you with this, because for all of it and in order that you may bear the usual insignia and enjoy the honors, favors, privileges, and liberties which are due to you, signed by my name and sealed with the seal of my arms, and countersigned by the secretary of government and war.[3]

Issued in the Villa of Santa Fe on the twenty-eighth day of the month of October of the year 1678. (Seal) Don Antonio de Otermín (rubric). By the order of his lordship, Francisco Xavier, secretary of government and war (rubric).

In the Villa of Santa Fe of New Mexico on the twenty-sixth day of the month of November of the year 1678, before don Antonio de Otermín, governor and captain general of this kingdom for His Majesty, this title was presented by the person mentioned in it, who asked for his honorable discharge and certification that he had served during the time the campaign lasted and fulfilled and executed the orders he received. His lordship states that the aforesaid is a very honorable soldier, valorous, and deserving that His Majesty honor him for having executed and fulfilled what he was ordered to do. He burned and destroyed more than 250 fanegas of maize, and it is public knowledge that he captured the wives and children of the infidel Apache enemies, put to rout an ambush they had prepared on a mesa, burned their settlements, and won many spoils, actions worthy of every reward. And in order that it may be of record, and at his petition, I issued the present writing, signed by my name, sealed with the seal of my arms, and countersigned by the secretary of government and war.

Done in the Villa of Santa Fe on the twenty-sixth day of the month of November of the past year 1678. Don Antonio de Otermín (rubric). (Seal) By order of the governor and captain general, Francisco Xavier, secretary of government and war (rubric).

Notes

1. BNE, Madrid, MSS 19258, photos 128–130.
2. The Apaches here mentioned were evidently the Navajo.
3. See Doc. 36, infra, Instruction as Lieutenant Captain General, Santa Fe, October 28, 1678.

Document 36

Instruction as Lieutenant Captain General
Santa Fe, October 28, 1678[1]

Don Antonio de Otermín, governor and captain general of the kingdom and provinces of New Mexico for His Majesty, etc.

To you, Maestre de Campo don Juan [Domínguez] de Mendoza, whom I have appointed as my lieutenant captain general in campaign, for the punishment and just war which is being waged at present: I order and command you to observe, fulfill, and execute the following instruction in its entirety.

In the first place, after holding the customary muster in the plaza de armas of the pueblo de Zía, you will march forth with all the enlisted force, taking your army in all good military order, following the most suitable direct route and the one by which you may go most concealed; always sending good guides and spies in advance of your main guard to see whether one or more of the enemies, who are wont to come and kill and rob, or to hunt, can be seized so that you may get information from them to ensure the success of your journey.

You will treat the Spanish soldiers and natives who follow you with kindness and courtesy so that all, united and in agreement, may execute your orders, as is my intent, employing themselves in the Service of God, our Lord, and of His Majesty as they have always done, because the desired end, which is so important, is the punishment of the atrocities and systematic robberies committed by the said enemies.

You will carry out the reprisal which may be necessary with all resolution and prudence, attacking the said enemies with great determination in order to achieve an exemplary punishment; and you will destroy all the grain and seeds of their maintenance, taking all possible precautions so that none may remain for them.

In all the assaults you make you will try to discover, find, and collect the things pertaining to the divine worship held by the holy temples; and you will give those you seize to the reverend father chaplain, as minister and priest, for safe-keeping, to whom they belong.

You will try to release from captivity all the Christian persons whom the said enemies are holding, and you will bring them to me to be set at liberty, congregating them in the pueblos of which they were natives. And because of the number of the attacks which are made, and since they can be given a lighter punishment than death, you will not permit them to be killed but rather allow them to receive holy baptism.

All the citizens and natives of this kingdom are serving His Majesty at their own cost, and in the continual warfare the enemies rob them of the animals which form the principal means for making war, and some of these [animals] usually fall in attacks which are made. Therefore, I order that if the beasts of those Spaniards and Indians who go on the campaign should tire, or if they should lose some of them in the service of His Majesty, you are to give them others from those you may seize. If anyone should recognize one which the said enemies have stolen from him, you will return it to him, with the understanding that it shall not be counted as part of the share of the spoils which are taken. And this is always to be observed, since it is applicable to everyone.

And because, in addition, many things may come up which cannot be foreseen now, obtaining the advice of the practiced and experienced persons under your command, you will act in everything as one who is on the scene, always attempting to inflict all the punishment necessary in such a manner that you may win reputation with friends and enemies. For all this I ordered the present writing issued to you, signed by my name and sealed with the seal of my arms, and countersigned by the undersigned secretary of government and war.

Issued in the Villa of Santa Fe on the twenty-eighth day of the month of October of the year 1678. (Seal) Don Antonio de Otermín (rubric). By order of his lordship, Francisco Xavier, secretary of government and war (rubric).

In the Villa of Santa Fe of New Mexico on the twenty-sixth day of the month of November of the year 1678, before don Antonio de Otermín, governor and captain general of this kingdom for His Majesty, the person mentioned in it presented this instruction and asked for his honorable discharge. His lordship gave it to him, certifying that he has fulfilled what is contained in it as is proved by the honorable discharge of the commission.[2] And he signed it before me, the present secretary. Don Antonio de Ortermín (rubric). By order of his lordship, Francisco Xavier, secretary of government and war (rubric).

Notes

1. BNE, Madrid, MSS 19258, photos 131–133.
2. See Doc. 35, supra, Commission as Lieutenant Captain General in Campaign, Santa Fe, October 28, 1678.

Document 37

Title of Encomienda of the Pueblo of Isleta
Santa Fe, November 26, 1678[1]

Don Antonio de Otermín, governor and captain general of the kingdom and provinces of New Mexico for His Majesty, etc.

Inasmuch as the death of Maestre de Campo Francisco de Valencia has left vacant the share of the encomienda which he enjoyed by favor of His Majesty, who makes such grants for three lives to those who continually serve him in this kingdom, giving them by way of salary and recompense the tributes which the settled Christian Indians owe His Majesty in recognition of vassalage; and since the said Maestre de Campo Francisco de Valencia died without leaving a legitimate son to succeed in the said encomienda, his share became vacant and may be conferred in the name of His Majesty on suitable and deserving persons who have rendered services, [and] who shall be obliged to occupy themselves in the royal service in the defense of this kingdom.[2]

Maestre de Campo don Juan Domínguez de Mendoza has performed many [services] for more than twenty-eight years in this region, serving in all the military operations which have been necessary, both as commander and subordinate, in which he has given a very good account of himself as a soldier of valor and experience. On account of his actions my predecessors have employed him in the posts of alférez, captain, sargento mayor, maestre de campo, commander of different troops, lieutenant of the governor and captain general in campaign, and as such he has executed two important reprisals on the infidel Apache enemies [who inhabit] the mountain ranges of Casa Fuerte, Navajo, Río Grande, and other jurisdictions. In the first engagement he inflicted upon them general destruction of their fields and grain, killed many of the said enemy, and captured a number of their women and children, not counting other damages they received. On the second occasion he also burned a large quantity of their maize, beans and other plants, and killed many of the said enemies, putting them to rout on a stronghold where they had prepared an ambush, and capturing some of their women and children; and he burned and demolished their settlements and houses, and restored some Christian captives whom the said enemies had carried off in the raids they are wont to make on the settled Christians.

All these services are worthy of reward. In remuneration of which, and honoring the aforesaid, in the name of His Majesty, for the three lives which are conceded, I grant to you, the said Maestre de Campo don Juan Domínguez de Mendoza in perpetuity for the said three lives the tributes which the Christian Indians of the pueblo of Isleta must pay to His Majesty, which the said Francisco de Valencia, by whose death they remained vacant, held and enjoyed. In order that you may enjoy and possess them as is customary and under obligation of an encomendero to be equipped with all arms and horses, to defend the said natives from their enemies and [assist them] in their litigations and other matters I order them to hold and consider you as such encomendero and to bring you the tribute they must pay at the customary times and dates, informing them of this title and grant by which I give you authority so that by virtue of it you may take possession and hold the said encomienda. For all the purposes mentioned above I order the present writing issued to you, signed by my name and sealed with the seal of my arms, countersigned by the secretary of government and war.

Given in this Villa of Santa Fe on the twenty-sixth day of the month of November of 1678. Don Antonio de Otermín (rubric). (Seal) By order of his lordship, Francisco Xavier, secretary of government and war (rubric).

Notes
1. BNE, Madrid, MSS 19258, photos 137–138.
2. Francisco de Valencia was a native of the Villa de Santa Fe about age fifty-four in 1665, indicating he was born around 1611, and held the position of *teniente del capitán del Río Abajo* (Lt. Captain of the Río Abajo jurisdiction). He married his comadre María López Millán, which caused scandal that was mentioned as such in testimony before Inquisition officials in the early 1660s. During this time, Valencia and his wife lived at their estancia located one league (approximately three miles) from the Pueblo de Isleta. AGN, Inquisición, vol. 507, f. 300r, Testimony of Maestre de Campo Francisco de Valencia, April 10, 1665, Villa de Santa Fe; and AGN, Inquisición, vol. 587, f. 171r, Testimony of Francisco de Valencia, June 17, 1661, Villa de Santa Fe. In the eighteenth century, the remains of this estancia became the site of the town of Valencia, now in Valencia County, New Mexico.

On May 24, 1661, María López Millán testified before Inquisition officials in the case against Governor Bernardo López de Mendizábal, declaring she was forty-eight years of age (born circa 1613). She made mention of her sister Sebastiana López de Gracia, who lived one league from the Pueblo of Quarac, and thus was also a sister of Captain Andrés López de Gracia. Francisco de Valencia was said to be mulatto, and in his own testimony before Inquisition authorities he declared he was *medio mulatto*, indicating he was part Caucasian and part African. He wife was mestiza, being part Caucasian and part Indian. AGN, Inquisición, vol. 593, f. 120r, Testimony of María López Millán, May 24, 1661, Convento de San Antonio de Isleta. Francisco de Valencia was described as being a castizo (one-fourth Indian and three-fourths European) by don Fernando Durán y Chaves. AGN, Inquisición, vol. 587, exp. 1, f. 169v, Testimony of Fernando Durán y Chaves, June 16, 1660, Villa de Santa Fe. (E & S)

Document 38

Commission as Maestre de Campo in Campaign

Santa Fe, August 17, 16[79][1]

Don Antonio de Otermín, governor and captain general of the kingdom and provinces of New Mexico for His Majesty, etc.

The infidel Apache enemies who surrounded this kingdom have joined in the attempt to destroy Christianity here and have committed many robberies, atrocities, and sacrileges, even attacking the holy temples and barbarously capturing and killing innocent women and children. As soon as I took office I ordered severe reprisals against them. The fields and crops of the Apache Indians ["*indios apaches navaho*"] of Navajo, Casa Fuerte, Río Grande, and other western mountain ranges were laid waste, and in a second occasion I sent a force to burn such grain as might have remained. Maestre de Campo Juan Domínguez [de Mendoza] carried out these reprisals [torn: text for the rest of the page is missing] . . .

In the name of His Majesty I now name him maestre de campo, chief and commander to take charge of a force to be assembled at the plaza de armas in the pueblo of Zía. On the twenty-fifth day of this month he will march with this detachment to the cordilleras of Navajo, Casa Fuerte, and Río Grande. This force is to proceed under military discipline, inflicting all the reprisals and destroying all the crops they are able, until they meet another division which will set out from the plaza de armas of the pueblo of Taos under Maestre de Campo Francisco Xavier. Each division is to try to keep informed as to the location of the other, and the first to discover the enemy will make three great smokes to show their whereabouts, whereupon the other division will reply in the same way. After the two divisions have joined, the two commanders will order whatever action seems best at the time. Every effort is to be made to inflict the same punishment on the Indians of the sierra and cordilleras of Acoma in order to reduce them to submission.[2]

All those under Domínguez's command, including the Spanish officers and soldiers and the Christian Indians, are to obey him and execute his orders under the legal penalties, which he will execute against the disobedient. Therefore this title is issued to him signed and sealed by the governor, and countersigned by the secretary of government and war.

Given in the Villa of Santa Fe of New Mexico on the seventeenth day of the month of August, 16[79].[3] [The signatures were on the lower half of the verso page, now torn away.]

Notes

1. BNE, Madrid, MSS 19258, photos 96–97. This document is written on the recto and verso of one leaf. The lower half is torn away, resulting in the loss of about one-third of the text. The phraseology of the parts that remain is so involved and repetitious that it would be difficult to give a clear, straightforward translation. Thus, it seemed best to give only a summary. The contents of the missing portion may be surmised from the parts that remain. Apparently, the reprisals carried out by Domínguez de Mendoza in 1678, to which reference is made in the first section of the summary, had not achieved permanent results. Consequently, Otermín had found it necessary to organize another expedition, to be comprised of two detachments. The first, under Juan Domínguez de Mendoza, was to march from Zía, and the second, under Francisco Xavier, was to set out from Taos.

2. This may refer to the Navajos who lived in the mountains north of Acoma, or to Apaches who inhabited ranges to the south.

3. The second half of the phrase giving the year was on the part of the manuscript now missing. But the year could only be 1679.

Document 39

Commission as Lieutenant General of the Cavalry

Ancón de Fray García, November 9, 1681[1]

Don Antonio de Otermín, governor and captain general of this kingdom, provinces, and presidio of New Mexico for His Majesty, etc.

At present I am on campaign in this post called the Ancón de Fray García,[2] where I halted to muster and review all the armed force, horses, and other provisions in order to form squadrons, give ammunition to the soldiers, and do the other things necessary before continuing the march which by express order of His Majesty I am making to the provinces of New Mexico for the punishment, reduction, pacification, and conquest of the traitorous, rebellious Indians, apostates of the Holy Faith.[3] By virtue of and in execution of the orders I have received, I have appointed officers of war and the other commanders and captains necessary; and for the better management of everything and in order that with my authority all the matters that may offer themselves in sieges, forays, incursions, and all the other dispositions which war necessitates may be attended to, it is fitting to appoint a person as my lieutenant general of the cavalry who shall possess the requisite qualities of experience, sufficiency, merits, quality and services, [and be] capable in matters of war and zealous in the service of His Majesty.

These and many other [qualities] are found in you, Maestre de Campo don Juan Domínguez de Mendoza, because you have served His Majesty in those provinces for the past forty years, beginning as ordinary soldier. On account of your merits and praiseworthy services the governor, my predecessors have employed you in the posts of alférez, captain, sargento mayor, and maestre de campo, in different campaigns, also occupying you in the office of lieutenant of the governor and captain general, not to mention other civil and military duties, commissions, and other orders which have been committed to you, of which you have given a praiseworthy account, distinguishing your person to great advantage. All this is evident from your papers, patents, and other documents, to which I refer.

In view of the foregoing and because on the present occasion is important to entrust to you the matters which may arise in this conquest and active war, for the present, in the name of the king, our lord, I elect, name, and appoint you as my lieutenant general of cavalry so that you may perform everything pertaining to the service of God and the king with the required vigilance, issuing, transmitting, and executing without restriction all [orders] that may be necessary for the great service of both Majesties. And I order the whole army to hold, consider, esteem, and obey you as such, to observe and fulfill your orders and commands under penalties imposed by law, which you will execute on the disobedient and transgressors, for such is the royal will and mine in his royal name. For which, and in order that the secretary may make this title known, and in order that you may enjoy . . . [the privileges, etc.],[4] which are due you by reason of the said office and bear the usual insignia, I order the present writing issued to you, signed by my name and sealed with the seal of my arms, and countersigned by the secretary of government and war.

Given in this campaign at the Ancón de Fray García on the ninth day of the month of November of the year 1681. Don Antonio de Otermín (rubric). (Seal) By order of the governor and captain general, Francisco Xavier, secretary of government and war (rubric).

The lieutenant general of cavalry mentioned in this title, don Juan Domínguez de Mendoza, served this office in the campaign which by order of His Majesty I made to the provinces of New Mexico for their reduction and the conquest of the traitorous and rebellious Indians, which lasted three months and five days. During this time the said lieutenant performed everything entrusted to him with all reputation and served with all promptness and care, executing and obeying my orders as he has done in all that has been necessary in the royal service. By virtue of this he asked for honorable discharge from the post, which I gave him with the necessary military ceremonies which I performed with my own hands. And in order that it may be evident to the royal councils, at his petition I issued the present writing to him in this plaza de armas of Guadalupe del Paso on the fourteenth day of the month of the year 1682, signed by my name and countersigned by the secretary of government and war. Don Antonio de Otermín (rubric). By order of the governor and captain general, Francisco Xavier, secretary of government and war (rubric).

Notes

1. BNE, Madrid, MSS 19258, photos 94–95.
2. The Ancón de Fray García was located five leagues (approximately fifteen miles) north of El Paso del Río del Norte on the Camino Real. Kessell, Hendricks, and Dodge, eds., *To the Royal Crown Restored*, 380. (E & S)

3. The muster roll has been published in Hackett and Shelby, *Revolt of the Pueblo Indians*, 2:191–201.

4. The photograph of this document in the Library of Congress cuts off most of this line, which is at the top of the verso page of the original.

Document 40

Certification of Services
El Paso, October 13, 1683[1]

General don Antonio de Otermín, former governor and captain general of this kingdom, provinces, and presidio of New Mexico for His Majesty, etc.

I certify to the king, our lord, in his royal councils and tribunals, to the governors and captains general there may be of this kingdom, and to all the royal ministers of His Majesty where the present writing may appear that Maestre de Campo don Juan Domínguez de Mendoza, citizen of these said provinces, has served His Majesty in this region for many years with great approbation from my predecessors, beginning with the post of simple soldier, occupying the posts of alférez, captain, sargento mayor, maestre de campo, commander and chief of different troops in campaign, lieutenant general of the kingdom, and alcalde ordinario of the cabildo of the villa, not to mention other orders and commissions which have been committed to him in the royal services. He has given a praiseworthy account of all, distinguished himself as a loyal vassal of His Majesty, a soldier of valor, credit, and reputation, all of which is shown by his titles and patents, to which I refer. During my government I employed the aforesaid in punitive expeditions and just wars of the greatest importance against the infidel enemies, the Apache nation, perturbers of the public tranquility, on whom he has inflicted many damages and severe punishments, killing many of them, capturing a large number of people, destroying their sowings, not to mention other things of much consequence which the aforesaid has carried out with all courage and reputation. On the occasion when I entered the said New Mexico against the rebellious apostates, he was at my side in the siege of the pueblo of San Antonio de Isleta; and I appointed him commander and chief of sixty picked soldiers with whom he marched to the stronghold and assembly of rebellious nations in the cordilleras of Cochiti. And he has acted in everything as an obedient man, assisting in this post in the defense of this holy temple and Christianity and the royal standard as my lieutenant, observing my orders with all judgment, vigilance, and care.

Therefore I find him praiseworthy and deserving of all the honors which His Majesty, and the governors and captains general in his royal name, may be pleased to do him. And by his petition and in order that it may be of record, I order the present writing issued to him, signed by my name and sealed with the seal of my arms, with declaration that it goes on ordinary paper because stamped paper is not current in this kingdom.

Given in this pueblo of Nuestra Señora de Guadalupe del Paso on the thirtieth day of the month of October of the year 1683.
(Seal) Don Antonio de Otermín (rubric).

Notes

1. BNE, Madrid, MSS 19258, photos 122–23.

Document 41

Statement Made by Juan Sabeata before Governor Jironza Petríz de Cruzate

El Paso, October 20, 1683[1]

In the pueblo of Nuestra Señora de Guadalupe del Paso, on the twentieth day of the month of October of the year 1683, I, don Domingo Jironza Petríz de Cruzate, governor and captain general of the kingdom, province, and presidio of New Mexico for His Majesty [state]:[2]

There has arrived in this said pueblo an Indian of the Jumano nation called Sabeata in his language, and Juan in Castilian, for he was baptized in San Joseph del Parral according to what he has said. Before I reached this post, he had been here and had returned to his land, which, according to what he says, must be about six or eight days' journey from this said pueblo. He was sent from there by all the captains of various nations who have their territories toward the east.

In order that the most excellent lord viceroy of this New Spain may be informed of the story told by the said Indian called Don Juan and his companions, who are six in number, I ordered them to appear before me, and through the interpretation of Captain Hernán Martín Serrano, citizen of these provinces, who is well versed in the language the said Indian called don Juan speaks, I administered the oath to him, by God, our Lord, and the sign of the cross, in legal form, in accordance with which he promised to tell the truth concerning all he may know, by whom he was sent, what he has seen and heard in all those territories, the distance from one another, and which nations carry on commerce and friendly relations with his.[3] He made the following statement:

He is a Christian and knows that God helps him who tells the truth and punishes him who does not. The place where he now lives with many of his Jumano nation is at the junction of the Río del Norte with the Conchos. From here to there is about eight days' journey. He was sent from there by six captains, who are Christians and are called Don Juan, Alonso, Bartolomé, Luis, don Francisco, and Joseph. These, together with this declarant, being troubled because, although they are Christians, they have no minister to teach them the things of God, decided in a council they held that this declarant should come to this pueblo of El Paso to ask for a priest to console them when they are ill, to give Christian burial to those who die, and to baptize the rest of the people as Christians. According to what this declarant says, there are more than ten thousand souls who ask for baptism, and these are Julimes and Jumanos; and he was sent jointly by the said people to ask the favor of the Spaniards so that they might defend them against their enemies, the Apaches, for there is a *ranchería* [of Apaches] very near theirs. The friendship of such long standing which their Jumano nation has maintained with the Spaniards from New Mexico gave them strong courage to make this petition.

He was asked how long a journey it is from where this declarant lives to where the rest of the Jumano people of his nation are, and he said it is about six days' journey; that the bison are three days from the ranchería where this declarant lives; and the river called Río de las Nueces is three days' journey. There is such an abundance of pecans that they are the sustenance of many nations who maintain friendly relations and trade with his. [These nations] are: those of the Long Member Nation, which is a very extensive nation and is innumerable; and another nation, which is called the Grinder Nation;[4] and another, that of the Ugly Arrows,[5] and another they call the People of Fish;[6] another they call the People Who Eat;[7] another they call the People of the Dirty Water;[8] and another they call Tuxaxa; and another nation called the Peñunde People; and another they call the Tijemu People; and another they call the Pecan People;[9] and another they call the people of the alligators;[10] and another they call Joapa; and another they call Quioboriqui; and another nation they call Joapazi; and another they call Geabori; and another they call Borobamo; and another they call Obori; and another they call Camecara; and another they call Beán; and another they call Arihuman; and another they call Utaca;[11] and another they call Tumposogua; and another they call Mana; and another they call the Left Handed Ones;[12] and another they call Quide; and the great kingdom of the Texas; and the Bowmakers;[13] the great kingdom of Quivira; the very extensive nation of the Yutas; the extensive nation of Jumanos; which makes thirty-six nations,[14] not counting very many others who trade with them and maintain permanent friendly relations with them. He considers it certain that they will receive the priests and the Spaniards with the greatest affection, because they are expecting them from one hour to the next, and if the [Spaniards] do not go on this occasion, they will give up hope and all will scatter.

This declarant left two Indians of the Tejas nation in the place where he lives now, waiting for the reply this declarant will take, in order to carry the news to the people of their nation. The latter have told this declarant that in that eastern region Spaniards come by water in wooden houses and they have carried on trade and commerce with the said nation of the Texas. In the said kingdom of the Texas they sow in large quantities and harvest in abundance; and there are many different fruits. The acorn is of the size of a large egg, and the fields are full of very many plum trees of many different varieties; and on all the rivers there are many grapevines that bear many grapes in their season. And, setting out from the place where they now live, which is at the Junta de los Ríos, and traveling toward the kingdom of the Texas, it will be reached within fifteen or twenty days at the longest. This declarant is of the opinion, because of what he has heard from the people of this nation, that they will receive the Spaniards and priests with great kindliness and love, for they have been longing for them and expecting since Sargento Mayor Diego del Castillo and other Spaniards were there.[15] The one who came to see the said Sargento Mayor Diego [López] del Castillo when he was there was not their king but his lieutenant, because the king never goes out and lives in great state. This declarant has learned that there among the Tejas there is an Indian belonging to the Teguas nation of New Mexico, who is well versed in the Castilian language and will be able to serve as interpreter if the Spaniards go there, because he has been there many years and must know the language of the Texas, which is a very powerful kingdom in numbers and this king rules them all. His kingdom borders on Gran Quivira, and they have such frequent dealings with one another that some of them visit the others every day. In this kingdom of the Texas such a large amount of provisions is harvested that they feed even the horses and mares maize, for they have a great many herds of mares which they have bred.

Four years ago, while they were living in great tranquility in their houses and ranches, they saw a cross fall from the sky. It swayed from side to side as it came, although the day was so calm that it was impossible that the wind should do it, for it was not blowing; rather [the cross] seemed a living thing. And the people, overcome with wonder, talking about what God's will with them was, stood to watch the said cross until it came down to earth. Falling upon some wood, it continued to move for a long time like a living thing. It was about nine *cuartas* in length, pure scarlet in color, and of form sketched in the margin.[16] This declarant took it in his hands with great veneration and all the people kept on looking at it, and they saw it was made of one piece. They then realized that God wishes them to become Christians. On this occasion when this cross descended, it happened that a great multitude of their enemies had come to their land, and, finding themselves with this precious thing in their possession, all those of his nation took heart and went forth following the track [of the enemies], and when they were already near the ranchería of the said enemies they wrapped the said holy cross on a tall staff, and, fastening it very securely, they raised it as a banner, each one of them painting another cross on their forehead. They attacked their enemies in their ranchería, which was composed of seventy-eight tents, destroying it entirely and attaining by means of the holy cross the greatest victory they have ever had, without loss of a single man. This declarant has the said cross in his possession, and the Spaniards who go there will see it. On another occasion after this one, when the hostile Apaches came to attack them in their own land, they actually carried off the cross among the things they stole from them. And when they [Sabeata's people] returned later, for they had gone, in pursuit of the enemies, weighed down by the theft of the holy cross, they unwrapped the banners which had remained in their possession here in their land and found the said cross wrapped in one of them. Therefore they rejoiced exceedingly, for since they have had it no evil things have befallen them.

He was asked whether traveling through all those regions which he has mentioned, both the rancherías which are friendly to them and the kingdoms of the Texas and Quiviras, there are watering places near to one another. He replied in the affirmative and said that there is pasturage in great abundance even if very many herds of horses are taken.

The only thing that has moved him to come is to seek for friars and Spaniards in order that [his people] may become Christians and that [the Spaniards] may settle in their lands.

The cross he has is decorated in different colors on the red.

This is the truth as he swore by the holy cross. He did not know how to sign. I, the said governor and captain general, signed it, together with the interpreter, in the presence of the said Indian Sabeata,[17] and they signed it in the presence of the said secretary of government and war. Don Domingo Jironza Petríz de Cruzate (rubric). Hernando Martín Serrano (rubric). Juan Lucero de Godoy (rubric). Diego López Sambrano (rubric).

Notes

1. AGN, Provincias Internas, vol. 35, exp. 2, ff. 30–32v.

2. Domingo Jironza Petríz de Cruzate served as governor of New Mexico from 1683 to 1686. See Supp. Doc. 9, infra, for an account of the merits and services of Jironza Petríz de Cruzate.

3. Captain Hernán Martín Serrano, b. ca. 1606–1607, New Mexico, and a resident of Santa Fe for many decades, appears in many records of seventeenth-century New Mexico as a witness in numerous cases. He consistently identified himself as mestizo, indicating Spanish and Indian parentage. Martín Serrano was referred to in 1626 as el mozo, the young one, and the son of doña Inéz, "*india mui ladina que se trata como española de nacion tana*" ("an acculturated Tano Indian woman whom they treat as a Spanish woman"). His father was the elder Hernán Martín Serrano, who accompanied don Juan de Oñate into New Mexico in 1598.

In the 1650s, Captain Hernán Martín Serrano was the operator of an *obraje*, a textile factory, which relied on Indian labor. Twenty years earlier, on September 25, 1632, at Santa Fe, he had declared that he was a mestizo, a soldier, and a vecino of the Villa de Santa Fe, and gave his age as twenty-five (b. ca. 1607). At Santa Fe, on March 7, 1662, he declared he was fifty-six years old and a "*vecino y natural*" (citizen and native) of Santa Fe, indicating he was born circa 1606. He named his wife as Isabel de Monuera. According to fray Angélico Chávez, Martín Serrano was a widower in 1664. His wife, Isabel de Monuera, must have died sometime between 1662 and 1664.

In the 1660s Captain Hernán Martín Serrano was an encomendero, although the name of the pueblo from which he received tribute has not been identified. His proficiency in Indian languages made him a valuable member of the expedition into the Jumano territory under the command of Juan Domínguez de Mendoza. AGN, México, Inquisición, vol. 304, exp. 26, f. 181r, Testimony of Hernán Martín Serrano, May 24, 1632, Villa de Santa Fe; AGN, México, Inquisición, vol. 356, exp. 140, f. 314r, Testimony of Francisco de Anaya Almazán, May 29, 1626, Villa de Santa Fe; AGN, Real Audiencia, Concurso de Peñalosa, Vol. 1, leg.1, no. 1, f. 74v, Testimony of Nicolás Durán, the younger, February 4, 1659, Villa de Santa Fe; Chávez, *Origins of New Mexico Families*, 72. (E & S)

4. "*La Nazion que muele.*"
5. "*La de las fechas feas.*"
6. "*La gente del pescado.*"
7. "*La gente q. come.*" Perhaps a noun following the word *come* has been omitted, so that the phrase should read, "the people who eat [a certain kind of food]."
8. "*La gente del agua suzia.*"
9. "*La gente del nuez.*"
10. "*La gente de los caimanes.*"
11. Also known as *hediondos*, "stinking people."
12. "*Los zurdos.*"
13. "*Los que hacen arcos.*"
14. Only thirty-five are named.
15. Reference to the expedition of Diego López del Castillo and Hernán Martín Serrano in 1650.
16. Nine *cuartas* is about seventy-two inches.
17. "*Chauiato*" in the manuscript.

Document 42

Commission as Commander of the Expedition to Texas

El Paso, November 29, 1683[1]

Don Domingo Jironza Petríz de Cruzate, governor and captain general of these provinces and presidio of New Mexico for His Majesty, etc.

Juan Sabeata, Christian Indian of the Jumano nation, and others from their settlements have represented to me the fervent desires of their people to become Christians because they have come to realize the benefits it brings to them in saving their souls. They have learned this from some of their nation who already are [Christians] and from many other things which have happened to them which have inclined them to abandon their heathenism. For example, some of the Christians, including don Juan Sabeata himself, because of their knowledge of God, our Lord, have invoked Him and carried the sign of the Holy Cross as a banner on occasions when they have found it necessary to go against their enemies, the Apaches, and they have obtained fortunate victories. They tell me that many other different nations with whom they are on friendly terms and carried on trade and commerce have the same desire, and that because of the lack of evangelical ministers they have not achieved it. Since I occupy this government in the name of the king, our lord, the said Sabeata asked me to give him evangelical ministers to baptize and instruct them in our Holy Catholic Faith. Having seen his narrative, I had him make a statement under oath, and I submitted it to the king, our lord, in the person of his viceroy and royal tribunal of the city of Mexico.[2]

I conferred about the case with the reverend fathers preachers, fray Nicolás López, custodian, ecclesiastical judge ordinary of these provinces, fray Juan de Zavaleta, commissary of the Holy Office, and fray Antonio de Acevedo. Having acquainted themselves with the said statement, they have decided to go apostolically to the conversion of these souls. Knowing this, I ordered an edict promulgated to the effect that all the citizens dwelling in this country who wished to go to the said discovery voluntarily to assure the safety of the said priestly ministers should appear before me within a certain period, which I designated, and present themselves with the provision of arms and horses which each had, in order to perform a great service to the king, our lord, in extending his royal Crown by bringing under obedience to him that great number of nations about which the said don Juan Sabeata informs us in his declaration, to which I refer, as well as by gaining true knowledge of the two powerful kingdoms of Gran Quivira and the Texas and seeing whether it might be possible to conquer them by this method.

The said soldiers who go voluntarily as guard and escort for the said priests and to the reconnaissance and demarcation of the said lands and settlements need to take a person to command and govern them, who should be of exemplary character, a soldier of valor and experience, merits, and quality. These and other good qualities converge in the person of Maestre de Campo don Juan Domínguez de Mendoza, in consideration of how well he has served His Majesty in the provinces of New Mexico from a very tender age, as simple soldier, squadron commander, alférez, captain of cavalry, sargento mayor of that kingdom, and maestre de campo. In many expeditions and punishments which were inflicted on the enemy, the governors, my predecessors, employed him as commander and chief, alcalde mayor and captain of war in some of those frontiers, as well as in the post of lieutenant general of those provinces. He was one of those who went to the conquest of New Mexico in the year 1681, on which journey he occupied the post of lieutenant captain general, taking under his command all the military officials. He was lieutenant of the governor and captain general of that kingdom during the absence of General don Fernando de Villanueva. Of all this he has always given a very good and praiseworthy account, as is evident from his titles, patents, and certifications which he presented before me.

Because I hope that as one so zealous in the royal service he will continue in the same way henceforward, I have thought it well to appoint and name him, as for the present I do elect, name, and appoint the said Maestre de Campo Juan Domínguez de Mendoza, in the name of the king, our lord, as such captain, commander, and chief of all the troop of Spaniards and Christian Indians who go to the said discovery, in order that as such he may command and govern them in good style and military policy in all the cases and matters which may present themselves, making all the soldiers under him respect and venerate the evangelical ministers who go on the said journey, and making the said soldiers set a good example in everything, observing in every way the obligations of Catholics, in order that the infidel Indians, seeing their mode of life, may become favorably inclined toward the Spanish nation. He is to take particular care that the soldiers do not swear, on account of the bad example which results from this practice. And I order all the soldiers of his company and the Christian Indians who go to the said discovery to hold and consider the said Maestre de Campo Juan Domínguez de Mendoza as such their captain, commander, and chief, to esteem, respect, and obey all the orders he may give them, orally or in writing, in the terms and periods designated, and under the penalties he may impose upon them, which he will execute on the rebellious and disobedient, because for it and what pertains to and concerns it, and in order that he may wear the usual insignia, I give him as much power and authority as is required by law. He will observe the instruction which I have issued to him for this occasion, enjoying well and fully all the honors, privileges, and liberties which by reason of the said office pertain and belong to him and as all the discoverers of the new kingdom and provinces have enjoyed and enjoy them, for such is the will of His Majesty and mine in his royal name.[3] Therefore I ordered the present writing issued to him, signed by my name and sealed with the seal of my arms and countersigned by the undersigned secretary of government and war, who will record it in the books in his charge.

Given in this pueblo of El Paso on the twenty-ninth day of the month of November of the year 1683. (Seal) Don Domingo Jironza Petríz y Cruzate (rubric). By the order of the governor and captain general, don Pedro Ladrón de Guevara (rubric).

His lordship appointed Maestre de Campo Juan Domínguez [de Mendoza] as captain, commander and chief.

Notes

1. BNE, Madrid, MSS 19258, photos 8–11.
2. See Doc. 41, supra, Statement of Juan Sabeata before Governor Jironza Petríz de Cruzate, El Paso, October 20, 1683.
3. See Doc. 43, infra, Instruction for the Expedition to Texas, El Paso, November 29, 1683.

Document 43

Instruction for the Expedition to Texas
El Paso, November 29, 1683[1]

Instruction to be observed by Maestre de Campo Juan Domínguez de Mendoza, whom I have appointed as captain, commander, and chief of all the volunteer force going to the new discovery of the Jumano nation and all the other nations friendly to them.

1. First, he will go marching forth with the Spanish soldiers and Christian Indians under his command in the order usual in this country, taking his route toward the east, which is the destination of the said discovery. The day before he is to march he will make all his soldiers and Christian Indians pass general muster so that he may know the provisions they are taking on beasts of burden as well as offensive and defensive arms and all the other supplies of war which are ordinarily used for the said purpose according to the custom of the country. And when this has been done, he will give sufficient ammunition to them, carrying in reserve for occasions of greater need the powder and balls left over after the distribution of a sufficient amount.
2. He will see to it that the priests who go on the said journey to win souls for God are treated with all respect, politeness, and good courtesy in such a way that both infidels and Christians acknowledge

them, and so that it may serve as an example to the [infidels] and they may do the same in imitation. Whenever the holy sacrifice of the Mass is celebrated, all the soldiers and Christian Indians who attend it are to hear it on their knees and without turning their glance away in any direction. And when the Mass is over, after the priest has made a prayer, all are to draw near and ask his benediction with a profound obedience, kissing the sleeve of his habit, in order that the infidels may see the respect which is due the [ministers].

3. From the day he leaves the plaza de armas he will take great care that each stopping place he reaches is set down in writing, with the distances in leagues there is from one to another, and the route he takes, giving names of saints to the said stopping places and to the rivers, springs, lakes, and other watering places, making an itinerary and good demarcation of the lands and roads for the better knowledge of all of it.[2]

4. Whenever he is to advance, with the information he has he will take expert and discriminating guides; and whenever he reaches any settlement of infidels he will take note of the nation, setting it down in writing, with all the distinguishing characteristics they may have and their way of life, and how they are governed. He will try to treat them kindly in such a way that, feeling love for the Spanish nation, they may give obedience to His Majesty and receive our Holy Faith.

5. Whenever he halts and makes camp, he will have it placed upon an eminence in military form, in order that, if the occasion arise (may God not permit it) that it is assaulted by the infidels, they may not be able to injure it, and our forces may be masters of the field and able to defend themselves in such a manner that the Spanish arms win good repute.

6. He will take great care that the Spanish soldiers and Christian Indians live righteously, and he will not allow anyone to cohabit with infidel women, giving this order under penalty of their lives; and in order to prevent so grave an offense against the Majesty of God, he will order under the same penalty that no one dare to remain outside his camp nor enter the settlements of the infidels at night; and that when they go to barter, it is to be in public so that cise more particular care than in any other thing, seeing that it is observed inviolably.

7. He will reconnoiter the river called "*de los Nueces*" which they say is that of the pearls, and bring me the signs of both which can be

obtained, and he will also bring me information concerning the temperature, climate, and customs, as well as about the fruits and food supplies he finds, and especially concerning the pecans and acorns, in order to inform His Majesty with the same.

And because there are events which may happen that cannot be foreseen from here, in any that may befall he will call a council of all his soldiers, receiving their opinions in writing. He will decide it, always inclining toward the greater service of both Majesties, for thus it befits the exaltation of Our Holy Faith and the aggrandizement of the royal Crown of His Majesty.

Done in this pueblo of El Paso on the twenty-ninth day of the month of November of the year 1683. Signed by my name and countersigned by the secretary of government and war, who will set it down to the letter in the books in his charge.

And inasmuch as he is mortal, in case the said Maestre de Campo Juan Domínguez de Mendoza may be lacking, by death or other accident (may God not permit it), I order Sargento Mayor Diego Lucero de Godoy to take his place with the same authority which has been given by me to the said maestre de campo, and for lack of him, Captain Felipe Romero.[3] Done ut supra. Domingo Jironza Petríz de Cruzate (rubric). By order of the governor and captain general, don Pedro Ladrón de Guevara (rubric).

Notes

1. BNE, Madrid, MSS 19258, photos 152–54.

2. It was standard practice of the Spaniards to keep a daily log that recorded leagues traveled, names of campsites, and descriptions of events while on expedition. A league is 2.6 miles. See Doc. 45 (1683–1684) for the itinerary of the journey into Texas recorded by Juan Domínguez de Mendoza.

3. Diego Lucero de Godoy was the son-in-law of Juan Domínguez de Mendoza and doña Isabel Durán y Chaves and was a son of Pedro Lucero de Godoy. Archives of the Archdiocese of New Mexico, Diligencias Matrimoniales, 1683, February 18, no. 3, El Paso del Norte; and Chávez, "New Mexico Roots, Ltd.," 891. As early as 1663 he held the rank of alférez, and he was a sargento mayor residing as a widower in Taos in 1680. He survived the 1680 Pueblo Revolt, and on February 16, 1681, he married María Domínguez de Mendoza, a daughter of Juan Domínguez de Mendoza and Isabel Durán y Chaves. Chávez, *Origins of New Mexico Families*, 25–26, 60. Captain Felipe Romero, born circa 1639–1641, was a son of Matías Romero and doña Isabel de Pedraza, who married doña Jacinta

de Guadalajara Bernardo y Quiros, born circa 1640, Santa Fe, daughter of don Diego de Guadalajara and doña Josefa de Zamora. AGN, Inquisición, vol. 610, exp. 7, f. 63r, Carta a Fray Alonso de Posada, 1667; AGN, Inquisición, vol. 608, f. 419r, Testimony of Doña Jacinto de Guadalajara, April 17, 1667 Estancia de San Antonio; Chávez, *Origins of New Mexico Families*, 43, 97. (E & S)

Document 44

Certification

June 23, 1684[1]

Maestre de Campo Juan Domínguez de Mendoza, captain, commander, and chief of this detachment which was formed for the new discovery of the east and conquest of the kingdom of Tejas, etc.

Insofar as I can, I certify to the royal and Catholic Majesty of the king, our lord, and to all the viceroys, governors, presidents, and *oidores* of all his kingdoms and dominions who may see the present writing, that on the first day of the month of December of the year 1683 the reverend fathers preachers, fray Nicolás López, custodian and ecclesiastical judge ordinary of these provinces, father fray Juan Zabaleta, commissary of the Holy Office, and father fray Antonio de Acevedo set forth from this post of El Paso del Río del Norte de Nuestra Señora de Guadalupe, apostolically, on foot, with their staffs in their hands, barefooted, and with their breviaries under their arms, and they went toward the east, downriver. At a distance of a hundred leagues, which the said fathers had traveled on foot among many barbarous nations, I overtook them and found them at the junction of the Río de Conchos with the Río del Norte. There they had already built two chapels and reduced seven nations, to whom they were administering the holy sacraments which don Juan Sabeata, an Indian of the Jumano nation, gave, saying that inland toward the east there were many more nations who were asking for the water of baptism, the said father custodian, fray Nicolás López, decided to leave father fray Antonio de Acevedo alone there apostolically in order that he might carry on the administration of the said seven nations.

We set out from there marching on the twenty-eighth of the said month of December, and the said reverend fathers fray Nicolás López and fray Juan

Zabaleta accompanied me. I appealed to these reverend fathers that they should desist from going on foot because of the rigors of the winter and the length of the journey, and because their feet were sore and their habits torn by the roughness of the country; as well as for the greater safety of their lives since upon their preservation the reduction of the many souls to our Holy Catholic Faith might depend. The said fathers, seeing that my petition was just, assented to it. We traveled inland more than three hundred leagues toward the east, undergoing insufferable hardships of hunger and wars which the Indians of the Apache and Salineros nations waged against us, there being only myself and ten men accompanying the said reverend fathers. They took vocabularies they had made of the language of the Indians of the Jumano nation, and they went preaching the Holy Gospel to the infidels in their language, and to many other nations who rendered obedience to God, our Lord, and to the royal and Catholic Majesty, which are the said sixty-six nations.

All of these asked the said reverend father fray Nicolás López for the water of baptism, and we also learned from ambassadors whom the Indians of the kingdom of Tejas sent that they were asking for the water of baptism, but, because of the small forces I had, I could not proceed to such important matter as offered themselves in the service of both Majesties, in whose name, divine and human, possession was taken on the river which was given the name San Clemente; and a pact was made with the said sixty-six nations and with many others whose ambassadors were present. On this occasion, during the period we waited there, which was a month and a half, a suitable chapel was built by the hands of the said reverend father custodian and fray Juan Zabaleta, the fathers working in person aided by the infidel Indians of the Jumano and other nations. Among the latter there were some Christian Indians. There, after the chapel had been finished, the holy sacraments and the offices of the Holy Week were celebrated in it. They were celebrated with great solemnity before the eyes of all the nations, the Christian Indians alone entering the said chapel when the holy sacrifice of the Mass was celebrated, attending it with great punctiliousness and devotion. During all the said stay, all who died, both adult and children, became Christians, the said fathers baptizing them; and some who died were buried in the said chapel. We returned from there, making, as I have already said, a pact with the said nations that within a year or so a return would be made and all that offered itself in the service of both Majesties would be put into effect. There the said nations took their leave, showing great regret because we were returning.

This took place on the first day of the month of May of the 1684, and our arrival at the said Río del Norte was on the fourth of the month of June.

There we found the said father preacher fray Antonio de Acevedo very pleased with the good way in which the said seven nations had acted in the service of both Majesties and their punctiliousness in the things pertaining to divine worship, and because he had already baptized more than five hundred persons, large and small, and married many according to our true law, rescuing them from their barbarisms and evil abuses. All the people of the said seven nations and of many neighboring ones came there to welcome us, especially the said reverend father custodian. In my presence and in that of all the soldiers who were with me, they asked his reverend to give them six priests whom they needed then for the good and profit of their souls. For this purpose they had already built six churches. All of them, and especially the captains, pointed out their good behavior toward the said father fray Antonio de Acevedo and the fact that more than five hundred souls in different pueblos were already baptized. The said reverend father custodian replied to this and affirmed for their consolation that at the present time such friars were not available until he should bring them from Mexico along with the other friars who were needed. They received great consolation from this and accepted it.

During the days we spent with the said seven nations I saw that the said reverend father custodian never stopped going to different pueblos, administering the holy sacraments, on his own initiative and many other times summoned by different pueblos.

We left there on the thirteenth of the said month of June and took the route up the Río de Conchos, finding it settled on both sides by different nations, all agricultural as are the said seven nations. Emulating the latter, they asked for the water of baptism generally, alleging that they had been asking for it for many years and that no one had wished to grant it, for their said nations are about are about one hundred leagues from the jurisdiction of [Nueva] Vizcaya.

At the petition of the said reverend father custodian fray Nicolás López, I issued the present writing, with the declaration that it is on ordinary blank paper because sealed paper is not current in this kingdom, with my corroborating witnesses who signed it with me in person as juez receptor, commander, and chief.

Done on June 23 of the year 1684. Juan Domínguez de Mendoza (rubric). Diego Lucero de Godoy (rubric). Hernando Martín Serrano (rubric). Baltasar Domínguez de Mendoza (rubric).

Notes

1. AGN, Provincias Internas, vol. 37, exp. 4, ff. 81–82.

Document 45

Journal of the Expedition to Texas
1683–1684[1]

Journal of the expedition of the east to the Tejas and Jumano [Indians], drawn up by the Maestre de Campo Juan Domínguez de Mendoza.

When all the soldiers of this expedition had assembled at the Real de San Lorenzo, which is apparently twelve leagues to the east of the pueblo of Nuestra Señora de Guadalupe del Paso del Río del Norte, we set out from here on the 15th day of the month of December of the year 1683, for the discovery of the east and the kingdom of the Tejas, in the company and for the protection of the reverend father fray Nicolás López, fray Juan de Zabaleta, and fray Antonio de Acevedo. Juan Sabeata, an Indian of the Jumano nation, who had come with other captains of the same nation to ask for evangelical ministers, acted as our guide. After we had traveled five leagues toward the east, we halted where Maestre de Campo Tomé Domínguez formerly lived. There is good pasturage here on the plains of the Río del Norte, and an abundance of wood. We named it San Bartolomé. Today, 5 leagues. From here the reverend fathers went on ahead with Sabaeta.

On the 16th day of December we left here, traveled seven leagues, following the river, and reached another place which we named Santísima Trinidad. Here the river runs through a narrow canyon. A watering place for the horses was found opposite a high hill upon which there was a ranchería of Suma Indians. Here a cross was set up. Today, 7 leagues.

On the 17th we went on, and after traveling eight leagues down river we halted at a place which we named Nuestra Señora del Pilar de Zaragoza. Here there was a populous ranchería of Suma Indians, poor people, who sustain themselves on mescal, which is the same as cooked palms.² This [ranchería], and others belonging to the same nation which we found today, asked me for aid against the common enemies, the Apache nation. Some of these Sumas alleged that they were Christians, even though they were living among infidels; others, that they desired to become [Christians], and for this reason I promised to give them aid upon my return journey. 8 leagues.

On the 18th we traveled eight leagues from the place called Nuestra Señora del Pilar and reached another which we named La Purísima Concepción. It is a deep arroyo which forms a stony beach where it enters the Río del Norte. This serves as watering place. There is a sheltered corner with good pasturage and sufficient wood. I placed a cross on a nearby hill. Today, 8 leagues.

On the 19th we set out from the place called La Purísima, leaving the river, and after traveling about eight leagues we stopped by an arroyo with plenty of good water which we named [Nuestra Señora] de la Soledad. It is found by traveling from west to east about three leagues away from the river, which we had left to the south of us. 8 leagues.

On the 20th we traveled four leagues over broken country as far as a hot spring. From here we traveled another four leagues until we reached the Río del Norte again and halted, naming the place Nuestra Señora del Tránsito. Here there are good plains abounding in pasturage and wood. Several rancherías of pagan Sumas dwell in the vicinity. Today, 8 leagues.

On the 21st we traveled four leagues over good country and halted near the canyon which the Río del Norte makes here. We named the place Nuestra Señora del Buen Suceso. Today. 4 leagues.

On the 22nd we left the river, traveling along a trail which leads west from here and turns east within a short distance over rough land with many thickets of mesquite, cat's claw, and *lechuguilla* until it reaches the river again. We halted on its bank, having traveled about eight leagues with great difficulty. We named the place Nuestra Señora del Rosarío. In this region there are several rancherías of the aforesaid nation. Today, 8 leagues.

On the 23rd we went on, and after traveling eight leagues we halted. Here the river runs through a beautiful plain and there is a good watering place.

On the 24th, after going eight leagues, we reached a place which we named for Nuestra Señora de Belén because of a great rock on the summit of a nearby sierra which forms a kind of portico with its window. Today, 8 leagues. The watering place is good.

On the 25th, after traveling eight leagues along the course of the river, we halted on a plain which we named Nuestra Señora del Pópulo. On the south bank of the river there is a great rock, with buttresses on the sides, which at first glance resembles a church. There is an abundance of pasturage and a leafy grove. Today, 8 leagues.

On the 26th, we traveled three leagues over hills covered with a great deal of prickly pear. Some horses were lost and for this reason we went no further. The place where we stopped was called Nuestra Señora de Atocha. There is good pasturage. 3 leagues.

On the 27th we traveled seven leagues to another place, which we named Nuestra Señora de los Remedios. The Río del Norte flows east in this region. It has great plains with much pasturage and good watering places. Nearby, toward the north, there is a high sierra. 7 leagues.

On the 28th we went on to another place which we named Nuestra Señora de Guadalupe, traveling seven leagues from Los Remedios. To the north of this place, very near, there are two sierras. The river waters two groves of cottonwoods and plains covered with a great abundance of canebrake. I placed a cross on a height.

On the 29th we reached the junction of the Río del Norte and the Conchos. Here we found several rancherías of Indians belonging to the Julimes nation, people versed in the Mexican language. They sow maize, wheat, and other grains. Here we overtook the reverend father vice-custodian, fray Nicolás López, and the reverend fathers preachers, fray Juan de Zabaleta and fray Antonio de Acevedo, who had gone in advance from El Paso. All the Indians of these rancherías asked for holy baptism and more than 100 persons were baptized. The reverend father fray Antonio de Acevedo remained in the same place called La Junta de los Ríos, which we named La Navidad en las Cruces because of the [crosses] which these Indians had already erected on both banks of the Río del Norte, to instruct and minister to them. These broad plains abound in pasturage and plenty of good cultivated lands. There is also wood in abundance and the climate is good. We remained here one day.

On the 31st we went on, and after traveling seven leagues from La Navidad en las Cruces we halted near an arroyo which runs from north to south. On its plains and nearby there is good pasturage. We named it Santiago. Today, 7 leagues.

On the first day of January of the year 1684, we set out from the arroyo of Santiago. Before we left, the reverend fathers vice-custodian fray Nicolás López and fray Juan de Zabaleta celebrated mass. After traveling seven leagues we halted in a place which we named for Our Father San Francisco. There is a hot spring here, and there is also good drinking water. There is little wood. 7 leagues.

On the 2nd day of January, after traveling seven leagues, we halted on the point of a mesa which extends toward the north. We called the place San Nicolás. The watering place is a great reservoir of rainwater which is caught by a large cavity in a rock, around which there are some ash trees and other kinds of trees and a great deal of maiden-hair fern.[3] On the west there is a great plain abounding in pasturage of crouch-grass. From here we took the trail to the north. 7 leagues.

On the 3rd we set out from San Nicolás, and at a distance of three and a half leagues over flat country we reached some depressions, all of which contained brackish water. Around them white and yellow *tequezquite* grows in abundance.[4] All the rest of the terrain of this day's journey is salinitrous, and in the midst of the saltines there is a little spring of fresh and potable water. We went on for another three and a half leagues and halted among some hills where there is a reservoir of good water, sufficient for many people and horses. It is in a hollow in the living rock, and its inlet is an arroyo which runs west. A number of oaks grow on its sides, and higher up there are cedars. We named the place San Antonio. 7 leagues.

On the 4th we set out from here, following the same trail; and after going four leagues over land rough in parts and with some hills, and in other parts flat and without stones, we halted at the foot of a hill which we named San Lorenzo because of an unexpected fire which placed us in considerable danger. From this hill a spring of good water, sufficient for many people and horses, arises. There is also good pasturage. Today, 4 leagues. On the fifth we set out from San Lorenzo after the two reverend fathers had celebrated mass, and, leaving the trail about half a league we halted by an arroyo which runs through it. It has no permanent water but holds it in some pools. We named the place Los Reyes. Today, 5 leagues.

On the 6th, after the holy sacrifice of the Mass had been celebrated, we left the place called Los Reyes for another which we named San Pedro de Alcantará. We traveled six leagues. We spent the seventh here at the petition of the Jumano Indians, who were accompanying us and no longer had any food supply, in order that they might hunt deer and other animals. 6 leagues. Here there is a great plain, and a spring of good water, sufficient for many horses, arises from a nearby hill. [There is] little wood.

On the 8th we set out from San Pedro de Alcantará, traveled eight leagues over flat country, and camped for the night without water at a place we named San Bernardino de Sena. 8 leagues.

On the 9th we went on, and found water four leagues away. We stopped here, naming the place San Francisco Javier. It is on a plain with good pasturage and mesquite wood. Toward the west there are three little hills, and toward the north, a cliff from which a spring of alkaline, though potable, water arises. 4 leagues.

On the 10th we set out from the placed called San Francisco Javier, and after traveling four leagues we halted, naming the site San Juan del Río. It is a broad plain which has four mesas around it. From the smallest, which is toward the north, a spring arises; and at a distance of about three gunshots more to the south five more large springs arise. Half a league below they form a fair-sized river of very clear but somewhat alkaline water which breeds fish in abundance. There are no trees whatsoever on its banks, and only in parts are there patches of *camalote*. By now the whole army was very short of food, and since bison tracks had been seen, beginning the preceding-day, we remained here the 11th and killed three bulls, thus providing ourselves with meat. 4 leagues.

On the 12th we set out from the place called San Juan del Río, and after traveling two and a half leagues we found a spring of beautiful water which flows north. We went on for another two and a half leagues and halted on a waterless plain which has a range of mesas toward the east. We named the place San Anselmo. Today, 5 leagues.

On the 13th we reached the Río Salado, which comes from New Mexico. It flows from northwest to southeast. [In the original it says from north to east.] It also carries as much water as the Río del Norte. The water is muddy and rather alkaline, but potable. On its banks there are no trees except mesquite, but there is good pasturage. 6 leagues. (Place called San Cristóbal.) [In the margin: This river must be the Pecos joined to the Salado.]

On the 14th we remained here hunting bison, and we killed six. To the east of the Río Salado and about a league from this place, between a mesa and a hill, there is a great saline abounding in good, white, granulated salt.

On the 15th we set out from the place called San Cristóbal on the Río Salado, traveled three leagues following the same river and halted on its banks. Name: place of Santo Domingo Soriano. Here the water of the river is already better. About four leagues to the east of the river there is a little sierra from which a long mesa juts out, and upon the latter another small one rises. It is very temperate country. 3 leagues.

On the 16th we continued along the shore of the same river through flat country, and after traveling six leagues we halted, naming the place San Juan de Dios. 6 leagues.

On the 17th we set out from here after hearing Mass. When we had gone one league, we reached the ranchería of the Indians they call the Hediondos, among whom there were also Jumanos and some Indians belonging to other nations. The captains and other people came out to receive us with demonstrations of great joy, some on foot and others on horseback, bearing a large holy cross about two and one-half *varas* long, of wood, well made, and painted red and yellow. They also brought out a taffeta banner a little less than a vara long, which had in the middle two crosses, one after the other, made of blue taffeta. Don Juan Sabeata came forth leading them, for he had arrived before us, and upon meeting us he used a fuse to fire a harquebus without a lock which he was carrying. I had our men return the salute with two shots. I did not permit any soldier to dismount. The reverend fathers fray Nicolás López and fray Juan de Zabaleta dismounted and kissed the holy cross. Upon reaching the ranchería, which was on a *peñol* on the east bank of the river, we crossed the river by a good ford. Immediately, the women and children came forth to receive us with many shouts as an expression of joy, and all kissed the holy habits of the reverend fathers. Although they wanted to lodge us within the ranchería itself in huts of tule they had prepared beforehand for this purpose, I excused myself with good reasons and pitched camp a short distance from the ranchería on a little height according to military usage during campaign. Place of San Ignacio de Loyola. 1 league.

Here we remained seven days in order that the horses might gain strength and that the army might be provided with food supplies. This was accomplished, for they killed twenty-seven bison during those days. We found the Indians docile and affectionate. They were expecting an incursion by the Apaches, and all the captains of this ranchería, Hutacas, or Hediondos, as well as Jumanos begged me to attack the aforesaid Apaches. I consulted with the commanders and men of experience who were under my command, and because they were all of the opinion that it was proper to do so, I granted the petition. The Indians were very pleased by [my decision] and they presented us with some deerskins to make leather jackets, which I distributed to the most needy.

Several soldiers and squadron leaders, who had been clamoring to return from the time we were at La Junta de los Ríos, rebelled against the commander. They caused some disturbances among the other citizens and great consternation on the part of these Indians. The discord became so serious that two of the malcontents put their hands to their swords with the intention of wounding their commander and made it necessary for him to defend himself. Therefore he proceeded against them according to the usage of war and sentenced them to be shot. But the father vice-custodian and his companion, seeing that this might result in general aversion toward Christianity on the part of all these infidels, as a result of the [behavior of the Christians] who were there, appealed in behalf of the criminals, and their lives were granted to them. Some days later they fled with seven other citizens and a number of Indians and reached El Paso much sooner than the others. So it is recorded in the journal itself, folios 13–45.[5]

While we were in San Ignacio the reverend fathers celebrated the holy sacrifice of the Mass every day.

On the 24th day of January we set forth from the place and ranchería of San Ignacio, traveled five leagues, and halted without water on a plain with little pasturage which we named La Conversión de San Pablo. Here we learned that Juan Sabeata and other captains were going in pursuit of the Apaches, who were carrying off the horse herds. Train toward the east, 5 leagues.

On the 25th we set out from La Conversión de San Pablo, and after traveling five leagues over flat country, killing five bison on our way, we halted near a flat on which we found a spring of pure and good water, sufficient pasturage and wood, and many bison. We named the place San Onofre.

We remained here two days in order that the horses might recuperate, and during that time we killed thirty-four bison. Here the infidel Indians whom they call the Arcos Tuertos joined us.[6] They resemble the Sumas in their clothing and other characteristics. Five leagues.

On the 28th we left San Onofre, and after traveling three leagues we halted near a spring of good water which we named San Marcos. There is good pasturage and sufficient wood. Some horses lost and for this reason we remained here twenty-ninth and thirtieth. We killed thirty-one bison. 3 leagues.

On the 31st we set out from San Marcos, and after going four leagues we halted at an arroyo which we named San José. There is a large pool of good water in it, and in the environs there is sufficient wood and good pasturage. Because of these advantages we remained here the first day of February. From here we went on to another place which we named Nuestra Señora de la Candelaria, having traveled six leagues from the place called San José. 6 leagues.

This is the place where the Río de las Nueces, the course of which is toward the east, arises from several springs. It abounds in fish and we caught some catfish. It is a pleasant place, with a great deal of wood and good pasturage.

On the second day of February of the year 1684, day of Nuestra Señora de la Candelaria, the reverend father fray Nicolás López sang mass and the reverend father fray Juan de Zabaleta said another. Then we continued our march, and after we had gone three leagues we halted on the bank of a river carrying much water. We do not know its source because a short distance to the northwest it flows hidden and near here it issues between rocks, on the crest of which I placed a holy cross. Water dogs (so they are called around here) of various colors and of the same species and size as tame dogs, breed there, and although they are bred in the water, these Indians say that they are so fierce that when the bison come down to drink they attack and bite them. The course of this river is toward the east and it joins the [Río] de las Conchas. It breeds a variety of fish, and there are also many shells on its banks. It has extensive plains abounding in pasturage and dense groves of very tall, thick oaks, and also large pecan trees and fruit-bearing trees in such a great abundance that the whole army was supplied with good nuts which were still lying on the ground. Around here there are also many game birds. We named the place El Arcángel San Miguel. Today, 3 leagues.

We remained here two days and a half, pasturing the horses. During this time the Apaches stole nine animals from us, seven belonging to the Jumanos and other Indians who were accompanying us, and two of ours. We could not follow them because they had seized too great an advantage.

On the 6th we left San Miguel and the Río de las Nueces, and after traveling six leagues we reached a little river and halted in a plaza formed by a nearby grove of pecan trees and oaks. We named the place San Diego. 6 leagues.

Here we learned that there was a ranchería of Apaches nearby. We sent spies to see whether it was true and delayed four days, waiting for them; it was useless, for they were not found. During these days we killed sixty bison.

On the 11th we set out from San Diego, and because it was raining a great deal, we halted four leagues away in a place which we named El Santo Ángel de la Guarda. 4 leagues.

It is on the shore of another river which joins the principal one called the Río de las Nueces, or [Río] de las Perlas. There is an abundance of catfish, *boquinete*, *matalote*, and other fish in it. On its banks there is also a variety of sweet-singing birds and game birds, and many herds of bison come there, of which we killed eighty head during the ten days we were detained in that place because Sabeata deceived us at each step, saying that the Apaches were near. We also delayed in order that the horses might recover strength.

On the 21st we traveled three leagues and halted on the shore of the aforesaid river, which we named San Vicente. Here it has broad plains, pecan and other trees, wild grapes, and good pasturage. 3 leagues.

On the 22nd we set out from San Vicente and at a distance of five leagues reached the river they call [Río] de las Nueces, or, for another name, [Río] de las Perlas, into which all the others except the Río Salado empty. Although there is an abundance of pecan trees on the banks of the others, and shells in some of them, this alone is one that is called the Río de las Nueces, or [Río] de las Perlas, and now by the new name of San Pedro. It is the very one to which the governor and captain general, don Domingo Jironza Petríz de Cruzate, ordered me to go in his instructions. Therefore his order has now been carried out. We are about eight leagues from the place which don Diego de Guadalajara reached.[7] There is an abundance of pecans and other trees on its banks. 5 leagues.

On the 23rd we remained on the Río de San Pedro. On the 24th we went on and halted after six leagues, naming the place San Pablo. There is no permanent water here. What we found was rainwater. Because of the bad weather we remained here the 25th and 26th. 6 leagues.

On the 27th we continued toward the east as far as another place which we named San Sebastián, and halted there, having traveled three leagues.

On the 28th we traveled five leagues in the same direction. We received information from the Jumano Indian spies, who were going in advance, that the Apaches were on the road, and we halted at a watering place of rainwater which we named Los Desamparados. 5 leagues.

Here our greatest difficulty occurred, for several of our malcontents declared themselves. The two mentioned above had been sentenced to death; and their lives having been granted them at the insistence of the reverend fathers, they fled, taking with them a number of the best horses and many of the friendly infidels who had come with us. This resulted in such ill feeling among those who remained that the reverend father fray Nicolás López and fray Juan de Zabaleta had great difficulty in pacifying them, since they now considered false all they had heard from their reverences about evangelical doctrine and all that I had told them about the royal service and protection. So bad a storm came up that for ten days we could not travel nor did we see the sun. As a result the horses grew thin and several horses died. Because most of the latter belonged to the friendly infidels, their ill feelings increased.

On the 9th day of March we left this place called Los Desamparados, and after traveling five leagues we reached a beautiful river abounding in shells. There are many pecans and other trees on its banks. We named it San Roque. 5 leagues. We remained here until the 14th.

On the 14th we went on, over flat country abounding in pasturage, trees, and turkeys or wild hens. After traveling eight leagues we reached the source of another river which we named San Isidro Labrador. There are many pecan trees here. In the preceding place about 200 bison were killed. 8 leagues.

On the 16th we set out from San Isidro, traveled five leagues, and halted on the bank of another river which we named San Clemente. In this region it has no shells whatsoever, but six days' journey farther down, according to what I heard, it produces extremely large ones, in many of which there are pearls. It flows toward the east, and on both banks there are pecan trees in abundance, wild grapes, berries, and plums. In this region, there is also an abundance of game birds, bears, deer, a few pronghorn antelope, and a great many herds of bison.[8] 5 leagues.

In addition to the Indians who accompanied us and belonged to the following nations: the Jumanos, the Orasos, the Beitonojanes, Chubates, Cujacos, Taremes, Hediondos, Siacuchas, Suajos, Isuchos, Caucas, Chinches, Llames [Ilames?] Cunchucos, Quitacas, and Cuicuchubes; in addition to these, I say, we were expecting various other nations, who, through their ambassadors, had promised to come to meet us. Therefore, we remained on this Río de San Clemente from the 16th day of March until the first day of May. On a height near the camp we built a fortified tower of adobe with two rooms. In one of them, Mass was said every day and the offices of Holy Week were celebrated with all possible decorum, to the wonderment of the infidels who were with us. During this time the Christians and pagans of the army together killed 4,300 large head of bison, not counting many which were left for lost in the field and a large number of calves which were caught and which are not included in the aforesaid number.

The nations whom we were expecting could not come; and they all belonged to the Tejas, with these names: Huicaciques, Ayelis, Aguidas, Amichienes, Tujujos, Amomas, Manaques, Durjaquitas, Chuncotes, Anchimos, Colabrotes, Unojitas, Chinsas, Quaysabas, Payubunas, Pahuachianes, and others. Seeing that we were no longer able to sustain the war which the Apaches from the north were waging against us in this place, and that which the enemies from [Nueva] Viscaya, whom they call Salineros, were making from the opposite direction, because both had made various attacks upon us and done us great harm, in accordance with the opinions of the reverend fathers fray Nicolás López and fray Juan de Zabaleta, and of the squadron leaders and others, I decided to dispatch to their lands all those who were not to accompany us, telling them that we would return the following year of 1685 and return from here to report to the governor. Only Juan Sabaeta remained behind with a few families of all those who had accompanied us to here, because he feared that he would be punished for his misconduct, and impelled by this same fear, he approached some of these nations to conspire with him to take our lives, according to what they themselves assured us, but they behaved with fidelity toward us.

On the 1st day of May we began our return journey and traveled four leagues. We halted on the same Río de San Clemente and we named the place San Atanasio. 4 leagues.

On the 2nd we traveled three leagues and halted, naming the place Santa Cruz. We remained here during the 3rd and the following night with our arms in our hands because we had received information that the enemies were coming to attack us, but they did not do so. 3 leagues. Route to the southwest and west.

On the 4th we set out from Santa Cruz, and after three leagues we halted in a valley with many great rocks, where a river which we named San Agustín de las Cuevas, flows west. 3 leagues. Here there is an abundance of berries, plums, and maiden-hair fern. We remained here two days, during which Mass was celebrated, and we killed 120 bison.

On the 7th we set out from here and went to another little river which we named La Ascención del Señor. On this happy day our Very Reverend Father Zabaleta said another Mass. We remained here four days, waiting for some men who had gone to explore the country. We killed 250 bison. On the banks of this river, which flows toward the east, there are many berries, pecan trees, and grapevines.

On the 11th day of May we set out from La Ascención, traveled five leagues, and halted near some *bateques* of rainwater which are the only watering places around here. We named it San Lázaro. 5 leagues. We remained here one day.

On the 13th we went on. Within a short distance a youth got lost while following bison. When he did not reappear that day, we spent six days traveling only 14 leagues, in order to search for him. And even yet, in this place which we named Nuestra Señora de la Piedad, we do not know whether they have killed him or whether he is wandering lost. His name is Francisco de Archuleta. In this place the Reverend Father López sang a mass to San Antonio in order that this poor youth might reappear. From San Lázaro to here there is no permanent watering place in the region through which we traveled. The country is mountainous and broken. From San Lázaro, 14 leagues.

On the 18th we set out from La Piedad, and after going eight leagues we halted, naming the site the place of the Espíritu Santo. We remained here the 20th. There is no permanent water. 8 leagues.

On the 21st we went on, and after five leagues we halted at another place which we named San Jerónimo. 5 leagues.

On the 22nd we went on, and at sunset we reached the Río Salado, much farther down than where we had left it because from the place called San Ignacio to here we have taken another route, always leaving to our right the one we took on the outward journey. The one we have been following now is toward the west, with a slight inclination toward the south (west southwest). Here the Indians whom they call Hediondos left us, without asking permission or informing us. And in this same place we at last found the track of Francisco [de] Archuleta, who had wandered away from us. We named the place San Pantaleón. From the time we left the Río de San Clemente we entered much less pleasant land.

On the 23rd we left San Pantaleón, and after going five leagues we stopped by a river formed by two springs, from each one of which a great amount of good water gushes.[9] It flows from north to south and joins the Salado within a short distance. There are great meadows with abundant pasturage, and its groves are of willows and tangles of rockrose. We were there on the twenty-fourth, which was Corpus Christi, and we gave the place this name. 5 leagues.

On the 25th we set out from here, and after going ten leagues we again reached the Río Salado and took the road of our outward journey at the place called San Juan de Dios. We halted at another place which we named Santo Tomás de Villanueva. Here God was pleased, through the intercession of His Most Holy Mother and the glorious San Antonio, that we should find Francisco de Archuleta alive and uninjured. 10 leagues.[10]

On the 26th of May we went on, leaving the road of our outward journey for another route which they told me was shorter, and within eleven days we reached La Junta where the Río del Norte and the Conchos join. I am not setting these stopping places down individually because it is rough land, with little water, and almost impassable. On the 6th day of June we reached La Junta where the aforesaid Río del Norte and Conchos join.

And in order that it may be of record, I signed it as head and commander of this detachment, together with my corroborating witnesses,[11] on June 6, 1684. Juan Domínguez de Mendoza. Diego Lucero de Godoy. Hernando M[artín Serrano].

[Domínguez de Mendoza's diary continues:]

Insofar as I can, I certify to don Domingo Jironza Petríz de Cruzate, governor and captain general of the provinces and presidio of New Mexico, and to the other ministers of His Majesty who may see the present writing, that on the twelfth day of the aforesaid month of June, the governors and captains gathered and assembled with more than five hundred Indians, all of whom belong to the seven nations who have rendered obedience to His Majesty and are subject to the yoke of our Holy Catholic Faith. Unanimously and of one accord they asked our very reverend father fray Nicolás López, custodian and judge ordinary of the provinces of New Mexico, for six priests to administer the holy sacraments to them, alleging that the two ministers who remained with them were not sufficient, because their pueblos are not near one another and there are many people, and as a result the two friars were burdened with a great deal of work. Therefore, in order that it might be possible to minister to them, they have already built six churches of wood and straw, and later they would make them of adobe. At the petition of the aforesaid reverend father custodian I set down the present writing because, for the lack of paper, his reverence did not put the petition in writing. And in order that it may be of record, I signed it as captain, commander, and chief, and my corroborating witnesses signed it along with me in my presence on the said day, month, and year. Juan Domínguez de Mendoza. Diego Lucero de Godoy. Hernando Martín Serrano.

In this place and new conversion of the aforesaid La Junta where the Río de Conchos joins the Río del Norte, on this other side of the Río del Norte, on the thirteenth day of the month of June of the year 1684: When all the governors and captains of that jurisdiction had assembled, I asked them whether they knew or had any information whether at any time any Spaniards or ministers of justice had entered the aforesaid jurisdiction and taken possession. They replied in the negative, unanimously and of one accord, and [said] that all they knew, because they saw it, [was] that the Reverend Father García de San Francisco had reached their pueblos. He said Mass and left them a summons for a later occasion. And after many years had passed, another friar of the same Order of Our Father San Francisco called fray Juan de Sumeta arrived. He came only as far as the first pueblo and returned the following day. Since then they have not seen any Spaniards or any more friars, except those who are here today. Therefore, seeing that it belonged to New Mexico, I took possession in the name of the royal and Catholic Majesty with all the necessary formalities, explaining the significance of my act to the said governors and captains. They asked me to name four captains for them, in order that they might better procure the service of both Majesties, in whose name I entrusted and gave to them the rods of office. And in order that it may be of record, I signed it as captain, commander, and chief, along with my corroborating witnesses, who signed it in my presence on the said day, month, and year. Juan Domínguez de Mendoza. Diego Lucero de Godoy. Hernando Martín Serrano.[12]

The reverend fathers preachers fray Juan de Zabaleta and fray Antonio de Acevedo remained here to minister these conversions, and I, with the reverend father vice-custodian and the rest of the party, left for El Paso on the 14th day of June by way of the Río de Conchos, the Sacramento, Tabaloapa, Encinillas, etc., and I arrived on the 18th day of July of 1684.

[In the margin]: From La Junta de los Ríos to the pueblo of El Paso, 100 leagues by the Río del Norte. From the same to Tabaloapa, 42 leagues.

[The Escalante version of the itinerary ends at this point. The certified copy in Archivo General de la Nación, México, Provincias Internas, vol. 37, exp. 4, contains the following account of the journey from La Junta to El Paso.]

On the 14th day of the month of the year 1684, we left the said Junta de los Ríos, taking the route of the Río de Conchos to the Río Sacramento, because of information we had received concerning the route of the Río del Norte, which goes to the Conversion of the Mansos and El Paso del Río del Norte, which is about one hundred leagues from the aforesaid junction of the Río de Conchos with the Río del Norte, over rough land in parts, with many narrow passes. It was necessary to cross the Río del Norte four times and it is swollen and very dangerous to cross. In addition to the said information, we were told that the whole region of the barbarous nations who frequent the Río del Norte was in revolt, especially the nation of the Sumas, along with many other nations, and that they were lying in wait for us to make war upon us. Therefore, I thought it best, in accordance with the opinion of all the soldiers, to take the aforesaid route, because my forces were small, in order to prevent the said enemies from consummating their evil plans and increasing in daring.

Following the said route [upstream] along the Río de Conchos toward the [Río] del Sacramento, we reached a place with many people about eight leagues from the said Junta. It was given the name Santa Catalina. Thence we set forth again and halted at a foot of a sierra, crossing the said Río de Conchos a third time without any danger. [The place] was given the name Santa Juana de la Cruz, and we reached a very populous ranchería. The distance from the said place called Santa Juana to Santa Catalina is about eight leagues. [The ranchería] was named Santa Apolónia. We set out from there, and after crossing the Río de Conchos two more times, we reached other rancherías which were near one another. [This place] was given the name Santa Teresa. It is about eleven leagues from the preceding place. We left there and traveled all day from sunrise to sunset and halted in a ravine, where a spring served as a watering place. [The ravine] is about twelve leagues from the place called Santa Teresa. It was given the name Santa Brígida. We set out from there and traveled all day—water was scarce—and reached the Río de Conchos at the junction of the said Río del Sacramento, which is about fourteen leagues from the place of Santa Brígida. Here we crossed the said Río de Conchos for the last time. Counting the first, the aforesaid Río de Conchos was crossed thirteen times. This place was given the name Santa Mónica. We left there and reached the pueblo of San Antonio de Julimes, inhabited by Christian Indians very proficient in the Mexican language, who received us with many flattering attentions. We remained there four days because of the weakness of our mounts. The said pueblo of San Antonio de Julimes has an adobe church. We left there June 21 and reached a spring the call El Tule, which is about six leagues from the said pueblo. We left there and reached the hacienda of Tabaloapa, which is about fourteen leagues from the place called El Tule over waterless country. We set out from there and reached the house of Sargento Mayor don Pedro Durán y Chaves where we spent a week pasturing the horses. We left on July 2, and from there we went to the place called Los Sauces to the house of Maestre de Campo Tomé Domínguez de Mendoza, which is about eight leagues from the said house of don Pedro Durán y Chaves. We remained there six days, pasturing the horses and laying in provisions. Then we left and reached the estancia they called Las Encinillas, which is about six leagues from Los Sauces. We left the place called Las Encinillas for El Ojuelo, where we stayed one day. It is about six leagues from Las Encinillas. We left the aforementioned Ojuelo and went to El Gallego, which is about seven leagues; and from there we went to El Portesuelo, which is about ten leagues. From there we set out for Ojo Caliente, which is about six leagues from the preceding place. Then we set out for the place called Los Patos, which is a distance of about eight leagues; and from there to the place called

La Ranchería, where we overtook the mail wagons and their escort. In the middle of this place we found many tracks of livestock which had been carried off, for the enemy is in direction of the Río del Norte. Leaving the said ranchería we reached the place called Los Médanos, which is nine leagues away. We set out from there and reached this haven of the presidio, a distance of nine leagues away, and tomorrow, with God's favor, we shall reach El Paso del Río del Norte and Conversion of the Mansos, which will be on July 18 of the year 1684.[13] And so that it may be of record, I signed it as captain, commander, and chief, together with my corroborating witnesses. Juan Domínguez de Mendoza. Diego Lucero de Godoy. Hernando Martín Serrano.

[Here follows the certification of the copy signed by don Pedro Ladrón de Guevara, secretary of government and war, and dated at El Paso on October 7, 1684.]

Notes

1. The translation derives from a copy of Domínguez de Mendoza's Itinerario, or Log of the Jumano Expedition, which was originally in the Spanish Archives at Santa Fe. Fray Silvestre Vélez de Escalante found it there in 1777 when he was making a compilation of documents relating to the history and geography of New Mexico. He summarized the Itinerario and incorporated it his manuscript collection titled Extracto de Noticias, now located in the Biblioteca Nacional, México, Archivo Franciscano, volumes 19 and 20. Eleanor Adams used the Vélez de Escalante copy for this translation. The original Santa Fe Itinerario disappeared sometime after Adolph F. Bandelier saw it in the late 1890s. Ralph Emerson Twitchell states, "Just when or who carried this archive away is not known." Ralph Emerson Twitchell, *The Spanish Archives of New Mexico* (Cedar Rapids, IA: Torch Press, 1914), 2:77. Four pages of the Itinerario are still part of the collection of the Spanish Archives of New Mexico (SANM II, Roll 21, frs. 126–29).

Bolton's translation of the Domínguez de Mendoza Itinerary, published in *Spanish Explorations in the Southwest, 1542–1706* (New York: Charles Scribner's Sons, 1916), 320–43, was made from a different version found in AGN, México, Provincias Internas, vol. 37, exp. 4. This account was incomplete, the log ending with the entry of May 25 at the crossing of the Salado River. The Vélez de Escalante version continues into July and the return of the expedition to El Paso del Norte. Bolton consulted still another copy of the Itinerario, this one in AGN, México, Historia, vol. 298. Comparing it with the Provincias Internas copy, he stated: "There are few essential differences between the two versions." *Spanish Explorations*, 319. The Vélez de Escalante copy, on the other hand, varies significantly in a number of instances, and readers may wish to compare the Adams translation of this copy with the one presented by Bolton.

Brian Imhoff transcribed and edited a critical edition of the Spanish text of two additional copies of the journal of the Domínguez de Mendoza expedition into Texas. The main text presented by Imhoff is also from the Biblioteca Nacional de México, Archivo Franciscano (caja 21/4431, 1, ff. 1r–33v; 2). Imhoff provides copies of the original pages of this text with a transcription and a comparative analysis with six other known versions. In addition Imhoff includes a facsimile copy and transcription of the Domínguez de Mendoza journal preserved in the collection of the Center for American History, University of Texas at Austin (2Q234, 731, ff. 1r–14v). Brian Imhoff, *The Diary of Juan Domínguez de Mendoza's Expedition into Texas, 1683–1684: A Critical Edition of the Spanish Text with Facsimile Reproductions* (Dallas, TX: William P. Clements Center for Southwest Studies, Southern Methodist University, 2002). (E & S)

2. With regard to mescal, the fleshy heart or bulb of various species of agave were collected in season by Indians, roasted in pit ovens, and served as a sweet and nutritious food.

3. The Spanish term used in the journal is "*culantrillo del pozo*," specifically, *adiantum capillus-veneris*.

4. *Tequesquite* is a crude bicarbonate of soda that forms on the edge of mineral springs and was used for medicinal and culinary purposes. (E & S)

5. This paragraph is apparently an abridgment by Vélez de Escalante of the record of this affair found in folios 13 to 45 of the original journal. This incident is not mentioned in the certified copy of the itinerary found in AGN, Provincias Internas, vol. 37, exp. 4, and translated by Bolton in *Spanish Explorations*, 320–43.

6. Arcos Tuertos means "twisted bows."

7. Reference to Diego de Guadalajara's expedition to the Río de las Nueces in 1653. Domínguez de Mendoza was a member of that expedition.

8. The word used in the text is "*berrendos*," which to this day remains the word for pronghorn antelope in New Mexican Spanish. (E & S)

9. "*Mas de un buey de buena agua*," in the original. The term *buey* is applied to an approximate hydraulic measurement used in some localities to estimate the volume of water issuing from a spring when the quantity is large.

10. Bolton's translation of the itinerary ends here, with the entry for May 25, and does not have the entry covering the period from May 26 to the arrival at La Junta on June 6. (E & S)

11. "*Testigos de asistencia*": this form of attestation was used in the absence of a qualified notary.

12. This paragraph and the preceding one are given in the Bolton translation in the same form as in the Vélez de Escalante version.

13. This account of the journey from La Junta to El Paso is also omitted in Bolton's translation.

Document 46

Certification of Documents Showing the Services of Maestre de Campo Don Juan Domínguez de Mendoza

El Paso, October 3, 1684[1]

The cabildo justicia y regimiento of the Villa of Santa Fe, capital of the provinces of New Mexico, residents in El Paso del Río del Norte, etc.[2]

We certify and attest to the king, our lord, God keep him many years, and to his royal Council of the Indies, and to the viceroys of New Spain and other ministers of His Majesty who may see this, that we know the Maestre de Campo don Juan Domínguez y Mendoza,[3] citizen of these provinces, and that he has served His Majesty in them at his own cost and expense since the year of 1640,[4] when he entered this kingdom to serve His Majesty, and has continued to do so up to the present year of 1684. The aforesaid is the legitimate son of General don Bartolomé [sic] Domínguez who was among the first conquerors of this kingdom, and the said son, in conjunction with his said father, has brought twelve families to this said kingdom at his own cost and expense, important service which he has done His Majesty as is shown by his titles and certifications from thirteen generals who have governed this said kingdom, which he has presented before this cabildo in order that they might be reviewed and registered by it for their greater validation.[5] They are as follows:

A title of alférez real of the kingdom in active war, issued by General Alonso Pacheco when he was governor and captain general, signed by his name and sealed with the seal of his arms, countersigned by his secretary of war and government.[6]

Also an appointment as captain of infantry for the defense of the royal standard and service of His Majesty, signed by General don Fernando de Argüello and sealed with the seal of his arms, and countersigned by his secretary of war and government.[7]

Also, a title of captain and commander in active war, issued by General don Luis de Guzmán when he was governor and captain general, signed by his name and sealed with the seal of his arms, and countersigned by his secretary of war and government.[8]

Also, a title of lieutenant general of the kingdom, issued by General Hernando de Ugarte y la Concha when he was governor,[9] and a certification [issued] after he ceased to be governor,[10] signed by his name and sealed with the seal of his arms, the title being countersigned by his secretary of war and government.

Also, a title of captain of cavalry;[11] a certification in which the services he has rendered His Majesty at his own expense in active war are attested;[12] and a patent of *hidalguía* and privileges from the king, our lord on twelve sheets of paper;[13] issued by General don Juan Samaniego y Jaca, Knight of the Order of St. John, when he was governor and captain general of this kingdom, signed by his name and sealed with the seal of his arms, and countersigned by his secretary of war and government.

Also, a title of maestre de campo, commander, chief, and visitor-general in active war [mentioning the] services which the aforesaid rendered in accoutering for an expedition of fifty men with two hundred horses and the other provisions necessary, issued by General don Juan Manso when he was governor and captain general, signed by his name and sealed with the seal of his arms, and countersigned by his secretary of war and government.[14]

Also, two titles: one of captain of infantry in active war; and the other of alcalde mayor and lieutenant of the captain general in the jurisdiction of the Río Abajo and Salinas; issued by General don Bernardo López de Mendizábal when he was governor and captain general, signed by his name and sealed with the seal of his arms, and countersigned by his secretary of war and government.[15]

Also, three titles: one of encomienda;[16] another of visitador general of the kingdom and lieutenant captain general;[17] and a decree;[18] issued by general don Diego de Peñalosa when he was governor and captain general, signed by his name and sealed with the seal of his arms, and countersigned by his secretary of government and war.

Also four titles: one of lieutenant of the governor and captain general in the Río Abajo; and another title of visitador of the wagons and property of His Majesty; also, a title of visitador of the wagons which left this kingdom with property of private individuals; also, a title of lieutenant of the governor and captain general of the kingdom, presented in the cabildo; issued by General don Fernando de Villanueva when he was governor and captain general of this kingdom, signed by his name and sealed with the seal of his arms, and countersigned by his secretary of war and government.[19]

Also, a certification of the oath of allegiance to the king, our lord, whom God keep;[20] and three titles, the first of maestre de campo of campaign and active war, the second of encomienda, and a title of sargento mayor of the kingdom;[21] issued by General don Juan de Medrano when he was governor and captain general, signed by his name and sealed with the seal of his arms, and countersigned by his secretary of war and government.

Also, four titles: the first of maestre de campo general of the kingdom, and the second of lieutenant of the governor and captain general of the kingdom; two titles of maestre de campo of campaign in active wars; issued by general don Juan de Miranda when he was governor and captain general of this kingdom, signed by his name and sealed with the seal of his arms, and countersigned by his secretary of war and government.[22]

Also, an appointment as captain and commander in active war, issued by the Maestre de Campo don Tomé Domínguez de Mendoza by order of the governor and captain general.[23]

Also, a title of leader, commander, and chief [and] certified; issued by General don Juan Francisco Treviño when he was governor and captain general of this kingdom, sealed with the seal of his arms, and signed by his name and countersigned by his secretary of war and government.[24]

Also, four titles of lieutenant captain general with their instructions and certifications; also, a title of encomienda, and a certification after he [Otermín] ceased to be governor.[25] All the four titles mentioned and that of the encomienda were issued by General don Antonio de Otermín when he was governor and captain general of this kingdom.

And having seen and registered all the said titles and certifications and patent of *hidalguía* and privileges of His Majesty, the Sargento Mayor Lorenzo de Madrid[26] and Captain don Juan Severino de Zuballe,[27] alcaldes ordinarios, and Captain Francisco de Anaya Almazán,[28] *alguacíl mayor* and *procurador general*, and Captain Joseph Telles Jirón, and the Alféreces Sebastián González[29] and Pedro de Sedillo,[30] regidores, certify and attest that the signatures and seals of the arms of the said generals are authentic and genuine as are those of their secretaries, as is evident to us and is publicly known, general knowledge and report.

It is also well known that in the general uprising which occurred in this kingdom in the year 1680, the said Maestre de Campo don Juan Domínguez de

Mendoza collected and assisted all the people of the kingdom as well as eight priests who escaped, to all of whom he gave lodging in his house and hacienda of Atrisco, giving then all that was necessary for their sustenance until Governor don Antonio de Otermín arrived. And all the people having been succored and made ready for the journey at the expense of the said Maestre de Campo, from whose house they set out for El Paso del Río del Norte, which was one hundred leagues away, feeding with his herds all the company who went, giving them a free hand to kill for their sustenance, as they did until they reached the place called Salineta, four leagues from the aforesaid El Paso, where the reverend padre predicador fray Francisco de Ayeta, custodian and procurador general of the wagons of His Majesty, which he was on that occasion, was waiting. And we found the said father with a good supply of provisions and dry goods in order that those in need, who were the majority, might be clothed. [This was] a very pious deed and service which he did His Majesty, for the said herds and other supplies of the said Maestre de Campo had already been exhausted, the said Maestre de Campo having lost and spent his fortune in the royal service of His Majesty.[31]

Therefore, we find him worthy and deserving of the favors His Majesty may be pleased to grant him. And at his petition we order the present writing issued to him with the declaration that it goes on ordinary white paper, as are all the said titles and certifications and patent, because stamped paper is not current in this kingdom.

Signed by our hands and sealed with the seal and arms of the said Villa of Santa Fe, and countersigned by our notary. Done in this pueblo of Nuestra Señora de Guadalupe del Paso del Río del Norte on the third day of the month of October of the year 1684. (Seal) Lorenzo de Madrid (rubric). Juan Severino Rodríguez de Zuballe (rubric). Francisco de Anaya Almazán (rubric). Joseph Telles Jirón (rubric). Sebastián González (rubric). Pedro de Sedillo (rubric). By order of the cabildo, Francisco Romero de Pedraza, notary of the *cabildo* (rubric).[32]

Notes

1. BNE, Madrid, MSS 19258, photos 2–5.

2. The contents of this document do not match what is purported to be an attested copy of the same document bearing the same date and also listing the title and offices of Juan Domínguez de Mendoza presented below as Doc. 52, Attested Copy . . . by the Cabildo of Santa Fe Certifying the Titles of Offices of Juan Domínguez de Mendoza, Mexico City, April 23–24, 1686, which contains

an attested copy of a similar act of the cabildo also dated October 3, 1684. The most important differences relate to the titles that are believed to be fraudulent or reconstructions, as discussed in the preface of this book. Doc. 46 lists thirty-six documents, including one patent of nobility and two documents of *probanzas* (proof of lineage). Eleven of the listed documents are not accounted for in the attested copy in Doc. 52. Of these eleven, nine are found in the collection of documents that make up the Servicios Personales of Juan Domínguez de Mendoza preserved in the Biblioteca Nacional de Madrid (Doc. 2, Doc. 3, Doc. 4, Doc. 6, Doc. 9, Doc. 13, Doc. 14, Doc. 26, Doc. 32). Eight of these nine are documents under question as either fraudulent or reconstructions of lost records, as discussed in the preface. Also, two of the eleven documents not accounted for in the attested copy in Doc. 52 are the patent of nobility issued under Governor Samaniego y Jaca and a certification of oath of allegiance under Governor Medrano, which are also not found in the preserved Servicios Personales. Moreover, a comparison of the signatures of the cabildo on Doc. 46 with those on the genuine documents of 1684 in the Archivo General de la Nación in Mexico City reveals evidence of forgery. For example, the rubrics of Lorenzo Madrid and Sebastián González on Doc. 46 are unlike the rubrics on a genuine original dated October 4, 1684, only a day later. Likewise, in the genuine signature of the clerk, Francisco Romero de Pedraza, the name Romero is written out all on the same line and not as Rome^{ro}, which is the form used in Doc. 46. It seems, therefore, that the certification of the cabildo presented by Domínguez de Mendoza in Mexico City in 1686, and of which we have an attested copy in Doc. 52, was the authentic original, and that Doc. 46 was forged in order to record the additional or fraudulent titles of appointment.

3. This form of the surname written with "y" instead of "de" may be additional evidence of forgery.

4. This date also constitutes possible additional evidence of forgery. All of Domínguez de Mendoza's own statements indicate that he came to New Mexico in 1642 or 1643. Doc. 2 (October 12, 1643) and Doc. 3 (December 7, 1664) contain certain statements in favor of the 1640 date, but they belong to the questionable series of documents. For discussion of the date of his arrival, see Doc. 2 n. 3 and Doc. 3 n. 3.

5. Juan Domínguez de Mendoza was a son of Tomé Domínguez, and thus it is odd that the name of his father is given as Bartolomé Domínguez. This is a blatant error, since Tomé is a distinct given name derived from the name Tomás, not Bartolomé.

6. Doc. 2 (October 12, 1643), believed to be either a fraudulent or reconstructed record. This document is not listed in Doc. 52.

7. Doc. 3 (December 7, 1664), believed to be either a fraudulent or reconstructed record. This document is not listed in Doc. 52.

8. Doc. 4 (April 14, 1646), believed to be either a fraudulent or reconstructed record. This document is not listed in Doc. 52.

9. Doc. 5 (April 15, 1650). The act of the cabildo certified in Mexico City (Doc. 52) listed two certifications by Governor Ugarte y la Concha. Doc. 5, which purports to be an appointment as lieutenant governor and captain general, was probably substituted for one of these certifications.

10. This document is listed in an attested copy found in Doc. 52 and is presented as Doc. 7 (January 12, 1653). Doc. 7 appears to be an example of a reconstructed record, since it falls into Group B of the questionable documents by comparison of handwriting to the other questionable documents.

11. Doc. 6 (November 10, 1652), believed to be either a fraudulent or reconstructed record. This document is not listed in Doc. 52.

12. This appears to be the same document mentioned in Doc. 52 as the certification by Samaniego y Jaca after he left office, which is found in Doc. 8 (September 13, 1653), supra.

13. The patent of hidalguía is missing in the Domínguez de Mendoza Servicios Personales manuscript found in B.N. Madrid, 19258. The foliation of the manuscript jumps from 113 to 121 at this point, and my notes made in 1928, when I examined the manuscript in Madrid, state that there is a break in the binding at this point. So presumably the patent of hidalguía and four other leaves were taken out at some undetermined date. By a royal cédula, dated at San Lorenzo (El Escorial), July 2, 1602, persons who served for five years in the conquest and pacification of New Mexico were eligible for the rank and privileges of hidalgo. Original cédula in AGN, México, Reales Cédulas Duplicadas, tomo 4, printed in Gaspar Pérez de Villagrá, *História de Nuevo México* (Mexico, 1900), 2:6–8.

14. Doc. 9 (October 15, 1658), believed to be either a fraudulent or reconstructed record. This document not listed in Doc. 52, but the title of maestre de campo is mentioned in Doc. 11 (November 19, 1659).

15. Doc. 10 (August 30, 1659) and Doc. 11 (November 19, 1659). Both documents are also listed in Doc. 52.

16. Doc. 12 (May 7, 1662), which is also listed in Doc. 52.

17. Doc. 13 (October 6, 1663), believed to be either a fraudulent or reconstructed record. This document is not listed in Doc. 52.

18. Doc. 14 (January 7, 1664), which is not listed in Doc. 52 but is undoubtedly genuine.

19. Doc. 15 (June 25, 1665), Doc. 16 (October 16, 1665), Doc. 17 (December 16, 1666), and Doc. 18 (February 10, 1667). Each of these is listed in Document 52.

20. This document is not part of the collection found in B.N. España 19258.

21. Doc. 22 (September 11, 1670), Doc. 20 (May 1, 1669), and Doc. 23 (June 27, 1671). Each of these is listed in Doc. 52.

22. Doc. 24 (July 27, 1671), Doc. 25 (August 2, 1671), Doc. 28 (July 15, 1673), and Doc. 30 (July 5, 1675). Each of these is listed in Doc. 52.

23. Doc. 32 (July 1, 1676). This document is not listed in Doc. 52 but appears to be genuine.

24. Doc. 31 (September 24, 1675). This document is listed in Doc. 52.

25. Doc. 33 (July, 12, 1678), Doc. 34 (July 12, 1678), Doc. 35 (October 28, 1678), Doc. 36 (October 28, 1678), and Doc. 37 (November 26, 1678). Doc. 52 identifies "five titles as lieutenant of the captain general in campaign during various military expeditions, [issued] by General don Antonio de Otermín with their [respective] discharges and certifications," instead of four. The fifth title is Doc. 39 (November 9, 1681).

26. Lorenzo de Madrid's second wife was Ana de Anaya Almazán, a daughter of Francisco de Anaya Almazán and Juana López. Madrid was thus a brother-in-law of fellow cabildo member Captain Francisco de Anaya Almazán. In early 1693, Madrid declared he had served His Majesty in New Mexico since 1652 and had been an encomendero. With his wife and children, Madrid returned to resettle Santa Fe in December 1693 under the leadership of Governor don Diego de Vargas and was still living as late as 1715, when he recorded his last will and testament, mentioning his third wife, Juana Domínguez. Chávez, *Origins of New Mexico Families*, 66, 216; Esquibel, "Francisco de Madrid II," 12–14, and "Founders of the Villa de Santa Fe: Francisco de Madrid, Part 3," *El Farolito* 12, no. 3 (Fall 2009): 5–25. (E & S)

27. Don Juan Severino Rodríguez de Zuballe, born circa 1650–1653, was a native of Sevilla, Spain. In 1677 he was forced to serve as a soldier in New Mexico as part of a sentence for a crime he had committed in Mexico City. After his term of sentence had ended, he remained as a citizen of New Mexico. In 1680 he was serving as alcalde of the jurisdiction of Sandia in the Río Abajo region. He married Ana María Varela. Chávez, *Origins of New Mexico Families*, 95. (E & S)

28. Francisco de Anaya Almazán, born circa 1633 in New Mexico, was a son of Francisco de Anaya Almazán and Juana López de Villafuerte. He first married Gerónima Pérez de Bustillos and then Francisca Domínguez de Mendoza, a sister of Juan Domínguez de Mendoza. Prior to the Pueblo Revolt of 1680, Francisco served as alcalde mayor of the Tanos Pueblos. When the revolt occurred, he was in the Santa Clara jurisdiction, where he was attacked and escaped with five other soldiers. His second wife and his children, except one son, were killed during the Indian uprising. According to his own testimony in 1681, he declared he had served His Majesty as a soldier since 1643. He held positions on the Santa Fe cabildo for many years. In 1693, he was *alcalde ordinario de primer voto* of the cabildo and held the rank of sargento mayor. His third wife was Felipa Cedillo Rico de Rojas, daughter of fellow cabildo member Pedro Sedillo, and with their children they returned to New Mexico under the leadership of Governor don Diego de Vargas in December 1693. Chávez, *Origins of New Mexico Families*, 4, 125, 285; Kessell, Hendricks, and Dodge, *To the Royal Crown Restored*, 49. (E & S)

29. There were two men with the name Sebastián González living at this time, both of whom resided in the area of La Cañada prior to the Pueblo Indian

Revolt of 1680. The Sebastián González who was a member of the cabildo of Santa Fe was born circa 1654, held the post of adjunct in 1680, and was married to Josefa Rico de Rojas, very likely a daughter of fellow cabildo member Pedro Sedillo Rico de Rojas. In early 1693 he held the rank of sargento mayor, declaring he had served His Majesty since 1643, and was accounted for with his wife and eight children. The other was also known as Sebastián González Bas, who later resettled in Santa Fe with his seventy-year-old mother, Polonia Varela, and several orphaned children; thus, he was a son of Juan González Bernal (see Doc. 20 n. 4). Kessell, Hendricks, and Dodge, *To the Royal Crown Restored*, 51, 54, 87n61; and Chávez, *Origins of New Mexico Families*, 39–40, 189. (E & S)

30. Pedro Sedillo, also known as Pedro Sedillo Rico de Rojas, was born circa 1610 in Querétaro, New Spain. He married Isabel López de Gracia in New Mexico, and they resided in the Río Abajo jurisdiction prior to the Pueblo Indian Revolt of 1680. Pedro Sedillo was still living in early 1693, when he registered his intent to return as a settler of New Mexico. At that time he was a widower with two sons and an Indian woman servant as part of his household. Chávez, *Origins of New Mexico Families*, 103; Kessell, Hendricks, and Dodge, *To the Royal Crown Restored*, 50. (E & S)

31. This account of Juan Domínguez de Mendoza's services at the time of the Pueblo Revolt does not appear in the certification in Doc. 52.

32. Francisco Romero de Pedraza, born circa 1632–1634 in New Mexico, held the post of alcalde of Santo Domingo in 1664. He was a son of Matías Romero and doña Isabel de Pedraza and married Francisca Ramírez de Salazar. Chávez, *Origins of New Mexico Families*, 98; and AGN, Inquisición, vol. 586, exp. 1, f. 71v, Audiencia primera del Capitán Diego Romero, May 1663, Mexico City. (E & S)

Document 47

Certification of the Personal Appearance and Services of Maestre de Campo Don Juan Domínguez de Mendoza and His Two Sons, Don Baltasar and Don Juan, Issued by the Cabildo, Justicia, and Regimiento of the Villa de Santa Fe

El Paso, October 8, 1684[1]

The cabildo, justicia, and regimiento of the Villa de Santa Fe, capital of the provinces of New Mexico, resident in this Paso del Río del Norte:

The Maestre de Campo don Juan Domínguez y Mendoza, citizen of these provinces, appeared before this cabildo and presented a petition in which he makes presentation of his person and also of that of his two sons, Captain

Baltasar Domínguez y Mendoza and don Juan Domínguez de Mendoza, both his sons out of legitimate matrimony. In the said petition, stating and alleging that in the first certification that this cabildo issued to him, dated on the third day of the present month of October of 1684, his person, the features of his face, and other signs of his person were not described, nor were those of his two sons, neither those of the said don Baltasar nor those of the said don Juan, he requests that this said cabildo, on account of the incidents that might occur, grant him the favor of doing so, as he has requested and petitioned. They are as follows:

The said Maestre de Campo is a tall man, although not excessively so, of good stature, black-haired of goodly countenance, somewhat dark in complexion and going gray, has a good mustache, and appears to be about sixty years of age. He has three wounds, all on the left side. The first is in a shoulder blade, which was broken at the Peñol de Acoma and as a result he has a withered shoulder. The second is in his left hand, the whole span of the said hand being cleft. The third is above the knee on the said left side, across the thigh, and he has another wound on the right side of his head. He received these in active wars, and this cabildo knows it was in the royal service of His Majesty, serving him at his own cost and expense, as is proven by his papers, which he presented for the second time, with two additional titles, one of alférez real of the kingdom and the second as captain of infantry in active wars, both titles of his said son, Baltasar, issued by General Juan de Miranda at the time he was governor and captain general of this kingdom, signed by his name and sealed with the seal of his arms, and countersigned by his secretary of war and government, in order that they may be certified by this cabildo for their greater validation. And thus this said cabildo certifies.

And the marks of the said son, don Baltasar, are as follows: He is youthful of pleasing person, of the same stature as his said father, of goodly countenance and with ruddy and fair complexion, chestnut brown hair. There is a little mark on his forehead. In his right eye at one side of the pupil there is a small light blue mark.[2] He is twenty-five years of age, as we know from his baptismal certificate.

And his son don Juan is a taller youth than the said don Baltasar, somewhat dark-complexioned, of goodly countenance, robust, black-haired, and he has another light blue mark in the same form except that it is on the left side. He is few months less than twenty years of age.

Both brothers have served His Majesty in active wars, and especially in the expedition of the east which they made with their said father by order of General don Domingo Jironza in the year 1684, at their father's expense. He presented them, as has been said, before the Sargento Mayor Lorenzo de Madrid and don Juan Severino de Zuballe, alcaldes ordinarios, and before Captain Francisco de Anaya Almazán, alguacil mayor and procurador general, and Captain Joseph Telles Jirón and Captain Sebastián González and Captain Pedro Sedillo, regidores. We certify and attest to the king, our lord (God keep him many years) and to his Royal Council of the Indies, and to the viceroys and other tribunals and ministers of His Majesty who may see this, and in order that it may be known to be certain and true, we order the present writing issued to him, signed by our hands and sealed with the seal and arms of the said Villa of Santa Fe, countersigned by the undersigned notary, with the declaration that it goes on ordinary white paper, for sealed paper is not current in this kingdom, as has been said. Done in this pueblo of El Paso de Nuestra Señora de Guadalupe on the eighth day of the month of October of the year 1684. (Seal). Lorenzo de Madrid (rubric). Juan Severino Rodríguez de Zuballe (rubric). Francisco de Anaya Almazán (rubric). Joseph Telles Jirón (rubric). Sebastián González (rubric). Pedro Sedillo (rubric). By order of the cabildo, justicia, and regimiento, Francisco Romero Pedraza, notary of the cabildo (rubric).

Notes

1. BNE, Madrid, MSS 19258, photos 6–7.
2. Scholes sought the opinion of Dr. J. Albert Henderson of New Orleans in regard to a medical explanation of a "small light blue mark" on a pupil, as mentioned in the physical descriptions of Baltasar Domínguez de Mendoza and his brother, Juan Domínguez de Mendoza. Dr. Henderson consulted three individuals on the matter. The first individual that Henderson consulted was the renowned Dr. Rudolph Matas (1860–1957), known as "the father of vascular surgery." The next individual was Dr. Womack, an oculist, and the third was a man who managed the Spanish business of the Whitney Bank. Dr. Womack diagnosed the blue mark of the iris as a form of heterochromia iridis, referring to the condition of having more than one color in the iris. Dr. Henderson composed an undated letter that he sent to Scholes at the Carnegie Institute in Washington, D.C.; the letter reads as follows:

#1231 North Dorgenois St
New Orleans, La.

Professor Frances [sic] Scholes
Carnegie Institute
Washington, D.C.

Dear France,

    Yesterday I visited Dr. Rudolph Matas, and brought your letter to see if he could shed any light on the optics of Domínguez de Mendoza.
    Matas is of the opinion that the expression means "he has in the right eye to one side of the pupil a small fleshy mole." The word *sarco* is of popular usage and may mean several things.
    Then I went to a chap who handled the Spanish business of the Whitney Bank and he believed that it reads as follows . . . "and has, in the right eye, alongside of the pupil, a small sea green mole." He stated that the word *sarco* in Spanish is employed when one refers to a person whose eyes are of a color similar to green. The other expression he believes should be read as follows . . . "and has another sea green mole of the same shape, except that it is on the left side."
    Then I went to an oculist who believes that these boys had what they call hetrochromia [sic] iridis. A condition in which there is more than one color in the iris.
    I believe Matas stated that the word *misma* meant in the very centre, if so I doubt that a small fleshy mole would exist there, although it is in the realm of possibility. According to Matas the mole is to the right of the eye. I am inclined to believe that the oculist is probably correct and the expression being used for mole may be a spot or something of that type, being a popular expression. I believe *sarco* can be meant as blue as well as green.
    I do not know if I have been of any help to you. It was remarkable that the farther I went the more confusing were the results.

All at home are well.
Sincerely,
Alfred (with signature)

Document 48

Excerpt from a Letter of Governor Domingo Jironza Petríz de Cruzate to the Viceroy

El Paso, August 26, 1685[1]

With regard to the Jumano expedition, I have already informed Your Excellency in a previous letter that the story of the holy cross turned out to be false.[2] From this it must be inferred that all the rest contained in the journal is probably the same. Your Excellency has already been informed of the behavior of the individual who made it, for having summoned extrajudicially the soldiers who went on the said journey, when I showed them what the itinerary said, they told me that [the truth is] very contrary to its content, and for this reason I sent Captain Diego de Luna to the capital so that he might inform Your Excellency orally, as will be seen by my letter.[3]

I have received information that the Very Reverend Father fray Nicolás López has gone so far as to propose that this governorship should be granted to Juan Domínguez de Mendoza, who was the commander and chief of the said expedition, in remuneration of the work he had. This individual is the one mentioned against whom Your Excellency ordered me to institute proceedings, along with don Pedro Durán y Chaves, against both of whom cases have been remitted by my predecessors which are preserved in the archive of the supreme government.[4] The said don Pedro is the one whom Your Excellency informed me was present at the death of don Luis de Rosas, which they say was so ignominious, although I did not find the proceedings that were fulminated with regard to this matter because they must have been lost in the general uprising in New Mexico.[5] And his said son-in-law, Juan Domínguez de Mendoza, is the one who had Alonso Catití and other chiefs and instigators of that uprising in his hand, communicating and trading with them, and let them go free, as is shown by what my predecessor wrote concerning this matter.[6] Although it is true that I have twice been ordered to fulminate cases against them, I have already informed Your Excellency that I have not done so because of the disadvantages and because the military operations of this time do not permit it if greater difficulties are to be avoided, for the said individual is widely related and his father-in-law is now in the jurisdiction of Parral.[7]

I am informed that when General don Fernando de Villanueva left the said Juan Domínguez de Mendoza to act as his lieutenant general during his absence, he fabricated a royal standard and appointed ministers of justice and war. He had a large number of infidel Apache beheaded in cold blood and under pledge of peace, and he seized their children and wives. For this reason General don Juan de Medrano sentenced him to death but because of appeals he stayed execution. I understand that the proceedings with regard to the aforesaid are preserved in those archives [of the supreme government]. In this kingdom it is so public and notorious that the rumors which have reached here of the pretension he has with regard to this government have troubled all the citizens and they have been scandalized to see that such an individual should have the audacity to pretend to what he cannot obtain because he is a citizen of this kingdom and suffers the impediments which have been related here. My predecessor, General don Antonio de Otermín, Sargento Mayor Bartolomé Gómez Robledo, Maestre de Campo Francisco Xavier, Sargento Mayor Luis de Quintana, and other citizens of this kingdom who are in that capital will be able to inform Your Excellency about everything. I, most excellent sir, have made this relation to Your Excellency because of seeing these citizens so notably afflicted, for as far as I am concerned, any successor Your Excellency may be pleased to send me will be very well received as Your Excellency's choice.

El Paso, August 26, 1685. Most excellent lord, humble servant of Your Excellency, who kisses your feet, don Domingo Jironza Petríz de Cruzate (rubric).

Notes

1. AGN, México, Provincias Internas, vol. 35, exp. 4, ff. 120–23.
2. In a letter to the viceroy, dated July 25, 1684, Petríz de Cruzate wrote as follows: "I have already informed Your Excellency that the fathers preachers fray Nicolás López, vice-custodian of these provinces, fray Juan de Zabaleta, and fray Antonio de Acevedo set out apostolically [to investigate] the reports of the new discovery of the Jumanos and other nations, and that for this reconnaissance and for the security of the said fathers I sent a troop of soldiers with a chief to command them. These persons, sir, have now returned to this land. They bring reports of many and diverse nations and other details which I omit in order not to tire Your Excellency. I will only state that with regard to the cross said to have fallen from heaven this proved to be false, because of the form it had and [the material] of which it was made. It was of a very ordinary, fragile material, and it was almost worn out." AGN, México, Provincias Internas, vol. 35, exp. 2, ff. 25v–26.
3. This letter has not been found. Diego de Luna was identified as a son of María Jaramillo when he registered his intent in early 1693 to resettle New

Mexico. At that time his wife was Elvira García, and he had three children: Gerónima, age twenty-four; Antonio, age fifteen, and Nicolás, age five. Kessell, Hendricks, and Dodge, *To the Royal Crown Restored*, 59. (E & S)

4. Pedro Durán y Chaves was born around 1627, being a son of Pedro Durán y Chaves, the elder, and doña Isabel de Bohórquez. The name of his first wife is not known, but a daughter from this union, doña Isabel, became the wife of Juan Domínguez de Mendoza. Pedro Durán y Chaves then married Elena Domínguez de Mendoza, a daughter of the elder Tomé Domínguez and his wife doña Elena de la Cruz (aka Ramírez de Mendoza), and a younger sister of Juan Domínguez de Mendoza. Don Pedro and doña Elena lived at their estancia located along the Río Grande about eleven miles north of Isleta Pueblo. Chávez, *Origins of New Mexico Families*, 19, 21, 25–26; Gloria M. Valencia y Valdez, José Antonio Esquibel, Robert D. Martínez and Francisco Sisneros, eds., *Aqui se comienza: A Genealogical History of the Founding Families of La Villa de San Felipe de Alburquerque* (Albuquerque: New Mexico Genealogical Society, 2007), 184–85. (E & S)

5. This administration of Governor Luis de Rosas (1637–1641) and his violent death on January 9, 1642, are described in Scholes, *Church and State*, chaps. 5 and 6.

6. Alonso Catití was a leader of the Santo Domingo Pueblo Indians during the Pueblo Indian Revolt. He was referred to as a *coyote*, a reference to being part Indian and part Spanish. He was related to the Márquez family, specifically being a brother of Pedro Márquez. Chávez, *Origins of New Mexico Families*, 70. (E & S)

7. Governor Domingo Jironza Petríz de Cruzate finally instituted proceedings against Juan Domínguez de Mendoza in the autumn of 1685. See Doc. 51 (September 28–October 6, 1685), supra. (E & S)

Document 49

First Memorial of Juan Domínguez de Mendoza to the Viceroy
Mexico City, November 18, 1685[1]

Most Excellent Sir: Maestre de Campo Juan Domínguez de Mendoza states that he has been informed that His Majesty (God keep him) is asking for detailed, clear, and precise information about the lands in the east and north which the most Christian king hopes to settle because of the report which don Diego de Peñalosa has given concerning their great wealth and fertility. [Peñalosa] has not spoken falsely in this respect, for he is acquainted with the whole of New Mexico and when he was governor of those provinces, he traveled over the entire kingdom as far as the provinces of Zuñi and Moqui, surveying all the places of the kingdom. He has detailed information concerning the powerful kingdom of Teguayo because he questioned a Christian Indian of the Jemez nation who had been a captive in the aforesaid kingdom. He also has information about the kingdom of Gran Quivira and the kingdom of the Texas, as well as about the Cerro del Azul, the metals of which have been assayed and found to be very rich in gold and silver.[2] The said Peñalosa wanted to make an expedition to the said Cerro de Azul and had already laid in many stores, but because of the wars with the Apaches and other accidents, he did not carry it through. If the said Peñalosa puts his plan into effect, great misfortunes are to be feared in this New Spain, for those lands are the most fertile and abundant in this New World and they hold promise of very great wealth because of the abundance of minerals. Moreover, the Real del Parral is in those regions, three hundred leagues from the Levant sea, by which Peñalosa intends to enter.

I ascertained their distinctions in the year 1684 during the expedition I made to the north and east, of which I kept a very full itinerary. I entered all those nations alone with twenty men, fighting with the hostile Apache and forcing the Salineros, Tobosos, Acodames, and Gabilanes nations, who are dangerous to Nueva Vizcaya, to flee from their rancherías. Finding myself, sir, with knowledge and experience of those countries, because I have made two expeditions to the aforesaid lands in the east, it is necessary for me to make representations to Your Excellency—as a loyal vassal of His Majesty and one who has served him at his own cost and expense in that kingdom for forty-two years, which is on record in the papers I presented to Your Excellency, as is my having made the said expeditions to those lands—and to warn you of the harm that is threatening those regions. On this occasion, most excellent sir, I therefore obligate myself anew for the aforesaid expedition, and to explore and discover the north sea and to bring back detailed information about the inhabitants of those lands, and to find out the conveniences or drawbacks which the settlements in that region may have, and, at the same time, to find out the wealth of Gran Quivira and of the kingdom of the Texas, for in the year 1684 I set foot upon the threshold of the latter [kingdom] since it is not twenty-four leagues distant from their settlements, being sixty, or seventy leagues from Gran Quivira, crossing the land of the Aijados nation. At the same time I obligated myself to make a map of all that land and coast, just as it is, and remit it to this royal audiencia in order that His Majesty may have the true, clear, and precise information he asks for and may then apply the most suitable measures in order to bring about the reduction of so great a multitude of souls and temporal profits of which the abundance of those lands show so much promise.

[I speak] as one who saw, traveled through, and marked out the confines of the greater part of them.

All this, sir, I can attain in this occasion with great facility, for in the name of the royal and Catholic Majesty I took possession of all those lands, giving His Majesty a multitude of vassals, because I made seventy-five nations render obedience to him,[3] winning all of them to my friendship, as is on record in legal form in the itinerary I made during the said journey. When for seven months I accompanied three friar-priests of St. Francis, who entered those conversions on foot and barefoot to protect them, lending them my personal assistance in building the churches, as they will swear if it be necessary since two are in this city today. On their account I set the example that a matter so pleasing to God, our Lord, demanded. And, having, most excellent sir, already accomplished something and furthered these projects among the said friendly nations, it is very easy to enter all those so abundant lands and to extract their wealth, because I obligated myself to remit the fruits of everything to this royal audiencia. Then what His Majesty so greatly desires will be put into effect, since this is his royal will, without resultant cost to his royal treasury, for it promises great saving henceforward and another new world in those regions. And this, sir, can be accomplished if Your Excellency is pleased to order that I be given two hundred men, even though they are from prisons, provided with arms, and with maintenance as far as the river they call the Río de las Nueces, which must be less than four hundred leagues from this city. Once they are in the said place, thereafter His Majesty will not spend one real on their sustenance, for not only two hundred men, but two hundred thousand, can be maintained with the fruits of the land itself because of the great abundance in those lands of herds of buffalo, extremely large deer, turkeys, quail, and partridges, very many fruit-bearing trees, with nuts, extremely large acorns, blackberries, plums, piñons, dates and other kinds of wild fruits. The rivers abound in fish and are full of mother-of-pearl. All this, sir, I have just seen in the year 1684, and if I should deviate from the truth in this respect, let Your Excellency order that my head be cut off as a bad vassal. In addition, I obligate myself to build two well-fortified presidios in the most suitable locations, for when the aforesaid nations see me, all of them will settle, because they have already petitioned in the year 1684, and a pact was made with them to return to their lands within a year.

All the aforesaid, most excellent sir, I guarantee with my head, if what I proposed should not be put into effect, since my only aim is to assure Your

Excellency of this truth, because I have had experience of that land. At the same time I am inspired by the desire that His Majesty may have this true information, since solely from my occupying myself in his royal service and state in El Paso del Norte, with no few calamities, while waiting for the latest decision with regard to that kingdom and with regard to carrying out the aforesaid journey, many benefits and safeguards result to Nueva Vizcaya, because I have explored the lands of the nations which are dangerous to it. In the year 1684 I reconnoitered their comings and goings, and if they are caught from behind in that region, either they will give themselves up peacefully or they will withdraw to a great distance, or they will perish in the war waged on them. Finally, sir, I obligated myself to find out whether the French are settled in that region, for with the said friendly nations I will assemble a multitude of soldiers, sustained without expense to the royal treasury.

I petition and beg Your Excellency, with your great zeal, to be pleased to decide as is most fitting with regard to this serious matter, since the accomplishment of this proposal can be effected during the fortunate government of Your Excellency and His Majesty given another new world in those regions. In everything I hope to receive favor from the greatness of Your Excellency. Juan Domínguez de Mendoza (rubric).

This memorial was presented on November 18 of the year 1685.

[Endorsement]: It came with the letter of fray Nicolás López of the Order of St. Francis, dated April 25, 1686. Number 8, 1.o.

Notes

1. A transcription of this record appears in Cesáreo Fernández Duro, "Don Diego de Peñalosa y su descubrimiento del reino de Quivira. In Memorias de la Real Academia de la História" (Madrid: Imprenta y Fundación de Manuel Tello, 1882), *Memorias de la Real Academia de la História* (Madrid: Imprenta y Fundación de Manuel Tello, 1885), vol. 10, 74–77.

2. José Manuel Espinosa, "The Legend of the Sierra Azul," *New Mexico Historical Review* 9 (1934): 113–118.

3. Nine at La Junta and sixty-six in the interior.

Document 50

Second Memorial of Juan Domínguez de Mendoza
[Mexico City], November 18, 1685[1]

Maestre de Campo Juan Domínguez de Mendoza states that he has served His Majesty in the provinces of New Mexico for forty-two years at his own cost and expense with his arms and horses. During the aforesaid time he has exercised military offices from the rank of simple soldier to those of alférez, captain, sargento mayor, maestre de campo, and governor ad interim for a period of one year and four months, inflicting punishments on the rebels, pacifying the disobedient and winning them to friendship with us, and surveying all those provinces and places. This is all of record in papers and certification which he has presented to Your Excellency.

Finally, in the entrada which was made in the year 1681 for the purpose of pacifying the apostate, he was appointed lieutenant general of cavalry by order of don Antonio de Otermín, who was governor at that time. On this occasion he performed and fulfilled all the orders which were issued to him as a loyal vassal of His Majesty, as is of record in a certification which the aforesaid don Antonio de Otermín gave him, in which he attested to his conduct as well as in other certifications and appointments [issued] during the period of his government and afterward.[2]

The aforesaid pacification and settlement which His Majesty had ordained to be made, subsidizing one hundred fifty settlers, was undertaken. When they sighted the first pueblo, which is Senecú, the aforesaid don Antonio de Otermín ordered that it be burned along with three other pueblos which were farther on. In his company of the aforesaid governor the supplicant went on to the pueblo of Isleta where the Indians gave themselves up with great docility. One, who was very ill, asked for confession, and, having received the holy sacrament, he rendered his soul to God the following day.

By order of the aforesaid governor I was appointed leader of sixty men, and I went on to the pueblos of Alameda, Puaray, and Sandia, whence I sent reports to the aforesaid governor together with many silver valuables which the aforesaid Indians had preserved with great decency and cleanliness, and told him that he should make his headquarters between Puaray and Sandia because there were in the aforesaid pueblos more than ten thousand fanegas of maize, beans, wool, hides, and other necessities of life with which the aforesaid army could maintain itself for two years, even if it should be active in war.

After sending the aforesaid reports, as is of record in letters signed by my name, I went on to the pueblo of Cochiti where I found the majority [of the Indians] of the kingdom assembled with all their leaders and chieftains. And when I had reproved them as His Majesty commands by repeated cédulas, they appealed to me three times for peace in the name of God and His Most Holy Mother, and of the king, our lord. And when I granted it to them in the name of the royal and Catholic Majesty, everyone was joyful over the happy outcome and both Spaniards and apostates wept. The aforesaid apostates took off their leather jackets and voluntarily presented them to many soldiers. The supplicant sent many apostates to their pueblos with letters.

[At this juncture], an Indian came from the pueblos down [river] to give the news that the governor was burning the pueblos of Alameda, Puaray, and Sandia. This stirred up the whole community, which had already been pacified, and when the supplicant saw the state of affairs, he came to remonstrate with the governor for his blunder in having burned all those pueblos and supplies, for the king, our lord, had sent them to settle, not to despoil, and he had contravened royal cédulas. As a loyal vassal of His Majesty the supplicant was ready to lose his life over the matter, since the Catholic zeal had come to naught and so many souls[3] . . . [illegible] . . . now reduced to Satan's power.

And when the aforesaid governor took a formal juridical statement from them, the supplicant stated that the Indians said they had risen in revolt because they were not treated with justice and on account of three individuals, lieutenants of the aforesaid governor. And this was the public report and opinion current among them. And by this statement and other representations I made to the aforesaid governor [I urged] him not to leave the kingdom, for he had spent only twelve days in the aforesaid conquest, since the apostates were sighted on December 6 and on the nineteenth of the same month the order to leave the kingdom was given.

It appears, sir, according to what has come to my attention, that false writings against my person have been made, to the effect that I failed to fulfill the orders which were given me. The truth is that I have these [orders] in my possession, certified by the aforesaid don Antonio de Otermín himself, with the statement that I did my duty as a loyal vassal of His Majesty. Your Excellency can order this verified by the aforesaid order, which I have presented, in order that the manner in which His Majesty's vassals are harassed and wronged may be known, and that without recourse, because of the great distance.

[This], sir, is the motive which has inspired me to place myself at Your Excellency's feet, so that if I have failed in any respect as a loyal vassal, Your Excellency may order that my head be cut off. On the contrary, in order to await His Majesty's decision, in spite of these misfortunes and hardships I have remained in El Paso del Río del Norte so as not to abandon that kingdom. Moreover, I have been consistently engaged in the royal service, for in the year 1683 I set out as commander of twenty men to the new conversion of the Jumanos and many other nations. There I discovered for His Majesty the richest land in all New Spain, for it abounds in grapes, pecans, acorns, berries, plums, bison, rivers of mother-of-pearl, and hills rich in minerals. All this is legally recorded in the itinerary, which according to what I have been informed, has been remitted to Your Excellency. I surveyed the land of the enemies who threaten Nueva Vizcaya, and made some attacks upon them, forcing them to flee from their rancherías. And this was accomplished with the help of only twenty men and some friendly Indians, as is well known. We were serving as escort of three priests who were engaged in ministering to those infidels. I personally helped to build the churches, as the aforesaid ministers, two of whom are in this city, will testify. My only motive was to give vassals to His Majesty and to safeguard those of Nueva Vizcaya from that direction for the king, our lord; and I did this risking my life daily in order to occupy myself in the royal service, as I will do whenever the occasion offers.

It is necessary for me to bring to Your Excellency's attention so that the reward I have received after serving His Majesty for forty-two years, losing my fortune, which was not small, as is well known, and losing more than sixty-six of my kin, may be seen and recognized. Moreover, as a royal vassal of His Majesty I feel obliged to make representations and inform Your Excellency of these facts because I know that the preservation of this New Spain depends upon settlement of that kingdom, and I see the facility with which it can be accomplished. Therefore, if it should be necessary, I will guarantee on my life to settle it, provided His Majesty makes a grant to aid those citizens and send some men from this city because of the lack which that kingdom suffers; and provided that new orders are issued to the effect that all the inhabitants of those provinces who have gone to [Nueva] Vizcaya shall return. If this is not put into effect on this occasion, within a short time universal ruin can be expected in the provinces of Sonora and [Nueva] Vizcaya, for the losses are already being felt both in the royal *quintos* and the haciendas.

I beg and implore Your Excellency to be pleased to reward my services with your usual Christianity, and that they may have the seal of approval from the greatness of Your Excellency; and that orders may be given to observe the honors due me, since His Majesty grants me such prerogatives by royal cédulas. And I hope to receive justice in everything from the zeal and greatness of Your Excellency. Juan Domínguez de Mendoza (rubric).

This memorial was presented on November 18 of the year 1685.

Notes

1. AGI, Guadalajara, 138; Hackett, *Historical Documents*, 3:354–56.
2. Doc. 33 (July, 12, 1678), Doc. 34 (July 12, 1678), Doc. 35 (October 28, 1678), Doc. 36 (October 28, 1678), Doc. 37 (November 26, 1678), Doc. 38 (August 17, 1679), and Doc. 40 (October 13, 1683).
3. The photocopy of the original document is illegible at this point.

Document 51

Criminal Case against Maestre de Campo Juan Domínguez de Mendoza and the Others Who Fled with Him, Guadalupe del Paso, September 28–October 6, 1685[1]

Initiation of Proceedings [*Cabeza de proceso*]

In the pueblo of Our Lady of Guadalupe del Paso on the 28th day of the month of September of the year 1685, Governor and Captain General don Domingo Jironza Petríz de Cruzate said that inasmuch as yesterday, Thursday, the 17th [*sic*; 27th] day of this month at about five o'clock in the afternoon, he received word that Maestre de Campo Juan Domínguez de Mendoza, Sargento Mayor Diego Lucero de Godoy, Regidor Lázaro de Misquía,[2] Baltasar Domínguez, Juan de Anaya,[3] and don Alonso Rael de Aguilar,[4] soldiers of the presidio of Nuestra Señora de Pilar and San José, captain of the guard of the royal standard and for the defense of this holy temple of El Paso and present secretary of government and war of these provinces all united, allied and convened by the said Maestre de Campo Juan Domínguez [de Mendoza] and the said don Alonso [Rael] de Aguilar, with little fear of God and with scorn of royal justice, without regard for the edict promulgated and the penalty imposed by it, which is capital and of as traitor to the king in him who abandons this province and royal standard, have fled these provinces, violating the said edict and incurring the penalty imposed on it. And his lordship was also informed that Jacinto Sánchez de Iñigo was a party to the said flight and remained behind by accident.[5] And in order to learn the truth about the said flight he ordered that the said Jacinto Sánchez de Iñigo be seized and brought into his presence. When this had been done he administered the oath to him so that under it he might state what he knew of this matter or had seen, heard, or understood about the said flight and who was aware of it or parties to it so that this case may be pursued according to what comes out [of his statement]. The said governor and captain general so provided, ordered, and signed before me. Don Pedro Ladrón de Guevara, secretary of government and war. Don Domingo Jironza Petríz de Cruzate. Before me, Don Pedro Ladrón de Guevara, secretary of government and war.

Statement of Jacinto Sánchez de Iñigo, twenty-two years of age. Immediately thereafter on the said day, month, and year, the said governor and captain general, in fulfillment of the edict, initiating proceedings, ordered a prisoner to appear before him, to whom he administered the oath which he took by God our Lord and [the] sign of the cross in legal form, under which he promised to state the truth of what he knows and is asked.

1. Asked what he is called and where he is a native, and whether he knows the reason for his imprisonment, he said that he is called Jacinto Sánchez de Iñigo and that he is a native of these provinces of New Mexico, that he is about twenty-two years old, and that he has no trade, and he knows that they seized him because he wished to flee with Maestre de Campo Juan Domínguez de Mendoza and other persons.
2. Asked whether he was not aware of the edict made public that no one should leave without express permission of the governor and captain general under capital penalty as traitor to the king: He said that yes, he knows about it and that it was made public, but one day when he was on horseback passing in front of Maestre de Campo Juan Domínguez de Mendoza's house the latter was lounging at his

door, and calling this witness he urged him to flee with him, telling him that the father procurador fray Nicolás López had written him in a letter summoning him to go to Mexico [City] on business he has there. And he also told him that he had already enlisted don Alonso [Rael] de Aguilar, Diego Lucero [de Godoy], his son-in-law, the regidor Lázaro de Misquía, and his son Baltasar Domínguez, and Juan de Anaya; but this declarant, being young, was frightful of the edict promulgated and this is his reply.

3. Asked who and how many others have been aware of the said flight and whether the said fugitives were given provision for the journey by other persons: He said that the reverend father fray Pedro Gómez ordered this declarant to go to the king's herd and bring three mules and a horse he was keeping in the said herd for greater safety, and the beasts he was to bring were a sorrel-colored he-mule, a she-mule they call "la Respinsona," another gray he-mule, and a curly roan horse. And in fact this declarant went and brought the said animals to the pueblo of Isleta and handed them over by order of the said father in the presence of Matías Luján and Juan de Anaya, who had come for them.[6] In addition, the said father fray Pedro Gómez ordered this declarant to go to the herd of Maestre de Campo Alonso García, since he knows all the horses, and choose the best so that they might take them on the said journey, for it was so ordered by don Alonso [Real] de Aguilar since they belonged to his father-in-law. This declarant was unwilling to do it, fearing he might encounter someone. Therefore the said father wrote to don Alonso [Rael] de Aguilar that this declarant was unwilling to go for the horses and this declarant brought the letter. When he reached the aforesaid Juan Domínguez de Mendoza's house, his wife told him that he had already gone. When this declarant learned this, he gave her the said letter. She told him that her husband said he had not been able to let him know because his flight was already being suspected in the pueblo and therefore it had been necessary for him to make haste before they should know about it and prevent it. And this is his reply.

4. Asked whether he knows what route the said fugitives are taking and from whom they are taking letters of dispatches, where they are going or what word they are taking: He said that what they said Juan Domínguez [de Mendoza] told this declarant the day he talked to him about his flight was to say to him: "I will let you know the day we are to start, for now we are busy since Francisco Gómez is

unwilling to give the seal of the cabildo to seal the dispatches we are to take to Mexico [City]." This witness also says that when he came to find out whether the said fugitives had gone, Juan Domínguez [de Mendoza]'s wife told him that her son Baltasar had already brought the dispatches the said father fray Pedro Gómez was sending to father fray Nicolás López. And when the said Juan Domínguez [de Mendoza] talked to this declarant about his flight he told them they were to go by the coast, so that if the governor sent after them, they would not find them and if they went via Parral, he would write to the governor there and they would seize them. And asking him other questions and cross-examining him about the case, he said he knows no more than he has told, which is the truth by the oath he made, which he affirmed and ratified when his statement was read to him and *de verbo ad verbum*. He said he did not know how to sign. The governor and captain governor signed it before me, don Pedro Ladrón de Guevara, secretary of government and war. Don Domingo Jironza Petríz de Cruzate. Before me, don Pedro Ladrón de Guevara, secretary of government and war.

In the pueblo of Nuestra Señora de Guadalupe del Paso on the first day of the month of October of the year 1685, Governor and Captain General don Domingo Jironza Petríz de Cruzate, having seen Jacinto Sánchez de Iñigo's statement, said that in order to proceed in this case ex officio as royal justice and so that those mentioned in it, in view of their flight, should not escape the punishment their crimes deserve, an interrogatory should be drawn up for the examination [of witnesses] by the questions that should be put to them.

1. In the first place, let them be asked whether they know Maestre de Campo Juan Domínguez de Mendoza, don Alonso [Rael] de Aguilar, Sargento Mayor Diego Lucero de Godoy, Regidor Lázaro de Misquía, Baltasar Domínguez, and Juan de Anaya, and whether they know where they have gone or where they are. Let them say what they know.
2. Item, if they know that the said Maestre de Campo Juan Domínguez de Mendoza has received any injury or grievance from the governor and captain general and whether the said don Alonso [Rael] de Aguilar was current secretary of government and war, captain of the guard, of the royal standard, and for the defense of this holy temple of El Paso and whether he was drawing salary from his majesty, and

whether the others referred to had any grievance, let them say what they know.

3. Item, whether they know that the said Maestre de Campo Juan Domínguez de Mendoza, when he made the expedition to the province of New Mexico, went as *cabo y caudillo* of sixty men to the pueblo of Cochiti where the assembly of the tribes had been made, and whether he had in this group Alonso Catití and all the other ringleaders of the uprising and if he could have seized them and did not do so. On the contrary he traded and had dealings with them and let them go free, and let them say what also they may know about this matter and also whether they know or have heard that the said Alonso [Rael] de Aguilar violated the secrecy of what passed before him in secret.

4. Item, if they know whether the said Juan Domínguez de Mendoza and the said don Alonso [Rael] de Aguilar and the other fugitives have been dispatched by some person or persons and whether they are taking any dispatches and from whom, and who have been parties to it and where the said dispatches have been made and on what authority, each then say all they may know about this question.

5. Whether they know or heard about an edict which was made public in this pueblo of El Paso, in the presidio and the Real de San Lorenzo under the capital penalty as traitors to the king for those who might dare to leave this kingdom without express permission from this governor and captain general. Let them say who has broken it and those who have been accessories and everything else they may know about the question.

6. Item, whether they know or have heard that the said Juan Domínguez de Mendoza has been stirring up the citizens and Indian natives by saying he is to come to this kingdom as governor and captain general and has made threats that he will hang certain citizens of it, and whether they know the kind of treatment the said Juan Domínguez [de Mendoza] gave the veteran soldiers who went with him to the discovery of the Jumanos. Let them say what they know about this question.

7. Item, if they know or have heard that in the time of my predecessors the said Juan Domínguez de Mendoza had any criminal cases against him, let them say what they know and which of my predecessors presented them and what sentence was imposed on him. Also, let them state the reputation of the said Juan Domínguez [de Mendoza] and the said don Alonso [Rael de Aguilar] and the others

who fled with them. And I order that all the witnesses necessary be examined with the *autos* that are being made regarding this matter in the absence and rebellion of the aforesaid so that the proceedings against them may be as valid as if they were present and let all the necessary decrees be ratified in the courts where the said governor and captain general usually hold hearings. He so provided, ordered and signed.

Witness: Felipe Serna.[7]

In the pueblo of Nuestra Señora de Guadalupe del Paso on the 1st day of the month of October of the year 1685, the governor and captain general said that in order to proceed with this case he ordered to appear before him Felipe Serna, to whom, being present, the oath was administered by God our Lord and a sign of the cross in legal form, under which he promised to tell the truth of what he knows and may be asked.

1. The first question of the interrogatory having been put to him he said that he knows all those mentioned in the said question, and that he knows because he has heard so that they dare flee and are going to Mexico [City] and this is his reply.
2. This witness replied to the second question that he does not know nor has he heard that the governor and captain general has done any injury to the said Juan Domínguez de Mendoza. Indeed, he knows that he honored him by appointing him captain, cabo y caudillo of all the Spaniards and Indians who went to the discovery of Jumanos. And this witness knows that he honored the said don Alonso Rael de Aguilar with the post of captain of the guard of the royal standard and defense of this holy temple, which he is exercising at present, as well as that he was a paid soldier of the presidio, and that the others mentioned in the said question were treated kindly by the said governor and never received any injury. And this is his reply.
3. This witness replied to the third question that he knows it is so, for he was one of those who went under the said Juan Domínguez [de Mendoza]'s command and that it is true that he had all the ringleaders of the revolt in his group and could have seized them, but he let them go free, which resulted in great harm. And in regard to don

Alonso Rael de Aguilar, the content of the question has not come to his attention. And this is his reply.

4. This witness replied to the fourth question that he knows because he heard so, that some members of the cabildo came by night to the said Juan Domínguez [de Mendoza]'s house. Therefore, this witness is of the opinion that they must have come to draw up some dispatches. And this is his reply.

5. This witness replied to the fifth question that because he heard it he knows that an edict was made public imposing the capital penalty as traitors to the king on all who should leave this country without permission of the governor and captain general, and he knows that the said Juan Domínguez [de Mendoza] and the others who fled with him have incurred the said penalty because of their flight. And this is his reply.

6. This witness replied to the sixth question that he knows because he has heard many persons say so, that the said Juan Domínguez [de Mendoza] has been saying in many quarters that the government is to come to him; and in particular, a few days ago when this witness was harvesting his milpas, a serving woman of the said Juan Domínguez [de Mendoza] went where this witness's wife was, and the said wife asked the Indian woman whether her master was harvesting much maize. The said Indian woman replied that it mattered nothing to her master if he didn't harvest maize because her mistress had told her that they were very happy because the said Juan Domínguez [de Mendoza] was to come as governor and then he would have much maize and he would have all those who returned from the Jumanos. And this witness knows because he has heard it said generally that he mistreated the men who went to the Jumanos with him, for every day he wanted to slap and beat them and he has also heard tell that the night the said Juan Domínguez [de Mendoza] fled he told a servant of his called Cristóbal to take great care of his wife and horse because Father fray Nicolás López had summoned him to go to Parral to receive the office of governor and captain general and therefore that he should assemble the Indians and tell them so. And this is his reply. And this witness also heard tell that when the said Juan Domínguez [de Mendoza] was very wicked that it was best for them all to go to Julimes to live, and others replied that it was better to join and ask the governor's permission and go to see the king. And this witness knows that this has caused great scandal among Spanish citizens and Indians. And this is his reply.

7. This witness replied to the seventh question that he knows because it was public in New Mexico that General don Juan de Samaniego presented a criminal case against the said Juan Domínguez [de Mendoza], which he was told concerned his having killed one or two Indians who were in his service. And this witness knows, because it was public, that the said governor sentenced him to make campaigns and escorts at his own cost and expense. And he also knows because it was also public that General don Juan de Medrano sentenced the said Juan Domínguez [de Mendoza] to death because he had fabricated a royal standard and killed in cold blood and under pledge of peace many infidels of the Apache nation and had taken their children and wives captive and made an allotment of them. And they ordered this witness to go to the execution, and realizing that it was not a great injustice he excused himself. And he knows that the said Juan Domínguez [de Mendoza] is considered in this kingdom to be in ill repute, and that mostly the citizens and natives hate him. And this is the truth under the oath he has taken which he affirmed and ratified when this statement of his was read to him. And he is about forty years old and the general questions of the law do not concern him. And he signed it together with the governor.

Summary of Additional Testimonies

On October 1, 1685, at the Pueblo del Paso, Captain Juan Luis, age eighty-four, and a resident of the provinces of New Mexico declared that he had known Maestre de Campo Juan Domínguez de Mendoza for more than thirty years, don Alonso Rael de Aguilar for nearly three years, and Lázaro de Misquía for seven years, and all the others mentioned in this question since they were born in New Mexico.[8] He attested to the fact that all those mentioned have fled to the City of Mexico, and agreed with the answers of the previous witness. He specifically mentioned that Domínguez de Mendoza had gone to the pueblo of Cochiti with sixty men, and confirmed that Governor Samaniego y Jaca brought forth charges against Domínguez de Mendoza for the deaths of two Indian servants and that Governor Villanueva charged him with fabricating a royal standard and an appointment as alférez real. Domínguez de Mendoza also killed many Apache Indian captives in cold blood and had been given to death by Governor Miranda but was pardoned (*hubo lo perdono*). Juan Luis signed his statement.

On the same date, Salvador Holguín gave testimony declaring he was a resident of the provinces of New Mexico, living in the Pueblo del Paso.[9] He stated he was about forty-six years of age and married to the sister of the wife of Juan Domínguez de Mendoza. He had known Domínguez de Mendoza for thirty years, Lázaro de Misquía for more than six years, don Alonso Rael de Aguilar for the past three years, and the others who fled to Mexico City he had known since birth because he was a native of New Mexico. He provided the same testimony as the above witnesses, attesting to the fact that he was one of the soldiers that accompanied Domínguez de Mendoza on the expedition to the pueblo of Cochiti. He had heard from others that the fugitives were taking dispatches from the cabildo justicia and regimiento, without the participation of the alcalde, Francisco Gómez Robledo, Francisco de Anaya, and don Fernando de Chaves.[10] He further stated that it was well known that Domínguez de Mendoza caused much scandal and agitation between the Indians and the Spaniards by saying he was returning to New Mexico as governor and captain general of the kingdom and would be granted the post for three lives with succession going to his sons, Baltasar Domínguez de Mendoza and Juan Domínguez de Mendoza. If this were to be the case, many Spaniards and Indians had said they would leave the kingdom. Salvador Holguín did not sign his testimony because he declared he did not know how to sign his name.

On October 2, 1685, Guadalupe del Paso, *Ayudante* Diego Barela, about age thirty, gave his testimony.[11] He declared he was a resident of Nuestra Señora de Guadalupe del Paso and he agreed with the testimony of the above witnesses. In addition, he mentioned that padre fray Nicolás López was in Mexico City soliciting for the appointment of Juan Domínguez de Mendoza as governor and captain general of the kingdom of New Mexico. He ratified his statement and acknowledged that he was a compadre of Domínguez de Mendoza. He did not know how to sign his name.

On the same date, Sargento Mayor Diego López Sambrano gave his testimony.[12] He declared he was about thirty-five years of age, a resident of the Pueblo del Paso, and a compadre of don Alonso Rael de Aguilar. He further stated that he knew all of the men in the case and his statements agreed with the statements of the previous witnesses. He was also one of the soldiers who accompanied Domínguez de Mendoza to the pueblo of Cochiti. He recalled that an Indian named Lorenzo, the brother of don Luis Tumpatio of the Picurís nation, told Domínguez de Mendoza that all the leaders, except for two who were quite old, were at the pueblo of Cochiti.[13]

López Sambrano further declared that he knew the language of the Indians. When Domínguez de Mendoza was incarcerated by Governor Medrano, López Sambrano was one of the guards. López Sambrano ratified and signed his statement.

On the same date, Ayudante Antonio Lucero de Godoy, about age thirty-eight, began his testimony by declaring he was a resident of the Real de San Lorenzo.[14] His statement agreed with those previously recorded. In addition, he had served as ayudante de maestre de campo under Maestre de Campo Juan Domínguez de Mendoza in the expedition into New Mexico that encountered the Pueblo Indian leaders at the Pueblo of Cochiti. Lucero de Godoy concluded his testimony by stating that Domínguez de Mendoza was the blood uncle of his first wife, that Diego Lucero was his uncle, and that don Alonso Rael de Aguilar was married to a first cousin of his current wife. He ratified and signed his statement.

On the same date, Diego Montoya, a soldier of the presidio of Nuestra Señora del Pilar y San José and about age twenty-two, gave a testimony that agreed with that of the above witnesses.[15] He did not go on the expedition to the Pueblo of Cochiti because he had remained at the pueblo of Isleta with Governor Otermín. He concluded his statement by acknowledging that he was related to the wife of Domínguez de Mendoza by affinity. Montoya did not sign his statement.

On the same date, Antonio Montoya provided his testimony.[16] He declared he was about forty years of age and a resident of the Pueblo del Paso. His testimony agreed with that of the above witnesses. In addition, he mentioned that an Indian servant of Juan Domínguez de Mendoza had told him that his master would be returning to New Mexico as governor and that the Indians were very upset and sad about this news. Montoya declared he was related to Domínguez de Mendoza by affinity, and he ratified and signed his statement.

The testimony of Captain Hernando Martín Serrano was recorded on October 3, 1685, at the pueblo de Nuestra Señora de Guadalupe del Paso. He declared he was about eighty-eight years old. His testimony agreed with that of the above witnesses. He also stated that on the journey to the Jumanos Domínguez de Mendoza had mistreated the soldiers and Juan Sabeata, and had hit Antonio Jorge with a harquebus (*que tubo para alcabusear*). He, like the other witnesses, considered Domínguez de

Mendoza to be a man of bad reputation. Martín Serrano ratified and signed his statement.

On the same date, Captain Diego de Luna, about age forty-eight and a resident of the jurisdiction of the Pueblo del Paso, gave his testimony which agrees with that of the above witnesses.[17] Luna had accompanied Domínguez de Mendoza on the expedition to the Pueblo de Cochiti and on the expedition to the Jumanos.

Sargento Mayor Roque de Madrid, about age forty-three, *capitán cabo y cuadillo* of the Presidio de San José provided testimony on the same date.[18] His statement agreed with that of the above witnesses. Madrid had been one of the sixty soldiers that went with Domínguez de Mendoza to the Pueblo of Cochiti. He had heard that Lázaro de Misquía, a regidor of the cabildo, had taken the dispatches of the cabildo to Mexico City in the company of Domínguez de Mendoza. Madrid ratified and signed his statement.

On the same date, the testimony of José Madrid was recorded.[19] Madrid, about age twenty-nine, was a soldier of the presidio of Nuestra Señora del Pilar y San José. His statement agreed with that of the other witnesses. Furthermore, he declared he had gone with Domínguez de Mendoza to the pueblo of Cochiti. He did not sign his statement because he did not know how to sign his name.

Governor Otermín, finding just cause and guilt of the fugitives, ordered a decree of the formal charge to be posted in the customary places. Done at Nuestra Señora del Guadalupe del Paso del Río del Norte on October 3, 1685.

On the same day, month and year, the secretary of government and war, don Pedro Ladrón de Guevara, read and gave notice of the decree of guilt and accusation that resulted from the summary of information collected against Maestre de Campo Juan Domínguez de Mendoza, Sargento Mayor Diego Lucero de Godoy, Capitán don Alonso Rael de Aguilar, Regidor Lázaro de Misquía, Baltasar Domínguez, and Juan de Anaya, who were found guilty as charged in absentia.

Statements of the witnesses were read and ratified as follows.

> On October 6, 1685, Guadalupe del Paso, Jacinto Sánchez de Iñigo ratified his statement.

On October 6, 1685, Guadalupe del Paso, Felipe de la Serna ratified his statement and signed the statement of ratification.

On October 6, 1685, Guadalupe del Paso, Juan Luis ratified his statement and signed the statement of ratification.

On October 6, 1685, Guadalupe del Paso, Captain Salvador Holguín ratified his statement.

On October 6, 1685, Guadalupe del Paso, Ayudante Diego Barela ratified his statement.

On October 6, 1685, Guadalupe del Paso, Sargento Mayor Diego López ratified his statement and signed the statement of ratification.

On October 6, 1685, Guadalupe del Paso, Ayudante Antonio Lucero ratified his statement and signed the statement of ratification.

On October 6, 1685, Guadalupe del Paso, Diego Montoya ratified his statement.

On October 6, 1685, Guadalupe del Paso, Antonio Montoya ratified his statement and signed the statement of ratification.

On October 6, 1685, Guadalupe del Paso, Captain Hernán Martín Serrano ratified his statement and signed the statement of ratification.

On October 6, 1685, Guadalupe del Paso, Captain Diego de Luna ratified his statement.

On October 6, 1685, Guadalupe del Paso, Captain Roque de Madrid ratified his statement and signed the statement of ratification.

On October 6, 1685, Guadalupe del Paso, José Madrid ratified his statement and signed.

The entire document was certified by don Pedro Ladrón de Guevara as an exact copy of the original document filed in the government archives. The copy was made on October 11, 1685, and the witnesses to this action were Ayudante José López and Sargento Lázaro de Artiaga y Pedraza. Signed don Pedro Ladrón de Guevara (rubric).

Notes

1. Spanish Archives of New Mexico (SANM) II, no. 35.
2. Lázaro de Misquía, born circa 1653, came to New Mexico in 1677 as a volunteer soldier. He was a native of the Villa de Mortrico in the Basque province of Guipúzcoa. Misquía enlisted in Mexico City on February 2, 1677, and traveled in

the company of other soldiers who were forced by law to serve in New Mexico. Hackett, *Historical Documents*, 3:317. (E&S)

3. A nephew of Juan Domínguez de Mendoza, Juan de Anaya was a son of Cristóbal de Anaya Almazán and doña Leonor Domínguez de Mendoza. (E&S)

4. Alonso Rael de Aguilar, a native of Lorca, Spain, was a son of Juan Osca y Alzamora and Juliana Rael de Aguilar. He was baptized in the church of San Patricio on February 14, 1661. His mother, Juliana Rael de Aguilar, made her last will and testament on April 24, 1703. In this document she identified her parents as Juan Rael de Aguilar and Ana Soler y Riguelme. She also mentioned that her son, "Alphonso de Osca Rael de Aguilar," was a resident of "Parral de Indias." Apparently, Alfonso Rael de Aguilar made his way to Parral in Nueva Vizcaya before coming to New Mexico as a soldier by 1683. For information on family background of Alonso Rael de Aguilar and primary source citations for the will of Juliana Rael de Aguilar, see Stanley M. Hordes, *To the End of the Earth: A History of the Crytpto-Jews of New Mexico* (New York: Columbia University Press), 2005, 180–87. Alfonso Rael de Aguilar married Josefa García de Noriega at El Paso del Norte in 1683. Chávez, *Origins of New Mexico Families*, 263. (E&S)

5. Jacinto Sánchez de Iñigo, a native of New Mexico born circa 1663, was apparently a brother of Pedro Sánchez de Iñigo, who was a son of Juana López. Curiously, Jacinto claimed he did not know the names of his parents when he sought to marry his second wife, María Rodarte de Castro Xabalera, in 1696. Chávez, *Origins of New Mexico Families*, 280. There is evidence that suggests that Jacinto and Pedro were natural sons of fray Francisco Muñoz (b. ca. 1629), who was a native of Puebla de los Ángeles in Nueva España and a son of Jacinto Muñoz and doña Magdalena Sánchez de Iñigo. Muñoz ministered in New Mexico from as early as 1660, and he survived the Pueblo Indian uprising of 1680. In 1663, Muñoz was accused of living scandalously with Juana López de Aragón. Esquibel, "The Sánchez de Iñigo Puzzle: New Genealogical Considerations," *El Farolito* 6, no. 3 (Winter 200): 8–17. (E&S)

6. Matías Luján, born circa 1652–1656, was a native of La Cañada, which later became known as Santa Cruz de la Cañada. He, his wife, Francisca Romero, and their children escaped the Pueblo Indian uprising of 1680 and after thirteen years of exile they returned to settle the area of La Cañada. Chávez, *Origins of New Mexico Families*, 63, 213. (E&S)

7. Felipe Serna, born circa 1641, escaped the Pueblo Indian uprising with his wife, Isabel Luján, and their eight children. Chávez, *Origins of New Mexico Families*, 103. (E&S)

8. Juan Luis Luján was a native of New Mexico, whose wife was Isabel López del Castillo. They were the parents of Ana María Luján, who married Juan López Olguín, son of Captain Salvador Holguín and Magdalena Fresqui, at El Paso del Norte on May 30, 1682. Archives of the Archdiocese of Santa Fe (AASF), Diligencia Matrimoniales (DM) 1682, May 30, no. 8. See also Chávez, *Origins of New Mexico Families*, 62. (E&S)

9. Salvador Holguín was a native of New Mexico, being a son of Cristóbal Holguín and Melchora de Carvajal. Salvador married Magdalena Fresqui, and their son, Juan, married a daughter of Juan Luis Luján. Chávez, *Origins of New Mexico Families*, 81–82; AASF, DM 1682, May 30, no. 8. (E&S)

10. Don Fernando de Chaves, also known as Fernando Durán y Chaves, a native of New Mexico, born circa 1647–1651, was the son of Pedro II Durán y Chaves, and a brother-in-law of Juan Domínguez de Mendoza. José Antonio Esquibel and Patryka Durán y Chaves, "Pedro Durán y Chaves and doña Juana de Montoya," in *Aqui se comienza: A Genealogical History of the Founding Families of La Villa de Alburquerque* (Albuquerque: New Mexico Genealogical Society, 2007), 184–85. (E&S)

11. Ayudante Diego Barela, also known as Diego Varela de Losada, accompanied Juan Domínguez de Mendoza on the expedition into Téjas. He and his wife, Ana María Fresqui, remained residents of Guadalupe del Paso after New Mexico was restored to the Spanish Crown in 1692. Chávez, *Origins of New Mexico Families*, 111. (E&S)

12. Sargento Mayor Diego López Sambrano appears to have been the same man of this name who escaped the Pueblo revolt with his wife, María Suazo, and their six children. In 1680 he gave his age as forty, and thirty-eight in 1681, indicating he was born circa 1640–1643. This is in contrast to the age of thirty-five (born circa 1650), which he gave as part of his testimony in the case against Juan Domínguez de Mendoza. Chávez, *Origins of New Mexico Families*, 58. (E&S)

13. Don Luis Tumpatio and his brother, Lorenzo, appear to be the same persons who played critical roles as Pueblo leaders during the restoration of New Mexico to the Spanish Crown from 1694 through 1697. Don Luis was known as Luis, El Picurís, and Luis Tupatú. Governor don Diego de Vargas appointed don Luis as governor of the Tewa Nation in December 1694, governing from San Juan Pueblo. Don Lorenzo was known as Don Lorenzo of Picurís and was appointed by Vargas as governor of the pueblo of Picurís. Kessell, Hendricks, *By Force of Arms*, 509; and Kessell, Hendricks, and Dodge, *To the Royal Crown Restored*, 402, 416. (E&S)

14. Ayudante Antonio Lucero de Godoy, born circa 1647, was a son of Juan Lucero de Godoy and Juana de Carvajal. The name of his first wife, who was a niece of Juan Domínguez de Mendoza, is unknown. Antonio's uncle, Diego Lucero de Godoy, married María Domínguez de Mendoza in 1681, she being a daughter of Juan Domínguez de Mendoza and doña Isabel de Chaves y Bohórquez. Antonio's second wife, Antonia Varela de Losada, was a first cousin of doña Josefa García de Noriega, a daughter of Captain Alonso García and Teresa Varela. Chávez, *Origins of New Mexico Families*, 26, 33–34, 60, 209.

15. Diego Montoya, born circa 1661–1663, was the husband of Josefa de Hinojos. He was very likely the brother of Antonio Montoya, a known son of Diego de Montoya and doña María de Vera. Doña María de Vera was a second cousin of Pedro Durán y Chaves, the father of doña Isabel de Chaves y Bohórquez, the wife of Juan Domínguez de Mendoza. Chávez, *Origins of New Mexico Families*, 78, 236, and 377.

16. Antonio Montoya, born circa 1645, was a son of Diego de Montoya and doña María de Vera, and the husband of María Hurtado. Antonio Montoya and doña Isabel de Chaves y Bohórquez, the wife of Juan Domínguez de Mendoza, were both descendants of Captain Juan López Holguín, who came to New Mexico in 1600. Chávez, *Origins of New Mexico Families*, 14–15, 20, 78, 81, 235, 376. (E&S)

17. Captain Diego de Luna, born circa 1637, and his wife Elvira García, raised a family of at least two sons (Antonio and Nicolás) and one daughter (Gregoria). Although the name of his father is not known, Diego de Luna's mother was María Jaramillo. Kessell, Hendricks, and Dodge, *To the Royal Crown Restored*, 59. Two decades earlier, Diego de Luna gave testimony on May 29, 1662, at the pueblo of Sandia in which he declared he was a vecino of the jurisdiction of Sandia, thirty-one years old (b. ca. 1631) and a native of La Cienega in New Mexico. He named his wife as Elvira García and identified Tomás García as his brother-in-law, apparently the brother of Elvira García. AGN, Inquisition, vol. 593, f. 247r–247v, Testimony of Diego de Luna, May 29, 1662, Convento de San Francisco de Sandia. (E&S)

18. Roque de Madrid, born circa 1642, was a son of Francisco de Madrid II. Roque could speak the Towa and Tano languages of the Pueblo Indians and served as an interpreter. Chávez, *Origins of New Mexico Families*, 66; Kessell, Hendricks, and Dodge, *To the Royal Crown Restored*, 402 and 437. (E&S)

19. José Madrid, born circa 1656, a nephew of Roque de Madrid, was a son of Lorenzo de Madrid and Antonia Ortiz. Chávez, *Origins of New Mexico Families*, 68. (E&S)

Document 52

Attested Copy of a Document Issued by the Cabildo of Santa Fe, October 3, 1684, Certifying the Titles of Offices of Juan Domínguez de Mendoza

Mexico City, April 23–24, 1686[1]

In the city of Mexico on the twenty-third day of the month of April, 1686, before Captain don Pedro de Escalante y Mendoza, alcalde ordinario therein for His Majesty, this petition was read:

Petition

I, Maestre de Campo Juan Domínguez de Mendoza, citizen of El Paso del Río del Norte de Nuestra Señora de Guadalupe of the provinces of New Mexico and resident in this city, appear before Your Honor and state that it accords with my rights that I should be given one, two, or more copies of the certification of offices [I have held] given and executed by the cabildo, justicia y regimiento of the Villa of Santa Fe of said New Mexico and resident in the said Paso del Río del Norte and which I present in due form, so that I may issue them wherever and however it may suit my interest. I beg and pray that Your Honor may be pleased to order the present notary, or any other royal [notary], to give me the said copies of the certification of offices wherewith I shall receive favor, etc. Juan Domínguez de Mendoza (rubric).

Decree

[This petition] having been examined by His Honor, he ordered the present notary, or any other royal [notary] to give to this party one, two, or more copies of the certification of offices which he presents. For this purpose he interposed his authority and judicial decree, and thus he ordered and signed it. Don Pedro de Escalante y Mendoza. Juan Díaz de Rivera, royal and public notary.

In fulfillment of the aforesaid decree, I, the said Juan Díaz de Rivera, one of the royal and public proprietary notaries *del número* in this city of Mexico,[2] made a copy of the certification of offices referred to in the petition and presented before me by the said Maestre de Campo Juan Domínguez de Mendoza, of which the literal content is as follows:

Certification[3]

The cabildo, justicia y regimiento of the Villa of Santa Fe of New Mexico, resident in this pueblo of El Paso del Río del Norte, etc.

We certify and attest that Maestre de Campo Juan Domínguez de Mendoza, citizen of these provincias, has served His Majesty in them (as appears from his titles and certifications) for many years past, and that the aforesaid is the legitimate son of Captain Tomé Domínguez, whose letters patent of nobility he enjoys because of his many services to His Majesty (God keep him) which are shown, as has been said, in the commission which he presented to this cabildo so that they may be certified for their greater validation. They are as follows:

Two certifications [issued] by General Hernando de Ugarte y la Concha, one when he was governor, and the other after he left office.[4]

Another [issued] by General don Juan de Samaniego y Jaca, Knight of the Order of St. John, after he ceased to be governor.[5]

Two titles [issued] by don Bernardo López de Mendizábal, one as captain of infantry and the other as alcalde mayor and lieutenant captain general.[6]

A title of encomienda [issued] by General don Diego de Peñalosa.[7]

Four titles [issued] by general don Fernando de Villanueva; one as lieutenant of the governor and captain general of the jurisdictions of the Río Abajo, two as visitador, and the other as lieutenant governor and captain general of the whole kingdom, accepted by the cabildo.[8]

Three titles [issued] by general Juan de Medrano; one as maestre de campo of campaign in active war and certified [by the said governor]; another as sargento mayor of the kingdom; and a title of encomienda.[9]

Four titles [issued] by General Juan de Miranda; one as maestre de campo of the kingdom; another as lieutenant governor and captain general of the kingdom; two others as maestre de campo of campaign in active war and service of His Majesty.[10]

Another title of leader, commander, and chief in campaign [issued] by general don Juan Francisco Treviño, [and] certified [by him].[11]

Also, five titles as lieutenant of the captain general in campaign during various military expeditions, [issued] by General don Antonio de Otermín with their [respective] discharges and certifications;[12] also, another title of encomienda [issued by Otermín]; and a certification by the said governor after he left office.[13]

And besides, a copy of a probanza and privileges of His Majesty in five folios, executed and issued when General Francisco Martínez de Baeza was governor and signed by his name, sealed with the seal of his arms, and countersigned by his secretary of government and war.[14]

We certify that the signatures of the said governors as well as those of their secretaries are those which they were accustomed to make, as is publicly known.

Therefore we find him [Domínguez de Mendoza] worthy and deserving of any honor that His Majesty may be pleased to confer upon him, and by his petition we order the present writing issued to him, signed by our hands, sealed with the seal used by the cabildo, and countersigned by our secretary, with the declaration that it goes on ordinary white paper because sealed paper is not current in these parts.

Done in the pueblo of Nuestra Señora de Guadalupe del Paso on the third day of the month of October of the year 1684. Lorenzo de Madrid. Juan Rodriguez de Suballe. Sebastián González. By order of the cabildo, justicia y regimiento, Francisco Romero de Pedraza, clerk of the cabildo.

It agrees with the certification of offices mentioned above, to which I refer, and which are the titles mentioned therein, which I saw and examined and together with the [certification] I returned to the petitioner the originals, to which I attest. And in order that the said petition and order may be of record, I issued the present [writing] in the city of Mexico on the twenty-fourth day of the month of April of the year 1686, the witnesses being Juan de Monzón, Joseph de Bustos, and Diego Díaz, citizens of Mexico.

I affix my signum.[15] (Signum) In testimony of the truth, Juan Díaz de Rivera, royal and public notary (rubric).

We make oath that Juan Díaz de Rivera, by whom it appears that the above copy is marked ["*signado*"] and signed, is one of the royal and public proprietary notaries del número of this city of Mexico, and that as such complete faith and credit, judicially and extrajudicially, should be given the writings, decrees, copies, and other documents that have passed and do pass before the aforesaid.

Done in the city of Mexico on the twenty-fourth day of the month of October of the year 1686. Juan Jiménez de Navarro, royal and public notary (rubric). Joseph Cabellero, notary of His Majesty (rubric), Joseph Soni, royal notary (rubric).

It came with the letter of fray Nicolás López of the Order of St. Francis [dated] April 25, 1686. Number 8. 3.0

Notes

1. Another translation of this record was published in Hackett, *Historical Documents*, 3:357–58. Hackett cites the document as being preserved in the collection of the Bancroft Library but does not provide a specific source citation. Scholes also did not provide a specific source citation. His translation varies

slightly from that of Hackett. A handwritten note in Scholes's typewritten draft of this document refers to "Cf. Hackett trans," an apparent reference to the translation of the same document published in *Historical Documents*, vol. 3.

2. "*Escribano del Rey nuestro señor y publico en propiedad de los del número desta ciudad de Mexico.*" The *escribanos del número* constituted a limited number of notaries, licensed by royal authority. Their books, in which were recorded copies of deeds, wills, mortgages, and other legal documents that they drew up and attested, constituted in colonial times the equivalent of our present-day public archives and registry administered by county and city clerks.

3. This is undoubtedly a copy of the authentic original certification issued by the cabildo on October 3, 1684, whereas the certification of the same date found in the Domínguez de Mendoza Servicios Personales manuscript in the Biblioteca Nacional, Madrid, is apparently fraudulent. See Doc. 46 (October 3, 1684) and notes, supra.

4. The Domínguez de Mendoza Servicios Personales manuscript contains two papers issued by Ugarte y la Concha. One of these (Doc. 5, April 15, 1650) belongs to the groups that are not authentic. It is an appointment as lieutenant governor and captain general, dated April 15, 1650, and was probably substituted for the certification by Ugarte y la Concha during his term of office and listed above. The second (Doc. 7, January 12, 1653) is actually a certification of services, issued by Ugarte y la Concha after he left office, and undoubtedly corresponds with the second certification noted here.

5. The Domínguez de Mendoza Servicios Personales manuscript contains two papers (Doc. 6, November 10, 1652; and Doc. 8, September 13, 1653) supposedly issued by Samaniego y Jaca. Both are apparently fraudulent or reconstructed records. One is a certification of services but is dated January 12, 1653, before Samaniego y Jaca took office and not after he ceased to be governor, unless it was backdated. It was probably substituted for the one noted here.

6. Doc. 10 (August 30, 1659) and Doc. 11 (November 19, 1659). Doc. 10 is a commission as captain of mounted harquebusiers but is undoubtedly the title of captain of infantry mentioned here.

7. Doc. 12 (May 7, 1662). The Domínguez de Mendoza Servicios Personales manuscript has another title issued by Governor Peñalosa (Doc. 13, October 6, 1663), but this belongs to the group of suspect documents. Doc. 14 (January 7, 1664) was also issued by Peñalosa. It is merely an order to Domínguez de Mendoza to bring in certain individuals and was not listed here. It is undoubtedly genuine.

8. Doc. 15 (June 25, 1665), Doc. 16 (October 16, 1665), Doc. 17 (December 16, 1666), and Doc. 18 (February 10, 1667).

9. Doc. 20 (May 1, 1669), Doc. 22 (September 11, 1670), and Doc. 23 (June 27, 1671).

10. Doc. 24 (July 27, 1671), Doc. 25 (August 2, 1671), Doc. 28 (July 15, 1673), and Doc. 30 (July 5, 1675).

11. Doc. 31 (September 24, 1675).

12. Here the scribe wrote "*teniente de gov.^{or} y capp.^{an} general*," but there is a correction at the end to strike out the words "*gov.or y*."

13. The Domínguez de Mendoza Servicios Personales manuscript has eight documents issued by Governor Otermín (Docs. 33–40). The title of encomienda and the certification of services are Docs. 37 and 40, respectively. Four of the five titles of lieutenant captain general noted here are apparently Docs. 33, 35, 38, and 39, although the commissions do not call Domínguez de Mendoza lieutenant captain general in all cases. Docs. 33, 35, 38, and 39 all have the decrees of discharge, and a similar decree may have been recorded in Doc. 38 in the lower half of the leaf now torn away. Docs. 34 and 36 contain Otermín's instructions issued in connection with the appointments made in Docs. 33 and 35, respectively.

14. Francisco Martínez de Baeza was governor of New Mexico from 1634 to 1637. Consequently, the document "probanza and privilege" mentioned here was not related to Juan Domínguez de Mendoza, for his services in New Mexico did not begin until 1642–1643. The document was a probanza of the services of his father, Tomé Domínguez, the elder, and a patent of hidalguía issued to him by virtue of the royal decree of 1602. Tomé Domínguez, the elder, had not actually resided in New Mexico for the required five years prior to the end of Martínez de Baeza's term of office, but between 1631 and 1636 he had made three trips to New Mexico, and on such occasions may have brought colonists to the province. Governor Martínez de Baeza, who was apparently on friendly terms with the elder Domínguez, may have interpreted this journeying back and forth as the equivalent of the five years of service necessary before the privilege of hidalguía could be granted. The probanza of Tomé Domínguez was at one time part of the collection of documents that were part of Juan Domínguez de Mendoza's records of services, but the probanza is now missing from the collection.

15. "*Signo*," the special mark or scroll employed by each notary, the equivalent of the modern notary's seal.

Document 53

Petition of Fray Nicolás López to the Viceroy with the Reply of the Fiscal and Decision of the Junta General

Mexico City, March 26, 1686[1]

Most Excellent Sir: Fray Nicolás López, friar of the Order of St. Francis, missionary, preacher, present custodian, and legate of His Holiness in the provinces of New Mexico, and its procurador general, states:

He has expressed to Your Excellency and to the royal audiencia his motives for coming to this capital, leaving that custodia during the time while he was prelate as the result of a council and decision of all the missionary friars, and coming to this city to describe the wretched state of that kingdom and what its inhabitants are suffering from hunger and nakedness because of the unfavorable nature of the country. And at the same time the supplicant made known in a memorial, which he has given to Your Excellency, the number of nations so well inclined toward our Holy Catholic Faith that they are asking for the water of baptism, availing themselves of expedients pertaining to our holy law in order to bring ministers to their lands, feigning that a cross fallen from the sky had appeared to them, for the aforesaid infidels saw a small intention there was on the part of the Spaniards to make a journey to their lands, and with this portent of the aforesaid cross, [they hoped] to induce them to make the journey. The nation they call Jumanos took the lead, because this nation had always maintained friendship with the Spaniards.

And at the solicitations of the aforesaid barbarians, the supplicant went down, accompanied by two friars, on foot and barefoot, until he reached the place they call La Junta de los Ríos, where he found two chapels built by the aforesaid infidels. There the aforesaid friars immediately began to catechize and to build four more chapels, where nine nations were assembled and were already being ministered to, as is all on record in legal form in the instruments he has presented to Your Excellency. More than five hundred souls were baptized and many babes saved who died at that time.

And, because of the lack of ministers, leaving a single friar for the administration of these nine nations, the supplicant went on, accompanied by another friar, at the supplications and petition of many other nations who are asking for baptism. And, surveying and traveling through their lands both on the north and east, with sixty-six more nations in the interior, he set foot upon the threshold of the extensive and powerful kingdom of the Tejas and trod the lands of the nation they call Hayjados near the great kingdom of Quivira. All this land abounds in pecans, plums, blackberries, piñon, grapes, and very many herds of bison, as is all on record in legal form in the certifications he has presented, as well as in the itinerary which was kept by the commander and chief, Maestre de Campo Juan Domínguez de Mendoza.

And in consideration of the fact that the supplicant has shown the need for missionaries, he asked for twenty priests for the aforesaid conversion, and, as a result of his aforesaid petition, his superior prelate dispatched a patent for all the provinces, informing the friars on behalf of the aforesaid conversions because of the pact which had been made with the aforesaid nations to return to their lands within one year, which, sir, was the reason why they permitted us to leave their lands.

And now again, notwithstanding the decision of the junta general, the supplicant finds it necessary to point out the manifest dangers threatened by delay in putting the remedy into effect, especially when the danger threatens from all sides. And upon this occasion much can be accomplished, because seventy-five nations who rendered obedience to both Majesties when legal possession was taken of all those lands and nations are friendly toward the Spaniards. They are ready to receive baptism, if it is his royal will not to fail them with regard to the ministers necessary. This is evident from his royal decrees which I have presented, and from the last one, newly issued, its date August 2, 1685, in which His Majesty asks to be informed whether there is any friar who is ready to go to the aforesaid conversions, from which his royal will is clear and manifest. And in that connection, the supplicant, in the name of his sacred order, not only offers the twenty friars for whom he has asked and pointed out were necessary at that time, but again asks for and offers the fifty-one friars to make up the number of those His Majesty has assigned to that custodia. And for the accomplishment of a work so pleasing to God, our Lord, and in the service of His Majesty and increase of his royal treasury because of the great promise of that land with its abundance of minerals and fruits, the supplicant offers to go to the aforesaid conversions as prelate of that custodia, for he has already communicated with and known the aforesaid nations and knows the Jumano language. He has preached in it to those barbarians and has made up a very extensive vocabulary of the aforesaid language, as is on record in legal form because he has been heard to preach in it. Moreover, one of the friars whom he took with him as his companion was already versed in it, although not with entire perfection.

And now once more the supplicant represents to Your Excellency in the name of his order and in accordance with what he knows from the aforesaid royal decree that if the most Christian king [does not] win the friendship of these docile nations, whose [docility and friendliness] the supplicant knows by experience (for it seemed that they had been on friendly terms for many years), a great disaster is imminent, and one that it will be impossible to repair afterward with millions. And on this occasion with two hundred men it is possible to prevent their passage since seventy-five nations are friendly toward us. These nations asked for aid against the Apache nation. His Majesty can accomplish all this on this occasion at very little expense, because once the aforesaid soldiers have been led into those lands, His

Majesty will not spend even one *maravedí* on the sustenance of the people, because the great numbers of herds of bison, the tenancy of the people, the variety of fruits, diversity of fish, and abundance of turkeys, quail, and partridges, and especially the vines and grapevines, cannot be described or expressed. The supplicant and other persons who went on the said expedition are eyewitnesses to all this. And since the supplicant is aware that His Majesty should be informed with all detail, clarity, and precision concerning all these lands, he has thought it proper to place this map in the hands of Your Excellency as one who represents the king, our lord, to whom it is dedicated and inscribed. It has been faithfully prepared according to his knowledge and understanding as one who has traveled over the greater part of the land and who reconnoitered the trails of those kingdoms, since it is twenty-five leagues from the kingdom of the Tejas, treading the land of the Ayjados nations, which lies between it and the kingdom of Gran Quivira. The supplicant had this reason, sir, for making the foregoing representation to Your Excellency, in consideration of which:

He petitions and begs Your Excellency with your exalted intelligence to be pleased to decide what is most fitting with regard to a matter of such great consequence, for his intention and that of his sacred order is solely the services of God, our Lord, and that of His Majesty. And in order that the vigilance which his aforesaid order has maintained and maintains in fulfillment of its rule may be of record for all time, let Your Excellency be pleased to order that he be given a certified copy, or as many certified copies as may be necessary, of all the representations he has made concerning this weighty matter from August 3, 1685, including the decision of the junta general of May 8 of the aforesaid year, and also of the certifications he has presented on behalf of his order and of all the replies and decisions in the junta general.

And I swear *in verbo sacerdotis* that what I have related and represented is the truth, considering only the service of both Majesties. In everything I hope to receive favor from the greatness and zeal of Your Excellency. Fray Nicolás López (rubric).

Mexico [City], March 26, 1686. To the fiscal, together with the map, and with his reply, to the junta general. (rubric)

Reply of the Fiscal

Most Excellent Sir: The fiscal of His Majesty has seen this petition of Father fray Nicolás López, friar of St. Francis, missionary, custodian of the provinces of New Mexico, and the enclosed map which he presents of the lands and nations which he says he has explored and seen in the aforesaid provinces. He went into the interior with other friars and soldiers who went to this discovery, as he has represented on another occasion when he presented the diaries. He now presents the matter and again offers his services to return to these conversions with fifty-one friars. He also propounds the theory that if the most Christian king [does not] win them to friendship with him, great disaster will follow, which it will be impossible to remedy afterward at little expense, but today, placing two hundred men there will not cost His Majesty anything because of the abundance of provisions.

And [the fiscal] says that all the foregoing is fantastic and [are] ideas that must not be evaluated solely because the aforesaid father believes and reasons they will be effective without taking into consideration the fact that even in the place on the Río del Norte to which the citizens who fled at the time of the uprising of the aforesaid New Mexico have withdrawn they cannot maintain themselves without great difficulty, and also the disturbed state of all the nations of that whole area. And if some expenditure were to be made and any operations undertaken, it would be better to recuperate what was lost in the aforesaid New Mexico. His Majesty has been amply informed on this point and his decision concerning what is to be done is expected. Here the point is reached that the propositions which some of the aforesaid Indians have made have turned out to be false, as regards both peace and conversions.

Therefore, in view of all the forgoing, Your Excellency should be pleased to declare that the offers and proposals of the aforesaid father are inadmissible. Let him be given the certified copies of his petitions and instruments which he has presented, albeit with the insertion of this reply and other replies the fiscal has given with regard to this matter, so that if perchance he should have recourse to His Majesty, he may not be deceived and may be in possession of this information, and so that whatever decision he may make, if he be so pleased, may be preceded by reports from Your Excellency or your successors and from the fiscales. Your Excellency will order what is best. Mexico [City] and May 22 of the year 1686. Licenciado Pedro de la Bastida (rubric). Mexico [City], May 29, 1686. As the fiscal asks. (rubric)

Notes

1. AGI, Guadalajara, 138. See also Hackett, *Historical Documents*, 3:360–63.

Document 54

Copy of the Sentence Pronounced in the Proceedings against Maestre de Campo Juan Domínguez de Mendoza

Mexico City, April 30, 1687[1]

Presentation

In the City of Mexico on the twelfth day of the month of March of the year 1693, this petition was presented before Licenciado don Francisco Fernández Marmolejo, of the Council of His Majesty, his oider in this royal audiencia, and auditor *general de la guerra* of this kingdom.

Petition

Maestre de Campo Juan Domínguez de Mendoza says that in support of his legal rights it is necessary that the notary of war give him a copy of the sentence pronounced in the proceedings against the aforesaid with regard to certain charges made against him. This [copy] should be authorized in legal form because it is for the purpose referred to. He petitions and begs Your Excellency to be pleased to order that the said attested copy be given him by the said notary, and to interpose your authority and judicial decree, which he will receive as a favor, with justice. Juan Domínguez de Mendoza.

Edict

Seen by the auditor general, he acknowledged it and ordered the present notary to give this party the attested copy he asks for of the sentence he mentions, authorized in legal form; let him make use of it as is permitted by law. Signed with a rubric. Before me, Sebastián de las Fraguas, royal notary and [notary] of war.

In fulfillment of the above edict, I, Alférez Sebastián Sánchez de las Fraguas, notary of His Majesty of the chamber of justice, [notary] general of bienes de difuntos of this New Spain, and of war in this kingdom, made a copy of the sentence to which the petition refers, the literal contents of which are as follows:

Sentence

In the proceedings and criminal case which was prosecuted de oficio [by] don Domingo Jironza Petríz de Cruzate when he was governor and captain general of the provinces of New Mexico, against Maestre de Campo don Juan Domínguez de Mendoza, Baltasar Domínguez, his son, Juan de Anaya, his nephew, and other defendants, for having abandoned the post of El Paso and left that kingdom without license from the said governor, in contravention of an edict which forbade it.[2] Having seen them and the other charges made, especially against the said maestre de campo; and the statements, allegations, and proofs made by the aforesaid and by Baltasar Domínguez and Juan de Anaya, and the other things it was fitting to consider, I find that in view of the proceedings and the merits of the case I should and do decide it in the following manner:

With regard to the charge made against the said Maestre de Campo don Juan Domínguez de Mendoza concerning the circulation of rumors in that kingdom that he had been appointed as its governor, which had occasioned horror and discontent among its natives on account of their terrible condition, in view of his answers I absolve and free him.

With regard to the charge made against him that having gone with the title of chief, commander, and captain of the Spaniards and Indians who went to the discovery of Jumanos, he did not behave with the prudence, zeal, and energy which he should have displayed in an affair of such great importance and gravity, in view of his answers I absolve and free him [of this] and the rest which it contains.

With regard to the charge made against him that having been appointed by Governor don Antonio de Otermín as chief and commander of sixty men during the entrada to recover that kingdom, he did not fulfill the orders of the said governor, and as a result the attempt failed, [of this] and the rest contained in it I also absolve and free him in view of the allegations of the aforesaid and the instruments and certifications he presented.

And for the guilt which results against the said Maestre de Campo Juan Domínguez de Mendoza and Baltasar Domínguez, his son, and Juan de Anaya, his nephew, for having abandoned the post of El Paso and left without license from the said governor in contravention of the edict prohibiting it under penalty of life and treason to the king, I should and do condemn them to the costs of this case and warn them that henceforth they are not to fail to execute and fulfill with punctiliousness the orders of their superiors, nor are they to leave that kingdom without permission on any pretext, under penalty of being punished most severely.

And by this my sentence, handing down judgment definitely, I so declare, pronounce, and order, in accordance with the opinion of my auditor general of war. Conde de la Monclova. Licenciado don Francisco Fernández Marmolejo.

Pronouncement

In Mexico City on April 30 of the year 1687, the most excellent Conde de la Monclova, viceroy, governor, and captain general of this New Spain, and president of his royal audiencia, gave and pronounced the preceding sentence according and as appears in it, in accordance with the opinion of Licenciado don Francisco Fernández Marmolejo of the council of His Majesty, his oider in the royal audiencia, and audito general of war of this kingdom. And they signed it in my presence, to which I attest. Miguel de Múxica, royal and provincial notary.

[Certification of copy, etc., follows here.]

Notes

1. BNE, Madrid, MSS 19258, photos 98–104.
2. Lawsuits were of two classes, de oficio and de parte. The first were suits in which the state was a party; the second were between private parties.

Document 55

Testimony Concerning the Conduct of Juan Domínguez de Mendoza during the Expedition of 1681–1682

[El Paso del Norte], May 19–June 12, 1687[1]

[To] Father Preacher Fray Pedro Gómez, definitor and minister guardian of the holy convent of El Paso:

For the service of God, our Lord, and the good repute of our holy habits, it is necessary to verify and know for certain everything that happened in the pueblo of Cochiti of New Mexico at the time General don Antonio de Otermín entered to pacify and reduce those provinces, because certain ill-founded rumors have arisen which detract from and are contrary to the good name and reputation of Maestre de Campo don Juan Domínguez de Mendoza. Therefore, in order that all that happened in the said pueblo of Cochiti may be known with certainty, and so that the truth of all the above may be stated, he has requested and petitioned me that the declaration of father preacher fray Antonio Guerra, who assisted and accompanied him in all the operations that occurred, be taken, both with regard to what the said Maestre de Campo don Juan Domínguez de Mendoza did and the reports he gave the said General don Antonio de Otermín, and with regard to how he had the kingdom reduced and the reason why the reduction was not carried into effect nor achieved, and what the Indians said on that occasion. And in addition, let the said father preacher fray Antonio Guerra state whether he did or did not remit some silver belonging to the churches, or whether he knew or saw that the said Maestre de Campo don Juan Domínguez de Mendoza misappropriated anything, either some of the valuables belonging to the churches and convents or those found in the pueblos in the possessions of the Indians. Because it is most essential that the truth concerning all which has been set forth be declared, I, therefore, by authority of the present writing, signed by my hand, grant your fathership all my authority so that you may summon into your presence the said father fray Antonio Guerra, whom you may compel by virtue of holy obedience, charging his conscience in this matter, to declare and state the exact truth about all the above and about what he heard and saw as an eyewitness, omitting nothing which may be useful for the good repute of our holy habit. I have confidence in his great religiosity and in yours that you will do your utmost in a matter so greatly in the service of God with the rectitude of spirit which the case requires.

Issued in this our new conversion of Santa María Magdalena of the Suma Indians on the nineteenth day of the month of May of this present year of 1687. Fray Nicolás López, Custodian (rubric).

In this convent of Nuestra Señora de Guadalupe del Paso, on the twenty-second day of the month of May, 1687, I, fray Pedro Gómez, received the above decree. And, obeying the command of our reverend father custodian, fray Nicolás López, I state that I accept the said commission and that I will do and fulfill everything as I am ordered by it. And so that it may be of record, I signed it on the said day, month, and year ut supra. Fray Pedro Gómez (rubric).

In this convent of the Immaculate Conception of Socorro of the Piro Indians, on the twenty-sixth day of the month of May, 1687, I notified father fray Antonio Guerra, preacher, and minister president of the said convent, in person, of the above decree and decision of our reverend father fray Nicolás López, preacher, procurador general, custodian, ecclesiastical judge ordinary of these provinces and custodia of the Conversion of St. Paul of New Mexico. And having heard and understood it, he said that he promised to make a true statement under oath about all he saw and heard, and he made it in verbo sacerdotis under oath and understood it, his hand on his breast. I enjoined holy obedience upon him by virtue of the Holy Spirit.

First, he was asked whether he knows Maestre de Campo Juan Domínguez de Mendoza, and he said that he has known him since the year 1680 when the resident force set out.

Asked whether he went to the pueblo of Cochiti with the said Maestre de Campo Juan Domínguez de Mendoza when he was sent by General don Antonio de Otermín the past year of 1681, he said that he accompanied him from the pueblo of Isleta and that they left the said pueblo of Isleta on the eighth day of December of the said year of '81 and that he always accompanied him in all the operations, and by this he means that he never left him, even for an hour.

Asked if he knows whether [Domínguez de Mendoza] sent any reports to General don Antonio de Otermín, [he said] that he dispatched a message to the said general from the pueblo of Alameda and sent with it a chalice and its paten, and a bronze crucifix which was on a chest in the house of an [Indian?].[2] And he also declares that in the said pueblo of Alameda he issued a strict order to the soldiers who accompanied him to bring to the middle of the plaza all the valuables found in the houses of the Indians, because the said Indians were in the sierras. All [the valuables] were to be placed there and examined, and the property of the churches set apart, and this order was observed in all the pueblos they reached. Likewise the said Maestre de Campo Juan Domínguez [de Mendoza] sent another message to the said General don Antonio de Otermín from the pueblo of Sandia, and these messages concerned the conditions he was finding in all the settlements, because the said general had told him that, depending upon circumstances, he would follow with wagons and men. He also informed him that there was a large amount of food supplies in the pueblos in order that for this reason the said general and the force which was with him might be encouraged to advance, since it was feared that they might not be able to do so because if provisions were lacking, hunger would be serious. There was a large quantity [of provisions] there. He saw him dispatch these two messages to the said General don Antonio de Otermín. And he also declares that they buried along the way in places known and marked all the treasures belonging to the church, both silver and other valuables such as vestments, crosses, missals, and other things. And this was done by [order]³ of the said father witness and by that of the said Maestre de Campo Juan Domínguez [de Mendoza].

Asked whether he saw him misappropriate any valuables belonging either to churches and convents or to private individuals, he said that by no means did he see him misappropriate or seize anything; indeed, he observed that he was very scrupulous on this point and that he was most insistent that the soldiers should hide nothing. And he also declared that the gossip that the said Maestre de Campo Juan Domínguez began to trade and barter with the apostate Indians is false; indeed he observed the contrary, and by no means did he see trade or barter.

Asked whether he saw or knew that the said Maestre de Campo Juan Domínguez de Mendoza had reduced the apostate Indians to submission so that they were ready to return to our holy evangelical law, [he said] that according to what he saw and believed, [Domínguez de Mendoza] had everything under control in the pueblo of Cochiti where they spoke and talked with the [apostates]. The said father witness found in all the Indians great susceptibility, and remorse for what they had done, since the first word the said apostate Indians spoke and the first request they made to the said Maestre de Campo Juan Domínguez [de Mendoza] was to ask him to grant them peace, invoking God and St. Mary; except for one called Alonso Catití, of the Queres nation, who was their captain, who said that it was not possible that God would pardon him for the terrible atrocities he committed such as the murders of so many priests and Spaniards, and such cruel profanities of the temples and holy vessels, and that for this reason he did not want peace, because he knew they would hang and kill him because of them. When he heard such talk, the said father witness left the army and went to him, where he admonished him and by means of the divine word tried to bring him back to recognition of evangelical law. And this short discourse had so great an effect that he fell from his horse to the ground weeping, as one in a swoon; and then he asked for peace, and with one accord all of them did likewise. Then the said maestre de campo gave and granted them peace in the name of His Majesty, and they all embraced one another tenderly with many tears and sobs. And when they saw the said father alone on a *loma* where the apostate Indians were, they all knelt, and especially, Alonso, el Catití, who was the greatest [sinner?],⁴ who threw himself at his feet, weeping so copiously that he dampened them with his tears, for although he tried to put them away, he was unable to do so because he held his feet with great strength. At this point the said Maestre de Campo Juan Domínguez [de Mendoza] went up to the loma accompanied by all his men, and he made them a speech, exhorting them, and ordered them to go down to the plain. They obeyed him and descended, and when they had done so, he proposed that they should go to the pueblo, for they were about two leagues from it, and that he would tell them there what they were to do. They replied that they were keeping all the women in the sierra and that it was necessary to go for them, and therefore they asked for a term of a day and a half, which was the time they might spend in going and coming down and going to the pueblo. This was granted them, and most of their people went to the sierra and only a few principals of all the nations remained behind. The latter accompanied the Spaniards and soldiers to the pueblo of Cochiti, because most of the kingdom had gathered in that place. And there they conversed, asking them why they had left the pueblos and gone fleeing through the sierras. They said [they had done so] because don Antonio de Otermín and Francisco Xavier were coming. To this the said Maestre de Campo Juan Domínguez [de Mendoza] replied that the said don Antonio de Otermín did not intend to do them harm; and that Francisco Xavier was no longer in the governor's confidence and did not hold any command but came with his arms like any poor fellow. The Indians replied to this that if he no longer gave orders nor was in the governor's confidence, why did he begin to pick on them and revile them as soon as they reached the pueblo of Isleta to . . . ?[5] And why did he strike an Indian cantor called Parraga? Thereupon the said Maestre de Campo Juan Domínguez [de Mendoza] tried to dissuade them and said that perhaps they had been deceived, but they said it was not possible because they had already been informed from Isleta of all that was going on and that it was the truth, which indeed it was.

The said father preacher fray Antonio Guerra, declarant, also states that he called upon and requested the said Maestre de Campo Juan Domínguez [de Mendoza] to ask all the apostate Indians whether the reason for their having rebelled had anything to do with the friars or not, in order that in this way the truth might be declared and all the soldiers might serve as witnesses to it. He also called upon them to state the truth at all times whenever the occasion might arise and tell what they had heard from the Indians themselves. This was done, for whenever an opportunity of talking to the Indians presented itself, the first question which the said maestre de campo put to them was to ask whether they had rebelled on account of the friars or because of any private individual, either the governor or anyone else in the kingdom. And all said and stated that by no means had they rebelled on account of the friars nor any one [of them] in particular; rather they all found consolation in the friars since there were many [friars] who paid the tribute for them in order to be free from vexation. [They said] that the reason why they rebelled was [the conduct of] the governor, don Antonio de Otermín, because he never did them justice and [because he] kept them burdened with labor so that they had no opportunity to sow [their own fields].[6] Likewise, [they said that the use of] their estufas had been prohibited on the grounds that they performed idolatries in them; and that if this was true, why had they not been forbidden in Taos, where the Indians were allowed to keep them because of bribery; and that if the estufas were evil, why had they been tolerated in that pueblo, because if they were used for idolatrous purposes, then the Taos [people] had idolatrized?[7] Moreover, the said don Antonio de Otermín had issued an edict forbidding any Indians of the pueblos to barter with the friendly Apaches at the times when they came, and had ordered grave penalties that when the said Apaches came, the said General don Antonio de Otermín should be informed so that he might be first [to trade with them], and he did so, because through Francisco Xavier he bartered for all they brought and they (the Pueblo Indians) were left with nothing, and they resented this because it was their means of livelihood.

The Indians also said that Francisco Xavier was the reason for their rebellion, since he caused them many vexations using the power the governor gave him; and whenever he saw that an Indian possessed any local merchandise, he accused the [said Indian] of being a sorcerer, and they said that Xavier did so in order to take what the Indians had. By virtue of the rod of office which he always carried, although he was not an alcalde mayor, he molested them greatly in their pueblos, and he never paid them for their bodily labor, for when they went to the governor to ask for it, he referred them to Xavier, who immediately reviled and abused them so that out of fear they no longer wanted to ask for anything. So little by little they began to discuss rising in rebellion.

The said father preacher fray Antonio Guerra concluded by saying that the Indians kept the promise they gave that they would return within a day and a half, and that all but two or three, who reached the pueblo of Cochiti, came to about a half league from the pueblo. And they said that all the people were now returning to the sierras because the Spaniards who were coming with the governor were already burning the pueblos. Astonished by this, the said father and the said maestre de campo and all the forces went up to the *azotea*, and they saw that a great cloud of smoke was issuing from the pueblo of Sandia itself and that this was the reason why all the people had not come, since they feared they would be killed. In view of this, the maestre de campo immediately arranged to return to meet Governor don Antonio de Otermín, and then they found that it was true that the pueblos had been burned and a quantity of provisions in them. And they never took out the silver and other things they had hidden for safekeeping because they had always understood that wagons would come. At the time they met the governor, which was in the pueblo of Puaray, the said governor decided to leave and to burn the pueblos he had left standing as he came to them, and in effect he did so.

He declared that this was the truth of what happened and he observed that he might tell many more things, but since it happened some time ago, he decided not to certify [to them] but only to what he has declared, which he saw and heard and remembers with entire [certainty].[8] And this is the truth under the oath he made as he was enjoined by virtue of holy obedience. His entire statement having been read to him de verbo ad verbum, he said that it was according and as he had made it and that it is in accordance with what he finds in his conscience happened. He declared all this in my presence, and he signed it with his name on the said day, month, and year ut supra. Fray Pedro Gómez, judge commissary (rubric). Fray Antonio Guerra (rubric).

In accordance with the command of our reverend father custodian, Fray Nicolás López, I remitted this statement to his reverend fathership so that he might dispose of it as is most fitting. El Paso, June 2 of the year 1687.

In this new conversion of Santa María Magdalena of the Sumas on the twelfth day of the month of June of this year of 1687, our reverend father fray Nicolás López, preacher, procurador, custodian, and ecclesiastical judge of these provinces and kingdom, having seen the above statement, ordered that it be given just as it stands in the original to the representative of Maestre de Campo Juan Domínguez de Mendoza, and in order that it may serve as evidence in his behalf, it goes sealed with the great seal of the office and countersigned by me, the above-mentioned secretary. Thus he provided, ordered, and signed on the said day, month, and year ut supra. (Seal) [The document is not signed.]

Notes

1. BNE, Madrid, MSS 19258, photos 142–45.
2. Illegible text.
3. Illegible text.

4. Illegible text.
5. Illegible text.
6. "*Atareados en vales*," i.e., kept busily occupied as a result of the *vales*, or permits authorizing the use of Indian labor.
7. *Estufa* is the term used by the Spaniards of the seventeenth century to refer to what is more popularly known today as a kiva: a round, underground room used mainly for religious ceremonies.
8. Illegible text.

Document 56

Permission for Maestre de Campo Don Juan Domínguez de Mendoza to Bring His Wife and Family from El Paso del Río del Norte

Mexico City, July 23, 1688, and Presentation of License of Baltasar Domínguez de Mendoza, Nuestra Señora de Guadalupe del Paso del Río del Norte, March 1, 1689[1]

Don Melchor Portocarrero Laso de la Vega, Conde de la Monclova, of His Majesty's Council of War and Junta de Guerra de Indias, his viceroy, lieutenant governor, and captain general of this New Spain, and president of the royal audiencia.

Inasmuch as this memorial was presented before me:

Most Excellent Sir: Maestre de Campo Juan Domínguez de Mendoza, resident in this city, states that he has been informed that doña Isabel Durán y Chaves, the petitioner's wife, who is now in El Paso del Río del Norte, has fallen so seriously ill that she needs a very long cure, and this cannot be accomplished in the said place, for there is no physician or apothecary there, and she will never be able to regain her health. Therefore he begs and entreats Your Excellency to grant him permission for her to leave the said Paso del Río with a married daughter of theirs and a son, and other people in service in the household, such as some Indian girls whom she has brought up and who assist her, for this petitioner so hopes from Your Excellency's magnanimity.

I ordered that the above be shown to His Majesty's fiscal, and in view of his reply, for the present I grant permission to the said Maestre de Campo Juan Domínguez de Mendoza so that he may take his wife and family from the aforesaid El Paso del Río del Norte. As for the married daughter he says he has, the representative of her husband will be heard, for he is the one who has to speak for her. And I ordered His Majesty's ministers and magistrates not to place any hindrance or impediment to the use of this license. Mexico, July 23, 1688. El Conde de Monclova (rubric). By order of His Excellency, Joseph de Bustos (rubric).

In the pueblo of Nuestra Señora de Guadalupe del Paso del Río del Norte, on March 1, 1689, before Governor and Captain General don Domingo Jironza Petríz de Cruzate, this petition was presented with a license issued by the most excellent lord viceroy of New Spain.

Sr. Governor and Captain General:

I, Baltasar Domínguez de Mendoza, resident in El Paso del Río del Norte, state that having been sent from the City of Mexico with permission from the most excellent lord viceroy of this New Spain to take from this kingdom my mother, doña Isabel Durán y Chaves, and also her family, I make this presentation of this license before your lordship in the form which best befits my legal rights. And in order to carry it into effect, I need the aid and patronage of your lordship and also that that you grant me permission for the servants my mother has in her service to go with her for her assistance and help on the journey in accordance with the aforesaid.

I petition and beg that for my security the said license which has been presented before your lordship be returned to me together with your lordship's provision, for thus I hope in the good zeal, Christianity and love of your lordship, etc.

Baltasar Domínguez de Mendoza (rubric)

And [the foregoing] having been seen by the governor and captain general, he said that he acknowledged its presentation together with that of the said license from the most excellent lord viceroy of this New Spain; and since it is a mandate of the supreme government he obeyed and rendered obedience to it; and in its fulfillment the one mentioned in it may leave and take his family as stated in the said license; and that both the said license and this petition are to remain in the archive of this government, and license is to be issued to the petitioner, stating what His

Excellency grants to him. Thus he provided, ordered, and signed, before me, the present secretary of government and war.

Domingo Jironza Petríz de Cruzate (rubric). Before me, Alfonso Rael de Aguilar, secretary of government and war (rubric).

Notes
    1. SANM II, nos. 47 and 48.

Document 57

Decree of Governor Domingo Jironza Petríz de Cruzate

El Paso, March 1, 1689[1]

General don Domingo Jironza Petríz de Cruzate, governor and captain general of the kingdom and provinces of New Mexico and its presidio for His Majesty, etc.

The most excellent lord viceroy, on recommendation of the fiscal, has conceded license to Maestre de Campo don Juan Domínguez de Mendoza and his family [to leave New Mexico] on condition that it should not create a precedent. This [license] was presented before me and I obeyed it as an order of the supreme government. By virtue thereof, the said Maestre de Campo Juan Domínguez [de Mendoza] may leave this country with his family, and in order that he may not be detained and in order that it may be of record, I ordered the present [writing] issued. The said license and the petition that was presented before me remain in the archive of this government.[2]

Done in this Real del Paso del Río del Norte on the first of March of the year 1689. Signed by my name and countersigned by the undersigned secretary of government and war. Domingo Jironza Petríz de Cruzate (rubric). By order of the governor and captain general, Alfonso Rael de Aguilar, secretary of government and war (rubric).

Notes
    1. BNE, Madrid, MSS 19258, photo 105.
    2. See Doc. 56, supra, Permission for Maestre de Campo don Juan Domínguez de Mendoza to Bring His Wife and Family from El Paso del Río del Norte to Mexico City, July 23, 1688.

Document 58

Information Given by Maestre de Campo Don Juan Domínguez de Mendoza

Mexico City, June 6, 1693[1]

In the City of Mexico on June 6, 1693, Lord don Theobaldo de Gorráez Beaumont y Navarra, Comisario General de la Caballería of this kingdom, corregidor of this city, by His Majesty's will, read this petition.

I, Maestre de Campo don Juan Domínguez y Mendoza, a citizen of this city, present myself before your lordship and I say that it is within my rights for you to receive from me information [confirming] that I am the one mentioned in the papers and documents of nobility, which I present with the necessary solemnity and oath so that I may have the originals returned to me.

I plead and supplicate to your lordship to have the said papers and other representations [*recaudos*] served and presented, receiving from you the information that I offered before the present public scribe or other royal [scribe], and to deliver them to me original in order to protect my rights with the said papers and the rest. I ask for justice and swear to God and the cross that what is referred to is true, etc.

Bachiller Buenaventura del Guijo (rubric) Don Juan Domínguez y Mendoza (rubric)

Decree

And for his favor, which was evident in the papers of services and documents of nobility that are referred to in the petition, I order that he be given the information that he offered in writing before the present public scribe to whom it was commissioned. For him they are proof of the said accounts of the witnesses, and copies were made in order to deliver back to him the originals that were authorized in public form and manner, as certified. And they are to carry this out and return the said representations, and as such I decide and I sign. Theobaldo de Gorráez (rubric). Gerónimo Ruiz Cabal, public scribe (rubric).

Brief

Don Nicolás de Tapia y Sosa, sixty-seven years of age.
The personal questions do not apply to him.

In the City of Mexico, on the sixth day of June 1693, Maestre de Campo don Juan Domínguez de Mendoza, concerning the information that he has offered and is order to receive, presented as a witness Captain don Nicolás de Tapia y Sosa, present alcalde mayor of His Majesty of the mines of Tetela del Río, resident of this city, who took the oath before God, Our Lord, [in the presence of] me, the scribe, to tell the truth and was questioned about the said petition:

He said he has known the said Maestre de Campo don Juan Domínguez de Mendoza for a period of thirty years, and he knows and is certain that the papers that he has and that were shown to this witness refer to and pertain to the above said [Domínguez de Mendoza], and in each of the papers the contents refer to the said maestre de campo, and [the papers] are, and they contain [an account] of his personal services, and he has remitted the said recaudos [taxes/fees/bonds]. This is the sworn truth that he makes and affirms and ratifies it as such. He declared to be the age of sixty-seven years, and the legal personal questions of the law did not apply to him, and he signed it. D. Nicolás de Tapia y Sosa (rubric). Before me, Gerónimo Ruiz Cabal, public scribe (rubric).

Don Melchor Fernández, sixty years of age.
The personal questions do not apply to him.

In the City of Mexico, on the sixth day of June 1693, the said Maestre de Campo don Juan Domínguez de Mendoza, concerning the said brief, presented as a witness don Melchor Fernández, taxpaying citizen of this said city, who through me, the scribe, swore before God, Our Lord, and the sign of the cross in due form to tell the truth, and he was asked about the said petition:

He said that he has known the said Maestre de Campo don Juan Domínguez de Mendoza in this part [of the country] for twenty-five years, and what he knows is that the papers pertain to the proof of nobility and services presented by him [Domínguez de Mendoza] and at his own cost, and [the witness] knows that he was occupied in all the things expressed in the papers, which is public knowledge and well known. [The witness] swore what he had to say is the truth and so affirmed and ratified [this statement]. He declared to be the age of sixty years, and the personal questions of the law did not apply to him. He signed it. Melchor Fernández (rubric). Before me, Gerónimo Ruiz Cabal, public scribe (rubric).

Don Antonio Sarmiento, fifty-two years of age.
The personal questions do not apply to him.

In the City of Mexico, on the ninth day of June 1693, the said Maestre de Campo Juan Domínguez y Mendoza on his behalf presented as a witness Captain and Sargento Mayor don Antonio Sarmiento Jirón, a taxpaying citizen of this city from whom I, the scribe, received his oath made before God, Our Lord, and the sign of the cross in due form, promising to speak the truth, and was asked [the questions] according to the petition of the previous page:

He said that he has known the said Maestre de Campo don Juan Domínguez de Mendoza more that forty years in this part [of the country], and he knows and confirms that the papers shown to this witness, and which refer to the executoria and personal services, pertain to the said Maestre de Campo don Juan Domínguez de Mendoza, having been acquired at his cost and in the service to His Majesty in the [kingdom of] New Mexico. This witness has seen him [Domínguez de Mendoza] carry out the said charges that are described in the said papers, since this witness has served His Majesty in the said New Mexico along with him [Domínguez de Mendoza]. What he [the witness] presents here is the truth under the oath he has made and he affirmed and ratified [this statement]. He declared to be the age of fifty-two years of age, more or less, and the personal questions of the law did not apply to him. He signed it. Don Antonio Sarmiento Jirón Guerrero de Luna (rubric). Before me, Gerónimo Ruiz Cabal, public scribe (rubric).

Captain Don Pedro Ramírez de Cañizares, sixty-seven years of age.
The personal questions do not apply to him.

In the City of Mexico, on the ninth day of June 1693, the said Maestre de Campo Juan Domínguez y Mendoza on his behalf presented as a witness Captain Pedro Ramírez de Cañizares, a tax-paying citizen of this city from whom I, the scribe, received his oath made before God, Our Lord, and the sign of the cross in due form, promising to speak the truth, and was asked [the questions] according to the petition of the previous page:

He said that he has known the said Maestre de Campo don Juan Domínguez de Mendoza for the period of forty years, more or less, and he knows that the papers that were shown to this witness pertain to the said Maestre de Campo don Juan Domínguez de Mendoza because he saw them and recognized them to be the executoria and personal services that the said Maestre de Campo don Juan Domínguez de Mendoza made at his cost in the [kingdom of] New Mexico. This witness has seen him [Domínguez de Mendoza] carry out the said charges that are described in the said papers and has served His Majesty in the company of the said maestre de campo in the said New Mexico. What he had to say here is what indeed has occurred and is the truth under the oath he has made, and he affirmed and ratified [this statement]. He declared to be the age of sixty-seven years of age, more or less, and the personal questions of the law did not apply to him. He signed it. Don Pedro Ramírez de Cañizares (rubric). Before me, Gerónimo Ruiz Cabal, public scribe (rubric).

Notes

1. BNE, Madrid, MSS 19258, photos 155–61. Translation by José Antonio Esquibel and Marc Simmons.

Document 59

License for Maestre de Campo Juan Domínguez de Mendoza to Go to Spain

Mexico City, June 12, 1693[1]

Don Gaspar de Sandoval Cerda Silva y Mendoza, Conde de Galve, gentleman of His Majesty's chamber, Comendador de Zalamea and Ceclavin of the Order and Knighthood of Alcántara, viceroy, governor, and captain general of this New Spain, and president of its royal audiencia.

Inasmuch as the following memorial was presented before me:

Most Excellent Sir: Maestre de Campo don Juan Domínguez de Mendoza, citizen of this city, states that it is necessary for him to go to the kingdoms of Castile on urgent business which absolutely requires personal attention.

Therefore, in order to be able to do so, I petition and beg Your Excellency to be good enough to grant me your permission and consent, which the supplicant will receive as a favor, trusting in the greatness of Your Excellency. Juan Domínguez y Mendoza.

Having seen the [foregoing], I ordered that it be given to the fiscal of His Majesty, who replied as follows:

Most Excellent Sir: The fiscal of His Majesty says that if it please Your Excellency, you may grant the supplicant the license he seeks to go to the kingdoms of Castile provided that he presents certifications that he is not a debtor of the real hacienda and that he has no lawsuits pending in any of the offices of this superior government and royal audiencia to prevent it. With regard to this matter Your Excellency will order what is best and most suitable, as always. Mexico [City], May 28, 1693. Dr. don Juan de Escalante y Mendoza.

And provisions having been made that he should present all the certifications which the fiscal mentions in his reply and also one from the notary of war that he has no lawsuit [pending], and that all of them have been drawn up they should be brought to me for my decision, he presented the said certifications to me with the following memorial.

Most Excellent Sir: Maestre de Campo don Juan Domínguez y Mendoza says that Your Excellency saw fit to order him to present the certifications proving that he owes nothing to His Majesty and the other [certifications] which are usually presented for the purpose of obtaining the license to go to Spain for which he has petitioned Your Excellency. And in fulfillment of Your Excellency's order he makes presentation of the aforesaid certifications with due solemnity.

Therefore he petitions and begs Your Excellency to be pleased to grant him the license to go to Castile for which he asks, since he is not a debtor to His Majesty in any quantity whatsoever nor as one who has put up bind for another, nor are there any claims against him, which the governor of New Mexico instituted and which the most excellent Conde de la Monclova decided, absolving and freeing him, as is of record in one of the aforesaid certifications. Such an order from Your Excellency will be received by the supplicant as a benefactor and favor. Juan Domínguez y Mendoza.

And having seen the foregoing, for the present I grant permission to the aforesaid Maestre [de Campo] Juan Domínguez y Mendoza to go to the kingdoms of Castile in the present fleet now anchored in the port of San Juan de Ulloa, and I order all the judges and justices of His Majesty not to put any difficulty or impediment in the way of his using the license, provided he first obtains the usual one from the tribunal of the Holy Office of the Inquisition of this New Spain. Mexico [City], June 12, 1693. El Conde de Galve (rubric). By order of His Excellency, Don Pedro Velásquez de la Cadena (rubric).

Insofar as it concerns the Holy Office of the Inquisition of this New Spain, let him who is mentioned in the license go [to Spain]. Inquisition of Mexico, and June 12, 1693. By order of the Holy Office, don Diego de V . . . [illegible] Gaviria (rubric).

He presented the certifications (rubric).
Recorded (rubric).
Your Excellency grants Maestre de Campo don Juan Domínguez de Mendoza license to go to the kingdoms of Spain in the present fleet, pending the usual [authorization] by the tribunal of the Holy Office of the Inquisition.

Notes
1. BNE, Madrid, MSS 19258, photos 82–84.

Document 60

Résumé of Papers Presented by Baltasar Domínguez de Mendoza
Madrid, August 19, 1694[1]

Don Baltasar Domínguez de Mendoza, resident in this capital.

While he was serving as a soldier in the kingdom of New Mexico in the imitation of his father, don Juan Domínguez de Mendoza, who had done so more that forty years, the governor of New Mexico, on December 27, 1672, appointed him alférez real of all that kingdom, and on October 20, 1674, captain of cavalry for the war against the rebellious Indians.

He is the grandson of Bartolomé Domínguez de Mendoza [sic], [one of the] first conquerors and settlers of that kingdom, which he entered with thirty families whom he took at his own expense.[2]

His father began to serve at his own expense and cost in the year 1642 in the conquest of the New Kingdom of Mexico, where he was alférez real; twice captain of infantry; sargento mayor of the kingdom and its provinces; alcalde mayor of the jurisdiction of Sandia and pueblo of Isleta; and lieutenant captain general, holding this post of captain general on seven more occasions, both as an administrative office and going on campaign; four times commander of various troops which were formed for the reduction and punishment of the rebellious Indians and new conquests; on another occasion he was lieutenant captain general for the visita of the whole kingdom; twice inspector of His Majesty's wagons, which go from Mexico [City] with the allowances for the presidios of New Mexico and its provinces; and six times maestre de campo of war and campaign; all by commissions from the governors of the said New Mexico. Finally, in the year 1683, he was appointed commander and head of the force and evangelical ministers which Governor don Domingo de Jironza Petríz de Cruzate raised for the conversion of the Indians of the Jumano nation and many other [nations] who asked for baptism, and to attempt the discovery of the kingdom of Gran Quivira and the Tejas, which expedition he carried out at his own expense.

Governors Hernando de Ugarte y la Concha, don Juan de Samaniego y Jaca, don Juan Francisco Treviño, don Antonio de Otermín, and the above-mentioned don Domingo Jironza certify that the said don Juan Domínguez de Mendoza entered to serve in those conquests in the year 1642, from which time up to 1680 he continued serving with outstanding zeal, application, and toil, maintaining cuerdas, arms, and horses. Being one of the persons of whose services they have availed themselves on occasions of danger [and] expeditions into the lands of infidel and rebellious Indians, he attained the offices and commissions which have been listed. In the war which was carried out with the Escanjaques Indians and their protégés, they killed 1,600 of them and ransomed twenty-five Christians whom they were holding captive, and in the expedition which was made to the Sierra Blanca he also ransomed twenty-seven women and children. In the entrada for the punishment and reduction of the Apache Indians of the cordilleras of the west and that which was made into New Mexico, he went with the first as head of troop and division. He killed fifteen of their men and captured thirty-five and rescued the persons they were holding as slaves. And in the second in which he was put in charge of a division of sixty soldiers, he destroyed more than 2,500 fanegas of maize belonging to the natives, capturing the Apache Indians. And on several occasions he burned, sacked, and destroyed their milpas, houses, and sowings, which brought about the submission of various nations. In these encounters he received two wounds, running great risk, all of which I related in the certifications mentioned, [and in] the original titles and commissions which are authorized and verified by the cabildo of the villa of Santa Fe, capital of the kingdom of New Mexico. [The cabildo] relates that the said don Baltasar de Mendoza is a legitimate son of don Juan Domínguez de Mendoza who performed the services which are described, and that he has a brother, and that both of them together with their father have served as soldiers in that kingdom and its provinces in its conquest, pacification, and reduction. In particular all three [served] in the expedition of the east which was made in 1684 by order of General don Domingo de Jironza. Madrid, August 19 of the year 1694.

Notes

1. BNE, Madrid, MSS 92581, photos 88–91.
2. In the version of this document preserved in AGI, Indiferente, 133, N. 142 (Relación de méritos y servicios de Baltasar Domínguez de Mendoza), this statement appears later in the document, and the entire statement is crossed out, indicating an error in the statement and the need for its deletion.

Document 61

Report of the Council of the Indies Concerning Petitions Made by Baltasar Domínguez de Mendoza

Madrid, October 1, 1694[1]

Duque de Montalbo. Conde de Villaumbrosa. Conde de Cifuentes. Don Bernardino de Valdes.

Sir: By decree of August 2 last of this year Your Majesty was pleased to remit a memorial of don Baltasar Domínguez y Mendoza in order that we might take it under consideration and report our opinion to Your Majesty.

He relates in the memorial that his father, don Juan Domínguez de Mendoza, served for forty-four years in the wars of New Mexico, where he himself served as a soldier. When they were both coming to these kingdoms, they were shipwrecked on the sea, losing everything they had with them, and afterward his father died. And, for the services of both, he begs Your Majesty to be pleased to grant him a future right to succeed the governorship of New Mexico when it becomes vacant, or to the *alcaldía mayor* of Sonora.

With regard to this representation, the cámara, in view of the state of the two offices the future right to which this party seeks, finds that by Your Majesty's favor the first is being served by don Diego de Vargas Zapata y Luján, and that don Pedro [Rodríguez] Cubero holds the right to succeed him, and that both made a pecuniary contribution for it. The alcaldía mayor of Sonora was also granted to Captain don Melchor Ruiz in return for a pecuniary consideration; and because he arrived in Mexico in poor health, he resigned it. The viceroy had received an order from Your Majesty to employ don Domingo Jironza Petríz y Cruzate in the governorship of New Mexico (because of the excellent progress he made with regard to the reduction of various Indian nations who were in revolt) and, being unable to put this into effect because don Diego de Vargas is serving there, as has been said, he placed don Domingo Jironza in possession of the alcaldía mayor of Sonora. In the past, this [office] has been at the disposal of the governor of Nueva Vizcaya. At the petition of don Juan Bautista de la Rea, upon whom Your Majesty has conferred this office, it has been conceded that during the time he may govern no appointment to this alcaldía mayor is to be made. For these reasons, and in particular because it is against the royal orders of Your Majesty to present candidates for the right to succeed to office when they become vacant, pecuniary considerations alone, because of the powerful motive of public necessity, can obligate any dispensation from these orders. It is to be regretted that the cámara is in a state which permits the possibility of quick action upon the claims of this party. On the basis of this information, Your Majesty will decide as it may please you. Madrid, October 1694.

Cámara de Indias. October, 1694. Decided on the eleventh. It is in response to a decree of Your Majesty, together with which you were pleased to remit a memorial of don Baltasar Domínguez y Mendoza in which he asks to be granted the right to succeed to the governorship of New Mexico or the alcaldía mayor of Sonora; and, with regard to this pretension, it sets forth the reasons which exist for not allowing it.
Seen. (Rubric of don Bernardino Antonio de Pardiñas)[2]
Done. Don Bernardino Antonio de Pardiñas.

Notes

1. AGI, Guadalajara, leg. 73.
2. Don Bernardino Antonio de Pardiñas Villar de Franco was Secretary of the Council of the Indies from October 5, 1694, to July 1697. Ernesto Shäfer, *El consejo real y supremo de las Indias: su historia, organización y labor administriva hasta la terminación de la Casa de Austria*, vol. 1: *História y organización del Consejo y de las Casa de Contratación de las Indias* (Sevilla: Centro de Estudio de America, Universidad de Sevilla, 1935), 371. (E & S)

Document 62

Petition of Baltasar Domínguez de Mendoza to the Crown Asking for the Corregimiento of Tlajomulco and Caxititlan

[Madrid, November] 1694[1]

Sir: Captain don Baltasar Domínguez y Mendoza, son of Maestre de Campo don Juan Domínguez y Mendoza, citizen of the provinces of New Mexico, states that his aforesaid father served Your Majesty for more than forty-four years in the conquest of the aforesaid New Mexico and the reduction of other provinces. His aforesaid father, his grandfather, and the supplicant himself and his brother brought in different numbers of families, always at the expense of their own private means, and [underwent] the very many hardships and dangers which can be believed of such costly and dangerous enterprise, as is all on record in authentic papers which have been presented in the secretariat, and in the report of services which has been drawn up from them.

When his aforesaid father and he were coming to place themselves at Your Majesty's feet in order to give you the information which they had him acquire by their experience in those regions, the ship in which they were coming was wrecked and they lost the residue of their fortune. And after they had reached land and came to this capital, his aforesaid father died immediately in its general hospital where, for lack of means, it had been necessary for him to take shelter.

By virtue of his own services and those of his father and grandfather, the supplicant petitioned Your Majesty to appoint him the *gobierno* of New Mexico or the alcaldía mayor of Sonora, but he has not obtained either because of the interdict against granting rights to succession to offices before they become vacant. The corregimiento of the pueblo of Tlajomulco and Caxtitlan in the jurisdiction of Nueva Galicia is vacant because the person upon whom it was conferred has not been able to go to serve the office.

Therefore, in remuneration of the services which have been described and out of compassion for his need and family responsibility, since he has been left destitute of resources and without any means of supporting himself or returning to his household as a result of the loss of his father and the resources they had with them, for everything perished in the sea, I beg Your Majesty to be pleased to incline your royal clemency to all the aforesaid by granting him the above-mentioned corregimiento of Tlajomulco and Caxititlan for five years, issuing an order to the president and Audiencia of Guadalajara to give him possession as soon as he arrives, for since no appointment has been made by Your Majesty, there will be no reason to prevent them from doing so. By this means the supplicant will find himself rewarded by the royal hand of Your Majesty, and others will be inspired with great zeal and fervor for the royal service in the hope of the reward, as his father confidently expected an even greater one, if he had not died before placing himself at the feet of Your Majesty, from whom he hopes to receive favor, etc.

Baltasar Domíngues y Mendoza (rubric).

Cámara

Sir: Captain don Baltasar Domínguez de Mendoza relates that his father served for more than forty-four years in the wars of New Mexico, where the supplicant's grandfather, the supplicant, and a brother of his have also served as soldiers. While coming to these kingdoms they were shipwrecked, losing everything they had with them, and a few days after they reached Madrid his father died in the hospital. Because of the service mentioned he asked to be honored with the governorship of New Mexico or the alcaldía mayor of Sonora, but consent has not been given because of the interdict against granting rights to succeed to offices before they become vacant, which was the case with regard to those he desired. And because the corregimiento of the pueblos of Tlajomulco and Caxititlan in the jurisdiction of Guadalajara is now vacant, he asks to be granted this office for five years, with an order to the president and Audiencia to give him possession as soon as he arrives.

Let the report of services, which records those performed by the supplicant's father and his own appointments as alférez real and captain of cavalry against the rebellious Indians of New Mexico, be brought.

His Majesty remitted a memorial of the aforesaid don Baltasar in order that his petition for the governorship of New Mexico or the alcaldía mayor of Sonora might be considered. It was found to be against orders to grant future rights to offices before they become vacant, and His Majesty accepted the report.

The corregimiento for which he now asks is vacant; and the first time it was conferred it brought two thousand pesos *escudos*, which have been ordered returned to the party because he is unable to serve.

Let the report made by don Baltasar be brought.

Cámara. November 29, 1694.

Being resolved that the appointment to the offices shall be for pecuniary consideration, the favor or remuneration to which he pretends cannot be allowed.

Notes
  1. AGI, Guadalajara, leg. 40, Cartas y expedientes de personas seculars, 1675–1698.

Document 63

Petition of Baltasar Domínguez de Mendoza Asking for Admission to One of the Military Orders

[Madrid], March 1695[1]

Sir: Captain don Baltasar Domínguez y Mendoza, son of Maestre de Campo don Juan Domínguez y Mendoza, says that his aforesaid father served Your Majesty for more than forty-four years in the conquest of the aforesaid New Mexico and reduction of other provinces. His aforesaid father, as well as his grandfather, the supplicant himself, and a brother of his, brought different families there, and always at the expense of their private means, [undergoing] the very great hardships and dangers which can be believed of such costly and dangerous enterprises, as is all on record in authentic papers which have been presented in the secretariat, and in the report of services which has been drawn up from them.

And when he and his aforesaid father were coming to place themselves at Your Majesty's feet in order to give you the information they had acquired by their experience in those regions, the ship on which they were coming was wrecked and they lost the residue of their fortune. And after they had reached land and come to this capital, his aforesaid father died immediately in its general hospital, where he had been obliged to take shelter for lack of means.

And the supplicant, in virtue of his own services and those of his father and grandfather, petitioned Your Majesty to grant him the governorship of New Mexico or the corregimiento of Tlajomulco. He has not obtained either one because of the interdict against granting rights of future vacancies and also because Your Majesty has ordered that all [such appointments] be made for a pecuniary consideration.

Therefore, their aforesaid services have never been rewarded because they were performed in the farthest limits of the world of New Spain and because they have never before been able to come to place themselves at Your Majesty's feet as the supplicant has done. Nevertheless, at the end of a year of pressing his claims, he has not even obtained a grant of aid with which to support himself, although his aforesaid father spent all his patrimony in the royal service of Your Majesty.

Therefore, since at the present time he has no money to offer for the appointment to the aforesaid governorship, nor any means of receiving the reward for his services, he begs Your Majesty, in remuneration of the services which have been described and out of compassion for his need and family responsibilities, because he has been left destitute of resources and without any way of being able to maintain himself or to return to his household as a result of the loss of his father and the slender means they had with them, which were all lost in the sea, that Your Majesty be pleased to incline your royal clemency to all the aforesaid, granting him one of the three military habits for himself or his son, and for a brother of his who has also served Your Majesty in the aforesaid provinces at the expense of the aforesaid maestre de campo, his father. By this means the supplicant and he will find themselves rewarded by the royal hand of Your Majesty and others will be inspired with great zeal and fervor in the hope of the reward, as his father was confident of an even greater one, if he had died before placing himself at Your Majesty's feet.

He also begs you to be pleased to order that the patent and privilege of nobility [*ejucutoria y privilegio*] which his aforesaid father won be revalidated for its greater validation, as he hopes from the greatness of Your Majesty. Baltasar Domínguez y Mendoza (rubric).

Junta. Sir: Captain Baltasar Domínguez y Mendoza relates that his father served for more than forty-four years in the wars of New Mexico, where the supplicant and a brother of his, and his grandfather have also served as soldiers. While on their way to these kingdoms they were shipwrecked, losing everything they had with them, and a few days after their arrival in Madrid his father died in the hospital. In consideration of his own services and those of his father and ancestors, he has asked for the various offices which he has not obtained because appointments to them are for a pecuniary consideration and he does not possess the means to apply for them.

Therefore he begs to be granted the habit of one of the three military orders for himself or a son, or for a brother who has also served in the aforesaid wars.

Let the report of services which records those performed by the supplicant's father and his own appointments as alférez real and captain of cavalry against the rebellious Indians, although without verification of the length of time he served, be brought.

His Majesty, by two decrees, one of August 28, 1686, and the other of September 1, 1692, has ordered in the first that [granting] habits shall not be considered except in favor of one who has served for at least six years in the active wars; and in the second, that [granting the habit] of any of the three orders shall not be considered in the case of any person who has not served in war, for it is his royal will that they be reserved for soldiers, and that of Santiago for those who serve in armies, armadas, presidios, and frontier areas.

Junta. March 17, 1695. Let him be given a cédula of recommendation so that the viceroy may favor him and hear his claims.[2] (rubric of don Bernardino Antonio de Pardiñas)

Notes

1. AGI, Guadalajara, leg. 40, Cartas y expedientes de personas seculars, 1675–1698.
2. See Doc. 64, infra, Royal Cédula to the Viceroy of New Spain Recommending don Baltasar Domínguez de Mendoza, Madrid, April 21, 1695. (E & S)

Document 64

Royal Cédula to the Viceroy of New Spain Recommending Don Baltasar Domínguez de Mendoza

Madrid, April 21, 1695[1]

Conde de Galve, my kinsman, gentleman of my chamber, viceroy, governor, and captain general of the provinces of New Spain, and president of the royal audiencia of Mexico, or to the person or persons in charge of their government.

In consideration of the fact that don Juan Domínguez de Mendoza served me for more than forty years in the wars of New Mexico, achieving by his zeal and intelligence fortunate successes in those conquests, having been badly wounded on two occasions; and because don Baltasar Domínguez de Mendoza, his son, has also striven to deserve well in this kingdom, where he has been alférez real and captain of cavalry,[2] all by appointment of the governors of New Mexico; and in consideration of his lack of means, because when he was on his way to Spain accompanying his father, they were shipwrecked, losing all they brought, his father having died thereafter in this capital, I have desired to recommend his person to you in order that in consideration of what both have done worthy of reward in my service, you may keep him in mind and accommodate him in the offices and employments under your provision and favor him in everything else which may offer itself in the kingdom so that he may attain the relief and alleviation which his straitened circumstances necessitate, which I will consider a service.

Done in Madrid on April 12, 1695. I the King (rubric). By order of the king, our lord, don Bernardino Antonio de Pardiñas Villar de Francos (rubric). (Three rubrics).

Notes

1. BNE, Madrid, MSS 19258, photos 92–93. There is a draft of this cédula dated April 16, 1695, in AGI, Guadalajara, leg. 73.
2. See Doc. 27, supra, Commission as Alférez Real Granted to Don Baltasar de Mendoza, Santa Fe, December 27, 1672, and Doc. 29, supra, Commission as Captain of Calvary Granted to Baltasar Domínguez de Mendoza, Santa Fe, October 20, 1674.

Document 65

Papers Concerning the Return of Baltasar Domínguez de Mendoza to New Spain

May 26–July 8, 1695[1]

[Summary]

Royal cédula to the officials of the Casa de Contratación in Seville ordering them to permit don Baltasar Domínguez de Mendoza to return to New Spain in the fleet which is about to sail. Aranjuez, May 26, 1695.[2]

Order of the officials of the Casa de Contratación to the masters of ships of the fleet going to New Spain to receive Domínguez as a passenger by virtue of the above cédula. Cádiz, July 8, 1695.

Memorandum of the above order in the passenger list of the ship *Nuestra Señora de los Dolores*, owner, don Jerónimo Mier del Tojo. Cádiz, July 8, 1695.

Notes

1. BNE, Madrid, MSS 19258, photos 86–87.
2. There is a draft of this cédula, in AGI, Guadalajara, leg. 73, Minutas reales cédulas, reales provisiones consultas, 1691–1696.

Document 66

License Granted to Baltasar Domínguez de Mendoza to Travel in the Fleet of General Don Ignacio de Barrios Leal

July 8, 1695, Cádiz[1]

1695

Don Baltasar Domínguez de Mendoza seeks to return to the Provinces of New Spain from which he came by virtue of a decree from His Majesty. Before don Juan Baptista de Aguinaga and don Francisco Lorenzo de San Millán.

July 8. Don Baltasar Domínguez de Mendoza appeared and presented a royal license from His Majesty dated May 26 of this year in Aranjuez in order to return to the Provinces of New Spain from which he came to these kingdoms in the year of 1693. The royal decree being validated by señor don Bernardino Antonio de Pardiñas Villa de Francos. Accordingly, don Baltasar Domínguez was given the dispatch necessary for his boarding of any ship of the fleet that is being dispatched to the Provinces of New Spain under the command of General don Ignacio de Barrios Leal. Cádiz, July 8, 1695.

Transcription of the royal license presented by don Baltasar Domínguez for passage to the Provinces of New Spain from where he came. It is as follows:

> The King. President and Official Judges of the Casa de Contratación, of the City of Sevilla. I order that don Baltasar Domínguez y Mendoza, who came from New Spain in the fleet of 1693, is permitted to return to those provinces, boarding as soon as he can to make the voyage. He can carry with him his clothing and necessary personal belongings. Dated in Aranjuez, May 26, 1695.
>
> I, the King. By order of the king, our lord. Don Bernardino Antonio de Pardiñas Villar de Francos. At the bottom there are two rubrics.

This transcription concurs with the original royal license that don Baltasar carries in his possession along with the dispatch for boarding. Cádiz, July 6.

On this day, I gave clearance to don Baltasar Domínguez de Mendoza for boarding whichever ship of the fleet [that is bound] for New Spain.

Corregidor [rubric]

Notes

1. AGI, Contratación, 5457, N. 152. Translation by José Antonio Esquibel.

Document 67

Certification of Services of Don Juan Domínguez de Mendoza, the Younger
Santa Fe, September 18, 1701[1]

Castellan don Pedro Rodríguez Cubero, governor and captain general of the provinces of the kingdom of New Mexico for His Majesty, etc.

I certify to the king, our lord, in his royal audiencia of Mexico City, and to other judges and justices of His Majesty that with manifest danger to his life, don Juan Domínguez y Mendoza took part in carrying out the campaign I undertook in the months of June and July against the apostate Indians of the pueblo of Aguatubi. He took under his charge and as his responsibility all the provisions and stores for the war being waged against them. Although he was in the midst of so large a number of enemies and surrounded by them, he did not lose any part of the very necessary things he was bringing, availing himself of the experience he has had of the kingdom; and he fought with all courage and valor as a good vassal of His Majesty; all of which was common knowledge and known to everyone. And in order that this may be of record in favor of the said don Juan Domínguez y Mendoza, I issue the present writing in this villa of Santa Fe on the eighteenth day of the month of September of the year 1701, signed by my hand and sealed with the seal of my arms and countersigned by the present secretary. Pedro Rodríguez Cubero (rubric). By order of the governor and captain general, Pedro de Morales, secretary of government and war (rubric).

Notes

1. BNE, Madrid, MSS 19258, photo 85.

PART TWO

SUPPLEMENTAL DOCUMENTS

Translations by
France V. Scholes, Eleanor B. Adams,
and José Antonio Esquibel

Supplemental Document 1

The State of the Conversions, Churches and Conventos of the Custodia de San Pablo in New Mexico in the Matter of Granting Forty Friars

Circa 1641[1]

Certification of the notices that exist for the Custodia of the New Mexico, part of the Province of the Santo Evangelio of Mexico [City]; the state of the conversions, churches, conventos, and divine worship, which are noted above by [the] relation and notices that were given of that custody by the father predicador fray Gerónimo de Zarate Salmerón, exemplary minister in that custody, remitted to the very reverend father fray Francisco de Apodaca, Father of the Province of Cantabria and *Comisario General* of the [Provinces] of New Spain, from the year 1538 until the year 1626.

[1] The Villa de Santa Fe, the head of the said Custodia, where the governor and the Spaniards are assisted, [which] has a very good church in which is kept the Blessed Sacrament. Everything pertaining to divine worship is very complete and well arranged. It has a reasonable convento and 200 Indians under its administration capable of receiving sacraments.   200

The said Villa also has one visita at the pueblo of Tesuque with a church and 170 Indians under its administration.   170

[2] The pueblo of San Ildefonso has a very good church in which is kept the Blessed Sacrament, that which is necessary for divine worship, a music chapel and an organ, with two pueblos that are visitas and 400 Indians under its administration.   400

[3] The pueblo of Santa Clara has a very good church, that which is necessary for divine worship, a music chapel and an organ, a reasonable convento with one visita at the pueblo of San Juan. In addition it also has eight estancias and farms [*labores*] and their service people, and it has 553 souls under its administration.   553

[4] The pueblo of Nambé with a very good church and convento and everything for divine worship, music chapel and organ, with one pueblo as a visita that is called Cuyamungue, and 300 Indians under its administration.   300
[subtotal at bottom of page 85]   1,623

[5] The pueblo of Santo Domingo has a very good church in which is kept the Blessed Sacrament, a music chapel, an organ, and many musical instruments; everything for divine worship is very complete. [It has] a good convento and this pueblo has one visita called Cochiti, with a church; and there are 850 souls under its administration.   850

[6] The pueblo of San Felipe has a good church and is well adorned for divine worship; with a chapel, an organ, and other musical instruments. It has 350 souls under its administration.   350

[7] The pueblo of Pecos has a very good church, [provisions for] divine worship, an organ and music chapel; there are 1,189 souls under its administration. Distinct nation [note in margin].   1,189

[8] The pueblo of Galisteo has a church with good [provisions for] divine worship, an organ and a music chapel, and a good convento. In addition it has one visita called San Cristóbal with a good church and living quarters. There are 1,000 souls under its administration.   1,000

[9] The pueblo of San Marcos has an ordinary church and things for divine worship are poor. The convento is not finished. It has two visitas called San Lázaro and La Cienega, each poor. There are 777 souls under its administration.   777

[10] The pueblo of Chilili has a very excellent church and convento, chapel and organ. In this pueblo there have been assembled many people from other pueblos. It has 250 souls under its administration.   250

[11] The pueblo of Taxique has a very good church and convento, a music chapel and an organ, with 484 souls under its administration.   484

[12] The pueblo of Cuarác has a very good church, an organ and chapel, very good [provisions for] divine worship, with 698 souls under its administration.   698

[13] The pueblo of Abó with a church and convento, an organ, chapel and [provisions for] divine worship, with two visitas, one at Las Humanas, the other at Tabirá. It has 1,580 souls under its administration.   1,580
[subtotal at bottom of page 86]   8,961

[14] The pueblo of Jemez has a very attractive church, a good convento, chapel and organ, with 1,860 souls under its administration. Distinct nation [note in margin].   1,860

[15] The pueblo of Zía has a church, convento, chapel and organ, and one visita called Santa Ana, with 800 souls under its administration.   800

[16] The pueblo of Sandia has an excellent church in which the Blessed Sacrament is kept. There is a chapel and an organ, and very complete [provisions for] divine worship. It has visitas and *estancias de labor* [farming estancias], the visita of the pueblo of [Puaray],[2] and 640 souls under its administration. Distinct nation [note in margin, apparently referring to Puaray].   640

[17] The pueblo of Isleta has a very excellent church and convento. It has very fine music and an organ, with fourteen estancias de labor. In this pueblo there is kept the Blessed Sacrament, and it has 750 souls under its administration.   750

[18] The pueblo of Alameda has a reasonable church and convento, music and organ, poor [provisions for] divine worship, and it has 400 souls under its administration.   400

[19] The very beautiful Peñol de Acoma has on its summit the church, which is very beautiful, abundant and rare [provisions for] divine worship, a music chapel and an organ. There are 600 souls under its administration.   600

[20] The pueblo of Oraibi has a very good church, very good [provisions for] divine worship, a music chapel with many instruments, a good convento, and 1,236 souls under its administration.   1,236

[21] The pueblo of Aguatobi has a church and convento and one visita called Gualpi, with 900 souls under its administration.   900

[22] The pueblo of Xongopabi and its visita of Moxainavi have churches, a good convento, well adorned for divine worship, with 830 souls under its administration.   830

[23] The pueblo of Socorro has a church with two visitas, El Alamillo and Sevilleta. With very good [provisions for] divine worship, and 400 souls under its administration.   400

[subtotal at bottom of page 87]   17,387

[24] The pueblo of Picurís has a very good church and convento, [provisions for] divine worship and music, with 564 souls under its administration. Distinct nation [note in margin].   564

[25] The pueblo of Taos rebelled, killed its minister, destroyed a very beautiful church and convento, and profaned everything relating to divine worship; a very barbarous people—and of them 600 souls are reduced. Distinct nation [note in margin].   600

[26] The province of Zuñi severely punished for having destroyed churches and conventos and killing a minister among those working at conversion. In this province there are 1,200 Indians who have often requested a minister. Distinct nation [note in margin].   1,200

[27] The pueblo of San Pedro, which is being repopulated anew and has 200 converted souls.   200

[Total]   19,951

All the churches and conventos with all things pertaining to divine worship were built by the evangelical ministers of the Province of Santo Evangélio of Mexico [City] without avoiding the hardships of those places, attending only to the spiritual end of so many converted souls who now live peacefully in those conversions of this Custodia, and in such holy ministry is known the service of God, Our Lord, the spiritual fruit and the attention to fulfilling that which His Majesty (God protect him) has ordered of us for advancement of Our Holy Catholic Faith.

I, fray Bartolomé Márquez, secretary-general of the Indies, certify that at the request of padre fray Antonio de Aristoi, Procurato-general of the Province of Santo Evangélio of Mexico [City], this transcription was extracted from the original that is in the archive of the Secretariat of the Indies, and it concurs with it. Madrid, May 24, 1664.

Fray Bartolomé Márquez (rubric).

Secretary-general of the Indies.

Notes

1. AGI, Audiencia de México, 304, Cartas y expedientes de personas eclesiásticas, 1636. A translation of this record by France V. Scholes was originally published in the *New Mexico Historical Review* 4 (January 1929): 45–51, with some errors. Scholes prepared a new translation with corrections, which was

intended for this volume since 1944; see *New Mexico Historical Review* 19 (July 1944): 246. The following conclusions are those of Scholes. One of the errors is in the opinion that this record was a missing part or supplementary to the 1626 *Relación* of fray Gerónimo de Zárate Salmarón. Despite the inexplicable reference to Zárate Salmarón in the preamble to the list of pueblos, churches, and conventos, further investigation shows that the list comes from a slightly later period, circa 1641–1644. First, the record accounts for the killing of a friar of the province of Zuñi, undoubtedly being a reference to the murder of fray Francisco de Letrado in 1632. Second, the record indicates that the Indians of Taos had rebelled, killed their minister, and destroyed the church and convent. This appears to be a reference to events in 1639, when fray Pedro de Miranda was killed at Taos (Scholes, "Church and State in New Mexico, 1610–1650," *New Mexico Historical Review* 11 (October 1936): 137). As such, the list of churches, conventos, and the number of Indians was prepared no earlier than 1639.

Several factors lead to the conclusion that the above list of pueblos was apparently written in 1641, but certainly no later than 1644. The entry for the pueblo of Taos records that six hundred souls had been "reduced," implying that action had already been taken to restore authority in that area. We learn from a decree of Governor Juan Flores de Sierra y Valdes, dated July 16, 1641, that soon after his arrival in the spring of that year he had "subjected" the Indians of Taos. AGI, Patronato Real, 244, R. 7, exp. 7, Decree of Flores de Sierra y Valdés, July 16, 1641, Santa Fe. The reference in the above list of pueblos to six hundred souls "reduced" at Taos may be a reference to the campaign of Flores de Sierra y Valdés. It should be noted, however, that the list of pueblos does not indicate that the Taos convento was reestablished.

A letter of the Franciscan commissary general of New Spain to the commissary general of the Indies, dated March 12, 1642, makes reference to the return of the supply caravan to Mexico City, which left New Mexico in the autumn of 1641, and a *memoria* relating to the conventos of the custodia of New Mexico. Finally, there was testimony recorded in New Mexico in 1644 to the effect that there were twenty-eight doctrinas, with their churches and conventos, in the province, besides other churches and visitas (AGI, Patronato, 244, exp. 7, Testimony of Alférez Alonso Varela, Santo Domingo, August 11, 1644). The list of pueblos accounts for twenty-four conventos, not including Senecú, Taos, and Zuñi. If Senecú was established, and Taos and two more conventos at Zuñi were reestablished, between 1641 and 1644, as seems likely, then there would have been twenty-eight in 1644, as the testimony of Varela in 1644 indicates. All of this seems to indicate that the list of pueblos, churches, and conventos was written in 1641.

On August 6, 1643, Governor don Alonso Pacheco de Heredia reported that there were forty-three pueblos with twenty thousand "Christians, minus 130," and "in all the said pueblos churches and conventos were established," but twenty of the doctrinas were without ministers, leaving a count of twenty-three pueblos with ministers; AGI, Patronato, 244, R. 7, B16, f. 2r, Account of the circumstances in the death of Governor Luis de Rosas, August 6, 1643, New Mexico. (E & S)

2. The name of the visita is partially illegible. Inasmuch as the pueblo of Puaray is not mentioned elsewhere in the document, it is reasonable to assume that the word is *Puaray*.

Supplemental Document 2

List of Administrators of Justice and War during the Tenure of Governor Don Bernardo López de Mendizábal

Santa Fe, 1659–1661

List of the administrators of justice and war who were appointed by myself [Bernardo López de Mendizábal] during the said office [as governor], which is as follows:

> Alcalde mayor of Isleta and Sandia and lieutenant captain general of the Río Abajo and Salinas, Captain Juan Domínguez de Mendoza.
>
> Alcalde mayor and war captain of the Piros, Francisco Pérez Granillo, and in his absence, his brother, Alonso Pérez Granillo.
>
> Alcalde mayor of Las Salinas and war captain, Captain Pedro de Leyba, and after him, Nicolás de Aguilar.
>
> Alcalde mayor and war captain of the Provinces of Moqui, Diego de Trujillo, and after him with title as lieutenant captain general, Andrés López Sambrano.
>
> Alcalde mayor and war captain of Cochiti, Miguel de Hinojos, and after him, Toribio de la Huerta.
>
> Alcalde mayor and war captain of the Tanos, Diego González Bernal, and in the interim, Antonio de Salas.
>
> Alcalde mayor and war captain of the Tewas, Juan Luján.
>
> Lieutenant general, the Maestro de Campo Pedro Lucero [de Godoy].
>
> Secretary of governor and war, Miguel de Noriega, and after he resigned, Bartolomé Gómez Robledo.
>
> Squadron leaders of the expeditions and chastisements [*cabos de entradas y castigas*] were appointed to Maestre de Campo Francisco Gómez [Robledo], Captain Juan Domínguez [de Mendoza], Captain Miguel de Hinojos, Sargento Mayor Francisco de Madrid, Captain Juan Luján, and Captain Luis Martín [Serrano].

Certification of the notification of officials, October 2, 1661: Juan Domínguez, Pedro Lucero, Captain Pedro de Leyba, Toribio de la Huerta, Alférez Bartolomé Gómez Robledo, Captain Juan Luján, Captain Diego González Bernal, Captain Antonio de Salas, Captain Miguel de Noriega, Captain Miguel de Hinojos, Captain Nicolás de Aguilar, Captain Diego de Trujillo, Captain Andrés López Sambrano of the Moqui frontier, [and] Captain Alonso Pérez Granillo of the Piros frontier.

Notes

1. AGN, Real Audiencia, Concurso de Peñalosa, vol. 1, leg. 1. no. 2, f 6r. Translation by José Antonio Esquibel.

Supplemental Document 3

List of Papers of Merits and Services of New Mexico Vecinos

Santa Fe, July 11, 1662[1]

The papers of merits for some [vecinos] are in the possession of the said General don Bernardo López de Mendizábal, and they are as follows:

    Papers of Capitán Miguel de Ynojos [Hinojos] in 90 pages.[2]

    Papers of José Telles Girón in 6 pages.[3]

    Papers of Capitán Juan Griego in 26 pages.[4]

    Papers of Francisco Xavier in 30 pages.[5]

    Other papers of Capitán Juan Griego in 44 pages.

    Papers of Capitán Antonio de Salas in 23 pages.[6]

    Papers of Diego González Lobón in 25 pages.[7]

    Papers of doña Ana Baca in 20 pages.[8]

    Papers of Roque Cadimo in 10 pages.[9]

    Papers of Capitán Juan Luis in 4 pages.[10]

    Papers of Diego de Archuleta in 4 pages.[11]

    Papers of Francisco de Ortega in 4 pages.[12]

    Papers of Agustín Griego in 4 pages.[13]

    Papers of Francisco Ramírez in 3 pages.[14]

    Papers of Felix de Carabajal in 2 pages.[15]

    Papers of José Gutiérrez in 3 pages.[16]

    In addition, 17 petitions of different persons in 17 pages

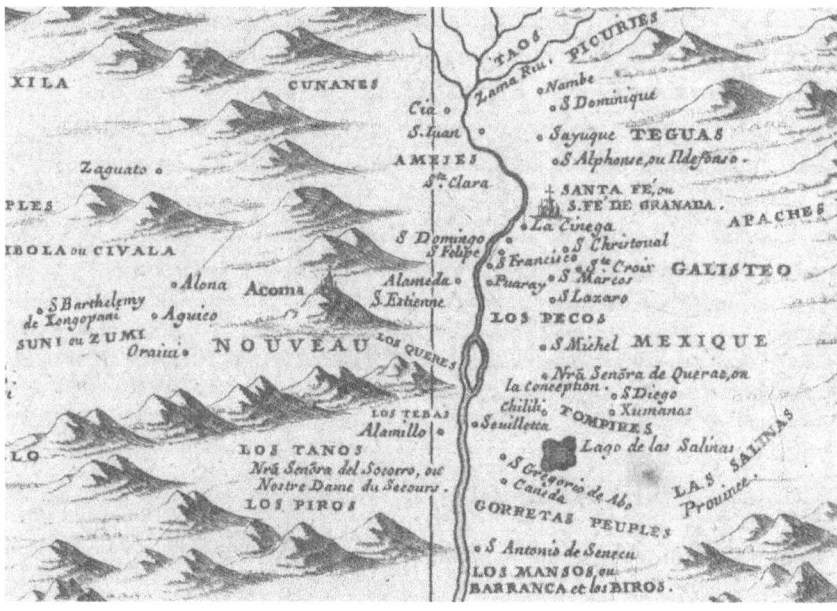

MAP 3 Las Provincias del Nuevo México. Detail of the Coronelli-Tillemon map of seventeenth-century New Mexico. In 1661 Governor don Bernardo López de Mendizábal provided this description of New Mexico: "... the Villa de Santa Fe is the only town, which consists of only thirty-eight houses of adobe, including those of nine widows and the others belonging to the vecinos. Most of the encomenderos, going against their obligation, reside away from the Villa de Santa Fe as far as fifty leagues to the south on ranches where they plant fields and raise cattle, sheep, and goats.... and there are thirty-seven Pueblo communities in the said fifty leagues to the south and another nine that are one hundred leagues to the west called the Provinces of Zuñi and Moqui." AGN, Real Audiencia, Concurso de Peñalosa, vol. 1, leg. 1, no. 2, f. 166r/313r. Fr. Vicenzo María Coronelli (1650–1718), augmented by Jean Nicolás du Tralage, Sieur de Tillemon (d. 1699), and published by Jean Baptiste Nolin (1648–1708), *Le Nouveau Mexique appele aussi Nouvelle Grenade et Marata; Avec partie de Californie*, ca. 1688, Paris. Library of Congress, Geography and Map Division, Washington, D.C.

Witnesses: Diego del Castillo (rubric) and Juan de Mondragón (rubric) before Juan Lucero de Godoy (rubric), secretary of the governor.

Notes

1. AGN, Real Audiencia, Concurso de Peñalosa, vol. 1, leg. 1, no. 1, ff. 37v–38r. Translation by José Antonio Esquibel. In the Villa de Santa Fe, during the summer of 1662, all the possessions of don Bernardo López de Mendizábal, governor of New Mexico (1659–1661), were embargoed as part of a formal investigation by royal

authorities into allegations of abuse of power related to conflicts with Franciscan missionaries and New Mexico citizens. A detailed and exhaustive inventory was carefully made on July 11, 1662. Included in this inventory were many personal papers and letters of don Bernardo. Also among the documents in his possession were papers relating to the merits and services of fifteen New Mexico citizens (fourteen men and one woman), consisting of a combined total of 299 pages.

It was customary for men of honor to submit *"papeles de méritos y servicios"* to royal authorities for the purpose of seeking recognition for personal and honorable service to the Crown and receiving special privileges, especially in being granted an encomienda, or an appointment to an important civil position, or promotion to a higher military rank. Since the list is small, it presumably represents papers of merits and services submitted during the tenure of López de Mendizábal as governor in New Mexico. It is very likely that papers of merits and services of other seventeenth-century citizens of New Mexico were submitted to other New Mexico governors before and after López de Mendizábal's tenure. If so, additional research into this potential resource of valuable personal information would prove to be quite fruitful. Unfortunately, no copies of papers of merits and services of seventeenth-century New Mexico citizens have survived among the Spanish Archives of New Mexico, and apparently no such records have been uncovered to date among existing archival collections in Mexico and Spain. In particular, it would be of great interest to read the paper of merits and services submitted under the name of doña Ana Baca.

It is not unreasonable to assume that copies of these papers were made and forwarded to royal officials in Nueva España, perhaps to officials of the Audiencia de Nueva España. If so, this could open a new avenue of research in the continued documentation of New Mexico colonial genealogies and family histories. Papers of merits and services contain a varying degree of valuable personal information. They always include noteworthy service to the Crown and sometimes provide family lineage information. Additional research into the bureaucratic protocol for processing papers of merits and services could help to identify the possible archival location of such records that may have survived to the present. (E & S)

2. Miguel de Hinojos was a son of Hernando de Hinojos and Beatriz Pérez de Bustillo. He held the encomienda of Humanas Pueblo in 1661. Chávez, *Origins of New Mexico Families*, 48. (E & S)

3. In 1661, José Telles Jirón held the encomiendas of San Felipe and Cochiti. He was a native of Los Altos de San Jacinto at Cuyoacán in Nueva España, b. ca. 1631–1632. Chávez, *Origins of New Mexico Families*, 106. (E & S)

4. Capitán Juan Griego is named frequently in the documents relating to the case against López de Mendizábal and his wife. In 1662, he was referred to as an encomendero and a vecino of the Villa de Santa Fe. AGN, Real Audiencia, Concurso de Peñalosa, vol. 1, leg. 1, no. 1, f. 38r, Deposit of the Embargoed Property of don Bernardo López de Mendizábal, July 17, 1662, Villa de Santa Fe. (E & S)

5. A native of Sevilla, Francisco Xavier arrived in New Mexico with the retinue of López de Mendizábal and became an encomendero. He married Graciana Griego, daughter of Capitán Juan Griego and Juana de la Cruz. Chávez, *Origins of New Mexico Families*, 113. (E & S)

6. Capitán Antonio de Salas was born circa 1617. He was a natural son of Petronila de Zamora and a stepson of Maestre de Campo Pedro Lucero de Godoy. His encomienda was Pojoaque Pueblo. Chávez, *Origins of New Mexico Families*, 100. (E & S)

7. Diego González Lobón was a son of Domingo González. Diego sided with the party that opposed López de Mendizábal. In fact, he was the courier for Governor Peñalosa, for whom he carried the papers relating to López de Mendizábal's residencia to Mexico City. Chávez, *Origins of New Mexico Families*, 39. (E & S)

8. This doña Ana Baca may be the same woman of this name who was widowed of her husband, Francisco López de Aragon, by 1661. She resided at her Estancia del Alamo about twelve miles from Santa Fe. Chávez, *Origins of New Mexico Families*, 54. (E & S)

9. Roque Cadimo is not accounted for in Chávez, *Origins of New Mexico Families*. (E & S)

10. Capitán Juan Luis Luján was a native of Santa Fe and married Isabel López del Castillo. Chávez, *Origins of New Mexico Families*, 62, 212, and 369–70. (E & S)

11. Diego de Archuleta is not accounted for in Chávez, *Origins of New Mexico Families*. (E & S)

12. Francisco de Ortega was identified by fray Angélico Chávez as a native of Zacatecas, born circa 1614, and living in the jurisdiction of Sandia in 1667. The presence of his papers of merits and services in the possession of Governor López de Mendizábal indicates he was in New Mexico as early as 1662. Chávez, *Origins of New Mexico Families*, 82. In April 1668, Captain Francisco de Ortega, was described as "*color pardo*," age fifty-three, married to Isabel de Zamora. AGN, Inquisición, vol. 608, f. 392v, Testimony of Capitán Francisco de Ortega, April 5, 1668, Convento de San Antonio de Isleta. In June 1670, Ortega described himself as a vecino of the jurisdiction of Sandia, age fifty-five, and married to Isabel de Zamora, when he testified in the case against Bernardo Gruber. AGN, Inquisición, vol. 666, exp. 5, f. 407r, Testimony of Captain Francisco de Ortega, June 30, 1670, Convento de San Francisco de Sandia. Tiburcio de Ortega was identified as a son of Captain Francisco de Ortega in 1670. AGN, Inquisición, vol. 666, exp. 5, f. 413r, Declaration of Athanacio, Indio Apache, July 8, 1670, Convento de San Francisco de Sandia. (E & S)

13. This Agustín Griego appears to be the elder man of this name who was identified as the father of Agustín Griego (born circa 1657). The elder Agustín Griego was married to Francisca Montoya. Chávez, *Origins of New Mexico Families*, 42 and 361. (E & S)

14. Francisco Ramírez was a native of New Mexico, born circa 1628. He was married to María López de Gracia, daughter of Captain Andrés López de Gracia. Chávez, *Origins of New Mexico Families*, 55, 90. (E & S)

15. Felíx de Carabajal (Carvajal), son of Juan de Vitoria Carvajal, was an encomendero. His wife was Juana de Arvizu. Chávez, *Origins of New Mexico Families*, 15. (E & S)

16. José Gutiérrez is not accounted for in Chávez, *Origins of New Mexico Families*. (E & S)

Supplemental Document 4

Merits and Services of Don Diego de Guadalajara Bernardo de Quirós, Lieutenant Governor of Nueva Vizcaya

Madrid, January 4, 1664[1]

It is recorded that don Francisco de Guadalajara, his father, a vecino of Zacatecas, arrived in the Provinces of New Mexico on December 13, 1628, in order to serve His Majesty with arms and horses at his own expense, with don Diego de Guadalajara and don Juan de Guadalajara, his sons. They were admitted by don Francisco Nieto de Silva, Knight of the Order of Alcántara, who governed those provinces.

The said don Diego de Guadalajara began to serve as a *soldado* on the 28th of the said month and year [of December 1628] and continued to do so with all approbation and satisfaction of those who governed the said provinces, taking part in all the occasions that presented themselves [to serve as a soldado] until the year 1634, in which, by consideration of [his] demonstrated valor, he was given the post of alférez. In the year of 1635, don Francisco Martínez de Baeza, who governed those provinces, appointed him as ayudante de sargento mayor after returning from [a campaign] in the pacification of [the provinces]. He was made capitán de caballos, appointed by those persons who governed [those provinces], and squadron leader of different incursions, battles, and assaults that presented themselves. Other governors appointed him as lieutenant, and he was favored with political positions of the most importance for having actively participated in many successful [campaigns] in the pacification and chastisement of [the provinces].

During the four years that don Luis de Rosas served as governor and captain general of the said provinces of New Mexico, he always served with his arms and horses and in particular in the discovery of the Gran Reino de Quivira, a service of great importance and augmentation for the royal Crown. And, in the sixteen months that the mutineers caused riots in the provinces of New Mexico and at length situated themselves in the Villa de Santa Fe, he was always in that [villa] assisting in service to the royal standard with all loyalty, and throughout this period of mutiny he maintained the causes of His Majesty as his cornerstone [*piedra fundamental*]. And, in consideration of his good actions, the said governor assigned him to deliver a set of papers to the viceroy of New Spain regarding the succession [of leadership] in those provinces, and following his journey the mutineers left and withdrew. In such, he defended [the Crown] with notorious risk to life and he delivered [the set of papers] to the viceroy as ordered.

In the year 1644 don Fernando de Argüello Carvajal gave him title as sargento mayor of the kingdom and provinces and of the army. In the year 1645 he was appointed as squadron leaders of the encomenderos and people who went to the province of Zuñi to collect the tributes, which is very far from the Villa de Santa Fe, and he had to pass through territory occupied by enemies. He elected to visit that province and to see how the natives were receiving the doctrine [of the Catholic faith]. In the year 1647, don Luis Guzmán, who governed those provinces and kingdom [of New Mexico], appointed him as his lieutenant of different pueblos to administer justice in which he complied and gave very good satisfaction in all he was charged to do in service to His Majesty. And, in the year 1649, he was given various commissions related to the chastisement of the Indians of the Apache nation because of their excesses that were done in the territory of Acamache.

In the year 1653, don Juan de Samaniego, who governed that kingdom and provinces, gave him title as his lieutenant governor of all the [kingdom] and he was commissioned to represent [the governor] on the journey to the territories of the east with the people that were convened, conforming to the order that was given by the viceroy of New Spain for the discovery of the Ríos de Perlas and other riches. And, in the year of 1657, the same governor appointed him as cabeza capitán y cabo of the Spanish people and natives that went to chastise the Apache Indians for their many robberies and atrocities they committed in the kingdom, and he was given authority so that with all rigor he could ruin and finish them.

He is a son of don Francisco de Guadalajara, a native of this Villa de Madrid, confirmed as a hidalgo as shown in the pedigree sent to the *Real Chancillería* of Valladolid, [and] litigated by the course of the law on March 11, 1546.

And, in 1623 his said father was elected as alcalde of the Santa Hermandad, as accorded to those of hidalgo status [to serve] in the position as protectors. He [Francisco de Guadalajara] served as administrative judge of the alcaldes of Zacatecas by appointment of the Marqués de Cerralvo, viceroy of New Spain, in the year of 1626. In 1629, the king sent a decree of His Majesty to the viceroy of New Spain in commendation of don Francisco de Guadalajara,[2] and in 1630 the said Marqués de Cerralvo gave him title as alcalde mayor of Guatulco in which he continued [in that post] in various commissions of His Majesty's service in which he performed with all approbation and zeal for royal service until 1633.[3]

This relation [of services] was extracted from that which is signed by don Felipe Morán de la Serda, scribe of government and war in New Spain, dated in Mexico [City] on March 2, 1661.

Madrid, January 4, 1664.

A decree of His Majesty sent to the viceroy of New Spain, dated January 30, 1635, was presented as attestation in which it was made understood that those soldiers who serve His Majesty in the provinces of New Mexico receive gratitude for their services, and that to each of them they be honored in accordance to their merits and that they be assured that if they come forward to ask for *mercedes*, that they be so duly consigned. It is a copy of that [original] which is signed by Juan de Pinedo, official of the secretariat of New Spain.

Notes

1. AGI, Indiferente, 120, N. 44, Relación de méritos y servicios de Diego de Guadalajara Bernardo de Quirós, Teniente de Gobernador de Nueva Vizcaya, 4 de enero de 1664. Translation by José Antonio Esquibel. Don Diego de Guadalajara, a native of Oaxaca, New Spain, married in New Mexico doña Josefa de Zamora, a daughter of Maestre de Campo Pedro Lucero de Godoy and doña Petronila de Zamora. Guadalajara's estancia was situated about eighteen miles from the pueblo of Alamillo, a Piro Pueblo settlement along the Rio Grande just north of modern-day Socorro. He was granted the encomienda of the nearby pueblo of Sevilleta, which was located about one league from his hacienda. Guadalajara cooperated in business transactions with Governor López de Mendizábal in the trade of salt. Don Diego de Guadalajara and doña Josefa de Zamora were also the parents of don Francisco de Guadalajara Bernardo de Quirós and doña Jacinta de Guadalajara Bernardo de Quiros. Don Francisco de Guadalajara Bernardo de Quiros, born circa 1638, a "*vecino del Nuevo México*," was residing in the province of Chalco in 1665 and traveled to Mexico City in that year to provide testimony in the Inquisition's

case against his first cousin (*primo hermano*), Nicolás de Aguilar, and his uncle, Sargento Mayor Diego Romero. Doña Jacinta de Guadalajara Bernardo y Quiros, born circa 1640, Santa Fe, married Felipe Romero, born circa 1639–1641, son of Matías Romero and doña Isabel de Pedraza. By 1661, doña Jacinta and her husband resided at their Estancia de San Antonio de Sevilleta, located in the area of the pueblo of Alamillo in the Río Abajo.

   It appears that after his wife's death don Diego de Guadalajara also left New Mexico. By 1679, he was residing in New Spain, where he was serving as alcalde mayor of Metepec in the Valle de Toluca. See Esquibel, "Romero Family of Seventeenth-century New Mexico," 11:3, 2–20. (E & S)

   2. This royal decree, dated September 6, 1629, is preserved in AGI, Indiferente, 452, L.A. 12, f. 122v–123, Real cédula al Marqués de Cerralvo, Virrey de Nueva España, recomendándole a Francisco de Guadalajara, September 6, 1629, Madrid. (E & S)

   3. The order to conduct the residencia of don Francisco de Guadalajara as alcalde mayor of Guatulco was issued in 1634. The order is preserved in AGN, Indiferente Virreinal, Alcaldes Mayores 6474, exp. 54, and consists of two pages. (E & S)

Supplemental Document 5

Certification of the Number of Friars Serving in the Conventos of the Custody of New Mexico

Mexico City, December 6, 1667[1]

Fray Domingo Cardoso of the Order of the Friars Minor of the Regular Observance of Our Seraphic Father St. Francis, preacher, and minister provincial of this Province of the Holy Gospel, Custodies of Tampico [and] New Mexico, nuns of Santa Clara, and Brothers of the Third Order, etc.

I certify to you the *jueces oficiales* of the royal treasury of this New Spain, who reside in this city of Mexico, that from August 3 of the year 1663 until August 3 of last year, 1666, the [number of] friar priests which will be stated have assisted and assist in the convents of the conversions of the Custody of New Mexico. And they have served during the aforesaid three years, occupying themselves in the administration of the Holy Catholic Faith and catechizing innumerable others of different nations who are being converted to it by means of their teaching and preaching. And in the same they will serve throughout the following triennium in the same activity, fulfilling insofar as pertains to us the ministry to which His Majesty (God keep him) has appointed the aforesaid friars, for which purpose he aids them with his royal alms in advance.

Therefore, in consideration of the above, there is owing to the aforesaid friars the [alms] for the three years which began to run and be counter from the third day of August of the past year of 1666 and which will cease to accrue on the third of the aforesaid month of the coming year 1669,[2] provided the number of friars which is included in this certification of ours in each one of the convents if the aforesaid Custody is maintained. And, in addition, [it certifies] the extremely urgent need there is of a larger number of priests for the greater honor and glory of both Majesties, as follows:

1. In the convent of La Concepción of the Villa of Santa Fe there are and will be three friar-priests who administer the villa itself, three visitas, and several estancias, and it is necessary that there should be five friars, four priests and one lay brother.
2. In the convent of Nuestro Padre San Francisco of Nambé there are and will be two friars, one priest and one lay brother. The priest administers the pueblo, two visitas, and several estancias. There is need of another priest.
3. In the convent of San Ildefonso there is and will be one friar-priest who administers the pueblo and six estancias, and, for lack of friars, he visits the convent of Santa Clara of Tetehuas [Tewas] and that of San Juan, which belongs to the same nation, distant and distinct pueblos. And, at the very least, three friars, two priests and one lay brother are needed.
4. In the convent of San Lorenzo of the pueblo of Picurís there are and will be two friars, one a priest who administers the pueblo. And because the aforesaid pueblo is in the sierra, and in addition to the distance, has the disadvantage that from the beginning of October until the end of April it is inaccessible because of heavy snow and the rigorous climate of the region, and because the number of natives is large, at least four friars, three of them priests, are needed for their spiritual consolation and that of the friars who are in the aforesaid pueblo.
5. In the convent of San Jerónimo of the pueblo of Thaos [Taos] there is and will be one friar-priest who administers the pueblo, which is behind all the sierras. Therefore it is indispensable that there should be two priests.

6. In the convent of Nuestra Señora de los Ángeles of the pueblo of Pecos, established in the sierra, there are and will be two friar-priests for its administration.
7. In the convent of Santa Cruz of the pueblo of Galisteo there is and will be one friar-priest who administers it and also another [pueblo] visita, and of necessity he begs for another priest.
8. In the convent of San Marcos of the pueblo so called there is and will be one friar-priest who administers it along with two visitas and three estancias. And in the aforesaid pueblo, which belongs to the nation called Tanos, at least two are needed.
9. In the convent of San Miguel of the pueblo of Taxique there is and will be one friar-priest for the administration of the aforesaid pueblo who also takes care of administering the pueblo of Chichili [Chililí] where a convent has been established under the title of La Natividad de Nuestra Señora. Both are in the sierra and there is extreme need that two friar-priests at the very least should be there.
10. In the convent of La Limpia Concepción of the pueblo of Cuarac there is and will be one friar-priest to administer it, and because it is also on the ruggedness of the sierra it is necessary that there should be at least two priests.
11. In the convent of San Gregorio of the pueblo of Abó, founded in the sierra and with like disadvantages, there is and will be one friar-priest who administers it, and there is indispensable need for the services of two priests.
12. In the convent of San Buenaventura of the pueblo of Jumanas there is and will be one friar-priest for the administration of the holy sacraments in it and in a visita which is also in within the sierra, for which reason it is obvious that the presence of two more priests is indispensable.
13. In the convent of Nuestro Padre Santo Domingo (so called), established in the aforesaid *peaje* [sic] of the sierra, there is and will be one friar-priest for the aforesaid administration in it and in a visita. And for lack of friars, he also administers the pueblo of Cochiti in which the convent of San Buenaventura is. In the convent of Nuestro Padre Santo Domingo there is a sanctuary with a lamp always lighted; and there the father custodian with a lay brother as the companion of the aforesaid father serve. There should be at least three priests in addition to the lay brother.

14. In the convent of San Diego of the pueblo of Jemez there are and will be two friars, one a priest who administers the pueblo; and it is necessary to add one more priest.
15. In the convent of La Asunción de Nuestra Señora of the pueblo of Zía there is and will be one friar-priest who administers it and a visita as well, and it is necessary that there should be two priests there.
16. In the convent of Nuestro Padre San Francisco of Sandia there are and will be two friars, one a priest who administers the aforesaid pueblo, two visitas, and about thirty estancias. For this reason three priests and a lay brother are indispensable.
17. In the convent of San Antonio of the pueblo of Isleta there is and will be one priest for the administration and custody of the sanctuary which is there with a lamp perpetually lighted. And he also has the care of fourteen estancias. Therefore the constant presence of two priests for the continuation of administration is indispensable.
18. In the convent of Nuestra Señora del Socorro (as it is called), there are and will be one friar-priest for the administration of the (convento), two visitas and two estancias, and one more priest is necessary.
19. In the convent of the glorious San Antonio of the pueblo of Senecú there are and will be two friars, one a priest who administers the aforesaid pueblo, and at the very least there is need of one more priest.
20. In the convent of San Esteban of the Peñol de Acoma, which is twenty-four leagues from the nearest settled place, there is and will be one friar-priest for its administration, and it is absolutely necessary that there be three priests.
21. In the convent of Nuestra Señora de la Candelaria of the pueblo of Alonas [Halona] there is and will be one friar-priest who administers the holy sacraments in it and one visita; and in addition, because of the great need, he attends to the pueblo of La Purísima Concepción of Hahuico [Hawikuh] as well as another visita which is thirty-six leagues from the nearest settled place. For these reasons it is impossible almost to abandon going to it and it is necessary that there should be at least three friars to administer them.
22. In the convent of San Miguel of Oraybi there is and will be one friar-priest who administers it and also a visita, as he also, for lack of a friar, takes care of the pueblo of Mojagnabi [Mishongnovi] in which there is a convent, and also a visita. And it is necessary to add another priest.

23. In the convent of Xongopavi [Shongopovi] there is a friar-priest who administers it and also a visita, and it is necessary to add another priest.
24. In the newly founded convent of Nuestra Señora de Guadalupe in El Paso del Río del Norte there are and will be two friar-priests who administer more than seven hundred new Christians and a large number of catechumens.
25. In the new conversion of the nation of the Sumas a chapel with a dwelling place has been built, the title of which is Las Llagas de Nuestro Seráfico Padre San Francisco. There is and will be one friar-priest who administers a single family of Christians and some catechumens of this nation, reducing a large number of heathens to our Holy Catholic Faith with great hope that they will receive holy baptism. He asked for another friar to help him.

And in order that the aforesaid may be evident to the aforesaid jueces oficiales of the royal treasury who reside in this city of Mexico and the usual alms given which His Majesty (God keep him) gives in advance of the aforesaid friars of our holy order for all three years which began to run, are now current, and will come to an end on the aforesaid third day of the month of August of the year dated 1669, as has been told and expressed at more length on the first page of this paper, I issue the present certification, and I swear in verbo sacerdotis with my hand on my breast that in the aforesaid conversion of the above mentioned Custody no friar has been admitted to them by me or by the reverend fathers provincial, my predecessors, who have come from the kingdoms of Castile with stipend from the king, our lord (God keep him), assigned to the Philippine Islands or specifically for other parts of these kingdoms, nor will I admit such. And I also swear in the same form mentioned above that in all the convents, visitas, and estancias of this aforesaid Custody of ours to which reference has been made, where it is customary to offer the holy sacrifice of the mass, I know that there are vestments, chalices, and other things necessary to celebrate it with decency, and also that in the convents there are books in which the natives of the aforesaid Custody are set down and written, with individual records of those who are baptized, marry, and die; and in the convents which are said in this certification to possess a sanctuary they are there, with lamps that are customarily kept lighted continually before the most holy sacrament. And I certify that this is true by the present writing, signed by our hand, sealed in this city of Mexico on December 6 of the year 1667.[3] Fray Domingo Cardoso, Minister Provincial (rubric). By order of his reverence, fray Félix de Zandategui, secretary (rubric).

Notes

1. Museo Nacional, México, Asuntos de conventos y colegios, vol. 191, ff. 21r–22v, Certificación de los religiosos del Nuevo México, 1667. A translation by Scholes of this document was published in *New Mexico Historical Review* 4 (January 1929): 51–58. Scholes made a new translation intended for the present volume. In regard to the mention of estancias, one interpretation is that these were vecino estancias within the ecclesiastic jurisdiction of the conventos. In this respect, since the friars administered to the vecinos within their jurisdiction, the estancias were mentioned to strengthen the argument for the need of additional friars. Another interpretation is that the friars, or Pueblo Indians, managed estancias that were part of the doctrinas. However, where there are numerous references in other historical documents to vecino estancias, there are no clear references to estancias run by the Pueblo Indians. In 1660, Governor don Bernardo López de Mendizábal offered this revealing description: "Each pueblo is an estancia [of] heavy labor, and every *doctrinero* [friar] is a farmer of all kinds of seeds and a livestock raiser of cattle, sheep and goats. The Indians of the pueblos labor for them without pay, and as a community they all farm the land and card wool. The *doctrineros* benefit from the fruit of the labors of one hundred of more Indians who do not enjoy any liberty or much time to care for their wives and children. The laborers are divided into troops or squadrons, each with its own leader that they call '*mayor*,' such as eight or ten *cocineros* [cooks] with a *cocinero mayor* [head cook] to serve the friar. Others included *pastores* [shepherds] with their *pastor mayor*, *gañanes* [stock raisers] with *gañan mayor*, *caballerizas* [horse herders] with their *caballerizo mayor*, *porteros* [porters] with their *porter mayor*, *fiscales* [accountants] with their *fiscal mayor*, and many *cantores* [cantors] and sacristans with their *mayores* that sing and help with the masses. Just as with the men, numerous woman are divided into groups with their *mayores* for making bread [*panaderas*], for laundry [*lavanderas*], for tailoring [*tejadoras*] and stocking makers [*medieras*]." Basically, the Franciscan friars operated a well-organized system of labor [*maquina*] centered around their convento, utilizing the Indians of the Pueblo community to run a large estancia enterprise. López de Mendizábal offered some amazing details about the convento operations, but made no mention of multiple estancias as part of the system of the conventos. López de Mendizábal further characterized the relationship of the friars with the Pueblo Indians as that of lord and slave. AGN, Real Audiencia, Concurso de Peñalosa, vol. 1, leg. 1, no. 2, ff. 177r–177v, Testimony of don Bernardo López de Mendizábal, October 24, 1660, Villa de Santa Fe. (E & S)

2. Reference is here made to the payments for the triennial mission supply service. The amount expended for each triennium depended on the number of friars serving in the province. See France V. Scholes, "The Supply Service of the New Mexican Missions in the Seventeenth Century," in *New Mexico Historical Review* 5, no. 1 (1930) : 93–115; no. 4, 386–404.

3. A note to the 1929 translation, made from a typewritten transcript of the original, states that the month was omitted. A photograph of the original in the library of the University of New Mexico, Southwest Research Center, reveals, however, that the date was December 5. The copyist who made the transcript apparently misread the abbreviated form of December as "*dias*." (E & S)

Supplemental Document 6

Account of the Services of Don Fernando de Villanueva, Governor and Captain General of the Provinces of New Mexico by Appointment of the Marqués de Mancera, Viceroy of New Spain

October 30, 1671[1]

He began to serve His Majesty in the year 1630 with the post of soldado and two escudos de ventaja in the royal armada of the ocean sea in which he continued until 1634 at which time he was promoted to alférez in the Army of Cataluña where he was at the site of Leocata until the army was retired. He was then part of the company reformed under license of the Duque de Cardona, the general of the company, which went to serve the Royal Armada of the Indies under the command of don Carlos de Ibarra. Being given the post of soldado in April 1637, he advanced and participated in the pacification of Los Algarbes, Kingdom of Portugal, attached to the army and afterward he went on at his own expense to the Presidio de la Isla de San Martín with a set of documents with regard to his royal service to present to the governor of [the presidio], who ordered that he remain there as a soldado, in which post he was given. For his part and valor, the said governor appointed him alférez and later as sargento mayor of that presidio in which he performed to all satisfaction, participating in specific services such as going to the island of Puerto Rico four times to aid with provisions, which were necessary for conducting the siege, fighting three times with the enemy engaged within the plaza, and on one occasion he left [the island] in bad condition with two wounds and retreated to the island of Anguillas, taking away two pieces of artillery from the enemy. He went various times to reconnoiter the perimeters of island, in which he brought good notice of an enemy supply ship in a bay of the said island of San Martín. The governor went out in a launch with one hundred and fifty-two soldiers and fought with the enemy with valor and *le rindio a escala vista* and they carried back eight pieces of artillery to the port and they were sold at Puerto Rico for the gain of His Majesty, and the proceeds went into the royal treasury of that city.

Afterward he went to Nueva Vizcaya where he was justicia mayor and war captain of the Real de Minas de Guanazevi y San Pedro, the frontier of the Tepeguanes. By means of his prudence and at his own cost he [helped to] pacify many barbarous Indians who were in revolt, reducing them to the peace of Our Holy Faith, which helped to increase the amount of the royal fifth. In the occasions in which there was war with the rebellious Indians of that frontier, he attended to what was ordered with satisfaction, and in the review of his tenure that was taken regarding his duties he was declared as being a good judge. With the license of the governor of Nueva Vizcaya he went to serve in the Armada de Barlovento and having returned to these kingdoms [of Spain] he went to Cataluña and took part in the assistance of Lerida.

In the year 1645, he served as an adventurer at his own cost and in return His Majesty honored him with a royal decree in which he was commended for vacant posts. And in March 1646 he returned with the post of soldado in the said Armada de Barlovento and arrived at Veracruz very ill.[2] He left there with license granted by the general of [Veracruz]. Later the Conde de Salvatierra, the viceroy of New Spain, appointed him on September 14, 1647, as alcalde mayor and war captain of the Provincias de Autlán and Puertos de la Navidad and squadron leader of the southern coast. For these services His Majesty commended his person by a decree dated May 14, 1651, to the Conde de Alba de Aliste, viceroy of those provinces, *mandandole le tubiese* by his commission and provided and occupied in offices and duties of royal service in which he served honorably.

On August 26, 1653, the viceroy Duque de Alburquerque appointed him as captain of the soldiers of the Presidio de la Villa y Provincias de San Sebastián Chiametla y Acaponeta in Nueva Vizcaya where there were some people of fierce war bordering with other provinces that were taken in possession on November 21 of the following [year]. While exercising this post, he went forth from the said Villa de San Sebastián with some soldiers of the presidio in the years 1664 and 1655 and made an inspection of the pueblos of his jurisdiction, covering all of the province where the religious doctrineros of that [jurisdiction] had been among the rebellious Indians working with those that are tranquilly pacified and left in peace as is certified by the said doctrineros, in particular those of the Company of Jesus [Jesuits]. In the course of twenty-three years there had not been a single inspection of the said pueblos by any of his predecessors; the terrain having severe waters and rivers and rugged roads, as known by the zeal in which he complied with his obligations.

On September 12, 1659, the viceroy appointed him as capitán juez protector of the Guachiciles and the Caltecos Indians that are settled in the Villa de Santiago del Saltillo, in which charge he served from November 15 when he took possession of the post until December 1, 1661, without being absent from his territory, assisting and complying with all that was expected [of him] in his duties. With the Reales Almazenes he maintained this work with vigilance of all the frontier Indians in peace and justice and defended the [frontier] from great invasions of the rebellious Indians who were responsible for some deaths and robberies. For their punishment he dispatched and went out with five companies of Spaniards and Indians that were divided up to cover those territories and there was not enough [?]. He went in his pursuit and punishment of some of [the rebellious Indians], having apprehended some of their children through which they were obligated to ask for peace, which he gave to them and returned their children. He carried out all that is here referred to without cost to the royal treasury and spent his own amount of pesos. And, to further secure peace he distributed a quantity of clothes to forty-five people and the necessary provisions so that they would return in peace to their land and without any more vexations in all of that frontier and territory, and because of this they left in peace, which he did for the greater service to His Majesty.

In concession to what is referred to above, and because of the knowledge and experience required in military affairs, which concurred in his person, the viceroy, the Marqués de Manzera, appointed him as governor and captain general of the Provinces of New Mexico on January 14, 1665, in which duties he served three years and 265 days from March 10 [1665] until November 29, 1668. The review of his tenure [residencia] is on file with the Audiencia Real de México, taking into account that he served this government and was declared to have done very well as an honest and just judge and never failed at the obligations of his offices in governing, justice and war, and all that was required of his duties seeking from His Majesty the favor of other offices to occupy. From the time he entered to govern the said Provinces of New Mexico, he was always alert with particular watchfulness and vigilance in his conservation and defense. And he discovered the general collusion that the natives of the provinces had organized and arranged with the Apache enemies for ten years, intending to cause universal damage to that kingdom and its vassals and bringing the Christian Indians to idolatry, and [this was] confirmed afterward. They stole herds of horses and other items of sustenance with their provisions from the conventos, committing those crimes with such dissolution, which it was well known publicly in various pueblos. Because of this, some of the religious doctrineros had to forsake the doctrinas and withdraw to their conventos.

And having come to agreement, the idolatrous Indians planned to kill the said governor and all of the Spaniards and religious. They had named an Indian as their captain general and worshipped another, following the bad doctrine of their ancestors, which they had arranged with such art that had not the said governor discovered their plans they would have executed a very sad ruin in that [land of] Christianity, having already killed five Spanish soldiers and six Christian Indians. He engaged the enemies in the Sierra de Magdalena, helping to kill them, where they surrendered, and also another six persons were killed together and others lost their minds in order to intercept this destruction. As soon as there was news of the events, the instigators of the insurrection were apprehended.[3] And without consideration given either to the inconveniences of time or to his many years, he took to the road with all possible secrecy and swiftness. And he went to the pueblo of Senecú where the major danger emanated and he had six of the principal heads of the mutiny executed by harquebuses and he punished other delinquents who were the keepers of many idols and instruments of witchcraft and rancor. In this way he prevented their intentions from taking place. And he also punished the Indians of the pueblo of Socorro who were allied in it and afterward he pacified and calmed the rest of the accomplices with much friendly treatment, conceding to them a general pardon in the name of His Majesty and he left them pacified.

He then returned to the said Villa de Santa Fe, which is the capital of the said Provinces of New Mexico, working in complete and tireless watchfulness and without regard to inconveniences, inspecting all of the pueblos of his governing jurisdiction, calming its residents, and through his diligence and good friendly treatment he left those provinces tranquil and pacified, clear of the abominable idolatry and the referred-to treacheries as was certified by the cabildo y regimiento of the Villa de Santa Fe and the religious guardians and doctrineros of the pueblos of his jurisdiction on February 20, and November 11 and 22, and December 12 of the past year of 1667.

Considering the grand service that he has provided for both Majesties he should be rewarded with the recompense he deserves as the restorer of that kingdom.

All this is further recorded in full length by the original papers that appear in this Hacienda of New Spain from which this information was extracted and the papers returned.

Madrid, October 30, 1671.

Notes

1. AGI, Indiferente, 123, N. 59, Relación de méritos y servicios de Fernando Villanueva, Gobernador y Capitán General de Nuevo México, October 30, 1671. Translation by José Antonio Esquibel.

2. There is a certification of the services of Sargento Mayor don Fernando de Villanueva with the Armada de Barlovento dated March 22, 1646. As certified by Captain don Pedro Alonso de Valdivieso, veedor and contador of the Armada de Barlovento, Villanueva held the post of soldado in the company of Captain don Favián de Ávila y Salazar beginning March 7, 1646. The Armada de Barlovento, the Windward Fleet, protected Spain's coastal region and the Caribbean Islands from foreign intrusion and was in port at San Lucar de Barrameda at the time of the certification of Villanueva's services. AGI, Indiferente, 113, N. 8, 2ff, Relación de méritos y servicios de Fernando Villanueva, March 22, 1646. (E & S)

3. In December 1681, Diego López Sambrano provided testimony regarding this particular incident when six Indians were hanged and others were sold and imprisoned. According to López Sambrano, a group of Piro Indians were ambushed with their Apache allies in the Sierra Magdalena, and in the ensuing skirmish five soldiers were killed. The captured leaders were hanged, which resulted in the rebellion within the Piro nation. This appears to correlate with Villanueva's reference to having to go to the pueblos of Senecú and Socorro to quell "the mutiny." In regard to this action, López Sambrano related that the Indian governor of Las Salinas, Esteban Clemente, headed a general conspiracy to drive away the herds of horses of the Spanish citizens and take them by surprise on the night of Holy Thursday in an attempt to completely destroy the vecino population and the Franciscan friars. See John L. Kessell, *Kiva, Cross and Crown: The Pecos Nation and New Mexico, 1540–1840* (Washington, D.C.: National Park Service, 1979), 225. (E & S)

Supplemental Document 7

Letter of the Viceroy to the King Regarding Aid to New Mexico to Quell the Invasion of the Apache Nation

Mexico City, January 13, 1678[1]

The Viceroy of New Spain gives an account to His Majesty of the aid that has been made for the Provinces of New Mexico because of the great jeopardy of loss due to the invasions that are continually made by the Apache Nation.

Having been consulted by the *definitorio* of the custodia and mission of the Order of San Francisco in the Provinces of New Mexico with a report made at the request of the procurador general of the Villa de Santa Fe, the *cabezera* [capital] of that kingdom and a report made by its governor, by which it is evident that those provinces are at great risk of being lost due to the continuous invasions that are made by the Chichimecas of the Apache nation, who are banded in confederation with other pagan nations that had been in a state of peace until the present times, returning to their insolence. They have destroyed five settlements, setting fire to the churches, making off with the holy vessels, profaning the holy images, some taken as trophies, especially an image of Nuestra Señora that they bring out for their customary dances. They have killed many Christians without reservation to children. They murdered father fray Pedro de Ayala, minister at the pueblo of Axuico [Hawikuh], on October 7 of the past year of 1672 and father fray Alonso Gil de Ávila, minister of the Pueblo of Senecú, on January 23 of the past year of 1675.

While in the past there was much veneration [by the Indians], now, fearing the loss of respect caused by the undertaking of similar and major cruelties, the religious petitioned me for aid for those provinces with people, arms and horses because there are no more than five Spanish men for each frontier post and there are only ten [men] that can remain in the *cabezera* Villa de Santa Fe. Many of the Spaniards are without any arms and almost all are without horses to chase the enemy. All this has been reviewed by my auditor of war, as well as by the fiscal of Your Majesty, and through consultation with the junta general de Hacienda, and all agree in the necessity of this aid and that it is best to do so immediately for the conservation of those provinces, since [on this aid] there hangs [the conservation] of the other places nearby and one upon the other that of all of New Spain.

The aid is arranged through the *real caxa* [royal treasury], which consists only of the people, arms, horses and munitions that are requested, with accounts of the expenses being handled through royal officials of Your Majesty and the auditing of accounts by the procurador general of that custody [of New Mexico]. In order that everything be economical and is of consequence to the Royal Hacienda of your majesty, [the aid] is comprised of the following arrangements and purchases. Recruit the people, either compelled or voluntary, to be delivered to the said procurador general in order that they be conducted in the wagons as is proposed, going at the responsibility and risk of those custodias, delivering that which is precisely needed for their sustenance until they reach New Mexico, where they will remain. In order that the people are sustained in advance by account of the said missionaries, the governor of those provinces will supervise the delivery of the people and supplies so that the people, as well as the arms and horses, are all accounted for with the obligation to give [a report] of the success from one to another [official] to the viceroys to acknowledge the good ends and progress of this mission.

In order to carry out this instruction, there will be various *diligencias* to show the prices and total amount of cost for the merchandise that will be bought for this aid, the conduction of the fifty men and their sustenance, being regulated and audited by the agreement and regulation of the fiscal of Your Majesty. This will be brought forward for review by the junta general for determination in making the aid, which in effect will consist of fifty men, some compelled and some volunteers, selected and intended for this purpose, for whom it is commanded that they be assisted by six months of salary in advance, four months being paid immediately and the remaining two, complementing the six, when they arrive in those provinces.

Eight persons will be paid to go with the wagons specifically for making the tortillas [*morelerles las tortillas*] and to care for the sustenance [of the fifty men]; an indispensable point in these journeys. One hundred *arquebuses de chispa* are intended to be taken to that land, one hundred swords and daggers with dressings [*aderezos de espadas y dagas*], and three thousand pesos to purchase one thousand horses in Guadiana, five hundred that are bridle-tamed in order to be handled in service immediately. In addition, twelve men will be paid and sustained as guards. And there will be named a squadron leader and commissary so that from this city [of Mexico] all the people are protected and managed so that everything will be delivered to the father procurador general of these missions under obligation of his syndic for the best assurance of this aid. In regard to the people and wagons, they will pass muster in my presence, to be held outside the walls of this city, and supported until those provinces have been judged to have attained relief and their lives secured and settled in [those provinces], including the conservation of the religious missionaries.

Of their good account, I hope to have very brief reports to notify Your Majesty, although I have had none until this time with respect to the great distance from this city to those provinces, in which the wagons take six months going and six months to return, not counting the time to prepare the wagons with supplies in delivering the various aids, charity, and stipends to the missionaries, who are also separated from each other by the distances.

Notwithstanding the above aid, which is very necessary, there is the additional cost of four thousand and seven hundred pesos, as appears from the attached attested edicts, which Your Majesty has commanded to see. God protect the Catholic and royal person of Your Majesty, since Christianity depends on you.

Mexico [City], January 13, 1678. Don Payo [Enríquez de Rivera] Archbishop of Mexico [rubric].

Notes

1. AGI, Audiencia de México, 50, R.1, N.3, ff. 1r.–3r, Cartas del Virrey Payo Enríquez de Rivera, El Virrey a Su Majestad, socorros a las provincias de Nuevo México, 13 de enero de 1678. Translation by José Antonio Esquibel.

Supplemental Document 8

Excerpt from a Petition of Fray Nicolás López to the Viceroy

Mexico City, June 7, 1685[1]

At this time [the supplicant] found himself with twenty-six captains of different infidel nations and three Christians, who were begging for the water of baptism, once, twice, and three times. The supplicant scrutinized the desire they had to become [Christians] because he had informed at considerable length by Licenciado Antonio de Salaices, commissary of the Holy Office in the Real del Parral, that many of those nations had repeatedly petitioned for the water of baptism in the said real, but it had not been granted to them on account of the long distance to the junction of the Río de Conchos with the Río del Norte. In order to learn whether the petition was sincere, the supplicant propounded to the said infidel Indians the difficulty that they did not have a church where mass could be said to them. The following day the said captains dispatched couriers, taking measurements of the altars of the church of El Paso, and they went to order a church made. And within twenty days the couriers returned with more than thirty persons, men, women, saying that all the people were at work building two churches. At the same time, they pretended that a cross had fallen down to them from the sky in order to further obligate us to [make] the said journey, as the captains by whose order the first ones had gone declared afterward. The said Indians alleged that they had been serving the king in the mines and farms of the citizens of Parral and they [the latter] had never given them ministers, although they had asked for them many times. For this reason they went to El Paso de Río del Norte, realizing its proximity and knowing that there were Spaniards residing there.

When the supplicant saw that the said Indians facilitated the journey, he decided to set forth, apostolically, on foot, with two friars, in the company of the said infidels, as is recorded in a certification. He spent thirteen days on the journey, because of going little by little, finding great numbers of heathen Suma Indians on his way to La Junta de los Ríos. When he reached the first nations, the supplicant found an adequate church built of *sacate* with its altar in accordance with the measurements the couriers had taken, and good enough to make it possible to say mass. Going six leagues farther, he found another church, much larger and more elaborate, where a halt was made; and there was also a house that the said Indians had built for the minister to live. Realizing that their desires were sincere, we began without the least delay to catechize and to baptize many babies because their parents asked for this with great importunity. The supplicant found very many Christian Indians, who, desirous of Our Holy Faith, had gone out to Parral to be baptized and had returned to their lands afterward. All of these, most excellent sir, the supplicant rescued from a simulated, involuntary apostasy, and even if nothing else had been accomplished, the journey would have been most successful. Afterward, seven other nations built their churches on their own initiative, in order that [the friars] might say mass to them, and many other nations, their neighbors, asked them to minister to them. Because the supplicant found himself short of ministers, he did not grant the spiritual nourishment to so many souls, giving them only hopes that more fathers would come later on, trying for the time being to keep them friendly to us because of the benefits that would result to the kingdom of [Nueva] Vizcaya, since once those settlements were won over, it was a safeguard to the aforesaid kingdom and its environs because it is traveled by the malevolent nations who are so prejudicial to it; and because of the great distance it is impossible to bridle their daring from Parral even though His Majesty should spend many thousands.

Seeing that the nations who were already being administered to were settled, and that they sow a great deal of maize, wheat, beans, squash, watermelons, melons, and tobacco, he immediately dispatched a courier to Governor don Domingo Jironza [Petríz de Cruzate], so that, being informed of the abundance of the land, he might be able to put into effect the establishment of a better post for those citizens. He asked him for sixty men in order that when the latter had been won over by the fatness of that country, they might settle in a good central place and be sustained without expense to His Majesty. His sole aim was to retain the said citizens in order that they might not abandon that kingdom, but he could not bring it about.

Leaving a single friar for the administration of six pueblos, the supplicant went on inland toward the north and east at the insistence of a summons from other nations who were asking for baptism, in order to keep them friendly toward us and not to displease them; and also in order to make a demarcation of the land. He made the said journey, seeing very many nations, for counting those who were already being administered, those who rendered obedience to both Majesties, wishing to detain us for the administration of holy baptism, reached the number of seventy-five.[2] Many souls were won then since some who died on that occasion received the water of baptism. And in order not to leave them unconsoled, the supplicant made a pact with the said nations that within a year or a little more a return would be made to their lands, so abundant and fat in fish, all of which is recorded in the autos which the governor of that kingdom remitted.

When the supplicant returned to the said Junta de los Ríos, father fray Antonio de Acevedo already had six churches built because of the docility of that people. The said Indians insisted that they should ask the said father whether they had taken care of him, for they had been sustaining him with maize and wheat; and the supplicant found the said friar most content at seeing the winning over of so many souls. The said Indians again asked for six more priests, because they said the father could not say mass to all the pueblos even if the supplicant left father fray Juan de Sabaleta with him. He told them that more fathers would come from Mexico [City] and that for the time being they should remain with those two.

While they were being administered in this pacific fashion, more than five hundred souls having been baptized and more than seventeen hundred rescued from apostasy, on account of the disturbance which occurred in the Real del Parral because sentence of death had been executed on eighteen Indians, and many of the latter were connected with those of La Junta del Ríos, very many nations became disaffected, and those [Indians] of the said Junta, fearing that the other malevolent nations might kill their ministers, or [kill them] for defending them, took the said fathers near to the Real del Parral, sustaining them on the journey. All its citizens and those of the environs were astonished to see that barbarians should take so much care of their priests, as is known to be truth by the governor of the said Real and all its inhabitants. Likewise, the said Indians took the vestments and chalices with which they ministered to them, keeping some images in the said Junta de los Ríos against the time when their ministers may return again, remaining with these hopes.

The said father fray Juan de Sabaleta and fray Antonio de Acevedo certified to this truth, for with no few tears they signified to the supplicant the grief of those souls already attracted to the lap of our Holy Mother Church. This, most excellent sir, is manifest proof of the love those nations have for our Holy Catholic Faith, and the docility of all of them. The writings of Madre María de Jesús [de Ágreda] show it very clearly, grieving that so many souls are damned when they are so docile. This and other cases, most excellent sir, are worthy of consideration, since it seems that for the sake of justice the said nations should be aided, and especially when they offer to make war at their own expense on the malevolent ones who endanger the citizens and miners of Parral, as is recorded in the autos which Governor Don Domingo Jironza [Petríz de Cruzate] remitted. And if necessary, the supplicant will present letters from one of the ministers in which he relates special incidents that have happened to him with the said barbarians in the administration of the holy sacraments, which verify the love these people have for our Holy Catholic Faith. He will do so whenever he is asked and it may be necessary.

[Here follows an account of the desperate situation at El Paso and on the northern frontier in the summer and autumn of 1684. López appeals for sufficient aid to maintain the settlers at El Paso, or at some more suitable place, and to carry forward the missionary labors at La Junta de los Ríos and among the tribes of the interior visited in 1683–1684. A specific request for twenty more friars is made.]

Fray Nicolás López (rubric)

Notes

1. The original of this letter and the opinion of the fiscal are in AGN, Provincias Internas, vol. 37, exp. 4, ff. 84–91. Translation by Eleanor B. Adams. In the first part of the petition, fray Nicolás López described his efforts to improve the conditions in the El Paso area after his return from Mexico City in 1683. He referred briefly to the reorganization of the Spanish and Indian settlements affected at that time. He also reported that messages of peace were received from the pueblo area and that Governor don Domingo Jironza Petríz de Cruzate considered the possibility of making an entrada. In the name of the friars, López offered food and livestock for such an expedition, which he believed might have had success, but Jironza Petríz de Cruzate finally abandoned the idea. López stated that subsequently he directed efforts to improving the desperate situation of the settlers at El Paso, but without success, and that he then seized the opportunity to engage in new missionary enterprises, as described in the following excerpt. (E & S)

2. Nine Indian nations at La Junta de los Ríos and sixty-six in the interior.

Supplemental Document 9

Letter of Fray Nicolás López to the Secretary of the Council of the Indies, Don Antonio Ortiz de Otalora

Mexico City, April 24, 1686[1]

Señor Secretary don Antonio Ortiz de Otalora. My dear Sir: The obligation of my office compels me to place myself at the feet of your lordship, offering myself as a servant of your house. Moreover, two royal cédulas of His Majesty, the one of August 2 and this last one which came in the latest dispatch-boat in April, have moved me to do so. In the first one His Majesty urgently requests detailed information from the viceroy of this New Spain concerning the lands which the most Christian king hopes to settle. At the same time His Majesty ordered that the reports and dispatches that were remitted concerning this matter should be placed in the hands of your lordship. Since at the present time I am custodian of New Mexico, procurador general of that kingdom, and legate of His Holiness in those provinces. I am sending a report to His Majesty with very detailed, clear, and precise information concerning the said lands in the east, for in the year 1683 I went to the said lands at the petition of many nations who were asking for the water of baptism and I left the said regions during the month of July of the year 1684.[2] Coming to this capital the following year of 1685, I made representations concerning all that His Majesty asks in the said royal cédula, ordering that he be given a clear and true report about all those lands. Therefore I have thought it proper to send this dispatch through the hands of your lordship, knowing your ever-present zeal in the services of both Majesties, for I have consolation that my desires will be attained if I have your lordship's patronage.

I am sending a map, which I dedicated to His Majesty, of all those eastern lands and provinces of New Mexico, because I have learned that the one I submitted to the viceroy of this New Spain was not sent to His Majesty. Moreover, another was remitted to my commissary general of the Indies in order that by some route it might reach His Majesty's hand.

Although I have asked for a certified copy of all the representations made by me, it has not been given to me, for what reason I do not know. All the information which I am giving to His Majesty will be found on record in legal form in the instruments that are now in the office of this government.

Therefore, I beg your lordship, for the love of God and our father St. Francis, to have compassion for this New Spain, so vulnerable on all sides, since your lordship's personal zeal is very well known in these parts. I am consoled by the hope of being admitted as one of your lordship's servants, and henceforward I will not fail to keep your lordship informed of whatever may happen.

The early departure of the ship does not permit me to write at greater length. I hope to find occasions when my worthless person may be fortunate enough to accomplish things pleasing to you. May God, our Lord, grant your lordship a long life and keep you for me many years, as we all have need. Mexico, April 24, 1686. Your most devoted and faithful chaplain, who kisses your hand. Fray Nicolás López (rubric).

[Endorsement]
Mexico, April 24, 1686. To the Secretary.
It came by post on November 11 of the [same year]. Number 7.

Fray Nicolás López of the Order of St. Francis, Custodian of New Mexico and Its Procurador General.

Council: It says that by virtue of two royal cédulas in which the viceroy of New Spain is ordered to give detailed description of the lands which the most Christian king hoped to settle in the provinces of New Mexico, he is giving His Majesty clear and definitive information because he entered them in the year 1684 at the petition of very many nations who were asking for baptism. After returning to Mexico [City] the following year of 1685, he made representations in the audiencia concerning all that occurred to him with regard to this matter. He is remitting a map, which he dedicated to His Majesty, of all the aforesaid lands. And because he learned that the one he submitted to the viceroy was not being sent, he remitted another to the commissary general of the Indies in order that it might reach His Majesty's hands. Although he has asked for a certified copy of the representations he has made, it has not been given to him, and he does not know the reasons why. All the information he gives will be found on record in the instruments which are now in the offices of [that] government.

The map to which he refers did not come with this letter.

Notes

1. Translation by Eleanor B. Adams. Another translation is found in Hackett, *Historical Documents*, 3:359–60. The original source is apparently part of AGI, Guadalajara, 138. (E & S)
2. See next Supp. Doc. 10, Memorial of fray Nicolás López to His Majesty, Mexico City, April 24, 1686.

Supplemental Document 10

Memorial of Fray Nicolás López to His Majesty

Mexico City, April 24, 1686[1]

Sir: On this occasion I cannot excuse myself from informing you of the wretched state in which the kingdom of New Mexico finds itself at the present time, for it has been in a bad way since the year 1680 (when its lamentable loss occurred); and, no less important, of the evil consequences which have followed and which have affected the citizens of Nueva Vizcaya and the provinces of Sonora. Therefore, I say, Sir, that many reasons impel me to take up my pen on this occasion; the first, that I am a vassal of Your Majesty; the second, because I am at present custodian and legate of His

Holiness in those provinces, and because my sacred order gave the Custodia into my charge, entrusting to my worthless person a burden so weighty for my insufficiency. Although I felt hesitant to give this information to your royal Council of the Indies, because I had already set it forth in this capital to your viceroy and fiscal, warning them of the damages, losses, and injuries that have followed since the aforesaid loss of New Mexico, as the key to all this New Spain. I was also dismayed, Sir, to see that, having presented a memo on March 24 of this year, asking for [a copy of] all my representations and warnings drawn up in the interests of your royal services and the preservation of what has been acquired, there has been unwillingness to give me the said certified copy, for what reasons I do not know. The reason, Sir, why I hesitated to report on what is happening in that kingdom at the present time is that I wanted legal documents themselves, which I have presented to state the truth which I am expressing on this occasion.

But, having been informed of your royal cédulas, one of August 2, 1685, and the latest one which has come in this last dispatch-boat, they have served to encourage me, for in the first one Your Majesty asks for detailed, clear, and precise information about the lands in the east and their inhabitants; a relation made by fray Alonso de Benavides, a former custodian of those conversions, being mentioned in the said royal cédula. The most Christian king wishes to settle these lands because of the reports that don Diego de Peñalosa has given about their great wealth, concerning which, I assure Your Majesty, he has not fallen short of the truth. Therefore I say, Sir, that it is going on seven years that I have been a missionary in those conversions, and I am an eyewitness to all that has happened since the fatal event. When I came to this city at the end of 1682, this holy province appointed me procurador general and prelate of that already destroyed custodia, not taking into consideration my insufficiency.[2] Leaving this capital for that kingdom in 1683, with the alms for the missionary friars, whom Your Majesty succors with paternal affection. God, our Lord, was pleased that I should reach the convento of El Paso, the only one that survived the uprising, although other conversions have since been made in which twelve friar-priests are occupied.

At that time, I found there thirty-three infidel captains of the Jumanos nations and others who had come to ask for baptism. This nation, Sir, was the one which, accompanied by others, came to ask for the same thing in the time of fray Alonso de Benavides, and the said father sent friars to these conversions. In these lands there was a very numerous flock of Christians, but everything came to naught for lack of support; the hour must not have arrived.

And since I was now custodian,[3] seeing that the said infidels had come on this embassy three times, I made a decision in the matter, and, accompanied by two friars, we set out, traveling on foot and barefoot, in the company of the aforesaid infidels without an escort of Spaniards, until we reached the La Junta de los Ríos, which is a distance of one hundred leagues, where the aforesaid infidels had already built us two clean and decent chapels and a house for the ministers to live in. In view of this docility and the eagerness they felt to become Christians, we immediately began to baptize the babes, because their parents offered them with extraordinary love for our Holy Law. There are nine parent nations who live in this place, all settled people; they sow maize and wheat, squash, beans, tobacco, watermelons, and melons. At times these [nations] go out to work in Parral.

Leaving a single friar for the administration of these nations, I went on, accompanied by the other, at the summons of many other nations who had sent their couriers to wait at La Junta de los Ríos so that they might go to give the news of our arrival. Although I realized, Sir, that it was not possible to give them the spiritual nourishment, because of the great lack of missionaries with which I found myself, I went on for the sole purpose of not displeasing them and of winning them to friendship with us, as I did, penetrating and surveying their lands, both on the north and on the east. I was in sixty-six nations, all docile and well inclined toward the Spaniards, who asked for the water of baptism and at the same time that we should settle them wherever we thought best. I made no decision for the reason mentioned, but, in order that they might remain assured of our friendship, a pact was made with them to return to their lands within a year and to take friars in order that they might minister to them; and as a result of this artifice they allowed us to leave.

We had been in their lands six months, sustained by the aforesaid infidels with the produce of the land alone, for all of it has such an abundance of herds of bison, which is the cattle that Captain Martín de Echaragai [sic; Echagaray][4] says grows wool like sheep, trees bearing nuts, grapevines, vines, blackberries, plums, and piñon, all in abundance; turkeys, quail, partridges, deer [in herds] like cattle;[5] everything in abundance; extremely large acorns and other kinds of wild fruits. What their hills offer in minerals is great; the abundance of rivers, great, all with diversity of fish and abounding in mother-of-pearl, from which many pearls were taken in years past. The reason why we did not do so on that occasion was so that the aforesaid infidels might not think that we were led on by greed, trying only for the time being to give them knowledge of the true God and to secure their friendship for the future.

And beside these nations, we received ambassadors from the Tejas, a powerful kingdom where Mother María de Agreda catechized many Indians, as is related in her writings. Through her intercession two friars of my order reached that kingdom in years past and baptized many Indians, their prince himself being the first to receive baptism. We received ambassadors from this kingdom and set foot upon the thresholds of the first settlement of this nation since it is not twenty-five leagues distant from the nation [where we were]. This was in the month of May of the year 1684, and we had entered in 1683. At the same time we set foot in the lands of the Aijados nation, adjoining the great kingdom of Quivira. Fray Alonso de Benavides mentions them.[6] Because the said Aijidos were at war with the nations that were friendly to us, I did not communicate with them although they were already negotiating a reconciliation with one another. It is not seventy leagues distant from Gran Quivira. I speak, Sir, with this assurance because Captain Hernando Martín, who in years past was in the first settlements of that kingdom, went with me.[7]

Moreover, Sir, I traveled over and saw the lands of many enemy nations who are dangerous to [Nueva] Vizcaya and its environs. They have their dwelling place forty leagues beyond La Junta de los Ríos on the south and east; and, in order to carry out their attacks, they take up temporary residence in the sierra they call the Sierra del Diablo, and after they have done their mischief, they withdraw to their aforesaid dwelling place. And when [the Spaniards operating] from Parral seek to remedy [the situation], it is an impossible undertaking because of the difficult mountains to be crossed. Concerning all this, Sir, I speak from experience as an eyewitness, for when I was in those lands in the year 1684, the aforesaid enemies committed many robberies in Parral, and we learned this truth by experience. This is the reason, Sir, why I solicited with your viceroy and fiscal, with extraordinary urgency, the support of those conversions of La Junta de los Ríos, because I knew the insecurity of the Real del Parral and its environs. But I have not been able to accomplish anything, for the decision in this matter was remitted to your royal Council of the Indies, even though I warned of the harm that could result from delay. This has been known by experience since the year 1684, because very many herds of horses and mules belonging to both carters and miners have been carried off from Parral, very large cattle haciendas destroyed, and many people killed, for it has reached the point that in the jurisdiction of Parral the area from the pueblo they call

Carretas, which is thirty leagues beyond the pueblo of Casas Grandes, to San Francisco de Conchos and the pueblo of Julimes has been abandoned. Concerning all this I have made representations to your viceroy and fiscal in repeated memorials, and at the same time I have pointed out the risk to New Spain once those kingdoms are lost, since as a result of the bad example of New Mexico, both friendly and enemy nations became bold.

All this truth, Sir, Your Majesty will find legally on record, if you will send for all the memorials I have presented on behalf of my order concerning this serious matter since the year 1685 in the month of May up to this present year of 1686 in the month of March. These documents are now in the office of this government. And seeing, Sir, that seventy-five nations rendered obedience to God, our Lord, and to your royal and Catholic Majesty with extraordinary docility when legal possession was taken of all those lands in your royal name by General Juan Domínguez de Mendoza, commander and chief of twenty men who later entered for our protection, overtaking us at the aforesaid Junta de los Ríos, the aforesaid commander and chief made a very detailed itinerary in which he gives information about the said expedition and records in legal from what I have related.[8]

Considering, Sir, the benefit of those souls, I thought it well to leave my two friar-companions for the administration of nine nations and to proceed to the pueblo of El Paso to communicate to the other missionaries the importance of this serious matter; I held a council of all the friars, and they were all of the opinion that I should go in person, as present prelate of that custodia and as one who had communicated with those nations and had seen and marked out the confines of their lands, to inform your viceroy and fiscal of the greatness and opulence of those lands. Since a matter of such great consequence and seriousness demanded immediate action, I set out at once to make the journey to this capital. When I arrived, I described the multitude of nations who had rendered obedience to your royal and Catholic Majesty, asking your viceroy and fiscal for twenty missionary friars for the said nations, because as a result of the petition I made to my commissary general of this New Spain, he immediately and without delay dispatched a patent for all the provinces, telling them of the said conversions and delegating his authority to me so that they may apply to me with the notice of those who might wish to go. As a result of the said patent, forty-six friars of my order responded, voluntarily asking to go to the aforesaid conversions, as a work so pleasing to God, our Lord, and in advancement of your royal Crown. But your fiscal, don Pedro de la Bastida, depreciated not only the gravity of the matter but also my person, replying that the situation was not to be evaluated according to what I represented or according to what father fray Alonso de Posada, present definitor of this holy province and former custodian of New Mexico with fourteen years' residence in those provinces, reported,[9] but that it must be judged in accordance with what General don Antonio de Otermín said. He was the governor of New Mexico during whose government that kingdom was lost, for the reasons, Sir, which the apostates proclaim this day. My failure to express them is because of the purity of my condition; but I console myself, Sir, that it is God's cause and that he will open the most fitting road.

I am inspired only by my Catholicism, by being a loyal vassal of Your Majesty, and by having seen with my own eyes the doleful loss of so many souls, for I have been present at everything. When your fiscal should have sought the reasons for the loss of that kingdom from persons of conscience, he avails himself of the very person and individual during whose government it was lost, as Your Majesty will see by the replies given by your aforesaid fiscal, don Pedro de la Bastida, of which he has been unwilling to give me a certified copy so that I might not remit them on this occasion to your royal Council of the Indies, and because I knew that I had given and expressed the clear, precise, and detailed information that is asked for in your royal cédula of August 2, and that it had been seen in junta general on August 3 of the same year of 1685, as will all be found on record in my aforesaid memorials which are now in the office of this government; and seeing that I was not going to obtain the legally certified copy, I thought it best to remit, as I do remit, to your oider, don Lope de Sierra Osorio,[10] the simple uncertified copies, although signed by my name, of two memorials, one seen in junta general on August 3, 1685, and the other presented on March 24 of the present year, which I place in Your Majesty's hands signed by my name; and by them the warnings and representations I have made will be recognized. At the same time I made a map of all those lands and nations in the east, marking on it the loss of New Mexico and the temples which the fire grievously destroyed, which I dedicated to Your Majesty because you asked for clear and precise information about all those lands; I handed it over personally to your viceroy with the enclosed memorial, and I have learned that it is not being remitted to your royal council. Therefore I am also remitting the aforesaid map, prepared by me as one who traveled through and saw, marked out and penetrated the lands of the east and reconnoitered the trails of these lands that the most Christian king hopes to settle, and I do not doubt that as a result of the good qualities of the country and the docility of the nations he may bring it to pass.

I have also represented on behalf of my sacred order the advantage of moving the post to which the citizens of Santa Fe have now retired, in order that they might find sustenance without expense to your royal treasury, for in the former pueblos of New Mexico, now lost, there was plenty of irrigated land that could be sown to provide maintenance; but at the post where the said citizens are today, they cannot accomplish this because of the unsuitability of the land. The said citizens have made representations to this effect two or three times in this capital and have also warned that, harassed by need, they were abandoning the kingdom. They asked to be given very limited financial assistance to transport their families to a suitable place where they might maintain and keep themselves without expense to your royal treasury, and this need should be succored without delay because at the time it would be assured to Your Majesty, always occupied in your royal service. Because your fiscal did not assent to my proposition, more than two hundred men capable of bearing arms have abandoned that kingdom, whom Your Majesty might have kept at the price of only the trifling aid of fifteen thousand pesos, for at that time the transportation of their families was easy. Now it will cost ten times more and time will attest this truth. I believe, Sir, that the same thing is bound to happen as did with regard to the drainage of this city, when although the harm that was threatened was foreseen, it was not believed, so that the expense is being felt to this day. I speak so plainly, Sir, because I am a loyal vassal of Your Majesty and heed only the considerations due my God and my king; and if I should deviate from the truth in any way with regard to the gravity of this matter, I beg Your Majesty once and many times for due correction and punishment, for because I know how vulnerable this New Spain is on all sides and the facility the most Christian king can have in settling those eastern regions, I find it necessary to speak about the seriousness of this matter without regard for any earthly power since it pertains to our services of both Majesties; keeping in mind, Sir, on this occasion the Catholic determination of the primitive missionaries of this New Spain when they ask for a remedy of many things from our kings and lords, predecessors of Your Majesty, with whose support they were able to spread the faith in this New World and reduce its inhabitants, attracting them to knowledge of the true God.

I, Sir, shall leave this city at the end of the coming month for that custodia. I am prepared in spirit to enter the aforesaid nations for the second time because I already know the Jumano language, have preached in it to those barbarians, and have made an extensive vocabulary of the aforesaid language, as is legally on record in the documents I have presented; and this truth will be more evident when it is given to the press, as I will do.¹¹ I hope in His Divine Majesty to harvest some fruit, although I go destitute of human support.

Finally, Sir, desirous that the aforesaid conversation should be encouraged, I communicated this matter to two brothers I have in this New Spain, miners and discoverers of the Minas del Rosario (they give them this title),¹² who have paid more than a million pesos and some thousands of marks in gold and silver in the fifth to your royal coffers (for if it should be necessary, I will remit certifications from your royal coffers), because the abundance of the aforesaid mining post is well known in this New Spain. These men, Sir, offered to allow me five hundred fanegas of maize, three hundred head of cattle, and two hundred horses. In accordance with this offer, I presented a memorial asking for one hundred men from the prisons, offering the aforesaid quantity for the sustenance and provisioning of the said people, taking into account only the saving to your royal treasury and finding out whether by this means I might be able to attain the desired end. When your fiscal saw my proposition, he scorned it, as is on record in his reply, for in all of them he had little esteem for the matter, replying at the same time that not one missionary should be granted. Since your royal cédula of August 2 has been seen, they have tried to give some appearance of activity in the matter, although nothing has actually been done to put it into effect.

All the aforesaid will be legally on record for all time and therefore I speak plainly, for although I do not deserve the happiness of placing myself at Your Majesty's feet, I am consoled by the possibility that these letters of mine may attain the good fortune of Your Majesty's ordering that they be read; for although I have well disburdened the conscience of my sacred order by making representations and giving information with regard to what befits your royal service, as will be on record for all time, I also wish to keep it completely secure in every way by giving this information to Your Majesty as present custodian and procurador general of that kingdom, and as legate of His Holiness in those provinces, since even though I might know that I should suffer many hardships, I will not fail to report whatever befits the service of both Majesties.

May God, our Lord, keep the royal and Catholic person of Your Majesty very happy and lengthy years, as all your vassals have need and we desire. México, April 24 of the year 1686.

Fray Nicolás López (rubric)

Notes

1. Translation by Eleanor B. Adams. A transcription of this memorial appears in "Don Diego de Peñalosa y su descubrimiento del reino de Quivira, Informe presentado á la Real Academia de la História por el capitán de navío, Cesáreo Fernández Duro" (Madrid: Imprenta y Fundación: Imprenta y Fundación de Manuel Tello, 1882), published in *Memorias de la Real Academia de la História* (Madrid: Imprenta y Fundación de Manuel Tello, 1885), vol. 10, 67–74. The transcription ends with this notation: "Archivo de Indias. Secretaría de España. Audiencia de Guadalaxara. Expediente sobre la conquista del Nuevo México. Años de 1639 á 1686. Copia en la Biblioteca de la Academia."

2. According to the extracts from the *Libros de Decretos* of the Franciscan Province of the Holy Gospel, now in the Biblioteca Nacional de México, legajo 9, no. 8, fray Nicolás Hurtado was elected custodian at the chapter meeting held on August 15, 1682. Soon after the arrival of Governor Jironza Petríz de Cruzate and fray Nicolás López in New Mexico in August 1683, Hurtado returned to Mexico and López was left in charge as vice-custodian. It is possible that the chapter designated López as alternate in case of Hurtado's death or absence, but the record does not say so. López served as vice-custodian until his departure in the autumn of 1684. At the meeting of the intermediate chapter on January 22, 1684, fray Salvador de San Antonio was elected custodian to replace Hurtado. Then, at the triennial chapter meeting held on June 23, 1685, fray Nicolás López, who had returned to Mexico City, was elected custodian. Finally, on June 12, 1688, fray Francisco de Vargas was named to succeed López.

3. To be exact, López was vice-custodian at the time.

4. Captain Martín de Echagaray served as many as thirty years at the Presidio de Florida before coming to New Spain. AGI, Contratación, 5460, N. 5, R. 6, f. 3r, Expediente de información y licencia de pasajeros a Indias del capitán Martín de Echagaray, a Nueva España, 5 de Julio de 1704. Over the years he served as a mariner, a *piloto mayor*, and *capitán de marigría* of the ships and frigates. In 1685, Echagaray proposed to royal officers to reconnoiter the area of Bahía del Espíritu Santo. AGN, Gobierno Virreinal, Reales Cédulas, vol. 20, exp. 111, 5 ff. Proposición del Capitán Martín de Echagaray, 1685. He was serving in the area of the mining town of Azogue near Temascaltepec around 1695–1697. He traveled to Spain, where he attained from the king the title of corregidor of Cheitla in New Spain for a period of five years and at a salary of two hundred pesos a year, as confirmed in a royal decree dated March 2, 1704. In July 1704 he was in Cádiz seeking to obtain the necessary clearance to obtain passage on a ship bound for New Spain after having been granted license. AGI Contratación, 5460, N. 5, R. 6, 10 ff. (E & S)

5. The text reads "*venados como reses vacunas.*"

6. Fray Alonso de Benavides identified that Aixaos (Aijados) as living thirty to forty leagues east of the province of Quivira, possibly in eastern Texas. George P.

Hammond, ed., *Fray Alonso de Benavides' Revised Memorial of 1634* (Albuquerque: University of New Mexico Press, 1945), 319–29. (E & S)

7. In 1650, Captain Hernán Martín Serrano and Captain Diego López del Castillo led a small troop of soldiers with a large number of Pueblo Indian warriors on an expedition to the area of modern-day Texas, following the Concho River of south-central Texas, in the region of the Jumano Indians. AGI, Indiferente, 120, N. 44, f. 1v, Relación de méritos y servicios de Diego de Guadalajara, 1664. See Supp. Doc. 4 above. (E & S)

8. Nine nations at La Junta de los Ríos and sixty-six in the interior.

9. For the report by fray Alonso de Posadas, see S. Lyman Tyler and M. Darrel Taylor, eds. and trans., "The Report of Fray Alonso de Posadas in Relation to Quivira and Teguayo," *New Mexico Historical Review* 33 (October 1958): 285–314. (E & S)

10. Licenciado don Lope de Sierra Osorio was a member of the Council of the Indies from 1684 to 1702. Ernst Schäfer, *Las rúbricas del Consejo Real y Supreme de las Indias desde la fundación del Consejo en 1524 hasta la terminación del reinado del los Austrias* (Sevilla: Universidad Publicaciones del Centro de Estudios de História, 1934), 43.

11. There is as yet no evidence that the vocabulary was ever printed.

12. This phrase is not translated because its meaning is not clear.

Supplemental Document 11

Account of the Services of Don Domingo Jironza Petríz de Cruzate, Former Governor and Captain General of the Provinces of New Mexico

January 12, 1693[1]

I, José del Castillo, public proprietary scribe del número of this City of Mexico of New Spain, give faith and true testimony in the form that I can.

Having reviewed the papers and instruments that General don Domingo Jironza Petríz de Cruzate exhibited before Captain don Alonso de Morales, justicia mayor of the Estate and Marquesdao del Valle, alcalde ordinario of this City of Mexico by [appointment of] His Majesty, and before me, to formulate this certification. First, there is recorded a testimony in brief, sealed and signed, it appears, by Carlos de Sigüenza, scribe of His Majesty, dated January 16 of the past year of 1688 in this City of Mexico.

Having asked for a memorial, that the said General don Domingo Jironza presented to the Most Excellent Señor Conde de la Monclova, viceroy, governor, and captain general of this New Spain, and president of the Real Audiencia of [New Spain], forming an narrative account of his merits and military services. And, by decree dated July 24 of the referred-to year, it was ordered to be formed. And according to the accounts that were exhibited, it appears to have been made. His Majesty, may God protect, through a royal decree, legalized by don José de Beitia Linaje, his secretary in the royal Supreme Council of the Indies, appointed the said General don Domingo Jironza as captain of the royal sealed papers (pliegos) in one notice that was dispatched to this Kingdom of New Spain, and the presidios of Santo Domingo, Puerto Rico, Havana and Cuba, in the past year of 1688, also being appointed as visitador of those [places]. For this the lord president and lord judge of the royal casas de contratación [of the Indies] in the City of Sevilla provided him with instructions for the mission of his voyage and the distribution of the sealed papers, giving him the title of captain of infantry of fifty soldiers that were enlisted for the purpose of security and defense of the said ship. And it appears from the said testimony that his said charge was completed with all punctuality, delivering all of the sealed papers. His Majesty directed the Most Excellent Señor Viceroy don fray Payo de Rivera, to whom he commended the person of the said General don Domingo Jironza, entrusting [in him] a request to Your Excellency, that as soon as he arrived with the said sealed papers, he was to accommodate him with one of the offices of his royal provisions; and if no opportunity existed, he would enlist him in one of those [offices] of Your Excellency. For his performance he was provided with the alcaldía mayor of Mestitlán, being dispatched a title in due form. He gave a good account of himself, delivering the royal tributes and other effects of the Royal Hacienda, which he administered in the two years of exercising his duties, and for which he went through a judicial review. In this review the president and oidores of this Royal Audiencia, by means of the judgment pronounced in the review, assessed him as a good, honest and just judge, worthy so that His Majesty and the Most Excellent Lord Viceroys, in his royal name, would occupy and honor him in major positions, as is recorded in the testimony of the said judicial review, which was shown and authorized by José de Anaya, royal scribe of the said Royal Audiencia.

It also appears in the papers, that with the occasion that the Indians of the Provinces of New Mexico rebelled in the past year of 1680, executing the atrocities that are recorded in the official reports remitted by the governor of those provinces, the Superior Government, the Most Excellent Señor Conde de Paredes, Marqués de la Laguna, viceroy, governor and captain general of New Spain and president of this Royal Audiencia, as resolved in three general councils, especially the council of June 20, 1682, where the account of the said reports was reviewed, appointed the said General don Domingo Jironza as governor and captain general of the said provinces of New Mexico.[2] The royal title, dated January 25, 1683, as it appears, was signed by the Most Excellent Señor Viceroy, countersigned by don Pedro Velásquez de la Cadena, principal scribe of government and war of this New Spain. By reason of his many activities and military knowledge, he was charged with the recovery from the loss [of the provinces], the pacification and reduction of the nations that were left, the founding of missions, the maintenance of the taxpaying citizens, the settlement of a new villa, and other necessary activities.

It is apparent from the papers that he took possession of his post on August 28 of the referred-to year of 1683 in the Real y Plaza de San Lorenzo en la Toma del Río del Norte, whose royal title was presented before the cabildo, justicia y regimiento, which they obeyed and ordered to give full complement, as appears in the original document signed by those who promulgated [the royal title], as well as by the certification sealed and signed by the said cabildo, justicia y regimiento dated November 25, 1690, in which the following were referred to:

- By order of the said General don Domingo Jironza dated November 18, 1683, a company of thirty men went with Maestre de Campo Juan Domínguez de Mendoza, captain and squadron leader, on the discovery of the Jumanos Indians and engaged the Apache nation in war, all of whose arrangements, provisions and people were supported at the cost of the said General don Domingo Jironza.[3]
- Also, it appears [in the certification] that on November 25, 1683, another company left with Captain Antonio Domínguez de Mendoza as squadron leader, against the enemy Apache, with people, arms and munitions, at the cost of the said General don Domingo Jironza.[4] Arriving at the Cerro Hueco, this company punished the enemy and returned with captives and sang Victory.
- Also, it appears [in the certification] that on the 14th of the said month of November 1683, a company went forth under [the command] of Captain Salvador Holguín as squadron leader with people, arms and munitions to reconnoiter the intentions of the apostate Indians, going as far as the Paraje de las Barrancas, eighty leagues into the interior land, punishing the Apache enemy. Although the

apostate Indians did not accept peace, all went according to what was ordered, and at the cost of the said don Domingo Jironza.

- Also, it appears [in the certification] that in April 1684 General don Domingo Jironza made the first aid with thirty men with arms and munitions, assigning as squadron leader the maestre de campo, Alonso García, lieutenant governor and captain general, and they fought at a Peñol, which they call Los Janos, from which the said maestre de campo left injured, and one assistant of the said General don Domingo Jironza was killed. This was on the occasion that the enemy Indians laid waste to the mission of Los Janos, named Nuestra Señora de la Soledad in the jurisdiction of Nueva Vizcaya, killing a religious missionary. The provisions [for this expedition] were made by the said General don Domingo Jironza.

- Also, it appears [in the certification] that in September 1684, Captain Francisco Ramírez and Captain Juan Hernández came to request help to go out against the barbarous [Indians], and the said General don Domingo Jironza responded with fifty men and provisions, later sending new reinforcements to the jurisdiction of Nueva Vizcaya. And all of this was done at the cost of the said don Domingo Jironza.[5]

- Also, it appears [in the certification] that in September 1685, while negotiating peace with those nations, to bring about a conclusion to the forces of war, he received notice that in the pueblo of Casas Grandes, in the jurisdiction of [Nueva] Vizcaya, the Indians planned to mobilize and kill the minister of doctrine during the celebration [of mass] as well as all of the Spaniards that were in the church. Upon receiving this notice, the said General don Domingo Jironza sent fifteen armed men with Maestre de Campo Alonso García as squadron leader, having arrived in good time to punish the intended treachery, exacting justice on fifty-six Indians, all at the cost of the said General don Domingo Jironza.

- Also, it appears [in the certification] that in October of the said year of 1685, the said General don Domingo Jironza sent the aid of one hundred Indian allies of war and the company alférez, Alonso García, the younger, as squadron leader, to the pueblo of Casas Grandes in the jurisdiction of Nueva Vizcaya to search for the enemy who was fortified in a mountain range with the livestock of cattle, sheep and goats that they had made off with.[6] And, on October 14, of the said month, they gave battle at daybreak, fighting the entire day until the coming of night, putting the enemy to flight, leaving behind many of them dead and restoring the livestock to their owner. This good outcome was fitting to the response and swift aid of the said General don Domingo Jironza, making it at his own cost.

- Also, it appears [in the certification] that in the year 1684, he, the said General don Domingo Jironza, went out in person with thirty-six men of arms, provisioned at his own cost, to search for the enemy allied with the Manso nation and others. Having arrived at the Paraje de Doña Ana, there was a battle in which they were defeated and their ranchería burned. And having returned with the company in August, he brought all the leaders of the uprising to justice. And as a result of this punishment, the enemy retreated as far as the Sierra Florida and the Provinces of Sonora, from where they came to ask for peace.

- Also, it appears [in the certification] that in September of the said year of 1684, Captain Roque de Madrid was sent on campaign with fifty men of arms, provisioned at the cost of the said General don Domingo Jironza, in search of the enemy Apache pursuing them and defeating them as far as the Sierra Florida, the soldiers returning with victory.

- Also, it appears [in the certification] that on September 21 of the said year of 1685, the said General don Domingo Jironza went out on campaign with seventy men of arms and one hundred and thirty friendly Indians, provisioned at the cost of the said General don Domingo Jironza. The military camp [plaza de armas] was set up at the ranch of Maestre de Campo Alonso García, having received notice that fourteen nations of barbarous Indians were conspiring with the intention of laying waste to the Christians of these provinces. Upon holding a war council, it was determined to give battle at daybreak to the enemies and in doing so they were defeated and victory was sung.

- Also, it appears [in the certification] that in the month of October of the year 1685, Captain Felipe de la Serna went forth on two campaigns to the Cerro Hueco where the enemy Apache were fought. [The campaigns] were provisioned at the cost of the said General don Domingo Jironza, both with twenty men and thirty friendly Indians in the same form, and at the same Paraje [of Cerro Hueco] the Apache nation was defeated, and victory was sung.

- Also, it appears [in the certification] that on November 25 of the said year of 1685, the said General don Domingo Jironza went forth in person on campaign with seventy men of arms and one hundred friendly Indians, all provisioned at the cost of the said don Domingo Jironza, in search of the nations of the Sumas, Conchos, Jolomes, Hunares, Julimes and Jumanos, and having encountered them, he engaged them in battle on the eighth day of December of the referred-to year, defeating them and killing and apprehending many of them. This punishment obligated them to ask for peace, which was given to them the following year of 1686.

- Also, it appears from a testimony, sealed and signed by Miguel Moxica, royal scribe of the province and war, dated January 16, 1687, of the judgment given in the official review [residencia] of the tenure of the General don Domingo Jironza during the time he was governor and captain general of the said Provinces of New Mexico, appraised by the lord general assessor of war, by the Most Excellent Señor Conde de Monclova, viceroy, governor and captain general of this New Spain. He was declared a good, honest and just judge worthy for His Majesty to occupy and honor him in major positions, and from this there resulted no finding of fault many charge against the said [General don Domingo Jironza].

- Also, it appears [in the certification] that on July 3, 1688, the said Most Excellent Señor Viceroy Conde de la Monclova reappointed the said General don Domingo Jironza as governor and captain general of the provinces of New Mexico, in order to return and prevent a second uprising of the Indians of those provinces and to calm the said nations, and in recognition of his relevant service to His Majesty. According to a royal title, this charge was dispatched on the said day, month and year, and he took possession [of the post] in the Real de Nuestra Señora de Guadalupe del Paso del Río, on January 23 of the following year 1689, and the cabildo, justice y regimiento marked their obedience to the possession [of the governorship] with their signatures.

- Also, it appears [in the certification] that on August 10, 1689, the said General don Domingo Jironza went forth in campaign in person, setting up a military camp [plaza de armas] on the other bank of the of the Río del Norte, bringing eighty men and one hundred and twenty friendly Indians and making war against the apostates of

New Mexico. On the day of the beheading of San Juan Baptista [August 29], they engaged in a bloody battle that lasted from daybreak until eight o'clock at night, with much resistance on the part of the apostate Indians, many choosing to be burned rather than surrender. And, according to the declarations taken by those who were captured, as recorded, more than six hundred of the enemy apostates died in the fray. With this terror, the other nations, with the enemy Apache, left the road to ask for peace from the said General don Domingo Jironza. This operation was supported at his own cost.

- Also, it appears [in the certification] that on October 21, 1691, the said General don Domingo Jironza went forth in person on campaign with seventy men of arms and one hundred friendly Indians to give war to a congregation of more than ten nations of barbarous Indians who intended to lay waste to the Christians of those provinces. With this news, General don Domingo Jironza went in search of them and on November 2 of the said year he engaged them in battle, defeated them and took women and children as captives. On this occasion they surrendered and asked for peace, which was conceded to them and the said general released the prisoners. All of this was performed at his own cost.

The said cabildo, justicia and regimiento concluded the said certification with an account of the documentation of all of these operations, [submitted] to the Most Excellent Señor Viceroy so that His Majesty would honor the said General don Domingo Jironza and Your Excellency [the viceroy] in his royal name since he is worthy of greater employment, recognizing him for his capabilities in those [positions] as a faithful minister [of justice] and great soldier.

Also there are two other certifications, sealed and signed by the said cabildo, justicia y regimiento, both made in the Pueblo del Paso del Norte. The first is dated October 27 of the said year 1684, in which it was certified that as soon as he took possession of the position as governor and captain general of those provinces the said General don Domingo Jironza mounted a horse along with several vecinos that accompanied him, especially two leaders and alcaldes ordinarios, whose names are given in the said certification, desirous to find a convenient place to establish and found a villa, and he went up and down one and then the other side of the Río del Norte. He was not able to find an appropriate place or site for the said purpose because of the reasons expressed in the said certification. By means of the zeal that attended the said General don Domingo Jironza to comply with the obligations as a loyal vassal of His Majesty, and desirous that the vecinos sow and harvest their crops, he planned to establish a settlement a little more than one league from the said Pueblo del Paso where an *acequia* could be expanded in order for [the vecinos] to avail themselves of water, and discovering that the vecinos were without means to start the founding [of the settlement], the said General don Domingo Jironza had much timber cut and other necessities, and in reconsidering the obstacle in the lack of wood and pastures they did not have the desire to establish the settlement, which was not due on any part to the said General, since it was the vecinos who formerly promoted the foundation.

Since the time he entered to govern, he assisted them with a considerable sum of his estate, without hope of collecting what he gave. And, having taken lodging in the Real de San Lorenzo, he provided aid to the many people who were in need of clothes, corn and meat, responding to public and individual needs. In the repeated occasions of commotion by those Indians, the said General don Domingo Jironza assisted the soldiers with weapons, horses and munitions, all at his own cost. All of which is reproduced in the said certification in addition to those referred to in regard to the campaigns and instances of aid that were previously expressed.

The other [certification] is dated August 23, 1685, in the Pueblo de Guadalupe del Paso, in which the said cabildo, justicia y regimiento certified the operations that the said general carried out from the time he immediately entered as governor in the said year of 1683, having founded the presidio of fifty soldiers, being quartered in the part that was built. And, when some of the men who were not from the area had fled, the said General don Domingo Jironza consulted the veterans and set up military camp in the said presidio, spending his time recruiting enlistments to fill the ranks of the fifty soldiers, naming the war officials, and exercising [the soldiers] in military discipline. He paid their salaries and equipped them with weapons and horses. And, to intervene in the above-mentioned incursions and attacks, the said General don Domingo Jironza went forth in campaign to provide aid where it was asked, pacifying the nations in revolt and securing the roads to Parral, Casas Grandes and Sonora, keeping commerce open, which before had been closed because of the invasions of these Indians.

The said General don Domingo Jironza worked in this means as well as with the assistance of his wealth to meet the needs of the soldiers and vecinos, not as a governor but as a father, according to the many great deeds referred to in the said certifications. And all of the said aid he provided was in the province of Parral and the Reyno de la Nueva Vizcaya.

Also, a command of the Most Excellent Señor Conde de Galve, Viceroy, Governor and Captain General of this New Spain, dated January 20 of the past year of 1690, was dispatched in accord with the Council of [the Royal] Hacienda to the said General don Domingo Jironza, governor and captain general of the said provinces, in which it was ordered for him to execute the points of the Council in the referred-to command. Wherein, as seen in the letters of the said general, soldiers, vecinos and representatives, he gave resolution to each one of the said points. And especially in that he gave account of the war he made against the apostate Indians of the pueblo of Zía and the risks to which the said General don Domingo Jironza exposed himself, his acknowledged valor and courage and that of the soldiers, motivated only by his Catholic zeal, and his ability to successfully discharge his obligation against the multitude of such an uncivilized nation. The said General don Domingo Jironza repeatedly gave thanks in the royal name of His Majesty. It is acknowledged that by the orders, mode and disposition which belong to such a person who honors his obligations and military manner, watchfulness and solicitude and attention, which speaks of his punctuality, and behaves in a way very worthy for Your Majesty to reward and honor him with the positions that correspond to his services, since he attended [his services] with particular consideration to both Majesties, he endeavored to punish the rebels and to bring them to our religion with considerable Christian persuasion. He carried out all of the orders of the said Council with particular estimation, because he approved the peace that was conceded to the rest of the referred-to nations. The said general attended to the conservation of peace through all measures possible, always avoiding violence and war except in the most necessary occasions.

As such, take notice of his great understanding and useful expertise. And he placed seventy Indians with the vecinos and soldiers, so that they were able to sell their personal service in search of enemy factions. [He performed all this] in observation of the points included in this resolution.

Also, it appears from a title of a letter written by the said General don Domingo Jironza to the Most Excellent Señor Viceroy Conde de Galve, dated November 15, 1690, that when the order of Your Excellency arrived to place the seventy Indians among the soldiers and vecinos, and because they were already placed in a mission, the said General don Domingo Jironza did not remove the said Indians, in order for them to remain in the said mission [to be taught] the [Christian] doctrine.

Also, it appears from a testimony, sealed and signed by Sebastián Sánchez de las Fraguas, scribe of His Majesty and of war of this kingdom, dated July 4, 1691, of the sentence given and pronounced by the said Most Excellent Señor Viceroy Conde de Galve, appraised by the lord auditor general of war, in the referred-to day, year and month, in which the said General don Domingo Jironza was declared a good, honest and just judge worthy of His Majesty to be occupied and honored in higher positions, as it was confirmed and declared in the residencia of his second term as governor of the said provinces of New Mexico.

Also, as it appears in various decrees that were dispatched by the Superior Government of this New Spain, General don Domingo Jironza was given the benefactions in the royal name of His Majesty because of the undertakings he made in the provinces of New Mexico and the kingdom of Nueva Vizcaya in service to His Majesty, according to the large volume of documentation in the said decrees.

Also, this is evident from two certifications, apparently sealed and signed by the said cabildo, justicia y regimiento. One is dated October 5, 1686, in the town of El Paso in which it is related that the said General don Domingo Jironza delivered the Provinces of New Mexico in a state of peace when don Pedro Reneros came as governor of the said provinces. And the other [certification] given in the said town of El Paso, dated November 25, 1690, also relates that the said general delivered the provinces of New Mexico in a state of peace when don Diego de Vargas Zapata y Luján entered to govern the said provinces.

Also, it appears from a testimony given and signed by don Francisco de Vargas Manuel de Lodeña, *Secretario de Cámara* of the said Most Excellent Señor Viceroy Conde de Galve regarding a royal decree of His Majesty, dated July 26, 1691, countersigned by don Juan de la Rea, his Secretary in the Royal Council of the Indies, directing the said Señor Most Excellent Viceroy, in which he gave an account of the letter of Your Excellency dated February 9, 1690, and a testimony of edicts that were remitted, regarding the work of the said General don Domingo Jironza in the provinces of New Mexico, along with the cited resolution of the Council of Hacienda. His

Majesty decided that in respect to the official approval that was made by Your Excellency, with the particular zeal and prudence in which he carried it out, that the said General don Domingo Jironza be commissioned at the referred-to occasion, which in his royal name he grants him the benefactions in order to encourage him to continue in [H]is [Majesty's] services, as is so offered.

Without hesitation, it is desired that His Majesty's intent and hope is the cooperation of Your Excellency, as is hoped for by his generous obligations, many encouragements, and preservation of the hope that his services will be attended to and rewarded. And in attention to these and that which His Majesty hopes to confer, and as a sign of gratitude for what he has executed up to this time, he asked His Majesty for the benefaction of a habit of one of the three military orders, which notice is communicated through Your Excellency. And such a favor corresponds with the conduct of the said General don Domingo Jironza as shown by his methods and the demonstration of his honor, and he is deserving of many other [rewards] for what he has accomplished up to the present. It was considered to be a convenient time for the said General don Domingo Jironza to continue governing in New Mexico, because of the good way he had conducted himself and the exercise of his good judgment in the functions he performed. However, Your Excellency instead appointed don Diego de Vargas Zapata y Luján, who entered [the kingdom] with qualifications to exercise [the post], notwithstanding that the term of the person serving [Jironza] had not expired.

And this notwithstanding, it was charged and ordered that if the referred-to don Diego de Vargas was not able to take possession, he [Vargas] would be accommodated and employed with another post, thus conserving the said General don Domingo Jironza in New Mexico. But even if he [Vargas] is able to take [possession of the post] as recognized by Your Excellency, having proceeded with equal satisfaction and good judgment in all, Your Excellency can yet decide to remove him and restore the said General don Domingo Jironza [to serve as governor]. In order for this to be done, it would need to be preceded by giving the said don Diego de Vargas a principal accommodation in another post. In this conformity Your Excellency has governed, giving a full account to His Majesty of the results. His royal decree of September 23 of this present year [of 1693] is obeyed by the said Most Excellent Lord Viceroy, commanding, as presently done so, that which follows with regard to the fulfillment of the royal decree, imposing much authorization through the edicts of this material, and entered into the government books, and brought to the lord fiscal, as it appears in [the government books] and by the other papers, titles and documents which are exhibited by the said General don Domingo Jironza for the purpose of forming this certification. The originals, which I reviewed, were returned to his possession.

Accordingly, he did all of what is mentioned at his own cost, as it appears in the titles, certifications, and other original documents exhibited before me to conduct this certification by the said General don Domingo Jironza, who returned to give power of attorney, of which I give faith. And, of his said request and writ, I give the present [documentation] and certification. [Done] in Mexico [City], on January 10, 1693. Witnesses: Bachiller Juan de Guadalupe and don Antonio de Morales Pastrana, citizens of this City. In attestation of verification, José del Castillo, public scribe, signed it, consisting of six folios all on sealed paper [sello tercer] and [made in] duplicate.

We give faith that José del Castillo, who sealed and signed the attached testimony, is a public scribe propietario del número of this City, and as such he uses and exercises his office in regard to all the documents that are handed and have been handed to him, and he gives full faith and judicial credit, and extrajudicially. And to make it of record, we give the present [attestation]. In Mexico [City], on January 12, 1693. I sign it, Diego de Marchena, Royal Scribe. I sign it, Juan Díaz de Ribera, Royal and Public Scribe. I sign it, Gerónimo Ruiz Cabal, Public Scribe.

Notes

1. AGI, Indiferente, vol. 133, N. 58, exp. 2, ff. 1r–9v, Relación de méritos y servicios de Domingo Gironza Petris de Cruzati, Gobernador y Capitán General de Nuevo México, 1693. Translation by José Antonio Esquibel.

2. Don Domingo Jironza Petríz de Cruzate submitted a petition dated August 26, 1682, to the viceroy requesting an advance equaling three years' salary, in order to assist with recruiting and sustaining soldiers for New Mexico. He was granted an advance of two years' salary. By the late summer of 1683 he was able to enlist only twenty of the fifty soldiers he was required to recruit. After arriving at Guadalupe del Paso in late August 1683, he completed his contingent of soldiers by enlisting soldiers of New Mexico and established the Presidio de Nuestra Señora del Pilar y el Glorioso San José. Anne E. Hughes, *The Beginnings of Spanish Settlement in the El Paso District*, in University of California Publications in History, vol. 1, no. 3 (Berkeley: University of California Press, 1914), 324 and 327. (E & S)

3. See Doc. 45, supra, *Journal of the Expedition to Texas, 1683–1684*. (E & S)

4. There were two contemporaries, cousins, named Antonio Domínguez de Mendoza. The one referred to as captain was most likely the son of Francisco Dominguez de Mendoza and Juana de Rueda, who married Juana García de Noriega, the daughter of Maestre de Campo Alonso García and Teresa Varela. Chávez, *Origins of New Mexico Families*, 26, and 33–34. (E & S)

5. Captain Francisco Ramírez was most likely the same person as Captain Francisco Ramírez de Salazar, a native of New Mexico and longtime resident of the jurisdiction of El Paso del Río del Norte before taking command at Casas Grandes in Nueva Vizcaya. Ramírez de Salazar was a son-in-law of Andrés López de Gracia, who served as the first alcalde mayor of Guadalupe del Paso. Chávez, *Origins of New Mexico Families*, 55–56 and 90. In mid-August 1684, Captain Francisco Ramírez de Salazar set out from Casas Grandes in pursuit of raiding Indians, mainly of the Manso nation. Petríz de Cruzate provided fifty soldiers to join Ramírez de Salazar's force, but the soldiers were unable to successfully track the Indians. Hughes, "Beginnings of Spanish Settlement in the El Paso District," 353. (E & S)

6. Alonso García, the younger, also known as Alonso García de Noriega, was born circa 1651, being a son of Maestre de Campo Alonso García and Teresa Varela. He married Ana Jorge de Vera. Chávez, *Origins of New Mexico Families*, 33–34. (E & S)

PART THREE

IN SERVICE TO THE SPANISH CROWN
THE FAMILY OF JUAN DOMÍNGUEZ DE MENDOZA

José Antonio Esquibel

Background

The first genealogical account of the Domínguez de Mendoza family was researched, compiled, and written by fray Angélico Chávez, representing the second-longest family section of the first part of *Origins of New Mexico Families in the Spanish Colonial Period*. Chávez extracted bits and pieces of information about the Domínguez de Mendoza family from scattered references among copies of original Inquisition documents housed at the University of New Mexico, as well as from published translations of documents relating to the Pueblo Revolt of 1680. With the publication of *Origins of New Mexico Families* in 1954, Chávez presented the first comprehensive historical and genealogical account of the Domínguez de Mendoza family for interested historians and genealogists. He solidly documented three generations, beginning with Tomé Domínguez and Elena Ramírez de Mendoza.

Fray Angélico Chávez determined that the Domínguez de Mendoza family came to New Mexico from Mexico City by the mid-seventeenth century, and he documented that the children of Tomé Domínguez and Elena Ramírez de Mendoza used the extended surname of Domínguez de Mendoza. As adults these children occupied important military and civil posts and were economically and socially prominent citizens of New Mexico. The Domínguez de Mendoza children and grandchildren married into numerous other New Mexico families of the same social status, including Anaya Almazán, Carvajal, Durán y Chaves, García de Noriega, López Mederos, Lucero de Godoy, Márquez, Paredes, Romero, and Varela de Losada. Clearly, as related by Chávez, the multiple intermarriages between members of the Domínguez de Mendoza and the Durán y Chaves clan, along with the events of the Pueblo Indian Revolt of 1680, were most influential regarding the history the Domínguez de Mendoza family.

The military service records of Juan Domínguez de Mendoza contain valuable historical and genealogical information about the Domínguez de Mendoza family and their maternal ancestors. The single most illuminating document concerning this family's genealogy is the surviving record of the proof of lineage for Elena de la Cruz, also known as Elena Ramírez de Mendoza, the wife of Tomé Domínguez and the mother of Juan Domínguez de Mendoza. Apparently, the collection of military services records for don Juan Domínguez de Mendoza also included records of the proof of lineage for his father, Tomé Domínguez. France V. Scholes noted that the collection was missing a set of documents that he said were related to the proof of lineage of Tomé Domínguez. This set of records, torn from the collection, would have provided details about Tomé Domínguez's parents and grandparents and served as a genealogical treasure for descendants of the Domínguez de Mendoza family.

The information concerning the ancestry of Elena de la Cruz and the military service papers of Juan Domínguez de Mendoza were intended for publication in the 1940s, but the book Scholes proposed to the University of New Mexico Press as part of the Coronado Cuarto Centennial Celebration was not completed. Although Scholes and fray Angélico Chávez knew each other, the Domínguez de Mendoza genealogical information and the military service records in Scholes's possession apparently did not come to Chávez's attention. As such, none of the additional information from these important documents was incorporated into Chávez's account of the Domínguez de Mendoza family. Scholes enlisted Eleanor B. Adams to translate the documents from the military service records of Juan Domínguez de Mendoza and apparently did not have Adams work on a translation of the proof of lineage of Elena de la Cruz. Instead, Scholes wrote a very brief summary (see document 1 in part 1) providing only the basic genealogical information found in the record. A copy of this summary remained part of the Scholes collection housed at the Center for Southwest Research at the University of New Mexico. The photostat copy of the original proof of lineage remained in the possession of Scholes until it was passed on to Marc Simmons, along with the other documents relating to the military service of Juan Domínguez de Mendoza. The following section provides a detailed account of the information found in the proof-of-lineage document, which will prove to be invaluable to the interested genealogical researcher for extending the lineage of Elena de la Cruz into Spain. Subsequent sections offer a detailed historical account of the Domínguez de Mendoza clan in New Mexico.

Paternal and Maternal Ancestry of the Domínguez de Mendoza Clan

The progenitors of the Domínguez de Mendoza family of seventeenth-century New Mexico were Tomé Domínguez—also known as Tomás Domínguez—and Elena de la Cruz—also known as Elena Ramírez de Mendoza. Tomé was a native of the Villa de Cartagena, born circa 1587.[1] It is not clear whether his native villa was Cartagena in Spain or a villa of the same name in New Spain. It was very likely not the Ciudad de Cartagena, the port city in Columbia, which would not have been referred to as a villa, because of its official designation as a city (*ciudad*). Elena de la Cruz was a native of Antigua Villa Rica de la Vera Cruz, the port city along the Gulf of Mexico established by Hernán Cortés and his men in 1519. Perhaps Tomé resided in Vera Cruz or conducted business with relatives of Elena de la Cruz in that city and thus came to know her. More likely, they both become residents of the city of Puebla de los Ángeles, New Spain, by the summer of 1616, where the marriage between this couple occurred in August of that year.

On August 29, 1616, Tomé Domínguez and his prospective bride presented themselves before Bachiller José de Espinola in the *sagrario* chapel of the Catedral de Puebla, where a nuptial mass was conducted in the presence of witnesses to the sacramental union and formal blessings bestowed upon the couple according to the rites of the Roman Catholic Church. Following the ceremony, the priest entered this record of the event:[2]

tomas dominguez	*en beinte y nuebe de agosto de 1616 desposo*
y elena de la crus	*y belo el bachi ller Jusepe de espinola a tomas*
	Dominguez natural dela billa de cartagena hijo de
	tome dominguez y de leonor gonsalez su muger y a
	elena de la crus hija de benito de paris y de leonor
	francisca su mujer difuntos testigos gironimo
	riquerio e sebastian galeote y otros y lo frimo
	El B^r. espinola

According to this record, Tomé Domínguez was a native of the Villa de Cartagena and a son of Tomé Domínguez and Leonor González. The given name of Tomé is the Portuguese variation of the name Thomas. As seen clearly in the above marriage record, the priest identified Tomé by the Castilian version of the name, Tomás. Although the marriage record did not specify that the Villa de Cartagena was located in one of the realms of the Iberian peninsula, it is probable that Tomé was a native of Spain and had come to New Spain prior to 1616. A search of the records of passengers coming to the Americas between 1550 and 1599 did not uncover a record for Tomé Domínguez or his parents. Perhaps he or his parents sought passage between 1600 and 1616. Whether Tomé came to New Spain with his family is still a point that needs to be determined, although he did have a brother, Juan Mateo, who was later a resident of Mexico City.[3]

The parents of Elena de la Cruz were deceased by August 1616, as mentioned in the marriage record. She was a daughter of Benito Paris and Leonor Francisca de Mendoza, longtime residents of the Villa Rica de la Vera Cruz, New Spain. Information about her parents and grandparents comes from a document concerning the proof of her family lineage.[4] Proof of lineages were linked to statutes that restricted eligibility for public offices, and for entry into colleges, religious orders, and some trade guilds to individuals without an immediate ancestor who was tried and found guilty by the Inquisition. The restriction was particularly related to those individuals of Jewish backgrounds that converted to Christianity and then were discovered to have continued practicing their Jewish faith. In all likelihood, Tomé Domínguez was interested in obtaining a royal or public appointment or needed to prove his and his wife's lineage to be accepted into a trade guild, or perhaps in seeking a position of leadership within a trade guild.

The document relating to the proof of lineage of Elena de la Cruz was apparently recorded among the civil records of Pedro Fernández de Orduño, a royal scribe of Mexico City. A copy of this record, consisting of sixteen pages, was obtained by either Tomé Domínguez or Elena de la Cruz and passed on to Juan Domínguez de Mendoza. Alternatively, Juan Domínguez de Mendoza may have acquired a copy during one of his visits to Mexico City, requesting the papers for inclusion among his portfolio of documents relating to his service to the Crown, which he intended to present to royal officials in Spain. A document relating to the proof of lineage of Tomé Domínguez also existed at one time among the military papers of Juan Domínguez de Mendoza. Unfortunately, this document was missing from the collection at the time the photostat copies were made at the behest of Scholes.[5] A copy of the Domínguez proof of lineage may still exist among the civil records of one of the scribes of Mexico City, perhaps among the records of Pedro Fernández de Orduño.

In 1625, Tomé Domínguez and Elena de la Cruz completed preparations for initiating the formalities required in establishing a proof of lineage. The reason for taking this action is not given in the available documents but was most likely related to a desire to acquire privileges of *hidalguia*, given to people who could prove an "old Christian" lineage without any Moorish or Jewish lineages, or without any direct ancestor having been tried and condemned by the Inquisition, within three generations. In this year, Tomé Domínguez and Elena de la Cruz resided in Mexico City, where Tomé was occupied as a merchant. They enlisted the services of Francisco Franco, and on August 8, 1625, they officially granted Franco power of attorney to represent them and to collect information about the legitimacy and lineage of Elena de la Cruz, a process that apparently began in 1624.[6]

Elena declared she was "a legitimate daughter of Benito Paris and of Leonor Francisca, my parents who are both deceased, who were residents of the Nueva Vera Cruz and Puerto de San Juan de Ulloa, where my parents were married and veiled and live a married life and from this marriage they procreated me, their legitimate daughter from their legitimate union, raising me and teaching me all that was necessary for my person, and my said parents and grandparents, paternal and maternal, were old Christians of pure lineage and blood and were not descendants of Moors nor Jews nor penitents of the Holy Office of the Inquisition, nor of the newly converted to the Holy Faith."[7] The document was recorded by Pedro Fernández de Orduño, royal scribe of Mexico City, in the company of three witnesses, Juan Bernal, Sebastián González, and Juan Pérez Fernández, each vecinos (taxpaying citizens) of Mexico City. All three, plus Tomé Domínguez, were said to have signed the document, indicating they were literate men, although no signatures appear on the copy of the original. It was specifically mentioned that Elena de la Cruz did not know how to sign her name.

The document regarding power of attorney was certified on the same day by three additional royal scribes, Gregorio Sáenz, Diego Núñez, and Gines Vásquez.[8] The names of these scribes are important for future research regarding records pertaining to the Domínguez–de la Cruz family, since the civil archival records in Mexico City are catalogued by the name of the scribes. Of particular interest is a statement referring to "the decrees and documents (*autos y escripturas*) of the previous year," apparently related to the process of proving lineage, perhaps even relating to the proof of lineage of Tomé Domínguez.[9]

Francisco Franco made his way to Vera Cruz and on August 30, 1625, he officially presented the petition of Elena de la Cruz before Captain Juan Rodríguez Barrientos, Castellanos de las Fuerzas de San Juan de Ulloa and justicia mayor of the city.[10] Franco declared he held power of attorney for Elena de la Cruz, the wife of Tomé Domínguez, vecinos of Mexico City. In the petition Elena de la Cruz declared she was a legitimate daughter of Benito Paris and Leonor Francisca, who had raised her in the Ciudad de la Antigua Vera Cruz, where she was born. She then stated that her father was the legitimate son of Juan González and Isabel Gallega, who had also been vecinos of Antigua Vera Cruz. Elena then declared that her mother was the legitimate daughter of don Francisco de Mendoza and doña Leonor de Grimaldos, vecinos and natives of Puerto de Santa María in Andalucía, Spain. Elena once again claimed that her parents and grandparents were old Christians and not Moors or Jews, or penitents of the Inquisition, or newly converted to the Catholic faith. Francisco Franco asked for permission to conduct the investigation into the lineage of Elena de la Cruz by examining witnesses who had knowledge of her family. Captain Juan Rodríguez Barrientos formally authorized the request.[11]

The fact that Elena de la Cruz and her parents did not use their paternal surnames is not surprising, since social custom did not require people to do so. This is one particularly challenging aspect of colonial Spanish genealogy. The genealogical information provided by Elena de la Cruz in her petition clearly indicates that the Mendoza surname, which was used by her children in the extended family name of Domínguez de Mendoza, was drawn from her maternal grandfather, don Francisco de Mendoza, who was very likely a member of one of the many branches of the prominent Mendoza family of Spain. Harking back to this surname served not only to honor a distinguished maternal family line but also to bring a sense of distinction to the current generation. The Mendoza surname resonated with prestige in Spanish society, given the significant contribution of the Mendoza clan to fortifying the social and political dominance of the realm of Castile among the kingdoms of the Iberian Peninsula. The history and genealogy of the Mendoza family is intimately intertwined with the expansion of the Castilian Crown through the period of the reconquista from the eleventh century to the conquest of Granada in the 1490s. Over the centuries, branches of the Mendoza family settled throughout the various Spanish realms, particularly Andalucía. Additional research, particularly into records from Puerto de Santa María, may determine to which branch don Francisco de Mendoza belonged. Don Francisco de Mendoza and his wife, doña Leonor de Grimaldos, were residents of Puerto de Santa María and Cádiz, Spain, and did not settle in New Spain.[12] It is not certain where Leonor Francisca and Benito Paris were married or when they became residents of Antigua Vera Cruz.

The surname Grimaldos is also of some consequence, apparently being a Spanish variation of the Italian surname Grimaldi, a very prominent and large extended family originally from Genoa. Apparently, a branch of the Grimaldi family was established in Puerto de Santa María and possibly Cádiz, perhaps for purposes of trade. Additional research is required to further understand the genealogy and history of the Grimaldos family in Andalucía.

According to Elena de la Cruz, her paternal grandparents, Juan González and Isabel Gallega, resided in Antigua Vera Cruz.[13] Their place of origin is not given, and they may have emigrated from Spain sometime in the mid-1500s, although a record of passage from Sevilla could not be located in the published listing of passengers to the Spanish Americas. In testimony given by several witnesses, as seen below, Elena's paternal grandfather was also known as Juan González Magaña, and her paternal grandmother was also known as Isabel Gallego and Isabel Gallegos. Research into records for the city of Vera Cruz may uncover additional historical and genealogical information on the González Magaña–Gallega family.

A series of four questions, those customarily used in the process of any proof of lineage, were set forth by Francisco Franco to be asked of key witnesses who knew Elena de la Cruz and her family.[14] The first question asked whether the witnesses knew Elena de la Cruz, the wife of Tomé Domínguez, residents of Mexico City, whether they knew her parents, Benito Paris and

Leonor Francisca, who were deceased, former vecinos of Puerto de la Nueva Vera Cruz, and whether through their legitimate union procreated Elena de la Cruz as their legitimate daughter. The second question asked if the witnesses knew the paternal and maternal grandparents of Elena de la Cruz and where they were born. The next question asked the witnesses if they knew that the parents and grandparents of Elena de la Cruz were old Christians, without Moorish or Jewish lineage, and not penitents of the Inquisition, and not newly converted to the Catholic faith. The last question asked if the witnesses knew of any contrary public information that would draw into questions the legitimacy of the marriages of the parents and grandparents of Elena de la Cruz and their lineage as old Christians.

The first witness, Agustín Hernández, was interviewed in Vera Cruz on September 1, 1625.[15] Hernández gave his age as sixty-six (b. ca. 1559) and declared that he knew Elena de la Cruz and her parents, who were residents of Antigua Vera Cruz, where he witnessed the marriage and veiling of Benito Paris and Leonor Francisca. He further declared that he had known Juan González and Isabel "Gallega" in Ciudad de la Antigua Vera Cruz and had known don Francisco de Mendoza and doña Leonor de Grimaldos in the city of Cádiz, Spain. Hernández concluded his testimony by stating that he knew the parents and grandparents of Elena de la Cruz to be old Christians and that there was nothing known publicly that was to the contrary. As he was not related to Elena de la Cruz, he did not have to provide information about his background. Hernández did not sign his statement, as he did not know how to do so. The testimony was recorded and witnessed by Gines Alonso and Diego de Remoludo, both royal scribes.

On the same day, Salvador Ramírez, age eighty (b. ca. 1545) and a resident of Vera Cruz, provided his testimony, declaring he knew Elena de la Cruz and her parents, who had lived a married life in Antigua Vera Cruz.[16] He had also known Juan González and Isabel Gallego, who had lived in the city of Antigua Vera Cruz, and knew that Leonor Francisca, the mother of Elena de la Cruz, was a daughter of don Francisco de Mendoza and doña Leonor de Grimaldos. Beyond this, the only information he knew about the maternal grandparents was based on what he had heard from other people, in particular, that Mendoza and his wife had been residents of Puerto de Santa María and that they were people of honor and old Christians. He ended his statement by confirming that the family members of Elena de la Cruz were not of Moorish or Jewish descent, nor descended of a penitent of the Inquisition, nor of the newly converted. Diego Remoludo, royal scribe, who noted that Ramírez did not know how to sign his name, recorded the testimony. Ramírez declared he was not related to Elena de la Cruz.

The depositions of witnesses continued on the following day, September 2, 1625. Francisco de Jesús, a resident of Vera Cruz, who gave his age as around fifty-four (b. ca. 1571), declared that he knew Elena de la Cruz and had known her parents, former residents of Antigua Vera Cruz.[17] He stated that Elena was a legitimate daughter of a legitimate union, which was publicly known. He also had known the parents of Benito Paris, Juan González, who was also known as Magaña, and Isabel Gallegos (later referred to as Gallega in this same testimony), and he knew they had been residents of the city of Antigua Vera Cruz. Francisco de Jesús next stated that it was well known in the city that Leonor Francisca, the mother of Elena de la Cruz, was a daughter of don Francisco de Mendoza and doña Leonor de Grimaldos, residents of Puerto de Santa María. Like the witnesses before him, he also declared that all of these people were old Christians. Francisco de Jesús was not related to Elena de la Cruz, and he signed his testimony before the royal scribe, Diego de Remoludo.

The next witness, sixty-five-year-old Juan Silva (b. ca. 1560), a resident of Vera Cruz, was a master carpenter by occupation.[18] He also stated that he knew Elena de la Cruz and her parents, who had been residents of Antigua Vera Cruz, and that it was well known that she was a legitimate daughter of Benito Paris and Leonor Francisca. He then declared that he had known Juan González Magaña and Isabel Gallegos, the parents of Benito Paris, who had also been residents of Antigua Vera Cruz. Next he stated that he had only heard that Leonor Francisca was a daughter of don Francisco de Mendoza and doña "Ysabel" [sic; Leonor] de Grimaldos, who were from Puerto de Santa María, which he had heard from his wife. He had also heard that all of these people were old Christians. Silva was not a relative of Elena de la Cruz and did not know how to sign his name. Gines Alonso, public scribe, recorded his testimony.

The next witness was Hernando Ramírez, age forty (b. ca. 1585) and a resident of the Nueva Ciudad de la Vera Cruz, who gave his testimony on September 9, 1625.[19] His testimony was exactly the same as that of Juan Silva, even to the point of naming the paternal grandmother of Elena de la Cruz as Isabel Gallegos and the maternal grandmother as Isabel de Grimaldos. He was not a relative of Elena de la Cruz, and he signed his statement before Gines Alonso, public scribe.

The last witness was Francisco Romero, a councilman of Nueva Ciudad de la Vera Cruz, over forty years of age (b. ca. 1585).[20] He affirmed that Benito Paris and Leonor Francisca were married and veiled and raised Elena de la Cruz as their legitimate daughter. He named Juan González and Isabel Gallega as the paternal grandparents of Elena de la Cruz, and he did not know her maternal grandparents or anything about them. He had heard they were named don

Francisco de Mendoza and doña Leonor de Grimaldos. In this instance the name "Ysabel" was first written, then crossed out and replaced with the name Leonor. Like the other witnesses he concluded by stating that each of these individuals were old Christians. He signed his name to the statement before Diego Remoludo, royal scribe.

The exact social benefit acquired by Tomé Domínguez and Elena de la Cruz as a result of documenting proof of old Christian lineage is not known. They had been married a little over eight years when the process regarding Elena's proof of lineage was completed. The relationship with Francisco Franco was strengthened when he became the godfather of a child of Tomé and Elena in December 1625.[21] By 1632, Tomé and Elena were still residents of Mexico City, where he was a wine merchant, selling his wine on the Calle de Tacuba in Mexico City, next to the blacksmith.[22] Apparently, Tomé sold wine to the friars of the Franciscan order, in particular those of New Mexico. On March 4, 1633, fray Estéban de Perea, commissary of New Mexico, wrote a letter to his superior in Mexico City in which he mentioned a case he was submitting to officials of the Inquisition against Tomé Domínguez, a resident of Mexico City and the brother of Juan Mateo.[23] The nature of this denunciation was not specified in Perea's letter. Nonetheless, this brief reference indicates that Tomé Domínguez was very likely involved in commerce with New Mexico by 1631, having established an economic relationship that would eventually lead him to relocate his family to New Mexico.

The Domínguez de Mendoza Family in New Spain

Tomé Domínguez and Elena de la Cruz were the parents of fourteen known children, all born in New Spain. On July 4, 1617, this couple presented their firstborn son, Juan [sic; José] for baptism at the church of San José in Puebla de los Ángeles, New Spain, in the company of his godparents, Gerónimo Riguerio and his wife doña Antonia de Arcega.[24] Curiously, the name Juan was crossed out in the text of the baptismal record, and the name José was written in its place and again in the margin of the record. This is an unusual occurrence in sacramental records. There is no other account of Tomé Domínguez and Elena de la Cruz having a son named José, and thus this son may have died as a child. Clearly, this firstborn son was not the same person as Juan Domínguez de Mendoza, whose distinguished military career is preserved in his records of service, since the records indicated that he was born in May 1627. In the following year, Tomé and Elena's second child, Francisco Domínguez de Mendoza, received the sacrament of baptism on October 28, 1618, in the church of San

José in Puebla de los Ángeles, New Spain.²⁵ The next known child, María Domínguez de la Cruz, was baptized in the sagrario chapel of the Catedral de México in Mexico City on November 4, 1620.²⁶ The Domínguez family was back in Puebla de los Ángeles for the birth of Domingo Domínguez de la Cruz, who received the sacrament of baptism in the chapel of the Cathedral of Puebla de los Ángeles on January 23, 1622.²⁷

Tomé Domínguez and Elena de la Cruz apparently relocated permanently to Mexico City by 1623. During this year their fourth son was christened Tomé at the sagrario chapel of the Catedral de México on February 19, 1623.²⁸ The child's godfather was a man named Gaspar Rodríguez. Records indicate five of the next seven children of the Domínguez family were born in Mexico City between 1627 and 1636. Pedro Domínguez de la Cruz was christened on July 10, 1624.²⁹ A second daughter named María Domínguez de la Cruz was baptized December 31, 1625.³⁰ Juan Domínguez de Mendoza, the subject of this book, was baptized in the chapel of the Mexico City cathedral on May 30, 1627, and Damiana Domínguez de Mendoza received the sacrament of baptism on October 4, 1628.³¹ Four younger daughters of Tomé Domínguez and Elena de la Cruz were Leonor Domínguez de Mendoza (baptized March 5, 1630, Mexico City), Francisca Domínguez de Mendoza, Elena Domínguez de Mendoza, Baleriana Domínguez de la Cruz (baptized January 25, 1635, Mexico City), and Isabel Domínguez de la Cruz (baptized June 8, 1636, Mexico City).³²

The names of the children of Tomé Domínguez illustrate the custom of naming children after close relatives, particularly grandparents and great-grandparents. Juan Domínguez de Mendoza was named for his maternal grandfather. Tomé Domínguez de Mendoza was named for his father and paternal grandfather, and Francisco Domínguez de Mendoza for his maternal great-grandfather. Leonor Domínguez de Mendoza was named for her paternal and maternal grandmothers, Elena Domínguez de Mendoza was named for her mother, and Isabel Domínguez de la Cruz was named for her paternal great-grandmother.

The Domínguez de Mendoza Family in New Mexico

Tomé Domínguez's association with New Mexico can be traced to 1631, when fray Estéban de Perea, the comisario of New Mexico, sent some dispatches to Mexico City in the care of Domínguez, who was identified as a vecino of Mexico City.³³ On March 4, 1633, fray Estéban de Perea, again in his capacity as comisario of New Mexico, made reference in a letter to Inquisition officials to a lawsuit from 1632 against "a loyal taxpaying citizen of this city [Mexico

City] named Thomé Domínguez, brother of Juan Matheo, who sells wines on the Calle de Tacuba near the blacksmith's."[34] This brief reference identified Tomé Domínguez as a wine merchant who apparently conducted business with the Franciscans friars related to transporting wine to New Mexico, or perhaps he bought wine for export from New Mexico to be sold in New Spain.

On May 26, 1633, Domínguez presented himself at the Convento de la Concepción at Pueblo de Cuarác in New Mexico to have his testimony recorded in a case of bigamy against a mulatto name Juan Antón.[35] Domínguez declared he was vecino of Mexico City, and thus was not yet officially a resident of New Mexico. He recounted that he left New Mexico in July 1632 and that when he arrived at Cuencamé in Nueva Vizcaya, he went to a house of some tailors, where a miner by the name of Corea asked if Domínguez knew a mulatto named Juan Antón who had traveled with Maestre de Campo Pedro Durán y Chaves. Domínguez responded that he knew the mulatto, who was married in New Mexico to an Indian woman. Corea informed Domínguez that Juan Antón was also married to an African slave of his, who actually served the food in the house of the tailors, further revealing Juan Antón's bigamy. This testimony served as part of the denunciation of Juan Antón to the Office of the Inquisition.

Domínguez was back in Mexico City in 1634 when four separate lawsuits were brought against him by four men to whom he was in debt.[36] Two years later Domínguez was again in New Mexico, this time serving as a military captain of the frontier, being commissioned on December 15, 1636, at the pueblo of Socorro by Governor don Francisco Martínez de Baeza as "capitán y cabo" for a dispatch squadron to deliver papers to the viceroy, and thus Domínguez invested himself in a new occupation that became the way of life for his sons and grandsons.[37] It was probably around this time or soon after that Domínguez decided to settle in New Mexico, where he most likely utilized his skills as a merchant and maintained his commercial contacts in Mexico City.

In one record it was claimed that Tomé Domínguez brought thirty families as settlers of New Mexico and that he paid for the cost of their journey.[38] In another record the number of families was given as ten.[39] The assertion that he brought thirty families was again made many decades later, in 1694.[40] Lack of records makes it difficult to substantiate these claims with additional documentary evidence, but it is probable that Domínguez brought a few families to New Mexico and provided financial support.

It appears that several children of Tomé Domínguez and Elena de la Cruz did not come to New Mexico, either having died young or having remained in Mexico City. In fact, Domínguez maintained his home in Mexico City on

CHART 1

The Genealogy and Family of Tomé Domínguez and Elena de la Cruz y Mendoza

Researched and compiled by José Antonio Esquibel

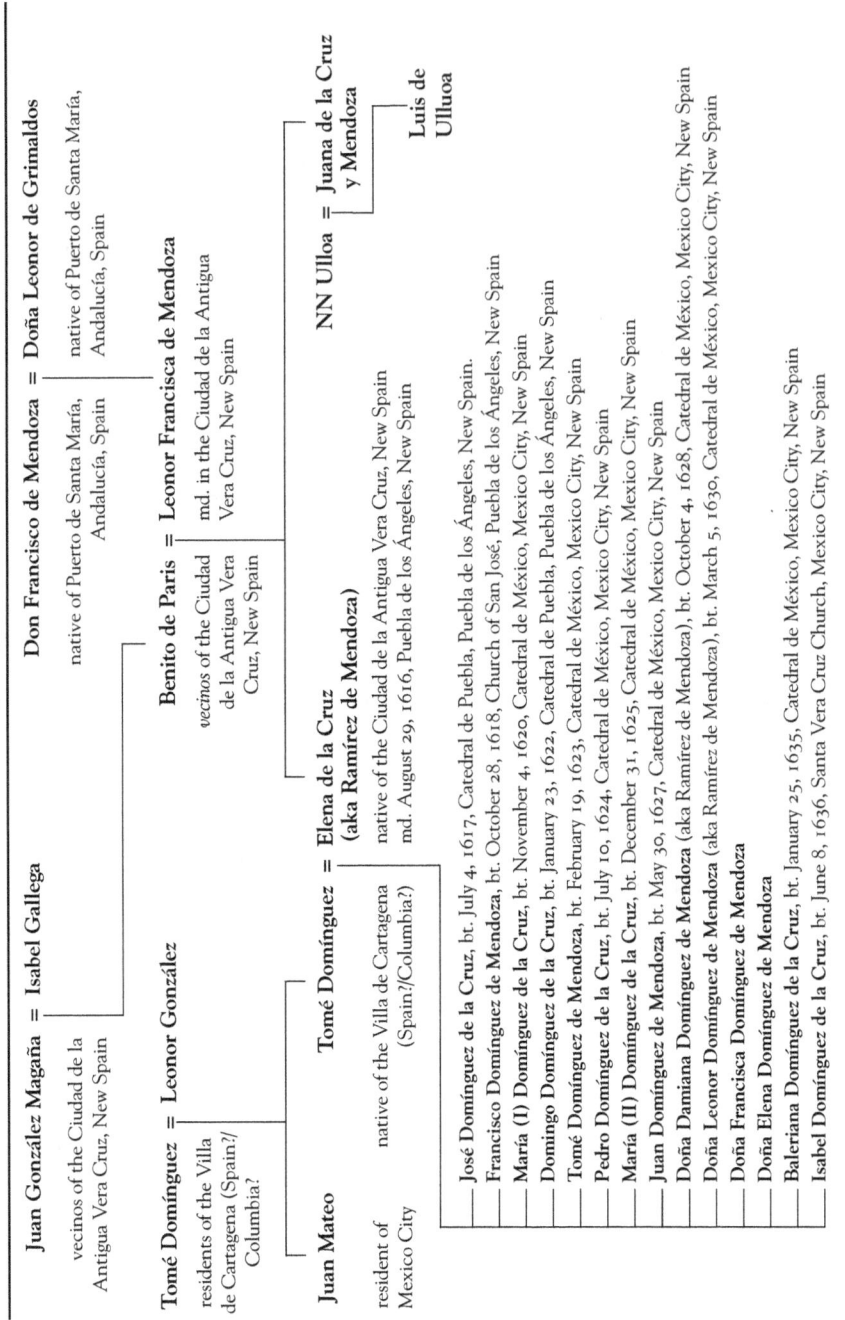

Juan González Magaña = Isabel Gallega
vecinos of the Ciudad de la Antigua Vera Cruz, New Spain

Don Francisco de Mendoza = Doña Leonor de Grimaldos
native of Puerto de Santa María, Andalucía, Spain — native of Puerto de Santa María, Andalucía, Spain

Tomé Domínguez = Leonor González
residents of the Villa de Cartagena (Spain?/Columbia?)

Benito de Paris = Leonor Francisca de Mendoza
vecinos of the Ciudad de la Antigua Vera Cruz, New Spain — md. in the Ciudad de la Antigua Vera Cruz, New Spain

Juan Mateo
resident of Mexico City

Tomé Domínguez = Elena de la Cruz (aka Ramírez de Mendoza)
native of the Villa de Cartagena (Spain?/Columbia?)
native of the Ciudad de la Antigua Vera Cruz, New Spain
md. August 29, 1616, Puebla de los Ángeles, New Spain

NN Ulloa = Juana de la Cruz y Mendoza

Luis de Ulluoa

- José Domínguez de la Cruz, bt. July 4, 1617, Catedral de Puebla, Puebla de los Ángeles, New Spain.
- Francisco Domínguez de Mendoza, bt. October 28, 1618, Church of San José, Puebla de los Ángeles, New Spain
- María (I) Domínguez de la Cruz, bt. November 4, 1620, Catedral de México, Mexico City, New Spain
- Domingo Domínguez de la Cruz, bt. January 23, 1622, Catedral de Puebla, Puebla de los Ángeles, New Spain
- Tomé Domínguez de Mendoza, bt. February 19, 1623, Catedral de México, Mexico City, New Spain
- Pedro Domínguez de la Cruz, bt. July 10, 1624, Catedral de México, Mexico City, New Spain
- María (II) Domínguez de la Cruz, bt. December 31, 1625, Catedral de México, Mexico City, New Spain
- Juan Domínguez de Mendoza, bt. May 30, 1627, Catedral de México, Mexico City, New Spain
- Doña Damiana Domínguez de Mendoza (aka Ramírez de Mendoza), bt. October 4, 1628, Catedral de México, Mexico City, New Spain
- Doña Leonor Domínguez de Mendoza (aka Ramírez de Mendoza), bt. March 5, 1630, Catedral de México, Mexico City, New Spain
- Doña Francisca Domínguez de Mendoza
- Doña Elena Domínguez de Mendoza
- Baleriana Domínguez de la Cruz, bt. January 25, 1635, Catedral de México, Mexico City, New Spain
- Isabel Domínguez de la Cruz, bt. June 8, 1636, Santa Vera Cruz Church, Mexico City, New Spain

the Calle de San Juan in the early 1640s even though he had settled in New Mexico.[41] One daughter who stayed in Mexico City, María Domínguez de la Cruz, married Nicolás González, a native of that city, on November 29, 1652, in Santa Vera Cruz Church, Mexico City.[42] The remaining children—Juan, Tomé, Francisco, Damiana, Francisca, Elena, and Leonor—came with their parents to New Mexico, where they formed matrimonial alliances with prominent families such as those of Anaya Almazán, Carvajal, Durán y Chaves, and Márquez. These alliances created a large extended family that was socially, politically, and economically influential in New Mexico. By 1680, this clan consisted of almost one hundred people.[43]

Tomé Domínguez and his family settled in the jurisdiction of Sandia, having established an estancia with a house and land for agriculture and the raising of livestock, located just north of Sandia Pueblo. In April 1662, fray José de Paredes, an in-law of the Domínguez de Mendoza family, mentioned that the house of Captain Tomé Domínguez was located two leagues "*arriva de Sandia*," and in the following year, Cristóbal de Anaya Alamzán gave the same information, indicating that the Domínguez house was about six miles north of the pueblo of Sandia.[44] Anaya Almazán specified that his own house was a quarter league's distance from the house of Domínguez to the north and east.[45] Anaya Almazán's property was referred to as the Estancia de San Antonio, which consisted of a house and property that he purchased from Tomé Domínguez. The property, locate in the area of modern-day Algodones along the Rio Grande just north of the pueblo of Sandia, contained "*tierras de labor y asequia*," irrigated farmland, and the house consisted of a living room or hall (sala), two rooms (aposentos), one kitchen (cosina), and one room (aposento) outside of the house with doors and windows made of timber with metal locks.[46] The room outside of the main house may very well have been a place of lodging for travelers. In fact, the property of Tomé Domínguez, which was located south of the Anaya Almazán property, may have had a similar arrangement. Fray José de Paredes, in his testimony to Inquisition officials in April 1662, mentioned that on the Domínguez property there was el aposento (the lodging) where people gathered and which was located beside the river, perhaps used as a stopping place for travelers on the Camino Real.[47]

Tomé Domínguez and other settlers of the Sandia jurisdiction, such as Diego de Trujillo, Fernando Durán y Chaves, Francisco de Ortega, Juan Estévan de Fagoaga (estancia de Santiago), Pedro Varela de Losada, Cristóbal Ruiz de Hinojos, Mateo Manzanares, and Andrés Hurtado (encomendero of Santa Ana), were responsible for establishing the northern part of the Río Abajo as the predominant region for commerce, agriculture, and livestock raising in New Mexico.[48] By 1667, the concentration of thirty estancias in the Sandia jurisdiction was greater than that of other New Mexico jurisdictions combined. The Isleta jurisdiction followed, with fourteen estancias. The entire Río Abajo region from below the pueblo of Isleta to just south to Cochiti Pueblo contained as many as forty-four estancias, while there were three estancias accounted for in the area of the pueblo of San Marcos, six in the area of San Ildefonso, and only "several" in the vicinity of Santa Fe and near Nambé.[49]

Also settling in New Mexico for a short while was a sister of Elena de la Cruz, Juana de la Cruz y Mendoza, who served in the household of Governor don Diego de Peñalosa y Briceño in the early 1660s. Juana's son, Luis de Ulloa, served as a page of the governor.[50] These members of the extended Domínguez de Mendoza family appear to have returned to Mexico City when Peñolasa y Briceño left New Mexico in 1664.

Tomé Domínguez died in New Mexico around the year 1656 and was very likely buried in the church of San Francisco at Sandia Pueblo. It is not known when Elena de la Cruz passed away. Their children maintained an influential position in New Mexico's seventeenth-century society until the Pueblo Revolt of 1680. During the 1660s members of the Domínguez de Mendoza extended family were occupied as soldiers and ranchers, and were actively and prominently involved in local and regional politics. Juan Domínguez de Mendoza received numerous appointments to civic and military positions and was granted at least three encomiendas. His brother Tomé Domínguez de Mendoza served as alcalde mayor of the Isleta jurisdiction and teniente general of New Mexico under Governor Peñalosa y Briceño. Along with that of their brother Francisco Domínguez de Mendoza, the testimonies of these men are scattered across various volumes of Inquisition records relating to the cases against Governor don Bernardo López de Mendizábal (1659–1661), Governor don Diego de Peñalosa y Briceño (1661–1664), and several citizens of New Mexico.

Juan Domínguez de Mendoza and Doña Isabel de Chaves y Bohórquez

The military service records of Juan Domínguez de Mendoza provide the most detailed historical account of any single individual of seventeenth-century New Mexico. Domínguez de Mendoza was born in May 1627, in Mexico City, and apparently began his military career in New Mexico at an early age, about twelve, in 1640.[51] He married doña Isabel Durán y Chaves, also known as doña Isabel de Chaves y Bohórquez, a daughter of don Pedro II Durán y Chaves and named after her maternal grandmother, doña Isabel de

Bohórquez.⁵² The name of the first wife of Don Pedro II is not known; he was also the father of don Fernando II Durán y Chaves. Don Pedro II Durán y Chaves was himself a son of Pedro I Durán y Chaves, a native of the town of Valverde de Llerena, Extremadura, Spain.⁵³

The estancia of don Pedro II Durán y Chaves was situated in the jurisdiction of Sandia between Sandia Pueblo and San Felipe Pueblo in the vicinity of present-day Bernalillo, and thus he was a neighbor of the Domínguez de Mendoza family.⁵⁴ In addition, his mother, doña Isabel de Bohórquez, had owned land in the vicinity of the Arroyo del Tunque, about twelve miles north of the pueblo of Sandia, that remained in the Durán y Chaves family during the seventeenth century.⁵⁵ Given the proximity of these families, it is not surprising that members of Domínguez de Mendoza and Durán y Chaves families created matrimonial alliances that served to strengthen the social, economic, and political standing of this clan in the Río Abajo region that lasted until the Pueblo Revolt of 1680.

Throughout the mid- to late 1600s, political and economic rivals were unable to topple the extended Domínguez de Mendoza family, even with charges of heresy that brought members of the clan under the scrutiny of the Office of the Inquisition. Juan Domínguez de Mendoza proved to be a valuable military leader and an adept government administrator under successive governors from the 1640s into the 1680s. He held the post of lieutenant governor of New Mexico in the early 1660s under Governor don Bernardo López de Mendizábal and again under Governor don Fernando de Villanueva.⁵⁶ He was serving on the cabildo of Santa Fe in the 1670s when additional provisions and soldiers were received in Santa Fe.⁵⁷ As a longtime resident and official of the jurisdiction of the pueblo of Isleta, Juan Domínguez de Mendoza resided with his family on his estancia de Atrisco, just north of Isleta, until the revolt of the Pueblo Indians in August 1680 forced his family to flee to the region of El Paso del Norte.⁵⁸ Over the course of his marriage with doña Isabel de Chaves y Bohórquez, they had four known children, all apparently born in New Mexico: Baltasar Domínguez de Mendoza, Juan Domínguez de Mendoza, María Domínguez de Mendoza, and a second daughter whose name is not known (see chart 2).⁵⁹

Baltasar Domínguez de Mendoza, born around 1659, accompanied his father in various expeditions against hostile Indians.⁶⁰ He was his father's companion on the ill-fated journey to Spain, which resulted in a shipwreck in 1693 and the death of his father soon after in Madrid.⁶¹ While in Spain, Baltasar represented his father and himself in the attempt to receive honors and privileges for the many decades of his father's service to the Crown, as well as for his own service. Baltasar requested royal appointment to the post

CHART 2

The Genealogy and Family of Juan Domínguez de Mendoza and Isabel Durán y Cháves

Researched and compiled by José Antonio Esquibel

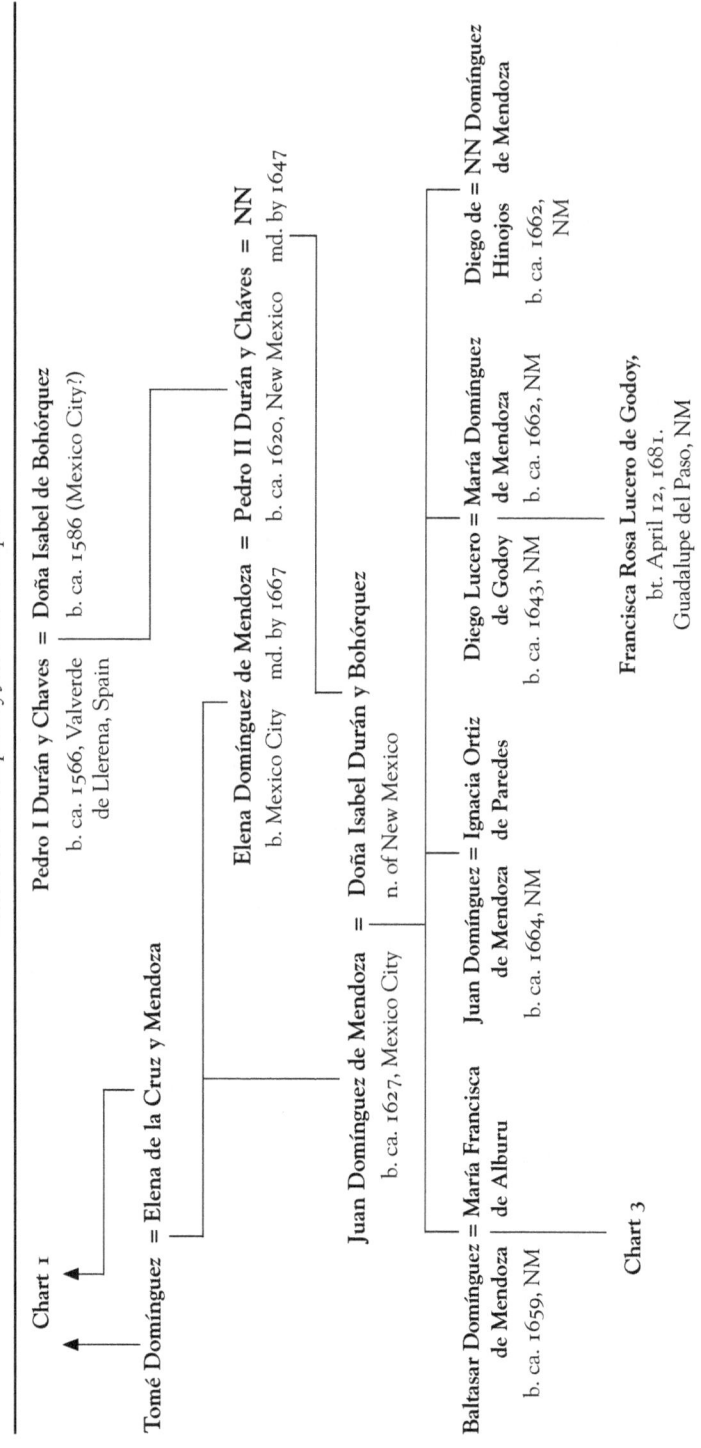

of either the governorship of New Mexico or the alcadía mayor of Sonora, both of which were denied him.[62] He then petitioned for the post as corregidor of the pueblo of Tlajomulco and Caxititlan in Nueva Galicia, and this too was denied.[63] Not one to give up easily, Baltasar then requested consideration by the king for the granting of one of the habits of the military orders for himself and for his brother.[64] This petition was summarily denied, and the royal court provided Baltasar with a decree of recommendation with which to seek the favor of the viceroy of New Spain.[65]

Baltasar Domínguez de Mendoza returned to New Spain and resided in Mexico City, where he married María Francisca de Alburu on August 11, 1697.[66] The ceremony took place in the chapel of the cathedral, located on the north side of the main plaza in Mexico City. Information has been located for three of their children born in Mexico City: Baltasar, born in September 1705; Joaquín Atanacio, born in May 1708; and Nicolás, born September 1709 (see chart 3).[67] Baltasar and his family apparently remained as residents of Mexico City, not seeking to return to New Mexico. Descendants of Baltasar Domínguez de Mendoza continue to live in the Mexico City area to this day.

The younger Juan Domínguez de Mendoza, the namesake of his father, was described in 1664 as "somewhat dark-complexioned, of goodly countenance, robust, black-haired."[68] He later returned to New Mexico, where he was apparently a soldier of the presidio of Santa Fe. In December 1701 and again in March 1702, he was a witness in Santa Fe on behalf of Governor don Pedro Rodríguez Cubero.[69] Juan Domínguez de Mendoza, the younger, settled in Nueva Vizcaya, living at the Real de Santa Eulalia by November 1708, along with several others who were also apparently originally from New Mexico, including Juan de Anaya, don José de Chaves, Sebastián de Herrera, and Juan de Perea.[70] Domínguez de Mendoza was one of the men who founded the Real de San Francisco de Cuéllar in 1709, the future San Felipe el Real de Chihuahua, modern-day Chihuahua City, Mexico.[71] He owned and operated the Mines of Carmen, San Alejo, and Nuestra Señora de la Piedad.

In November 1710, at about the age of thirty-five, he sought to marry doña Ignacia Ortiz de Paredes y Aguirre, born circa 1691. A prenuptial investigation record for this couple dated November 28, 1710, is preserved in the archives of the Catedral de Chihuahua.[72] Don Juan Domínguez de Mendoza gave his age as thirty-five, declared he was a native of New Mexico, and named his parents as General don Juan Domínguez de Mendoza and doña Isabel Durán y Chaves.[73] Doña Ignacia stated she was nineteen years old. The marriage record for this couple is dated December 8, 1710, San Felipe el Real (Chihuahua).[74]

Juan Domínguez de Mendoza and his wife resided at the Real de Santa Eulalia, where three of their known children were baptized in the local church:

CHART 3

Descendants of Baltasar Domínguez de Mendoza and María Francisca de Alburu

Researched and compiled by José Antonio Esquibel

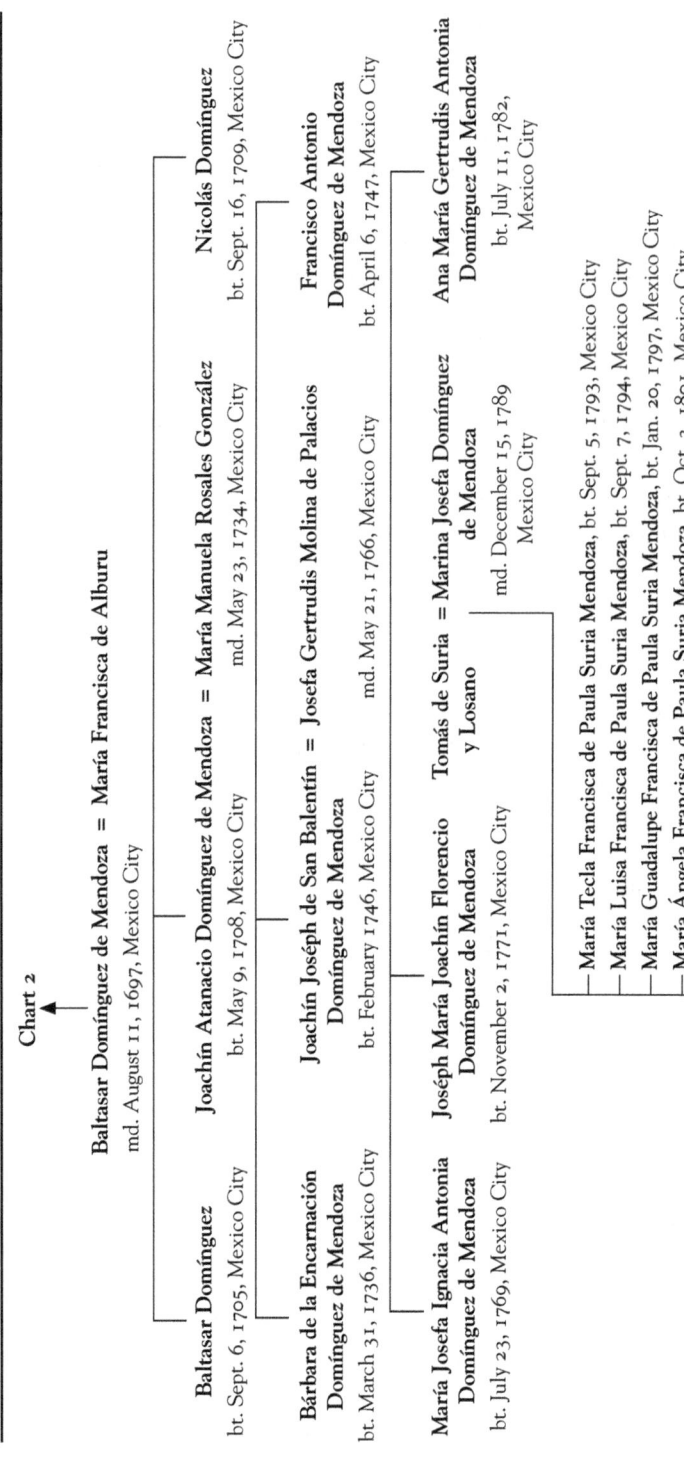

(1) Ana María, baptized May 3, 1713; (2) Isabel, baptized June 13, 1717; (3) Isabel Rita, baptized January 20, 1720.[75] Their fourth known child was José Domínguez de Mendoza.[76] Juan Domínguez de Mendoza was buried in the church of Santa Eulalia on February 12, 1733.[77]

María Domínguez de Mendoza, a daughter of Juan Domínguez de Mendoza and doña Isabel de Chaves y Bohórquez, married Diego Lucero de Godoy on February 16, 1681, at the church of Guadalupe del Paso in El Paso del Río del Norte.[78] One of their children, Francisca Rosa Lucero de Godoy, received the sacrament of baptism on April 12, 1682, in the church of Guadalupe del Paso, with her grandmother, doña Isabel de Chaves y Bohórquez as her godmother.[79] Fearing the child would die, the chrism and holy oil were placed on Francisca seven days after her birth. Another daughter of Juan Domínguez de Mendoza and doña Isabel de Chaves y Bohórquez, whose name is not known, was the wife of Diego de Hinojos.[80]

There were no known immediate descendants of Juan Domínguez de Mendoza and doña Isabel de Chaves y Bohórquez that remained in New Mexico. After serving the royal Crown for over fifty years in the rugged and hostile frontier of New Mexico, enduring many sacrifices and dangers, the immediate members of the Domínguez de Mendoza clan decided to raise their families elsewhere.

Francisco Domínguez de Mendoza and Juana de Rueda

Francisco Domínguez de Mendoza received the sacrament of baptism on October 28, 1618, in the Church of San José in the Ciudad de Puebla de los Ángeles.[81] At the age of almost twenty-five, he contracted marriage with Juana de Rueda, a native of Mexico City and a daughter of Manuel Rodríguez and María de Toro. The marriage and veiling of this couple took place on September 30, 1643, in the house of Francisco's father on the Calle de San Juan in Mexico City.[82] This record was entered into the book of marriages of Santa Vera Cruz Church and identified Francisco's parents as Tomé Domínguez and doña Elena Ramírez. The witnesses to the union were Tomás de los Reyes, Nicolás Lema, and Nicolás de Ávila, and the presiding priest was Francisco de Aguirre. Francisco Domínguez de Mendoza and Juana de Rueda may be the same couple recorded as Francisco Domínguez and Juana de Castañeda, whose son, Francisco, was baptized at Santa Vera Cruz Church on September 4, 1644.[83]

There is a reference to Francisco Domínguez de Mendoza as part of the armed escort for the wagon heading to New Mexico in October 1646. He was described as a son of Captain Tomé Domínguez, age twenty-six, a native of Puebla de los Ángeles, "tall, swarthy, with a small wound on his forehead."[84] It is assumed that he made the trip to New Mexico, one that he would come to know very well over the course of the next three decades. During June and July of 1659, he traveled from Mexico City to New Mexico in the company of Governor don Bernardo López de Mendizábal, along with an in-law of the Domínguez de Mendoza clan, Captain Cristóbal de Anaya Almazán, and as many as sixteen friars bound for New Mexico.[85] It was on this long journey that conflicts arose between López de Mendizábal and the Franciscan friars over the issues of whether he or the Franciscan leadership represented the "universal head" of authority in New Mexico. As such, Francisco Domínguez de Mendoza and Cristóbal de Anaya Almazán may have been involved in the thick of this political conflict from the time that López de Mendizábal came to New Mexico.

Within the first several months of his tenure as governor in New Mexico, López de Mendizábal effectively diminished the authority and political influence of the Franciscans, with the assistance of loyal supporters such as Francisco Domínguez de Mendoza, his brother Juan, and brother-in-law Cristóbal de Anaya Almazán, the last two falling prey to the enmity of the Franciscans because of their outspoken criticism. By contrast, Francisco managed to avoid the same treatment. Perhaps he was not as outspoken as his kin in disparaging the friars, although he later had cause to be a vocal critic.

Francisco Domínguez de Mendoza made the trip to Mexico City and back to New Mexico on several occasions. On March 15, 1662, he left for New Spain with dispatches from former Governor don Bernardo López de Mendizábal to be delivered to the governor's brother, Juan López de Mendizábal. The correspondences were in regard to the governor's imprisonment by the Inquisition, which began with his residencia, the customary review of one's tenure of royal service. Domínguez de Mendoza traveled with the four carros and the single carillo that Governor don Diego de Peñalosa sent to San José del Parral in the charge of Lucas de Villasante and Tomás Granillo.[86] The cargo consisted of piñon nuts, *fardos de gamuses, coletos, camisas Jubones, labrados, pinturas*, male and female Apaches, and fifty mules, all property that Peñalosa took from López de Mendizábal. In addition, nine hundred sheep belonging to Governor López de Mendizábal were placed in the charge of Captain Alonso García, a resident of the Sandia jurisdiction.[87]

Back in New Mexico by October 1662, Francisco Domínguez de Mendoza was at El Paso del Norte with his brother Juan, both having been charged by fray Alonso Posada with delivering dispatches addressed to officials of the Inquisition's tribunal in Mexico City.[88] They also received a set of documents from Governor don Diego de Peñalosa y Briceño addressed to officials of the Real Audiencia de Nueva España with complaints about the "extreme abuses" of fray Alonso de Posada as Franciscan custodian of New Mexico, who was characterized in the same vein as previous Franciscan leaders who had overstepped their ecclesiastical authority since the time of don Juan de Oñate.[89] Peñalosa y Briceño included certified copies of a royal provision dated January 9, 1621, addressed to fray Estéban de Perea, charging Perea in his role as custodian in New Mexico to exercise *jurisdicción ordinaria*, limiting his authority to church and spiritual matters and to attending to nothing more than the administration of the holy sacraments. Also included was a certified copy of the decree of Marqués de Guadalcazar, viceroy of New Spain, dated February 5, 1621, aligned with the king's royal provision and setting forth specific instructions to settle matters for the sake of peace, security, and quietude in New Mexico in response to the previous "very grave ruptures and scandals" resulting from conflicts of the Franciscan leaders with governors. Peñalosa y Briceño not only intended to discredit fray Alonso de Posada he also highlighted the persistent political struggle between ecclesiastical authority and secular governmental authority that underscored the denunciations and arrests of Governor don Bernardo López de Mendizábal and several of his main supporters by the Office of the Inquisition.

When the Domínguez de Mendoza brothers reached the community of San José del Parral in late January 1663, they were employed by General don Juan Manso on behalf of the Inquisition to provide mules to assist in transporting six prisoners from New Mexico: Diego Pérez Romero, Cristóbal de Anaya Almazán, Nicolás de Aguilar, Francisco Gómez Robledo, former governor don Bernardo López de Mendizábal, and his wife doña Teresa de Aguilera y Roche. This episode and the request for compensation from Inquisition officials are related in the introduction to this book.

Manso's task was to oversee and guide the transport of the six prisoners from New Mexico. On February 3, 1663, at Parral, the Domínguez de Mendoza brothers officially received sealed dispatches from don Juan Manso. The difficulties of the slow journey across the desert frontier necessitated additional wagons and beasts of burden. In Parral, Manso imposed upon the Domínguez de Mendoza brothers for assistance and they provided four carros, one carreta, and some mules to carry the belongings of López de Mendizábal, in addition to receiving the charge of carrying sealed documents to Inquisition officials in Mexico City.[90]

The Domínguez de Mendoza brothers were in Mexico City by the end of May 1663. On June 1, Francisco Domínguez de Mendoza and his brother Juan presented a petition to officials of the tribunal requesting recompense for their services in delivering the dispatches and for the wagon carts and animals they supplied.[91] With Francisco Domínguez de Mendoza serving as the principal petitioner, the brothers asked for ample payment to cover the cost of their return to New Mexico. General don Juan Manso was called to testify in the matter and appeared at a hearing on the morning of June 9 before one of the Inquisitors, Doctor don Pedro de Medina Rico. Manso confirmed that fray Alonso de Posada gave him the commission as alguacil mayor of the Inquisition in New Mexico. Manso also confirmed he made use of four carros and one carreta belonging to the Domínguez de Mendoza brothers, as well as some of their beasts of burden.

A second petition submitted by Francisco Domínguez de Mendoza on June 12 again requested compensation for the personal services he and his brother performed on behalf of the tribunal of the Inquisition. He repeated the reference to the services requested by fray Alonso de Posada and provided on behalf of General Manso, which they performed for a period of two months, indicating they apparently left El Paso del Norte with the dispatches as early as the first week of April. Domínguez de Mendoza referred to the danger of the long, drawn-out journey through uninhabited deserts, and the threat of attack from hostile Indians. He calculated the distance from Parral to Mexico City at 430 leagues, approximately 1,247 miles, a calculation of 471 miles more than today's mileage of about 776 miles. Diego Martínez Hidalgo, secretary of the Inquisition in Mexico City, reviewed the request and provided a summary of the case on June 14, ordering that witnesses be examined to attest to the facts presented in the petition of the Domínguez de Mendoza brothers.

On June 16, the Domínguez de Mendoza brothers provided an additional explanation of their circumstances. They recounted that by order of fray Alonso de Posada they were sent in the company of General don Juan de Manso with ten dispatches to be delivered in Mexico City to the tribunal of the Inquisition. Manso also appointed Juan Domínguez de Mendoza as receptor of the tribunal in the care of the large quantity of belongings of don Bernardo López de Mendizábal, and Francisco was appointed receptor on behalf of the former governor. The brothers again requested compensation for their services on behalf of the tribunal, including sufficient funds for each of them to return to New Mexico, "where we have children and wives, and where we serve the king."

Several residents of New Mexico came with the Manso party to Mexico City, and thus Francisco and Juan were able to present witnesses on their behalf. The first witness was thirty-three-year-old Captain Toribio de la Huerta, whose testimony was recorded on June 20 before Pedro de Medina

Rico. De la Huerta confirmed that the Domínguez de Mendoza brothers provided Manso with twelve mules in Parral at the order of fray Alonso de Posada. Because of the hardship of the journey through harsh terrain, some of the beasts died in route, and the rest arrived in Mexico City very haggard. De la Huerta indicated the trip from Parral was about twenty days in length, more or less.

The second witness, Juan González Lobón, gave his age as fifty-four and also attested to the fact that the Domínguez de Mendozas were acting on the order of fray Alonso de Posada. González Lobón confirmed that the Domínguez de Mendoza brothers delivered twelve mules to General Manso, whom they joined in Parral. According to González Lobón, the trip from Parral took one month. He also recounted that because of a great lack of water, some of the beasts died and of those that completed the journey from New Mexico, two or three were very thin and worn out. By June 25, the tribunal officials approved compensation for the Domínguez de Mendoza brothers in the amount of a little over one hundred pesos each. As there is no record of the receipt of the funds, it can only be presumed that they did indeed collect the money. Francisco Domínguez de Mendoza and his brother completed the long journey back New Mexico by early October 1663.[92]

The frequent trips made by Francisco Domínguez de Mendoza may have contributed to trouble in his marriage. In the early 1660s family members discovered that Francisco's wife, Juana de Rueda, was engaged in sexual relations with fray Salvador de Guerra, a friar at the pueblo of Sandia, where the family attended church services.[93] Compounding this relationship was the fact that fray Salvador was also a godfather to a daughter of Francisco and Juana. Family members discovered the affair, and although Juana received stern instruction to keep away from the friar, she managed to slip away from watchful eyes. How the insult to the family's honor was handled is not known from available records. However, the information about this affair was used by Cristóbal de Anaya Almazán, brother-in-law of Francisco Domínguez de Mendoza, in his testimony before Inquisition officials in Mexico City to discredit fray Salvador de Guerra.

In May 1663, in front of officials of the tribunal of the Inquisition in Mexico City, Cristóbal de Anaya Almazán recounted that fray Salvador Guerra engaged in an illicit affair with Juana de Rueda. When the two were discovered lying "together in indecency" by doña Damiana Domínguez de Mendoza, fray Salvador purportedly rose quickly and told doña Damiana not to say anything about the incident, and he would send her a loaf of sugar.[94] On another occasion, when the members of the Domínguez de Mendoza family were attending mass at the pueblo of Sandia, Juana de Rueda managed to slip away. When doña Damiana went looking for her, she encountered Juana coming out of the porter's lodge of the convento. Upon seeing a look of embarrassment on Juana's face, doña Damiana slapped her.[95] How Francisco Domínguez de Mendoza dealt with this affront is not known. However, according to Anaya Almazán, Juan Domínguez de Mendoza knew about the affair, which probably served to enflame his own animosity toward the Franciscan clerics, fray Salvador Guerra in particular. This knowledge became a source of political leverage for the Domínguez de Mendoza family used against the Franciscan friars.

In other aspects of his life, Captain Francisco Domínguez de Mendoza served well in his civil and military posts. He was appointed justicia mayor y capitán de guerra of the jurisdiction of Zía and Cochiti by Governor don Fernando de Villanueva and in 1665 was deemed worthy by his merits and services to be granted by the same governor the encomiendas of Zía and Cochiti, which were formerly in the possession of Diego Pérez Romero until his sentencing by the Inquisition in 1664.[96] Domínguez de Mendoza remained a trusted follower of Governor Villanueva and accepted the charge of carrying papers relating to the residencia of Villanueva to the royal audiencia in Mexico City, most likely traveling in early 1669, before the month of April.[97]

There is almost no documentation relating to the activities of Francisco Domínguez de Mendoza in the 1670s. The only known record is dated July 12, 1670, at San José del Parral, in which don Juan Manso, former governor of New Mexico, granted power of attorney to Captain Francisco Domínguez de Mendoza "in all legal causes, civil and criminal cases, and suits that I have and will have with whatever persons."[98] This brief record indicates that Francisco maintained a long-term relationship with don Juan Manso, who operated the wagons that ran between New Mexico and Mexico City until his death in 1672.[99] Beyond this record, there are no known accounts regarding the activities of Francisco.

Surviving records confirm that Francisco Domínguez de Mendoza and five members of his immediate family escaped the revolt of the Pueblo Indians in August 1680.[100] His name does not appear in records related to the period of exile in the region of El Paso del Norte, suggesting that he may have left the area or perhaps that he died sometime between late 1680 and early 1681. He and his wife, Juana de Rueda, were the parents of at least two known children, a son and a daughter. Their son Antonio Domínguez de Mendoza (also known as Domínguez de Rueda) married doña Juana García de Noriega, daughter of Captain Alonso García and doña Teresa Varela.[101] This union represented yet another matrimonial alliance with a prominent family of the Sandia jurisdiction. In late November 1683, Captain Antonio Domínguez de

Mendoza received the appointment as squadron leader of a successful campaign against the enemy Apache toward the east of El Paso in the area of Cerro Hueco.[102]

Antonio Domínguez de Mendoza and doña Juana García de Noriega were both deceased by March 1689; they were the parents of four daughters and one son: (1) doña Antonia Domínguez de Mendoza, first married on April 19, 1689, El Paso del Norte, to Andrés Hurtado, son of Andrés Hurtado and doña Bernardina de Salas y Orozco; widowed by 1694, doña Antonia on October 25, 1694, Santa Fe, Mexico City, married native Tomás Jirón de Tejeda; (2) María Domínguez de Mendoza married July 20, 1694, Santa Fe, to Antonio Godines, a native of Mexico City; (3) Teresa Domínguez de Mendoza, born circa 1688–1689, married in 1704 to Diego González de la Rosa, born circa 1685 in New Mexico; (4) doña Leonor Domínguez de Mendoza, married circa October 1707 to Miguel Martín Serrano, son of Captain Pedro Martín Serrano and Juana de Argüello; and (5) Antonio Domínguez de Mendoza, baptized November 21, 1681, El Paso del Norte.[103]

Tomé Domínguez de Mendoza and Doña Catalina López Mederos

The baptismal record of Tomé Domínguez de Mendoza, dated February 19, 1623, was recorded in the book of sacraments of the sagrario chapel of the Catedral de México in Mexico City.[104] His parents were identified as Tomé Domínguez and Elena de la Cruz, and his godfather was a man named Gaspar Rodríguez. The younger Tomé was about seventeen years of age when his father served as a soldier of New Mexico in 1640. As such, it is likely that the younger Tomé came to New Mexico in the company of his father, although the earliest known historical reference to Tomé, the younger, is from 1659. In that year he held the rank of sargento mayor and the prestigious post of alcalde mayor and lieutenant captain general of the Río Abajo region, in effect, lieutenant governor of New Mexico.[105] A well-established estancia owner by 1659, his house and property were located along the Río del Norte just four leagues south of the convento of Isleta Pueblo, and his property was considered the southern limit of the jurisdiction of Isleta.[106]

Tomé Domínguez de Mendoza was already married to Catalina López Mederos by 1643.[107] Her brother, Pedro López, a mestizo, lived on the Domínguez de Mendoza estancia.[108] Pedro's racial caste indicates that Catalina was also part Indian. Tomé and Catalina raised at least five known sons as well as several daughters: (1) Tomé Domínguez de Mendoza, who appears to have been the eldest; (2) Diego Domínguez de Mendoza, born circa 1643; (3) Juan Domínguez de Mendoza, a namesake of his uncle, born circa 1646; (4) Francisco Domínguez de Mendoza, a namesake of his uncle, born circa 1656; and (5) Antonio Domínguez de Mendoza, born circa 1661.[109] The names of the daughters of Tomé and Catalina are not known from the historical record, but mention was made in 1680 of his daughters who were killed by Pueblo Indians.

Tomé Domínguez de Mendoza, like his brother Juan, excelled in politics and military service. Governor don Juan Manso de Contreras (1656–1659) appointed Tomé Domínguez de Mendoza as alcalde mayor of the jurisdiction of Isleta and as lieutenant general of the Río Abajo region.[110] With the transition of administration from Governor Manso de Contreras to Governor don Bernardo López de Mendizábal in July 1659, Tomé continued to serve as alcalde mayor and lieutenant general until his positions were revoked and granted to his brother Juan in November 1659.[111] In leaving his posts, Tomé was required to "stand residencia" for the period of time for which he served. Although the residencia was customarily recorded, the documents of this process for Tomé have not come to light. The loss of his posts was most likely related to the fact that he favored the Franciscan friars politically and did not adhere to Governor López de Mendizábal's policy of restricting the authority of the friars. This was in contrast to his brother Juan, who became a loyal supporter of López de Mendizábal and was a vocal critic of the friars.

In November 1660, retired sargento mayor Tomé Domínguez de Mendoza and his neighbor, Captain Francisco Valencia, who resided one league south of the pueblo of Isleta, were in its communal house during a visit by Governor López de Mendizábal. On this occasion they witnessed the public dancing of the catzina by the pueblo residents, which shocked them. The matter of the catzina dances became a divisive political issue soon after López de Mendizábal took command as governor in New Mexico. When he received Indians from various pueblos in Santa Fe and listened to their concerns and complaints about the friars, one complaint was the prohibition of the catzina dances. Based on the descriptions given him, López de Mendizábal considered the catzina dances similar to some Spanish dances and granted permission for them to be performed for him to make a better judgment. A group of Pueblo Indians came to Santa Fe, where they changed into costumes in a newly constructed room of the casas reales de palacio and then performed a catzina dance on the plaza. López de Mendizábal did not see any idolatrous behavior that should cause the dance to be prohibited.[112]

While visiting pueblo communities to address concerns about the behavior of the friars, López de Mendizábal asked to watch the catzina dances to determine whether superstition was in any way manifested, as occurred at the pueblo of Isleta. Tomé Domínguez de Mendoza noted that López de Mendizábal did "not observe there were any superstitions connected with the catzina" and gave permission for the Indians to dance publicly, much to the chagrin and anger of the friars.[113] Traveling with López de Mendizábal to the pueblo of Isleta in November 1660 were Juan Domínguez de Mendoza, Miguel de Noriega, secretary of government and war, Pedro de Arteaga, and Juan Griego, identified as "Naguatlato of the Tewa nation," who spoke Indian languages, particularly Tewa.

When López de Mendizábal asked Tomé Domínguez de Mendoza if he had ever seen the catzina dances, Domínguez de Mendoza replied that "he had never seen them performed in his life because the religious had prohibited them as being evil, and always mentioned the catzinas when they spoke against the superstitions of the Indians."[114] Tomé informed the governor that the recent permission allowing public performance of the catzina caused scandal in the realm, because these kinds of dance had been previously prohibited as "idolatrous and diabolical." According to Tomé and others, these Indian dances had not been seen by citizens in the past, since the friars strongly restricted such dances. López de Mendizábal told Tomé that in his opinion the dances were no different than the dances of the Spaniards, comparing them to the zarambeque. Tomé Domínguez de Mendoza described the catzina dance he observed at Isleta Pueblo, which involved four Indians:

> The Indians went out wearing various evil costumes; one of them especially had an ugly costume, like a devil, with horns on the head, and a bear skin which he dangled by two fingers thrust through the eye socket—a horrible thing. They sang something which sounded like "hu-hu-hu," at which the governor said, "Look there, this dance contains nothing more than this "hu-hu-hu," and these thieving friars say that it is superstitious.[115]

With the governor's permission, the Indians of Isleta continued to dance the catzinas. These ceremonial dances were witnessed in January 1661 by a mulatto boy named Blas, a servant of María López Millán, the wife of Captain Francisco Valencia, who lived a league south of the pueblo of Isleta. Blas was at Isleta, where he observed the Indians performing ceremonial dances "in a council chamber underground, using all their ancient ceremonies, wearing costumes, and dancing this dance."[116]

Tomé Domínguez de Mendoza echoed the outrage and alarm of the friars that the license given by Governor don Bernardo López de Mendizábal negatively affected the Pueblo Indians' Christian moral behavior, causing them to neglect instruction in Catholic doctrine.[117] On the day of his deposition, Domínguez de Mendoza entered an "underground council chamber," a kiva, at Isleta Pueblo, and observed eleven catzina masks hanging "just as we have our holy images," with "a wreath of flowering grasses" set as an offering before one of the masks.[118] Domínguez de Mendoza stated emphatically that he came to have an aversion for don Bernardo and considered the governor's behavior to be detrimental to the faith of the Indians. He also refused to cooperate with a request made by López de Mendizábal to carry papers to Mexico City that contained information against the way the religious conducted themselves and lived in New Mexico.[119]

These episodes give a clear indication of Tomé Domínguez de Mendoza's loyal and unswerving support of the Franciscan friars, which was juxtaposed to that of his brother, Juan, who publicly disparaged the friars and treated them with contempt. In his own testimonies before Inquisition officials, López de Mendizábal acknowledged his disagreements with Tomé.[120] Domínguez de Mendoza provided testimony against López de Mendizábal as part of the case pursued by the Franciscan friars against the former governor in 1661 and 1662.[121] The favor with which the Franciscan friars regarded Tomé is illustrated in the description recorded about him concerning his *calidad* (quality or character) as a witness in which fray Alonso de Posada described Tomé as being "of good reputation" (*de bien credito*).[122] A decree of the tribunal of the Inquisition dated October 13, 1661, granted authorization of the release of embargoed possessions to Maestre de Campo Tomé Domínguez de Mendoza, but it is not clear to whom belonged the properties that were kept under the authority of fray Alonso de Posada.[123]

Tomé Domínguez de Mendoza came under the favor of Governor don Diego de Peñalosa y Briceño (1661–1664), receiving appointments as teniente de capitán general (lieutenant general of New Mexico), treasurer of the Santa Cruzada, and regidor perpetual of the Santa Fe cabildo, serving as such in December 1662.[124] In his capacity as lieutenant governor, Tomé was in the company of Governor Peñalosa y Briceño on May 1, 1662, on a visit of the pueblo of Isleta. Also with the governor, among others, were his brother Juan Domínguez de Mendoza, don Fernando Durán y Chaves, Captain Miguel de Noriega (former secretary of government under Governor López de Mendizábal), Captain Andrés López, Captain Diego Romero, and Captain Nicolás de Aguilar.[125] It was during this visit that Diego Romero and Nicolás de Aguilar, royalists and supporters of López de Mendizábal, were taken by surprise and arrested by order of the tribunal of the Inquisition.

In a deposition recorded on December 26, 1662, Tomé Domínguez de Mendoza, in his position as teniente de capitán general y tesorero de la Santa

Cruzada, made reference to "the paraje of Guadalupe del Paso del Río del Norte, which is in the jurisdiction of Nueva Vizcaya."[126] As a government official Domínguez de Mendoza considered El Paso to be within the jurisdiction of Nueva Vizcaya. However, the early work to establish missions and a small settlement was conducted by friars and vecinos of New Mexico. In particular, Captain Andrés López de Gracia was among the first citizens of New Mexico to maintain himself and his family at El Paso de Río del Norte. López de Gracia maintained wagons for transporting commercial goods, in addition to serving as the military commander of the El Paso area.[127] A document prepared by Governor don Fernando de Villanueva dated February 10, 1667, indicates that he regarded the El Paso region as part of the jurisdiction of New Mexico:

> Captain Andrés de Gracia of El Paso del Río del Norte of this jurisdiction wrote letters asking for aid because the Manso nation was in revolt, as a result of which the friars of that conversion were in danger. With regard to these letters, councils of the captains, cabildo, and retired officials were held and edicts [were pronounced] in which the said Paso del Río del Norte was declared to be of this jurisdiction. And in accordance with the said council I issued an order that Maestre de Campo Tomé Domínguez de Mendoza should go forth with twenty-five men, with powder and munitions, to help the said friars and make the said conversion safe and peaceful, and [to execute] the rest contained in the edicts. In the second dispatch from the said Captain Andrés de Gracia, he states that the said aid is unnecessary and the [men] should halt and turn back because he has hanged two Indians, abettors of the uprising. [He has done this] without remitting autos or knowing how to prepare them. By these letters he shows that he made himself judge without jurisdiction or authority from me.[128]

The 1670s was a decade of constant warfare with Apaches and Navajos aggravated by pestilence and famine. Petitions were sent to royal officials in Mexico City decrying the deplorable conditions in New Mexico and the need for additional soldiers to prevent the loss of New Mexico to the various Apache tribes. In 1676, Governor Juan Francisco Treviño appointed Maestre de Campo Tomé Domínguez de Mendoza as lieutenant governor of New Mexico. Acting on orders of Treviño in June 1676, Tomé organized an expedition to deal with Apache incursions in the area of Socorro and Senecú; he appointed his brother Juan as commander. In the following year of 1677, Tomé was elected to the cabildo of the Villa de Santa Fe.

By this year, the depredations of the Apache tribes and the severe impact of famine on livestock as well as grain production and supplies had taken such a toll on both Pueblo Indians and Spanish citizens that many feared the kingdom of New Mexico could not be preserved without vital assistance from the royal Crown. After several years of written requests and review of the conditions in New Mexico, royal officials finally authorized funds to purchase needed weapons and supplies to assist the citizens of New Mexico, and approved financial support for fifty soldiers, forty-two sentenced to serve in New Mexico and eight volunteers, all brought from Mexico City under the command of fray Francisco de Ayeta.[129]

The arrival of these supplies and soldiers in late 1677 presented an occasion for the majority of non-Indian inhabitants of the Villa de Santa Fe to attend an open council of the cabildo justicia y regimiento in which the civic leaders and the governor formally acknowledged their gratitude to His Majesty, the viceroy of New Spain, the fiscal, and the member of the royal council, as well as to fray Francisco de Ayeta. The cabildo was extremely pleased with the "punctuality" with which Ayeta performed the instructions given him. As a member of the cabildo, Tomé Domínguez de Mendoza, his brother Juan, and his son Diego signed the decree of appreciation issued by the cabildo in December 1677.[130]

Tomé Domínguez de Mendoza again served on the cabildo of the Villa de Santa Fe, being elected to a post on the council in the fateful year of 1680. In the face of the devastating and deadly Pueblo Indian uprising, his large immediate family consisting of fifty-five people, including servants, managed to escape to the south in the company of others who fled for their lives in August 1680. His estancia south of Isleta Pueblo stood abandoned for decades and was never reestablished by any of his descendants. Instead, new settlers established a small village christened Tomé on or near the site of his estancia in the 1700s.

After the survivors of the uprising were gathered and accounted for, Governor Antonio Otermín relied on the council of the most experienced soldiers of the kingdom. Tomé's cautious opinions regarding the feasibility of retaking New Mexico were sound and based on prudent judgment. Governor Otermín and others agreed with him in not attempting an expedition to engage the Pueblo Indians. Instead, it was decided to assemble the survivors in a place around El Paso del Norte until royal authorities were well informed and possible assistance received.[131]

Tomé Domínguez de Mendoza continued to serve in military and political posts into the 1680s. It is quite likely that he also kept a portfolio of papers similar to those of his brother Juan, documenting his accomplishments related to various appointments to military and political posts. To date, this portfolio has not been located, if it survived the passage of the centuries. For

Tomé, the prospect of regaining New Mexico and returning to former lands and homes became less attractive. He established a place of residence for his family about five leagues east of the Real de San Lorenzo in the El Paso area where there was good pasturage, but in 1682 he sought permission to leave New Mexico.[132] By June 1683 he was living in the kingdom of Nueva Vizcaya at a place known as Los Suaces, located north of the modern-day city of Chihuahua. His children and grandchildren continued to reside in the area that became the jurisdiction of Chihuahua.

Tomé Domínguez de Mendoza and Catalina López Mederos were the parents of five sons, and possibly one daughter. Tomé's son, Tomé III Domínguez de Mendoza, born circa 1648, was raised as a frontier soldier. Although there are few historical documents that mention him, Tomé III participated in an expedition to the west against hostile Indians, most likely in late 1668 or early January 1669. In the following year, the younger Tomé III held the rank of captain, no doubt having proven himself as an able commander while on campaigns in the tradition of his grandfather, father, and uncles.[133] The other children of Tomé Domínguez de Mendoza and Catalina López Mederos were:

- Juan Domínguez de Mendoza.[134]
- Diego Domínguez de Mendoza.[135]
- Francisco Domínguez de Mendoza, born circa 1656, who was married by 1681.[136] He may be the same person as Francisco Domínguez who settled in the Valle de San Bartolomé with his wife, María Vitoria de Carvajal, by December 1684.[137]
- Antonio Domínguez de Mendoza, who as a resident of La Toma near El Paso del Norte in 1681 sought to marry doña Juana Romero, daughter of Captain Felipe Romero and doña Jacinta de Guadalajara.[138]
- Apparently, Catalina Domínguez de Mendoza, who was married by 1664 to Cristóbal Durán y Chaves, son of Fernando II Durán y Chaves.[139] Cristóbal Durán y Chaves was killed near Acoma by Apache raiders in June 1669.[140]
- Apparently, Mateo Domínguez de Mendoza married Margarita Márquez and left many descendants.[141] This couple settled first in the San Bartolomé, then at Cusihuiriachic and eventually at Papigochi, now modern-day Ciudad Guerrero, all in the area of modern-day Chihuahua.

Maestre de Campo Tomé Domínguez de Mendoza entered into a second marriage with Catalina Varela de Losada, also known as Catalina Victoria

Carvajal, apparently prior to August 1680; they were the parents of at least six children, five of them born between 1687 and 1699.[142] He was deceased by October 1701, as described in the marriage record of his daughter doña Josefa Domínguez. Many of the immediate descendants of Tomé Domínguez de Mendoza settled in the communities of Cusihuiriachic, east of the modern-day city of Chihuahua, and the Valle de San Bartolomé, now known as the Valle de Allende.

Doña Damiana Ramírez de Mendoza and Álvaro de Paredes

The brief residency of Álvaro de Paredes in New Mexico spanned perhaps as many as five years or fewer, before his untimely death at the age of twenty-three in 1662. Born in February 1638 in Mexico City, Álvaro very likely came to New Mexico as a soldier in the company of his brother, fray José de Paredes (b. ca. 1631), in the late 1650s. Their grandfather, Álvaro de Paredes Espadero, emigrated from Cáceres, Spain, to New Spain in 1580.[143] An educated man with a university degree, Paredes Espadero managed to obtain a royal appointment as the alcalde mayor of the Villa de Colima (1587–1589) in Nueva España, now part of the Mexican state of Colima.[144] He acknowledged he was aided by the reputation of a relative who sat on the Council of the Indies, Licenciado Alonso Martínez Espadero, although this man never did anything specific to assist him.

After completing his term as alcalde mayor of the Villa de Colima, Álvaro de Paredes Espadero made his way to Mexico City, where he sought an advantageous marriage. He made a favorable impression on Licenciado Esteban de Porres, a *relator* (secretary) of the royal audiencia, who acted as the guardian of his sister, doña Beatriz Méndez de Sotomayor.[145] Álvaro wrote to a relative in Cáceres that although Porres "knows well of my poverty, he wanted my company, and he could have married his sister to wealthy men of quality, and knowing who our parents are, he thought it better to do it with me."[146] Porres provided a generous dowry of eight thousand pesos and some land, thus giving Álvaro and his bride a firm foundation for a life together. In fact, they prospered and became the parents of eight children, one of whom was don Estéban de Paredes, the father of the two brothers that came to New Mexico.[147]

Don Estéban de Paredes married doña Beatris Cortés on April 18, 1633, in the chapel of the Cathedral of Mexico City, she being a native of Mexico City and a daughter of Juan Andrés de Zaldívar and Andrea Rangél, previously residents of Celaya in New Spain.[148] Among the seven known children of this couple, each born in Mexico City, were fray José de Paredes and Álvaro de Paredes, both of who came to New Mexico.[149]

It is possible that these two brothers and their family were known to members of the Domínguez de Mendoza family in Mexico City. Whatever the circumstances that brought Álvaro de Paredes to New Mexico, he successfully engaged the male members of the Domínguez de Mendoza family in arranging marriage to doña Damiana Ramírez de Mendoza. The couple received the sacrament of marriage in a ceremony held at the house of Tomé Domínguez, the elder, in February 1660.[150] The occasion of this celebration also marked the occurrence of significant events that would eventually bring Juan Domínguez de Mendoza and his brother-in-law Cristóbal de Anaya Almazán under suspicion of heresy by the Inquisition.

Among those in attendance at the marriage and festivities were four friars, fray José de Paredes, fray Tomás de Alvarado, fray Miguel de Guevara, and fray Salvador de Guerra, this latter friar being the one who was engaged in an illicit affair with Juana de Rueda, the wife of Francisco Domínguez de Mendoza. At some point a conversation took place in which Cristóbal de Anaya Almazán imprudently and assuredly commented that a spiritual relationship, known as *parentesco*, was not formed between a godparent and the parents of a child with baptism, contrary to the teaching of the Roman Catholic Church. The reactions of the friars to this comment were not recorded, but if they did not engage in a heated exchange of theological discourse, they definitely made note of the comments, which in time were used to form a case against Anaya Almazán, leading to his arrest by the Inquisition in 1662 and subsequent trial in Mexico City in 1663. Also present at the wedding celebration was doña Ana Moreno de Lara who informed fray Tomás de Alvarado that Juan Domínguez de Mendoza made amorous advances toward her, which she rebuffed and reminded him of their parentesco, in response to which Domínguez de Mendoza also claimed that he did not believe that a spiritual relationship was formed between godparents, child, and parents when a child was baptized.

It was more than a differing view of parentesco that formed the enmity between the many members of the Domínguez de Mendoza clan and the Franciscan friars. The illicit affair between Juana de Rueda and fray Salvador de Guerra sullied the family honor. It was her sister-in-law doña Damiana Ramírez de Mendoza who encountered Juana and fray Salvador embraced in "indecency."[151] At the moment of discovery, he rose rapidly and, knowing that the elder Tomé Domínguez and his wife, Elena de la Cruz, were nearby, he attempted to bribe doña Damiana into silence offering to bring her a loaf of sugar. How doña Damiana exactly handled this situation is not known; however, she did discuss it with her brother Juan and apparently with Cristóbal de Anaya Almazán, who later related the brief details as part of his testimony before Inquisition officials. Adding insult to injury, it was also said that fray Salvador de Guerra carried on an affair with Josefa Montoya, a member of another family of the Sandia jurisdiction.[152]

Beyond these two incidents, there is very little known from surviving records about doña Damiana Ramírez de Mendoza and her husband Álvaro de Paredes. They resided on an estancia adjacent to that of Cristóbal de Anaya Almazán near Angostura, most likely property of the elder Tomé Domínguez that was given to Álvaro de Paredes as part of the marriage dowry. On May 29, 1662, at the Pueblo de Sandia, Álvaro de Paredes provided testimony before Inquisition officials and declared he was twenty-three years of age, a native of Mexico City, and married to doña Damiana Ramírez de Mendoza.[153] Within a couple of months of this testimony, Álvaro was an unfortunate victim of a lightning strike that ended his life.[154] Before his untimely death, he and doña Damiana were the parents of at least one child, María de Paredes, also known as María Domínguez, who married Felipe de Montoya.[155] Through the children of María de Paredes, the Paredes family descendancy continued in New Mexico. A man named Gonzalo de Paredes and his wife and five children were residents of New Mexico in 1680 and managed to escape the furious onslaught of the Pueblo Indian Revolt in August 1680. This man, originally thought to be a son of Álvaro de Paredes, was most likely the brother of the same name who was born in Mexico City in early June 1641.[156]

Doña Leonor Ramírez de Mendoza and Cristóbal de Anaya Almazán

The strategic matrimonial alliance of the Domínguez de Mendoza family with the politically influential Anaya Almazán family bolstered the integration and upward mobility of the more recently arrived Domínguez de Mendozas within New Mexico's social milieu. Like the Domínguez de Mendoza family, that of Anaya Almazán hailed from Mexico City. Francisco de Anaya Almazán established the family in New Mexico by 1626. His union with Juana López de Villafuerte was undoubtedly influenced by the fact that her parents were among the first settlers of New Mexico, and thus they were accorded special privileges that were advantageous to Francisco as their son-in-law.

An educated man, Francisco de Anaya Almazán served as the scribe of the cabildo of the Villa de Santa Fe in the 1630s and later served as a regidor of the cabildo, alcalde ordinario of Santa Fe, and secretary of government and war directly under the governor.[157] As a civil leader and a soldier, Francisco earned the grant of three encomiendas—the pueblos of Cuarác, Picurís, and La Cienega—which were later inherited by his sons, Cristóbal and Francisco. In fact, by 1660, the Anaya Almazán clan represented one of the three predominant encomendero clans of New Mexico. Seven members of the Anaya Almazán extended family held a vested interest in at least eight encomiendas, second only to the Romero-Gómez Robledo-Lucero de Godoy-Montoya clan. Given that the number of encomenderos was set at thirty-five, the Anaya Almazán clan occupied a fifth of these positions.[158]

A native of the Villa de Santa Fe born circa 1629, Cristóbal de Anaya Almazán received the sacrament of baptism from fray Alonso de Benavides and was confirmed in the Catholic faith by Benavides at a young age. He was taught to read and write by his father as well as by a friar, a skill that served him well in his own social, military, and political advancement but later caused him trouble with the Inquisition. Cristóbal claimed that he entered military service at age eleven, beginning as most soldiers did in the "*plaza de soldado*" (the post of soldier). He served his first four years in the frontier region between San José del Parral in Nueva Vizcaya and Sinaloa before returning to New Mexico, where he continued in his military service, progressing in rank from squadron leader to alférez to captain. As contemporaries, Cristóbal de Anaya Almazán and Juan Domínguez de Mendoza most likely served together on numerous campaigns. By his own account, Cristóbal participated as one of twenty-nine soldiers in the 1651 expedition to Quivira into south-central Texas that lasted nine months, according to his recollection many years later.[159] Among the other soldiers was Juan Domínguez de Mendoza.

By the time of the expedition to Quivira or soon after, Tomé Domínguez and Francisco de Anaya Almazán reached an agreement for the arrangement of the marriage of Tomé's daughter doña Leonor Ramírez de Mendoza with Cristóbal de Anaya Almazán. Part of the dowry apparently included land bought by Tomé and located along the Rio Grande between the pueblos of Santa Ana and San Felipe in the area of modern-day Angostura, New Mexico, and included three springs and land for farming and raising livestock. This property, which was a quarter league north of the house of Tomé Domínguez, became known as the Estancia de San Antonio, where Cristóbal and doña Leonor raised their family.[160] They were neighbors of doña Leonor's sister and brother-in-law doña Damiana Ramírez de Mendoza and Álvaro de Paredes. This property was later augmented by a donation of land from Juan Domínguez de Mendoza and his brother Francisco, located west of the Rio Grande in the mountain area.[161]

FIGURE 5   View of Santa Fe looking northeast, near the bank of the Santa Fe River, with the Sangre de Cristo Mountains in the background, ca. 1909–1915. Denver Public Library, Western History Collection, Horace Swartley Poley, P-1345.

The Anaya Almazáns belonged to the political faction known as "royalist," a group with allegiance to the governors versus the Franciscan leadership. However, a heated political conflict in 1658 initiated a chain of events that eventually caused members of the Anaya Almazán family to flee New Mexico, seeking recourse from royal officials in Mexico City. When some documents of the government archive in the Villa de Santa Fe turned up missing, Governor don Juan Manso (1656–1659) suspected the papers were in the possession of Francisco de Anaya Almazán.[162] Upon confrontation, Anaya Almazán denied concealing any government documents. The conflict intensified when Manso, either acting on knowledge obtained from informants about Anaya Almazán's culpability or with the intention of damaging the patriarch's social and economic standing, initiated a criminal case and ordered his arrest. Also charged and arrested was Anaya Almazán's son-in-law Captain Alonso Rodríguez. Both men were initially held in the jail of the *casas de cabildo*, the jail of the municipal building in the Villa de Santa Fe, and then were transferred to house arrest when bail was provided by Maestre de Campo Pedro Lucero de Godoy and his brother-in-law, Sargento Mayor Francisco Gómez Robledo, members of another prominent encomendero clan and also royalists.[163]

When Governor Manso left the Villa de Santa Fe to conduct an inspection of the Zuñi region in western New Mexico sometime around the spring of 1658, Anaya Almazán slipped out of the villa with his two sons, Francisco de Anaya Almazán (the younger) and Cristóbal de Anaya Almazán, and his son-in-law, Alonso Rodríguez.[164] The group of men fled south on the Camino Real with several supporters. By the time Governor Manso learned of the escape, Anaya Almazán and his sons were well on their way to Mexico City. In retaliation, Manso revoked the grants of encomienda of the Anaya Almazán family, confiscated their houses in the Villa de Santa Fe, and, undoubtedly, sent reports to royal officials in Mexico City.[165]

Apparently, Francisco de Anaya Almazán successfully convinced authorities in Mexico City that his actions—in particular the escape from house arrest—were in response to unfair treatment by Governor Manso. During the period of time he and his sons were in Mexico City, they learned of the appointment of don Bernardo López de Mendizábal as governor of New Mexico, making the new governor's acquaintance and developing an amiable relationship in the spring of 1659. Francisco's son-in-law Captain Alonso Rodríguez befriended López de Mendizábal's wife, doña Teresa de Aguilera y Roche, and regularly attended mass with her.[166] In short order, the Anaya Almazán family found themselves in good favor with the new governor and his wife and managed to win López de Mendizábal to their side of the political conflict with Governor don Juan Manso.

The Anaya Almazán men accompanied López de Mendizábal on his journey to New Mexico, and it was later commented that Francisco de Anaya Almazán traveled "*en grande amistad*," "in great friendship," with López de Mendizábal.[167] They engaged in frequent conversation, and undoubtedly López de Mendizábal was thoroughly briefed on the social and political milieu of New Mexico. Also joining this group of travelers was Alférez Francisco Domínguez de Mendoza, brother-in-law of Cristóbal de Anaya Almazán.

When the entourage of Governor don Bernardo López de Mendizábal reached the Río Abajo region of New Mexico, the group entered the pueblo of Senucú, the southernmost settlement of Pueblo Indians, which also served as a stopping place along the Camino Real.[168] By this time, Governor Manso was well aware that the Anaya Almazán men were returning to the Villa de Santa Fe in López de Mendizábal's favor. On the morning of July 10, 1659, Governor Manso traveled out of town to meet López de Mendizábal and escort him into the Villa de Santa Fe.[169] The transfer of authority was immediate, and one of López de Mendizábal's first acts as governor of New Mexico was to restore the houses and grants of encomiendas to the Anaya Almazán men and their immediate kin.[170]

The influence of the Anaya Almazán clan with the new governor translated into a keen bias against Governor Manso, who was immediately arrested by the order of López de Mendizábal. Manso was first held prisoner in the jail of the casas de cabildo and then was transferred to house arrest, where he remained throughout the customary residencia, the review of his tenure as governor.[171] Among the four men appointed by López de Mendizábal as guards of Manso was a member of the Anaya Almazán family, Captain Alonso Rodríguez, whom Manso considered a personal and political enemy. Manso later gave a statement in which he emphasized the fear he held for his life because his enemies were the main witnesses who testified in his residencia.[172]

For the Anaya Almazán clan, don Bernardo López de Mendizábal served as a conduit by which they exacted their political revenge on don Juan Manso. Nevertheless, the friendship and favor enjoyed by the Anaya Almazán clan with López de Mendizábal eroded into a strained relationship over the course of a few short years. By 1661, behaviors by the governor challenged the honor of the extended Anaya Almazán family.

With a consolidated and firm base of political supporters, Governor don Bernardo López de Mendizábal systematically diminished the authority of the Franciscan friars during the first year of his arrival in New Mexico. He first prohibited the exercise of ecclesiastical jurisdiction by the Franciscan custodian of New Mexico, in opposition to a royal decree granted to the order by the king. Then, through his ministers of justice, who included Juan Domínguez de Mendoza, he ordered that no Indians were to serve the friars, because of the abuses he perceived on the part of the friars, and also based on complaints made to him by some Pueblo Indians.

López de Mendizábal was in no way compelled by the protests of the friars and their political followers. All the friars could do was to complain among themselves and shoot off letter after letter to officials of their order in Mexico City seeking recourse from royal officials. This was the political circumstance in which Cristóbal de Anaya Almazán made the bold claim in the company of several friars in early 1660 that he did not believe that a spiritual bond, parentesco, was created through the sacraments of baptism, marriage and confirmation.[173] It may be that he was overconfident in the political edge that he and other royalists held as supporters of a governor who was not intimidated by the friars and their authority.

By July 1660, the friars had already sent an emissary to the viceroy of New Spain claiming they would abandon New Mexico if no political remedy was forthcoming in regard to the policies and behavior of López de Mendizábal as a representative of the royal Crown.[174] Whether the friars seriously considered leaving New Mexico or simply used these words to provoke royal officials into action, it is appears that the social and political strength of the Franciscans in New Mexico was seriously weakened by the actions of López de Mendizábal and his supporters.

The friars celebrated their first victory in their battle to regain lost political stature with the appointment of father fray Alonso de Posada as custodian, ecclesiastical judge, and commissary of the tribunal of the Inquisition in New Mexico. This success was accompanied by the acquisition of orders from the tribunal for the arrest of two supporters of López de Mendizábal, Captain Nicolás de Aguilar and Captain Diego Pérez Romero. Posada arrived in New Mexico on April 28, 1661, entering the pueblo of Senecú on the following day, and he proved to be an able administrator who was not easily intimidated.[175] He initiated proceedings to collect denunciations from friars and citizens against López de Mendizábal and his main supporters, which included, among others, Cristóbal de Anaya Almazán.

With the arrival of don Diego de Peñalosa y Briceño as governor of New Mexico in the summer of 1661, the residencia of don Bernardo López de Mendizábal was initiated with an edict read in the plaza of the Villa de Santa Fe on September 30, 1661, informing residents that they had thirty days to come forward in the review of López de Mendizábal's tenure as governor.[176] The scribe appointed by Peñalosa y Briceño for the residencia hearings was Francisco de Anaya Almazán, who by this time had developed an extreme dislike for López de Mendizábal.[177] This change of support appears to have been directly related to the fact that López de Mendizábal seduced two women of the Anaya Almazán family.[178]

The falling-out of the Anaya Almazán family with López de Mendizábal had no effect on the vengeance of the friars. After months of gathering testimony to implicate several men of the most prominent and economically successful families with charges of heresy, a review of the investigations garnered the arrest warrants for Francisco Gómez Robledo and Cristóbal de Anaya Almazán but failed to bring formal charges against Juan Domínguez de Mendoza.

Arrested in early May 1662 by the Office of the Inquisition, Cristóbal de Anaya Almazán was held in a cell of the convento of the pueblo of Santo Domingo without knowing the specific charges against him, which was a customary practice of the Inquisition.[179] All of his property was inventoried and sequestered to ensure payment for the cost of his imprisonment, and the rights to the various encomiendas were revoked, which served as a significant economic blow to the family's prosperity. Using the power of the Inquisition as their hammer of justice, the friars struck hard, intending to damage the reputation as well as the social and economic standing of the Anaya Almazán and Gómez Robledo-Romero families.

In the spring of 1663, Cristóbal was one of six prisoners of the Office of the Inquisition transported from New Mexico to Mexico City for trial. Doña Leonor Ramírez de Mendoza endured the separation from her husband for two and a half years, which included his imprisonment in a secret cell of the Inquisition in Mexico City from April 10, 1663 until his release on December 13, 1664.[180]

At the time of Cristóbal's trial in 1663, he and doña Leonor were the parents of four children, Cristóbal, age eleven, Catalina, age eight, Francisco, age five, and María, age two.[181] When asked by Inquisitors if he knew the reason for his arrest and imprisonment, Cristóbal stated that he had no idea of the specific charges and unequivocally affirmed he was a Catholic Christian, as were his parents and grandparents. In regard to his comments against parentesco, he related that he was taught by his father that no bond was formed between a sponsor and the baptized child and the child's parents. In this regard, he described his father as a very learned man, and his testimony reveals the respect and high regard that Cristóbal held for his father. Following numerous sessions before Inquisitors and a drawn-out process of review and determination of heresy, Cristóbal de Anaya Almazán was released in December 1664 with a light sentence of penitence to be made in the church of the pueblo of Sandia, and he was charged a total of 194 pesos and two and a half reales in expenses.[182]

Cristóbal de Anaya Almazán returned to New Mexico in the company of the new governor, don Fernando de Villanueva. In June 1665 Anaya Almazán was in the house of relatives in the Villa de Santa Fe explaining to them the charges that were leveled against him and discussing the embargo of his property that was made at the time of his arrest three years earlier.[183] The first order of business was getting all of his assets in order and regaining his previous lifestyle. By good fortune, the relationship Cristóbal forged with Governor Villanueva on the long journey northward resulted in several favors bestowed upon him. In particular, within the first three days of his arrival in Santa Fe, Villanueva appointed Cristóbal as Provincial de la Santa Hermandad, a prestigious position with the charge of serving as a police agent of the travel routes in New Mexico.[184]

Although Cristóbal complied with the sentence to make public penance for his faulty beliefs, his resentment toward certain friars was not diminished by his experience with the Inquisition. On Sunday, July 19, 1665, he attended mass at the church of Sandia in full regalia and arms. He took a seat at the head bench in the church on the side of the lectern (*espistola*) with Captain Andrés Hurtado, the alcalde mayor of the Sandia jurisdiction on the opposite side. When asked to remove the cane of his authority as Provincial de la Santa Hermandad from his hands and to take off his sword, Cristóbal refused, and for about fifteen minutes he displayed belligerence and expressed his resentment toward the friars. In reference to this incident, fray Rafael de Santa María described Cristóbal as "very rebellious and disobedient."[185]

When Governor Villanueva appointed Juan Domínguez de Mendoza as lieutenant governor of New Mexico, Cristóbal de Anaya Almazán served at the side of his brother-in-law. He was with Domínguez de Mendoza on patrol of the area near the pueblo of Acoma when reports of abuse by two friars of that community were received, and Anaya Almazán took part in the subsequent investigation against the friars, fray Nicolás de Freitas and fray Diego de Santander. These actions brought about a denunciation of Juan Domínguez de Mendoza to the Inquisition. As part of the initial investigation in this case, Cristóbal de Anaya Almazán once again faced interrogation by Inquisition representatives in New Mexico as an "enemy of the religious."[186]

In May 1666, less than a year from his return to New Mexico, Anaya Almazán was called before fray Juan de Paz, custodian of New Mexico and commissary of the Inquisition, to discharge his conscience. In his statement he placed direct blame on fray Salvador de Guerra for instigating the first denunciation against him and accused Guerra of wanting to have him killed. He admitted to his own anger toward the friars but declared he was a Catholic Christian, thus not a heretic. Fray Nicolás de Freitas described Anaya Almazán as having "little fear of God."[187] The statements of Anaya Almazán before officials of the Inquisition exhibit bitter disdain for several friars rather than "little fear of God."

While the Franciscans continued their proceedings against Juan Domínguez de Mendoza and Cristóbal de Anaya Almazán, hoping to have them both removed from positions of political authority, Anaya Almazán received the charge from Villanueva to preside over the transport of the possessions of former governor don Juan de Miranda in late 1666 or early 1667, traveling as far as San José del Parral. Returning to Santa Fe on September 24, 1667, Anaya Almazán was informed by the secretary of government and war, Juan Lucero de Godoy, that Governor Villanueva revoked his appointment of Provincial de la Santa Hermandad upon learning that Anaya Almazán "had been sentenced in the pueblo of Sandia."[188] It is not clear if the reference is to the sentence of the Inquisition from 1664 or the result of a second denunciation that was part of the denunciation of Juan Domínguez de Mendoza in 1667.

The house of doña Leonor Ramírez de Mendoza and Cristóbal de Anaya Almazán at the Estancia de San Antonio consisted of a living room or hall, two rooms, one kitchen, and one room outside of the house with doors and windows made of timber with metal locks.[189] Located about six miles south of the pueblo of San Felipe, it was at this estancia that they raised a family of as many as eight children of whom the names of only five are known: (1) Cristóbal II, born circa 1652; (2) Catalina, born circa 1655; (3) Francisco, born circa 1658; (4) María, born circa 1661; and (5) Juan.[190]

This family experienced the full fury of the Pueblo Indians during the August 1680 uprising. Taken completely by surprise at their estancia, Cristóbal, his wife, and five of their children were slaughtered and their bodies stripped of clothing. Two adult sons survived and another son was left for dead, only to be taken in by Pueblo Indians and reunited with his family many years later, in 1692.[191] The surviving sons were Juan de Anaya and Francisco de Anaya Almazán. Juan de Anaya remained close to his uncle, Juan Domínguez de Mendoza, with whom he left New Mexico without license in 1687.[192]

Doña Elena Domínguez de Mendoza and Don Pedro II Durán y Chaves

Of the eight daughters of Tomé Domínguez and Elena de la Cruz, Elena Domínguez de Mendoza was one of four that are known to have lived in New Mexico. By all appearances, Elena became the second wife of don Pedro II Durán y Chaves, son of Pedro I Durán y Chaves and doña Isabel de Bohórquez.[193] The name of don Pedro II's first wife is not known.

It is not surprising that don Pedro II Durán y Chaves and his daughter, doña Isabel Durán y Chaves, married into the Domínguez de Mendoza family, creating a strategic alliance with one of the more prominent social and political families of seventeenth-century New Mexico. The Domínguez de Mendoza family, with lands north of Sandia Pueblo in the area of modern-day Angostura, were neighbors of the Durán y Chaves family of nearby El Tunque.

Pedro I Durán y Chaves (b. ca. 1566) was a native of Valverde de Llerena in Estremadura, Spain, and resided in New Mexico by 1610.[194] The names of his parents are unknown, but he was apparently a relative of Pedro Gómez Rico, also a native of Valverde de Llerena, who died in New Mexico around 1606. Pedro I Durán y Chaves married doña Isabel de Bohórquez, born 1586 in Mexico City, who was a daughter of New Mexico settlers Captain Cristóbal Baca and Ana Ortiz.[195] Pedro I Durán y Chaves and doña Isabel participated in the founding of the Villa de Santa Fe in 1610, and they raised at least two children, don Fernando I Durán y Cháves (born circa 1617) and don Pedro II Durán y Chaves (born circa 1618–1620).[196]

Although Pedro I Durán y Chaves and doña Isabel de Bohórquez were vecinos of the Villa de Santa Fe, they came to own property in the fertile Rio Grande Valley of the Río Abajo region of New Mexico. Doña Isabel's landholdings in the area of the Arroyo del Tunque most likely came from the dowry given by her father.[197] El Tunque is located about ten miles north of the present-day town of Bernalillo. Pedro I also owned an estancia located south of Sandia Pueblo.[198] These farm and ranching landholdings formed an estate that was eventually inherited by their children and grandchildren, attesting to the firm roots of the Durán y Chaves family in the Rio Abajo region.

Politically, Pedro I established his family's longtime political affiliation with the Franciscan friars, and this family apparently prospered from the alliance until 1642. His brother-in-law, Antonio Baca, also an ally of the Franciscans, served as a leader of the group of men who murdered Governor Luis de Rosas and Alférez Sebastián de Sandoval in 1642. Baca and several other Durán y Chaves relatives and associates were convicted of the crime, branded as traitors to the Crown, and executed. This disgrace also stained the honor and social standing of living members of their families, whose social identity as respectable vecino landowners and encomenderos was maligned.

By kinship association, as "relatives of traitors," the Durán y Chaves family was stigmatized politically and socially, which also affected them economically.[199] In fact, with the sentencing and execution of the men accused of murdering Governor Rosas, don Pedro II Durán y Chaves and his brother don Fernando Durán y Chaves were declared traitors by Governor Alonso Pacheco Heredia, and their property and encomiendas were confiscated.[200] In an attempt to regain their family honor and the lost titles to land and encomiendas, the Durán y Chaves brothers, and two male relatives of the men who were executed, traveled to Mexico City to seek legal recourse before royal officials.

On November 14, 1643, in Mexico City, the first of several petitions was drawn up by the Durán y Chaves brothers, Alonso Baca and Juan Ramírez de Salazar. In these petitions the men went so far as to emphatically state that Nicolás Ortiz was the sole perpetrator of the murder of Governor Rosas and declared that they and their relatives were wrongly persecuted by Governor Pacheco y Heredia.[201] The Durán y Chaves brothers pleaded their case stating that their relative Antonio Baca and the other men who were identified as accomplices of Nicolás Ortiz were innocent of the crime for which they were convicted and executed.[202] As part of their plea for mercy from the Crown, they emphasized that their fathers and relatives served His Majesty in the "conquest and pacification, settlement and conservation" of New Mexico.[203]

Although the Durán y Chaves brothers retained the social honor associated with being hidalgos, including the use of the title of don, the loss of property and the grant of encomiendas diminished their social and political influence during the mid-1600s. The stain of association with those who murdered Governor Rosas remained with the Durán y Chaves family for decades. Writing to the viceroy in August 1685, Governor Jironza Petríz de Crusate mentioned that don Pedro II Durán y Chaves was "the one whom your Excellency informed me was present at the death of don Luis de Rosas, which they say was so ignominious . . ."[204]

The Durán y Chaves brothers returned to New Mexico by the late summer of 1644 when don Pedro II Durán y Chaves, a vecino of the Villa de Santa Fe, provided testimony on August 18, 1644, before the Franciscan custodian, fray Tomás Manso, at the convento of Santo Domingo.[205] This was part of an inquest to determine whether any Franciscan friars were involved in seditious activities and to formally describe the manner in which the friars were mistreated by Governor Rosas. Pedro II made a comment that indicated the long-standing support by the Durán y Chaves family of the Franciscan friars, stating that he knew all of the religious who served in New Mexico, especially those who had served for the past twenty years.

Don Pedro II Durán y Chaves, a native of Santa Fe, apparently had a first marriage for which there is no documentation, but this union produced a son, Fernando, and daughter, Isabel. By 1667 he and Elena Domínguez de Mendoza were married, and his daughter, doña Isabel de Chaves y Bohórquez, was married to Juan Domínguez de Mendoza.[206] Five years earlier, in 1662, Diego de Luna, a vecino of the Sandia jurisdiction, specifically mentioned that Captain don Pedro II Durán y Chaves was the "*suegro*," father-in-law," of Maestre de Campo Juan Domínguez de Mendoza.[207] Also, in later years, don Fernando II Durán y Chaves identified himself as a son of don Pedro II and referred to Juan Domínguez de Mendoza as his brother-in-law.[208] The fact that don Fernando II referred to Juan Domínguez de Mendoza as a brother-in-law instead of an uncle indicates that don Fernando was not a son of Elena Domínguez de Mendoza. This information clarifies relationships that fray Angélico Chávez left unclear when he published *Origins of New Mexico Families*.[209] This clarification is illustrated in following chart:

In Service to the Spanish Crown

CHART 4

DURÁN Y CHAVES–DOMÍNGUEZ DE MENDOZA

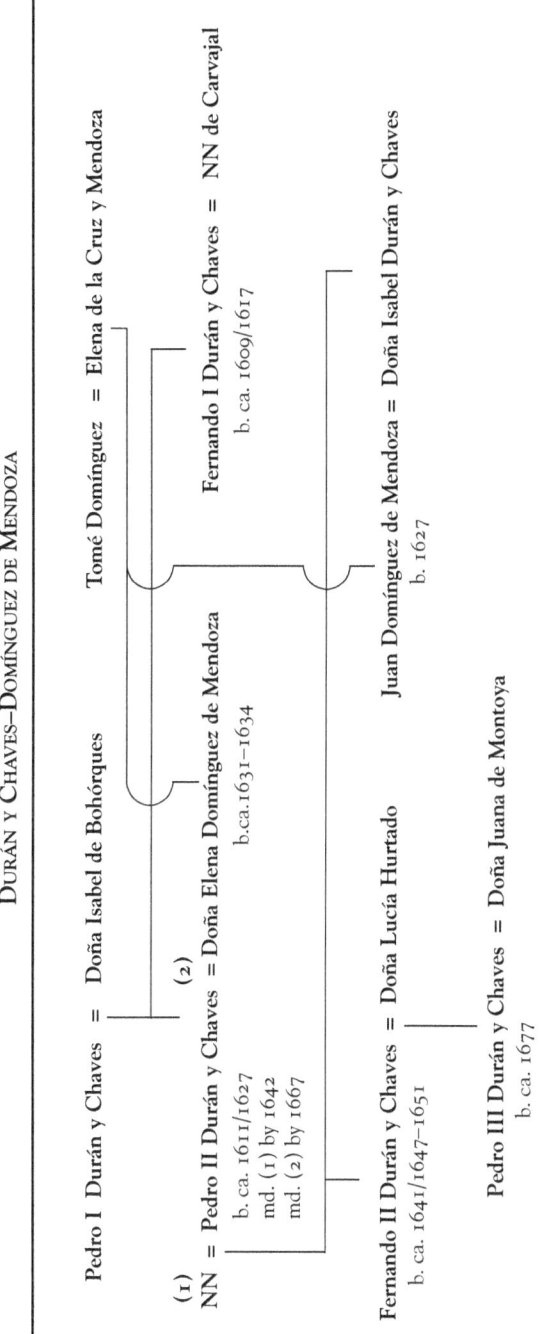

The political support and alliance of the Durán y Chaves family with the Franciscan friars offers a plausible reason that immediate members of this family are not featured frequently in the Inquisition documents of seventeenth-century New Mexico, the main surviving sources for genealogical and historical information about New Mexico families. This raises a curious question as to why a staunch royalist such as Juan Domínguez de Mendoza would marry into a family belonging to the faction of "protectors of religion." The answer most likely rests with the long-standing tradition of marriage unions arranged by male heads of household, usually fathers. Indications are that Juan's father, Tomé Domínguez, favored the Franciscans, since Tomé maintained commercial dealings with the Franciscans in New Mexico prior to relocating to the frontier. Perhaps Tomé's political ideology also leaned toward the religious. If so, it is very likely that Tomé arranged matrimonial alliances with other families of similar political ideology. This would explain the union of Juan and his sister Elena with two members of the Durán y Chaves family. For his own personal reasons, Juan did not follow in the political footsteps of his father the way his brother Tomé Domínguez de Mendoza did by remaining politically partisan to the Franciscans.

It is not surprising that, following the tragic events of the Pueblo Indian uprising of August 1680 and the failed attempts to reestablish Spanish presence in northern New Mexico, don Pedro II Durán y Chaves and his brother-in-law, Tomé Domínguez de Mendoza, left the exiled New Mexico colony at El Paso del Norte and migrated southward with their families. Rather than clinging to hopes of returning to their former homes, they sought opportunities for themselves and their families south of El Paso del Norte.

By June 1684, don Pedro II was already well established in the area that would eventually become the jurisdiction of Chihuahua. On his return from exploring Texas, Juan Domínguez de Mendoza arrived at the house of his father-in-law in late June 1684, located north of the hacienda de Tabalaopa and south of Los Suaces. It was here that Domínguez de Mendoza spent a week resting the horses before traveling eight leagues to the house of Tomé Domínguez de Mendoza at Los Suaces.[210]

In the aftermath of the Pueblo Revolt of 1680, Pedro II Durán y Chaves, at about age sixty, was accounted for with ten minor children, presumably grandchildren, but perhaps several were his own children. However, his wife, Elena Domínguez de Mendoza, was not listed among his household. The year of her death is unknown, having been lost in the records destroyed by Pueblo Indians. The loss of numerous other records also makes it challenging to identify any children of this couple.

Don Fernando Durán y Chaves, the one known son of don Pedro II, is the only known male member of this family that returned to resettle New Mexico in 1693. After settling at Santa Fe for a short while, don Fernando and his family established themselves in the area of Bernalillo in 1695. In time and through perseverance, he managed to reclaim some of his family's land in the area of Atrisco, which eventually became part of the jurisdiction of the Villa de Alburquerque in 1706.

José Domínguez de Mendoza and Juana Domínguez

No known male members of the families of Juan, Tomé, and Francisco Domínguez de Mendoza returned with the restoration of New Mexico under Governor don Diego de Vargas in 1693, although several female family members did resettle northern New Mexico. However, the Domínguez de Mendoza family name was reestablished in New Mexico by Ayudante José Domínguez de Mendoza, a mestizo man carrying the distinguished surname and whose exact relationship to members of the Domínguez de Mendoza family is unclear.

José Domínguez de Mendoza, born circa 1657–1666, may have been a natural son of one of the Domínguez de Mendoza men.[211] Alternatively, he may have derived his surname from an influential godparent of the Domínguez de Mendoza family. His mother, Ana Velásquez, also known as Ana Velasco, was an Indian woman and resident of the Villa de Santa Fe in the early 1660s, serving as cook and laundress at the casas reales de palacio (Governor's Palace) during the tenure of Governor don Bernardo López de Mendizábal.[212] In subsequent years, José Domínguez de Mendoza served with distinction as a frontier soldier, holding the rank of alférez in 1692, captain in 1705, and ayudante in 1707, and carrying forward the Domínguez de Mendoza tradition of military service to the royal Crown with valor, distinction, and unremitting dedication.[213]

In a petition presented to fray Nicolás Hurtado dated April 8, 1682, at El Real de San Lorenzo near El Paso del Norte, José Domínguez de Mendoza formally submitted his request to enter into the state of matrimony with Juana López Sambrano, a daughter of Sargento Mayor Diego López Sambrano and María de Suazo, all natives of New Mexico and originally residents of the Villa de Santa Fe.[214] Domínguez de Mendoza identified himself as a native of New Mexico and a son of Ana Velásquez and an unknown father. He and Juana received the sacrament of matrimony on April 19, 1682. From this union was born a son, Domingo Domínguez, and a daughter, María Domínguez.

María Domínguez married Dimas Jirón de Tejeda, born circa 1685, a native of Mexico City and a son of Tomás Jirón de Tejeda and Josefa González de Aragón.[215] María and Dimas became the progenitors of the Jiron (Girón) family of New Mexico.

A widower by 1692, José Domínguez de Mendoza, commissioned with the military rank of alférez, participated in the efforts of don Diego de Vargas to restore New Mexico to the Spanish Crown. In this endeavor he was reunited in October 1692 with his sister, Juana Domínguez, who had been taken captive by the Pueblo Indians during the uprising of 1680 with a son, Juan Luján (born circa 1678, Villa de Santa Fe), and four daughters, Antonia Luján Domínguez (born circa 1677, Río Abajo), Josefa Luján, Leonor Luján, and María Luján.[216] Juana's husband, Domingo Luján, escaped to El Paso del Río del Norte in August 1680 in the wake of attacks by Pueblo Indians.[217] Juana's reunion with Domingo Luján in 1692 lasted less than a year before he died in October 1693 near the paraje of Fray Cristóbal while on campaign with Governor Vargas.[218] She remained a widow for many years and carried on a long-term affair with Lorenzo de Madrid after the resettlement of the Villa de Santa Fe before their eventual marriage in 1707.

A list of soldiers of the presidio at El Paso del Río del Norte from April 1693 included the name of José Domínguez.[219] In May 1697, an account of settlers receiving livestock and supplies included the "orphan children of José Dominguez, Domingo and María."[220] Apparently, José Domínguez was away from New Mexico during this distribution. Soon after this time, he entered into his second marriage with Gerónima Varela de Losada, also known as Varela de Perea, by whom he had at least two known children before her death in April 1727: Ana María Domínguez, born circa 1698–1699, and Manuel Domínguez, born circa 1705.[221]

José Domínguez de Mendoza and Juana Domínguez remained residents of the Villa de Santa Fe until their deaths. He was still living in 1716, and she left a last will and testament before her death in 1717.[222]

There was another woman named Juana Domínguez who was a contemporary of José Domínguez de Mendoza and his sister. This second Juana Domínguez, born circa 1656–1657, sought in April 1680 to marry Sargento Mayor Diego Lucero de Godoy, the owner of a large tract of land in the Taos jurisdiction, who was associated with the Domínguez de Mendoza family, having been born in the house of Maestre de Campo Juan Domínguez de Mendoza.[223] Rumors were that Juana was a daughter of the elder Tomé Domínguez (born circa 1587, died circa 1660). Juana Domínguez declared this to be an untrue claim, as confirmed by her mother, an Apache woman of Tomé's household named

Josefa. Other allegations that Juana was a daughter of Maestre de Campo Juan Domínguez de Mendoza were flatly denied by him when he testified that Juana's father was man named Juan de Velasco, a vagrant and resident of Mexico City. Maestre de Campo Tomé Domínguez de Mendoza and his sisters doña Damiana Domínguez de Mendoza and doña Leonor Domínguez de Mendoza also denied any blood relationship with Juana Domínguez. According to Juan Domínguez de Mendoza, his mother, Elena de la Cruz y Mendoza, acted as Juana's godmother in a baptismal ceremony at the church of the pueblo of Sandia.

An impediment to the proposed marriage union put forward in force by members of the Domínguez de Mendoza family apparently succeeded in preventing the marriage of Sargento Mayor Diego Lucero de Godoy with Juana Domínguez. In February 1681, Lucero de Godoy instead married doña María Domínguez de Mendoza, daughter of Juan Domínguez de Mendoza and doña Isabel Durán y Chaves, and a person of the same social status as him.

Epilogue

The advent of the eighteenth century ushered in significant changes to New Mexico's frontier society. Between 1693 and 1695, new settlers from many regions of Nueva Vizcaya and Nueva España, as well as some from Europe, converged in northern New Mexico, reshaping the social structure that formed the foundation for the development of a *Nuevomejicano* heritage. Royal officials abolished the encomienda system of assigning Pueblo Indian communities to prominent residents for collection of tribute in exchange for military service. Instead, the government actively fostered an agrarian socioeconomic infrastructure that formed the basis for New Mexico's long-held land grant history. The government also established a presidio in the Villa de Santa Fe, which formalized the tradition of military service so characteristic of seventeenth-century New Mexico. Soldiers now received a salary, and military service became the main occupation for the one hundred soldiers that garrisoned the presidio located immediately adjacent to the casas reales de palacio in the Villa de Santa Fe.

In the last years of the seventeenth century, the Domínguez de Mendozas were no longer a leading family of New Mexico. Most male heads of the clan chose to improve their economic status in Nueva Vizcaya, mainly in the area of Chihuahua, and in Mexico City. Only Antonio Domínguez de Mendoza, son of Francisco Domínguez de Mendoza and Juana de Rueda, remained at El Paso del Norte with his wife, Juana García de Noriega, a daughter of the influential Maestre de Campo Alonso García, the former lieutenant governor of New Mexico at the time of the 1680 uprising of the Pueblo Indians.[224] Antonio was deceased by the end of 1692, when his widow declared her intention to resettle northern New Mexico with her two sons and three daughters.[225] She was not completely alone, since several of her immediate family members, including her parents, also intended to return to the land of their birth. As a result of this intention, the Domínguez de Mendoza lineage extended into eighteenth-century New Mexico, and into the present day, through several daughters of Antonio Domínguez de Mendoza and Juana García de Noriega.[226]

Whatever legacy Tomé Domínguez the elder may have envisioned for himself and his descendants in New Mexico, it waxed and waned in a period of about forty years but reemerged in other regions. Tomé's decision to settle New Mexico with his wife and some of his children transformed the social identity of his family and contributed significantly to the social, economic, and political history of seventeenth-century New Mexico. Members of his family persevered under harsh and dangerous frontier conditions while surrounded by the everyday threat of attack from hostile nomadic tribes. The military service records of Juan Domínguez de Mendoza and the accounts of his father and brothers documented above attest to the distinction with which members of this family served the Spanish Crown at their own cost, including the cost to their own legacy in New Mexico.

Notes

1. AGN, Inquisición, vol. 380, exp. 2, f. 250r–250v, Testimony and ratification of statement of Tomé Domínguez, May 26–27, 1633, Convento de la Concepción de Cuarác.

2. Family History Library, The Church of Jesus Christ of Latter-Day Saints (FHL-LDS), Mexico, Puebla, Puebla de Zaragoza, Sagrario (Catedral), Matrimonios 1585–1629, microfilm, #0227701.

3. AGN, Inquisición, vol. 304, exp. 26, f. 180r, Escrito de Fray Estéban de Perea, March 4, 1633, Convento del Pueblo de Cuarác.

4. Biblioteca Nacional de Madrid (BNM), 19258, ff. 106–20 (Prueba de Elena de la Cruz, 1625).

5. Folios 113–21 are missing from the collection of the service records of Juan Domínguez de Mendoza, see table 1 in the preface of this book.

6. BNE, Madrid, MSS 19258, f. 110.

7. Ibid., f. 108.

8. Ibid., f. 110.

9. Ibid.

10. Ibid., ff. 110–11.
11. Ibid., f. 111.
12. Ibid., f. 113.
13. Ibid., f. 111.
14. Ibid., ff. 106–7.
15. Ibid., ff. 112–14.
16. Ibid., ff. 113–15.
17. Ibid., ff. 115–16.
18. Ibid., ff. 117–18.
19. Ibid., ff. 118–19.
20. Ibid., ff. 119–20.
21. FHL-LDS, Mexico, Distrito Federal, Mexico City, Asunción Church (Catedral), Baptisms, 1612–1627, f. 201v, microfilm #0035169.
22. AGN, Inquisición, vol. 304, exp. 26, f. 180r, Escrito de Fray Estéban de Perea, March 4, 1633, Convento del Pueblo de Cuarác.
23. Ibid.
24. FHL-LDS, Mexico, Puebla, Puebla de Zaragoza, San José Church, Bautismos 1583–1956, microfilm #0227901. Geronimo de Riquerio was first married to Ana de Porras at the Catedral de Puebla on May 27, 1607. Gerónimo next married Antonia de Arcega, and they had a daughter, Juana, who was baptized at the sagrario chapel of the Catedral de Puebla, October 27, 1616.
25. Ibid.
26. FHL-LDS, Mexico, Distrito Federal, Mexico City, Asunción Church (Catedral), Bautismos, 1612–1627, f. 180r, microfilm #0035169. The godparents were Vibrán Martínez and Catalina Jonossa.
27. Curiously, his father's name was recorded as Juan Domínguez, rather than Tomé Domínguez, but his mother's name was recorded correctly as Elena de la Cruz. FHL-LDS, Mexico, Puebla, Puebla de Zaragoza, Sagrario Metropolitano, Bautismos, 1609–1623, microfilm #0227520.
28. FHL-LDS, Mexico, Mexico City, Asunción Church (Catedral), Bautismos, 1612–1627, f. 350v, microfilm #0035169.
29. Ibid., f. 77.
30. Ibid., f. 201v. As María de Mendoza, she married on November 29, 1652, Santa Vera Cruz Church, Mexico City, Nicolás González, native of Mexico City, son of José González and Catalina Enríquez. FHL-LDS, Mexico, Distrito Federal, Mexico City, Santa Vera Cruz Church, Matrimonios 1626–1667, microfilm #0035848.
31. The baptismal record of Damiana identified her as a daughter of Tomé Domínguez and Elena de la Cruz. Her godfather was recorded as Sebastián Pérez. The officiating priest was Francisco Gómez. FHL-LDS, Mexico, Distrito Federal, Mexico City, Asunción Church (Catedral), Bautismos, 1627–1639, microfilm #0035170.

32. The baptismal record of Leonor identified her parents as Thomé Domínguez and Elena de la Cruz. Her godfather was don Pedro Díes de la Banera, and the officiating priest was Bachiller Juan Barajo de Quintana. The baptismal record of Baleriana identified her parents as Captain Thomé Domínguez and doña Elena de la Cruz. Her godmother was doña Juana de Urquís. Ibid.; Chávez, *Origins of New Mexico Families*, 25.

33. AGN, Inquisición, vol. 372, exp. 19, f. 1r, Escrito de Fray Estéban de Perea, November 1631, Convento de San Francisco de Sandia.

34. AGN, Inquisición, vol. 304, exp. 26, f. 180r, Escrito de Fray Estéban de Perea, March 4, 1633, Convento del Pueblo de Cuarác.

35. AGN, Inquisición, vol. 380, exp. 2, f. 250r–250v, Testimony and ratification of statement of Tomé Domínguez, May 26–27, 1633, Convento de la Concepción de Cuarác.

36. AGN, Real Hacienda, Bulas de la Santa Cruzada, vol. 2, exp. 1, ff. 1–5, Litigio promovido por Miguel de Urquiola albacea del difunto Pedro de Ibarra contra Thomé Domínguez por una deuda, 1634, Ciudad de México; AGN, Real Hacienda, Bulas de la Santa Cruzada, vol. 2, exp. 2, ff. 6–8, Litigio promovido por Domingo de Barainca contra Thomé Domínguez, por una deuda, 1634, Ciudad de México; AGN, Real Hacienda, Bulas de la Santa Cruzada, 1634–1638, vol. 2, exp. 3, ff. 9–12, Juan de Rosas, mercader, entabla un litigio contra Thomé Domínguez, por una deuda, 1634, Ciudad de México, and exp. 4, ff. 13–92; AGN, Real Hacienda, Bulas de la Santa Cruzada, 1634–1638, vol. 2, exp. 4, ff. 13–92, Hernando Delgado, cirujano, promueve un litigio en contra de Thomé Domínguez, principal, y Tomás de Sein, fiador, pro usa deuda, 1634, Ciudad de México.

37. Spanish Archives of New Mexico, Series II, Reel 1, fr. 12, Commission of Tomé Domínguez as capitán y cabo, December 15, 1636, Socorro. Tomé Domínguez continued to run wagons between New Mexico and Mexico City. A record dated February 4, 1641, San José del Parral in Nueva Vizcaya, identified Tomé as "*dueño de sus carros de mulas y vecino de la Provincia del Nuevo México*" ("owner of his mule wagons and taxpaying citizen of the Province of New Mexico"), indicating that Domínguez had officially changed his primary residence from Mexico City to New Mexico by that date. Archivo Histórico del Parral, 1641A, G-102, Protocolos, f. 570ff, De escrituras públicas, correspondientes a los años de 1641, 1642 y 1643; Salvador Treviño Castro, *Del Chihuahua Colonial*, 32.

38. Doc. 9, supra, Title of Maestre de Campo, Santa Fe, October 15, 1658.

39. Doc. 11, supra, Appointment as Alcalde Mayor of the Jurisdictions of Sandia and Isleta and as Lieutenant Captain General in the Río Abajo, Santa Fe, November 19, 1659.

40. Doc. 64, supra, Résumé of papers presented by Baltasar Domínguez de Mendoza, Madrid, August 19, 1694.

41. The marriage record for Francisco Domínguez de Mendoza and Juana de Rueda specifically referred to the ceremony having occurred between eleven

and twelve o'clock in the house of Francisco's father on the Calle de San Juan. FHL-LDS, Mexico, Distrito Federal, Mexico City, Santa Vera Cruz Church, Matrimonios 1590–1668, microfilm # 0035848.

42. Nicolás González was a son of José González and Catalina Enríquez.

43. Chávez, *Origins of New Mexico Families*, 25.

44. AGN, Inquisición, vol. 582 exp. 2, f. 289r–289v, Testimony of Fray José de Paredes, April 23, 1662, Pueblo del Socorro; AGN, Inquisición, vol. 582, exp. 2, f. 323v, Summary of the Case against Capitán Cristóbal de Anaya Almazán, 1663, Ciudad de México.

45. AGN, Inquisición, vol. 582, exp. 2, f. 324r, Summary of the Case against Capitán Cristóbal de Anaya Almazán, 1663, Ciudad de México; AGN, Inquisición, vol. 582, exp. 2, f. 345v, Testimony of Alférez Alvaro de Paredes, May 1, 1662, Convento de San Francisco de Sandia.

46. AGN, Real Audiencia, Concurso de Peñalosa, vol. 3, leg. 1, no. 22, 44ff, Embargo of property of Captain Cristóbal de Anaya Almazán, May 25, 1662, Estancia de San Antonio.

47. AGN, Inquisición, vol. 582, exp 2, f. 289r–289v, Testimony of Fray José de Paredes, April 23, 1662, Pueblo del Socorro.

48. The estancia of Juan Estéban de Fagoaga was located twelve leagues from the Villa de Santa Fe in the Sandia jurisdiction, AGN, Inquisición, vol. 593, ff. 234v–235r, Testimony of Juan Estéban de Fagoaga, April 8, 1662, Convento de San Francisco de Sandia, and AGN, Inquisición, vol. 582, exp. 2, f. 287v, Testimony of Juan Estéban de Fagoaga, April 8, 1662, Convento de San Francisco de Sandia. The estancia of Diego de Trujillo was known as Las Huertas and was located in the area of Sandia Pueblo, AGN, Inquisición, vol. 596, f. 12r, Testimony of Diego de Trujillo, September 26, 1661, Villa de Santa Fe.

49. Supp. Doc. 5, supra, Certification of the Number of Friars in the Conventos of the Custody of New Mexico, Mexico City, December 6, 1667.

50. AGN, Inquisición, vol. 507, Ratification of the Statement of doña Francisca Gómez Robledo, May 19, 1664, Villa de Santa Fe; Chávez, *Origins of New Mexico Families*, 25.

51. See note 1 in Introduction, supra, for the transcription of the baptismal record of Juan Domínguez de Mendoza. Juan Domínguez de Mendoza gave his age as thirty-four in June 1663. AGN, Inquisición, vol. 507, exps. 1 and 2, f. 19r, Declaration of Juan Domínguez de Mendoza, June 20, 1663, Mexico City. See also, Hackett, *Historical Documents*, 3:234. For information about the early age of Domínguez de Mendoza's military service, see Doc. 46, supra, Certification of Documents Showing the Services of the Maestre de Campo Don Juan Domínguez de Mendoza, El Paso, October 3, 1684.

52. José Antonio Esquibel and Patryka Durán y Chaves, "Pedro Durán y Chaves and Juana Montoya," in Gloria M. Valencia y Valdez, José Antonio Esquibel, Robert D. Martínez, and Francisco Sisneros, eds., *Aquí se comienza: A Genealogical History*

of the Founding Families of La Villa de San Felipe de Alburquerque (Albuquerque: New Mexico Genealogical Society, 2007), 184–85.

53. Chávez, *Origins of New Mexico Families*, 19.
54. Hackett, *Historical Documents*, 3:231.
55. Chávez, *Origins of New Mexico Families*, 19.
56. Doc. 11 supra, Appointment as Alcalde Mayor of the Jurisdictions of Sandia and Isleta and as Lieutenant Captain General in the Río Abajo, Santa Fe, November 19, 1659; Doc. 15, supra, Appointment as Lieutenant of the Governor and Captain General in the Jurisdiction of the Río Abajo, Santa Fe, June 25, 1665.
57. Hackett, *Historical Documents*, 3:294.
58. AGN, Inquisición, vol. 610, f. 63v, Letter of Fray Diego de Santander to Fray Alonso de Posada, March 26, 1666; AGN, Inquisición, vol. 507, exp. 1 and 2, f. 19r, Declaration of Juan Domínguez de Mendoza, June 20, 1663, Mexico City; Doc. 46, supra, Certification of Documents Showing the Services of the Maestre de Campo don Juan Domínguez de Mendoza, El Paso, October 3, 1684.
59. Chávez, *Origins of New Mexico Families*, 26.
60. Doc. 47, supra, Certification of the Personal Appearance and Services of Maestre de Campo don Juan Domínguez de Mendoza and His Two Sons, El Paso, October 8, 1684.
61. Doc. 62, supra, Summary of the Petition of Baltasar Domínguez de Mendoza to the Crown, [Madrid], 1694.
62. Doc. 61, infra, Report of the Council of the Indies concerning Petitions Made by Baltasar Domínguez de Mendoza, Madrid, October 1, 1694.
63. Doc. 62, supra, Summary of the Petition of Baltasar Domínguez de Mendoza to Doc. 63, supra, Petition Asking for Admission to One of the Military Orders, Madrid, March 1695.
64. Doc. 63, supra, Petition Asking for Admission to One of the Military Orders, Madrid, March 1695.
65. Doc. 64, supra, Royal Cédula to the Viceroy of New Spain Recommending don Baltasar Domínguez de Mendoza, Madrid, April 21, 1695.
66. FHL-LDS, Mexico, Distrito Federal Mexico City, Asuncion Church (Cathedral), Matrimonios 1688–1701, microfilm #0035270. The banns of matrimony for don Baltasar Domínguez de Mendoza and doña María Francisca de Alburu were recorded on August 4, 1697, at the Catedral de México. He was identified as a native of the Villa de Santa Fe in the kingdom of New Mexico, son of don Juan Domínguez y Mendoza and doña Isabel Durán y Chaves. Doña Francisca was identified as a native of Mexico City and a daughter of Alférez don Diego de Alburu and doña Luisa de Rioja. FHL-LDS, Mexico, Distrito Federal, Mexico City, Asuncion Church (Cathedral), Información Matrimonial de Españoles, 1694–1734, microfilm #0035256. Alférez don Diego de Alburu, a native of the Valle de Oyarzun in Guipúzcoa, was a son of Juan de Alburu and Catalina de Ereros who arrived in Nueva España by 1664, when he married, on November 25,

Santa Vera Cruz Church, Mexico City, with Luisa de Rioja (baptized November 20, 1639, Santa Vera Cruz Church, Mexico City), daughter of Francisco de Rioja and Catalina de Villegas Ribera. FHL-LDS, Mexico, Distrito Federal, Ciudad de México, Santa Vera Cruz Church, Matrimonios, 1664–1726, microfilm #0035848; FHL-LDS, Mexico, Distrito Federal, Ciudad de México, Santa Vera Cruz Church, Bautismos, 1636–1668, microfilm #0035820.

67. FHL-LDS, Mexico, Distrito Federal, Ciudad de México, Asunción Church (Cathedral), Bautismos 1705–1713, microfilm #0035177. Information on one line of descent from Baltasar Domínguez de Mendoza was provided from a private correspondence with Luis Vera Prendes of Mexico City, who wrote in June 2004, "I have been conducting a genealogical research of my family lineage for about a year and a half, with many pleasant surprises in the way. One of the latest surprises is that I (with the help of my genealogist Ms. Luz Montejano Hilton) have discovered and documented that I am a descendant of Juan Domínguez de Mendoza." Luis Vera Prendes is a descendant of Marina Josefa Domínguez de Mendoza and Tomás de Suria y Losano (see chart 3).

68. Doc. 47, supra, Certification of the Personal Appearance and Services of Maestre de Campo don Juan Domínguez de Mendoza and His Two Sons, El Paso, October 8, 1684.

69. John L. Kessell, Rick Hendricks, Meredith D. Dodge, and Larry D. Miller, eds., *A Settling of Accounts: The Journals of Don Diego de Vargas, New Mexico, 1700–1704* (Albuquerque: University of New Mexico Press, 2002), 133, 165.

70. Salvador Treviño Castro, S. J., *Del Chihuahua colonial* (Ciudad Juárez: Universidad de Ciudad Juárez, 2000), 20.

71. Ibid., 33.

72. Ibid., 30–32.

73. Ibid., 30–32.

74. FHL-LDS, Mexico, Chihuahua, Sagrario, Matrimonios 1709–1785, microfilm #162689.

75. FHL-LDS, Mexico, Chihuahua, Aquiles Serdan, Iglesia de Santa Eulalia, Bautismos 1709–1726, microfilm #162596.

76. Treviño Castro, *Del Chihuahua colonial*, 31.

77. The name of the wife of Juan Domínguez de Mendoza appears in his burial record as doña Ignacia Zavala. FHL-LDS, Mexico, Chihuahua, Aquiles Serdán, Iglesia de Santa Eulalia, Defunciones 1727–1741, microfilm #162595.

78. Chávez, *Origins of New Mexico Families*, 60. Diego Lucero de Godoy was born in the house of Juan Domínguez de Mendoza. In 1680 he sought to marry Juana Domínguez, alleged by one party to be a daughter of Juan Domínguez de Mendoza, and alleged by another to be the daughter of Juan's father, Tomé Domínguez. Both claims were denied by members of the Domínguez de Mendoza family. Archives of the Archdiocese of Santa Fe (AASF), Roll 59, Diligencias Matrimoniales (DM) 1680, April 26, no. 1, Río Abajo. No marriage took place.

Instead, Diego Lucero de Godoy, who resided in the jurisdiction of Taos before the August 1680 Pueblo Indian uprising, married doña María Domínguez de Mendoza, daughter of Maestre de Campo Juan Domínguez de Mendoza and doña Isabel Durán y Chaves. In a prenuptial investigation document dated February 18, 1683, El Paso del Norte, doña Isabel Durán y Chaves was specifically referred to as the mother of doña María Domínguez de Mendoza and as the mother-in-law of Diego Lucero de Godoy. AASF, Roll 59, DM 1683, February 18, no. 3. El Paso del Norte.

79. John B. Colligan, comp., "Spanish Surnames Found in the First Book of Baptisms of Nuestra Señora de Guadalupe del Paso del Río del Norte, 1662–1688," manuscript in the possession of José Antonio Esquibel.

80. AASF, Roll 59, DM 1683, February 18, no. 3. El Paso del Norte; Chávez, *Origins of New Mexico Families*, 363.

81. FHL-LDS, Mexico, Puebla, Puebla de Zaragoza, San José Church, Bautismos 1583–1956, microfilm #0227901.

82. FHL-LDS, Mexico, Distrito Federal, Mexico City, Santa Vera Cruz Church, Matrimonios 1590–1668, microfilm #0035848.

83. FHL-LDS, Mexico, Distrito Federal, Mexico City, Santa Vera Cruz Church, Bautismos 1626–1668, microfilm #0035820.

84. Joseph Sánchez, *Between Two Rivers: The Atrisco Land Grant in Albuquerque History, 1692–1968* (Norman: University of Oklahoma Press, 2008), 191n7, citing AGN Hacienda, vol. 472, Lista de los soldados que van a la Nueva Mexico, October 31, 1446.

85. In September 1661, fray Miguel de Guevara testified that he had learned from Alférez Francisco Domínguez de Mendoza and other people that Francisco had overheard a mulatta on the camino from Mexico City to New Mexico say that Governor don Bernardo López de Mendizábal was a descendant of Jews. AGN, Inquisición, vol. 593, f. 186r–196r. Records of the Inquisition in Mexico City confirm that Governor don Bernardo López de Mendizábal's maternal great-grandfather Juan Núñez de León was denounced for practicing Judaism and found guilty of such in 1603. See Stanley M. Hordes, *To the End of the Earth: A History of the Crypto-Jews of New Mexico* (New York: Columbia University Press, 2005), 154. For information about Cristóbal de Anaya Almazán and the friars that accompanied López de Mendizábal to New Mexico in 1659, see Hackett, *Historical Documents*, 3:157.

86. AGN, Tierras, vol. 3268, leg. 2, no. 35, f. 256r–259v, Petition presented by Capitán Francisco Domínguez de Mendoza, November 18, 1662, Villa de Santa Fe. Captain Lucas de Villasante was born circa 1641, giving his age as twenty-two in 1663. In 1662 he was in the Villa de Santa Fe, where he was described as a vecino of Mexico City and a soldier of the guard for the wagons of His Majesty. See AGN, Tierras 3268, f. 254r, Testimony of Lucas de Villasante, August 19, 1662, Villa de Santa Fe. He appears to be the man of this name who was a son of Simón de Villasante and Casilda Martínez de Velasco, who married María de Tapia,

daughter of Juan de Tapia and Juana de Tapia, at Santa Catalina Martir Church, Mexico City, on March 7, 1666. AGN, Real Audiencia, Concurso de Peñalosa, vol. 3, leg. 1, no. 10, f. 20v–22v, Testimony of Capitán Lucas de Villasante, June 2, 1663, Mexico City; FHL-LDS, Mexico, Distrito Federal, Mexico City, Santa Catalina Martir Church, Matrimonios 1589–1671, microfilm #0036037. Tomás Pérez Granillo was an associate ("*persona de mi asitencia*") of don Juan Manso, who operated the wagons that ran between Mexico City and New Mexico. Pérez Granillo, a *carretero* (cart driver) and free mulatto, was a native of Santa Fe born circa 1603–1613. In 1661 he declared he was the son of an Indian woman and an African man. AGN, Inquisición, vol. 583, exp. 3, f. 278r, Testimony of Tomás Pérez Granillo, July 23, 1661, Mexico City; AGN, Real Audiencia, Concurso de Peñalosa, vol. 3, exp. 455, leg. 1, no. 1, f. 48v, Petición y Memoria de General don Juan de Manso, July 15, 1662, Villa de Santa Fe; AGN, Real Audiencia, Concurso de Peñalosa, vol. 3, leg. 1, no. 10, f. 22v–24v, Testimony of Tomás Granillo, June 2, 1663, Mexico City.

87. AGN, Tierras, vol. 3268, leg. 2, no. 35, f. 259v, Petition presented by Capitán Francisco Domínguez de Mendoza, November 18, 1662, Villa de Santa Fe; AGN, Concurso de Peñalosa, vol. 2, leg. 1, no. 8, 17ff, Sobre la provisión que traxo Francisco Domínguez de Mendoza y se presente al Custodio de Nuevo México, 1662.

88. AGN, Real Audiencia, Concurso de Peñalosa, vol. 3, leg. 1, no. 19, ff. 340r–354v, Pago de salaries a los capitanes Juan y Francisco Domínguez de Mendoza, June 1, 1663, Mexico City.

89. AGN, Real Audiencia, Concurso de Peñalosa, vol. 2, leg. 1, no. 8, 17ff, Sobre la provisión que traxo Francisco Domínguez de Mendoza y se presente al Custodio de Nuevo México, 1662.

90. AGN, Inquisición, vol. 587, f. 184r, Attestation of Francisco Domínguez de Mendoza and Juan Domínguez de Mendoza, February 3, 1661, San José del Parral.

91. Hackett, *Historical Documents*, 3:139; AGN, Real Audiencia, Concurso de Peñalosa, vol. 3, leg. 1, no.19, ff. 340r–354v, Pago de salaries a los capitanes Juan y Francisco Domínguez de Mendoza, June 1, 1663, Mexico City.

92. See Doc. 13, infra, Title of Lieutenant Captain General and Visitador General, October 6, 1663.

93. AGN, Inquisición, vol. 582, exp. 3, f. 327r, Response of Capitán Cristóbal de Anaya Almazán to Charges, 1663, Mexico City.

94. Ibid., f. 327v.

95. Ibid.

96. AGN, Inquisición, vol. 610, ff. 99r–100r, Testimony of Capitán Francisco Romero, October 21, 1666, Convento de Santo Domingo.

97. Hackett, *Historical Documents*, 3:272.

98. Archivo Histórico del Parral, Roll 1670A, ff. 251A–252A.

99. Archivo Histórico del Parral, Roll 1672B, f. 613B.

100. Chávez, *Origins of New Mexico Families*, 26.

101. Ibid.

102. Archivo General de las Indias (AGI), Indiferente, 133, N. 58, f. 2r, Relación de Méritos y Servicios de Domingo Gironza Petris de Cruzati, Gobernador y Capitán General de Nuevo México, 1693. Also, see Supp. Doc. 11, supra, Account of the Services of don Domingo Jironza de Cruzate, Former Governor and Captain General of the Provinces of New Mexico, January 12, 1693.

103. AASF, Roll 59, DM 1689, March 17 (no. 2), El Paso del Norte; AASF, Roll 59, DM, 1694, October 9 (no. 25), Santa Fe; AASF, Roll 59, DM, 1694 (no. 27), Santa Fe; AASF, Roll 60, DM 1704, October 16 (no. 1); AASF, Roll 60, DM 1707, October 3 (no. 1), Santa Fe; Walter V. McLaughlin, First Book of Baptisms of Nuestra Señora de Guadalupe del Paso del Norte" (master's thesis, Texas Western College, August 1962); Colligan, "Spanish Surnames Found in the First Book of Baptisms of Nuestra Señora de Guadalupe del Paso del Río del Norte, 1662–1688."

104. FHL-LDS, Mexico, Mexico City, Asunción Church (Catedral), Bautismos, 1612–1627, f. 201v, microfilm #0035169.

105. Doc. 11, supra, Appointment as Alcalde Mayor of the Jurisdictions of Sandia and Isleta and as Lieutenant Captain General in the Río Abajo, Santa Fe, November 19, 1659.

106. AGN, Inquisición, vol. 583, exp. 3, f. 281r, Testimony of Capitán Tomé Domínguez de Mendoza, Sargento Reformado, May 21, 1661, Convento de San Antonio de la Isleta; AGN, Inquisición, vol. 587, f. 91r, Testimony of Fray Nicolás de Freitas, February 26, 1661, Mexico City; Hackett, *Historical Documents*, 3:177–80, citing AGN, Inquisición, vol. 593, ff. 16r–21r, Deposition of Tomé Domínguez, Retired Sargento, May 21, 1661, Isleta.

107. AGN, Inquisición, vol. 583, exp. 3, f. 281v, Ratification of the Testimony of Capitán Tomé Domínguez de Mendoza, September 18, 1662.

108. AGN, Inquisición, vol. 586, exp. 1, f. 118r, Audiencia del Capitán Diego Romero, November 6, 1663, Mexico City.

109. Chávez, *Origins of New Mexico Families*, 25–26.

110. AGN, Inquisición, vol. 596, exp. 1, f. 153v, Statement of doña Teresa de Aguilera y Roche, 1663, Mexico City; Doc. 11, supra, November 19, 1659.

111. Doc. 11, supra, November 19, 1659.

112. Hackett, *Historical Documents*, 3:177.

113. Ibid., 3:178.

114. Ibid.

115. Ibid.

116. Ibid.

117. Ibid., 3:180.

118. Ibid.

119. Ibid., 3:162; AGN, Inquisición, vol. 587, ff. 91r, Testimony of fray Nicolás de Freitas, February 26, 1661, Mexico City.

120. Hackett, *Historical Documents*, 3:225, 262; AGN, Inquisición, vol. 594, exp. 1, f. 255v, Response of don Bernardo López de Mendizábal to Accusations before the Tribunal of the Inquisition, December 3, 1663, Mexico City.

121. AGN, Inquisición, vol. 583, exp. 3 f. 281r, Testimony of Capitán Tomé Domínguez de Mendoza, Sargento Reformado, May 21, 1661; AGN, Inquisición, vol. 583, exp. 3, f. 281v, Ratification of the Testimony of Capitán Tomé Domínguez de Mendoza, September 18, 1662; Hackett, *Historical Documents*, 3:177–80, citing AGN, Inquisición, vol. 593, ff. 16r–21r, Deposition of Tomé Domínguez, Retired Sargento, May 21, 1661, Isleta.

122. AGN, Inquisición, vol. 587, f. 201r, Names of witnesses in the form in which they are arranged, Fray Alonso de Posada, 1662. In this record, Maestre de Campo Tomé Domínguez was described as *"español y de bien crédito."*

123. Hackett, *Historical Documents*, 3:162; AGN, Inquisición, vol. 594, f. 310r, Notice of decree to release embargoed property to Maestre de Campo Tomé Domínguez de Mendoza, October 31, 1661, Mexico City; AGN, Real Audiencia, Concurso de Peñalosa, vol. 3, leg. 1, no. 10, f. 2r–6v, Diligencias de desembargo y autos seguidos por el Maestre de Campo Tomé Domínguez de Mendoza, July 23, 1663, Mexico City.

124. AGN, Real Audiencia, Concurso de Peñalosa, vol. 2, leg. 1, no. 8, f. 9r, Testimony of Maestre de Campo Tomé Domínguez de Mendoza, December 26, 1662, Villa de Santa Fe.

125. Hackett, *Historical Documents*, 3:235.

126. AGN, Real Audiencia, Concurso de Peñalosa, vol. 2, exp. 495, leg. 1, no. 8, f. 9r, Testimony of Maestre de Campo Tomé Domínguez de Mendoza, December 26, 1662, Villa de Santa Fe.

127. AGN, Tierras, vol. 3268, p. 5 mentions *"dho pueblo de Senecu hasta la casa del Cap^n Andres Lopez de Gracia que es en la toma del Norte ay mas de sesenta leguas"* ("from the said Pueblo of Sénecu to the house of Captain Andrés López de Gracia, which is at the hill of Del Norte, is more than seventy leagues").

128. Doc. 18, supra, Appointment as Lieutenant of the Governor and Captain General, Santa Fe, February 10, 1667.

129. Hackett, *Historical Documents*, 3:291.

130. Ibid., 3:293–94.

131. Ibid., 3:342.

132. Doc. 45, supra, Journal of the Expedition to Texas, 1683–1684.

133. Hackett and Shelby, *Revolt of the Pueblo Indians*, 1:138 and 2:145–51.

134. Chávez, *Origins of New Mexico Families*, 25.

135. Ibid.

136. Ibid.

137. Francisco Domínguez married María Vitoria de Carvajal; they were the parents of these known children:

> a. Francisca Domínguez Carvajal, bt. December 21, 1684, Valle de Allende, San Bartolomé. Godparents: Captain José Sapiain and his wife, María de Grados.
>
> b. Juan Domínguez Carvajal, bt. March 12, 1686, Valle de Allende, San Bartolomé. Godparents: Captain José Sapiain and María Grados, native of the Valle de San Bartolomé.
>
> c. Francisco Domínguez Vitoria de Carvajal, bt. December 1, 1687, Valle de Allende, San Bartolomé. The mother's name was recorded as Catalina Vitoria de Caravajal, and his godfather was Captain don Antonio de Maturana, vecino of San José del Parral.

See FHL-LDS, Mexico, Chihuahua, Valle de Allende, San Bartolomé Church, Bautismos 1662–1686 and 1692–1744, microfilm #162634.

138. Chávez, *Origins of New Mexico Families*, 25; AASF, Roll 59, DM 1681, November 13 (no. 2), Real de San Lorenzo.

139. Chávez, *Origins of New Mexico Families*, 20, 25. Fray Angélico Chávez refers to the wife of Cristóbal Durán y Chaves as Catalina and as Juana.

140. For the death of Cristóbal Durán y Chaves, see Doc. 21, supra, Documents concerning Provisions and Livestock Given by the Conventos for an Expedition against the Apache June 16–July 4, 1669.

141. Baptismal records were extracted for two children of Mateo Domínguez de Mendoza and Margarita Márquez: Simón Domínguez Márquez, bt. March 6, 1698, Valle de Allende, San Bartolomé; Tomás Domínguez de Mendoza y Márquez, bt. January 8, 1704, Cusihuiriachic. Dr. Encarnación Brondo Whitt makes references to a last will and testament of don Juan Mateo Domínguez de Mendoza, who died in 1730. According to Brondo Whitt's research, Juan Mateo, born circa 1670, was a son of Tomé Domínguez de Mendoza and Catalina López Mederos. Brondo Whitt identified the children of Juan Mateo and Margaríta Márquez as: Captain don Luis Domínguez; Simón Domínguez, who married doña Ignacia Fernández Morcillo; Juan Ignacio Domínguez, who married Bárbara de Agüero; Tomás Domínguez, who married Gertrudis Ramos; Diego Domínguez; Bárbara Domínguez, who married Bernardo Rodríguez; Elena Domínguez; Josefa Domínguez, who married Luis Cabeza de Vaca y Villaurrutia; Margarita Domínguez, who married Marcos Morcillo; and Isabel Domínguez, who married Pedro Estrada Bocanegra. Encarnación Brondo Whitt, *Los Patriarcas del Papigochi* (Chihuahua, Mex., 1952), 152–55.

142. The marriage and baptismal records for several of these children list Tomé Domínguez de Mendoza with the rank of maestre de campo and general. He and doña Catalina de Vitoria Carvajal were the parents of these known children:

a. Doña Josefa Domínguez, native of New Mexico, daughter of Maestre de Campo Tomé Domínguez, deceased, and doña Catalina Varela, married October 9, 1701, Valle de Allende, San Bartolomé Church, Simón Rojo de Soria, native of San José del Parral, son of General Nicolás de Rojo de Soria and doña Francisca de Lima. (Extraction by José Antonio Esquibel.)

b. Isabel Domínguez de Mendoza, bt. March 16, 1686, Valle de Allende, San Bartolomé Church. Her godparents were Captain José Sapiain and María de Prados, natives of the Valle de San Bartolomé. (Extraction by Henrietta Martínez Christmas.) Doña Isabel Domínguez de Mendoza, daughter of Maestre de Campo Tomé Domínguez and doña Catalina Varela de Losada, married January 7, 1703, San Bartolomé Church, Francisco Rojo Coronel, son of General Nicolás Rojo and doña Francisca Lima, both deceased. The sponsors of the couple were Somón Rojo and doña Josefa Domínguez. (Extraction by José Antonio Esquibel.)

c. Catalina Domínguez de Mendoza y Vitoria de Carvajal, bt. August 20, 1687, Valle de Allende, San Bartolomé Church. Her godparents were Captain José Sapiain and Angélica Sapiain. This baptismal took place in the hacienda of Pedro de Quesada, located six leagues, approximately eighteen miles, from the Church of San Bartolomé and very likely in the vicinity of the Domínguez de Mendoza hacienda at Los Suaces. (Extraction by Henrietta Martínez Christmas.)

d. Juana Domínguez de Mendoza y Varela de Losada, bt. March 28, 1690, Valle de Allende, San Bartolomé Church.

e. Salvador Bartolomé Domínguez de Mendoza, bt. August 1, 1696, Valle de Allende, San Bartolomé Church. His godparents were Bartolomé Sáens de Chaves and Ana Machado Rangel. (Extraction by Henrietta Martínez Christmas.)

f. Elena Domínguez de Mendoza y Varela, bt. May 19, 1699, Valle de Allende, San Bartolomé Church. (Extraction by Henrietta Martínez Christmas.) She married Nicolás Cano de los Ríos on February 12, 1716, Valle de Allende, San Bartolomé Church.

See FHL-LDS, Mexico, Chihuahua, Valle de Allende, San Bartolomé Church, Bautismos 1662–1686 and 1692–1744, microfilm #162634, and Matrimonios, 1686–1746, microfilm #162650.

143. AGI, Contratación, 5538, L.1, f. 281r: "*Primero de junio del 1580: alvaro de Paredes natural de la villa de caceres hijo de gonzalo mrnez Spadero y de doña*

estefana de paredes se despacho al Nueva Spaña Por solt⁰ [soltero] Por cᵃ [cedula] de su magᵈ [magestad]."

144. Ida Altman, *Emigrants and Society: Extremadura and America in the Sixteenth Century* (Berkeley: University of California Press, 1989), 128; José Miguel Romero de Solís, *Andariegos y pobladores: Nueva España y Nueva Galicia: Siglo xvi* (Colima: El Colegio de Michoacán, AC, 2001), 388.

145. Altman, *Emigrants and Society*, 129.

146. Ibid. The private letters of Álvaro de Paredes were donated to the Archivo del Monasterio de Guadalupe (AMG) by Vicente Barrante. The letters between Álvaro de Paredes Espadero and his family members in Cáceres are now part of the Fondo Barrantes Ms. B/3 in that archive. According to Ida Altman, a man named Juan Barrantes was a cousin of Álvaro de Paredes. Apparently, these private letters were preserved by the Barrantes family, eventually coming into the possession of the nineteenth-century bibliographer Vicente Barrantes, who donated the letters as part of his private collection to the Archivo del Monasterio del Guadalupe in Cáceres, Spain. See note 1 of chapter 4 in Altman, *Emigrants and Society*.

147. Ibid., 131. Álvaro de Paredes Espadero and doña Beatriz Méndez de Sotomayor were the parents of these known children:

> a. Estefanía de Paredes y Méndez de Sotomayor, bt. December 20, 1599, Catedral de México, Mexico City. FHL-LDS, Mexico, Distrito Federal, Mexico City, Asunción Church (Catedral), Bautismos, 1590–1611, microfilm #0035168.
>
> b. Álvaro de Paredes y Sotomayor, bt. March 22, 1604, Catedral de México, Mexico City. FHL-LDS, Mexico, Distrito Federal, Mexico City, Asunción Church (Catedral), Bautismos, 1590–1611, microfilm #0035168.
>
> c. Juana de Paredes y Sotomayor, bt. May 31, 1606, Catedral de México, Mexico City. FHL-LDS, Mexico, Distrito Federal, Mexico City, Asunción Church (Catedral), Bautismos, 1590–1611, microfilm #0035168.
>
> d. Estéban de Paredes, son of Álvaro de Paredes and Beatris de Sotomayor, married April 18, 1633, Catedral de México, Mexico City.

148. FHL-LDS, Mexico, Distrito Federal, Mexico City, Asunción Church (Catedral), Matrimonios 1620–1648, microfilm #0035267.

149. The known children of don Esteban de Paredes and doña Beatris Cortés were:

> a. Fray José de Paredes.
>
> b. Francisca de Paredes, native of Mexico City, md. December 17, 1651, Santa Vera Cruz Church, Mexico City, Antonio de

Robles Moctezuma, native of Mexico City, son of Acasio de Robles and Ana Cano Moctezuma. FHL-LDS, Mexico, Distrito Federal, Mexico City, Santa Vera Cruz Church, Matrimonios 1576–1666, microfilm #0035848. This couple were the parents of four known children: (1) María de Robles Moctezuma Paredes, bt. April 30, 1653, Santa Vera Cruz, Church, Mexico City; (2) Josefa de Robles Moctezuma Paredes, bt. February 23, 1655, Santa Vera Cruz, Church, Mexico City; (3) Ana de Robles Moctezuma Paredes, bt. June 12, 1657, Santa Vera Cruz Church, Mexico City; and (4) Sebastián de Robles Moctezuma Paredes, bt. February 1, 1660, Santa Vera Cruz Church, Mexico City. FHL-LDS, Mexico, Distrito Federal, Mexico City, Santa Vera Cruz Church, Bautismos 1636–1668, microfilm #0035820.

    c. Álvaro de Paredes, bt. February 23, 1638, Catedral de México. FHL-LDS, Mexico, Distrito Federal, Mexico City, Asunción Church, Bautismos 1627–1639, microfilm #0035170.

    d. Gonzalo de Paredes Cortés, by June 6, 1641, Catedral de México. FHL-LDS, Mexico, Distrito Federal, Mexico City, Asunción Church, Bautismos 1640–1652, microfilm #0035171.

    e. Estéban de Paredes Cortés, bt. March 4, 1643, Catedral de México. FHL-LDS, Mexico, Distrito Federal, Mexico City, Asunción Church, Bautismos 1640–1652, microfilm #0035171.

    f. Ignacio de Paredes Cortés, bt. August 14, 1644, Catedral de México. FHL-LDS, Mexico, Distrito Federal, Mexico City, Asunción Church, Bautismos 1640–1652, microfilm #0035171.

    g. Gregorio de Paredes Cortés, bt. March 25, 1646, Catedral de México. FHL-LDS, Mexico, Distrito Federal, Mexico City, Asunción Church, Bautismos 1640–1652, microfilm #0035171.

150. Fray Tomás de Alvarado provided testimony on April 5, 1662, at the Convento de San Francisco del Pueblo de Sandia as part of an investigation into the behavior of Cristóbal de Anaya Almazán and Juan Domínguez de Mendoza. Alvarado mentioned he had occasion to go to the house of Tomé Domínguez, the elder, two leagues from Sandia Pueblo, where doña Damiana Domínguez de Mendoza and Álvaro de Paredes were married in February 1660. He also mentioned that many people were present, including father fray Salvador de Guerra, father fray Miguel de Guevara, and father fray Joseph de Paredes. AGN, Inquisición, vol. 593, f. 123r, Testimony of fray Tomás Alvarado, April 5, 1662, Convento de San Francisco de Sandia.

151. AGN, Inquisición, vol. 582, f. 327r, Primer audiencia de Cristóbal de Anaya Almazán, April 26, 1663, Mexico City.

152. Ibid., f. 326v.

153. In 1662, Álvaro declared he was a native of Mexico City, age twenty-three. AGN, Inquisición, vol. 593, f. 245r, Testimony of Alférez Álvaro de Paredes, May 29, 1662, Convento de San Francisco de Sandia.

154. AGN, Inquisición, vol. 596, f. 153r, Statement of doña Teresa de Aguilera y Roche, 1663, Mexico City; Chávez, *Origins of New Mexico Families*, 85.

155. Chávez, *Origins of New Mexico Families*, 85. Felipe Montoya and his wife, María Domínguez, were the godparents of an orphaned child named Pasqual, who was baptized at Guadalupe del Paso Church on January 8, 1685. See Colligan, comp., "Spanish Surnames Found in the First Book of Baptisms of Nuestra Señora de Guadalupe del Paso del Río del Norte, 1662–1688."

156. See note 133 above.

157. Hackett, *Historical Documents*, 3:49; AGN, Inquisición vol. 582, exp. 2, ff. 309r–309v, Primer audiencia del Capitán Cristóbal de Anaya Almazán, April 22, 1663, Mexico City.

158. José Antonio Esquibel, "The Romero Family of Seventeenth-Century New Mexico," Part I, *Herencia* (Genealogical Journal of the Hispanic Genealogical Research Center of New Mexico) 11 (January 2003): 1–30.

159. AGN, Inquisición, vol. 582, exp. 2, f. 312r, Primer audiencia de Cristóbal de Anaya Almazán, April 26, 1663, Mexico City.

160. AGN, Inquisición, vol. 582, exp. 2, f. 324r; AGN, Inquisición, vol. 582, exp. 2, f. 345v, Response of Capitán Cristóbal de Anaya Almazán to Charges, 1663, Mexico City.

161. AGN, Real Audiencia, Concurso de Peñalosa, vol. 3, leg. 1, no. 22, 44ff, Embargo of property of Captain Cristóbal de Anaya Almazán, May 25, 1662, Estancia de San Antonio.

162. AGN, Real Audiencia, Concurso de Peñalosa, vol. 3, leg. 1, no. 1, f. 125r, Testimony of Sargento Mayor Francisco de Madrid, April 29, 1662, Villa de Santa Fe.

163. Ibid.

164. Ibid.

165. AGN, Real Audiencia, Concurso de Peñalosa, vol. 3, leg. 1, no. 1, f. 111r, Testimony of Capitán Juan Griego, August 17, 1662, Villa de Santa Fe.

166. AGN, Real Audiencia, Concurso de Peñalosa, vol. 3, leg. 1, no. 1, f. 96v, Testimony of Capitán Juan Varela de Losada, August 14, 1662, Villa de Santa Fe.

167. Ibid.

168. AGN, Real Audiencia, Concurso de Peñalosa, vol. 3, exp. leg. 1, no. 1, f. 113r, Testimony of Capitán Miguel de Hinojos, August 17, 1662, Villa de Santa Fe.

169. AGN, Inquisición, vol. 596, exp. 1, f. 228r, Statement of doña Teresa de Aguilera y Roche, 1663, Mexico City.

170. AGN, Real Audiencia, Concurso de Peñalosa, vol. 3, leg. 1, no. 1, f. 111r, Testimony of Capitán Juan Griego, August 17, 1662, Villa de Santa Fe; AGN, Real Audiencia, Concurso de Peñalosa, vol. 3, leg. 1, no. 1, 113r, Testimony of Capitán

Miguel de Hinojos, August 17, 1662, Villa de Santa Fe; AGN, Real Audiencia, Concurso de Peñalosa, vol. 3, leg. 1, no. 1, Testimony of Sargento Mayor Francisco de Madrid, April 29, 1662, Villa de Santa Fe.

171. AGN, Real Audiencia, Concurso de Peñalosa, vol. 3, leg. 1, no. 1, f. 126v, Testimony of Sargento Mayor Francisco de Madrid, April 29, 1662, Villa de Santa Fe.

172. AGN, Real Audiencia, Concurso de Peñalosa, vol. 3, leg. 1, no. 1, f. 128v, Petition of General don Juan de Manso, April 29, 1659, Villa de Santa Fe.

173. AGN, Inquisición, vol. 593, f. 232r, Testimony of fray Tomás de Alvarado, April 5, 1662, Convento de San Francisco de Sandia.

174. Hackett, *Historical Documents*, 3:154, 164.

175. Ibid., 3:231.

176. AGN, Real Audiencia, Concurso de Peñalosa, vol. 3, leg. 1, no. 2, ff. 3v–4r, Decree of Residencia of Governor don Bernardo López de Mendizábal Issued by Governor don Diego de Peñalosa Briceño y Berdugo, September 30, 1661.

177. AGN, Inquisición, vol. 596, exp. 1, ff. 155r and 161r, Statement of doña Teresa de Aguilera y Roche, 1663, Mexico City; AGN, Real Audiencia, Concurso de Peñalosa, vol. 3, exp. 455, leg. 1, no. 2, f. 2v, Appointment Made by Governor don Diego de Peñalosa Briceño y Berdugo in the Residencia of Governor don Bernardo López de Mendizábal.

178. Hackett, *Historical Documents*, 3:225, and AGN, Inquisición, vol. 594, exp. 1, ff. 253r–255r, Response of don Bernardo López de Mendizábal to Accusations before the Tribunal of the Inquisition, December 3, 1663, Mexico City.

179. Hackett, *Historical Documents*, 3:138.

180. AGN, Inquisición, vol. 582, exp. 2, f. 414r, Cuenta de los gastos por Cristóbal de Anaya Almazán, December 23, 1664,

181. AGN, Inquisición, vol. 582, exp. 2, f. 311r, Primer audiencia de Cristóbal de Anaya Almazán, April 26, 1663, Mexico City.

182. AGN, Inquisición, vol. 582, exp. 2, f. 414r, Cuenta de los gastos por Cristóbal de Anaya Almazán, December 23, 1664, Mexico City.

183. AGN, Inquisición, vol. 610, exp. 7, f. 66v, Denunciation made by Cristóbal de Anaya Almazán, May 3, 1666, Convento de Santo Domingo.

184. AGN, Inquisición, vol. 666, exp. 10, f. 534r, Declaration of Cristóbal de Anaya Almazán, October 21, 1667, Convento de Santo Domingo; see also Hackett, *Historical Documents*, 3:270.

185. AGN, Inquisición, vol. 666, exp. 10, ff. 434v–435v, Testimony of fray Rafael de Santa María, October 28, 1665, Convento de San Francisco de Sandia.

186. AGN, Inquisición, vol. 610, exp. 1, f. 63v, Denunciation made by fray Diego de Santander, March 26, 1666, Convento de San Estéban de Acoma.

187. AGN, Inquisición, vol. 666, exp. 10, f. 542r, Statement of fray Nicolás de Freitas, October 1, 1665, Villa de Santa Fe.

188. Hackett, *Historical Documents*, 270–71.

189. The house is described in the embargo of the property of Cristóbal de Anaya Almazán in AGN, Real Audiencia, Concurso de Peñalosa, vol. 3, leg. 1, no. 22, 44ff, Embargo of property of Captain Cristóbal de Anaya Almazán, May 25, 1662, Estancia de San Antonio.

190. Chávez, *Origins of New Mexico Families*, 4; AGN, Inquisición, vol. 582, exp. 2, f. 311r; Doc. 54, supra, Copy of the Sentence Pronounced in the Proceedings against Maestre de Campo Juan Domínguez de Mendoza, Mexico City, April 30, 1687.

191. Chávez, *Origins of New Mexico Families*, 4; Kessell and Hendricks, *By Force of Arms*, 430. At the time of the revolt in August 1680, Cristóbal de Anaya Almazán's house was said to be two leagues from the pueblo of San Felipe, where the Indians were said to have gone "to the narrow pass at the house of Cristóbal de Anaya," the area of modern-day Angostura. See Hackett and Shelby, *Revolt of the Pueblo Indians*, 1:22.

192. Doc. 54, supra, Copy of the Sentence Pronounced in the Proceedings against Maestre de Campo Juan Domínguez de Mendoza, Mexico City, April 30, 1687.

193. Chávez, *Origins of New Mexico Families*, 19.

194. As a witness in the case against Governor Juan de Eulate in the Villa de Santa Fe on May 22, 1626, Pedro Durán de Chaves, maestre de campo of the province, identified himself as a native of Llerena, age sixty (b. ca. 1566). AGN, Inquisición, vol. 316, f. 268r, Testimony of Pedro Durán y Chaves, May 22, 1626, Villa de Santa Fe. In previous research, Pedro Durán y Chaves was identified as the same person as Pedro Gómez Durán who came to New Mexico in 1600 and identified himself as a native of Valverde de Llerena, age fifty-five, and a son of Hernán Sánchez Rico. (See AGI, Patronato, 244, R. 7, exp. 20, ff. 8v–11r, Declaration of Pedro Durán y Chaves, August 18, 1644, Convento de Santo Domingo; Chávez, *Origins of New Mexico Families*, 19; José Antonio Esquibel and Patryka Durán y Chaves, "Pedro Durán y Chaves and Juana Montoya," in Valencia y Valdez, Esquibel, and Sisneros, *Aquí se Comienza*, 181–84.)

In 1616, fray Bartolomé Gómez, a priest of the Dominican order in Mexico City, submitted his proof of lineage in order to apply for a position with the Office of the Inquisition, declaring he was a son of Pedro Gómez Rico, who died in New Mexico around 1606–1607, and Catalina Cabezas, as preserved in AGN, Inquisición, vol. 484, exp. 1. Several witnesses confirmed that Pedro Gómez Rico died in New Mexico. Fray Bartolomé identified his paternal grandparents as Hernán Sanchez Rico and Leonor Duran, natives of the Villa de Valverde. It appears that Pedro Gómez Durán was the same person as Pedro Gómez Rico, but clearly this individual was not the same person as Pedro Durán y Chaves, who founded the Chaves family of New Mexico. As such, the identities of the parents of Pedro Durán y Chaves remain unknown.

In his proof of lineage, fray Bartolomé Gómez mentioned an uncle, Fernando Durán, who was a knight of the Orden de Santiago, and two cousins, Licenciado Pedro Gómez Durán of Salamanca and Juan de Chaves, who were also knights of the Orden de Santiago. The surnames of each of the men mentioned are similar to those used in the Durán y Chaves family of New Mexico. José Antonio Esquibel, "A Case of Mistaken Identities: Pedro Gómez Durán and Pedro Durán y Chaves," in *Herencia* 18, no. 3 (July 2010): 2–6.

195. Chávez, *Origins of New Mexico Families*, 9–10.

196. Ibid., 20–21; AGN, Inquisición, vol. 385, ff. 1r–2r, Testimony of Capitán don Fernando Durán y Chaves, July 27, 1638, Villa de Santa Fe; AGN, Inquisición, vol. 608, f. 379r, Testimony of don Pedro Durán de Chaves, July 6, 1667, Convento de San Diego de los Jemez.

197. Chávez, *Origins of New Mexico Families*, 19.

198. Hackett, *Historical Documents*, 3:231.

199. AGI, Patronato, 244, R. 7, exp. 14, f. 3v, Petition of Juan Hidalgo de Heredia in the name of Alonso Baca, don Fernando Durán de Chaves, don Pedro Durán de Chaves, and don Juan Ramírez de Salazar, November 27, 1643, Mexico City.

200. AGI, Patronato, 244, R. 7, exp. 14, f. 3v, Petition of Juan Hidalgo de Heredia in the name of Alonso Baca, don Fernando Durán de Chaves, don Pedro Durán de Chaves, and don Juan Ramírez de Salazar, November 27, 1643, Mexico City; AGI, Patronato, 244, R. 7, exp. 14, f. 35v, Petition of Juan Hidalgo de Heredia in the name of Alonso Baca, don Fernando Durán de Chaves, don Pedro Durán de Chaves, and don Juan Ramírez de Salazar, November 16, 1643.

201. AGI, Patronato, 244, R. 7, exp 14, ff. 1v–3v, Petition of Juan Hidalgo de Heredia in the name of Alonso Baca, don Fernando Durán de Chaves, don Pedro Durán de Chaves, and don Juan Ramírez de Salazar, November 27, 1643, Mexico City; AGI, Patronato, 244, R. 7, exp. 14, 36r–36v, Petition of Alonso Baca, don Fernando Durán de Chaves, don Pedro Durán de Chaves, and don Juan Ramírez de Salazar, November 14, 1643, Mexico City.

202. AGI, Patronato, 244, R. 7, exp. 14, f. 3r, Petition of Juan Hidalgo de Heredia in the name of Alonso Baca, don Fernando Durán de Chaves, don Pedro Durán de Chaves, and don Juan Ramírez de Salazar, November 27, 1643, Mexico City.

203. AGI, Patronato, 244, R. 7, exp. 14, ff. 2v–3r, Petition of Juan Hidalgo de Heredia in the name of Alonso Baca, Don Fernando Durán de Chaves, Don Pedro Durán de Chaves, and Don Juan Ramírez de Salazar, November 27, 1643, Mexico City.

204. Doc. 48, supra, Excerpt from a Letter of Governor Domingo Jironza Perríz de Cruzate to the Viceroy, El Paso, August 26, 1685.

205. AGI, Patronato, 244, R. 7, exp. 20, ff. 8v–11r, Declaration of Pedro Durán y Chaves, August 18, 1644, Convento de Santo Domingo.

206. AGN, vol. 608, exp. 6, f. 379r, Testimony of Pedro Durán y Chaves, July 6, 1667, Convento de San Diego de los Jemez; Chávez, *Origins of New Mexico Families*, 21, 25.

207. AGN, Inquisición, vol. 593, f. 247v, Testimony of Diego de Luna, May 29, 1662, Convento de San Francisco de Sandia.

208. SANM I, Roll 37, frs. 727–728. Private Land Claim Case 45, Town of Atrisco Grant.

209. Chávez, *Origins of New Mexico Families*, 19–23.

210. Doc. 45, supra, Journal of the Expedition to Texas, 1683–1684.

211. In April 1682, José Domínguez de Mendoza declared he was a native of New Mexico whose father was unknown, and he named his mother as Ana Velásquez. AASF, Diligencias, Roll 59, DM 1682, April 8, no. 5, Real de San Lorenzo. José Domínguez de Mendoza gave his age as twenty-four in May 1682. Fray Angélico Chávez, "New Mexico Roots, Ltd., Addendum," Part II, in *New Mexico Genealogist* 49 (June 2010): 74. In November 1719, José Domínguez de Mendoza gave his age as fifty-two. Fray Angélico Chávez, "New Mexico Roots, Ltd., Addendum," Part III, in *New Mexico Genealogist* 49 (September 2010): 146.

212. Chávez, *Origins of New Mexico Families*, 51. Ana Velasco served as the *cocinera y labandera* (cook and laundress) of Governor don Bernardo López de Mendizábal for eleven months in 1659–1660. In October 1661, she provided testimony on her behalf in regard to payment of thirty-seven pesos and two *tomines* she did not receive for work she did for López de Mendizábal. She identified herself as an "*India*" and declared she was a native of the Villa de Santa Fe and married to Francisco Cuaxinque. AGN, Real Audiencia, Concurso de Peñalosa, vol. 1, leg. 1, no. 2 f. 233v/380v, Testimonio en relación de la demandas públicas que sean puesto en los quince dias de la residencia del don Bernardo López de Mendizábal, 1661; AGN, Real Audiencia, Tierras, vol. 3268, leg. 2, f. 18r, Testimony of Ana Velasco, Villa de Santa Fe, October 21, 1661.

213. Chávez, *Origins of New Mexico Families*, 169–70; AASF, Roll 60, DM 1707, June 9, no. 3, Santa Fe.

214. AASF, Roll 59, DM 1682, April 9, no. 5, Real de San Lorenzo.

215. SANM I, 233, Dimas Jirón, litigation against José Domínguez, 1716, Villa de Santa Fe; Chávez, *Origins of New Mexico Families*, 200–201; Esquibel and Colligan, *The Spanish Recolonization of New Mexico*, 234.

216. Kessell and Hendricks, *By Force of Arms*, 525; Kessell, Hendricks, and Dodge, *Blood on the Boulders*, 1143; SANM I, 235, Will of Juana Domínguez, January 12, 1717, Villa de Santa Fe; AASF, Roll 59, DM 1698, January 20, no. 16, Villa de Santa Fe (Juan Luján and María Martín); AASF, Roll 59, DM 1696, May 16, no. 15, Santa Fe (José de Quintana and Antonia Luján Domínguez).

217. Chávez, *Origins of New Mexico Families*, 63–64, 212.

218. Kessell, Hendricks, and Dodge, *To the Royal Crown Restored*, 394.

219. Ibid., 166.

220. Ibid., 1150.
221. Chávez, *Origins of New Mexico Families*, 170.
222. SANM I, 233, Dimas Jirón, litigation against José Domínguez, 1716, Villa de Santa Fe; SANM I, 235, Will of Juana Domínguez, January 12, 1717, Villa de Santa Fe.
223. AASF, Roll 59, DM 1680, April 26, no. 1, Río Abajo.
224. Chávez, *Origins of New Mexico Families*, 33–34.
225. Kessell, Hendricks, and Dodge, *To the Royal Crown Restored*, 47.
226. Juana García de Noriega was deceased by July 1694, when her daughter María Domínguez de Mendoza, entered into marriage with Antonio Godines, a native of Mexico City who came to New Mexico in June 1694 with other settlers recruited in Mexico City. AASF, Roll 59, DM 1694, July 16, no. 27; Chávez, *Origins of New Mexico Families*, 186; Esquibel and Colligan, *Spanish Recolonization of New Mexico*, 207–9. Her other daughters that returned to northern New Mexico married as follows: (1) Antonia Domínguez de Mendoza was first married to Andrés II Hurtado and then married on October 25, 1694, Villa de Santa Fe, Tomás Jirón de Tejeda, a thirty-one-year-old widower from Mexico City who arrived in New Mexico in June 1694; AASF, Roll 59, DM 1694, October 9, no. 25; Chávez, *Origins of New Mexico Families*, 200–201; Esquibel and Colligan, *Spanish Recolonization of New Mexico*, 232–34; (2) Fifteen-year-old Teresa Domínguez de Mendoza married, in 1704, nineteen-year-old Diego González de la Rosa (also known as Diego Sayago), a native of Mexico City; AASF, Roll 60, DM 1704, October 16, no. 1, Santa Cruz; (3) Leonor Domínguez de Mendoza married, in 1707, Miguel Martín, a son of Captain Pedro Martín Serrano and Juana Argüello. AASF, Roll 60, DM 1707, October 3, no. 1, Santa Fe.

Works Cited

Archival Material

Archives of the Archdiocese of Santa Fe (AASF)

AASF, Roll 59, Diligencias Matrimoniales, 1678–1696.
AASF, Roll 60, Diligencias Matrimoniales, 1697–1710.

Archivo General de Indias Sevilla (AGI)

AGI, Audiencia de México, 50, R. 1, N. 3, Cartas del Virrey Payo Enríquez de Rivera, El Vierry a Su Majestad, socorros a las provincias de Nuevo México, 13 de enero de 1678.

AGI, Audiencia de México, 304, Cartas y expedientes de personas eclesiásticas, 1636.

AGI, Contaduría, leg. 728 (1626–1628), leg. 729 (1628–1630), leg. 740 (1646–1648), leg. 742 (1648–1650), leg. 747 (1652–1653), leg. 748 (1654–1658), leg. 750 (1656–1658), leg. 754 (1661–1663), leg. 755 (1663–1664), leg. 757 (1664–1666), leg. 759 (1667–1668), leg. 760 (1668), leg. 763A (1669–1671), leg. 766 (1674–1675), leg. 767 (1675–1676), leg. 768A-B (1676–1678), Caja de México, Cuentas de los oficiales reales de México; photostat copies located at the Southwest Research Center, University of New Mexico.

AGI, Contratación, 5432, N. 2, R. 11, Expediente de información y licencia de pasajero a indias de Juan de Miranda, Regidor perpetuo del Consejo de Tineo, vecino de Madrid, hijo de Juan de Miranda y de Magdalena Díaz, a Nueva España, 17 de abril de 1660.

AGI, Contratación, 5439, N. 115, Expediente de información y licencia de pasajero a Indias de fray Francisco de Ayeta, franciscano, predicador, a Nueva España, 7 de julio de 1673.

AGI, Contratación, 5457, N. 152, Expediente de información y licencia de pasajeros a indias de Baltasar Domínguez de Mendoza, a Nueva España, 8 de julio de 1695.

AGI, Contratación, 5460, N. 5, R. 6, Expediente de información y licencia de pasajeros a Indias del Capitán Martín de Echagaray, a Nueva España, 5 de julio de 1704.

AGI, Contratación, 5538, L.1, f. 281r, Libro de asientos de pasajero, Alvaro de Paredes, primero de junio de 1580.

AGI, Estado, 43, N. 1, Descubrimiento y situación de Quivira y Teguayo, Alonso de Posada, 14 de marzo de 1686, México.

AGI, Guadalajara, leg. 40, Cartas y expedientes de personas seculares, 1675–1698.

AGI, Guadalajara, leg. 73, Minutas reales cédulas, reales provisiones consultas, 1691–1696.

AGI, Guadalajara, leg. 138, Expediente sobre la conquista de Nuevo México, 1639–1686.

AGI, Indiferente, 113, N. 6, Relación de méritos y servicios de Fernando Villanueva, 22 de marzo de 1646.

AGI, Indiferente, 120, N. 44, Relación de méritos y servicios de Diego de Guadalajara Bernardo de Quirós, Teniente de Gobernador de Nueva Vizcaya, 1664.

AGI, Indiferente, 123, N. 59, Relación de méritos y servicios de Fernando Villanueva, Gobernador y Capitán General de Nuevo México, 1671.

AGI, Indiferente, 133, N. 58, Relación de méritos y servicios de Domingo Gironza Petris de Cruzati, Gobernador y Capitán General de Nuevo México, 1693.

AGI, Indiferente, 133, N. 142, Relación de méritos y servicios de Baltasar Domínguez de Mendoza, Teniente de Capitán General y Visitador de Nuevo México, 19 de agosto de 1694.

AGI, Indiferente, 452, L.A. 12, f. 122v–123, Real Cédula al Marqués de Cerralvo, Virrey de Nueva España, recomendándole a Francisco de Guadalajara, 6 de septiembre de 1629, Madrid.

AGI, Patronato Real, 244, R. 7, Papeles sobre la conducta y proceder de don Juan de Palafox y Mendoza, siendo Obispo de la Puebla de los Ángeles y visitador general, 1642–1650 (Decree of Flores de Sierra y Valdés, July 16, 1641, Villa de Santa Fe; and Testimony of Alférez Alonso Varela, August 11, 1644, Santo Domingo).

Archivo General de la Nación, México (AGN)

AGN, Gobierno Virreinal, Reales Cédulas Originales, vol. 20, exp. 111, 5ff, Que informe si conviene aceptar la proposición del Capitán Martín de Echagaray de descubrir dicha Bahía del Espiritu Santo, 2 de agosto de 1685.

AGN, Indiferente Virreinal, Alcaldes Mayores, 6474, exp. 54, Mandato de la Real Audiencia a las justicias para que tomen residencia al Alcalde Mayor de Guatulco don Francisco de Guadalaxara, 1634.

AGN, Inquisición, vol. 304, exp. 26, Información contra Antón, Mulato, por usar el peyote y ser casado dos veces, 1632.

AGN, Inquisición, vol. 304, exp. 27, Testificación contra Juan de la Cruz y su mujer por supersticiosos, 1631.

AGN, Inquisición, vol. 356, exp. 140, Testificación contra Diego de Vera por palabras, 1626.

AGN, Inquisición, vol. 356, exp. 144, Testificación contra Isabel Holguín por usas hierbas, 1626.

AGN, Inquisición, vol. 372, exp. 16 y 19, Información contra Gaspar Pérez, Armero, flamenco, por palabras mal sonatas, 1632.

AGN, Inquisición, vol. 380, exp. 2, Carta del Comisario de Nuevo México con la información contra Juan López por casado dos veces y contra Juan Antón por el mismo delito, 1634.

AGN, Inquisición, vol. 385, exp. 15, Del padre fray Estéban de Perea, comisario de Nuevo México con una information contra Luis de Rosas, Gobernador, por palabras mal sonatas, 1638.

AGN, Inquisición, vol. 425, exp. 23, Acusasción presentada por Apolonia Varela contra el gobernador de la provincial de Santa Fe, don Luis de Rosa, por haberle obligado a casarse contra su voluntad con Juan Bautista Zaragoza, 1641.

AGN, Inquisición, vol. 507, exp. 1 y 2, Proceso contra don Diego de Peñalosa Briceño y Verdugo por blasfemo, 1663.

AGN, Inquisición, vol. 582, exp. 2, Proceso y causa criminal contra Cristóbal de Anaya, por proposiciones heréticas, 1660–1666.

AGN, Inquisición, vol. 583, exp. 3, Proceso y causa criminal contra Francisco Gómez Robledo por sospechoso de judío y haber dicho proposiciones heréticas, 1661.

AGN, Inquisición, vol. 586, exp. 1, Causa contra el Capitán Diego Romero por hereje, 1660.

AGN, Inquisición, vol. 587, exp. 1, Segundo cuaderno del proceso contra don Bernardo López de Mendizábal, Gobernador de Nuevo México, por proposiciones heréticas, México, 1660.

AGN, Inquisición, vol. 590, exp. 3, Borrador de cartas que se escriben a diferentes personas del distrito de esta Inquisición del primero del presente año adelante, México, 1662–1669.

AGN, Inquisición, vol. 593, exp. 1, El fiscal del Santo Oficio contra don Bernardo López de Mendizábal, Gobernador de Nuevo México, por proposiciones heréticas y sospecho de judiazante, 1662.

AGN, Inquisición, vol. 594, exp. 1, Primer audiencia de don Bernardo López de Mendizábal, México, April 28, 1663.

AGN, Inquicisión, vol. 596, exp. 1, El fiscal del Santo Oficio contra doña Teresa de Aguilera y Roche, mujer de don Bernardo López de Mendizábal, por proposiciones heréticas y sospecho de judiazante, 1663.

AGN, Inquisición, vol. 598, exp. 7, Testificaciónes que se han sacado a pedimiento del señor fiscal contra Juan Gómez, vecino de Nuevo México, 1663.

AGN, Inquisición, vol. 608, exp. 6, Diferentes autos y papeles remitidos por el comisario de Nuevo México, 1667.

AGN, Inquisición, vol. 610, exp. 7, Denunciaciones contra Juan Domínguez de Mendoza, 1666–1667.

AGN, Inquisición, vol. 629, exp. 2, Causa contra Diego Romero, alias Diego Pérez, por poligamo, 1674.

AGN, Inquisición, vol. 666, exp. 5, Autos remitados por fray Juan Bernal, Comisario de Nuevo México, contra Bernardo Gruber, 1669.

AGN, Inquisición, vol. 666, exp. 10, Autos remitados de Nuevo México por fray Juan Bernal, Comisario del Santo Oficio, contra Cristóbal de Anaya, por proposiciones, palabras ofensas y calumnias a los ministros de Santo Oficio, 1669.

AGN, Inquisición, vol. 1551, exp. 28, El Señor Fiscal del Santo Oficio contra varias personas vecinos del Pueblo de Corpus Christi, Paso del Río del Norte, 1682.

AGN, Provincias Internas, vol. 35, exp. 2, Información levantadas por orden del fiscal de su Majestad en la Ciudad de México relativas por orden del Capitán Domingo Gironza Petris de Cruzate, Nuevo México, 1682–1683.

AGN, Provincias Internas, vol. 35, exp. 4, ff. 120–123, Excerpt from a letter of Governor Domingo Jironza Petríz de Cruzate to the viceroy, El Paso, August 26, 1685.

AGN, Provincias Internas, vol. 37, exp. 4, ff. 81–82, Certification of services of Juan Domínguez de Mendoza, June 23, 1684.

AGN, Provincias Internas, vol. 37, exp. 4, ff. 84–91, Petition of fray Nicolás López to the viceroy, Mexico City, June 7, 1685.

AGN, Real Audiencia, Concurso de Peñalosa, vol. 1, leg. 1, no. 1, 166ff, Embargo de los bienes de don Juan Manso y embargo de bienes que le hizo don Bernardo López de Mendizábal, 1660–1662.

AGN, Real Audiencia, Concurso de Peñalosa, vol. 1, leg. 1, no. 2, 247ff, Jucio de Residencia a don Bernardo López de Mendizábal, 1660–1661.

AGN, Real Audiencia, Concurso de Peñalosa, vol. 1, leg. 1, no. 3, 64ff, Prisión y embargo de bienes de doña Teresa de Aguilera, 1662–1674.

AGN, Real Audiencia, Concurso de Peñalosa, vol. 1, leg. 1, no. 10, 65ff, Autos remitados por el padre fray Juan Bernal, Custodio en las Provincias del Nuevo México y Comisario de Este Santo Oficio, a don Bernardo López de Mendizábal, 1673.

AGN, Real Audiencia, Concurso de Peñalosa, vol. 2, leg. 1, no. 8, 17ff, Sobre la provisión que traxo Francisco Domínguez de Mendoza y se present al Custodio de Nuevo México, 1662.

AGN, Real Audiencia, Concurso de Peñalosa, vol. 3, leg. 1, no. 10, 160ff, Diligencias de desembargo: Autos seguidos por el Maestre de Campo Tomé Domínguez de Mendoza, a nombre del Capitán don Diego de Peñalosa Briceño y el padre fray Alonso de Posada, 1663–1665.

AGN, Real Audiencia, Concurso de Peñalosa, vol. 3, leg. 1, no. 19, Pago de salaries a los capitanes Juan y Francisco Domínguez de Mendoza, 1663.

AGN, Real Audiencia, Tierras, vol. 3268, exp. 1–01 to exp. 1–14, Concurso a los bienes de Diego de Peñalosa y Bernardo [López] de Mendizábal y algunas autos hechos en el Nuevo México para la residencia que se tomo a dicho Mendizábal, 1660–1668.

AGN, Real Hacienda, Archivo Histórico de Hacienda, vol. 474, exp. 78, Fianzas, Antonio de Otermín, Gobernador y Capitán General del Presidio de Sinaloa, 1672.

AGN, Real Hacienda, Bulas de la Santa Cruzada, 1634–1638, vol. 2, exp. 1, ff. 1r–5r, Litigio promovido por Miguel de Urquiola albacea del difunto Pedro de Ibarra contra Thomé Domínguez por una deuda, 1634, Ciudad de México.

AGN, Real Hacienda, Bulas de la Santa Cruzada, 1634–1638, vol. 2, exp. 2, ff. 6–8, Litigio promovido por Domingo de Barainca contra Thomé Domínguez, por una deuda, 1634, Ciudad de México.

AGN, Real Hacienda, Bulas de la Santa Cruzada, 1634–1638, vol. 2, exp. 3, ff. 9–12, Juan de Rosas, mercader, entabla un litigio contra Thomé Domínguez, por una deuda, 1634, Ciudad de México.

AGN, Real Hacienda, Bulas de la Santa Cruzada, 1634–1638, vol. 2, exp. 4, ff. 13–92, Hernando Delgado, cirujano, promueve un litigio en contra de Thomé Domínguez, principal, y Tomás de Sein, fiador, por una deuda, 1634, Ciudad de México.

Archivo Histórico de Hidalgo del Parral (AHP)

AHP, Roll 1641A, G-102, Protocolos, f. 570ff, De escrituras públicas, correspondientes a los años de 1641, 1642 y 1643.

AHP, Roll 1670A, G-15, ff. 251A–252A, Protocolos, De escritas e instrumentos públicos.

AHP, Roll 1672B, G-18, f. 613B, Causas Civiles, Testimonio de las diligencias del testamento hecho por la señora Francisca Ezquerra de Rosas por poder de su esposo, el General Juan Manos, de los carros, quien murió en Querétaro viniendo a México.

Archivo Histórico Nacional (AHN)

AHN, Órdenas Militares, San Juan de Jerusalén, exp. 25285, Pruebas de Juan de Samaniego Díez de Ulzurrun Jaca y Roncal, 1637.

AHN, Órdenas Militares, Santiago, exp. 7503, Pruebas de Lorenzo de Samaniego Jaca y Díez de Ulzurrun, 1638.

Bancroft Library, California

Libro de contradas y profesiones de novicios de este convento de Padre San Francisco de México 1562–1680, Bancroft Library, Mexican Manuscripts 216–18.

Biblioteca Nacional de España, Madrid (BNE)

BNE, MSS/19258, Relación de servicios personales del Maestre de Campo don Juan Domingues y Mendoza hechos en las Provincias de la Nueva México, 1686.

Biblioteca Nacional de México (BNM)

BNM, leg. 1, no. 7, f. 482, Settlement of the Estate of Francisco Gómez de Torres; photostat copy located at the Southwest Research Center, University of New Mexico.

BNM, vols. 19/397 and 20/428.1, leg. 3, no. 1, Fray Silvestre de Escalante, Extracto de Noticias, 1777; photostat copies located at the Southwest Research Center, University of New Mexico.

Center for Southwest Research, University of New Mexico Library

France V. Scholes Collection, Box 1

Family History Library, The Church of Jesus Christ of Latter-Day Saints (FHL-LDS)

Mexico, Chihuahua, Aquiles Serdan, Iglesia de Santa Eulalia, Bautismos, 1709–1726, LDS microfilm #162596.

Mexico, Chihuahua, Aquiles Serdán, Iglesia de Santa Eulalia, Defunciones, 1727–1741, LDS microfilm #162595.

Mexico, Chihuahua, Chihuahua, Sagrario, Matrimonios, 1709–1785, LDS microfilm #162689.

Mexico, Chihuahua, Valle de Allende, San Bartolomé Church, Bautismos, 1662–1686 and 1692–1744, LDS microfilm #162634.

Mexico, Chihuahua, Valle de Allende, San Bartolomé Church, Matrimonios, 1686–1746, LDS microfilm #162650.

Mexico, Distrito Federal, Mexico City, Asunción Church (Catedral), Bautismos, 1590–1611, LDS microfilm #0035168.

Mexico, Distrito Federal Mexico City, Asunción Church (Catedral), Bautismos, 1612–1627, LDS microfilm #0035169.

Mexico, Distrito Federal, Mexico City, Asunción Church (Catedral), Bautismos, 1627–1639, LDS Microfilm #0035170.

Mexico, Distrito Federal, Mexico City, Asunción Church, Bautismos, 1640–1652, LDS microfilm #0035171.

Mexico, Distrito Federal, Mexico City, Asunción Church (Catedral), Bautismos, 1705–1713, LDS Microfilm #0035177.

Mexico, Distrito Federal, Mexico City, Asunción Church (Catedral), Información Matrimonial, 1620–1648, LDS microfilm #0035267.

Mexico, Distrito Federal, Mexico City, Asunción Church (Catedral), Información Matrimonial de Españoles, 1694–1734, LDS microfilm # 0035256.

Mexico, Distrito Federal, Mexico City, Asunción Church (Catedral), Matrimonios, 1620–1648, LDS microfilm #0035267.

Mexico, Distrito Federal Mexico City, Asunción Church (Catedral), Matrimonios, 1688–1701, LDS microfilm #0035270.

Mexico, Distrito Federal, Mexico City, Santa Catalina Martir Church, Matrimonios, 1589–1671, LDS microfilm #0036037.
Mexico, Distrito Federal, Mexico City, Santa Vera Cruz Church, Matrimonios 1590–1668, LDS microfilm #0035848.
México, Distrito Federal, Mexico City, Santa Vera Cruz Church, Bautismos, 1636–1668, LDS microfilm #0035820.
Mexico, Distrito Federal, Mexico City, Santa Vera Cruz Church, Matrimonios 1626–1667, LDS microfilm #0035848.
Mexico, Distrito Federal, Mexico City, Santa Vera Cruz Church, Matrimonios, 1664–1726, LDS microfilm #0035848.
Mexico, Durango, Church of Santiago Papasquiaro, Matrimonios, LDS microfilm #0654993.
Mexico, Puebla, Puebla de Zaragoza, Sagrario Metropolitano, Bautismos, 1609–1623, LDS microfilm #0227520.
Mexico, Puebla, Puebla de Zaragoza, Sagrario (Catedral), Matrimonios 1585–1629, LDS microfilm, #0227701.
Mexico, Puebla, Puebla de Zaragoza, San José Church, Bautismos 1583–1956, LDS microfilm #0227901.
Mexico, Zacatecas, Zacatecas, Sagrario, Matrimonios, 1606–1619, LDS microfilm #977702.

Museo Nacional, México

Asuntos de conventos y colegios, vol. 191, ff. 21r–22v, Certificación de los religiosos del Nuevo México, 1667.

New Mexico State Records Center and Archives

Spanish Archives of New Mexico (SANM), Series I.
Spanish Archives of New Mexico (SANM), Series II.

Other Works

Adams, Eleanor B. "The Historical Society of New Mexico Honors France Vinton Scholes for Outstanding Achievement in Spanish Colonial History, 1970." *The Americas* 27 (January 1971): 226.
Altamira y Crevea, Rafael. *Diccionario castellano de palabras jurídicas y técnicas.* Mexico: Instituto Panamericano de Geografía e História, 1951.
Altman, Ida. *Emigrants and Society: Extremadura and America in the Sixteenth Century.* Berkeley: University of California Press, 1989.
Applegate, Howard G., and C. Wayne Hanselka. *La Junta de los Rios del Norte y Conchos.* El Paso: Texas Western Press, 1974.
Archer, Christon I. *The Army in Bourbon Mexico, 1760–1810.* Albuquerque: University of New Mexico Press, 1977.

Bandelier, Adolph F. "Documentary History of the Zuñi Tribe." In *Journal of American Ethnology and Archaeology*, vol. 3. Boston: Houghton, Mifflin, 1892.

Barrett, Elinore M. *Conquest and Catastrophe*. Albuquerque: University of New Mexico Press, 2002.

Beckett, Patrick H., and Terry L. Corbett. "Indian Cultural Diversity in Southern New Mexico, A.D. 1581–1988." In *Current Research on the Late Prehistory and Early History of New Mexico*, edited by Bradley J. Vierra. Albuquerque: New Mexico Archaeological Council, 1992.

Bloom, Lansing B., ed. "Fray Esteban de Perea's Relación." *New Mexico Historical Review* 8 (July 1933): 211–35.

Bolton, Herbert Eugene. *Spanish Explorations in the Southwest, 1542–1706*. New York: Charles Scribner's Sons, 1916.

Brading, D. A. *Patriots and the Liberal State, 1492–1867*. New York: Cambridge University Press, 1991.

Brondo Whitt, Encarnación. *Los Patriarcas del Papigochi*. Chihuahua, Mex., 1952.

Casey, James. *Early Modern Spain: A Social History*. London: Routledge, 1999.

Castañeda, Carlos Eduardo. *Our Catholic Heritage in Texas*. Vol. 1. Austin, TX: Von-Boeckmann, 1936.

Chávez, Fray Angélico. *Chávez: A Distinctive American Clan of New Mexico*. Santa Fe, NM: William Gannon, 1989.

———. "New Mexico Roots, Ltd, Addendum, Part II." *New Mexico Genealogist* 49, no. 2 (June 2010): 74–79.

———. "New Mexico Roots, Ltd, Addendum, Part III." *New Mexico Genealogist* 49, no. 3 (June 2010): 145–52.

———. *Origins of New Mexico Families in the Spanish Colonial Period*. Rev. ed. Santa Fe: Museum of New Mexico Press, 1992.

Chipman, Donald E., and Harriet Denise Joseph. *Spanish Texas 1519–1821*. Austin: University of Texas Press, 1992.

Colligan, John B., comp. "Spanish Surnames Found in the First Book of Baptisms of Nuestra Señora de Guadalupe del Paso del Río del Norte, 1662–1688." Unpublished manuscript in the possession of José Antonio Esquibel.

Coronado Cuarto Centennial, What Will It Mean to New Mexico. N.p.: Cuarto Centennial Commission, ca. 1938. Pamphlet in the possession of Marc Simmons.

Espinosa, José Manuel. *First Expedition of Vargas into New Mexico, 1692*. Coronado Cuarto Centennial Publications, 1540–1940. Vol. 10. Albuquerque: University of New Mexico Press, 1940.

———. "The Legend of the Sierra Azul." *New Mexico Historical Review* 9 (1934): 113–18.

Esquibel, José Antonio. "A Case of Mistaken Identities: Pedro Gómez Durán and Pedro Durán y Chaves." *Herencia* 18, no. 3 (July 2010): 2–6.

———. "Esta gran familia: The Genealogy of the Lucero de Godoy Family of Mexico City." *El Farolito* 6, no. 3 (Fall 2003): 5–21.

———. "Founders of the Villa de Santa Fe: Francisco de Madrid, Part 1." *El Farolito* 12, no. 1 (Spring 2009): 5–18.

———. "Founders of the Villa de Santa Fe: Francisco de Madrid, Part 3." *El Farolito* 12, no. 3 (Fall 2009): 5–25.
———. "Francisco de Madrid II: New Genealogical and Historical Information from Seventeenth-Century Inquisition Records." *El Farolito* 4, no. 3 (Fall 2001): 11–14.
———. "The Leyva-Nevares Heredia Extended Family of Nueva Vizcaya, 1659–1710, Part I." *El Farolito* 3, no. 3 (Fall 2000): 5–15.
———. "The Leyva-Nevares Heredia Extended Family of Nueva Vizcaya, 1659–1710, Part II." *El Farolito* 3, no. 4 (Winter 2000): 21–26.
———. "The Leyva-Nevares Heredia Extended Family of Nueva Vizcaya, 1659–1710, Part III." *El Farolito* 4, no. 1 (Spring 2001): 17–21.
———. "López de Gracia: Clarifying Familial Relations." *Nuestra Raíces* 6, no. 3 (Fall 1994): 92–98.
———. "The Romero Family of Seventeenth-Century New Mexico, Part I." *Herencia* 11, no. 1 (January 2003): 1–30.
———. "The Romero Family of Seventeenth-Century New Mexico, Part II." *Herencia* 11, no. 3 (July 2003): 2–20.
———. "The Sánchez de Iñigo Puzzle: New Genealogical Considerations." *El Farolito* 6, no. 3 (Winter 2003): 8–17.
Esquibel, José Antonio, and Patryka Durán y Chaves. "Pedro Durán y Chaves and doña Juana de Montoya." In *Aqui se comienza: A Genealogical History of the Founding Families of la Villa de Alburquerque*, 184–227. Albuquerque: New Mexico Genealogical Society, 2007.
Fernández Duro, Cesáreo. *Don Diego de Peñalosa y su descubrimiento del reino de Quivira*. In *Memorias de la Real Academia de la História*, tomo 10. Madrid: Imprenta y Fundación de Manuel Tello, 1885.
Forbes, Jack D. *Apache, Navaho, and Spaniard*. Norman: University of Oklahoma Press, 1960.
Greenleaf, Richard E. "France V. Scholes: Historian's Historian, 1897–1979." In *New Mexico Historical Review* 75, no. 3 (July 2000): 325.
Hackett, Charles Wilson, ed. *Historical Documents Relating to New Mexico, Nueva Vizcaya, and Approaches Thereto, to 1773*. Vol. 3. Washington, D.C.: Carnegie Institute of Washington, 1923–1937.
Hackett, Charles Wilson, and Charmion Clair Shelby, eds. and trans. *Revolt of the Pueblo Indians of New Mexico and Otermín's Attempted Reconquest*. 2 vols. Coronado Cuarto Centennial Publications, 1540–1940, Vol. 9. Albuquerque: University of New Mexico Press, 1942.
Hammond, George P. *Coronado's Seven Cities*. Albuquerque: University of New Mexico Press, 1940.
Hammond, George P., ed. *Fray Alonso de Benavides' Revised Memorial of 1634*. Coronado Cuarto Centennial Publications, 1540–1940, Vol. 4. Albuquerque: University of New Mexico Press, 1945.
Hendricks, Rick, and Gerald Mandell. "Juan Manso, Frontier Entrepreneur." *New Mexico Historical Review* 75, no. 3 (2000): 339–67.

Hendricks, Rick, and John P. Wilson, eds. and trans. *The Navajos in 1705, Roque Madrid's Campaign Journal.* Albuquerque: University of New Mexico Press, 1996.

Himmerich y Valencia, Robert. *The Encomenderos of New Spain, 1521–1555.* Austin: University of Texas Press, 1991.

Hoberman, Louisa Schell. *Mexico's Merchant Elite, 1590–1660.* Durham, NC: Duke University Press, 1991.

Hodge, Frederick Webb. *Handbook of American Indians North of Mexico.* Vol. 1. Washington, D.C.: Smithsonian Bureau of American Ethnology, 1907.

———. *History of Hawikuh, New Mexico, One of the So-Called Cities of Cibola.* Los Angeles: Ward Ritchie Press, 1937.

Hordes, Stanley M. *To the End of the Earth: A History of the Crytpto-Jews of New Mexico.* New York: Columbia University Press, 2005.

Hughes, Anne E. *The Beginnings of Spanish Settlement in the El Paso District.* University of California Publications in History, vol. 1, no. 3, 295–392. Berkeley: University of California Press, 1914.

Imhoff, Brian, ed. *The Diary of Juan Domínguez de Mendoza's Expedition into Texas (1683–1684): A Critical Edition of the Spanish Text with Facsimile Reproductions.* Dallas: William P. Clements Center for Southwest Studies, Southern Methodist University, 2002.

Ivey, James E. *In the Midst of Loneliness: The Architectural History of the Salinas Missions.* Santa Fe: National Park Service, 1988.

Kessell, John L. *Kiva, Cross and Crown: The Pecos Nation and New Mexico, 1540–1840.* Washington, D.C.: National Park Service, 1979.

———. *Remote Beyond Compare: Letters of Don Diego de Vargas to His Family from New Spain and Mexico, 1675–1706.* Albuquerque: University of New Mexico Press, 1989.

———. *Spain in the Southwest.* Norman: University of Oklahoma Press, 2002.

Kessell, John L., and Rick Hendricks, eds. and trans. *By Force of Arms: The Journals of Don Diego de Vargas, 1691–1693.* Albuquerque: University of New Mexico Press, 1992.

Kessell, John L., Rick Hendricks, Meredith D. Dodge, José Ignacio Avellaneda, and Larry D. Miller, eds. *To the Royal Crown Restored: The Journals of Don Diego de Vargas, New Mexico, 1692–1694.* Albuquerque: University of New Mexico Press, 1995.

Kessell, John L., Rick Hendricks, Meredith D. Dodge, and Larry D. Miller, eds. *A Settling of Accounts: The Journals of Don Diego de Vargas, New Mexico, 1700–1704.* Albuquerque: University of New Mexico Press, 2002.

———. *That Disturbances Cease: The Journals of Don Diego de Vargas, New Mexico, 1696–1700.* Albuquerque: University of New Mexico Press, 2000.

Kessell, John L., Rick Hendricks, Meredith D. Dodge, Larry D. Miller, and Richard Flint, eds. *Blood on the Boulders: The Journals of Don Diego de Vargas, New Mexico, 1694–97.* Book 2. Albuquerque: University of New Mexico Press, 1998.

Knaut, Andrew L. *The Pueblo Revolt of 1680.* Norman: University of Oklahoma Press, 1995.
Kramer, Paul. "The Dynamic Ethnicity of the People of Spanish Colonial New Mexico." In *Transforming Images: New Mexican Santos In-Between Worlds,* edited by Claire Farago and Donna Pierce. University Park: Pennsylvania State University Press, 2006.
Leonard, Irving Albert, trans. and ed. *The Mercurio Volante of Don Carlos de Sigüenza y Góngora.* Los Angeles: Quivira Society, 1932.
Lockhart, Bill. "Protohistoric Confusion: A Cultural Comparison of the Manso, Suma, and Jumano Indians of the Paso del Norte Region." *Journal of the Southwest* 3 (Spring 1997): 130–40.
MacLachlan, Colin M. *Criminal Justice in Eighteenth Century Mexico.* Berkeley: University of California Press, 1974.
Martin, Thomas P. "Spanish Archive Materials and Related Materials in the Other National Archives Copied for the Library of Congress by the Rockefeller Project, 1927–1929." *Hispanic American Historical Review* 10 (February 1930): 96.
Martínez Cosio, Leopoldo. *Los caballeros de las ordenes militares en México.* Mexico: Editorial Santiago, 1946.
McLaughlin, Walter V., Jr. "First Book of Baptisms of Nuestra Señora de Guadalupe del Paso del Norte." Master's thesis, Texas Western College, August 1962.
Mendoza Castro de Ludwig, Patsy. "Domínguez de Mendoza." Unpublished manuscript in possession of the editors.
Parrott Hickerson, Nancy. *The Jumanos, Hunters and Traders of the South Plains.* Austin: University of Texas Press, 1994.
Preucel, Robert W. "Writing the Pueblo Revolt." In *Archaeologies of the Pueblo Revolt,* edited by Preucel. Albuquerque: University of New Mexico Press, 2002.
Reeves, Frank D. "Early Navajo Geography." *New Mexico Historical Review* 31 (October 1956): 295–96.
Riley, Carroll L. *The Kachina and the Cross: Indians and Spaniards in the Early Southwest.* Salt Lake City: University of Utah Press, 1999.
Romero de Solís, José Miguel. *Andariegos y pobladores: Nueva España y Nueva Galicia: Siglo xvi.* Colima: El Colegio de Michoacán, AC, 2001.
Sánchez, Joseph P. *Between Two Rivers: The Atrisco Land Grant in Albuquerque History, 1692–1968.* Norman: University of Oklahoma Press, 2008.
Schäfer, Ernst. *El Consejo Real y Supremo de las Indias: Su historia, organización y labor administriva hasta la terminación de la casa de Austria.* Vol. 1: *História y organización del Consejo y de las Casa de Contratación de las Indias.* Sevilla: Centro de Estudio de America, Universidad de Sevilla, 1935.

———. *Las Rúbricas del Consejo Real y Supremo de las Indias desde la fundación del Consejo en 1524 hasta la terminación del reinado del los Austrias.* Sevilla: Universidad Publicaciones del Centro de Estudios de História, 1934.
Scholes, France V. "Church and State in New Mexico, 1610–1650." *New Mexico Historical Review* 11 (October 1936): 340.

———. "Civil Government and Society in New Mexico in the Seventeenth Century." *New Mexico Historical Review* 10 (April 1935): 71–111.

——— "Documents for the History of the New Mexican Missions in the Seventeenth Century." *New Mexico Historical Review* 4 (January 1929): 45–58.

———. "Royal Treasury Records Relating to the Province of New Mexico, 1596–1683." *New Mexico Historical Review* 50 (January and April 1975): 5–24, 139–64.

———. "The Supply Service of the New Mexican Missions in the Seventeenth Century." *New Mexico Historical Review* 5 (January 1930): 93–115, 386–404.

———. *Troublous Times in New Mexico, 1659–1670*. (*New Mexico Historical Review*, 1937 to 1941, and afterward issued as a separate monograph.) Albuquerque: University of New Mexico Press, 1942.

Simmons, Marc. "The Pueblo Revolt: Why Did It Happen?" *El Palacio* 86 (Winter 1980–1981): 11–15.

———. *Spanish Government in New Mexico*. Albuquerque: University of New Mexico Press, 1990.

Simpson, Lesley Byrd. *The Encomienda in New Spain*. Berkeley: University of California Press, 1982.

Snow, David H. "A Note on Encomienda Economics in Seventeenth-Century New Mexico." In *Spanish Borderlands Sourcebooks*. Vol. 17, *The Spanish Missions of New Mexico I: Before 1680*, edited by John L. Kessell and Rick Hendricks, 469–79. New York: Garland, 1991.

Sonnichsen, C. L. *Pass of the North: Four Centuries on the Rio Grande*. 2 vols. El Paso: Texas Western Press, 1968, 1980.

Thomas, Alfred Barnaby. *After Coronado: Spanish Exploration Northeast of New Mexico, 1696–1727*. Norman: University of Oklahoma Press, 1935.

Thomas, Alfred Barnaby, ed. *Alonso de Posada Report, 1686*. Pensacola, FL: Presidio Bay Press, 1982.

Thomas, Alfred Barnaby, trans. and ed. *Forgotten Frontiers: A Study of the Spanish Indian Policy of Don Juan Bautista de Anza, Governor of New Mexico, 1777–1787*. Norman: University of Oklahoma Press, 1932.

Treviño Castro, S. J., Salvador. *Del Chihuahua colonial*. Ciudad Juárez: Universidad de Ciudad Juárez, 2000.

Twitchell, Ralph Emerson. *The Spanish Archives of New Mexico*. 2 vols. Cedar Rapids, IA: Torch Press, 1914.

Tyler, S. Lyman, and M. Darrel Taylor, eds. and trans. "The Report of Fray Alonso de Posadas in Relation to Quivira and Teguayo." *New Mexico Historical Review* 33 (October 1958): 285–314.

Valencia y Valdez, Gloria M., José Antonio Esquibel, Robert D. Martínez, and Francisco Sisneros, eds. *Aquí se comienza: A Genealogical History of the Founding Families of la Villa de San Felipe de Alburquerque*. Albuquerque: New Mexico Genealogical Society, 2007.

Velázquez, María del Carmen. *El estado de guerra en Nueva España, 1760–1808*. Mexico: El Colégio de México, 1950.

Vetancurt, Fray Agustín de. *Teatro mexicano: Descripción breve de los sucesos ejemplares, historicos, politicos, militares y religiosos del nuevo mundo occidental de las Indias, por. Fr. Agustin de Vetancurt.* Vol. 4. *Menológio franciscano de los varones mas señalados, que con sus vidas ejemplares, perfección religiosa, ciencia, predicación evangélica, en su vida y muerte ilustraron la provincia del Santo Evangélio de México.* Biblioteca Histórica de la Iberia, vol. 10. Mexico: Imprenta de I. Escalante, 1871.

Walz, Vina. "History of the El Paso Area, 1680–1692." PhD diss., Albuquerque, University of New Mexico, 1951.

Weber, David J., ed. *What Caused the Pueblo Revolt of 1680?* Boston: Bedford/St. Martin, 1999.

Weddle, Robert S. *The French Thorn, Rival Explorers in the Spanish Sea, 1682–1762.* College Station: Texas A & M University Press, 1991.

———. "Juan Domínguez de Mendoza." In *The New Handbook of Texas,* edited by Ronnie C. Tyler, Douglas E. Barnett, and Roy R. Barkley. Vol. 2. Austin: Texas Historical Association, 1996.

Weigle, Marta, with Samuel Larcombe, and Claudia Larcombe. *Hispanic Arts and Ethnohistory in the Southwest.* Santa Fe, NM: Ancient City Press, 1983.

Wozniak, Frank E. "The Location of the Navajo Homeland in the Seventeenth Century: An Appraisal of the Spanish Colonial Records." In *Current Research on the Late Prehistory and Early History of New Mexico,* edited by Bradley J. Vierra and Clara Gualtieri, 328–31. Albuquerque: New Mexico Archeological Council, 1992.

Závala, Silvio A. *La Encomienda indiana.* Mexico: Editorial Porrua, 1973.

Index

Page numbers in italic text indicate illustrations. The letters *ch* following a page number denotes a chart. The letter *t* following a page number denotes a table.

Abó Pueblo (New Mexico), 22, 140, 292, 306
Acevedo, fray Antonio: and building of churches, 42, 319; departs for La Junta, 40, 193, 196; and the Jumanos Indians, 39, 188, 226n2; leaves La Junta, 43; remains at La Junta, 41, 195, 198, 210, 320
Acoma Indians, killed by Apache, 132
Acoma Pueblo, *ii*, 387; attacked by Apaches, 132, 134, 137; attacked by Navajo Indians, 28, 171; church of, 293; convento of, 134, 307; as encomienda, 22, 24; population of, 293; provision requested of, 120. *See also* Peñol of Acoma
Adams, Eleanor B., collaboration with France V. Scholes, xvi–xvii, xviii, xxii, 348
Ágreda, Madre María de Jesús de, reference to, 320, 326
Aguatubi Pueblo (New Mexico), 293
Aguatubi Pueblo Indians, 287
Aguilar, Nicolás de, 18, 304n1; as alcalde mayor, 296, 297; arrest by Inquisition, 19, 101n5, 367, 374, 385
Aguilera y Roche, Teresa, 111n5, 383; arrest by Inquisition, 19, 96n4, 367
Alameda Indians, conspire against Spaniards, 77n6

Alameda Pueblo, *ii*, 5, 35, 56n19, 231, 232, 262, 293
Alamillo Pueblo (New Mexico), 125n3, 293, 303n1
Alburu, María Francisca de, 362ch, 364ch; children of, 363; marriage of, 363, 400n66
alcalde mayor: Alonso García (Sandia), 96; Alonso Pérez Granillo (Piros), 296; Andrés López de Gracia (El Paso), 116n2; Andrés López Sambrano (Moqui), 296; Antonio de Salas (Tanos), 296; Bartolomé de Cisneros (Zuñi y Moqui), 90; Diego de Trujillo (Moqui), 296; Diego González Bernal (Tanos), 296; Francisco Pérez Granillo (Piros), 296; Francisco Romero de Pedraza (Santo Domingo), 221n32; José Nieto (Las Salinas), 128n11; Juan Domínguez de Mendoza (Sandia, Isleta, and Río Abajo), 16, 96–98, 296; Juan García Holgado (Senecú and Alameda Pueblo), 114, 116n5; Juan Lucero de Godoy (Senecú), 147; Juan Luján (Tewas), 296; Miguel de Hinojos (Cohciti), 296; Nicolás de Aguilar (Las Salinas), 296; Pedro de Leyva (Humanas and Las Salinas), 155n3, 296; Tomé Domínguez de Mendoza (Isleta and Río Abajo), 96, 372; Toribio de la Huerta (Cohciti), 296
alcalde ordinario of Santa Fe: Bartolomé Romero as, 125n5; Francisco de Anaya Almazán as, 380; Francisco de Madrid as, 127n8; Francisco Gómez

Robledo as, 242; Juan Domínguez de Mendoza as, 23, 102, 104, 106, 145; Juan Rodríguez de Zuballe as, 223; Lorenzo de Madrid as, 223; Pedro de Escalante y Mendoza as, 248; Tomé Domínguez as, 97; Tomé Domínguez de Mendoza removed as, 18

Alvarado, fray Tomás, 19, 105n3, 379, 409n150; and council at Santo Domingo, 122–23; and Jemez convento, 135; origin of, 129n19

Anaya, Juan de, 246n3, 363, 386, 388; deserts El Paso, 234–37, 244, 246n3; sentenced for desertion, 258–60

Anaya Almazán, Ana de, 127n10, 220n26

Anaya Almazán, Cristóbal de (son of Francisco), 81n6, 110n2, 246n3, 365, 369, 379, 380; acquitted of charges, 386; arrest by Inquisition, 19, 70n3, 101n5, 367, 385; baptism of, 381; children of, 386, 388; death of, 388; defies Franciscans, 387; denies parentesco, 384, 386; as encomendero, 101n5, 381; encomienda revoked, 385; estancia and house of, 110n2, 359, 380, 381, 388, 412n189, 412n191; flees New Mexico, 383; marriage of, 381; military service of, 381; as provincial judge of the Santa Hermandad, 109, 387; and term of Inquisition imprisonment, 386; and trade wagons, 109–10

Anaya Almazán, Francisco de (father of Francisco and Cristóbal), 81n6, 117n6, 220n26, 220n28; arrest of, 382; and encomiendas restored, 384; flees New Mexico, 383; marriage of, 380; as residencia scribe, 385; as secretary of government and war, 79, 82, 380–81

Anaya Almazán, Francisco de (son of Francisco), 220n28; as alguacíl mayor and procurador general, 216; as member of the cabildo of Santa Fe, 115, 217, 220n26, 223, 380

Anaya Almazán, Francisco de (son of Cristóbal), 386, 388

Anaya Almazán, María de, 386, 388

Ancón de Fray García, 179–80, 180n2

Apache Indians, 4; Acodames Apache, 228; Apache de Navajo (see Navajo Indians); attack churches, 25, 29, 153, 315; attack estancias by, 144; attack Humanas Pueblo by, 22, 25, 140, 141; attack of Hawikuh Pueblo by, 90, 315; attack on Governor Miranda by, 25, 142; attack Pueblo communities by, 4, 17, 28, 29, 159; attack roads by, 112, 144, 148, 171; attack Santa Fe, 165; attacks by, 16, 25, 28, 36, 118, 121, 163, 375; barter with Taos Indians, 265; campaigns and wars against, 40, 74, 78–79, 88–89, 92, 118, 130, 137–38, 139–40, 144–45, 147–48, 153, 157, 277, 302, 334, 336, 375; captives of, 25, 90, 93, 132, 140, 141; as captives or slaves, 16, 17, 94, 110, 112n9, 226, 241, 277, 313, 366; as confederates of Jemez Indians, 77n6; as confederates of Pueblo Indians, 144–45; del Acho Apache, 78, 80n3; del Chilmo, 114; and expedition to Texas, 42; Faraon Apache, 154, 159n2; Gabilanes, 228; of Gila, 26, 142; grain fields of, 134, 136, 137, 165, 277; Jicarilla Apache, 80n3; killed or executed, 41, 145, 226, 241, 277, 313; and killing of people, 90, 93, 118, 119, 129–31, 132, 135, 137, 140, 142, 144–45, 148, 153, 165, 315; Lipan Apache, 80n3; Llanero Apache, 159n2; peace with, 93–94, 118; rancherías of, 183, 185, 204; Salineros, 42, 133, 138n5, 145, 206, 228; sentence of death against, 78; of Siete Ríos, 22, 25, 139–40, 142, 145; speak Spanish, 132; steal horses, 90, 118, 130, 132, 137, 144,

153, 163, 204; steal mules, 130, 142; steal or kill livestock, 90, 118, 132, 134, 136, 135–36, 137, 144, 147, 153, 163, 165; and territory of Acamache, 302; as threat to El Paso, 40; as threat to Jumano Indians, 38, 183, 185, 188, 197, 202, 204, 205, 206, 255; as threat to Pueblo Indians, 17, 140; Tobosos, 228; travelers robbed by, 148; Vaquero Apache, 159n2; and war at Sierra Blanca, 86

Archuleta, Diego de, 300n11; service papers of, 297

Archuleta, Francisco, 207, 208

Argüello Carvajal, Francsico de (governor), xxx, 8t, 72n3, 80n5, 144; commissions Juan Domínguez de Mendoza, 73–75, 214; and encomienda tributes, 302; takes office as governor, 76n3; term as governor, 75n2

Atrisco. *See* estancia and hacienda

Ayala, fray Pedro de (Ávila y Ayala), xxix; killed at Hawikuh Pueblo, 90, 92n3, 155n2, 315

Ayeta, fray Francisco de, 34, 38; brings provisions from Mexico City, 31; departs for Mexico City, 37; origin and parents of, 61n86; and request for military aid and soldiers, 28–29, 376; in Spain, 61n86

Baca, Ana: estancia of, 300n8; service papers of, 297

Baca, Cristóbal, 104, 105n3, 389

Barela, Diego. *See* Varela de Losada, Diego

Bastida, Pedro de la, 47, 257, 327, 328

Benavides, fray Alonso de, 324, 326, 331n6, 381

Bernal, fray Juan: chastised by Inquisition officials, 24; as commissary of Franciscans in New Mexico, 24; origin and parents of, 60n70

Bernal, Pascuala, 80n4, 131n4

Bohórquez, Isabel de, 227n4, 360–61, 362ch, 388–89, 391ch; estate of, 389

cabildo of Santa Fe, xxiii; accepts military aid, 376; accusations against Governor Jironza, 44–45; certifies services of Governor Jironza, 338; jail of 382, 384; members of, 115, 216, 217, 223, 242, 251; and Juan Domínguez de Mendoza, 47–48, 115, 247–51; and power of attorney, 53; at Real de San Lorenzo, 32, 334; request of Franciscans for grain, 121; request to abandon El Paso, 44; and sign of obedience of, 115

Cadimo, Roque, 300n9; service papers of, 297

Cañada. *See* La Cañada

Capitán Chiquito (Manso leader), 116n4; ranchería of, 112, 114

Cardoso, fray Domingo, 304, 308

Carvajal, Felix de: as encomendero, 301n15; service papers of, 297

Carvajal, Juana de, 93n4, 247n14

Carvajal, Luis de, 111n6; and military escort of wagons, 109

Carvajal, Melchora de, 149n3, 247n9

Caravan: inspection of, 109–10; and license of personnel, 109; royal support of, 107, 145; and trade, 109–10

Casa Fuerte, 26, 27, 28, 153, 165, 295; attack on, 28; mountain range of, 88n4, 160, 168, 171, 175; Navajos of, 87, 133, 138n5, 144, 145, 147n4, 153, 177

Casas Grandes (Nueva Vizcaya), 327, 338; battle at, 335

casas reales, 30, 73, 78, 119, 124, 126n6, 372, 393, 395

Carlos II (King of Spain), 150, 151n2

Castillo, Diego del. *See* López del Castillo, Diego

Castillo Betancur, Francisco del, 131, 138

Catití, Alonso, 35, 62n108, 225, 227n6, 238, 263

cattle. *See* livestock
catzina dances, 18, 19, 23, 372–73; masks, 19, 35, 374; suppression of, 18, 373
Cedillo Rico de Rojas, Pedro, 116n2, 221n30, 221n30; as member of the Santa Fe cabildo, 216, 217, 223
Cerro de Azul, gold and silver at, 228
Cerro Hueco: battle at, 40, 334, 371; paraje of, 336
Chaves, Cristóbal de. *See* Durán y Chaves, Cristóbal
Chaves y Bohórquez, Isabel. *See* Durán y Chaves, Isabel
Chepira, Cristóbal, as war captain of Pecos Pueblo, 78
Chilili Pueblo (New Mexico), 99n5, 292, 306
Chiquito. *See* Capitán Chiquito
churches, list of, 291–94
Cisneros, Bartolomé de: as alcalde mayor of Zuñi and Moqui, 90; as resident of Zuñi jurisdiction, 125n2
Cisneros, Vicente: and house raided by Apache, 118; as resident of Acoma parish, 125n2
Clemente, Esteban, as governor of Las Salinas, 314n3
Cochití Indians, 77n6
Cochiti Pueblo (New Mexico), 35, 97, 232, 238, 241, 242, 243, 244, 260, 262, 263, 264, 265, 306, 360, 370
Conchos River, 38, 41, 43, 183, 193, 194, 203, 210, 211; junction with Río del Norte, 198, 318
Conde de Galve. *See* Sandoval Cerda Silva y Mendoza, Gaspar
Conde de Monclova (Viceroy of New Spain), 49, 260, 267–68, 274, 337
convento, 6; of Abó (San Gregorio), 306; of Acoma (San Estebán), 134, 307; of Chilili, 292, 306; of Cochiti, 306; of Cuarac, 306; and distribution of food, 123, 134–35; of Galisteo (Santa Cruz), 135, 306; of Guadalupe del Paso, 308; of Halona, 307; of Hawikuh, 307; of Humanas, 306; of Isleta, 307; of Jemez (San Diego), 135, 307; list of, 291–94; livestock stolen from, 134, 137; of Mishongnovi, 307; of Nambé, 134, 305; number of, 295n1, 304–8; of Oraibi (San Miguel), 307; of Pecos, 135, 306; of Picurís, 135, 305; robbed by Apache, 134; ruined by Apache raids, 136; Sandia, 135, 306, 370, 409n150; of San Ildefonso, 134, 305; of San Juan, 134; of San Marcos, 292, 306; of Santa Clara, 305; of Santa Fe, 305; of Santo Domingo, 121, 122, 123, 135, 306, 390; of Senecú, 135; of Senecú (San Antonio), 134, 307; of Shongopovi, 308; of Socorro, 134, 135, 307; of Tajique (San Miguel), 306; of Taos, 135; of Zía, 135, 307
cordillera, 106, 107n3, 139, 142; of Acoma, 178; of Gila, 147; of Navajo, 177; of Siete Ríos, 147. *See also* mountain ranges
Coronado Cuarto Centennial Commission, xiii, xixn3
Coronado Historical Series, xiii–xiv, xxi, xxii
Cortés, Beatris, 378; children of, 408–9n149
Cruz, Elena de la, 54n1, 56n18, 70n3, 227n4, 358ch, 362ch, 371, 379, 388, 391ch, 395; children of, 1, 355–56; marriage of, 1, 349; origin and parents of, 1, 348–49; proof of lineage of, xxv, 1, 69, 347–48, 349–55
Cruz, Juana de la, 138n3, 300n5; as sister of Elena, 56n18, 70n3, 358ch, 360
Cuarac Pueblo (New Mexico), 292, 305, 381
Cuéllar, fray Nicolás, 122
Cuyamunque Pueblo (New Mexico): population of, 291; as visita, 291

Díaz de Rivera, Juan, 249, 251, 343
doctrineros, 309, 311, 313

Domínguez, Ana María, 394
Domínguez, Baltasar, 363, 364ch
Domínguez, Domingo, 393
Domínguez, Josefa, 378, 407n142
Domínguez, Juana, 220n26, 304, 401n78
Domínguez, Juana (daughter of Josefa), 394–95
Domínguez, Manuel, 394
Domínguez, María, 393–94
Domínguez, Nicolás, 363, 364ch
Domínguez, Tomé (father of Tomé), 349, 358ch
Domínguez, Tomé (son of Tomé), 54n1, 70n3, 94, 227n4, 248, 347, 352, 358ch, 362ch, 371, 379, 388, 391ch, 392, 394, 396; age of, 1; as alcalde ordinario of Santa Fe, 97; brother of, 349; children of, 1, 355–56; commission as captain, 3, 357; death of, 5, 56n18; debt and arrest of, 2–3, 357; estancia of, 2–3, 110n2, 359, 380; house of, 365, 409n150; as lieutenant governor of New Mexico, 94, 97; marriage of, 1, 349; as merchant, 1, 2, 5, 103n2, 357, 398n37; misnamed as Bartolomé, 91, 102, 103n2, 214, 276; in New Mexico, 2–3, 75n3; origin and parents of, 2, 103, 348–49, 355, 356–57; and fray Estéban de Perea, 2, 103n2, 356–57; and proof of lineage, 253n14; sponsors settlers of New Mexico, 3, 90, 97, 357; travels to Mexico City, 55n7
Domínguez de la Cruz, Baleriana, baptism of, 356, 358ch, 398n32
Domínguez de la Cruz, Domingo, baptism of, 356, 358ch
Domínguez de la Cruz, Isabel, baptism of, 356, 358ch
Domínguez de la Cruz, José, baptism of, 355, 358ch
Domínguez de la Cruz, María: baptism of, 356, 358ch; marriage of, 359, 397n30
Domínguez de la Cruz, Pedro, baptism of, 356, 358ch

Domínguez de Mendoza, Ana María Gertrudis Antonia, 364ch
Domínguez de Mendoza, Antonia, 371; marriage of, 415n226
Domínguez de Mendoza, Antonio (son of Francisco), 370–71, 395–95; leads campaign against Apaches, 40, 334
Domínguez de Mendoza, Antonio (son of Tomé), 5, 98n2, 372, 377
Domínguez de Mendoza, Baltasar, 361, 362ch; brings his mother to Mexico City, 50, 267–69; certification of personal appearance of, xxiiit, 221–23; children of, 363, 364ch; commission as alférez real, xxiv, xxviii, 7, 151–52, 222, 275, 280, 284; commission as captain of cavalry, xxiv, xxviii, 156–57, 222, 280, 284; deserts El Paso, 234–37, 242, 244; and donation of property, 381; and forgeries of service records, xxvii, xxviii, xxix, xxx, xxxi, 72n3; and Jumano expedition, 39, 276; and license to leave Spain, 53, 285–86; in Madrid, 53; marriage of, 363, 400n66; and papers to return to New Mexico, xxv; and petition for military order admission, 281–83, 363; petitions king of Spain, 53, 279–80, 281–83; physical description of, 222, 223n2; and report of Council of Indies, 277–78; and request as alcalde mayor of Sonora, 278, 363; and request for governorship of New Mexico, 278, 279, 282, 363; resumé of papers of, xxv, 275–77; and royal recommendation to viceroy, xxv, 283, 284; sentenced for desertion, 258–60; services in New Mexico, 276; and shipwreck, xxvii, xxxi, 51, 282, 283, 284, 361; as soldier, 150, 151n2; travels to Mexico City, 45, 53; travels to Spain, 51, 279, 282; as witness, 196; year of birth of, 6, 362
Domínguez de Mendoza, Catalina, 5, 138n4, 377

Domínguez de Mendoza, Damiana.
    See Ramírez de Mendoza, Damiana
Domínguez de Mendoza, Diego, 5, 372,
    376, 377
Domínguez de Mendoza, Elena, 1, 5,
    227n4, 356, 358ch, 359, 362ch,
    391ch, 392; marriage of, 388, 390
Domínguez de Mendoza, Francisca, 1,
    220n28, 356, 358ch, 359
Domínguez de Mendoza, Francisco
    (brother of Juan), 1, 40, 98n2, 344n4,
    359, 360, 379, 395; and armed
    escort, 365–66; baptism of, 355, 365;
    children of, 370–71; description of,
    366; and donation of property, 381; as
    encomendero, 370; granted power of
    attorney, 370; as justicia mayor of Zía
    and Cochiti, 370; marriage of, 365,
    398n32; and petitions to Inquisition,
    367–69; returns to New Mexico, 369,
    383; travels to Mexico City, 20, 366
Domínguez de Mendoza, Francisco (son
    of Tomé Domínguez de Mendoza), 5,
    372, 377; children of, 406n137
Domínguez de Mendoza, Francisco
    Antonio, 364ch
Domínguez de Mendoza, Isabel (daughter
    of Juan), 365
Domínguez de Mendoza, Isabel (daughter
    of Tomé), 407n142
Domínguez de Mendoza, Isabel Rita, 365
Domínguez de Mendoza, Joachín Joséph
    de San Balentín, 364ch
Domínguez de Mendoza, Joaquín
    (Joachín), 363, 364ch
Domínguez de Mendoza, José, 365
Domínguez de Mendoza, José (son of
    Ana Velásquez), 393–94, 414n211
Domínguez de Mendoza, Joséph María
    Joachín Florencio, 364ch
Domínguez de Mendoza, Juan, xxi, xxvii–
    xxviii, xxix, xxxi, 7, 152, 220n28,
    247n10, 247n11, 247n12, 247n14,
    247n15, 248n16, 360, 387, 390, 391ch,
    395; accused of amorous advances,
    105n3, 379; as acting governor, 26; as
    alcalde ordinario, 9–11t, 23, 102, 104,
    106, 145, 149; alleged natural daughter,
    401n78; as ally of López de Mendizábal,
    17–18, 20; and appointment as alcalde
    mayor, xxiii, 16, 96–98, 215, 250, 296;
    appointment as escuderos, xxiii, 9t, 21,
    22, 99–100, 101n5; appointment as
    visitador of the supply caravan, xxiv, 7,
    107–8, 109–10, 145, 215; appointment
    as visitor-general of New Mexico, 20,
    102–3, 215; arrival in New Mexico,
    6, 75–76n3; birth and baptism of, 1,
    54n1, 356, 358ch; brings settlers to
    New Mexico, 73, 74, 150, 281; certifi-
    cation of personal appearance, xxiiit,
    221–23; certification of services of,
    xxiii, xxiv, xxix, 8t, 11–13t, 48, 86–87,
    88–89, 162, 172, 174, 180, 181–82,
    193–96, 214–17, 248–51; and conflict
    with Franciscan friars, 19–20, 23, 24;
    death of, xxvii, 51, 282, 283, 284; as
    encomendero, 22, 129–31, 175–76,
    215, 216; estancia of, 5, 6, 217; and
    expedition against Manso Indians, 87;
    and expedition to Cochiti, 181, 238,
    242, 243, 244, 260–66; and expedi-
    tion to Quivira, 86, 89n3, 381; and
    expedition to Sierra Blanca, 86; and
    expedition to Texas (1654), 15–16, 86;
    and fabrication of royal standard, 225,
    241; family of, 360–65, 362ch; financial
    loss of, 32; found guilty of charges of
    desertion, 49; and governorship of New
    Mexico, 7, 44, 45, 48, 49, 50, 225, 238,
    244, 259; as hidalgo, 10t, 147, 149,
    216, 253n14; home at San Lorenzo of,
    40; hospitalized in Madrid, 51; and the
    Inquisition, 19–20, 23, 379, 387; as
    juez receptor, 104, 106; leads expedi-
    tion against Apaches, 16, 97, 130,
    141, 144–45; leads expedition against
    Navajo Indians, 14, 26–28, 153, 160,
    165, 168–70, 171–74, 175–76, 177–78;
    leads Jumano expedition into Texas,

41–43, 193–95, 196–212, 254, 327; and license to travel to Spain, xxiv, 49, 51, 273–75; as lieutenant governor of the Río Abajo, 104, 108, 145, 215, 250, 387; list of commission of, xxii–xxvt, 8–13t, 144–45; marriage of, 5, 360; memorial of, 46, 47, 227–30, 231–34; in Mexico City, 15, 46, 50, 51, 367–69; military ranks and offices of, 8–13t, 14, 97, 102, 107, 130, 140, 144–45, 154, 157, 175, 179, 181, 188–89, 231; in muster of 1680, 32; and patent of nobility, 249, 270, 282; and personal service records, 270–73; physical description of, 48, 222; and possession of Texas, 327; proof of lineage (probanza), xxv, 1, 69, 250, 347–48, 349–55; provides equipment and supplies for campaign, 102; and Pueblo Indian Revolt, 30, 31, 61n93, 216–17; and Pueblo Indians, 29; as a receptor of the Inquisition tribunal, 368; and restoration of New Mexico, 34–36, 45, 51, 231, 393; royal fiesta sponsored by, 25; seeks permission for family to leave El Paso, 50, 267–69; sentenced to death, 226, 241; sentenced for desertion, 258–60; and shipwreck, xxvii, xxxi, 51, 282, 283, 284; sponsors a fiesta, 149; as squadron leader, 296; and title of encomendero, xxiv, 9 and 11–12t, 145, 149, 250; travels to Mexico City, 14, 20, 45, 89n3; travels to New Spain, 73, 75n3, 86; tried in absentia for desertion, 45, 49, 234–45; wounded, 84

—commission of: as alférez real, xxiii, xxvii–xxviii, xxix, 7, 8t, 70–71, 214; as captain and commander, xxiii, 78–79, 214, 215; as captain of cavalry, xxiii, 7, 83–84, 215; as captain of infantry, xxii, 8t, 73–75, 214, 215, 250; as captain of mounted harquebusiers, xxiii, 8t, 93–95; as commander of the 1683 Texas expedition, xxiii, xxix, 38, 187–90; as lieutenant captain general, xxiv, xxv, 9t, 23, 25, 27, 164–67, 171–72, 250, 296; as lieutenant general of cavalry, xxv, 34, 179–80; as lieutenant governor, xxiii, xxiv, 7–11t, 16, 23, 25, 81–82, 105–7, 112–15, 216; as maestre de campo, xxiii, xxiv, xxv, 10–11t, 90–92, 139–41, 216; as military commander and chief, xxiv, 144–46, 153–55, 160–61, 163–64, 250; as sargento mayor of the kingdom, xxiv, 142–43, 216, 250

Domínguez de Mendoza, Juan (son of Juan), xxiii, 242, 361, 362ch; certification of personal appearance of, xxiiit, 221–23; certification of services, 286–87; children of, 365; death of, 365, 401n77; as founder of Chihuahua, 363; and Jumano expedition, 39; and letter of recommendation, 54; marriage of, 363; physical description of, 222, 223n2, 363; as soldier, 150, 151n2; travels to Mexico City, 45; year of birth of, 6

Domínguez de Mendoza, Juan (son of Tomé Domínguez de Mendoza), 5, 372, 377

Domínguez de Mendoza, Juan Mateo. See Domínguez de Mendoza, Mateo

Domínguez de Mendoza, Juana, 5

Domínguez de Mendoza, Leonor (daughter of Antonio), 415n226

Domínguez de Mendoza, Leonor (daughter of Tomé). See Ramírez de Mendoza, Leonor

Domínguez de Mendoza, María (daughter of Antonio), 371; marriage of, 415n226

Domínguez de Mendoza, María (daughter of Juan), 6, 192n3, 361, 362ch, 365, 395, 402n78

Domínguez de Mendoza, María Josefa Ignacia, 364ch

Domínguez de Mendoza, Marina Josefa, 364ch, 401n67

Domínguez de Mendoza, Mateo, 377; children of, 406n141

Domínguez de Mendoza, Salvador Bartolomé, 407n142
Domínguez de Mendoza, Teresa, 371, 415n226
Domínguez de Mendoza, Tomé (brother of Juan), 1, 63n112, 119, 133, 138n4, 359, 360, 394; and abandoned house in El Paso region of, 40, 63n125; account of family killed in Pueblo Revolt, 32; as alcalde mayor of Isleta, 372; baptism of, 356, 358ch, 371; birth of, 98n3; as cabildo member, 375, 376; and charges against Governor Miranda, 26; children of, 5, 371–72, 377–78; commissions Juan Domínguez de Mendoza, 163, 164, 216; estancia of, 5, 98n4, 371, 376; exile of, 36–37; houses of, 43, 97, 211, 371, 377, 392; leads expedition to El Paso, 112; as lieutenant governor, 147, 163–64, 371, 372, 374, 375; and Pueblo Indian Revolt, 30, 31, 376; removed as alcalde ordinario, 18; and support of Franciscans, 18, 374; testifies against López de Mendizábal, 19, 374; and trading, 33; wife of, 5, 98n3
Domínguez de Mendoza, Tomé (son of Tomé), 5, 371–72, 377
Domínguez de Mendoza y Varela, Elena, 407n142
Domínguez de Mendoza y Vitoria de Carvajal, Catalina, 407n142
Domínguez de Mendoza y Vitoria de Losada, Juana, 407n142
Doña Ana (New Mexico), paraje of, 335
Durán, Salvador, 148, 149n3
Durán y Bohórquez, Isabel. *See* Durán y Chaves, Isabel
Durán y Chaves, Cristóbal, 6, 138n4, 377; as escuderos, 101n5; killed by Apache, 132
Durán y Chaves, Fernando, 247n10, 359, 361, 374, 377, 389, 390, 391ch, 392; estate of, 5; member of the cabildo of Santa Fe, 242; and murder of Governor Rosas, 389–90

Durán y Chaves, Isabel (wife of Juan Domínguez de Mendoza), 192n3, 247n14, 247n15, 248n16, 388, 390, 391ch, 395, 402n78; children of, 6, 361, 362ch, 365; leaves El Paso, 50, 267–69; marriage of, 5, 360
Durán y Chaves, Pedro I (father of Pedro II), 227n4, 357, 362ch, 391ch; estancia of, 361; origin of, 388, 412–13n194
Durán y Chaves, Pedro II (son of Pedro I), 63n112, 225, 247n10, 247n15, 360, 362ch, 391ch; and death of Governor Luis de Rosas, 225; estate of, 5, 227n4, 289; exile of, 36–37; and house in Nueva Vizcaya, 43, 211; marriage of, 388, 390; and murder of Governor Rosas, 389–90; and support of friars, 390; and trade, 33

Echagaray, Martín de, 325, 331n4
El Chilmo (Apache leader): and attack on Senecú Pueblo, 147–48; ranchería of, 112, 114
El Muerto, paraje of, 25, 142
El Paso del Río del Norte, 31, 32, 34, 40, 43, 193, 267, 318; declared to be part of New Mexico, 112, 116n3, 375; distance from La Junta de los Ríos, 210; distance from Santa Fe, 114; distance from Tabaloapa, 210; as part of Nueva Vizcaya, 375; protection of, 375; request for aid for residents of, 320. *See also* Guadalupe del Paso
El Tunque, 5, 389
encomenderos: captain of horses of, 127n8; Cristóbal de Anaya Almazán as, 381; Diego Romero as, 370; Domingo López del Ocanto as, 117n8; escuderos of, 99–100, 101n5, 130; Felix de Carvajal as, 301n15; Francisco de Anaya Almazán as, 381; Francisco de Valencia as, 22, 175; Francisco Domínguez de Mendoza as, 370; Francisco Gómez Robledo as,

20, 21; Francisco Xavier as, 300n5; Hernán Martín Serrano as, 186n3; José Telles Jirón as, 126n6, 299n2; Juan González as, 129; Juan González Bernal as, 22, 129; Juan Griego as, 299n2; López del Ocanto family as, 22, 117n8; Miguel de Hinojos as, 118n9, 299n2; and military defense, 123, 130; military duty, 90, 130; military service of, 99; number of, 99, 381; obligation of, 176; summoned to muster of, 130. *See also* Domínguez de Mendoza, Juan

encomienda: of Abó, 22, 100n3; of Acoma, 22, 100n3; of Cochiti, 126n6, 299n2, 370; conflict over revenues of, 101n5; of Cuarác, 381; end of, 22; and Governor Peñalosa y Briceño, 101n5; of Humanas, 22, 129, 299n2; of Isleta, 22, 175–76; of Jemez, 22, 117n8; of La Cienega, 381; of Nambé, 117n8; in New Mexico, 21, 22; number of, 21; of Pecos, 22, 100n3; of Picurís, 381; of Pojoaque, 300n6; of Sandia, 22, 100n3; of San Felipe, 126n6, 299n2; of Sevilleta, 303n1; shares of, 22, 129; of Shongopavi, 22, 100n3; of Taos, 22, 100n3; of Tesuque, 22, 100n3; threat of revocation, 130; title granted to José Telles Jirón, 126n6; title granted to Juan Domínguez de Mendoza, 129–31, 175–76; title of, 129–31; tributes, 99–100, 130, 131, 175, 302; of Zía, 359, 370

Enríquez, fray Diego, 121, 122–23
Enríquez, fray Nicolás, 122–23, 129n17
Enríquez de Rivera, Payo (viceroy), 315–17, 333
Escalante y Mendoza, Pedro de, 248, 249, 274
Escallada y Castillo, Juan, 86n6; as secretary of government and war, 84, 87
estancia: of Alonso García, 98n2; of Álvaro de Paredes, 380; of Andrés Hurtado, 104; at Arroyo de Tesuque, 100n3; of Cristóbal de Anaya Almazán, 359, 380, 388; of Cristóbal Baca, 104; del Alamo, 300n8; del Yunque, 100n3; of Diego de Guadalajara, 14, 303n1; of Diego de Trujillo, 399n48; of Felipe Romero, 125n3, 304n1; of Francisco de Valencia, 116n2; of Francisco Gómez Robledo, 100n3; in Isleta area, 293; of Juan Domínguez de Mendoza (Atrisco), 5, 32, 217; of Juan Estéban de Fagoaga, 359; of Juan Luis, 104; of Las Barrancas, 100n3; of Las Huertas, 399n48; number of, 4, 359–60; of Pedro Durán y Chaves, 227n4, 361; pueblos described as, 309n2; of San Antonio, 98n2, 110n2, 359, 381, 388; of San Antonio de Sevilleta, 125n3, 164, 164n2, 304n1; in Sandia area, 293, 307, 307n3; in San Ildefonso area, 305; near San Juan Pueblo, 100n3; in San Marcos area, 306; of San Nicolás, 104; in Santa Clara area, 291; in Santa Fe area, 305; of Sebastiana López de Gracia, 116n2; in Socorro area, 307; in Taos area, 100; of Tomé Domínguez, 3–4, 359; of Tomé Domínguez de Mendoza, 5, 56n17, 98n4. *See also* hacienda
expedition to Texas. *See* Jumano expedition

Fagoaga, Juan Estéban, estancia of, 359, 399n48
famine, 25, 29, 121, 133, 134–35, 135–36, 137, 375–76
Faraón Apache Indians. *See* Apaches
Fernández, Alonso, death of, 27, 166, 170
food: acorns, 184; beans, 35, 232; biscuit, 138; bison, 200, 202; cooked palm, 196; corn (maize), 35, 121, 131, 135, 172, 185, 198, 232, 319, 330; distribution in pueblos of, 123; grapes, 184; mescal, 197; for military expedition,

123, 124; milk, 137; pecans, 183; piñon nuts, 366; plum trees, 184; for refugees, 31; shortage of, 17, 25, 37, 121, 135; for soldiers, 162; stored grain, 27, 121; wheat, 135, 136, 137, 198, 319; wine, 2. *See also* famine

Flores de Sierra y Valdes, Juan (governor), arrival in New Mexico, 295

Francisca, Leonor. *See* Mendoza, Leonor Francisca

Franciscans (Order of Friars Minor): bound for New Mexico, 36; as casualties of Pueblo Revolt, 30; convene a council, 122–23, 327; and conventos closed, 121; diminished authority of, 365, 367; and election of custodians of New Mexico, 331n2; at El Paso, 112; and expedition into Texas, 188, 190–91, 193–94, 209, 254; horses acquired and used by, 121; killed by Apaches, 153, 315; and missionary work, 77n3; number of, 304–8; provide grain for military expedition, 123, 124; provide livestock and horses for military expedition, 132–38; and pueblo Indian labor, 309n1; request for more friars, 255, 291–94, 320; request for settlers, 319, 330; sharing grain, 121; and supply caravan, 2; threaten to leave New Mexico, 384–85. *See also* doctrineros

Franco, Francisco, 349, 351, 352

Fray Cristóbal (New Mexico), 30, 394

Freitas, fray Nicolás de: and council at Santo Domingo, 122–23; and mistreatment of Pueblo Indians 23, 387; origin and parents of, 129n18

Fresqui, Magdalena, 246n8, 247n9

Galisteo Pueblo: church of, 292; convento of, 135, 306; population of, 292

Gallega, Isabel, 351, 352, 353–55, 358ch

García, Alonso (father of Alonso), 236, 247n14, 344n4, 344n6, 366, 370, 395; as alcalde mayor of Sandía jurisdiction, 96; as cabildo member, 115; cattle of, 133; as courier, 125; estancia of, 98n2; ranch of, 336; as squadron leader, 335

García, Alonso (son of Alonso), 344n6; as squadron leaders in campaign, 335

García, Francisco: as military official, 120; as protector de los indios, 128n11

García de Noriega, Juana, 98n2, 344n4, 370–71, 395–96; children of, 415n226

García Holgado, Juan: as alcalde mayor of Alameda Pueblo, 116n5; as alcalde mayor of Senecú, 114

Gila Apache. *See* Apache Indians

Gil de Ávila, fray Alonso, killed by Apache Indian, 315

Gómez, Francisco, 100n3, 117n7, 118n8

Gómez, Francisco (priest), 54n1, 397n31

Gómez, fray Bartolomé, proof of lineage, 412–13n194

Gómez, fray Pedro, 236, 237, 260–61

Gómez de la Cadena, fray Francisco: and council at Santo Domingo, 123; as guardian of Santa Fe convento, 124; letter of, 125, meets with Governor Villanueva, 124

Gómez Rico, Pedro, 388; as Pedro Gómez Durán, 412–13n194

Gómez Robledo, Bartolomé, 117n7; as military official, 120, 226; as secretary of government and war, 296, 297

Gómez Robledo, Francisco, xxiii, 381; acquitted by Inquisition, 22, 101n5; appointments of, 100n2; arrested by Inquisition, 19, 99–100, 101n5, 367, 385; as cabildo member, 115, 236; as encomendero, 21, 99–100; encomiendas of, 100n2; estancias of, 100n2; house in Santa Fe, 101n2; as lieutenant captain general, 158; as squadron leader, 296

González, Domingo, 111n4; 300n7

González, Juan: as encomendero, 129;

identity of, 132n5; and revocation of encomienda, 130
González, Leonor, 349, 358ch
González, Nicolás, 359, 397n30, 399n42
González, Sebastián (grandson of Sebastián), 131n4, 220n29, as member of the Santa Fe, cabildo, 216, 217, 218n2, 223, 251
González Bernal, Antonio: as sargento mayor of New Mexico, 142; as secretary of government and war, 141, 143, 149; as secretary of the cabildo, 142n4
González Bernal, Diego, 118n9; as alcalde mayor, 296, 297
González Bernal, Juan, 221n29; as encomendero of Jumanas Pueblo, 129, 142n4; and loss of encomienda, 22, 130; origin of, 131n4
González de Apodaca, Sebastiana, estancia of, 116n2
González de la Rosa, Diego, 371, 415n226
González Lobón, Diego, 111n5, 111n6, 300n7; and military escort of wagons, 109; papers of merits and services, 111n4; service papers of, 297
González Magaña, Juan, 351, 352, 353–55, 358ch
governors of New Mexico: annual salary of, 82–83n2; commission of offices, 7; signatures and seals of, xxx. *See also* Argüello Carvajal, Francisco de; Flores de Sierra y Valdés, Juan; Guzmán y Figueroa, Luis de; Jironza Petríz de Cruzate, Domingo; López de Mendizábal, Bernardo; Manso de Contreras, Juan; Martínez de Baeza, Francisco; Miranda, Juan de; Mora Ceballos, Francisco de la; Otermín, Antonio de; Pacheco de Heredia, Alonso; Peñalosa y Briceño, Diego de; Reneros de Posada, Pedro; Samaniego y Jaca, Juan de; Treviño, Juan Francisco; Ugarte y la Concha, Hernando de; Vargas Zapata y Luján, Diego de

Gracia, Esteban de, 111n7; as witness to inspection of trade wagons, 110
Granillo, Tomás. *See* Pérez Granillo, Tomás
Gran Quivira, 184, 185, 228, 254, 256, 301, 326, 331n6
Griego, Agustín (son of Agustín), 300n13; service papers of, 297
Griego, Graciana, 138n3, 300n5
Griego, Juan (son of Juan), 138n3, 300n5; as interpreter, 78, 373; as military official, 120; papers of merits of, 80n4; service papers of, 297
Grimaldos, Leonor de, 70, 351, 352, 353–55, 358ch
Guadalajara, Diego de, 193n3; appointed as sargento mayor, 14; as encomendero, 303n1; estancia of, 303n1; leads expedition to Texas, 14–15, 204; as lieutenant governor, 301; merits and services of, 301–3
Guadalajara, Francisco de: arrives in New Mexico, 301; as hidalgo, 302–3
Guadalajara Bernardo de Quirós, Francisco, 303n1
Guadalajara y Quirós, Jacinta de, 125n3, 192–93n3, 303n1, 377
Guadalupe del Paso, 31, 116n3, 182, 193, 196, 217, 234, 237, 239, 242–45, 251, 267, 337, 339, 344n5, 365, 375; convento of, 261, 308; number of Indians of, 308; as plaza de armas, 180. *See also* El Paso del Río del Norte
Gualpi Pueblo (New Mexico), 293
Guerra, fray Antonio, 34; testimony in support of Juan Domínguez de Mendoza, 49–50, 261–66
Guerra, fray Salvador de, 409n150; allegations of violence by, 20; blamed for denunciation, 387; and council at Santo Domingo, 122–23; criticizes encomenderos, 22; as definitor habitual, 122–23; description of Juan Domínguez de Mendoza, 20; and illicit affairs, 369–70, 372, 380; as secretary of custodian, 122, 123, 124

Guevara, fray Miguel de, 379, 402n85, 409n150
Gutiérrez, José, 301n16; service papers of, 297
Guzmán y Figueroa, Luis de (governor), xxix, 8t, 144; commissions Juan Domínguez de Mendoza, 78–79, 214; term as governor, 80n2, 80–81n5

hacienda: de Atrisco, 5, 6, 30, 32, 217, 393; of cattle destroyed, 326; of Luis de Carvajal, 111n6. *See also* estancias
Halona Pueblo (New Mexico), 307
Hammond, George P., xii–xiv, xv–xvi, xixn2, xxii
Hawikuh Pueblo (New Mexico), xxix; attacked by Apaches, 90; as capital of Zuñi and Moqui province, 90; convento of, 307; friars killed at, 153
Herrera, Juan de, death of, 27, 166, 170
Hinojos, Diego de, 6, 362ch, 365
Hinojos, Hernando de, 72n5, 118n9, 299n2
Hinojos, Hernando de (the younger), 118n9; as member of the cabildo of Santa Fe, 115
Hinojos, Miguel de, 72n5; as alcalde mayor and squadron leader, 296, 297; as encomendero, 118n9, 299n2; service papers of, 297
Holguín, Cristóbal, 149n3, 247n9
Holguín, Salvador. *See* Olguín, Salvador
Holy Office of the Inquisition. *See* Inquisition
Huerta, Toribio de la: as alcalde mayor, 296, 297; as witness, 368–69
Humanas Pueblo (New Mexico), 86n3, 99n5; attack and abandonment of, 22, 129–30; attacked by Apaches, 86, 140, 141, 145; convento of, 131n3, 306; as encomienda, 22, 129, 130, 299n2; as a visita, 292
Hurtado, Andrés (father of Andrés), 104, 104n2, 105n3, 371; as encomendero, 359

Hurtado, Andrés (son of Andrés), 371; marriage of, 415n226
Hurtado, fray Nicolás, 147, 331n2, 393

Indians: Aijados (Ayjados), 15, 16, 86, 87n2, 254, 256, 326, 331n6; attack Casas Grandes, 335; attack Los Janos, 335; and baptism, 38, 42, 193, 194, 254, 317, 318, 319, 320, 321; Caddoan confederacy, 42; Cuitaos, 15; Cutoas, 145; Escanjaques, 15, 16, 86, 87n2, 276; Julimes, 41, 183, 198, 211, 239, 327, 337; liberated from captivity, 15, 276; as military escorts of wagons, 109; as prisoners, 15, 86, 338; Tonkawas, 15. *See also* Apache Indians; Jumanos Indians; Manso Indians; Pueblo Indians; Suma Indians; Tejas Indians; Ute Indians
—of Texas: Arcos Tuertos, 203; Arihuman, 184; Beán, 184; Beitonojanes, 206; Borobamos, 184; Bowmakers, 184; Caltecos, 312; Camecara, 184; Caucas, 206; Chubates Conchos, 337; Cuicuchubes, 206; Cujacos, 206; Geabori, 184; Grinder Nation, 183; Guachiciles, 312; Hunares, 337; Hutacas, 202; Joapa, 184; Joapazi, 184; Jolomes, 337; Left Handed Ones, 184; Long Member Nation, 183; Mana, 184; Obori, 184; Pecan People, 183; Peñunde People, 183; People of the Alligators, 184; People of the Dirty Water, 183; People of Fish, 183; People Who Eat, 183; Quide, 184; Quioboriqui, 184; Texaxa, 183; Tijemu, 183; Tumposogua, 184; Ugly Arrow, 183; Utaca, 184; Yutas, 184
—of the Texas expedition: Chinches, 206; Cunchucos, 206; Hedindos, 201, 202, 206, 208; Isuchos, 206; Llames, 206; Orasos, 206, 206; Quitacas, 206; Siacuchas, 206; Suajos, 206; Taremes, 206

Inés, doña, 186n3
Inquisition, 2, 17, 19, 20, 22, 100, 138n3, 275, 350, 361, 366, 367, 369, 374, 379, 380, 381, 385, 386; Alonso de Posada as commissary of, 19, 385; charges against López de Mendizábal by, 19; denunciation of Juan Domínguez de Mendoza to, 23, 24, 387; fray Estéban de Perea as commissary, 355; fray Juan Bernal as commissary, 24; fray Juan Bernal chastised by, 24; fray Juan de Paz as commissary, 387; fray Juan de Zavaleta as commissary of, 188, 193; prisoners of, 99, 101n5, 386
interpreters: Fray Nicolás López (Jumano), 254, 329; Hernán Martín Serrano (Jumano), 38, 182–83; Juan Griego (Tewa), 373; Juan Griego (Towa), 78; Roque de Madrid (Tano), 248n18; Roque de Madrid (Tewa), 248n18; Tewa Indians as, 184
Isleta Indians, conspire against Spaniards, 77n6
Isleta Jurisdiction (New Mexico), 96–97, 360
Isleta Pueblo, 5, 30, 32, 34, 35, 40, 97, 231, 262, 371, 374; catzina dances at, 18, 372–73; church and convento of, 293, 307; muster of encomenderos at, 130; number of residents of, 36; population of, 293; provision requested of, 120; siege of, 181

Jacona Pueblo, *ii*
Jaramillo, María, 226n3, 248n17
Jemez Indians: conspire against Spaniards, 77n6, 85n4; hanged, 77n6; uprising of, 83
Jemez Pueblo, *ii*, 32, 97; church and convento of, 293, 307; as encomienda, 22; food from convento of, 135; as part of Río Abajo jurisdiction, 106, 108; as plaza de armas, 133, 137; population of, 293; provision requested of, 120

Jiménez, Francisco, 118n9; as cabildo member, 115
Jirón de Tejeda, Tomás, 371, 394; marriage of, 415n226
Jironza Petríz de Cruzate, Domingo (governor), xxv, 11t, 186, 204, 209, 225, 227n7, 268, 277, 278, 319, 320, 390; account of services of, 332–43; appointment as governor, 37–38, 333–34; approves license for Domínguez de Mendoza family to leave El Paso, 50, 269; and campaign against Pueblo Indians, 337–38; commissions Juan Domínguez de Mendoza, 187–90; funds the Jumano expedition, 39, 334; funds military campaigns, 334–38; organizes campaign against Suma and Manso Indians, 44, 335; organizes campaigns against Apaches, 40, 334; organizes the Jumano expedition, 38, 190–92; reappointed as governor, 50, 337; term as governor, 186n2; and trial of Domínguez de Mendoza, 234–45, 258–60
Jumano expedition, 41–43, 193–95, 254–56; and Apache raiders, 42; journal of, 196–212; organization of, 39; reference to map of, 257; soldiers desert the, 42, 202. *See also* Texas
Jumano Indians (Texas), 14–15, 41, 48, 193, 194, 201, 324, 337; captains of, 183, 317, 324; on expedition to Texas, 200, 204, 205; and Julimes Indians, 183; as military allies, 15; request baptism, 317, 324, 325; request for missionaries, 38, 182–86, 187

kachinas. *See* catzinas
Keres (Queres) Pueblo Indians, 106, 263; as part of Río Abajo, 108

La Cañada, 27, 95n3, 111n8; attacked by Navajos, 167
La Cienega Pueblo (New Mexico), 106, 292, 381

Ladrón de Guevara, Pedro, 190; as secretary of government and war, 212, 235, 237, 244, 245
La Junta de los Ríos (Nueva Vizcaya), 38, 41, 42, 43, 184, 198, 208, 210, 254, 318, 319, 320, 325, 326, 327; claimed as part of New Mexico, 209; and Suma Indians, 40
La Salineta, 31, 32
Las Barrancas (New Mexico), paraje of, 40, 334
Las Salinas (New Mexico), 96, 97, 99n5, 116n2, 128n11, 140, 145, 215
Leyva, Pedro de: as alcalde mayor of Jumanos, 155n3, 297; as alcalde mayor of Las Salinas, 296, as cabildo member, 155n3; as lieutenant governor of New Mexico, 153, 154, 155n3, 296; origin and parents of, 155n3
Librán, Lorenzo, 71, 72n6
livestock, 30, 32, 33, 359, 375, 381, 394; cattle, 4, 32, 33, 109, 112n9, 118, 132, 133, 134, 136, 138, 163, 298, 309, 325, 326, 330, 335; ganado mayor, 138n2; ganado menor, 137, 138, 138n2; goats, 309, 335, 298; herds, 90, 132, 134, 163, 330; sheep, 4, 33, 109, 134, 136, 138n2, 147, 163, 309, 335, 366; stolen or killed by Apaches, 29, 134, 135–36, 144, 147, 163, 335
Llanos y Posada, Alonso, 58n49
López, Andrés, 15, 374. *See also* López de Gracia, Andrés; López Sambrano, Andrés
López, fray Nicolás, 34, 49, 230, 261, 266; advocates for Juan Domínguez de Mendoza as governor of New Mexico, 44, 49, 225, 240, 242; brothers of, 330; departs for La Junta, 40, 193, 318, 325; elevated to custodian of New Mexico, 48, 325, 331n2; and expedition to Texas, 194, 195, 196, 198, 201, 203, 205, 206, 207, 226n2, 254; at La Junta, 209; letter of, 251, 321–23; and map of New Mexico and Texas, 322; memorial of, 46, 254, 323–30; in Mexico City, 45; petition to the king, 47; petition to viceroy, 253–57, 317–23; promotes Jumano expedition, 38, 188; proposes missionary work in Texas, 46; returns to El Paso, 43; as supporter of Juan Domínguez de Mendoza, 32–33, 39, 46, 48; as vice-custodian of New Mexico, 38, 331n2
López de Gracia, Andrés: as alcalde mayor of El Paso, 115n2; as alférez real, 131n4; and commercial trading, 375; at El Paso, 112, 177n2, 221n30, 301n14, 344n5; house of, 405n127; origins of, 115n2
López del Castillo, Diego: as brother-in-law of Pedro de Montoya, 111n6; leads expedition to Texas, 14, 184, 332n7; as witness, 298
López del Castillo, Isabel, 246n8, 300n10
López de Mendizábal, Bernardo (governor), xvii, 8t, 9t, 93–95, 111n5, 138n3, 145, 303n1, 366, 368; and Apache slaves, 16; arrives in New Mexico, 16, 383; and catzina dances, 18, 372–73; commissions Juan Domínguez de Mendoza, 16, 96–98, 215, 250; and conflict with Franciscan friars, 17, 18, 384–85; and crypto-Judaism, 402n85; death of, 19, 95n2; describes pueblos as estancias, 309n1; family of, 95n2; grievance against, 111n4; and the Inquisition, 19, 80n4, 367, 385; livestock and property of, 366; papers of merits and services of New Mexico soldiers in possession of, 111n4, 297, 298n1; restores Anaya Almazán encomiendas, 384; and revocation of encomiendas, 126n6; term as governor, 95n2

López de Ocanto, Domingo: as cabildo member, 115; as encomendero, 117n8
López de Ocanto, Juan, origin and marriage of, 117n8
López de Villafuerte, Juana, 81n6, 117n6, 220n26, 220n28, 380
López Mederos, Catalina, 5, 98n3, 138n8, 371; children of, 5, 371–72, 406n141
López Millán, María, 116n2, 176–77n2, 373
López Olguín, Juan, 246n8, 247n9
López Paredes (Pareja), Francisco, 81n6
López Sambrano, Andrés, 127n10; as alcalde mayor, 296, 297; as member of the cabildo of Santa Fe, 115; as military official, 120; origins of, 117n6
López Sambrano, Diego, 247n12, 393; testimony of, 242–43, 245, 314n3; as witness, 186
Los Janos (Nueva Vizcaya), 44; mission at, 335
Lucero de Godoy, Antonio, 247n14; testimony of, 243, 245
Lucero de Godoy, Diego, 6, 192n3, 196, 208, 209, 210, 212, 243, 247n14, 362ch, 365, 395; birth of, 401n78; deserts El Paso, 234–35, 237, 243, 244; and Jumano expedition, 39, 40, 192; and land at Taos, 394; travels to Mexico City, 45
Lucero de Godoy, Francisca Rosa, 362ch, 365
Lucero de Godoy, Juan, xxxi, 247n14; as alcalde mayor of Senecú, 147; and convento of Santo Domingo, 122; marriage of, 93n4; as secretary of government and war, 92, 99, 103, 109, 115, 119, 120, 122, 186, 298, 387
Lucero de Godoy, Pedro, 117n8, 192n3, 297, 300n6, 303n1, 383; family of, 126n7; marriage of 126n7; as military official, 120
Luis, Juan. See Luján, Juan Luis
Luján, Juan, 296, 297

Luján, Juan Luis, 105n4, 246n8, 247n9, 300n10; service papers of, 297; testimony of, 241, 245
Luján, Matías, 236, 246n6
Luján Domínguez, Antonia, 394
Luna, Diego de, 225, 390; family of, 226n3, 228n17; testimony of, 244, 245

Macha, Francisco, seeks aid of governor, 78
Madrid, Francisco de (father of Francisco), 127n10
Madrid, Francisco de (son of Francisco), 248n18; as alcalde ordinario of Santa Fe, 127n8; as commander of military expedition, 138; family of 127n8; as military official, 120; as squadron leader, 296
Madrid, José, 248n20; testimony of, 244, 245
Madrid, Lorenzo, 248n20, 394; as encomendero, 22n26; family of, 127n10, 220n26; as cabildo member, 216, 217, 218n2, 223, 251; as military official, 120
Madrid, Roque de, 248n18, 248n20; and Apache campaign, 336; testimony of, 244, 245
Manos, Juan (governor). *See* Manso de Contreras, Juan (governor)
Manso de Contreras, Juan (governor), xxx, 8t, 16, 145, 372, 382, 383, 403n86; as alguacíl mayor of the Inquisition, 368; commissions Juan Domínguez de Mendoza, 90–92, 215; grants power of attorney, 370; imprisoned, 384; and inspection of, Zuñi, 383; revokes encomiendas, 383; as supply caravan contractor, 107, 108n2; term as governor, 92n3; and transport of Inquisition prisoners, 367
Manso Indians, 31, 36, 88n6; as allies 33; hanged, 87, 375; military campaign against, 335, 344n5; rancherías of, 112, 114, 116n4, 335; and Suma

Indians, 40; threaten Franciscan friars, 87; uprising of, 44, 112, 114 116n4

Márquez, Margarita, 377; children of, 406n141

Márquez, Pedro, 62n108, 227n6

Martín, Domingo, 111n8; as witness to inspection of trade wagons, 110

Martín Barba, Alonso, 117n8

Martínez de Baeza, Francisco (governor), 3, 4, 77n4, 250, 301, 357

Martínez Espadero, Alonso, 378

Martínez Espadero, Gonzalo, 407n143

Martín Serrano, Hernán (father of Hernán), 95n3, 186n3

Martín Serrano, Hernán (son of Hernán): as encomendero, 186n3; and expedition to Texas, 14, 325, 332n7; as interpreter, 38, 182–83, 186; origins and parents of, 186n3; testimony of, 243, 245; as witness, 196, 208, 209, 210, 212

Martín Serrano, Luis: death of, 95n3; leads military expedition, 16, 94; as squadron leader, 296

Martín Serrano, Miguel, 371, 415n226

Martín Serrano, Pedro, 371, 415n226

Matanassa, Indians of, 145

Mateo, Juan, 349, 355, 357, 358ch

media anata, 75, 77n7, 140, 142n3, 154, 159

Medrano Messía, Juan Rodríguez de (governor), 9–10t, 226; and attack on Humanas Pueblo, 22; and certification of expedition, 141; and certification of services of Juan Domínguez de Mendoza, 149–50; commissions Juan Domínguez de Mendoza, 139–41, 142–43, 145, 216, 250; grants title of encomienda of Juan Domínguez de Mendoza, 129–31, 250; organizes expedition against Apaches, 137–38; and provisions for military expedition, 133–34, 135–37; term as governor, 131n2

Meju, Pedro, as governor of Pecos Pueblo, 78, 79

Méndez de Sotomayor, Beatriz, 378; children of, 408n147

Mendoza, Francisco de, 54n3, 70, 351, 352, 353–55, 358ch

Mendoza, Leonor Francisca, 1, 70, 349, 350, 351, 352, 353–55, 358ch

military: aid, 316, 376; alliance with Ute Indians, 169; armor, 90; battle at Casas Grandes, 335–36; battle of Cerro Hueco, 336; battle with Cuitaos Indians, 15, 145; battle with Ecanjaques and Aijados, 15, 86, 276; battle at the Peñol de los Janos, 335; battle with Pueblo Indians, 338; campaign against the Faraones Apache, 157; campaign against Pueblo Indians, 181, 262–66, 287; campaign against the Salineros Apache, 145; campaigns and war against Navajo Indians, 27, 144, 145, 153–54, 160, 162, 165–67, 168–70, 171–72, 173–74, 175–76, 177–78; campaigns and wars against the Apache, 22, 25, 27, 40, 74, 78–79, 88–89, 90, 92, 94, 137–38, 139–40, 141, 144–45, 147–48, 157, 162, 163–64, 228, 302, 312–13, 334, 336; casualties, 28; company of Spanish infantry, 140; council of war, 118–19; deserters, 42, 202; enlisting of soldiers, 33, 343n2; escort for friars, 77n4; expedition against the Cutoas, 145; expedition to El Paso, 112; expedition to Sierra Blanca, 86, 276; guard and escort for friars, 188; insignia, 74, 94, 98, 106, 141, 143, 146, 147, 148, 152, 156, 158, 161, 166, 172, 180, 189; instructions for campaign, 168–70, 173–74, 190–92; mounted harquebusiers, 16, 90, 94, 160, 165, 171; muster of encomenderos, 130; muster of soldiers, 22, 27, 32, 33, 130, 138, 164, 165, 173, 179, 190, 317; patrol to Acoma, 23; presidio at El Paso, 33, 234, 243, 244, 343n2; protection of El Paso, 375; provision shortage, 119, 133; ranks, 7, 8–13t; royal standard, 7, 8t, 70, 71, 73, 84, 142, 148, 152, 182, 214, 226, 234, 235, 237, 239, 241, 302; service in New Mexico, 6–7, 303, 395; soldiers recruited in Mexico City, 28, 316; soldiers wounded by Navajo, 133; Spanish and Indian troops, 14, 16, 25, 27, 28, 34, 90, 94, 97, 133, 137, 138, 140, 153, 157, 160, 163, 164, 165, 171, 173, 177, 189, 190, 191, 336, 337. *See also* plaza de armas; weapons

Miranda, fray Pedro de, killed at Taos, 295

Miranda, Juan de (governor), 10–11t; arrest and imprisonment of, 26; arrives in New Mexico, 25–26; attacked by Apaches, 25, 142, 148; commissions Baltasar Domínguez de Mendoza, 151–52, 156–57; commissions Juan Domínguez de Mendoza, 144–46, 153–55, 157–59, 216, 250; origin and parents of, 146–47n2; seeks passage to New Spain, 147n2; and sentence of death of Juan Domínguez de Mendoza, 241; terms as governor, 92n3, 146n2

Mishongnovi Pueblo (New Mexico), convento of, 307

Mizquía, Lázaro: as cabildo member, 45, 244; deserts El Paso, 234–37, 241, 244; origins of, 245n2

Montoya, Antonio, 247n15, 248n16; testimony of, 243, 245

Montoya, Diego, 247n15, 248n16; testimony of, 243, 245

Montoya, Felipe de, 380, 410n155

Montoya, Pedro de, 111n5, 111n6; and military escort of wagons, 109

Moqui, 90, 227, 296, 297, 298

Mora Ceballos, Francisco de la (governor), 117n8

Moreno de Lara, Ana, 105n3; accuses Juan Domínguez de Mendoza, 19

mountain ranges: of Acoma, 178; of Navajo, 26, 153, 160, 165, 167, 168, 175, 177; near Zía, 165; Piedra Lumbre, 166, 167n4, 170; Sierra Blanca, 86; Sierra del Diablo, 326; Sierra de los Ladrones, 164; Sierra de Magdalena, 164, 313; Sierra Florida, 335. *See also* Casa Fuerte; Cordilleras; Rio Grande

Moxainavi Pueblo (New Mexico), as a visita, 293

Nambé Pueblo (New Mexico), *ii*, 134, 136, 291, 360

Navajo Indians (Apache de Navajo), 26–28; Acoma Pueblo attacked by, 28; ask for peace, 87; captives of, 28, 162, 165, 167, 168, 174, 176, 177; captured by Spaniards, 28, 87, 145, 162, 167, 169, 172, 175; of Casa Fuerte, 133, 138n5, 144, 147n4, 153, 165; churches attacked by, 153, 177; fields of corn and milpas, 28, 153, 162, 165, 167, 168, 172, 173, 175, 177; geographic region of, 26, 162, 167n2; Jemez Pueblo attacked by, 87; kill people, 171, 177; La Cañada attacked by, 166; of Matanassa, 144; mountain range of, 88n4, 162; of Río Grande, 144, 147n4, 153; soldiers and horses wounded by, 133; steal horses and livestock, 165, 169, 171; and stolen church objects, 165, 168; Villa de Santa Fe attacked by, 27; and war against, 87, 89n2, 144, 145, 153, 160, 162, 165–67, 168–70, 171–72, 173–74. *See also* Casa Fuerte

New Mexico: census of, 73; commerce in, 2, 4; and conditions at El Paso, 254, 323; condition of refugees of, 37; description of, 298, 315; map of, *ii*, 2, 68, 298, 322; mutiny in, 84, 85n5, 302; and number of residents that left El Paso, 47; Otermín's attempted reconquest of, 179–80; and plague of locusts, 121; political rivalry in, xxi, 5, 17, 18, 366, 367, 372–74, 382; population of, 4, 29, 32; and proposed relocation of resident to Texas, 46–47; referred to as Tierra Nueva, 74, 77n5; royal aid requested for, 315–17; settlers brought to, 3, 73, 74, 91; supply caravan in, 107–8; territory of Acamache, 302. *See also* famine

Nieto, José, 116n2; as alcalde mayor of Las Salinas, 128n11; family of, 127–28n11; as military official, 120

Noriega, Miguel de, 95, 98, 96n4, 296, 297, 374

Nueces River. *See* rivers

Nueva Vizcaya, place names of: Carretas, 327; Chihuahua, 37, 43, 363, 377, 392, 395; Cusihuiriachic, 377, 378; El Gallego, 211; El Ojuela, 211; El Portesuelo, 211; El Tule, 211; La Ranchería, 212; Las Encinillas, 210, 211; Los Médanos, 212; Los Patos, 211; Los Suaces, 43, 211, 377, 392, 407n142; Ojo Caliente, 211; Papigochi, 377; San Antonio de Juilmes, 211; Santa Brigida, 211; Santa Catalina, 211; Santa Juana, 211; Santa Mónica, 211; Santa Teresa, 211; Tabaloapa, 210, 211, 392; Valle de Allende, 378; Valle de San Bartolomé, 377, 378. *See also* Casas Grandes; Chihuahua; La Junta de los Ríos; Los Janos; Parral, San José del; Peñol of Los Janos

Núñez de León, Juan, 402n85; and auto de fe, 95n2

Olguín, Salvador, 149n3, 246n8; leads campaign against Apache, 40, 147–48, 334; testimony of, 242, 245; wounded by Apaches, 148

Onorato, 75, 154, 159

Oraibi Pueblo (New Mexico): church and convento of, 293, 307; population of, 293

Ortega, Francisco de, 98n3, 300n12, 359; service papers of, 297

Ortega, Tiburcio de, 300n12

Ortiz, Antonia, 127n10, 248n20

Ortiz, Nicolás, and murder of Governor Rosas, 389–90

Ortiz de Paredes y Aguirre, Ignacia, 362ch, 363; children of, 365

Otermín, Antonio de (governor), 11t, 39, 46, 49, 139n2, 232, 327; and attack on Santa Fe by Navajo Indians, 27; commissions and certification of services of Juan Domínguez de Mendoza, 164–67, 171–72, 177–78, 179–80, 216, 231, 250, 259; and expiration of term as governor, 38; instructions for military campaigns, 168–70, 173–74; issues title of encomienda, 175–76; organizes expedition against Navajo Indians, 27, 28, 168–69, 173–74; and Pueblo Indian Revolt, 30–32; and restoration of New Mexico, 33–36, 260, 262, 264, 376; term as governor, 167n2; and trade with Apaches, 265

Pacheco de Heredia, Alonso (governor), xxvii, xxviii, 8t, 72n3, 74, 77n4, 85n5, 389; and account of pueblo churches and conventos, 295n1; commissions Juan Domínguez de Mendoza, 70–71, 214; and expedition to Zuñi, 76n3; term as governor, 71n2

Pardiñas Villar de Franco, Bernardino Antonio, 278, 279n2, 283, 284, 286

Paredes, Álvaro de, 381, 410n153; baptism of, 409n149; birth and parents of, 378; child of, 380; death of, 380; estancia of, 380; family of, 378–79; marriage of, 4, 379, 409n150

Paredes, Estéban de: children of, 408–9n149; marriage of, 408n147

Paredes, Francisca de: marriage and children of, 408–9n149

Paredes, fray José, 359, 379, 408n149, 409n150
Paredes, María de, 380; as María Domínguez, 410n155
Paredes Espadero, Álvaro, 378; children of, 408n147; private letters of, 408n146; record of passage, 407–8n143
París, Benito, 1, 70, 349, 350, 351, 352, 358ch
Parral, San Jose del (Nueva Vizcaya), 4, 17, 43, 46, 228, 317, 318, 320, 326, 339, 367, 369, 370, 387; trade wagons to, 109–10
Paz, fray Juan de, 23, 387
Pecos Pueblo, ii; church of, 292; convento of, 306; as encomienda, 22; food from convento of, 135, 137; as plaza de armas, 157, 159; population of, 292; and provisions for military campaign, 133; threatened by Del Acho Apache, 78–79; and trade with Faraon Apache, 159n2
Pedraza, Isabel de, 93n4, 125n3, 192n3, 304n1
Peñalosa y Briceño, Diego de (governor), ii, xxiv, xxxi, 9t, 21, 70n3, 145, 250, 360; appoints Juan Domínguez de Mendoza as escuderos, 99–100; arrives in New Mexico, 385; and Cerro de Azul, 228; commission Juan Domínguez de Mendoza, 102–3, 215; commissions Tomé Domínguez de Mendoza, 374; and confiscated property, 366; and conflict over encomienda revenues, 101n5; decree of, 104; dispatches of, 367; and inspection of pueblos, 102; and lands of the east, 227; and Teguayo, 228; term as governor, 100n2
Peñol de Acoma (New Mexico), 48, 171, 222
Peñol de Caquima (New Mexico), 73, 76n4
Peñol of Los Janos (Nueva Vizcaya), 43; battle at, 335

Peralta, Regina de, rescued from captivity, 87, 88n5
Perea, fray Estéban: and royal provision, 367; and Tomé Domínguez, 2, 103n2, 355
Pérez de Bustillo, Beatriz, 73n5, 299n2
Pérez de Bustillo, Simón, 71, 72n5
Pérez Granillo, Alonso, as alcalde mayor, 296, 297
Pérez Granillo, Francisco, 125n5; as alcalde mayor, 296
Pérez Granillo, Tomás, 366, 403n86
Pérez Romero, Diego. *See* Romero, Diego
Picurís Indians, 74, 77n6; uprising of, 83
Picurís Pueblo (New Mexico), 74, 77n6; attacked by Del Acho Apache, 78; church and convento of, 294, 305; encomienda, 381; food from convento of, 135; population of, 294
Piedra Alumbre, 27, 166, 177
Piro Indians, 29, 30, 32, 34, 36, 99, 261, 303n1, 314n3; as allies, 33
Plasencia, fray Juan de, 122
plaza de armas: Abó Pueblo as, 140; Guadalupe del Paso as, 180; Jemez Pueblo as, 133, 137, 138; Pecos Pueblo as, 157, 159; ranch of Alonso García as, 336; San Juan Pueblo as, 90, 155; Socorro Pueblo as, 164; Taos as, 178; Zía Pueblo as, 27, 28, 160, 165, 168, 171, 173, 177
Portocarrero Laso de la Vega, Melchor. *See* Conde de Monclova
Posada, fray Alonso de, 374; arrival in New Mexico, 19, 385; commissions Juan Manso, 368, 369; complaint against, 367; and conflict over encomienda revenues, 101n5; dispatches of, 366; and Inquisition, 101n5; and number of years in New Mexico, 328; origin and parents of, 58n49; report on expeditions to Texas, 15, 16, 46, 328
presidio, 46, 179, 181, 182, 187, 276, 311; of Cerro Gordo, 15n3; at El Paso,

33, 212, 234, 238, 239, 243, 244, 339, 343n2, 394; at Santa Fe, 29, 363, 395; of Sinaloa, 75n2; in Texas, 47, 229
Puaray Pueblo (New Mexico), 35, 231, 232, 266, 293, 296n2
Pueblo Indian Revolt, 29–31, 227n6; reported cause of, 264–65
Pueblo Indians: attacked by Apaches, 78, 141, 144, 147, 163; attacked by Navajos, 153; barter with Apaches prohibited, 265; battle with Spanish and Indian troops, 337–38; casualties of, 30, 233; as confederates with Apaches, 144–45, 313, 314n3; and dances of (see Catzinas); and deaths by famine, 135, 137; an division of labor, 309n1; killed by Apache, 87, 90, 93, 119, 129–31, 132; as military troops, 6, 14, 16, 25, 27, 28, 163 165, 189, 332; number of, 291–94; population of, 29, 291–94, 295n1; rescue of, 25, 27, 86, 87, 174; regarded as apostate, 40, 264, 287, 337–38; request Spaniards for aid, 78; in revolt, 73, 74, 181; sustained by Franciscan friars, 134–35; taken captive by Apache, 22, 25, 87; taken as captives by Navajos, 165

Quarai (Quarac) Pueblo, 99n5, 116n2, 177. See also Cuarac
Quintana, Luis de, 161, 226
Quirós, fray Cristóbal de, 77n4
Quivira, 86, 381. See also Jumanas Pueblo

Rael de Aguilar, Alonso: deserts El Paso, 234–44; origins and parents of, 246n4; as secretary of government and war, 269
Rael de Aguilar, Juan, 246n3
Rael de Aguilar, Juliana, 246n3
Ramírez, fray Juan: as Franciscan custos, 16–17; letter to López de Mendizábal, 17
Ramírez de Mendoza, Damiana, 1, 369–70, 381, 395; baptism of, 356, 358ch, 359, 397n31; child of, 380; marriage of, 4, 379, 409n150
Ramírez de Mendoza, Elena. See Cruz, Elena de la
Ramírez de Mendoza, Leonor, 1, 70n3, 81n6, 246n3, 386, 395; baptism of, 356, 358ch, 359, 398n32; children of, 386, 388; death of, 388; dowry of, 381
Ramírez de Salazar, Francisca, 221n32
Ramírez de Salazar, Francisco, 301n14, 344n5; requests military aid, 335; service papers of, 297
Ramírez de Salazar, Juan, 389
Real de San Lorenzo (New Mexico), 32, 34, 40, 196, 238, 377
Remoludo, Diego de, 353, 354, 355
Reneros de Posada, Pedro (governor), 48–49, 341
Riguerio, Gerónimo, 355; marriage of, 397n24
Río Abajo (New Mexico), 30, 31, 35, 145, 215; description of jurisdiction of, 97, 106; inspection of the pueblos of, 81
rivers: Pecos River (Tejas), 41, 42; Río de la Ascención del Señor (Tejas), 207; as Río de las Nueces, 14, 15, 16, 41, 46, 47, 183, 191, 203, 204, 229; Río de las Nuecas (Tejas), 41, 46, 183, 191, 203, 204, 229; Río de las Nuecas as Río de San Pedro (Tejas), 204, 205; Río de las Perlas (Tejas), 41, 204, 302; Río del Norte (New Mexico), 183, 193, 195, 197, 198, 200, 209, 210, 212, 318; Río de los Conchos (see Conchos River); Río de San Agustín de las Cuevas (Tejas), 207; Río de San Isidro Labrador (Tejas), 205; Rio Grande (New Mexico), 38, 40, 41, 42, 144, 147n4, 153, 165, 168, 175, 177; Río Sacramento (Nueva Vizcaya), 37, 43, 210, 211; Río Salado (Tejas), 41, 200, 204, 208; Río San Clemente, 43, 194, 206, 207, 208; San Juan River, 26, 27, 88n4, 147n3, 167n3

Robledo, Ana, 100n3, 117n7
Rodríguez, Alonso: accompanies Governor López de Mendizábal, 383; arrest of, 382; flees New Mexico, 383; as guard, 384
Rodríguez Cubero, Pedro (governor), 54, 159n2, 278; and certification of services of Juan Domínguez de Mendoza, the younger, 286–87
Rodríguez de Medrano Messía, Juan. See Medrano Messía, Juan (governor)
Rodríguez de Zuballe, Juan Severino de, 220n27; as cabildo member, 216, 217, 223, 251
Rodríguez Varela, Alonso, 71, 72n5
Romero, Bartolomé I (father of Bartolomé II), 125n3
Romero, Bartolomé II (father of Bartolomé III), 125n5
Romero, Bartolomé III (son of Bartolomé II): as alcalde of Santa Fe, 125n5; as sargento mayor of New Mexico, 119, 120
Romero, Diego, 125n3, 304n1; arrest by Inquisition, 19, 101n5, 367, 374, 385; as encomendero, 370; marriage of, 126n7
Romero, Felipe, 125n5, 192n3, 304n1, 377; estancia of, 125n2, 304n1; family of, 125n3; and house raided by Apache, 118; and Jumano expedition, 40, 192; and pueblo of Sevilleta, 120
Romero, Francisco, 354
Romero, Luisa, marriage of, 93n4, 126n7
Romero, Matías, 93n4, 125n3, 192n3, 221n32, 304n1
Romero de Pedraza, Francisco, 221n32; as notary of cabildo, 217, 218n2, 251
Rosas, Luis de (governor), 85n5, 131n4, 301; murder of, 17, 77n4, 127n8, 225, 389–90
Rueda, Juana de, 98n2, 344n4, 395; children of, 370; and illicit affair, 369, 379; marriage of, 365, 398n32

Ruiz Cabal, Gerónimo, 270, 271, 272, 273, 343

Sabaleta, fray Juan de. See Zavaleta, fray Juan de
Sabeata, Juan: accompanies friars to La Junta, 41, 193; comes to El Paso, 38, 182, 187; and expedition into Texas, 41, 193–95, 196, 201, 202, 204, 243; remains behind in Texas, 206; statement of, 182–86
Salas, Antonio de: as alcalde mayor, 296, 297; as encomendero, 300n6; service papers of, 297
Salas y Orozco Trujillo, Bernardina, 105n2, 105n3, 371
Salazar, fray Francisco de: and council at Santo Domingo, 122; origin and parents of, 128n16
Salinas jurisdiction. See Las Salinas
Samaniego y Jaca, Juan de (governor), xxviii, xxix, 8t, 85n3, 145; accompanied by Juan Domínguez de Mendoza, 86; and charges against Juan Domínguez de Mendoza, 241; commissions and certification of services of Juan Domínguez de Mendoza, 83–84, 86–87, 215, 249; organizes expedition to Texas, 14, 15, 302; origins and parents, 85n2; and term as governor, 84–85n2
San Antonio, fray Salvador de, 331n2
Sánchez de Iñigo, Jacinto, 235–37, 244, 246n5
San Cristóbal Pueblo (New Mexico), 292
Sandia jurisdiction (New Mexico), 96–97, 359
Sandia Pueblo (New Mexico), ii, 3–4, 5, 30, 35, 231, 232, 262, 266, 369, 387, 395; church of, 293, 386; convento of, 307, 370; as encomienda, 22; food from convento of, 135, 409n150; population of, 293
Sandoval Cerda Silva y Mendoza, Gaspar (Viceroy of New Spain), 340, 341;

and recommendation of Baltasar Domínguez de Mendoza, 284; and travel license for Juan Domínguez de Mendoza, 273–75
San Felipe Indians, 77n6
San Felipe Pueblo (New Mexico), *ii*, 35, 126, 292, 361, 381, 388, 412n191
San Francisco, fray García de, 209
San Ildefonso Pueblo (New Mexico), *ii*, 134, 136, 291, 360
San Juan Pueblo, as plaza de armas, 91, 100n3, 134, 136, 155, 291
San Lázaro Pueblo (New Mexico), 292
San Lorenzo. *See* Real de San Lorenzo
San Marcos Pueblo (New Mexico), 292, 306, 360
San Pedro Pueblo (New Mexico), 294
Santa Ana Pueblo (New Mexico), 293, 381
Santa Clara Pueblo (New Mexico), 291
Santa Fe, Villa de (New Mexico), *ii*, 30, 31, 217, 223 268, 360, 388; alcalde ordinario of, 9t; attacked by Navajo Indians, 27, 165, 171; church and convento of, 291, 305; Indian population of, 291; muster of encomenderos at, 130; population of, 4; royal fiesta celebrated in, 25, 149; war council at, 90. *See also* cabildo of Santa Fe
Santa Hermandad, 109, 111n3, 303, 386, 387
Santander, fray Diego de, 23, 387
Santo Domingo Indians, and famine, 121
Santo Domingo Pueblo (New Mexico), 17, 35, 227n6; church of, 292; convento of, 120, 121, 122, 123, 128n13, 135, 292, 306, 385, 390; food from convento of, 135; meeting of friars at, 122–23; population of, 292; as seat of Franciscan custodian, 120
Sayuque, *ii*
Scholes, France V.: and analysis of questionable documents, xxxiin1; career of, xvi; consults physicians on optics of Domínguez de Mendoza brothers, 223n2; and the Coronado Historical Series, xiv–xvi; death of, xvi; and new translation of state of churches and conventos, 294n1; researches in Madrid, xv
Sedillo, Pedro. *See* Cedillo Rico de Rojas, Pedro
Senecú del Paso (New Mexico), 44
Senecú Pueblo (New Mexico), 4, 34, 81, 231, 383; attacked by Apaches, 136, 147, 163; convento of, 134; food from convento of, 135, 295, 307; as part of Río Abajo jurisdiction, 97, 106; as place of inspection of wagons, 109–10; provision requested of, 120; rebellion of, 313, 314n3
Serna, Diego de la, as notary, 118n8
Serna, Felipe de la, testimony of, 239–41, 245, 246n7
service records of Juan Domínguez de Mendoza, 7, 52; list of, xxiii–xxvt; question of forgeries, xxvii–xxxii, 72n3, 75n3, 80n5, 83n3, 85n3, 93n3, 150n2, 218n2, 218nn3–4, 219nn10–11, 219n17; translations of, xxii
Sevilleta Pueblo (New Mexico): as encomienda, 303n1; as place of safety, 120; as a visita, 293
Shongopavi Pueblo (Hopi territory): church and convento of, 293, 308; as encomienda, 22, 100n3; population of, 293
Sierra Osorio, Lope de, 328, 332n10
Siete Ríos Apache. *See* Apache Indians
slave trafficking, 17, 110
Socorro Pueblo (New Mexico), 3, 30, 40; attacked by Apache, 136, 163; church of, 293; convento of, 307; food from convento of, 135; as place of safety, 120; as plaza de armas, 164; population of, 293; provision requested of, 120; rebellion of, 313, 314n3
Sonora, 33, 44, 53, 234, 278, 279–81, 323, 336, 339, 363
Suazo, María de, 247n12, 393

Suma Indians, 36, 40, 42, 197, 203, 210, 318, 337; and chapel of Las Llagas, 308; at La Junta, 40; ranchería of, 196, 197; at Santa María Magdalena, 261, 266; uprising of, 43
supply train. *See* caravan
Suria y Losano, Tomás, 364ch, 401n67

Tabirá Pueblo (New Mexico), 292
Tajique Pueblo, 99n5, 292, 306
Talabán, fray Juan: and council at Santo Domingo, 122–23; as custodian of Franciscans in New Mexico, 120, 121, 122, 123, 124, 132, 137; death of, 128n13; as ecclesiastical judge, 121, 122, 123, 124, 132, 138; origin and parents of, 128n13; and provision for military campaign, 134–35; summons friars to Santo Domingo, 122
Taos Pueblo (New Mexico), 28, 265, 295n1; attacked by Apaches del Acho, 78; and barter with Apache, 265; church and convento of, 294, 305; as encomienda, 22; food from convento of, 135; as plaza de armas, 178; population of, 294; revolt of, 294; Ute Indians at, 169
Teguayo, kingdom of, 228
Tejas Indians, 14, 38, 48, 184, 194, 196; Caddoan confederacy of, 42; and María de Ágreda, 326; receive baptism, 326; tribes of, 206
Telles Jirón, José: arrives in New Mexico, 126n6; as cabildo member, 216, 217, 223; and encomienda granted and revoked, 126n6; ordered to move to the pueblo of Socorro, 120; origins of, 126n6; service papers of, 297
Tesuque Pueblo, 22, 291
Tetela, mines of, 271
Tewa Pueblo Indians, in Texas, 184
Texas: expedition of 1651 into, 86, 89n3, 381; expedition of 1654 into, 14, 86, 332n7; expedition of 1683 into, 41–43, 190–92, 193–95, 196–212; French in, 46, 49; Indians of, 183–84, 206; kingdom of, 184, 228, 254, 256; legal possession of, 327; map of, 46, 65n145, 228, 256–57, 322, 323, 328; resettling New Mexico resident in, 47, 324. *See also* rivers
—place names of: Corpus Christi, 208; El Arcángel de San Miguel, 203, 204; El Santo Ángel de la Guarda, 204; Espíritu Santo, 207; Horsehead Crossing Ford, 41; La Conversión de San Pablo, 202; La Junta de los Ríos, 198, 208; La Navidad en las Cruces, 198; La Purísima Concepción, 197; Los Desamparados, 42, 205; Los Reyes, 199; Nuestra Señora de Atocha, 198; Nuestra Señora de Belén, 198; Nuestra Señora de la Piedad, 207; Nuestra Señora de la Soledad, 197; Nuestra Señora del Buen Suceso, 197; Nuestra Señora de los Remedios, 198; Nuestra Señora del Pilar, 197; Nuestra Señora del Pilar de Zaragoza, 196; Nuestra Señora del Pópulo, 198; Nuestra Señora del Rosario, 197; Nuestra Señora del Tránsito, 197; Nuestro Padre San Francisco, 199; San Antonio, 199; San Atanasio, 207; San Bartolomé, 196; San Bernardina de Sena, 200; San Clemente, 42; San Cristóbal, 201; San Diego, 204; San Francisco Xavier, 299; San Ignacio, 202, 208; San Ignacio de Loyola, 201; San Juan de Dios, 201, 208; San Juan del Río, 200; San Jerónimo, 208; San Lázaro, 207; San Lorenzo, 199; San Marcos, 203; San Onofre, 202; San Pablo, 205; San Pantaleón, 208; San Pedro de Alcantará, 200; San Roque, 205; San Sebastián, 205; Santa Cruz, 207; Santiago, 198; Santísima Trinidad, 196; Santo Domingo, 201; Santo Tomás de Villanueva, 208; San Vicente, 204
Tiwa Pueblo Indians, 5, 34, 35, 99n5

Tlajomulco, corregimiento of, 279–80, 282
Tompiro Pueblo Indians, 99n5, 129
Treviño, Juan Francisco (governor), 11t, 163; commissions and certifies services of Juan Domínguez de Mendoza, 160–62, 216, 250; expedition against Apaches organized by, 27, 375; term as governor, 163n2
Trujillo, Diego de, 105n2, 105n3, 359; as alcalde mayor, 296, 297; estancia of, 399n48
Trujillo, fray José, 135, 138
Tumpatio, Luis, 242, 247n13. *See also* Tupatu, Luis
Tunque. *See* El Tunque
Tupatu, Lorenzo, 242, 247n13
Tupatu, Luis. *See* Tumpatio, Luis

Ugarte y la Concha, Hernando de (governor), xxx, 8t, 77n6, 126n6; arrives in New Mexico, 80n2; certifies services of Juan Domínguez de Mendoza, 88–89, 249; commissions Juan Domínguez de Mendoza, 81–83, 214; an conspiracy of Apache and Pueblo Indians, 144–45; and inspection of Río Abajo pueblos, 81–82; organizes expedition to Texas, 14; term as governor, 82n2
Ute Indians, 169; alliance with Spaniards, 27; homeland of, 26

Valencia, Francisco de, 155n3; cattle of, 133; death of, 175–76; as encomendero, 22, 175; estancia of, 116n2, 176n2, 372, 373; as lieutenant captain of Río Abajo, 176n2; origin and marriage of, 176n2
Varela, Alonso (father of Alonso), 72n5
Varela, Alonso (son of Alonso), 72n5; as lieutenant governor, 117n8. *See also* Rodríguez Varela, Alonso
Varela, Apolonia, 131n4, 221n29
Varela, Teresa, 98n2, 247n14, 344n4, 344n6, 370

Varela de Losada, Diego, 247n11; testimony of, 242, 245
Vargas, fray Francisco de, 331n2
Vargas Zapata y Luján, Diego de (governor), 278, 341; appointed as governor of New Mexico, 51, 342; and Faraon Apache, 159n2; sued by cabildo of Santa Fe, 53–54
Velásquez, Ana, 393; as Ana Velasco, 414n211
Velásquez de la Cadena, Pedro, 275, 334
Vélez de Escalante, fray Silvestre, 212n1
Vera, María de, 247n15, 248n16
Villanueva, Fernando de (governor), 9t, 10t, 26, 122, 123, 124, 370, 386, 387; absent from New Mexico, 145; and charges against Juan Domínguez de Mendoza, 241; commissions Juan Domínguez de Mendoza, 105–7, 107–8, 109–10, 112–15, 113, 145, 189, 215, 226, 250; orders council of war, 118–19; request provisions from conventos, 119–20; residencia of, 370; services of, 310–14; term as governor, 107n2, 312
Villar, fray Nicolás, 123; origin of, 129n19
Villasante, Lucas de, 366, 402–3n86
Villegas Rivera, Catalina de, 401n66
Vitoria Carvajal, Juan, 111n6, 301n15
Vitoria de Carvajal, Catalina, 377, 406n137; children of, 406–7n142
Vitoria de Carvajal, María, 377, 406n137

weapons: bow and arrow, 90, 109, 153, 157, 160, 163, 169, 171; cannon balls, 190; carbine, 34; daggers, 316; harquebus, 90, 243, 313, 316; powder and munitions, 112, 170, 190; swords, 316

Xavier, Francisco, 226, 264; arrival in New Mexico, 138n3; as campaign leader, 178; as encomendero, 300n5; and notice of attack on Acoma, 132; as reason for Pueblo Indian revolt, 265; as secretary of government and war,

28, 34, 107, 108, 146, 148, 152, 155, 157, 166, 167, 170, 172, 174, 176, 180; service papers of, 297

Xongopauy Pueblo. *See* Shongopavi Pueblo

Ybargaray, fray Antonio de, 122; origin and parents of, 128n15

Yojeda, María de los Ángeles, 128n13

Zaguato, *ii*

Zamora, Catalina de, 93n4, 126n7

Zamora, Josefa de, 193n3, 303n1

Zamora, Petronila de, 93n4, 117n8, 126n7, 300n6, 303n1

Zarate Salmarón, fray Gerónimo de, 291, 295n1

Zavaleta, fray Juan de, 39; as commissary of Inquisition, 188; departs for La Junta, 40, 193, 196; and expedition to Texas, 198, 201, 203, 205, 206, 207, 226n2; leaves La Junta, 43; remains at La Junta, 210, 319, 320

Zía Pueblo (New Mexico), *ii*; battle at, 340; church and convento of, 293, 307; as encomienda, 359, 370; food from convento of, 135; as plaza de armas, 27, 28, 160, 165, 168, 171, 173, 177; population of, 293; provision requested of, 120

Zuñi Indians: expedition to, 77n4; kill fray Francisco Letrado, 76n4

Zuñi Pueblo, (New Mexico), 227, 295n1; church and convento of, 294; and encomienda tribute 302; population of, 294; revolt of, 73, 294

www.ingramcontent.com/pod-product-compliance
Lightning Source LLC
Chambersburg PA
CBHW081754300426
44116CB00014B/2117